Theory and Decision Library A:

Rational Choice in Practical Philosophy and Philosophy of Science

Volume 50

This series deals with practical and social philosophy and also foundational issues in philosophy of science in general that rely on methods broadly based on rational choice. The emphasis in the Series A is on well-argued, thoroughly analytical and philosophical rather than advanced mathematical treatments that use methods from decision theory, game theory and social choice theory. Particular attention is paid to work in practical philosophy broadly conceived, the theory of rationality, issues in collective intentionality, and philosophy of science, especially interdisciplinary approaches to social sciences and economics.

More information about this series at http://www.springer.com/series/6616

Wenceslao J. Gonzalez

Philosophico-Methodological Analysis of Prediction and its Role in Economics

Springer

Wenceslao J. Gonzalez
Faculty of Humanities
Department of Humanities
University of A Coruña
Ferrol, (A Coruña)
Spain

ISSN 0921-3384 ISSN 2352-2119 (electronic)
ISBN 978-3-319-08884-6 ISBN 978-3-319-08885-3 (eBook)
DOI 10.1007/978-3-319-08885-3
Springer Cham Heidelberg New York Dordrecht London

Library of Congress Control Number: 2014945648

Printed on acid-free paper

Springer is part of Springer Science+Business Media (www.springer.com)

Introduction

The Problem of Scientific Prediction and its Role in Economics

Among the most crucial topics in science is prediction. It is a concept of a very wide range of philosophico-methodological repercussions: prediction has a key role in basic science, applied science, and application of science.[1] Moreover, it has relevance throughout sciences: it appears in both formal and empirical sciences, because prediction has links with mathematical calculus as well as with empirical content. Prediction occupies a very central place, both in the way that scientists usually describe their own activity, and in the elements that different philosophers provide in order to consider a type of knowledge as "scientific."

1 Scientific Prediction as a Problem in Economics

Despite the importance of prediction in the natural sciences, the social sciences and the sciences of the artificial (Simon 1996; Gonzalez 2008), prediction frequently appears as a philosophico-methodological problem. This is especially the case in disciplines such as economics, which can be considered as social science and design science (Gonzalez 2012a). The dual character of economics as a science—social as well as artificial—is a focal epistemological component that increases the methodological complexity of economic predictions.

Historically, prediction has received special recognition by scientists and philosophers of science, at least in some ways. Thus, for many scientists, prediction has assumed considerable methodological prestige since its success in classical mechanics. This success has also given a prominent place to physics in science as a whole.[2] For many philosophers, scientific prediction also has a methodological prominence, although only some conceptions of the methodology of science give

[1] On the differences between "applied science" and "application of science" see Niiniluoto (1993, pp. 9 and 19) and Gonzalez (2013a, pp. 1508 and 1516). Some aspects of the limits to prediction from the point of view of application of science can be seen in Gejsen (2013).

[2] In spite of those successes, there is sometimes a difference between some views on prediction in physics and the actual historical events (Worrall 1989a). This can be seen also in the analysis of the periodic table of the elements of Dmitri Ivanovich Mendeleev, a key case in chemistry (Scerri

prediction a keynote role. Among them are Hans Reichenbach, Karl Popper and Imre Lakatos, of whom the last two have also had repercussions on the methodology of economics.

Moreover, the recognition of the importance of prediction by various scientists and philosophers, has not led so far to the attention that it deserves from a philosophico-methodological point of view. For even though prediction receives attention in publications on philosophy and the methodology of science (either in the general approach or in the specific perspective), it is only rarely the main topic of research in monographs related to science as a whole[3] or in books devoted to specific sciences.[4]

Regarding science in general, the comparison with the case of scientific explanation is clearly noteworthy. (a) There is a *quantitative* difference, because "scientific explanation" has an impressive amount of publications, whereas "scientific prediction" has a more limited range of specialized publications. (b) There is a *qualitative* difference, due to the diversity of types of scientific explanations that have been distinguished and recognized in science,[5] whereas there is no clear counterpart on behalf of scientific prediction, in terms of characteristic kinds of predictions commonly accepted.

However, in recent years prediction appears as the focus of interesting discussions in applied economics, in general, and in econometrics, in particular.[6] Until the analysis here reaches that point, there is a philosophico-methodological framework of scientific prediction and relevant aspects of methodology of economics to be considered. This book seeks to offer that framework of scientific prediction and its philosophico-methodological characteristics in economics. In this regard, this monograph tries to contribute to fill what seems to be a lacuna in the economic field,[7] using the methodological approaches of philosophers and economists.

Before that framework is offered, it should be emphasized that prediction is not a simple concept. It is generally considered as a source of a variety of methodological problems, mainly in the social sciences: "the nature and complexity of what

---

and Worrall 2001). On the Mendeleev case considered from the point of view of predictivism, see Barnes (2008, pp. 82–122).

[3] In the large list of references which can be seen at the end of each chapter of this book, it may be considered that, previous to my book *La predicción científica* (Gonzalez 2010a), there is only a monograph on scientific prediction based on a philosophico-methodological standpoint which—*sensu strictu*—develops a systematic presentation of the topic: Rescher (1998). Moreover, the book has a subtitle—*An Introduction to the Theory of Forecasting*—which may be understood as an expression of this phenomenon.

[4] On some issues, of particular relevance is the collection of papers on prediction in Mason et al. (1986). To lesser extent, there are also some interesting analyses in Howe and Wain (1993), and Mäki (2012), which includes Granger (2012).

[5] Cf. Salmon (1990), esp., pp. 196–219; and Gonzalez (2002b), esp., pp. 15–28.

[6] See Hendry and Ericsson (2001a); Clements and Hendry (2002a); Elliott et al. (2006); Clements and Hendry (2011); and Elliott and Timmermann (2013a and 2013b).

[7] In a well-known extensive bibliography on economic methodology there are only a couple of pages specifically on prediction: Redman (1989, pp. 77–79).

one extrapolates from, the precision with which the processes of development are thought to be known, whether the outcome predicted has a contaminating effect on the prediction in question and may thus modify it, how far into the future this extrapolation is intended to predict, the range of variables which can be accommodated in calculations: all these are some of the many and more obvious problems which make foretelling the future a hazardous business" (Howe 1993, p. 4).

Within the relations between scientific prediction and economics, there is a special emphasis on the issue of prediction as *a test* for economics as a science. In this regard, the *key question* is that economics undoubtedly needs predictions but, at the same time, these are frequently unreliable. In spite of this situation (an objective tension in the discipline),[8] should prediction be the requisite to assess that economics is *a science*? The most influential methodological tendency of mainstream economics has defended that crucial role of prediction for economics as a science,[9] but this view should be analyzed more deeply, going to the roots of the problem, and that requires starting with the consideration at a general level: the analysis of science as such made by philosophers. It is from there that the structure of the volume follows.

2 From the General Methodology of Science to the Methodology of Economics

The book seeks to combine the general methodology of science, usually developed by philosophers, and the methodology of economics, both of a wide spectrum—shared by philosophers and economists—and a restricted one (a field for economists).[10] Thus, the deliberations will begin with the general scope of science and the role of prediction within it, as a previous step to analyzing the conception of prediction in a concrete realm: economics. This approach emphasizes the methodological study—at the general and special levels—but it also considers aspects of several dimensions of the philosophy of science, mainly the semantics of science and the epistemology.

In moving from the general perspective to the particular, this book includes five parts: (I) the problem of prediction as a test for economics as a science; (II) the general orientation in methodology of science and the problem of prediction as a scientific test; (III) the methodological framework of social sciences and economics: incidence for prediction as a test; (IV) from epistemology to methodology of economic prediction: rationality and empirical approaches; and (V) methodological aspects of economic prediction: from description to prescription.

[8] This tension has been emphasized in Sen (1986), esp., p. 3.

[9] This influential methodological conception in economics has a very important precedent in the epoch-making paper by Friedman (1953).

[10] On the distinctions between these methodological approaches, see Gonzalez (1998a). Cf. Gonzalez (2000), esp., pp. 15–18.

First, philosophy should examine if prediction is a requisite of science itself (i.e., if it should be considered a constitutive element of scientific activity). Second, the study of the general orientation in the methodology of science should throw light on the problem of prediction as a scientific test. Third, within the methodology of social sciences, it should analyze if prediction in economics is a decisive element in considering economics as a scientific discipline. Fourth, the role of rationality and the empirical contribution should be assessed in an effort to elucidate the epistemology and methodology of economic prediction. Fifth, within the context of the difference between description and prescription, it is necessary to go more deeply into the methodological aspects of economic prediction.

Each of these analyses proceeds at a level interconnected with the others, according to an internal order that goes from the most general dimension—the science as such—to a particular methodological aspect in economics. These analyses of the problem of prediction in economics can be seen in two ways: the methodology of economics open to philosophical contributions, and the methodology of economics made by economists with no direct connection to philosophy. All these factors should be taken into account in order to reach a suitable solution for the problem.

Following such an overall perspective, Part I offers the basic framework: the philosophico-methodological standpoint as well as a characterization of scientific prediction and its varieties. Part II analyzes some influential general methodologies of science from the point of view of prediction: falsificationism and the methodology of scientific research programs. Part III deals with the methodological framework for prediction in economics within the social sciences (which includes also reflections on its role within the sciences of the artificial), the methodological approaches on prediction of some relevant economists (Nobel Prize winners), and the problem of prediction in economics from the perspective of action theory. Part IV focuses on rationality in economics and scientific prediction, with a study of the empirically grounded view and the perspective of experimental economics. Finally, Part V covers methods and limits of prediction in economics as well as the relation between prediction and prescription in economics.

This overall perspective demands a systematic reading of the whole text. The internal connection between the different chapters of every part of the book is emphasized at the beginning of the diverse parts. At the same time, each one of the chapters is, to some extent, "free standing," i.e., there is a sense of autonomy in the contents offered in them. This form of presentation has the deliberate purpose of helping the reader who wishes to focus on a particular aspect of a problem of prediction, in general, or economic prediction, in particular.

3 Sources and Acknowledgments

With hindsight, this book is the result of my interest in analyzing the topic of scientific prediction from different angles. During different periods over the years, I have worked on diverse aspects of the problem of scientific prediction, in general, and of economic predictions, in particular. In both cases the focus has been on the most influential perspectives, studying above all key philosophers of science and Nobel Prize winners in Economics. The main line of research has been methodological, but it also takes into account other factors (semantic, logical, epistemological, ontological, axiological, and ethical). Some of the ideas have been published in articles in international journals and in chapters of specialized books. Below are the references:

Gonzalez, W. J. 1994. Economic prediction and human activity. An analysis of prediction in economics from action theory. *Epistemologia* 17:253–294.

Gonzalez, W. J. 1995. Reichenbach's concept of prediction. *International Studies in the Philosophy of Science* 9 (1): 37–58.

Gonzalez, W. J. 1996. Prediction and mathematics: The Wittgensteinian approach. In *Spanish studies in the philosophy of science,* ed. G. Munevar, 299–332. Dordrecht: Kluwer.

Gonzalez, W. J. 1996. On the theoretical basis of prediction in economics. *Journal of Social Philosophy* 27 (3): 201–228.

Gonzalez, W. J. 1997. Rationality in economics and scientific predictions: A critical reconstruction of bounded rationality and its role in economic predictions. *Poznan Studies in the Philosophy of Science* 61:205–232.

Gonzalez, W. J. 1998. Prediction and prescription in economics: A philosophical and methodological approach. *Theoria* 13 (2): 321–345.

Gonzalez, W. J. 2001. Lakatos's approach on prediction and novel facts. *Theoria* 16 (3): 499–518.

Gonzalez, W. J. 2003. From *Erklären–Verstehen* to *prediction–understanding*: The methodological framework in economics. In *Realism in action: Essays in the philosophy of social sciences,* ed. M. Sintonen, P. Ylikoski, and K. Miller, 33–50. Dordrecht: Kluwer.

Gonzalez, W. J. 2003. Rationality in experimental economics: An analysis of Reinhard Selten's approach. In *Observation and experiment in the natural and the social sciences,* ed. M. C. Galavotti, 71–83. Dordrecht: Kluwer.

Gonzalez, W. J. 2003. Racionalidad y Economía: De la racionalidad de la Economía como Ciencia a la racionalidad de los agentes económicos. In *Racionalidad, historicidad y predicción en Herbert A. Simon,* ed. W. J. Gonzalez, 65–96. A Coruña: Netbiblo.

Gonzalez, W. J. 2004. The many faces of Popper's methodological approach to prediction. In *Karl Popper: Critical appraisals,* ed. P. Catton and G. Macdonald, 78–98. London: Routledge.

Gonzalez, W. J. 2006. Prediction as scientific test of economics. In *Contemporary perspectives in philosophy and methodology of science,* ed. W. J. Gonzalez and J. Alcolea, 83–112. A Coruña: Netbiblo.

Gonzalez, W. J. 2007. The role of experiments in the social sciences: The case of economics. In *General philosophy of science: Focal issues,* ed. T. Kuipers, 275–301. Amsterdam: Elsevier.

Gonzalez, W. J. 2008. Rationality and prediction in the sciences of the artificial: Economics as a design science. In *Reasoning, rationality, and probability,* ed. M. C. Galavotti, R. Scazzieri, and P. Suppes, 165–186. Stanford: CSLI Publications.

Some of these articles and chapters of books have a direct correlation with the contents of this volume. This is the case of Chaps. 3, 4, 5, 7 and 8. In other cases, the relation is only partial, as happens in Chaps. 2, 6, 9 and 12. In addition, Chap. 1 is connected with other aspects of my research, and Chaps. 10 and 11 are new. I am very pleased to mention explicitly the journals and books where some topics of this book have been published. Besides this recognition to the publishing houses, I would like to point out that the previous publications have been thoroughly revised and adapted to the purpose of this book. Thus, there are always in the chapters new elements compared to the previous texts.

Because of my interest in the sciences of complexity and economics as a science of design, new ideas have arisen to complement of the previous research on prediction and economics. These ideas can be seen in several papers of recent years that emphasize the relevance of the topic and have been used for some remarks in the present book:

Gonzalez, W. J. 2011. Complexity in economics and prediction: The role of parsimonious factors. In *Explanation, prediction, and confirmation,* ed. D. Dieks, W. J. Gonzalez, S. Hartman, Th. Uebel, and M. Weber, 319–330. Dordrecht: Springer.

Gonzalez, W. J. 2012. La Economía en cuanto Ciencia: Enfoque desde la complejidad. *Revista Galega de Economía* 21 (1). http://www.usc.es/econo/RGE/Vol21_1/castelan/bt1c.pdf. Accessed 26 June 2012.

Gonzalez, W. J. 2012. La vertiente dinámica de las Ciencias de la Complejidad. Repercusión de la historicidad para la predicción científica en las Ciencias de Diseño. In *Las Ciencias de la Complejidad: Vertiente dinámica de las Ciencias de Diseño y sobriedad de factores,* ed. W. J. Gonzalez, 73–106. A Coruña: Netbiblo.

Gonzalez, W. J. 2012. Complejidad estructural en Ciencias de Diseño y su incidencia en la predicción científica: El papel de la sobriedad de factores (*parsimonious factors*). In *Las Ciencias de la Complejidad: Vertiente dinámica de las Ciencias de Diseño y sobriedad de factores,* ed. W. J. Gonzalez, 143–167. A Coruña: Netbiblo.

Gonzalez, W. J. 2012. Methodological universalism in science and its limits: Imperialism versus complexity. In *Thinking about provincialism in thinking, Poznan Studies in the Philosophy of the Sciences and the Humanities,* vol. 100, ed. K. Brzechczyn and K. Paprzycka, 155–175. Amsterdam: Rodopi.

Gonzalez, W. J. 2013. The sciences of design as sciences of complexity: The dynamic trait. In *New challenges to philosophy of science,* ed. H. Andersen, D. Dieks, W. J. Gonzalez, Th. Uebel, and G. Wheeler, 299–311. Dordrecht: Springer.

I would like to thank to Hilary Putnam, Patrick Suppes, and Stephen Toulmin for the opportunity to have conversations on scientific prediction. In addition, I have benefited from talks with Donald Gillies and Ivor Grattan-Guinness. During my stays at *London School of Economics* I have had the chance to discuss problems of scientific prediction with John Worrall, Colin Howson, and Peter Urbach. At LSE, besides the clarification of Lakatos' conception of prediction and the Bayesian approach on this topic, I had the chance to use the facilities of the Centre for Philosophy of Natural and Social Sciences.

Meanwhile, at the *Center for Philosophy of Science* at the University of Pittsburgh I had conversations on prediction and its role in science with well-known philosophers, such as Adolf Grünbaum, John Earman, Wesley Salmon, and Nicholas Rescher. In the University of A Coruña, where I work, I have talked to Larry Laudan, Ilkka Niiniluoto, Daniel Hausman, and Philip Kitcher during the days of conferences that I have organized. These conversations have had a direct influence on the chapters on Salmon, Kitcher and Rescher in the book Gonzalez, W. J., *La predicción científica: Concepciones filosófico-metodológicas desde H. Reichenbach a N. Rescher*, Montesinos, Barcelona, 2010.

Among the economists, I must recognize the importance of the conversations with Herbert A. Simon—Nobel Prize in economic sciences 1978—in Pittsburgh during the years 1993–1994, 1996 and 1999, and later—in a conference in 2001 organized by the University of Bologna—the discussions in Bertinoro (Italy) with Reinhard Selten, Nobel Prize in economic sciences 1994.[11] Furthermore, my recognition goes to David F. Hendry, who accepted my invitation for a Workshop at the University of A Coruña, Ferrol Campus, on 2010. Both his paper at this event and his publications have had a clear influence on my approach.

Yet it is clear that none of these authors is responsible for the contents of the book. However, for me, some comments have been very influential, especially those made by Salmon, Worrall, Hausman, Gillies, Simon, Selten, and above all, Rescher. They have read some chapters of the book and they have made very interesting comments about different aspects. Among the Spanish colleagues, I would like to thank the economists José Ramón Cancelo de la Torre and Carlos Fernández-Jardón. In addition, in connection with the editing and other aspects of this book, I appreciate the collaboration for years of José Fco. Martínez Solano, and more recently by Amanda Guillan and Jessica Rey.

Finally, I would like to insist on my gratitude to the *Center for Philosophy of Science* and the Department of Philosophy of the University of Pittsburgh. Gerald Massey and James Lennox, the directors of the Center in the periods when I have been working there, have offered their support to my work, which was originally aimed to be a composition of some of the papers on which the book is based. In this regard, my deepest gratitude is to Nicholas Rescher, Co-chairman of the *Center*, who always has tried to give his best to me. His intellectual advice and friendly attitude have been especially important to me.

Helsinki, 28 August 2013

Wenceslao J. Gonzalez

---

[11] In the first place, successive grants of the Spanish Ministry of Science and Education and the Government of the Autonomous Community of Galicia (Spain) made possible the research in Pittsburgh. In the second case, it was the European Science Foundation the institution that contributed to the event.

References

Barnes, E. C. 2008. *The paradox of predictivism*. Cambridge: Cambridge University Press.

Clements, M. P., and D. F. Hendry, eds. 2002a. *A companion to economic forecasting*. Oxford: Blackwell.

Clements, M. P., and D. F. Hendry, eds. 2011. *The Oxford handbook of economic forecasting*. New York: Oxford University Press.

Elliott, G., and A. Timmermann, eds. 2013a. *Handbook of economic forecasting,* vol. 2A. Amsterdam: North-Holland.

Elliott, G., and A. Timmermann, eds. 2013b. *Handbook of economic forecasting,* vol. 2B. Amsterdam: North-Holland.

Elliott, G., C. W. J. Granger, and A. Timmermann, eds. 2006. *Handbook of economic forecasting,* vol. 1. Amsterdam: Elsevier.

Friedman, M. 1953. The methodology of positive economics. In *Essays in positive economics,* ed. M. Friedman, 3–43. Chicago: University of Chicago Press (6th repr., 1969).

Gejsen, M. D. 2013. Limits to prediction: Europeanizing technology in an expert forum. *European Journal of Futures Research* 1 (1). doi:10.1007/s40309-013-0024-3.

Gonzalez, W. J. 1998a. Philosophy and methodology of economics. *Theoria* 13 (32):235–239.

Gonzalez, W. J. 2000. Marco teórico, trayectoria y situación actual de la Filosofía y Metodología de la Economía. *Argumentos de Razón Técnica* 3:13–59.

Gonzalez, W. J. 2002b. Caracterización de la "explicación científica" y tipos de explicaciones científicas. In *Diversidad de la explicación científica,* ed. W. J. Gonzalez, 13–49. Barcelona: Ariel.

Gonzalez, W. J. 2008. Rationality and prediction in the sciences of the artificial: Economics as a design science. In *Reasoning, rationality, and probability,* ed. M. C. Galavotti, R. Scazzieri, and P. Suppes, 165–186. Stanford: CSLI Publications.

Gonzalez, W. J. 2010a. *La predicción científica: Concepciones filosófico-metodológicas desde H. Reichenbach a N. Rescher*. Barcelona: Montesinos.

Gonzalez, W. J. 2012a. La vertiente dinámica de las Ciencias de la Complejidad. Repercusión de la historicidad para la predicción científica en las Ciencias de Diseño. In *Las Ciencias de la Complejidad: Vertiente dinámica de las Ciencias de Diseño y sobriedad de factores,* ed. W. J. Gonzalez, 73–106. A Coruña: Netbiblo.

Gonzalez, W. J. 2013a. Value ladenness and the value-free ideal in scientific research. In *Handbook of the philosophical foundations of business ethics,* ed. C. Lütge, 1503–1521. Dordrecht: Springer.

Granger, C. 2012. The philosophy of economic forecasting. In *Philosophy of economics,* ed. U. Mäki, 311–327. Amsterdam: Elsevier.

Hendry, D. F., and Ericsson, N. R., eds. 2001a. *Understanding economic forecasts*. Cambridge: The MIT Press.

Howe, L. 1993. Predicting the future. In *Predicting the future,* ed. L. Howe and A. Wain, 1–7. Cambridge: Cambridge University Press.

Howe, L., and A. Wain, eds. 1993. *Predicting the future*. Cambridge: Cambridge University Press.

Mäki, U., ed. 2012. *Philosophy of economics*. Amsterdam: Elsevier.

Mason, J., P. Mathias, and J. H. Westcott, eds. 1986. *Predictability in science and society*. London: The Royal Society and The British Academy.

Niiniluoto, I. 1993. The aim and structure of applied research. *Erkenntnis* 38:1–21.

Redman, D. A. 1989. *Economic methodology. A bibliography with references to works in the philosophy of science, 1860–1988*. Westport: Greenwood Press.

Rescher, N. 1998. *Predicting the future: An introduction to the theory of forecasting*. Albany: State University of New York Press.

Salmon, W. C. 1990. *Four decades of scientific explanation*. Minneapolis: University of Minnesota Press.

Scerri, E. R., and J. Worrall. 2001. Prediction and the periodic table. *Studies in History and Philosophy of Science* 32 (2): 407–452.

Sen, A. 1986. Prediction and economic theory. In *Predictability in science and society,* ed. J. Mason, P. Mathias, and J. H. Westcott, 3–23. London: The Royal Society and The British Academy.

Simon, H. A. 1996. *The sciences of the artificial.* 3rd ed. Cambridge: The MIT Press (1st ed., 1969; 2nd ed., 1981).

Worrall, J. 1989a. Fresnel, Poisson and the white spot: The role of successful predictions in the acceptance of scientific theories. In *The uses of experiment,* ed. D. Gooding, T. Pinch, and S. Schaffer, 135–157. Cambridge: Cambridge University Press.

Contents

Part I
The Problem of Prediction as a Test for Economics as a Science

From the perspective of the theoretical basis of its methodological development, prediction in economics appears as a relevant problem connected with the realm of scientific prediction in general. In this regard, Part I of the book deals with the philosophico-methodological standpoint: it offers the *general elements* of science as well as of prediction which underlie the methodology of science. Thus, the analysis emphasizes what constitutes the basis for a later consideration of the methodology of economics.

This connection between the general domain of science and the particular sphere of economics is important, especially for focusing on the roots of the problem of prediction in economics. It is a pertinent question, due to the need for prediction this science has (both in descriptive terms as well as in prescriptive ones) and the associated problem of its frequently unreliable character. In addition, it is a key topic, insofar as prediction has been presented by important economists—among them, Nobel Prize winners—as the test as to whether economics is a science.

a. The *necessity* of economic predictions is clear in many branches of this field, and the planning of economic activity is *de facto* heavily dependent on predictions. There is a growing need for predictions in applied economics, in those areas most sensitive to improving profits, and in many institutions, both in microeconomics and macroeconomics, which require predictions to develop their normal activity. A direct consequence of this fact is the increasing number of models for predicting (or forecasting) the future outcome of those variables of interest for such institutions.

b. There is a consensus on the notorious *unreliability* of many predictions produced by experts in the different fields of economic activity, as we have seen especially in recent years, during the severe crisis. The continued unreliability of the predictions places their scientific character, and consequently economics as a science, in doubt. The frequency of "unexpected" economic phenomena has been a real challenge for predicting in this science over the last decades.

With its dependence on this tension—necessity and unreliability—economic prediction appears initially as a *theoretical problem*: can it be "truly" scientific and, therefore, reliable? The answer to this issue has direct repercussions on the economic activity in different areas. The roots of the theoretical problem are in the characterization of economics as a science, because prediction (its existence as well as its accuracy and precision) is a key point in establishing this discipline—economics—as scientific knowledge. This question is related to a central topic of the philosophy and methodology of science: what *de facto* science is, and what it *ought to be*.

Therefore, the central issue in this part of the book deals with the theoretical basis of prediction in economics. Within this intellectual setting, two chapters try to clarify the background for the problem of prediction as a *test for economics* as a science. Thus, Chap. 1 analyzes the issue of prediction as a requisite for science, taking into account the components of a "science." It deals with the role of prediction within the philosophico-methodological framework of science: presenting features and the relations between basic science and applied science. And Chap. 2 goes deeper into the characterization of "scientific prediction" and its kinds in economics.

Chapter 1
The Philosophico-Methodological Standpoint: The Issue of Prediction as a Requisite for Science

Prediction is habitually a central topic in economics, in both practical and theoretical terms.[1] The relevance of prediction is clear: on the one hand, it is a central notion in the characterization of *economic activity*, because economic affairs are closely related with statements about the future; and, on the other, it has a key role in the discussion on traits to determine whether economics is a *science*. This issue of prediction as a possible requisite for economics to be considered a science has received the attention of philosophers as well as of economists.

In effect, economic prediction is a key issue in the philosophical and methodological study of this discipline. From the epistemological point of view, prediction has frequently been the hub of the debate on *reliability* of economic knowledge and, therefore, for the *demarcation* of economics as a science. At the same time, prediction is also a *central notion* in the main methodological controversies held in economics, and especially so in the last 60 years.[2] Thus, even though the starting point of economics as a science is usually put at more than 200 years ago (Adam Smith 1776), there is still a debate on whether economics is a *science* in a strict sense. Moreover, there is a famous Nobel Prize in economics—John Hicks (1983c and 1986)—who maintains that economics is not a "science" precisely because of the role of prediction in it.

Within economics itself, prediction also affects the way of understanding the relationship between the two main traditional realms of the subject matter of this discipline: the *descriptive* and *normative* branches. These approaches have been important since the period of classical economics.[3] According to this distinction, the

---

[1] An indicator of the relevance for economics of the problems related to prediction is the number and quality of the journals devoted to this issue: *Journal of Forecasting*, *International Journal of Forecasting*, *Future*, *Technological Forecasting and Social Change*, *Journal of Time Series*, … From the point of view of economic theory, the importance of prediction has been emphasized in Sen (1986) and Granger (2012).

[2] In fact, the discussion has a turning point in a paper published 60 years ago: Friedman (1953).

[3] This distinction is frequently conceived in terms of "positive economics" as opposed to "political economy." As Terence Hutchison has pointed out, in the first half of nineteenth century—with John Stuart Mill and Nassau William Senior—there are explicit attempts to differentiate the "positive" propositions of economic science and the recommendations on economic policies to be followed, according to the aims to be achieved. He also maintains that this distinction has not been

W. J. Gonzalez, *Philosophico-Methodological Analysis of Prediction and its Role in Economics*, Theory and Decision Library A: 50, DOI 10.1007/978-3-319-08885-3_1

task of economic prediction in the first case—the descriptive or "positive" side—would have a different character than prediction in the second case—the normative or "political" facet—because they have initially diverse aims and also a different practical incidence for social life.

Actually, there are three philosophico-methodological spheres of economics at stake here regarding prediction instead of just two realms (descriptive and normative). These are (i) basic science, which is the domain where prediction is related to economic theory (or "theoretical economy," for Granger 2012, p. 312); (ii) applied science, where prediction gives information about the future that is needed for economic prescriptions (i.e., the guide for thinking of the policy-making);[4] and (iii) application of science, where the decision makers intervene in the actual economy (e.g., in the area of finance), which includes the consideration by the decision-maker of the future consequences of the decision (Granger 2012, p. 314).

1.1 The Theoretical Framework

When dealing with the problem of criteria to ascertain if economics is a "science," the issue of the role played by prediction immediately arises. This is not a mere result of the influence of modern science in general, and of Newtonian physics in particular, which looked for reliable predictions. It also has closer historical roots within economics, in the most influential paper in methodology of economics to date: "The Methodology of Positive Economics," where Milton Friedman maintains that prediction is the *main aim* of economics (1953, pp. 7–16). This might be thought of as an echo of the philosophico-methodological approach held earlier by Hans Reichenbach, who considered prediction as the central aim of science (1938). But there is no evidence of any direct influence of the leader of the Berlin school on the mentor of monetarism.[5]

However, the Nobel Prize in economics 1976 and the author of *Experience and Prediction* coincide in the acceptance of a methodological instrumentalism (Gonzalez 1994, 1995). Moreover, both conceive the scientific process as a necessary means to reach a previously foreseen aim, which is predicting. Thus, their meeting point lies precisely in the subordination of scientific knowledge to the attainment of *success* in predictions. Both authors also give preference to *empirical results* over the realism of the assumptions.[6] Furthermore, they are in tune with fallibilist thesis: they accept the revisability of scientific knowledge. This cognitive

clear enough and that not all economists have considered it as an adequate orientation for the methodology to be used (cf. Hutchison 1964).

[4] On the features of applied science, in general, and the role of prediction in it, see Simon (2001, p. 32) and Gonzalez (2007d, esp. pp. 184–185). On the issue of the application of scientific knowledge from a methodological perspective, there are some interesting remarks in Giere (1971).

[5] On the legacy of Reichenbach's logical empiricism, see Rescher (2006).

[6] Regarding the possibility of success in prediction, there exists a similitude between the approaches proposed by Friedman and Reichenbach, insofar as it does not need to be based in the realism of assumptions. This thesis is explicitly defended by Friedman, and it has been strongly criticized by other economists (see, for example, Simon 1963b). The correlate of this position on the absence of realism of assumptions is in the capacity of success that Reichenbach accepts in the *clairvoyant*

fallibilism has some nuances: in Friedman it seems to have a kind of falsificationist flavor, whereas in Reichenbach it is based on an empiricist component.[7]

To some extent, these authors can be seen as important figures of the work on methodology of prediction made by philosophers and by economists in twentieth century and the first decade of the twenty-first century. Both are influential and offer elements for a theoretical framework of the problem. Nevertheless, there is the need to start with something previous to their views: the analysis of the *characteristics of science* as such (i.e., the components of science itself), looking for their relation with prediction. Thus, the philosophico-methodological standpoint on the issue of prediction as a requisite for science begins here with an examination at the most general level.

These steps regarding the *theoretical framework* of the problem of prediction belong to the most general level of analysis and, gradually, less general aspects will follow them. The rationale of this structure is based on the existence of diverse methodological approaches. Actually, the *methodological studies* on science have initially two different lines: (i) the *general scope*, which belongs to philosophy and methodology of science; and (ii) the *special sphere* of philosophy and methodology of economics.

In addition, the latter approach takes two directions: (a) it considers the broad focus related to economics (i.e., the methodology of economics worked by philosophers and also by economists with philosophical background); and (b) it examines the restricted perspective on economics (i.e., the methodology of economics developed by economists). In this book, the study commonly follows the path from the general scope—the philosophy and methodology of science—towards the specific sphere of economics.

1.1.1 The General Scope in Philosophy and Methodology of Science

An initial basic bifurcation appears in the realm of philosophy and methodology of science: general and special. (1) There are studies of a *general scope*, which research the set of elements characteristic of the scientific activity—structural and dynamic—because they look for the factors of the scientific endeavor as a whole (and, hence, seek the traits of any scientific discipline, mainly the empirical ones). (2) There are reflections within a *special sphere*, which deal with the philosophical and methodological considerations about some sciences or a particular discipline, in order to go deeper into a specific scientific activity (either in itself or in its relations with a group of disciplines).

This double philosophico-methodological orientation on science—general and special—also distinguishes the kind of intellectual endeavor, because the general line belongs in a natural way to philosophers, open by definition to the wider domain, whereas the attention to the conceptual and empirical problems of the

(1938, p. 354), because a "clairvoyant" does not seem to need any assumptions with solid support, either theoretical or empirical.

[7] Wesley Salmon called my attention in 1999 to Reichenbach's cognitive fallibilism.

diverse sciences can also be of interest of scientists (such as economists) who work in each particular discipline.

Despite the fact that methodology of science is developed in a philosophical context, it has its *own status* as a subject matter, which makes it possible to distinguish it from other philosophical disciplines. In this regard, methodology of science has two main aims: (i) it analyzes how science progresses *de facto*; and (ii) it gives prescriptions about how science *ought to be* developed (Gonzalez 1990b, pp. 72–73). Both aspects—analyzing and prescribing—are like two sides of the same coin.

Thus, methodology of science works on what the scientists have done and, at the same time, it looks for the best possible methods to improve science. Certainly, this analytical-prescriptive subject connects with other philosophical studies of science (the semantics of science, the logic of science, the epistemology, the ontology of science, etc.); but it is different from all of them (the examination of the scientific language, the study of the internal structure of the science, the reflection on scientific knowledge, the status of the scientific activity, etc.).

Basically, in the study of science in general, the realm of scientific prediction appears directly associated with characteristic methodological problems. In effect, the sense and reference of "scientific prediction" have connections with the problem of scientific progress. As a *methodological concept*, prediction requires some previous elements. Thus, the content of scientific prediction (whatever it is) depends on several factors that prevent its consideration as something that can be grasped "by acquaintance" or in an immediate way. The reason is clear: methodology of science has its roots at a different level, because it supposes other studies, mainly semantics of science, logic of science and epistemology (Gonzalez 1990b, pp. 67–74). In addition, methodology of science is connected also to ontology of science, axiology of scientific research and, sometimes, even to ethics of science (Gonzalez 1999a and 2013a).

Commonly, the task of general methodology of science concerns the research on the process of improvement of scientific knowledge (in the intensive and extensive ways), something that already has a precise language, a logically well-formed structure and a more accurate kind of knowledge than the ordinary knowledge. Hence, there is a dependence of methodology of science on these philosophical studies on science mentioned. Likewise, general methodology has links with the status of scientific activity (the ontology of science) and with the aims of scientific research (the axiology of science). It can be also related to ethics of science, insofar as science is a free human activity and this endeavor may be assessed in terms of ethical values.

Consequently, if prediction is accepted as a methodological concept (i.e., as an element present *de facto* in scientific theories and as an important component for developing them), then its *possibility* in the scientific field is beyond doubt. Nevertheless, to the same extent, prediction needs an *epistemological* support to guarantee its legitimate presence as a scientific concept. This is the problem raised by those who deny the scientific character of economic prediction: the existence of a congenital uncertainty in the knowledge about future events; thus, the expectation of an event occurring in an upcoming time could "be modified by things that will happen in the future and which cannot now be foreseen" (Hicks 1983c, p. 366).

General methodology of science deals with some crucial issues for the problem of prediction as a *test* for a science. The research connects with the epistemological basis of prediction as a criterion of demarcation. Thus, the methodological approach needs to take into account the elements that constitute what a "science" *is* and how science can *be improved* in order to get progressive standards. These diverse aspects receive a modulation here according to the *methodological orientation* chosen. Part II of this book pays special attention to two important orientations: falsificationism and the methodology of scientific research programs. These have been developed by key figures of contemporary philosophy: Popper and Lakatos.

1.1.2 The Sphere of Philosophy and Methodology of Economics

The last decades have witnessed an enormous outpouring of work on philosophy and methodology of economics. The turning point can be located in the publication of Mark Blaug's book *The Methodology of Economics* (1980),[8] where for the first time a clear link is established between general methodology of science (the received view, Popper, Kuhn, Lakatos, and Feyerabend) and specific issues concerning economics (the theory of consumer behavior, general equilibrium theory, Gary Becker's economy of the family, etc.), which are treated by Blaug from a methodological approach. When he published his book, several authors were already working in the field: Daniel Hausman, Alexander Rosenberg, Martin Hollis, ... Since 1980, there has been an explosion of work in this field.[9] It has seen a proliferation of new journals established to deal, in one way or another, with philosophical and methodological problems in economics.[10]

There were two main consequences of this period regarding the characterization of the subject: first, it was a decisive step for constituting a new area—philosophy and methodology of economics—among the philosophers of science; and, second, it led to a greater interest among economists in economic methodology and the underlying philosophical problems (semantic, logical, and epistemological, but also ontological, axiological, and ethical). Thus, for philosophers, philosophy of economics is now a common subject in university courses at both an undergraduate and graduate level, and it is a frequent topic at conferences; and, among economists, economic methodology has achieved the status of a subdiscipline within economics.

Undoubtedly, this *special* methodology of science—the methodology of economics—can be developed according to two different possibilities: (a) the option of the *broad approach*, and (b) the choice of a *more restricted* perspective (Gonzalez 2001a, pp. 12–15). These views of the subject depend on the level of connection to

[8] Two years later appeared another influential book: Caldwell (1982).

[9] Hausman lists 50 volumes published in English between 1983 and 1993 (Hausman 1994a, pp. 447–461).

[10] *Research in the History of Economic Thought and Methodology* (1983), *Economics and Philosophy* (1985) and *Methodus* (1989), which became the *Journal of Economic Methodology* (1994).

the general scope and, therefore, they rely on how close or far apart they are with regard to philosophy. In the first case the links between the methodology of economics and the philosophical stance are clear, whereas in the second case the vinculum is implicit and indirect rather than explicit and direct.

Hence, on the one hand, there is a *broad approach* to methodology of economics. Economists and philosophers share this when they study economics from the point of view of problems concerning science in itself. (For example, what distinguishes sciences from non-sciences in order to know if economics is a science? What is the cognitive status of economics? What are the logical peculiarities of the concepts of economics and how do they compare with the concepts of other disciplines? How are economic claims established? How important is prediction in economics as a goal and as a means of testing?). Those who pursue this first approach are concerned with links between economics and the main positions in the methodological literature, be they verificationist, falsificationist, Kuhnian, Lakatosian, etc.

A broad approach is open to substantial philosophical problems. It can be followed in many ways (Backhouse 1994a): in positive terms, as in Blaug's defense of falsificationism and the methodology of scientific research programs[11] or in Hausman's revision of J. Stuart Mill's views (1992a), or one can adopt a critical attitude, such as in the "post-modern" critiques of D. N. McCloskey (1985, 1990, 1994), or Philip Mirowski (1988, 1989, 1992), or one can even (dis)solve the philosophical stance in favor of a sociological view, as in the work of Harry Collins (1983). Those who pursue this approach are usually philosophers with active research interests in economics, or economists with a broad philosophical training. Pursuing this approach does not, however, exclude the possibility of developing methodological analyses of concrete aspects of economics, too.

The methodological study developed by influential economists seeks to clarify some crucial aspects of economics, such as the descriptive and normative distinction, the relevance or irrelevance of unrealistic assumptions to the appraisal of theories, or the nature of economic laws. This kind of approach, which connects epistemological and methodological bases of economics, was dominant before 1980.[12] Specific inquiries of this sort have been made not only by mainstream economists, but also by economists of alternative schools: post-Keynesians (in their study of time and uncertainty), Austrians (in their work on the relation between action and knowledge), followers of the Carnegie Mellon School of business behavior (in the study of rationality in decision making), and (neo)institutionalists (in their research into the economy as a structure of power instead of a set of interconnected markets).[13]

[11] Before his famous book—Popperian in some senses—Blaug (1976) endorses Lakatos against Kuhn. On the influence of Popper's philosophy on Blaug's approach see Martínez Solano (2007).

[12] Classical works of this kind include works pointed out in this chapter, such as Hutchison (1938) and Friedman (1953). In addition, among the well-known works in this regard are Robbins (1935[1932]), Machlup (1963), Samuelson (1963), and Machlup (1978). Many papers written by Simon as well as some of his books also belong to this group. A thematic presentation of his bibliography is in Gonzalez (2003c).

[13] The methodological divergence between these economic schools can be related at least to three different kinds of issues: (i) the methodological *assumptions* of the discipline; (ii) the way of

But there is also a more *restricted perspective* of the methodology of economics. This specific realm seeks to comprehend the specificity of economics itself (its assumptions, models, goals, kind of rationality, testability, possibility of experimentation, and internal structure of its development), and only secondarily looks for the relevance of the economics features to science, in general, or to other sciences (either social or artificial). Thus, the methodological perspective is narrower in this second approach to economics than in the previous one. But it is the dominant line in the research in economics directly related with mathematical improvements, as can be seen in the methodological history of econometrics (Morgan 1990).[14] Usually those who follow this more specific approach are economists interested in reflecting on the process of their own discipline (accounting, financial markets, business organizations, etc.), and they put less emphasis on the connection of economics with more general problems concerning science.

Leading figures in the philosophy and methodology of economics, such as Blaug and Hausman, agree when they characterize the "methodology of economics" as a philosophical enterprise. Thus, the former suggests that this discipline should "be understood simply as philosophy of science applied to economics" (Blaug 1980, p. xi), and the latter points out that "methodological questions concerning economics (…) are all philosophical questions" (Hausman 1994, p. vii). In a way, this book connects with that tradition, insofar as it accepts that methodological problems are related to philosophical problems; but the present research draws a *conceptual distinction* between philosophy of science and methodology of science. In this regard, it is a book that looks for further implications of what has been done in the field while, at the same time, it seeks new aspects.

Philosophy of science studies components of science: its language, structure, knowledge claims, activity, aims, values, … They are analyzed in the semantics of science, the logic of science, the epistemology, the ontology of science, the axiology of research, the ethics of science, etc. Connected to these components is the scrutiny of scientific method, the inquiry on the features of a scientific process. Hence the *methodology of science* is bound up with the research of philosophy of science, as is the case of the study of economic predictions, which involves philosophical questions, such as is the economy deterministic or stochastic? (Granger 2012).[15]

Although non-philosophers—the specialists of each science—can of course study methodology, it belongs initially to the philosophical sphere. In fact, the methodological questions, which combine queries about what science *is* and what science *ought to be*, start from a philosophical stance, due to their metascientific

understanding the economic *processes*; and (iii) the features of *evidence* (mainly in the empirical testing) which can be used to accept economic statements (Gonzalez 2000, pp. 52–56).

[14] The formation of this important part of economics is studied in Qin (1993) and in Epstein (1987). On the methodology of econometrics, cf. Poirier (1994).

An important exception is the econometrician David Hendry, who uses terminology inspired by Lakatos (Backhouse 1997, p. 116). In addition, there are methodological studies of econometrics which are also focused on general methodological approaches, cf. Keuzenkamp (2000).

[15] Granger maintains that philosophers "often ask interesting and penetrating questions that deserve attention of forecasters, both to improve their understanding of what they are doing and possibly, in consequence, improve the quality of their output" (2012, p. 311).

character. However, within the ample philosophical realm, methodology of science has its *specific status* (in order to analyze and to prescribe the scientific processes), as has been pointed out in the section on the general scope in philosophy and methodology of science.

1.2 Perspectives on Prediction from the Components of a "Science"

Terence Hutchison, in his reflections in "Changing Aims in Economics," clearly presents the topic discussed here: "to predict or not to predict? (That *is* the question)?" (Hutchison 1992b). In effect, on the problem of prediction as *requisite* for science there is a Hamletian doubt. The solution concerns science as a whole, but it affects economics directly, where this controversy is particularly pertinent. The question comes in this case from a well-known economist, interested in the theoretical problems of the discipline (Hutchison 1960, 1977, 1981, 1992a), and it appears in a book dealing with philosophical and methodological issues raised by economic theory.

After half a century of publishing on epistemology and methodology of economics, Hutchison reflects on the changes in aims in economics. He looks back to the nineteenth century and analyzes the centenary of the publication of *The Wealth of Nations* by Smith. It was in that period when Robert Lowe, who was *Chancellor of the Exchequer* and accepted a kind of economics based on David Ricardo, stated the idea of prediction as a *test* to assess the existence of a science and assured that Smith fulfilled, in the main, that requisite.[16]

Implicitly, Hutchison seems to assume two relevant philosophico-methodological aspects: (i) prediction as an *aim* of science, in general, and economics, in particular; and (ii) prediction as a *test* to appraise the scientific character of economics.[17] In his presentation of the issue they are not so clearly distinguished. The first aspect is primarily axiological (i.e., in connection with the values accepted in science, mainly regarding the ends of research), while the second is predominantly methodological (i.e., related to the evaluation of scientific processes).

Unquestionably, the problem of prediction as a *requisite* for science is not confined to economics, because it has a general character: it concerns, in principle, any science (including formal sciences). It needs to be focused from a philosophical perspective that is attentive to pivotal factors. *De facto,* there are many sciences—natural sciences and social sciences as well as sciences of the artificial—[18] which make predictions and interpret them in order to ascertain if their knowledge is scientific

---

[16] See Hutchison (1992b, p. 72). Lowe's text, originally published in *Political Economy Club*, in 1876, reads on page 7: "The test of science is prevision or prediction, and Adam Smith appears to me in the main to satisfy that condition."

[17] The third relevant aspect is prediction as a guide for prescription, i.e., as a previous step to policy-making.

[18] On the characteristics of this domain, see Simon (1996).

or not. Thus, disciplines that are rather distant from economics (e.g., geology and biology)[19] and disciplines closer to it (e.g., psychology and sociology) include successful predictions as a guarantee of the scientific nature of the achieved knowledge within a specific realm.[20] Common to all of these are some *features* related to the general idea of something future that, according to our present knowledge, might happen (i.e., something which is rationally expected on the basis of that knowledge).

1.2.1 Characteristics of a Science

Whether "prediction" is decisive or not in order to have *science* depends firstly on the concept of "science" that is used. Thus, it is convenient to characterize the *constitutive elements* of a science. In this regard, the characterization should reflect what *de facto* a science *is*—its being—and also what it *ought to be*, because the realm of philosophy of science—and, above all, specifically methodology of science—is both analytical and prescriptive. In effect, the methodological study of science makes analyses of past and present elements of scientific procedures, and it orientates on how to achieve future scientific developments on the basis of the knowledge available.

Methodology of science is a realm that cannot be purely descriptive (a mere knowledge of the past or present situation of science, like a "science of science") or purely normative (in the sense of strict norms, which can be aprioristic regarding the future development of science). (a) There is the need to take into account the contributions on the concept of science in the past (classical, modern and contemporary views) and the *methods which have been used* to increase scientific knowledge; and (b) the knowledge of the past and the present should be considered as *starting point* for what scientific activity ought to be in order to achieve better standards (Gonzalez 1990a, pp. 16–20).

These two sides can be combined: science is a complex reality which condenses a trajectory of centuries and is open to improvement in the future. Thus, the *characteristics of a science* can be summarized in several elements: (1) science possesses a specific language (with terms whose sense and reference are precise); (2) science is articulated in scientific theories with a well patterned internal structure, which is open to later changes; (3) science is a qualified knowledge (with more rigor, in principle, than any other human knowledge); and (4) it consists of processes to develop methods of research (normally they are deductive, although some authors accept inductive methods [Niiniluoto and Tuomela 1973]), and science appears as a dynamic

[19] The *evolutionary economics* can be seen as a specific approach regarding the dynamics of economics that takes a notion originated in biology—"evolution"—but it is applied to many other branches of science (see Nelson and Winter 1982).

[20] *Scientific prediction* is a concept that is used in scientific publications in a wide number of cases: earthquakes, volcanic activity, photosynthetic productivity, protein structure and function, child development or job behavior, tsunamis, etc.

activity of a self-corrective kind, which seeks to increase the level of truthlikeness (basic science) or to solve particular problems (applied science).

Apart from these characteristics, there are other elements of science which have been emphasized in recent times: (5) the reality of science itself comes from a social action, and the features of this human activity are different from other activities in its assumptions, contents, and limits; (6) science has aims—generally, cognitive ones—for guiding its endeavor of researching (in the formal sphere and in the empirical realm); and (7) it can have ethical evaluations insofar as science is a free human activity, whose values are related to the processes of research (honesty, originality, etc.) or to its nexus with other activities of human life (social, cultural, political, etc.).[21]

Definitely, these components of a science, which present a complex reality, and the concept of "prediction," which is connected with them, are based in the human character of the science. Actually, science is not something purely abstract—"the" science—or merely sociological—scientists making science—but rather a *human activity* articulated around those constitutive elements (language, structure, knowledge, method, etc.). In this regard, it can be said that *the* science is *our* science (Rescher 1992). This affects the problem of the limits of science and, therefore, the boundaries and bounds of scientific prediction. On the one hand, the limits can be understood as "barriers" (*Schranken*), which—according to Immanuel Kant—distinguish the safe way of science and the non-scientific orbit; and, on the other hand, the "confines" (*Grenzen*) of scientific activity can be drawn, i.e., the ceiling or terminal limit that can be reached by science (Radnitzky 1978).

In the first place the issue of prediction as a requisite for science can arise within the "barriers"—the specific realm of scientific activity as different from other domains—and only afterwards may it be studied in the context of "confines" (see Gonzalez 2012b). Our science, insofar as it is our science, is open to the future. Moreover, due to the "principle of proliferation of questions" (where each response given raises a new question which needs to be answered), it is problematic to foretell which contents the science will have after several decades; there exists a congenital difficulty in predicting future science with some reliability, because of the emergence of new issues in domains already explored and the discovery of previously unknown areas which lead to new questions.[22]

If it is assumed that science is lacking clear terminal limits and, at the same time, that it is always open to a progressive revision, then it is possible to accept that, in principle, scientific prediction can in the future improve its level of reliability as soon as there exists an enlargement of our knowledge of the variables within a specific domain. However, this cannot always be the case, because it could be that

[21] On these seven elements of science, cf. Gonzalez (1997a, p. 265). See also Gonzalez (2005, pp. 10–11).

[22] This might lead to the unpredictability of future predictions, which could be the absence of confines—terminal limits—in science. Rescher sees the problem from the point of view of the impossibility—in his judgment—of present science saying how the future science will be, cf. Rescher (1984, Chap. 7, pp. 95–111).

the reality itself present features whose nature can make it "not predictable" or even "unpredictable" for our science[23] (in addition to the problem indicated of the predictability of the science itself of the future).

Even though there are relevant problems on prediction in the context of the confines of science, usually the basic problems arise from prediction within the barriers of science, which is commonly discussed under the label of "demarcation." To distinguish between the complex phenomenon of science and what it is not science is a controversial issue. Moreover, besides philosophers of science who—in one way or another—defend the existence of such a demarcation (with different criteria, as in the case of Reichenbach, Popper or Lakatos), there are other philosophers who propose the demise of the demarcation problem (like Larry Laudan 1983), or claim "anything goes" in methodological matters (like Paul Feyerabend 1975).

Regarding this issue, the criterion here is in favor of a *demarcation* between science and non-science, taking into account the constitutive elements already pointed out. Thus, the frontiers should be given by the characteristics of a science (language, structure, knowledge, method, dynamic activity in a social setting, aims, and values) insofar as they are different from the features of other kind of disciplines or human activities. This requires considering each one of those elements, although some of them have a clearer relation with the problem of prediction as a requisite for the science and, specifically, with prediction as a test for economics as a science.

1.2.2 Diversity of Philosophical Analyses of Science

Each of the characteristics of a science can be analyzed from a philosophical point of view. Semantics of science studies this specific language, which is more precise than an ordinary one; logic of science works on the internal structure of scientific theories; epistemology clarifies this qualified knowledge; methodology of science deals with the procedures followed by the scientists to increase the knowledge—the methods and their possible changes—and also prescribes the dynamic activity in order to improve the self-correctiveness; ontology of science sees scientific endeavor as a social action (a kind of entity in the social world); axiology of research considers the aims of science (mainly, cognitive ones); and ethics of science examines the values of this free human activity (Gonzalez 2001a, pp. 15–17).

Scientific prediction, in general, and economic prediction, in particular, cannot be unfamiliar to the diversity of analyses of science. In fact, the issue of prediction as a requisite for science—as an aim, as a test, and as a guide for prescription—may receive attention at diverse levels, although the crucial one is the methodological study insofar as the main issue is to examine prediction as a test of having science. Put differently, the initial question—*to predict or not to predict*?—can have different answers according to the characteristic to be considered, but the key problem

[23] On these notions—"not predictable" and "unpredictable"—see Chap. 2.

is mainly methodological (i.e., a test to ensure that something—a procedure—is "scientific" instead of "non-scientific").

As regards the main line of response to the question of prediction as a scientific test, there are at least two options: (i) prediction as a *strong demarcator*, when it is seen as an inherent factor of science itself (i.e., an indispensable element of scientific theories); and (ii) prediction as a *weak demarcator*, when it is used to warrant that a statement or knowledge claim is "scientific" instead of "non-scientific" (or even that something is more scientific than other conceptions which do not include predictions or which have no success in predicting). These options lead to the determination of whether prediction is a *necessary condition* (a strong demarcator) or only a *sufficient condition* (a weak demarcator). In this regard, the diversity of analyses is important.

Semantically, scientific language is more rigorous and demanding than ordinary language or any other language. The sense and reference of scientific terms guarantee the possible absence of equivocal content and also the identification of the referent. In the act of predicting, the statements that express scientific propositions have, in principle, sense (*Sinn*) but that they have reference (*Bedeutung*) is more dubious.

Hence, Gottlob Frege's criterion might be applied: if there is no reference—the semantic value of the referent—then there is no truth in the proposition or "thought" expressed (such as in poetry, where—in his judgment—a sense can be expressed without relation to the truth).[24] But this criterion might be problematic: it can be interpreted that it legitimates the explanatory language, where there is a guarantee of sense and reference of terms used, whereas it may question the predictive language (insofar as it deals with a future whose truth can be unknown or unsettled).

Nevertheless, this semantic approach based on Frege cannot be interpreted or utilized in a reductive manner, because otherwise the problems of "verification" principle, like in logical positivism, or the difficulties of "verifiability," like in logical empiricism, might return.[25] The semantic requirement, understood in a realist perspective and adjusted to statements on the future, allows that something can have *reference* (and, thus, the possibility of truth value of the proposition expressed by the statement), even though it might not be possible to make an identifying reference at the moment of saying the statement (and, thus, without making effective the semantic role of the reference). Therefore, the term "neutrino" could have reference, in addition to sense, even though an identifying reference to the particle neutrino would have been impossible when its existence was predicted by first time.[26]

---

[24] Cf. Frege (1892). On reference as "semantic role" and "semantic value," cf. Gonzalez (1986, pp. 131–136).

[25] To some extent, this objection can also have repercussion for the anti-realist semantics proposed by Michael Dummett and developed with some changes by Crispin Wright. The problem has its roots in the attempt to substitute the concept of "truth" by the notion of "proof," cf. Gonzalez (1998d).

[26] Among the Nobel Prizes in physics given in 1995 is Frederick Reines, who received the award by confirming the existence of neutrino, a particle predicted many years earlier by other physicists (Enrico Fermi, Wolgang Pauli, and Hans Bethe).

A similar case can appear in explanations whose referents originate problems due to the difficulty of ensuring their existence (in natural sciences, some theoretical terms—like "black holes"—and in social sciences several cases, such as the identification of the first inhabitants of certain civilizations). Hence the *predictive language* is not in an essentially different situation from the explanatory language: in both cases the acceptability of the *sense* of the terms behooves a cognitive content, and the *reference* appears basically as a relation to a referent, by means of which something is identified (and whose reality does not emerge with the use of the term). The semantics of prediction allows a predictive language about the future whose status of being true or false might not be specified on the basis of the knowledge available.[27]

Logically, the existence of well-structured scientific theories does not imply, in principle, that they should be predictive. In effect, that a theory and its models may have a well-formed structure and fulfill some formal properties, such as consistency, does not depend a priori on its having or not having predictive character. It is the nature of theory at stake that—in its statements or in its core and intended applications—it can adopt one form or another:

(a) Explanatory (e.g., historical theories or genetic studies that research past events); (b) explanatory and predictive (e.g., many theories in the empirical domain, either of natural sciences, of social sciences, or of sciences of the artificial); and (c) predictive (e.g., in cases of theories interested in astronomical phenomena, in certain studies about seismological movements or tsunamis, in lines of research about the climate change, etc.). Accordingly, not all theory includes—as a theory—the predictive component as a constitutive element, either in the *statements* of the theory or in the *components* of the core of the theory (in the case of an analysis following the structuralist conception).[28]

Hence, there are several possibilities. Among them two are basic. They can be represented by the economic theory of "rational expectations" of Robert Lucas—Nobel Prize in 1995—[29] which possesses statements of a predictive kind, and the biological theory of evolution by natural selection, proposed by Charles Darwin, which was not originally conceived with a predictive perspective (i.e., "prediction" is not among the *components* of the core of his evolutionary theory).[30]

In the first case, Lucas develops "rational expectations" in economics, where the dynamic economic models emphasize the role of rationality and the expectations of firms tend to be distributed about the prediction of the theory. These ideas were

[27] If prediction is understood as a "testable implication regarding the future"—as a projection towards the future of explanatory statements—, then there is no problem: not only the sense of the language is accepted but also its reference (at least as semantic role).

[28] The initial proposal by Joseph Sneed of a scientific theory—as a pair consisting of a core (a structure) and its intended applications—has been enlarged regarding the components of the core. The structuralist conception of theories accepts proper models, potential models, partial potential models, constraints, and links (cf. Balzer et al. 1987; Balzer and Hamminga 1989).

[29] Cf. Lucas (1977, 1978, 1988).

[30] According to Michael Scriven, a satisfactory explanation of the past is possible even when prediction of the future is not possible, cf. Scriven (1959, p. 477).

initially proposed by John Muth (1961), who presents a direct connection between rational expectations and economic predictions: "I should like to suggest that expectations, since they are informed predictions of future events, are essentially the same as the predictions of the relevant economic theory" (Muth 1961/1981, p. 4).

As for the second case, the theory of evolution by variation and natural selection does not require necessarily the existence of a predictive component as a specific element. Thus, Darwin figures among the best known scientists, even though this biological theory does not make explicit predictions on the future of actual species or does not foretell the coming into existence of creatures of some novel species.[31] Moreover, his conceptual revolution appears among the most important in the history of science.[32] Therefore, it is risky to stipulate as an indispensable requisite that a scientific theory should be *predictive* when it is not demanded by its own internal structure. In other words, it is problematic to insist on the scientific prediction as a necessary condition to demarcate what is or is not science.

Besides the well-articulated internal structure of scientific theories, the adequate *cognitive content* is required. That a theory be logically well structured (or even that it be completely axiomatized) is not a guarantee of the reliability of its cognitive content (and consequently of its predictions). Historically, this has been the case many times, including the famous sociological report of the Club of Rome in 1970, which had demographic predictions made on false premises.[33] It is now crystal-clear that the best theories can include mistakes and this feature has been stressed by the epistemological fallibilism.

Epistemologically, it is assumed that a common feature of scientific knowledge is its testability and, thus, there is a means of assuring its *reliability*. But this is problematic for future events of different kinds, either due to its intrinsic difficulty to be tested (e.g., in chaotic systems) or because the period of time required in this regard (as John Maynard Keynes liked to say "in the long run, we are all dead").[34] In addition, the variables that intervene in the process studied can change during its own development over time, which makes the success in predicting more valuable.

Thus, it is a difficulty for predicting (and for testing the predictions) which raises the question of giving more weight to prediction than to explanation (Gonzalez 2010a, epilogue). This discussion leads to the issue of the philosophico-methodological debate in science on "predictivism" (see Barnes 2008). In economics the emphasis on the success in predicting as the best *test* for the reliability of scientific

---

[31] In this regard, Toulmin maintains that many of the most powerful theories did not state "verifiable forecasts," like the Darwinian theory of evolution by means of variation and natural selection. On this issue, cf. Toulmin (1961, pp. 24–27; esp., p. 24).

[32] On the conceptual revolution introduced by Darwin, cf. Gonzalez (1996a, pp. 618–625). This paper revises the analysis made in Thagard (1992).

[33] This case of the Club of Rome report is pointed out in Simon (1990a). It is also analyzed in Simon (1996, pp. 147–148).

[34] An analysis of Keynes' views on economics can be found in Blaug (1991).

knowledge has been very influential. Led by Friedman, the predictivist orientation has set prediction as a test for economics as a science.[35]

With hindsight, it is not difficult to reconstruct historically the development of modern science from the point of view of prediction. It has had a singular acknowledgment among many philosophers and scientists. Thus, at the origin of modernity, Francis Bacon emphasized the role of prediction in the appraisal of scientific theories and rejected Aristotelian methodology as non-predictive. Afterwards, Isaac Newton's theory was reinforced due to the success of Edmund Halley's prediction of the comet's return. In nineteenth century, William Whewell stressed the importance of the prediction of new phenomena as evidence for or against a theory; and, for August Comte, the aim of all science was the prevision, because the laws established by means of the observation of phenomena should be used to anticipate their succession.

During the last century there have been well known repercussions of success in predictions, such as the prediction of the displacement of spectral lines towards the red by the gravitational potential, which was stressed by Einstein for his theory of relativity (1920, p. 132). In addition, it is well known that several philosophers (such as Reichenbach, Popper, or Lakatos) emphasized prediction in science (at least, in the general methodology of science). But it is also the case that other philosophers (such as Kuhn, Salmon or Rescher) have pointed out the epistemological and methodological importance of prediction.[36]

However, in spite of that relevance given to predictive knowledge, it is overdemanding—from an epistemological point of view—that every scientific theory should include statements on future events. It seems clear that not all scientific knowledge has a relation to the future or needs to call on prediction as a guarantee of reliability, because much scientific knowledge deals with the past and the present without the possibility of saying, in the strict sense, that they are "predictive."[37]

Likewise, there are many cases of explanatory theories that do not include *prima facie* a predictive dimension. In fact, it is frequent in social sciences that theories are produced to explain what has happened (not only in history, but also in anthropology, sociology, psychology, etc.). Moreover in economics not all theory is predictive; and descriptive (or "positive") economics present theories that are not thought

[35] Besides this line in the methodology of positive economics, there is a long-standing commitment in econometrics to validating causal inference through its predictive accuracy, i.e., Grangerian causality. In this regard, there is an analysis of causal inference from several disciplines: Sobel (1995). The quality of prediction (of new data) is not the only means of testing a hypothesis. A key question is also the appropriateness of the testing means to the terms and conditions of the hypothesis.

[36] See, in this regard, Gonzalez (2010a), where there is an analysis of eight philosophico-methodological conceptions on prediction, those proposed by Reichenbach, Popper, Toulmin, Kuhn, Lakatos, Salmon, Kitcher, and Rescher.

[37] There is an old discussion on the role of "retrodiction" and the so-called "prediction of the past," cf. Toulmin's chapter "Forecasting and Understanding," in his (1961), pp. 18–43.

of as predictive, because they deal, for example, with structural phenomena, both in microeconomics and in macroeconomics.[38]

Methodologically, scientific prediction originates problems in the general scope—methodology of science—that have repercussions for the sphere of methodology of economics. They require the previous elements (language, structure, knowledge, activity, etc.), because the method is a process to increase or to improve something already existing. Thus, the key issue is not merely the *success* in predicting but rather to grasp the *process* itself that makes it possible to get reliable predictions. "Scientific prediction" is not purely a kind of statement about the future. In this regard, it is implausible to maintain the possibility of scientific predictions without reasons.[39] Rationality is an essential ingredient of the process of increasing our scientific knowledge.[40]

Therefore, there is a rationally based methodological process, which distinguishes the scientific prediction from the non-scientific one. This evinces that a pure instrumentalist view—the emphasis on the success itself of the prediction made—is faulty, because in science the process itself is particularly relevant in increasing or improving our knowledge. Nevertheless, not all scientific method needs to be predictive, insofar as cognitive progress is made on the basis of the knowledge available and this does not need to be intrinsically connected to the future. Thus, it is perfectly legitimate that some kinds of methods (such as those related with history) do not have predictive character.

Ontologically, science possesses a specific kind of reality: it comes forth from a human activity of social character, and can be distinguished from other activities due to its assumptions, contents and limits.[41] Its ontological status allows science to deal with any variety of phenomena, either in the past and present or in the future. Insofar as prediction is a statement on future events, it literally works on what do not exist. "Ontologically speaking, the future is non-existing (as long as we leave the supernatural out of it—as, given our limited powers, we must). Nor can the future as such exert any causal influence on the present—though of course our *ideas* about it will have a major formative impact in what we think and do. All the same, prediction is *not* a matter of describing the utterly inexistent; rather it is an attempt to foretell what will be there when the time comes and what will have been there when the time has come and gone" (Rescher 1998, p. 70).

It seems clear that, from an ontological point of view, prediction is needed insofar as scientific activity requires describing the future (in basic science, in applied science, and in the application of science), something that literally has not yet

[38] Maybe this is the ultimate reason for finding very important books on philosophy and methodology of economics, such as Hausman (1992a), where there is no section on economic predictions and prediction does not appear in the final subject index.

[39] This can be found in Mellor (1979, p. 221).

[40] On scientific rationality and technological rationality, see Gonzalez (1998c).

[41] On the relations with technology and, specifically, the proposal of a "technoscience," cf. Gonzalez (1997a and 2005, pp. 8–13).

entered upon the scene (either in the natural realm, the social domain or the artificial sphere). Prediction deals with "novel facts," according to several criteria of novelty (strictly temporal, heuristic, regarding background theory, and for the individual). These novel facts, in several ways, have been emphasized by Lakatos. Their characteristics are analyzed later on (Chap. 4).

Axiologically, science has a set of values, factors that imbue at least the specification of aims or ends of scientific research. The scientific values can be classified in two different realms: (i) the *internal* values to the scientific activity itself, those which are present in the process itself of making science (mainly, cognitive values); and (ii) the *external* values to the scientific endeavor, those which connect science with the other aspects of human experience (social, cultural, ecological, etc.). This means that science is not "value-free" (*Wertfrei*) but rather "value-laden." In addition, the issue of aims in science is not so simple as the "received view" thought, because to choose an aim in science depends on the values accepted.

Laudan has contributed to this change in vision with *Science and Values* (1984). Since then, the axiology of research has gone deeper into the analysis of values in science and its role in establishing scientific aims. Prediction is commonly among the scientific aims based on cognitive values. In the case of economics, prediction is also related to other kinds of values (practical, social, etc.) due to its nexus with prescription. The problem then is not its existence as a scientific aim but rather if prediction could be the *main aim* in science, in general, or in economics, in particular.[42] On such an issue it seems more prudent to maintain that prediction is indeed a *very important* aim in science, but it is not, in principle, the main aim of science.

Ethically, science may receive attention insofar as it is a free human activity and involves decision-making. This is also partially recognized by Laudan: "ethical values are always present in scientific decision making and, very occasionally, their influence is of great importance" (1984, p. xii). The ethical values can appear in this social activity—science—due, basically, to three features: (a) science is a human activity developed *intentionally* (it is deliberately oriented to chosen aims); (b) it possesses a specific *content* distinct from any other human endeavor (with repercussions which could be both theoretical and practical); and (c) it is interconnected with a great variety of human activities (social, cultural, political, etc.) even though it preserves its *autonomy*, because science has specific mechanisms of self-correction (Gonzalez 1999a, esp., p. 143).

Following these three features, the ethics of science can be developed in two directions: (1) it can attend to "science as activity" in itself (aims, means, and results of the research process), which leads to an *internal* study of scientific endeavor; and (2) it can examine "science as one human activity among others" which emphasizes the *external* factors of the scientific research as such (social, cultural, political, etc.) within a historical setting. In both cases science appears as a social action

[42] As will be analyzed in Part II, several thinkers assume that prediction is a central aim in science or even the crucial aim. In addition, mainly in Part III, it can be seen that some influential economists insist on prediction as the basic aim of science.

performed by free agents. The problem for ethical evaluation is, generally, when the focus is in the first case, when aims, means, and results of the research process are considered. This is even more obvious in basic science than in applied science.

Nowadays, it seems clear that scientific *knowledge* as such—a pure cognitive content—cannot receive an ethical evaluation (Rescher 1999a). Ethics of science examines the values—or their absence—in scientific *activity*. In this regard, prediction as such—a descriptive content on the future—cannot be evaluated ethically insofar as it is only knowledge. The relation might be through the presence of prediction in the *research activity*, mainly when the ethical limits of science are discussed. Thus, in order to make a decision on the acceptability of a particular research (e.g., human cloning), we need to know what can happen if an experiment is made. This relation between prediction and decision could exist in basic science and, more clearly, in applied science. Economics present both dimensions, and the role of ethics in this science undoubtedly varies from some parts to others.[43]

1.2.3 Prediction as a Test of Science

Taking into account the contributions made by the diversity of philosophical analyses of science and having stressed the methodological character of the question, the main issue should be addressed as follows: can prediction be a test of science? The response is also clear: prediction could be *a test* but not *the* single test for a science. Thus, prediction is a requisite of science in general (and, therefore, of economics insofar as it is a science), but it is not an *intrinsic characteristic* of science itself.

Appropriately, prediction is a weak demarcator: it is a factor which can guarantee the scientific nature of language, structure, knowledge, method, ... used in a specific domain; nevertheless, in order to have "science," it is not indispensable to count on predictions. If prediction were a strong demarcator, the actual "barriers" between science and non-science should be moved to exclude positions usually considered as scientific (such as the theory of evolution by natural selection, which has been utilized in the large list of posterior evolutionisms, present in almost any social science).[44]

Given these criteria, the question raised by Hutchison—to predict or not to predict?—is answered in favor of the first possibility, but not in an exclusive manner: prediction is a sufficient condition for a science, not a necessary condition. Furthermore, that use of prediction—as a test—is not the only one used in science. There is

[43] "Moral insights will, to be sure, be more important to some parts of economics than others. Moral ideas will not help much in forecasting the price of wheat or in refining theories of exchange rate determination. (Exchange rates and wheat prices do however result from the choices of human beings—not profit-maximizing automatons—and the moral dimensions of their choices might sometimes have some significant impact)" (Hausman and McPherson 1996, p. 4).

[44] Interestingly enough, there are some reflection on whether "could economics be a biological science?" cf. Rosenberg (1992, pp. 152–199).

at least another dimension of prediction: that directly related to *prescription*.[45] This is especially the case in economics, where besides a "descriptive" (or "positive") branch it has another realm that is "normative" (or "applied").

Between these two options,[46] the different role of prediction is clear: in the first case, it belongs to the attempt to *describe* economic activity in the real setting (the agents in the transactions of goods and services, the decision-making regarding supply and demand, etc.), looking at the future; whereas, in the second case, prediction is put to the service of prescriptions—as a guide—which seek the *desirable* courses of action to achieve some specific ends. (These relations between "prediction" and "prescription" are explicitly analyzed in Chap. 12).

Understood as a scientific test, prediction depends on the *content* itself considered. Thus, according to the amplitude of the scientific content, prediction is easier or more difficult. There is a correlation established by Rescher, who considers that the more informative a prediction is, the less secure it is, and vice versa, the less informative a prediction is, the more secure it is.[47] In addition, regarding the future science, he also thinks that an important feature of scientific inquiry is the existence of *unpredictable trends*, which are of special significance just because of their unpredictability. Thus, the more important the scientific creativity is, the less predictable it is, because its very unpredictability is a component of crucial importance (Rescher 1999b, p. 102).

Suitably, prediction can be used as *a test* to establish something as scientific as opposed to non-scientific. The diverse *constitutive elements* of science (language, structure, knowledge, method, activity, aims, and values) have a relation to the future: in the natural sciences, in the social sciences, and in the sciences of the artificial. Economics is directly concerned with this feature—as can be appraised in several chapters of this book—and the controversy reaches its peak when Hicks denies that economics is a "science" (cf. Chap. 6).

Insofar as it is accepted that a science consists of those constitutive elements, the perspective to consider economics as a science is open, because it is assumed that

---

[45] Within the economic field, the uses of prediction as a scientific test and as an element connected with prescription are emphasized by Herbert Simon elsewhere, especially in (1990a).

[46] There is a third option: the use of prediction by the policy-makers in the variety of settings of the historical contexts.

[47] "Consider some applications of this principle: (1) It is easier and safer to forecast general trends than specific developments. (2) It is easier and safer to forecast over the near future than over the longer term; long-range forecasts are inherently more problematic. (3) The fewer and cruder the parameters of a prediction, the safer it becomes: it is easier and safer to forecast aggregated phenomena than particular eventuations (e.g., how many persons will live in a certain city 10 years hence as compared with how many will belong to a particular family). (4) The more extensively a prediction is laden with a protective shield of qualifications and limitations, the safer is the prediction. (5) The more vaguely and ambiguously a prediction is formulated, the safer it becomes; particularly equivocal predictions have an inherent advantage. (6) The prediction of possibilities and prospects is safer and more secure than that of real and concrete developments. (It is one thing to predict what will be feasible at a given 'state-of-the-art' and another to predict what will be actual.)" Rescher (1984, p. 99). In this regard, cf. Rescher (1984, pp. 79–83).

economics has all those factors. To point out that prediction is not a necessary condition of having "science" leads to the criticism of the extreme thesis defended by Hicks (i.e., economics as a "discipline" rather than a "science"). When the general components of science are considered, it cannot be asserted—in my judgment—that economics is only a mere discipline.

1.3 Prediction and Present Features of the Science

Besides the characteristics of a science—the constitutive elements—there are *additional features* of a science that are pertinent within a general scope. Some of them are frequently accepted in our time as traits of what *is* and *ought to be* a science: objectivity, critical attitude, autonomy, and progress.[48] These are built upon the constitutive elements and then serve to configure the present image of a developed science. They will be used here to analyze the way in which the constitutive elements of science are presented nowadays.

Objectivity, critical attitude, autonomy, and progress can be seen as supplementary factors to the constitutive elements (language, structure, knowledge, method, activity, values, ...). In this regard, they can be grasped as a particularization or specification of the characteristic constituents of a science. Furthermore, all of them directly affect to the general methodology of science, due their being related to the "self-corrected" nature of scientific inquiry.[49] In the case of prediction, these features can have a particular repercussion—mainly in practical contexts—when at stake is the difference between a scientific prediction and non-scientific one.

While every feature at stake—objectivity, critical attitude, autonomy, and progress—can raise philosophical controversy, insofar as each can be disputed by different orientations of science—especially by post-modern approaches—[50] they are actually very relevant in the development and evaluation of science. Moreover, they play a key role in the professional journals as criteria for publication and in the committees for evaluating research projects. *De facto,* they are commonly assumed as representatives of "mature science," "*well-ordered science,*" and the like (Gonzalez 2006a).

[48] Cf. Niiniluoto (1984, pp. 4–7). Among other places, this topic is analyzed in Gonzalez (1990a, pp. 19–20). A projection of these features on the case of the science of history is made in Gonzalez (1996e, esp., pp. 69–75).

[49] For Niiniluoto, these general features "seem to be inseparably connected with any reasonable conception of science" (1984, p. 4). New developments of his views on science are in Niiniluoto (1999).

[50] Sometimes in postmodern views the emphasis on "external" factors is so strong that it becomes controversial insofar as "internal" constituents are diluted, cf. Haack (1998), and Koertge (1998, 2000).

1.3.1 Objectivity

Prima facie, scientific research should be characterized nowadays by its *objectivity*. Certainly, "objectivity" is a complex notion within the scientific realm, and it can be connected with any of the constitutive elements of a science (language, structure, knowledge, method, activity, values, …). Usually, objectivity plays a key role in the semantic, epistemological, methodological and ontological views on science.[51] In recent decades, it has been highlighted in the controversies between scientific realism and its alternatives (e.g., Dummett's semantic anti-realism, Laudan's epistemological pragmatism and methodological instrumentalism, and the diverse ontological relativisms, both of historical roots or of sociological extraction). In addition, objectivity is also a central topic of the disputes between scientific realism and its antagonists (idealism, solipsism, and skepticism).[52]

Common features of "objectivity," which are valid for any level of analysis (e.g., semantic, epistemological, methodological or ontological), are presently these:[53] (i) objectivity is a factor that, in principle, is *accessible to any person* (i.e., objective is something which potentially could be grasped by any scientist); and (ii) it is a component that, in principle, has an *existence independent* of a singular mind (i.e., objective is a trait which cannot be reduced to the possession of the mind of an unique scientist).

Both ideas are already in Frege's remarks on *Objectivität*, but he tends to emphasize the second one, going beyond realism to reach out to Platonism.[54] His main focus was on language (especially mathematical language), whereas here the interest is broader: the analysis also pays attention to epistemological questions and, above all, to methodological issues. (The analysis can be enlarged with the problem of the objectivity of the values in science, which is a topic discussed by Rescher 1999a).

Nonetheless, those features of "objectivity"—potential accessibility and independence from a singular mind—originally thought of as scientific language, are also compatible with other aspects that are usually pointed out in epistemological and methodological contexts. These features of objectivity are related with the

[51] On the characterization of scientific objectivity, cf. Gonzalez (1993a, esp., pp. 33–35).

[52] The controversies between scientific realism and its alternatives as well as the disputes between scientific realism and its antagonists are analyzed in Gonzalez (1993a, pp. 23–30). See also Gonzalez (2006a).

[53] According to Nicholas Rescher, "the objective/subjective distinction has undergone a curious inversion in the history of thought. In pre-Kantian days—from the time of Scholastics such as Suarez to that of Descartes, Spinoza, and Berkeley—for something to obtain *objectively* was for it to exist as on object of thought (as an idea or other item of mental representation), while for it to obtain *subjectively* or *formally* was for it to exist as an actual subject in the real world, independently of whatever mental representation might be connected to it. (…). For Descartes 'objective' meant being an object to a thinking mind, and 'subjective' meant being a mind-independent subject of thought. However, Immanuel Kant reversed this situation. For him subjectivity involves a correlativity to thinkers—to subjects who carry on an inquiry—and objectivity implies a thinker-independent, self-sustaining object of possible consideration" (Rescher 1997, p. 215).

[54] Regarding scientific objectivity and Gottlob Frege's approach, cf. Gonzalez (1993a, pp. 33–35).

process, the contents, and the results of scientific activity. They assume an ontological factor: there are characteristics that belong to something with properties different from the researcher.

Properly speaking, objectivity can be related to three aspects: (a) the *process* of grasping those contents should be of a public character, which leads to the principle of publicity and avoids a "private validity"; (b) the *contents* of that knowledge are the basis for an impartial judgment regarding natural phenomena, social events or human artifacts; and (c) the *results* of the research require severe tests in order to avoid subjective aspects and also merely intersubjective factors.

Scientific research is a *process* that should be characterized by its *objectivity*. For Ilkka Niiniluoto, this means that, in order to be scientific, an inquiry has to be objective in two senses: "First, the object of investigation has to be real in [Charles S.] Peirce's sense, i.e., its characteristics should be 'independent of what anybody may think them to be'. Secondly, the object should be allowed to influence the formation of the result of inquiry, and this influence should be intersubjectively recognizable" (1984, p. 4). Thus, an information *process* based upon private intuitions or instincts of the investigators, non-repeatable experiments, or any kind of phenomena that is not intersubjectively testable possesses no weight of evidence.

Although there are subjective factors in science (motives, tastes, desires, beliefs or personal suppositions), it should emphasize the objective level: the *contents* of science, in general, and scientific prediction, in particular, should be based on what is obtained from the object investigated. A form of balancing the subjective facet (or even "subjectual:" it belongs to the subject, but it does not need to be purely individual) is in the principle of publicity, because only what is put to critical discussion within the scientific community can be accepted as an outcome of research.

Appropriately, scientific prediction—in the natural sciences, in the social sciences or in the sciences of the artificial—should be under critical discussion in the context of scientific community. This does not mean that objectivity can be reduced to mere intersubjectivity (such as shared beliefs of the scientists at a given moment in history), but rather that the latter makes the former easier: objectivity is something accessible to the researches (properties of the object) and not a mere agreement or consensus among them.

This epistemological mode of objectivity is clearly connected with the methodological objectivity and has to do with the *justification* of a scientific claim.[55] "It pivots on the way the claim is substantiated and supported—namely without the introduction of any personal biases or otherwise distortive individual idiosyncrasies, preferences, predilections, etc." (Rescher 1997, p. 4). It is a sort of probative objectivity which leads to results coordinating with rational cogency.

Accordingly, scientific *results* must show a rational appropriateness insofar as scientists proceed in a way that will lead to the same knowledge which can be possessed by other scientists. This is clear in the case of simultaneous discoveries (such

[55] "Neither the fact that major scientific controversies are protracted nor our inability to delineated a precise account of scientific evidence should undermine our confidence that the resolution of scientific debate on the basis of evidence is possible. The ideal of objectivity need not be dismissed as a fond delusion" (Kitcher 2001, p. 41).

as the prediction of the boson that has the name of Peter Higgs, even though the mechanism on how mass can be generated was simultaneously predicted in 1964 by Francois Englert with the collaboration of Robert Brout), where the objectivity of the result shows also the rational character of the scientific process.

In addition to the objectivity in the epistemological and methodological realms, there is—in principle—an *ontological objectivity*. Science is—in one way or another—object-oriented: it is focused on real things instead of mere appearances. The scientific claims deal with objects in the real world (past, present, and future) rather than with ephemeral phenomena (or impressions or speculative possibilities) and comparable things of the mind. It is an ontological objectivity that separates what is, in some way, connected with existing things from what is somehow ideational and mind-bound (Rescher 1997, pp. 3–4). This issue is particularly relevant in the case of scientific prediction, which deals with future events and requires considering the reality of the future and the kind of ontological objectivity that could be pertinent to it.

Within the general philosophy and methodology of science, objectivity has been a feature stressed by Popper in the realms of epistemology and methodology as well as in the ontological dimension, but he did not pay attention to semantic objectivity. Lakatos went beyond him, insofar as he emphasized the role of the *historicity* in his methodology of scientific research programs.[56] Lakatos connected historicity—not merely temporality—and objectivity as elements of the scientific programs. Thus scientific theories are not purely temporal, in the chronological order of succession, but rather historical insofar as they undergo deep changes through time (Gonzalez 2001c). This revocability of past knowledge can be connected with the search for epistemological and methodological objectivity.

Historicity is not incompatible with objectivity. Moreover, human reality and scientific activity are historical in an objective way. Each one of the constitutive elements of science (language, structure, knowledge, method, activity, values, …) is *historical* insofar as can have changes that modify its status through the time. A key issue is how to harmonize historicity and objectivity in any science, including mathematics,[57] as well as in the diverse levels of science (at least in the semantic, epistemological, methodological and ontological levels). This connection between historicity and objectivity is at the bottom line of important controversies on scientific processes, such as the dispute between Worrall (1988, 1989b and 1998), and Laudan (1984, 1989, 1998a) about the status of the methodological principles.[58]

[56] On the role of historicity in science, see Gonzalez (2011b).

[57] The issue of historicity also appears in mathematics, cf. Lakatos (1976). Cf. Gonzalez (1998d, esp., pp. 311, 316–317, 339 and 342–343).

[58] On the changes in Laudan's epistemological and methodological views, cf. Gonzalez (1998e).

1.3.2 Critical Attitude and Autonomy

Insofar as objectivity in science is not understood as a timeless feature, because science is a human activity developed through historical contexts, it seems easier to connect objectivity and the three additional factors of critical attitude, autonomy and progress. In this regard, the search for scientific objectivity is—and should be—lead by a critical attitude, which seeks to differentiate it from subjective elements and merely intersubjective aspects. Moreover, the critical attitude that looks for objectivity may also serve to search the truth-seeking aim (basic science) or the adequate solution of concrete problems (applied science).

Epistemologically, objectivity is accepted commonly by scientific realists (in their different versions), but it is also something that certain pragmatists do (Laudan 1990, 1996, 1998b; see Gonzalez 1998e). Methodologically, objectivity in science requires that one assume a *self-corrective* capacity in scientific activity, in general, and in making predictions, in particular. The reason is clear: there does not exist an authority that can claim a permanent position or may offer a final report. Thus, each scientific knowledge is in principle under revision, which brings about the need for revising the predictive knowledge. Therefore, the prediction made can be modified insofar as there is more information or new contents about some phenomenon or event.

As a common feature of science, this preference in favor of a *critical attitude* in contemporary science is especially important for the social sciences and the sciences of the artificial in order to refine their aims, processes, and results. Moreover, the existence of a succession of positions (either explanations or predictions) to improve our comprehension of the reality should not be seen as an intrinsic deficiency of a science. This explicit option in favor of the critical attitude comes from Popper, who considers it as the axis of his methodological orientation (cf. Chap. 3). In effect, falsificationism relies on the critical attitude, which eventually is seen as decisive to determine whether or not a statement is scientific.

Critical attitude is seen by Popper as a requisite both to rational attitude and to scientific attitude. He insisted, although not from the very beginning,[59] that *falsification*—the methodological pattern to test our own theory or hypothesis seeking actively its flaws in order to see if it is false—and *refutation*—the consideration of a theory or hypothesis as untenable, because it is false, due to the available evidence or what the "crucial experiment" has laid out—rely on the knowability of what is false and the critical attitude to discharge it.[60] Later on, mainly in the period of evolutionary epistemology (1960–1972), his view was that, following the use of the

[59] "In 1919–1920, there was still much that Popper found confusing about science and philosophy. Contrary to his autobiographical accounts, he had not yet settled on testability, or falsifiability, as the demarcation between science and pseudoscience, or science and metaphysics" (Hacohen 2000, p. 96).

[60] For Lakatos, falsifications do not behave automatically as a refutation like in the case of Popper, cf. Lakatos (1974a).

critical attitude, we can know that a statement (or set of statements) is true or at least closer to the truth than other statements (i.e., "verisimilitude" or "truthlikeness").

Additionally, the *radical character* that Popper gives to the critical attitude constitutes a point of collision with the authors of the "historical turn." For Kuhn (1962, 1977, 2000), Lakatos (1970), and Laudan (1977), scientific practice teaches us that scientists act based on some previous assumptions that they do not argue (at least, for a while). Furthermore, the "paradigms" (or the "disciplinary matrix" and the "exemplars"), the "research programs" and the "research traditions" emphasize the *historicity* in science instead of a logico-methodological process. These authors assume that historicity in science carries out a kind of critical attitude that is not something "instantaneous," because it is connected with a sort of rationality that is not static.[61]

According to that scientific rationality embedded in historicity, the critical attitude is developed in a historical setting. The acceptance or rejection of a scientific claim is a process done through time and is not merely a punctual phenomenon (like Popper's rationality of a "crucial experiment"). Even the evaluation of a scientific prediction is not, in principle, a process done following a rationality of "all-or-none." The critical attitude in science requires *revision* within some margins and, eventually, the results can also be revised at a later moment. In this regard, the strong criticism of "historicism" made by Popper, rejecting the existence of a logical basis for social prediction, comes from a radical critical attitude that does not correspond to actual scientific activity (cf. Chap. 3).

However, Popperian fallibilism fits well with another feature of present science: *autonomy*. Scientific endeavor has a character that is primarily internal: the revision of scientific progress and its results cannot be done from any authority external to scientific community.[62] The autonomy of science attains its constitutive elements (language, structure, knowledge, method, etc.). Consequently, it belongs to science as an institutional activity. When the autonomy of science is perturbed, the specificity of scientific activity disappears: "the community of investigators ceases to be a scientific community if it gives up—or is forced to give up—this principle of autonomy" (Niiniluoto 1984, p. 6). From this point of view, it is risky to adopt

[61] Lakatos insists on the need of combining scientific rationality as historical and objectivity (cf. Chap. 4). Laudan wants to preserve that combination but he declines to seek true theories, considering the process as a "quixotic enterprise." This affects directly to his criticism of relativism, cf. Gonzalez (1999b).

[62] Historically, "the original use of the term *autonomy*—literally *self-legislation*—in antiquity referred to a property not of persons, but of polities. Autonomous city-states made their own laws; colonies were given laws by their mother cities. And (…) Kant ascribes autonomy not to persons, but to the will or, more accurately, to determinations of the will or principles" (O'Neill 2003, p. 3). "The context of Kant's account of autonomy is a distinctive view of action. Kant looks at action from the agent's standpoint; that is, from a practical point of view. He depicts agents as having a *power of choice* (*Willkür*) that they can use in innumerable ways" (O'Neill 2003, p. 7). For Kant, "there are some principles of action that are not derivative from supposed, but ultimately arbitrary 'authorities'" (O'Neill 2003, p. 16).

positions such as the finalization thesis,[63] where the external factors to science can determine the course of the scientific dynamics.

In the case of social predictions, in general, and economic predictions, in particular, there is more concern about the relations between internal and external factors than in natural predictions. In fact, there is an ingredient uncommon for prediction in natural sciences: the possibility of predictions made which can affect the course of the predicted phenomena themselves. This reflexive possibility has been analyzed by philosophers, such as Popper (1957) in his book *The Poverty of Historicism* (like an "Oedipus effect"), as well as social scientists in different fields (economists, sociologists, political scientists, etc.). Among them, there are some economists, such as Emile Grunberg and Franco Modigliani,[64] who is also the 1985 Nobel Prize in economics, who have studied this issue.

Grunberg and Modigliani have analyzed the aft-remarked assertion that after a prediction has been published, there is a reaction of the economic agents that can modify the course of the events and, thereby, they may falsify the prediction. In the conclusion of their paper, these economists consider that it "establishes the falsity of the proposition that the agents' reaction to public prediction necessarily falsifies all such prediction and that therefore social scientists may never hope to predict both publicly and correctly. But it demonstrates no more than that correct prediction if the possibility of correct private prediction is accepted."[65]

Both in public predictions and in private ones, it is assumed that the predictive process derives from mechanisms that are distinct from science itself. Moreover, predictability depends on the capacity of scientific knowledge as such—insofar as it is *our science*—to grasp the reality that it studies. Thus, the limits of science from a predictive point of view depend on the knowledge of the variables. The limits of predictions have their roots in the *self-corrective* character of science as such.[66] For this reason, it is certainly risky to establish the predictive limits of future science on the basis of the present stage of scientific knowledge.[67]

When this question is looked at backwards in the history of science, it is clear that, in the origin of modern science, scientists were aware of the predictive fecundity of that new science (mainly in physics), but *de facto* they did not predict very important phenomena (e.g., the advancements made by quantum theory, the achievements of the theory of relativity, etc.). And, looking forward on this issue, we should be careful to disregard *a priori* the future predictability of some phenomena or events, even in the case of social events (including economic ones),

[63] This thesis was defended by a research group at Starnberg (Germany): Gernot Böhme, Wolfgang van den Daele and Wolfgang Krohn. On this view and, in general, on the issue of the autonomy of science, cf. Niiniluoto (1984, pp. 226–243); and Gonzalez (1990c, pp. 100–104, 108–109).

[64] Cf. Grunberg and Modigliani (1954). From another angle, there is an analysis of the role of a published prediction in Simon (1954).

[65] Grunberg and Modigliani (1954, p. 478).

[66] The self-corrective nature of science is emphasized in Rescher (1978).

[67] The idea of unpredictability of future science is a recurrent theme in Rescher's writings, cf. Rescher (1999b, Chap. 7, pp. 94–110), and Rescher (2012). The openness of future social science is stressed in Rosenberg (1993).

which are usually more complex than physical happenings.[68] In this regard, when scientific prediction is possible, the success in predicting will depend on, above all, internal factors to science (the language that identifies the reality, the structure of scientific theories, the depth of the scientific knowledge, the rigor of methods used, the quality of the scientific activity, etc.).

1.3.3 Progress

Through the feature of progress, our present science embraces the existence of improvements (mainly in the cognitive contents) but combined with the possibility of variations. Scientific progress, which was intensely studied three decades ago,[69] is now open to conceptual revolutions. Today the conception of *scientific progress* is quite different from that tendency in favor of the idea of advancement of science as linear and accumulative, such as the positivists in nineteenth century or the neopositivists in the last century used to think. The criticisms of the authors more attentive to the history of science (Kuhn, Lakatos and Laudan)[70] have shown that scientific progress does not follow that way.

Nowadays it is generally accepted that there are deep changes in science (in "paradigms," "research programs," "research traditions," etc.). Thus, there are some challenges to harmonize historicity in science with the existence of a variety of values (coherence, cognitive cumulativism, truth, truthlikeness, etc.) that can be used to warranty the scientific progress.[71] Some of these challenges affect the possibility of progress in scientific prediction. It seems to me that after the "historical turn," it is not possible anymore to talk of a view of "scientific prediction" as purely linear and accumulative, because the progress of prediction is under the same kind of changes as science is as a whole.

Following this framework for the relations between scientific progress and prediction, the concept of *progress* should be characterized in dynamic terms.[72] (i) Progress is something related to a *goal* or *aim*. It cannot be restricted to present developments of science—a descriptive role—because it should give indications (or "normative standards") to assess the decisions of the scientific community. (ii) The goal or aim of science is not one-dimensional or unidirectional, but *multidimensional*

[68] In the case of economic activity, this aspect is analyzed in Chaps. 7 and 8 (mainly, the Sect. 8.4).

[69] From 1975 to 1985, it was the central topic in the general scope (philosophy and methodology of science). Thus, besides the publications of Rescher (1978), Laudan (1977), and Niiniluoto (1984), already pointed out, there are another relevant books on "scientific progress" in that period: Harré (1975), Radnitzky and Andersson (1978), Dilworth (1981), Shäfer (1983), and Pitt (1985).

[70] In the criticism to the concept of progress of the "received view" the key publication was Kuhn (1962). On the issue of "scientific revolutions," cf. Gonzalez (1996a, 2004a).

[71] That is the main concern of the chapter "Realism and Scientific Progress" in Kitcher (1993, pp. 127–177).

[72] This presentation follows Gonzalez (1990c, pp. 99–100). The analysis is based on Niiniluoto (1987, pp. 151–154).

or *multidirectional*: there does not exist a concept that can embrace all aspects of scientific progress. Nevertheless, the improvement of knowledge is particularly important. Moreover, a theory of scientific progress should start from the criteria of *cognitive* progress.

Furthermore, there are other features of scientific progress. (iii) The goal or aim used to measure the progress should be *accessible*, i.e., it should be possible to achieve it following a limited number of steps, within a finite time. The crucial question for the theory of scientific progress is: how is it possible to make rational assessments on the advancement towards the truth? (iv) The goal or aim must be *recognizable in an effective way*, because there should be tests to show that it has been reached or, at least, that there is an approximation to it. (v) For many activities oriented to goals or aims, it is important to distinguish between quality and progress. In the teleological domain, *quality* concerns ability and competence in doing a task: it is a concept related to the activity itself (and it could be the case of efficiency); whereas *progress* is a notion connected to an outcome: it deals with the product that is obtained seeking a goal (and it might be the case of efficacy).[73] Thus, there are no intrinsic conjunctions of quality and progress in science.

Finally, there are another two features of scientific progress: (vi) The goal or aim can be seen in a *retrospective* way but also in a *prospective* manner. To define "progress" in prospective terms emphasizes the cognitive distance towards the final end. When the goal is not known, then the stress goes to the appraisals of progress based on retrospective considerations. (vii) The failures in the proposals of "scientific indicators" to establish progress in science are due to avoiding the consideration of *semantic content* of scientific publications. Scientific progress is a *quantitative* concept ('the transit from the theory A to the theory B is progressive in such and such degree'), but it also allows for *comparative* judgments ('the transit from A to B is more progressive than the path from A to C').[74]

Clearly, this presentation of the features of "scientific progress" interconnects on at least three levels: semantic, epistemological, and methodological. (1) "Progress" belongs to a language with some specific characteristics: it possesses a *sense*—a content—of objective advance towards a goal or aim which may be achieved, and the *reference* is a reality which could be better known than previously. (2) There is an *epistemic advancement* in comparison with the initial situation. (3) The content of *improvement*—both semantic and epistemological—connects with methodological concepts, such as "testability," "truthlikeness," "corroboration," "accuracy," "precision," etc., and eventually with "explanatory power" and "predictive power." At the bottom, there is a notion of science which combines a dynamic activity—oriented towards something actively sought: to increase the level of truthlikeness—with a clearly propositional vision, where the statements can be used to express contents which eventually could be true.

[73] "Scientific progress" and "technological innovation" has some coincidences and also some differences, cf. Gonzalez (1997a, esp., pp. 261–265). See also Gonzalez (2013b).

[74] The comparative character of scientific progress is stressed by Lakatos (cf. Chap. 4). It can be found in other authors as well (Laudan 1998b).

From the perspective of scientific prediction, this approach to progress is useful: it can highlight the semantic, epistemological, and methodological aspects of prediction in science, in general, as well as in economics, in particular. Furthermore, this teleological presentation of progress can support a better comprehension of the nexi between prediction and prescription, because cognitive progress on scientific prediction serves to the prescriptive task, which belongs to normative economics. Thus, *descriptive economics* can reflect the presence of scientific progress as a matter of fact (in tune with some criteria, mainly epistemological and methodological), and *normative economics* can use predictions to think of the change of the course of events or how to steer them towards specific aims (something very common in applied economics, as a previous step for the application of economics through an actual political economy).

Prediction is a factor of scientific progress insofar as it includes a cognitive upgrading of the "research programs" or the "research traditions" in comparison with previous programs or traditions. This increase of content is assessed in comparative terms, analyzing if the succession of the theories in the research programs or research traditions brings in conceptual, empirical or heuristic advancement on "novel facts." (Their characteristics and different kinds are pointed out in Chap. 4.) In this regard, there is still an open discussion on what is more progressive: to predict in advance future phenomena, or to accommodate already known facts.

This issue, which will appear in different ways in this book, is a boundary question between the authors in favor of the predictive thesis and their opponents.[75] For the former, success in predicting is a guarantee of reliability of scientific knowledge, because it is assumed that predictions are methodological harder than accommodations; whereas, for the latter, the accommodations (either in the context of *Erklären* or even within the circle of *Verstehen*)[76] could be good enough for the purpose of scientific progress.

However, science in itself does not cease when it is unable to make predictions. It could be the case of scientific domains where *explanation* or *understanding* of phenomena (natural, social, or artificial) was sufficient without the need for predictions on future events. Thus, some theories may be scientific even though they do not make any explicit prediction (as it happens with the initial theory of evolution based on "natural selection," developed by Darwin).

But their character as a "complete" scientific theory ordinarily will demand them to project towards the future the scientific knowledge available[77] (as it has been the case with evolutionism in biology during last century). Therefore, although prediction may not be an indispensable component of science, it seems inconvenient to leave making predictions unattended, because scientific explanation might often be

[75] On the strong and weak versions of predictivism, see Barnes (2008, pp. 24–27). In addition, he distinguishes four types of predictivism (2008, pp. 80–82).

[76] This issue affects directly to social sciences, in general, and to economics, in particular. The analysis is made in Chap. 5.

[77] A special case is history, because its primary domain is past events. However, one of the main concerns of Popper's thought is precisely "historical prediction," cf. Chap. 3.

insufficient for scientific purposes without the presence of predictions (mainly in economic contexts).

Still, the impossibility of making predictions genuinely scientific can be argued (Gilbert and Berger 1975). Basically, these arguments can follow two main lines: the *strong* view and the *weak* option. The first one is of a *logical* or *methodological* nature: there does not exist any possibility of predicting future events scientifically on the basis of present knowledge, because it is not possible to infer logically or methodologically the coming phenomena based on actual situation. And the second one is the impossibility conceived in *practical* terms: we are not able to predict the future with the support of existing knowledge at every moment.

Those lines in favor of the impossibility of making predictions genuinely scientific do not exclude the possibility of having scientific progress. (a) Not all scientific theory needs *eo ipso* to make predictions (as it can be seen in the history of science or even nowadays); and (b) scientific progress comes primarily from *conceptual* changes, related to scientific creativity and technological innovation, which can be increased by social factors around scientific activity (Gonzalez 2004a and 2011b).

Moreover, the kind of logical or methodological argument against predictability, which is used, for example, by Popper in his rejection of "historicism," has received strong criticisms (see Chap. 3, Sect. 3.3); and the practical impossibility of predicting should be reconsidered, because there is a conceptual innovation which comes with the new questions after answering the previous queries, and this could be a sign of scientific advance, of whose contents we do not know which will be right now.[78] Thus, this novelty opens the door for a scientific progress, which is a historical process. And scientific prediction is above all a methodological concept, directly associated with the problems raised by scientific progress.

1.4 The Relations Between Basic Science–Applied Science and the Role of Prediction

Another key issue for the role of prediction for science is the distinction between *basic science* and *applied science*, which has a particular relation to the issue of scientific progress, both in theoretical terms (i.e., the characterization of the advancement of science) as well as in practical terms (i.e., science oriented to policy, in order to solve particular problems). Thus, in the present vision of science, the differentiation can be seen from the point of view of the internal contents but also from the external repercussions for society as a whole.

Yet the difference is sometimes neglected—both conceptually and pragmatically—arguing that it is either imprecise or unnecessary. In addition, the instrumentalist approach insists on the subordination of basic science to applied science, which moves science towards a strong connection with technology. This situation is also

[78] The topic is analyzed in Rescher (1983).

related to an external factor, which is the economic support of the projects of research and development (R&D),[79] because the endorsement tends more frequently to those projects that have economic consequences (such as patents). Nevertheless, some international institutions related with this issue, such as the OECD, recognize the existence of differences between basic science and applied science.[80]

1.4.1 The Distinction Basic Science–Applied Science

Conceptually as well as pragmatically, there are differences between basic science and applied science.[81] Moreover, the distinction can be seen in both internal and external terms. From an *internal perspective*, basic science and applied science are human activities with differences in three levels: (i) the aims or goals which they search; (ii) the means or processes which they use; and (iii) the kind of results or outcomes that they obtain. Also from an *external orientation*, basic science and applied science can have also differences on institutions (both in the case of approving and funding the research projects and to develop them) and on social evaluation (insofar as applied science commonly affects more directly to the persons and the society).[82]

Considering the *internal perspective*, it seems clear to me that the *aims* or goals of basic science are different from those of applied science (which should not be identified with "the applications of science").[83] The research in basic science is oriented directly towards achieving new knowledge or to increasing the present knowledge, in order to arrive in a systematic way at explanation of the natural happenings, or to understand the social events, as well as to predict novel facts. Meanwhile the research in applied science has a more specific goal: to grasp new knowledge in order to resolve a concrete problem (natural, social, or artificial) or to increase the efficacy in its solution. This second case receives a special weight from the nexus between prediction and design (Niiniluoto 1995a, pp. 127–130).

Concerning the *means*, there are also differences between both varieties of science. The distinction of the kind of process depends initially on the type of aims or goals that are sought. In effect, in basic science the scientific method (usually

[79] There are some countries that think of research, development, and innovation (R&D&I).

[80] Cf. OECD (1996, pp. 89–90). (This book was published in English with the title of *R&D Statistics and Output* and in French as *Manuel de Frascati 1993*).

[81] On the need of the distinction, cf. Sintonen (1990). A detailed analysis of the distinction, with special emphasis in the features of applied science, is developed in Niiniluoto (1993). See also Niiniluoto (1995b).

[82] The distinction between basic science-applied science from the internal perspective and the external orientation can be seen clearly in the case of ethical values in science, cf. Gonzalez (1999a).

[83] "It is important to distinguish *applied* science from the *applications* of science. The former is a part of knowledge production, the latter is concerned with the use of scientific knowledge and methods for the solving of practical problems of action (e.g., in engineering or business), where a scientist may play the role of a consult" (Niiniluoto 1993, p. 9).

hypothetical and deductive) seeks preferentially to increase the cognitive contents: the relevant knowledge claims should be empirically grounded (i.e., the epistemic components should be superior to the knowledge claims possessed by the alternative scientific theories). Scientific progress may be then comparative: commonly it involves a cognitive advancement in comparison with competitive theories. In applied science there are additional factors: the means are operative insofar as have a direct relation with specific ends. Thus, practical knowledge should allow us to get more efficient processes to solve the concrete problems that arise (those problems which were the very origin of applied science).[84] Efficiency—economy of means—is assessed in the simplicity and manageability of the processes used as well as in the parsimonious factors. Therefore, applied sciences look for efficacy with few means and low costs (both in terms of effort and economy).

Respecting the *results*, there are also differences between basic science and applied science. The roots are in the structure of the relevant knowledge claims. Basic science (e.g., fundamental biology or economic theory) brings about results that are assessed according to the *growth* in the scientific knowledge available (i.e., the augmentation of the cognitive contents or the accretion in the truthlikeness) (Niiniluoto 2002) without considering its possible utilization for a present problem. However, applied science (e.g., pharmacology or applied economics) involves results that are evaluated within *cognitive parameters* (the adequacy of a piece of information to resolve a specific issue risen) and *practical* ones (the ability to overcome in operative terms—simple and manageable—a concrete difficulty). The evaluation of results, even though it can also be related to truthlikeness (in the domain of its applicability, i.e., a practical knowledge),[85] is then more pragmatic or instrumental than in basic science; and the testability in applied science is in principle more immediate than in the other, insofar as it uses less general statements and knowledge claims.

With regard to the *external perspective* (science in the social context), there could also be variations in the kind of institutions (public and private) that develop basic science or work on applied science. The differences are rooted in the intellectual status of applied science, which is usually located between basic science and technology. Commonly, the external and functional criteria is not clear cut, because applied science could be elaborated in specific research centers (e.g., in the field of business administration), but frequently the institution moves on towards one side or the other, according to its needs.

It happens that applied science is sometimes done in research centers where the main focus is basic science (e.g., in many university departments), whereas in other

[84] In applied science, insofar as the factor of design is crucial, the interest is in controlling natural and artificial systems. Furthermore, "they do not describe reality, but rather tell what we ought to do in order to realize our goals" (Niiniluoto 1995a, p. 128).

[85] Niiniluoto maintains that there is a difference between "truth" and "practical success." For him, practical success does not prove the truth of a theory: it is only an indicator of its truthlikeness, cf. Niiniluoto (1995a, pp. 138–139). The truth of the theory of applied science only would imply its *potential* pragmatic success (i.e., it could be the case that is actually never implemented), cf. Niiniluoto (1993, p. 6).

cases it is matured in institutions specifically interested in technology (e.g., industrial corporations), which undertake applied science due to its links with the technological endeavor (e.g., pharmacology used by pharmaceutical enterprises). This situation has its bedrock in the fact that the *linear process of research* is not very common (i.e., from basic science to applied science, and from this to technology), because the interaction processes are predominant due to the needs of the concrete institution (e.g., in university hospitals).

Altogether there are differences—conceptual and pragmatic—between basic science and applied science, both internally and externally, even though there is a *practical interaction* in many institutions devoted to scientific research. In addition, they are also connected with technology, which is scientifically supported and which, at the same time, can improve science (e.g., the calculating procedures run by computers to make economic predictions in the macroeconomic sphere).[86] In each case of science—basic or applied—it seems that predictions, in general, and economic predictions, in particular, can have some distinctive characteristics from epistemological and methodological viewpoints. This can be seen in the different approaches to prediction within economic theory (both in microeconomics and in macroeconomics) and within the several branches of applied economics (such as statistical economics and econometrics).

To assume merely that there is a difference between basic science and applied science (e.g., economic theory and applied economics) is not good enough in order to characterize scientific prediction (mainly in the field of economics). A bifurcation should be emphasized: prediction as a utility for *describing* economic phenomena and prediction as a tool in connection with *prescription* (e.g., in design science). Thus, prediction can be pursued in order to *increase our knowledge* (basic science) or to *resolve practical problems* in a concrete area (applied science). Meanwhile, technological prediction is oriented towards a *creative transformation of reality* (either natural, social, or artificial), according to a design, which is followed by an activity and a subsequent artifact (or final product).

Therefore, these possibilities should be taken into account in a wider analysis of scientific prediction in the field of economics.[87] (1) *Basic science* is mainly "descriptive science:" commonly it seeks explanation and prediction of natural phenomena (e.g., a tsunami), social events (e.g., future business cycles) or artificial dealings (e.g., the impact of new financial products). Ultimately the research seeks the aim of truth in scientific claims or at least to increase the truthlikeness (to get

---

[86] Technology is an activity that is developed in an intersubjective doing in order to *transform* the previous reality (natural, social, or artificial), based on scientific knowledge as well as specific technological knowledge. As a consequence of this process, there is an expected product that should be tangible: a visible artifact or a new kind of social reality. This final product of technology might be registered in a patent, which could hardly be the case in the final outcome of science (even in applied science). On the features of "technology," cf. Gonzalez (2005, p. 12); and Gonzalez (2013c).

[87] This analysis differs from Niiniluoto's approach insofar as "predictive science" could be "basic research" (e.g., in astronomy) and basic science can go beyond "descriptive science." Cf. Niiniluoto (1993, p. 14).

epistemic goals or ends with scientific theories, which are structured independently of the solution of concrete problems or specific practical applications). (2) *Applied sciences* seek manageability and practical suitability (the pursuit of knowledge to obtain a specific goal in a delimited terrain). In this sense, applied research includes prediction and prescription: it can combine *predictive science* and *design science*[88] (i.e., predictions connected with prescriptions in order to get a goal, such as to diminish inflation). Then prediction could be a relevant point of connection between basic research and applied research, which is certainly the case in economics, where economic theory and econometrics should not be disconnected. (3) *Technology* based on scientific *problem solving*, which is located beyond the focus of attention here, should be seen in the context of the relations between science and technology (Gonzalez 1997a, pp. 266–269).

1.4.2 Predictive Science: From Basic Research to Applied Research

Usually, the tasks of *descriptive science* include—at least for the authors keen on scientific realism—"systematic studies and explanations of the present state of reality and its lawlike regularities, historical or postdictive studies about the past, and predictive studies about the future" (Niiniluoto 2001, p. 372). Frequently, theories of physics or economics, in addition to initial conditions about the present and boundaries conditions about the environment, can yield predictions about observable happenings or events of the future.

Obviously, these phenomena are not commonly necessary facts based on previous ones (e.g., the trajectory of planets) but rather contingent events of the future (e.g., supply and demand of goods). However, in both cases—necessary facts and contingent events—there are, in principle, *ceteris paribus* assumptions, because even a deterministic system could be unstable insofar as it is sensitive to the variations in its initial conditions (Earman 1986), as the theory of chaos has insisted for at least two decades.

Basic science can have a relevant descriptive role, but "description" alone does not fit well with all the tasks of explanation (or understanding) and prediction. Scientific explanations are answers to "why-questions" and the replies can go beyond the mere descriptive aim.[89] In fact, there are a variety of scientific explanations that search different purposes (e.g., functional explanations and genetic or historical explanations). Scientific predictions are statements on future events based on the present stage of human knowledge. Predictions can be made for different aims: to test a theory, to prevent undesired events or outcomes, etc. Some of them have a relevant descriptive content whereas others are prescriptively oriented.

[88] The most important book in this regard is Simon (1996). On the topic of the sciences of design, and economics as a science of design, see Gonzalez (2007b and 2007d).

[89] That is also the case in the approach based on "understanding," cf. Chap. 5.

This includes that "basic sciences are *descriptive* in the sense that they primarily describe, with sentences in the indicative mood, singular and general facts about the world. They seek to establish theories which express true and lawlike (nomic) connections between properties or types of events" (Niiniluoto 1993, p. 7; e.g., 'X causes A in situation B' or 'X tends to cause A with probability *p* in situation B'). Laws—deterministic or probabilistic—and other kind of general statements can be used for prediction. Moreover, in some cases (such as celestial mechanics), the same laws can be used for explaining past phenomena (e.g., eclipses) and also for predicting future events. But descriptive aims are not the only ones to be pursued (i.e., not all cognitive values of basic science are descriptive).

Predictive science has a rather complex position, which includes basic research and applied research: (a) prediction can have a descriptive aim of a basic science (e.g., astronomy, economic theory, etc.); and (b) predictive science is essential for applied science that works on a design (e.g., pharmacology, applied economics, etc.). Following this twofold status, both aspects should be emphasized:

(i) Predictive science as basic research offers *descriptive knowledge* about the future. So, "many 'ordinary' scientific disciplines—like physics (…), psychology, and economics—have futuristic relevance in the sense that their theories, together with initial conditions about the present and boundary conditions about the environment, yield predictions about observable events in the future" (Niiniluoto 2001, p. 372). (ii) Predictive science in the area of *applied science* is based on the interest in successful predictions for various practical reasons. Thus, "a scientific theory, which is able to produce reliable predictions about future events, has *predictive power*. Practical astronomy, meteorology, and social statistics are examples of applied sciences which have predictive power as their central epistemic utility" (Niiniluoto 1993, p. 7).

Therefore, predictive science can progress in the case of basic science as well as in applied science. Regarding the first aspect, it seems to me that there are no good reasons to distinguish *basic research* and *predictive science* as distinct endeavors that are associated under the label of "descriptive science." (1) It is not sufficiently clear the possible difference between "basic research" and "predictive science" within "descriptive science;" and (2) the expression "descriptive science" is not good enough to reflect the kind of activity developed by the scientists. The aim of this type of research and the structure of the knowledge claims in this domain are more "explanatory" or "predictive" than "descriptive." To explain (to answer "why-questions") is a more complex activity than to describe, and to predict usually has more aspects than to describe (to test, to control, etc.).[90]

Sometimes a distinction is used to evaluate research projects, which may be useful here: "non-oriented basic research" (i.e., a kind of research that ultimately will

[90] According to Wesley Salmon, "there are at least three—probably more—legitimate reasons for making predictions. First, we are sometimes curious about future happenings, and we want to satisfy that curiosity without waiting for the events in question to transpire. (…) Second, we sometimes make predictions for the sake of testing a theory. (…) Third, we sometimes find ourselves in situations in which some practical action is required, and the choice of an optimal decision depends upon predicting future occurrences" (Salmon 1981, pp. 115–116).

not lead to applied research) and "oriented basic research" (i.e., a type of research that eventually can be linked to applied research). This distinction, which belongs commonly to science policy, can intervene not only in internal factors (epistemological, methodological, etc.) but also in external values (social, economic, etc.). The reason is clear: the *oriented basic research* can lead to applied science and, in some countries, it receives more attention than basic science. Consequently, these nations are more reluctant to support *non-oriented basic research*, giving a superior value to pragmatic aims over cognitive aims. In spite of this external consideration, it seems obvious that some predictions are "non-oriented basic research" (e.g., predictions on "black holes" in distant galaxies) and other are "oriented basic research" (e.g., predictive medicine connected with genetic studies), which is usually the case of economic predictions.

Categorically, future studies cannot be limited to the sphere of "descriptive science," because applied science also deals with the future phenomena (unobserved events) and should consider what should be done (i.e., "prescription"). In this regard, the object to be studied in *future studies* is like a branching tree with different possibilities, where chance events and human choices have a role towards a future still open. Thus, the study of the alternative scenarios to be realized or to be avoided should consider several aspects, such as (i) how to *construct alternative* possible futures, (ii) how to *assess the probability* of alternative futures, and (iii) how to *evaluate the preferability* or desirability of alternative futures (Niiniluoto 2001, p. 373).

1.4.3 Applied Research: Predictive Science and Design Science

Within the realm of applied research, prediction appears as a common methodological tool: the need to anticipate knowledge of what seems possible should precede the rules on what should be, or can be, done (e.g., in applied economics). The progress in scientific prediction is central to improve in the area of prescription. This can be seen in any *design science* and, therefore, in economics as a science of design. The emphasis is then on the relation between prediction and prescription, which will receive special attention later on in this book (cf. Chap. 12). In order to design something in science, the common path is to consider in advance if the project is possible (i.e., prediction), before we give the indications about how to resolve the problem that is foreseen (i.e., prescription). Thus, to make a prediction is, in principle, chronologically prior to establishing a prescription when the problems involved are in the realm of design science (e.g., operations research in business).

Design science has been emerging since the mid-1970s. Around 1975 a Design Research Center was created at Carnegie Mellon University, and since 1985 it has been the "Engineering Design Research Center." Thus, this field started in the domain of the sciences of the artificial. "In substantial part, design theory is aimed at broadening the capabilities of computers to aid design, drawing upon the tools of artificial intelligence and operations research. Hence, research on many aspects of computer-aided design is being pursued with growing intensity in computer science, engineering and architecture departments, and in operations research groups in business schools" (Simon 1996, p. 114).

Indeed, designing is a teleological activity: commonly, design "is concerned with how things ought to be, with devising artifacts to attain goals" (Simon 1996, p. 114). Habitually, the number of alternatives is not unlimited and it can be a serious problem to optimize. Thus, according to Simon, "we cannot within practical computational limits generate all the admissible alternatives and compare their respective merits" (1996, p. 120).

The science of design is directly connected to prescribing: the design looks for courses of action whose aims are to change existing situations into preferred ones, and those processes require that some paths be prescribed to be followed. This characteristic affects prediction, because "design like science is a tool for understanding as well as for acting" (Simon 1996, p. 164). In both cases—understanding and acting—the design has consequences in the future.

For this reason, it seems that *prediction* is an unavoidable part of every design process and "the quality of design is likely to depend heavily on the quality of the data available. The task is not design without data but to incorporate assessments of the quality of the data, or its lack of quality, in the design process itself" (Simon 1996, p. 146). This is the case of data for social planning as happens in the much discussed Club of Rome report, where the understanding of the phenomena and the suggestions for acting have been a failure.

Simon has considered that the main failure is in what the Club of Rome report predicted (1996, pp. 146–147).[91] For him, "good predictions have two requisites that are often hard to come by. First, they require either a theoretical understanding of the phenomena to be predicted, as a basis for the prediction model, or phenomena that are sufficiently regular that they can simply be extrapolated. (…) The second requisite for prediction is having reliable data about the initial conditions—the starting point from which the extrapolation is to be made. Systems vary in the extent to which their paths are sensitive to small changes in initial conditions" (Simon 1996, p. 147). On the one hand, Simon thinks that the condition of extrapolation (i.e., phenomena that are sufficiently regular) is seldom satisfied by data about human affairs, and, on the other, he considers that we have reasons to admit that social phenomena are also sensitive to initial conditions.

Niiniluoto sees Simon's account as ambiguous insofar as he does not distinguish clearly between "design" (which appears in many professions) and "scientific design" (which adds new factors). "Scientific design is a species of design, i.e., the activity of solving design problems by using scientific methods and scientific knowledge. Operations Research (OR) provides methods for finding optimal or satisfactory solutions to design problems (e.g., game theory, decision theory, linear programming). In this sense, scientific design is the result of the 'scientification' of art, technology, management, or development" (Niiniluoto 1993, pp. 8–9).

In this regard, there is initially a professional activity (i.e., a practice according to some implicit or explicit rules) and, later on, the emergence of scientific design,

[91] The Club of Rome report is also analyzed in Simon (1997, pp. 110–111, 118–119, 123, 419).

within a scientific context. It belongs to the applied research: scientific design generates "instrumental knowledge for the production and manipulation of natural and artificial systems. Design science produces knowledge which may then be applied within scientific design" (Niiniluoto 1993, p. 9).

When Niiniluoto analyzes this issue of design science and prediction in the context of future studies, he considers that *future studies* are seeking its identity as a new academic discipline (2001, pp. 371–377). In this context, it seems clear to me that future studies cannot be reduced to the model of "descriptive science," and they require that the design sciences (the main branch in the field of the sciences of the artificial) be included.

But "design" should not be identified with "planning in the broad sense," because there are conceptual and pragmatic differences between them (cf. Chap. 2), especially when planning emphasizes the role of direction of human action and the temporal dimension of the activities to be developed. In addition, I consider that Simon rightly points out that human rationality follows the path of "satisfacing" rather than the "optimal means" for reaching—in a systematic way—accepted ends.

Nowadays it is clear that progress in applied sciences should include the development of design sciences, where the aim is not properly to tell how the things are, but rather how they *ought to be* in order to achieve some goals. This involves a relation between means and ends (i.e., efficiency and effectiveness), which should be considered in present sciences, such as economics, that deal with human and social practice. The science of design always looks at the future and requires prediction and prescription: it is a kind of *future studies*, which combines the tasks of exploring *probable* and *preferable* futures.

Meanwhile, in doing both tasks, design science is a mixture of theoretical and empirical research. Moreover, a science of design can go beyond the philosophico-methodological analysis to reach out to the sphere of political action (Niiniluoto 2001, p. 377), which is the application of science. This is the case in economics, where applied economics deals with macroeconomic phenomena searching for what should be done regarding public policy (the patterns for the solutions of problems), which later on might be implemented in national economy and in international economy.[92]

References

Backhouse, R. E., ed. 1994a. *New directions in economic methodology*. London: Routledge.

Backhouse, R. E. 1997. *Truth and progress in economic knowledge*. Cheltenham: Elgar.

Balzer, W., and Hamminga, B., eds. 1989. *Philosophy of economics*. Dordrecht: Kluwer (reprinted from *Erkenntnis* 30(1–2), 1989).

Balzer, W., Moulines, C., and Sneed, J. 1987. *An architectonics for science*. Dordrecht: Reidel.

Barnes, E. C. 2008. *The paradox of predictivism*. Cambridge: Cambridge University Press.

[92] The relation between applied economics and political action is emphasized in Joseph E. Stiglitz, Nobel Prize in 2001, cf. Stiglitz (1991).

Blaug, M. 1976. Kuhn versus Lakatos, or paradigms versus research programmes in the history of economics. In *Method and appraisal in economics*, ed. S. Latsis, 149–180. Cambridge: Cambridge University Press (reprinted in Blaug, M. 1986. *Economic history and the history of economics*, 233–264. Brighton: Harvester Press).

Blaug, M. 1980. *The methodology of economics: Or how economists explain*. Cambridge: Cambridge University Press.

Blaug, M. 1991. Second thoughts on the Keynesian revolution. *History of Political Economy* 23:171–192.

Caldwell, B. J. 1982. *Beyond positivism: Economic methodology in the twentieth century*. London: Allen and Unwin (revised edition 1994. London: Routledge).

Collins, H. M. 1983. An empirical relativist programme in the sociology of scientific knowledge. In *Science observed: Perspectives in the social study of science*, ed. K. D. Knorr-Cetina and M. Mulkay, 85–100. London: Sage.

Dilworth, G. 1981. *Scientific progress: A study concerning the nature of the relation between successive scientific theories*. Dordrecht: Reidel.

Earman, J. 1986. *A primer on determinism*. Boston: Reidel.

Einstein, A. 1920. *Relativity: The special and the general theory*. London: Methuen (reprinted in London: Routledge, 1994).

Epstein, R. J. 1987. *A history of econometrics*. Amsterdam: North-Holland.

Feyerabend, P. K. 1975. *Against method: Outline of an anarchistic theory of knowledge*. London: New Left Books (3rd ed., London: Verso, 1993).

Frege, G. 1892. Über Sinn und Bedeutung. *Zeitschrift für Philosophie und philosophische Kritik* 100:25–50.

Friedman, M. 1953. The methodology of positive economics. In *Essays in positive economics*, M. Friedman, 3–43. Chicago: The University of Chicago Press (6th repr., 1969).

Giere, R. N. 1971. The structure, growth and application of scientific knowledge: Reflections on relevance and future of philosophy of science. In *In memory of Rudolf Carnap*, ed. R. C. Buck and R. S. Cohen, 539–551. Dordrecht: Reidel.

Gilbert, M., and Berger, F. 1975. On an argument for the impossibility of prediction in the social sciences. In *Studies in epistemology*, ed. N. Rescher, 99–111. Oxford: Blackwell.

Gonzalez, W. J. 1986. *La Teoría de la Referencia. Strawson y la Filosofía Analítica*. Salamanca-Murcia: Ediciones Universidad de Salamanca and Publicaciones Universidad de Murcia.

Gonzalez, W. J. 1990a. La Ciencia y los problemas metodológicos. El enfoque multidisciplinar. In *Aspectos metodológicos de la investigación científica*, 2nd ed., ed. W. J. Gonzalez, 15–46. Madrid-Murcia: Ediciones Universidad Autónoma de Madrid and Publicaciones Universidad de Murcia.

Gonzalez, W. J. 1990b. Ámbito y características de la Filosofía y Metodología de la Ciencia. In *Aspectos metodológicos de la investigación científica*, 2nd ed., ed. W. J. Gonzalez, 49–78. Madrid-Murcia: Ediciones Universidad Autónoma de Madrid and Publicaciones Universidad de Murcia.

Gonzalez, W. J. 1990c. Progreso científico, autonomía de la Ciencia y realismo. *Arbor* 135(532):91–109.

Gonzalez, W. J. 1993a. El realismo y sus variedades: El debate actual sobre las bases filosóficas de la Ciencia. In *Conocimiento, Ciencia y realidad*, ed. A. Carreras, 11–58. Zaragoza: SIUZ-Ed. Mira.

Gonzalez, W. J. 1994. Economic prediction and human activity. An analysis of prediction in economics from action theory. *Epistemologia* 17:253–294.

Gonzalez, W. J. 1995. Reichenbach's concept of prediction. *International Studies in the Philosophy of Science* 9(1):37–58.

Gonzalez, W. J. 1996a. Towards a new framework for revolutions in science. *Studies in History and Philosophy of Science* 27(4):607–625.

Gonzalez, W. J. 1996e. Caracterización del objeto de la Ciencia de la Historia y bases de su configuración metodológica. In *Acción e Historia. El objeto de la Historia y la Teoría de la Acción*, ed. W. J. Gonzalez, 25–111. A Coruña: Publicaciones Universidad de A Coruña.

Gonzalez, W. J. 1997a. Progreso científico e innovación tecnológica: La "Tecnociencia" y el problema de las relaciones entre Filosofía de la Ciencia y Filosofía de la Tecnología. *Arbor* 157(620):261–283.
Gonzalez, W. J. 1998c. Racionalidad científica y racionalidad tecnológica: La mediación de la racionalidad económica. *Agora* 17(2):95–115.
Gonzalez, W. J. 1998d. "Verdad" y "prueba" ante el problema del progreso matemático. In *Filosofía actual de la Ciencia*, ed. P. Martínez Freire, 307–346. Málaga: Publicaciones Universidad de Málaga.
Gonzalez, W. J. 1998e. El naturalismo normativo como propuesta epistemológica y metodológica. La segunda etapa del Pensamiento de L. Laudan. In *El Pensamiento de L. Laudan. Relaciones entre Historia de la Ciencia y Filosofía de la Ciencia*, ed. W. J. Gonzalez, 5–57. A Coruña: Publicaciones de la Universidad de A Coruña.
Gonzalez, W. J. 1999a. Ciencia y valores éticos: De la posibilidad de la Ética de la Ciencia al problema de la valoración ética de la Ciencia Básica. *Arbor* 162(638):139–171.
Gonzalez, W. J. 1999b. El giro en la Metodología de L. Laudan. Del criterio metaintuitivo al Naturalismo normativo abierto al relativismo débil. In *Progreso, pluralismo y racionalidad en la Ciencia*, ed. Homenaje a Larry Laudan, 105–131. México: Ediciones de la Universidad Nacional Autónoma de México.
Gonzalez, W. J. 2000. Marco teórico, trayectoria y situación actual de la Filosofía y Metodología de la Economía. *Argumentos de Razón Técnica* 3:13–59.
Gonzalez, W. J. 2001a. De la Ciencia de la Economía a la Economía de la Ciencia: Marco conceptual de la reflexión metodológica y axiológica. In *Ciencia económica y Economía de la Ciencia: Reflexiones filosófico-metodológicas*, ed. A. Avila, W. J. Gonzalez, and G. Marques, 11–37. Madrid: FCE.
Gonzalez, W. J. 2001c. La Filosofía de I. Lakatos, 25 años después: Del "giro histórico" a la incidencia metodológica en Economía. In *La Filosofía de Imre Lakatos: Evaluación de sus propuestas*, ed. W. J. Gonzalez, 13–103. Madrid: UNED.
Gonzalez, W. J. 2003c. Herbert A. Simon: Filósofo de la Ciencia y economista (1916–2001). In *Racionalidad, historicidad y predicción en Herbert A. Simon*, ed. W. J. Gonzalez, 7–63. A Coruña: Netbiblo.
Gonzalez, W. J. 2004a. Las revoluciones científicas y la evolución de Thomas S. Kuhn. In *Análisis de Thomas Kuhn: Las revoluciones científicas*, ed. W. J. Gonzalez, 15–103. Madrid: Trotta.
Gonzalez, W. J. 2005. The philosophical approach to science, technology and society. In *Science, technology and society: A philosophical perspective*, ed. W. J. Gonzalez, 3–49. A Coruña: Netbiblo.
Gonzalez, W. J. 2006a. Novelty and continuity in philosophy and methodology of science. In *Contemporary perspectives in philosophy and methodology of science*, ed. W. J. Gonzalez and J. Alcolea, 1–28. A Coruña: Netbiblo.
Gonzalez, W. J. 2007b. Análisis de las Ciencias de Diseño desde la racionalidad limitada, la predicción y la prescripción. In *Las Ciencias de Diseño: Racionalidad limitada, predicción y prescripción*, ed. W. J. Gonzalez, 3–38. A Coruña: Netbiblo.
Gonzalez, W. J. 2007d. La contribución de la predicción al diseño en las Ciencias de lo Artificial. In *Las Ciencias de Diseño: Racionalidad limitada, predicción y prescripción*, ed. W. J. Gonzalez, 183–202. A Coruña: Netbiblo.
Gonzalez, W. J. 2010a. *La predicción científica: Concepciones filosófico-metodológicas desde H. Reichenbach a N. Rescher*. Barcelona: Montesinos.
Gonzalez, W. J. 2011b. Conceptual changes and scientific diversity: The role of historicity. In *Conceptual revolutions: From cognitive science to medicine*, ed. W. J. Gonzalez, 39–62. A Coruña: Netbiblo.
Gonzalez, W. J. 2012b. Methodological universalism in science and its limits: Imperialism versus complexity. In *Thinking about provincialism in thinking, Poznan Studies in the Philosophy of the Sciences and the Humanities*, vol. 100, ed. K. Brzechczyn and K. Paprzycka, 155–175. Amsterdam: Rodopi.

Gonzalez, W. J. 2013a. Value ladenness and the value-free ideal in scientific research. In *Handbook of the philosophical foundations of business ethics*, ed. Ch. Lütge, 1503–1521. Dordrecht: Springer.

Gonzalez, W. J. 2013c. The roles of scientific creativity and technological innovation in the context of complexity of science. In *Creativity, innovation, and complexity in science*, ed. W. J. Gonzalez, 11–40. A Coruña: Netbiblo.

Granger, C. W. J. 2012. The philosophy of economic forecasting. In *Philosophy of economics*, ed. U. Mäki, 311–327. Amsterdam: Elsevier.

Grunberg, E., and Modigliani, F. 1954. The predictability of social events. *Journal of Political Economy* 62:465–478.

Haack, S. 1998. *Manifesto of a passionate moderate*. Chicago: The University of Chicago Press.

Hacohen, M. H. 2000. *Karl Popper-The formative years, 1902-1945*. Cambridge: Cambridge University Press.

Harré, R., ed. 1975. *Problems of scientific revolution: Progress and obstacles to progress in the sciences*. Oxford: Oxford University Press.

Hausman, D. M. 1992a. *The inexact and separate science of economics*. Cambridge: Cambridge University Press.

Hausman, D. M., ed. 1994a. *The philosophy of economics. An anthology*, 2nd ed. Cambridge: Cambridge University Press.

Hausman, D. M., and McPherson, M. S. 1996. *Economic analysis and moral philosophy*. Cambridge: Cambridge University Press.

Hicks, J. 1983c. A discipline not a science. In *Classics and moderns. Collected essays on economic theory*, vol. III, ed. J. Hicks, 364–375. Cambridge: Harvard University Press.

Hicks, J. 1986. Is economics a science? In *Foundations of economics. Structures of inquiry and economic theory*, ed. M. Baranzini and R. Scazzieri, 91–101. Oxford: Blackwell.

Hutchison, T. W. 1938. *The significance and basic postulates of economic theory*. London: Macmillan.

Hutchison, T. W. 1960. *The significance and basic postulates of economic theory*, 2nd ed. New York: Kelley.

Hutchison, T. W. 1964. *"Positive" economics and policy objectives*. London: Allen and Unwin.

Hutchison, T. W. 1977. On prediction and economic knowledge. In *Knowledge and ignorance in economics*, T. W. Hutchison, 8–33, 145–151. Oxford: Blackwell.

Hutchison, T. W. 1981. *The politics and philosophy of economics: Marxians, Keynesians and Austrians*. Oxford: Blackwell.

Hutchison, T. W. 1992a. *Changing aims in economics*. Oxford: Blackwell.

Hutchison, T. W. 1992b. To predict or not to predict? (That *is* the question)? In *Changing aims in economics*, T. W. Hutchison, 71–88 (notes in 158–167). Oxford: Blackwell.

Keuzenkamp, H. A. 2000. *Probability, econometrics and truth. The methodology of econometrics*. Cambridge: Cambridge University Press.

Kitcher, Ph. 1993. *The advancement of science: Science without legend, objectivity without illusions*. New York: Oxford University Press.

Kitcher, Ph. 2001. *Science, truth and democracy*. New York: Oxford University Press.

Koertge, N., ed. 1998. *A house built on sand: Exposing postmodern myths about science*. New York: Oxford University Press.

Koertge, N. 2000. "New age" philosophies of science: Constructivism, feminism and postmodernism. *The British Journal for the Philosophy of Science* 51:667–683.

Kuhn, T. S. 1962. *The structure of scientific revolutions*. Chicago: The University of Chicago Press (2nd ed., 1970).

Kuhn, T. S. 1977. *The essential tension. Selected studies in scientific tradition and change*. Chicago: University of Chicago Press.

Kuhn, T. S. 2000. *The road since* structure. *Philosophical essays, 1970-1993, with an autobiographical interview*, edited by James Conant and John Haugeland. Chicago: University of Chicago Press.

Lakatos, I. 1970. Falsification and the methodology of scientific research programmes. In *Criticism and the growth of knowledge*, ed. I. Lakatos and A. Musgrave, 91–196. Cambridge: Cambridge University Press (Reprinted in Lakatos, I. 1978. *The methodology of scientific research programmes. Philosophical papers*, vol. 1, 8–101. Cambridge: Cambridge University Press).
Lakatos, I. 1974a. Popper on demarcation and induction. In *The philosophy of Karl Popper*, Open Court, La Salle, IL, vol. 1, P. A. Schilpp, 241–273. Reprinted in Lakatos, I. 1978. *The methodology of scientific research programmes. Philosophical papers*, vol. 1, 139–167. Cambridge: Cambridge University Press.
Lakatos, I. 1976. *Proofs and refutations. The logic of mathematical discovery* (ed. J. Worrall and E. G. Zahar). Cambridge: Cambridge University Press.
Laudan, L. 1977. *Progress and its problems. Towards a theory of scientific growth.* Berkeley: University of California Press. (Edited in UK by Routledge and K. Paul, London, 1977).
Laudan, L. 1983. The demise of the demarcation problem. In *Physics, philosophy and psychoanalysis*, ed. R. Cohen and L. Laudan, 111–128. Dordrecht: Reidel (Reprinted in Ruse, M., ed. 1988. *But is it science? The philosophical question in the creation-evolution Contoversy*, 337–350. Buffalo: Prometheus).
Laudan, L. 1984. *Science and values. The aims of science and their role in scientific debate.* Berkeley: University of California Press.
Laudan, L. 1989. If it ain't broke, don't fix it. *The British Journal for the Philosophy of Science* 40:369–375.
Laudan, L. 1990. *Science and relativism: Some key controversies in the philosophy of science.* Chicago: The University of Chicago Press.
Laudan, L. 1996. *Beyond positivism and relativism: Theory, method and evidence.* Boulder: Westview.
Laudan, L. 1998a. Naturalismo normativo y el progreso de la Filosofía. In *El Pensamiento de L. Laudan. Relaciones entre Historia de la Ciencia y Filosofía de la Ciencia*, ed. W. J. Gonzalez, 105–116. A Coruña: Publicaciones de la Universidad de A Coruña.
Laudan, L. 1998b. Una Teoría de la evaluación comparativa de teorías científicas. In *El Pensamiento de L. Laudan. Relaciones entre Historia de la Ciencia y Filosofía de la Ciencia*, ed. W. J. Gonzalez, 155–169. A Coruña: Publicaciones de la Universidad de A Coruña.
Lucas, R. E. 1977. Understanding business cycles. In *Stabilization of the domestic and international economy*, ed. K. Brunner and A. Meltzer, 7–30. Amsterdam: North-Holland.
Lucas, R. E. 1978. Assets prices in a exchange economy. *Econometrica* 46:1429–1445.
Lucas, R. E. 1988. On the mechanics of economic development. *Journal of Economic Development* 22:3–42.
Machlup, F. 1963. *Essays on economics semantics.* Englewood Cliffs: Prentice Hall.
Machlup, F. 1978. *Methodology of economics and other social sciences.* New York: Academic.
Martínez Solano, J. F. 2007. La influencia de la Filosofía de Karl Popper en la Metodología de la Economía de Mark Blaug. *Laguna* 27:9–28.
McCloskey, D. N. 1985. *The rhetoric of economics.* Madison: University of Wisconsin Press.
McCloskey, D. N. 1990. *If you're so smart. The narrative of economic expertise.* Chicago: The University of Chicago Press.
McCloskey, D. N. 1994. *Knowledge and persuasion in economics.* Cambridge: Cambridge University Press.
Mellor, D. H. 1979. The possibility of prediction. *Proceedings of the British Academy* 65:207–223.
Mirowski, Ph. 1988. *Against mechanism: Protecting economics from science.* Totowa: Rowman and Littlefield.
Mirowski, Ph. 1989. *More heat than light: Economics as social physics, physics as nature's economics.* New York: Cambridge University Press.
Mirowski, Ph. 1992. Three vignettes on the state of economic rhetoric. In *Post-Popperian methodology of economics*, ed. N. Marchi, 235–259. Boston: Kluwer.
Morgan, M. S. 1990. *The history of econometric ideas.* Cambridge: Cambridge University Press.
Muth, J. 1961. Rational expectations and the theory of price movements. *Econometrica* 29:315–335 (Reprinted in Lucas, R. E., and Sargent, Th. J., eds. 1981. *Rational expectations and econometric practice*, 3–22. London: G. Allen and Unwin).

Nelson, R. R., and Winter, S. G. 1982. *An evolutionary theory of economic change*. Cambridge: Belknap.

Niiniluoto, I. 1984. *Is science progressive*? Dordrecht: Reidel.

Niiniluoto, I. 1987. Progress, realism, and verisimilitude. In *Logic, philosophy of science and epistemology*, ed. P. Weingartner and G. Schurz, 151–161. Vienna: Hölder-Pichler-Tempsky.

Niiniluoto, I. 1993. The aim and structure of applied research. *Erkenntnis* 38:1–21.

Niiniluoto, I. 1995a. Approximation in applied science. *Poznan Studies in the Philosophy of the Sciences and the Humanities* 42:127–139.

Niiniluoto, I. 1995b. The emergence of scientific specialties: Six models. *Poznan Studies in the Philosophy of the Sciences and the Humanities* 44:211–223.

Niiniluoto, I. 1999. *Critical scientific realism*. Oxford: Clarendon.

Niiniluoto, I. 2001. Future studies: Science or art? *Futures* 33:371–377.

Niiniluoto, I. 2002. Truthlikeness and economic theories. In *Fact and fiction: Foundational issues on economics and the economy*, ed. U. Mäki, 214–228. Cambridge: Cambridge University Press.

Niiniluoto, I., and Tuomela, R. 1973. *Theoretical concepts and hypothetico-inductive inference*. Dordrecht: Reidel.

OECD. 1996. *Manual de Frascati. Propuesta de norma práctica para encuestas de investigación y desarrollo experimental*, 5th ed. México: Centro de Publicaciones y de Información de la OCDE.

O'Neill, O. 2003. Autonomy: The emperor's new clothes. *Proceedings of the Aristotelian Society* 77:1–21.

Pitt, J. C., ed. 1985. *Change and progress in modern science*. Dordrecht: Reidel.

Poirier, D. J., ed. 1994. *The methodology of econometrics*. vol. 2. Aldershot: Elgar.

Popper, K. 1957. *The poverty of historicism*. London: Routledge (reprinted by Routledge in 1991).

Qin, D. 1993. *The formation of econometrics*. Oxford: Clarendon.

Radnitzky, G. 1978. The boundaries of science and technology. In *The search for absolute values in a changing world. Proceedings of the VIth International Conference on the Unity of Sciences*, vol. II, 1007–1036. New York: International Cultural Foundation Press.

Radnitzky, G., and Andersson, G., eds. 1978. *Progress and rationality in science*. Dordrecht: Reidel.

Reichenbach, H. 1938. *Experience and prediction. An analysis of the foundations and the structure of knowledge*. Chicago: The University of Chicago Press.

Rescher, N. 1978. *Scientific progress. A philosophical essay on the economics of research in Natural Science*. Oxford: Blackwell.

Rescher, N. 1983. The unpredictability of future science. In *Physics, philosophy and psychoanalysis*, ed. R. S. Cohen, et al., 153–168. Dordrecht: Reidel.

Rescher, N. 1984. *The limits of science*. Berkeley: University of California Press.

Rescher, N. 1992. Our science as our science. In *A system of pragmatic idealism,* vol I: *Human knowledge in idealistic perspective*, N. Rescher, 110–125. Princeton: Princeton University Press.

Rescher, N. 1997. *Objectivity. The obligations of impersonal reason*. Notre Dame: University of Notre Dame.

Rescher, N. 1998. *Predicting the future: An introduction to the theory of forecasting*. Albany: State University of New York Press.

Rescher, N. 1999a. *Razón y valores en la Era científico-tecnológica*. Barcelona: Paidós.

Rescher, N. 1999b. *The limits of science* (revised edition). Pittsburgh: University of Pittsburgh Press.

Rescher, N. 2006. The Berlin school of logical empiricism and its legacy. *Erkenntnis* 64:281–304.

Rescher, N. 2012. The problem of future knowledge. *Mind and Society* 11(2):149–163.

Robbins, L. 1935. *An essay on the nature and significance of economic science*, 2nd ed. London: Macmillan (1st ed., 1932).

Rosenberg, A. 1992. *Economics-mathematical politics or science of diminishing returns*? Chicago: The University of Chicago Press.

Rosenberg, A. 1993. Scientific innovation and the limits of social scientific prediction. *Synthese* 97:161–182.
Salmon, W. C. 1981. Rational prediction. *The British Journal for the Philosophy of Science* 32:115–125. Reprinted in Grünbaum, A., and Salmon, W. C., ed. 1988. *The limitations of deductivism*, 47–60. Berkeley: University of California Press.
Samuelson, P. 1963. Problems of methodology—discussion. *American Economic Review* 53(2):231–236.
Scriven, M. 1959. Explanation and prediction in evolutionary theory. *Science* 130(3374):477–482.
Sen, A. 1986. Prediction and economic theory. In *Predictability in science and society*, ed. J. Mason, P. Mathias, and J. H. Westcott, 3–23. London: The Royal Society and The British Academy.
Shäfer, W., ed. 1983. *Finalization in science: The social orientation of scientific progress*. Dordrecht: Reidel.
Simon, H. A. 1954. Bandwagon and Underdog Effects and the Possibility of Election Predictions. *Public Opinion Quarterly* 18:245–253. Reprinted in Simon, H. A. 1982a. *Models of bounded rationality*, vol. 1: *Economic analysis and public policy*, 460–468. Cambridge: The MIT Press.
Simon, H. A. 1963b. Problems of methodology—discussion. *American Economic Review* 53:229–231. Reprinted in Simon, H. A., 1982. *Models of bounded rationality*, vol. 2: *Behavioral economics and business organization*, 369–371. Cambridge: (The MIT Press); also reprinted as Simon, H. A., 1984. Testability and approximation. In *Philosophy of economics*, ed. D. M. Hausman, 1st ed., 245–248. Cambridge: Cambridge University Press.
Simon, H. A. 1990a. Prediction and prescription in systems modeling. *Operations Research* 38:7–14. Reprinted in Simon, H. A., 1997. *Models of bounded rationality*, vol. 3: *Empirically grounded economic reason*, 115–128. Cambridge: The MIT Press.
Simon, H. A. 1996. *The sciences of the artificial*, 3rd ed. Cambridge: The MIT Press. (1st ed., 1969; 2nd ed., 1981).
Simon, H. A. 1997. *Models of bounded rationality*, vol. 3: *Empirically grounded economic reason*. Cambridge: The MIT Press.
Simon, H. A. 2001. On simulating Simon: His monomania, and its sources in bounded rationality. *Studies in History and Philosophy of Science* 32(3):501–505.
Sintonen, M. 1990. Basic and applied sciences-Can the distinction (still) be drawn? *Science Studies* 3(2):23–31.
Smith, A. 1776. *An inquiry into the nature and causes of the wealth of nations*. London: W. Strahan and T. Cadell (Edited by Edwin Cannan with a preface by George J. Stigler (1976). Chicago: The University of Chicago Press).
Sobel, M. E. 1995. Causal inference in the social and behavioral sciences. In *Handbook of statistical modeling for the social and behavioral sciences*, ed. G. Arminger, C. C. Clogg, and M. E. Sobel, 1–38. New York: Plenum.
Stiglitz, J. E. 1991. The economic role of the state: Efficiency and effectiveness. In *The Economic Role of the State*, ed. T. P. Hardiman and M. Mulreany, 37–59. Dublin: Institute of Public Administration.
Thagard, P. 1992. *Conceptual revolutions*. Princeton: Princeton University Press.
Toulmin, S. 1961. *Foresight and understanding. An enquiry into the aims of science*. Bloomington: Indiana University Press/London: Hutchinson.
Worrall, J. 1988. The value of a fixed methodology. *The British Journal for the Philosophy of Science* 39:263–275.
Worrall, J. 1989b. Fix it and be damned: A reply to Laudan. *The British Journal for the Philosophy of Science* 40:376–388.
Worrall, J. 1998. Realismo, racionalidad y revoluciones. *Agora* 17(2):7–24.

Chapter 2
Characterization of Scientific Prediction and its Kinds in Economics

After the analysis of the philosophico-methodological framework of science, this chapter focuses on problems that concern the empirical sciences and, among them, economics. The first step considers the shift regarding the vision of the structure of science: from the thesis of symmetry between explanation and prediction to the position of asymmetry. After of emphasizing the structural divergence between "scientific explanation" and "scientific prediction," there is a second step: a characterization of scientific prediction itself. It pays attention to central aspects, predominantly semantic and methodological: the concept of "prediction" and its main uses in the social sciences as well as in the sciences of artificial.[1]

Thereafter, the third step is the distinction between qualitative prediction and quantitative prediction. In this regard, the structural components of science as well as the dynamic traits of scientific activity are relevant. Both are needed to characterize complexity in economics (Gonzalez 2011a and 2013c).[2] These elements will lead to a fourth step: the diversity of economic predictions. (a) There are some relevant types of predictions that can be used in economics as a "descriptive science" and, especially, as an applied science (where prediction is commonly connected to prescription). These types of economic predictions center on important factors, such as the *length of time* and the *kind of event* predicted. (b) This diversity of economic predictions can be deepened towards an interesting semantic and methodological distinction, according to the degree of *control* of economic variables: "foresight," "prediction," "forecasting," and "planning."

[1] The remarks on prediction in the context of the sciences of artificial are made insofar as economics is a science of design. See, in this regard, Gonzalez (2008 and 2012a).

[2] An analysis of the complexities of complex economic dynamics is in Rosser (1999). Other studies on complexity in economics, both structural and dynamic, can be found in the three volumes edited by Rosser (2004a, 2004b, and 2004c).

W. J. Gonzalez, *Philosophico-Methodological Analysis of Prediction and its Role in Economics*, Theory and Decision Library A: 50, DOI 10.1007/978-3-319-08885-3_2

2.1 Scientific Explanation and Scientific Prediction

Scientific prediction has been frequently compared with scientific explanation in different ways, mainly in the logical and methodological contexts. The comparison is at least related to two well-known problems: (i) the *structural discussion* concerning the symmetry or asymmetry between scientific explanation and scientific prediction; and (ii) the *methodological dispute* concerning whether explanation or prediction has more weight in *testing* science or characterizing *scientific progress.* Commonly, this debate is seen in terms of the confirmatory value of accommodation—to fit the available facts—versus the prediction of unobserved phenomena.

When the discussion is in the first case (the *symmetry* or *asymmetry* between scientific explanation and scientific prediction), the issue belongs to logic of science, and is connected with the epistemology and methodology of science. It is a problem of similitude or dissimilitude between the reasoning in support of a hypothesis in both cases, with the feature of a temporal difference (i.e., the assumption that an hypothesis of explanation concerns the past and an hypothesis of prediction looks towards the future). This question about the empirical sciences has been discussed largely in natural sciences, but it has also a clear relevance for social sciences. The intellectual movement has been clear: from the dominance of the thesis of symmetry between explanation and prediction to the predominance of the view of asymmetry.

Within the second case (the dispute about the scientific weight of explanation and prediction or the level of confirmatory value of accommodation and prediction), the question raised is mainly methodological, but it is also linked to epistemological considerations. This debate has *prima facie* a less clear solution than the previous one. Even now, some views maintain that accommodation and prediction have a similar weight from the point of view of the confirmatory value. However, other perspectives hold that this methodological comparison to advance the future (i.e., prediction) has in principle more weight than accommodation to available facts.

2.1.1 From the Symmetry to the Asymmetry

The features of "scientific explanation" have been discussed for more than six decades.[3] After such a long time, it now seems difficult to accept a structural symmetry between *explanation* and *prediction.* Carl G. Hempel and Paul Oppenheim supported this thesis (1948), and it has been very influential.[4] As a logico-methodological view, it has had a special repercussion, because it has inspired well-known philosophers, such as Adolf Grünbaum (1969), who has defended the logico-methodological similitude between "explanation" and "prediction."

---

[3] See Salmon (1990), and Gonzalez (2002b). Both include an extensive bibliography on "scientific explanation" as well as its relations with "scientific prediction."

[4] He was also influential through Hempel (1966).

According to Grünbaum's analysis, the difference between both explanation and prediction has, above all, a temporal trait. The distinction depends on whether an event *E* is before or after the "now" of the person deriving *E* from a given set of conditions *C* in conjunction with suitable laws (the difference does not depend on whether the conditions precede or follow the event). Thus, following this view, there is not an authentic structural divergence between them. There does not exist a genuine logico-methodological separation between explaining and predicting (Grünbaum 1962, pp. 146–170; esp., p. 156).

But this position is something that Wesley Salmon has rejected (1993).[5] It is a perspective that he has criticized in a very respectful way, because he was well aware that it is a conception that has been defended for many years by one of his best friends. In this view, the alleged temporal anisotropy of scientific explanation does not allow it to reach a structural symmetry between explanation and prediction.

Thus, taking into account the problem raised by Grünbaum, Salmon went to the roots and has examined both parts of Hempel's *thesis of symmetry*: (1) Each scientific explanation could, under suitable circumstances, serve as a prediction (i.e., to give an argument explaining an event of the past—for example, an eclipse of the sun—can serve to predict an event in the future); and (2) each legitimate scientific prediction could, under suitable circumstances, serve as an explanation (Salmon 1993, pp. 231–232).[6]

This second part is clearly problematic. Salmon accepted Israel Scheffler's idea of prediction as a *statement* about the future (1957). It is a position that he compared with Hempel's approach, where explanation was understood as an *argument*[7] (and, therefore, containing premises and a conclusion). Hence, according to Salmon, prediction has its own logico-methodological characteristics, which are different from an explanation. It cannot be an explanation from the structural point of view. For him, the most that could be maintained is that legitimate scientific predictions are the *conclusions* of arguments that conform to specific schemes of explanation (such as the deductive-nomological or the inductive-statistical models). This is a conception that Salmon considered was adopted by Grünbaum when he was defending the symmetry thesis between explanation and prediction (Salmon 1993, p. 232).

Yet, regarding the phenomena of natural sciences, Salmon considered that the thesis of symmetry explanation-prediction is really *groundless*: "the alleged temporal anisotropy of scientific explanation is also the actual temporal anisotropy of scientific explanation" (Salmon 1993, p. 245). For him, this can be seen in the case of causal explanations, mainly in natural sciences: "causes can explain their effects,

[5] Within the sphere of scientific explanation, Wesley Salmon has developed influential views on causal explanation. See, for example, Salmon (2002a, and 2002b). His conception has repercussions for the social sciences through Merrilee Salmon (2002).

[6] The issue of the symmetry between explanation and prediction was considered by other thinkers, such as Hanson (1959). A few years later, in Scriven (1962), there are some interesting remarks on the conditions for successful explanations.

[7] "As such, a prediction could not be an explanation, for an explanation, according to Peter [Carl G. Hempel] is an argument" (Salmon 1993, p. 232). His initial ideas on prediction are in Salmon (1953 and 1957).

but effects cannot explain their causes, only the derivation of the occurrence of the eclipse [which occurred in Principe on 29 May 1919] from antecedent conditions can qualify as an explanation. The inference from subsequent conditions can qualify only as a retrodiction—not as an explanation as well" (Salmon 1993, p. 230).

In other words, there are three different *anisotropies* that go together: time, causality, and scientific explanation. This triple is compatible with the fact of having laws of nature that are time-symmetric (as is the case in Newtonian mechanics). Thus, "the temporal anisotropy of explanation has nothing to do with the reversibility or irreversibility of the physical process involved in the situation. The fact that there might be or might have been a solar system just about the same as ours, but with rotations reversed, is, to my mind, irrelevant to the fact that in our solar system the 1919 solar eclipse was a result of conditions in its past but not those in its future" (Salmon 1993, p. 244). Therefore, from a logical point of view, "explanation" and "prediction" are *asymmetrical* processes. The difference between "explanation" and "prediction" goes beyond the mere temporal anisotropy to reach the level of a difference in the structural level.

As many philosophers—among them, Rescher (1998, pp. 165–167 and 271–272)—hold today, there is an *asymmetry* between the scientific task of explaining and the scientific endeavor of predicting. The logical asymmetry is connected with epistemological-methodological aspects of a science, either natural or social: "in adequate explanatory arguments the premises must support the conclusion firmly—if not with decisive certainty, then with very high probability—whereas with cogent predictive arguments we often do (and are entitled to) settle for much lower degrees of probability. For a perfectly cogent prediction can rest on considerations to the effect that the predicted outcome is substantially more likely than any other possibility within the pertinent range of alternatives. Thus between prediction and explanation there is not just a temporal difference but also a significant epistemic difference in the degree to which the causal linkage at issue must be evidentiated" (Rescher 1998, p. 166). The methodological differences between them can be seen in sciences like economics (cf. Chaps. 10 and 11).[8]

2.1.2 *The Question of the Methodological Weight: Accommodation and Prediction*

Regarding the confirmatory value, whether explanation as *accommodation* to the available facts or *prediction* of future events has more weight from the methodological perspective is still a controversial issue (Harker 2006). The divergence is visible in the present day after the second half of the twentieth century when, according to Salmon, the scientific level of *description* was overcome, and it is clear that "scientific explanation" is seen commonly as a plausible methodological process. To

[8] "In economics is well-known that the best model for explaining is not necessarily the best model for predicting the future," José Ramón Cancelo, *Personal Communication*, January 2007.

emphasize the role of scientific explanation might suggest that the accommodation of evidence that is known when the theory is proposed is at least equal in value to the prediction of new evidence by a theory.

Prior to the mid-twentieth century, there was a predictivist tendency, which included influential authors who belonged to quite different philosophical traditions (empiricist, rationalist, Kantian, conventionalist, etc.), such as Francis Bacon (1620/1994), Gottfried W. Leibniz (1678/1969, p. 188), William Whewell (1860, p. 273), and Pierre Duhem (1914/1974, p. 28). Later on, for several decades, the key figures were influential philosophers: Reichenbach, with his well-known *Experience and Prediction* (1938);[9] Popper, with many faces in his approach to prediction (Gonzalez 2004b); and Lakatos (1970), which has a complex articulation of prediction and novel facts (Gonzalez 2001e).

Commonly, the *predictivist view* assumes that the prediction of new phenomena or evidence lends greater confirmational value than the accommodation of evidence available when the theory is proposed. In his characterization of the philosophical usage, Eric Barnes stresses novelty: "predictivism asserts that, when E is evidence for T [Theory], E supports T more strongly when it is a novel confirmation of T than when it is not" (2008, p. 1).[10] But this novelty, as can be seen in Chap. 4 on the analysis of Lakatos' conception of "novel facts," can be understood in different ways (Sect. 4.3.2).[11]

Predictivism assumes an evidential superiority of prediction over accommodation. This *prominence* can be seen mainly in three ways: (i) as a matter of logico-methodological preeminence (something that it is in principle, and thus it will not change); (ii) an epistemological-methodological advantage in the sense of a "practical supremacy" (due to the "intrinsic" difficulty of knowing the future); or (iii) as a heuristic enhancement of a successful prediction in comparison with a successful accommodation, because of the new routes to scientific research opened by this kind of search.

As regards the content of "predictivism," there are many options available.[12] Some of these philosophico-methodological possibilities are in Christopher Hitch-

---

[9] Reichenbach's approach is analyzed in Gonzalez (1995), where his whole production is considered in this regard.

[10] He also offers us a heuristic account of this issue: "Predictivism now proclaims that, where E is evidence for T, E confirms T more strongly when T was not built to fit E" (Barnes 2008, p. 2).

Among the critics of predictivism in terms of novelty, based on his perspective on history of science, is Stephen Brush: "The predictivist thesis gains little empirical support from the history of science. Any attempt to rescue it by redefining novelty in terms of what the theorist knew, when he knew it, and what he did or could have done with the information puts the philosopher in the position of a Watergate investigator without Deep Throat" (Brush 1995, p. 41). His analysis of scientific prediction based on historical grounds can also be seen in Brush (1989).

[11] On Lakatos' predictivism, see Sect. 4.4.2. *An Overemphasis on the Role of Prediction?*

[12] In this regard, some distinctions can be found in Lipton (1990, 1991). More recently, Barnes has proposed four "species" of predictivism: (1) "unvirtuous thin predictivism," (2) "unvirtuous tempered predictivism," (3) "virtuous thin predictivism," and (4) "virtuous tempered predictivism" (2008), p. 81.

cock and Eliot Sober, who have offered a taxonomy with several characterizations. Among them are those related to the *scope*—"global" versus "local" predictivisms—and to the *intensity* of the proposal ("strong" versus "week" predictivisms). For these authors, on the scope we have that "global predictivism maintains that a theory which successfully predicts some observation will always be superior to one that accommodates the same observation. Local predictivism maintains only that prediction is sometimes superior to accommodation" (Hitchcock and Sober 2004, pp. 3–4). In this regard, they endorse a version of local predictivism.

Meanwhile, regarding the intensity of the content, they propose a distinction between strong and weak predictivisms. "According to strong predictivism, prediction is intrinsically superior to accommodation. The fact that one theory predicts a phenomenon while another merely accommodates it is, by itself, a mark in favor of the former theory. According to weak predictivism, the difference between prediction and accommodation is epistemically relevant only because it tracks or is symptomatic of other differences that are themselves of evidential support" (Hitchcock and Sober 2004, p. 4). In this opposition, they defend a version of weak predictivism.

We can move from the thematic sphere to the historical context. Then we have that, during the period of the *four decades* of scientific explanation analyzed by Salmon (from 1948 to 1987), prediction was particularly relevant in some methodological orientations, such as Popperian falsificationism (mainly, in his general approach to science rather than in his view of the social sciences) and Lakatos's methodology of scientific research programs. The latter approach gives a clear methodological relevance to prediction in the sphere of scientific progress: it considers openly that predictive knowledge has more cognitive value than explanatory knowledge. Moreover, Lakatos used this for an interesting proposal of a nexus between prediction and "novel facts" (Gonzalez 2001e, pp. 505–508; Chap. 4, Sect. 4.3).

More recently, there have been other authors who, either in tune with empiricist positions (which many times follow the lines of naturalist conceptions) or in line with a Bayesian interpretation of probability of a personalist or subjectivist kind, tend to reject that prediction can have more weight from the confirmatory point of view than scientific explanation.[13] Furthermore, there is also an emphasis on the history of science defending that, in general terms, prediction does not have more cognitive relevance than explanation.[14] Accepting this view is equivalent to assuming that, in an overall perspective, the accommodation to available facts made through scientific explanation has, in principle, the same methodological value as the prediction of novel facts (either "novel facts" understood in the temporal sense or in other senses of this expression).

Even though this topic has been analyzed very frequently, due to its relevance in order for understanding *scientific progress*, today there is no real consensus about whether a successful prediction has *more confirmatory* character than the value pos-

[13] Cf. Achinstein (1995) and Howson (1989, 1990). The situation of the Bayesian camp is rather complex, due to the positions on the "problem of old evidence," see for example Earman and Glymour (1980). On this problem seen from a different perspective: Worrall (2002).

[14] Cf. Brush (1995). In this regard it is useful to use case-studies: cf. Worrall (1989a), Scerri and Worrall (2001), and Worrall (2005).

sessed by the accommodation to the facts (which a scientific explanation can give). The proposal of the methodological superiority of prediction above explanation is still under discussion. Nevertheless, in this ongoing dispute, many philosophers think that, on average, there is tendency in favor of a moderate version of predictivism, either "pragmatic" or "weak," i.e., the theories from which successful prediction had been made would be better supported by the total evidence than the theories that have merely accommodated existing data (McIntyre 2001; White 2003).

On the one hand, it seems that the *insight* persists in favor of considering it more difficult to anticipate the future than to explain the past. This option gives more relevance to the success—accuracy or precision—in the knowledge of the *future* (what still is not yet and can or not be) than to the process of accommodate our explanations to the present and the past (what it is or it has been and possesses a reality which is not going to change as such). But, on the other hand, the study of real cases of the *history of science* seem to suggest—at least in some cases, such as the "Periodic Law"—an equal role of prediction and accommodation, instead of a primacy of foretelling the future in comparison with explaining the past or present phenomena (e.g., Scerri and Worrall 2001).[15]

2.2 Characterization of Scientific Prediction

Following the acceptance of the asymmetry between scientific explanation and scientific prediction, it seems then that prediction is a *statement about the future* rather than an argument. The future could be about some phenomena or events that have not yet occurred (i.e., an ontological sense: a future from now), but it might be also about consequences that have not yet been observed (i.e., an epistemological sense: the phenomenon or event might already exist, but has not been observed so far).[16] Thus, in comparison with the accommodation to available evidence, prediction commonly includes the assumption of *anticipation* of something possible, either in the literal sense (e.g., a phenomenon in the next year) or in the epistemological content (e.g., economic consequences not yet observed of the euro as European currency or the economic effects of a tsunami).

If "scientific prediction" is seen above all as a methodological concept, then it should be considered in relation to the *progress* of scientific knowledge. This factor is sometimes used to argue that "in actual scientific practice prediction *is* preferred over accommodation" (McIntyre 2001, p. 309), which is certainly the case in mainstream economics. From the point of view of scientific progress, it is acceptable that "prediction" is more epistemological than ontological: predicting something is to do

[15] On this issue of Mendeleev's predictions, see also Barnes (2005a, 2005b, 2008); Worrall (2005); and Scerri (2005, 2007).

[16] There are more options in the context of "novel facts," such as the heuristic approach and the individual perspective, as can be seen in Chap. 4.

so before it is definitively known to happen, instead of doing so before it happens (Mellor 1979, p. 208).

Nevertheless, regarding the status of what is predicted, it should be considered a feature of the influential ontological tradition: if the prediction is successful, the new events happen after they are predicted,[17] but that reality does not depend, in principle, on the prediction.[18] Usually, the aim of scientific prediction—as of science as a whole—is not to produce or to transform a reality (as technology does) (Gonzalez 2005); rather it seeks to improve the accurate and precise knowledge of a reality that has been predicted or to offer useful knowledge about the future in order to solve concrete problems (in nature, the society, or in the artificial world).

2.2.1 The Concept of "Prediction"

Until now, within the methodology of economics there has been no general characterization of "prediction" which is approved by all economists. There does not exist *de facto* a general methodological framework about prediction that could be shared by the main experts in this discipline. In fact, as Hausman has pointed out,[19] it is possible to distinguish prediction as (a) testable implications regarding the future; (b) testable implications whose truth is not already known; and (c) testable implications. The view of prediction as disconnected from temporality—and, therefore, separated from the future (like option (c) here)—is adopted by some economists, such as Herbert Simon (cf. Chap. 8) or Frank Hahn.[20]

However, if prediction were the mere drawing of *testable implications* independently of the time factor, then it could be the case that scientific prediction might be almost indiscernible with respect to scientific explanation, because explanation cannot exclude *a priori* the bringing about of some consequences. Moreover, it is not the most frequent sense of "prediction" in economics, which tends to see prediction primarily as testable implications regarding the future (i.e., option (a) in Hausman's list). But, not all predictions require ontological novelty, because there are other forms of novelty (epistemological, heuristic, for the designer, etc.).

The use of prediction connected with the future is more characteristic of what prediction is in science (natural, social, and artificial). Thus, the usage of "prediction of novel phenomena" is common (Hitchcock and Sober 2004, pp. 1, 2 and 5). Also "predicting the future" reflects the ordinary language better than the others

[17] This should be understood as a conceptual difference with "retrodiction," even though the notion of "novel fact" is clearly more sophisticated than the temporally new event. On the diversity of new facts, cf. Gonzalez (2001e), esp., pp. 505–508.

[18] Popper was manifestly interested in the problem of the interdependence between prediction and the predicted event in social sciences, cf. Chap. 3, Sect. 3.5.3.

[19] This distinction is drawn by Hausman in a personal communication (21 January 1996) and clarified afterwards (20 January 1998).

[20] "It is important to recognise that not all predictions involve the future" (Hahn 1993, p. 79). Regarding the topic of "Prediction without the time dimension," cf. (Hahn 1993, pp. 79–81).

options do.[21] In addition, it fits well with two different problems: (i) prediction of those phenomena which, while known, are affected by *uncertainty* (such as the economic activity as a whole); and (ii) prediction of *novel facts* whose truth could be difficult to assess at the moment of making the economic prediction.[22]

These aspects conjoin with the constitutive *features of prediction* recognized in the general methodology of science. (1) Prediction establishes a connection with an event that can happen in the *future*, with it being almost a redundancy to asseverate that link between "prediction" and "future," but some authors do consider the possibility of "prediction of the present" (Mellor 1979, p. 207), or—like Friedman—even accept the "prediction of the past."[23] (2) There is a *reasonable basis* on our present knowledge to state in advance what will happen; so, in principle, the prediction is essentially corrigible if new knowledge appears that modifies the earlier situation. Some predictions are better than others, because they are correct in a greater number of cases. (3) Predicting implies something *possible* and, therefore, a kind of knowledge of *anticipation* which includes uncertainty. What is predicted is a reality that is possible rather than a reality that we are experiencing now or have experienced in the past. In this way, predictive knowledge is less certain or definitive than knowledge about the past or the present: generally, there is—in some way—an incomplete knowledge about the phenomenon or event. When the knowledge is "complete," the level of knowledge is commonly "explanation" rather than "prediction."[24] (4) Prediction is open to the possibility of "unobservable things" (i.e., a phenomenon not yet observed occurs), as well as to several kinds of *novel facts* (for example, facts discovered only as a result of testing some already articulated theory).[25]

Consequently, "scientific prediction" is not just any prediction: it is a statement about the future, epistemologically grounded and open to the possibility of ontologically new facts, which seeks to contribute to scientific progress. From this point

---

[21] Predicting the future is also a usage in papers related to physics, such as Hogarth (1993): "Predicting the future in relativistic spacetimes."

[22] According to this characterization of prediction, to state that the rate of inflation in the first half of 1910 in USA was 3.5 % is not to make a prediction of a "novel fact": that is not a future event.

The position held here is open to a Lakatosian sense of "novel fact": it includes the possibility that "Newtonian scientists predicted the existence and exact motion of small planets which had never been observed before. Or … Einstein's programme … made the stunning prediction that if one measures the distance between two stars in the night and if one measure the distance between them during the day (when they are visible during an eclipse of the sun), the two measurements will be different. Nobody had thought to make such an observation before Einstein's programme" (Lakatos 1974b, p. 5).

[23] "The 'predictions' by which the validity of a hypothesis is tested need not be about phenomena that have not yet occurred, that is, need not be a forecast of future events; they may be about phenomena that have occurred but observations on which have not yet been made or are not known to the person making the prediction. For example, a hypothesis may imply that such and such must have happened in 1906, given some other known circumstances. If a search of the records reveals that such and such did happen, the prediction is confirmed; if it reveals that such and such did not happen, the prediction is contradicted" (Friedman 1953, p. 9).

[24] On the characteristics and types of scientific explanations, cf. Gonzalez (2002b, pp. 21–28).

[25] These traits are dealt in Gonzalez (1996c, p. 207).

of view, it is not acceptable to sustain that "predictions don't need reasons" (Mellor 1979, p. 221).[26] *Rationality* is an ingredient in science and accompanies scientific progress, which is the core of methodological studies. At the same time, having well founded reasons, scientific predictions might be wrong, because they—along with the best theories in science—are *fallible* (Urbach 1987, p. 27). By contrast, it seems in principle too drastic to defend that there are clearly some events that are "literally unpredictable: such that it is impossible to anticipate the statement of a perception" (Mellor 1979, p. 221).

What is actually *unpredictable* of science—now and in the future of humankind—could be difficult to state.[27] In this regard, the probability of saying in advance that something will happen could be extremely low; but, in principle, it is not reasonable to exclude *a priori* any chance. A quite different question is to be able to offer the details of the event: when, where, how, what intensity, etc., it will occur. So, we can distinguish between "unpredictable" and "not predictable."[28]

Clearly, the first perspective is the complete impossibility of predicting (a methodological–ontological thesis: the reality itself does not allow the prediction). The second outlook is the impossibility of predicting on the basis of present knowledge (an epistemological–methodological position: a future knowledge can overcome present difficulties). If economic agents and economic markets were "unpredictable," then economic activity and economics as activity would break down altogether.[29] But this does not exclude the possibility of "not predictable" economic events, either in microeconomics or in macroeconomics.

2.2.2 Two Uses of Prediction

Regarding the social sciences and the sciences of the artificial, there are two fundamental *uses of prediction*: (i) as *a tool for testing* scientific theories, in general, and hypotheses, in particular; and (ii) as *an instrument* for giving information oriented to the *prescriptions for public policy* (i.e., knowledge the direction of human actions in the social world, which includes orientations for political economy). The third use is prediction in the actual practice of implementing the available knowledge, i.e., prediction in the decision-making of the policy-makers in the context of some given circumstances.

In the first case, the methodological character is emphasized: the progress in science is measured according to the criterion of reasonability in the process of making

[26] The interest in the relation between reason and prediction appears in Blackburn (1973).

[27] The dynamic status of scientific knowledge, which involves historicity, makes it more difficult to give timeless examples of unpredictable phenomena. A possible example is to state the impossibility of the full knowledge of the composition of the planets in the very distant galaxies.

[28] This distinction was suggested to me by Patrick Suppes at Stanford University. *Personal communication*, 18 November 1993.

[29] It is also the case that social predictions can have consequences in decision-making that are clearly described, cf. Simon (1954).

predictions and the success of the results predicted. To use prediction for orientation of the public policy highlights another aspect of the methodological dimension of prediction in the social sciences and sciences of the artificial (especially in economics): the direct repercussion in the sphere of social actions and the enlargement of the human possibilities. In this case, prediction leads usually to the introduction of mechanisms for predicting, mainly in the field of political economy. Both uses of prediction need to take into account the problem of regularity in human affairs, because it affects the question of the predictability of social events and human-made products (e.g., financial products), and therefore the predictability of economic actions.[30]

Both main uses of prediction—a tool for testing theories and an instrument for guiding public policy—have a long tradition in economics, because they are related, respectively, to the "positive" and "normative" branches of this science. In my judgment, it is more important to emphasize that what the role of prediction in economics is and ought to be depends on the *reality* that it is predicting. That reality is the outcome of human actions that involve at least some qualitative factors. Thus, economic predictions may require quantitative and qualitative considerations. Even more, besides the quantitative predictions produced by mathematical calculations, economics can need qualitative predictions (for example, in areas such as welfare economics). Both quantitative and qualitative predictions can predict *objective* aspects of economic reality (i.e., the *actions* but not the "acts").[31]

From this point of view, it is easier to understand Friedman's emphasis on the objective dimension of the phenomena studied by economics, Hick's comparison with the natural sciences (which are usually considered much more objective than the social ones), Buchanan's distinction between subjective (non-predictive) and objective (predictive) economics, or Simon's insistence on empirical grounding for economics (see Chap. 6). In one way or another, all of them seek to guarantee *objectivity* in economics by linking prediction with objective knowledge. Moreover, it seems that all agree on something basic: only an objective science could be really *predictive* (i.e., be capable of offering reliable knowledge about future events).

Frequently, the requirement of objectivity appears in a rather narrow sense, connected only with quantitative predictions. According to the conception of economics based on the analysis of economic activity, which is proposed in this book, one should recognize the existence of qualitative predictions in economics (and in the social sciences, in general), which complement the quantitative predictions. They exist *de facto* in economics and they ought to be used in this science, insofar as economics works on economic actions, which include qualitative factors (which

[30] "I should like to observe that there appear to be two quite distinct sorts of regularity in human affairs—the one represented by prediction of the arrival of a train, the other represented by prediction of the number of people who will die in auto accidents over Labor Day weekend. The latter depends, in one form of another, upon the law of large numbers; the former, upon a strict determination of behavior by program" (Simon 1958/1982, p. 390).

[31] The distinction between "acts," "activity," and "actions" is developed in Gonzalez (1994). See Chap. 7, Sect. 7.3.1.

affect human decision-making). Their characteristics can establish a difference with predictions present in physics, in particular, and in the natural sciences, in general.

2.3 The Distinction between Qualitative–Quantitative

Initially, the characterization of scientific prediction and the two main uses of prediction can be connected with the distinction between qualitative and quantitative. It is a methodological difference that is related to semantic aspects as well as epistemological factors. The distinction can be linked to two kinds of problems: (a) the *scientific status* of economics, which is cognate to the central question "are the generic predictions enough?," and (b) the issue of the *divergence* between social sciences and natural sciences, because of the query about the reliability of predictions: "are quantitative predictions in economics similar to quantitative predictions in other sciences?"

2.3.1 Qualitative Prediction and the Issue of Generic Predictions

Qualitative prediction is usually described with three components, which are interconnected: (1) the predictions do not follow, in principle, clear rules, because they commonly rely on an intuitive point of view; (2) the role of the subjects which propose the predictions can be emphasized, because they state in advance the future events on the basis of their own experience (e.g., the "experts" in fields as microeconomics or education) or their own capacities to grasp some kind of events (e.g., sociologists with social planning views or historians with historicist conceptions); and (3) the prediction habitually does not detail explicitly how the available information is incorporated into prediction, and it is possible that several people, given the same information, will end up with different predictions (e.g., stockbrokers or government advisers).

Paul Samuelson recognizes the *need* for qualitative predictions in economics: "in the absence of complete quantitative information concerning our equilibrium conditions, it is hoped to be able to formulate qualitative restrictions on slopes, curvatures, etc., of our equilibrium equations so as to be able to derive definite qualitative restrictions upon responses of our system to changes in certain parameters. It is the primary purpose of this work to indicate how this is possible in a wide range of economic problems" (Samuelson 1947, p. 20). This means the legitimacy of predictive economic hypotheses that are not quantitative, and require a sort of empirical test.

Besides the legitimacy of these predictions, there is another reason to consider them: their *usefulness* in grasping economic changes (such as economic turning points in the supply and demand relation in some markets). For Rosenberg, "the qualitative predictions which we can test against data are roughly the signs, positive or negative, of the partial differentials of the changes in the values of economic variables we set out to measure. (…) In general, qualitative predictions purport to identify the direction in which changes move, without however, identifying the magnitude of these directions" (1989, p. 53). This could be used in cases such as the analysis of an increase in the tax rate that can lead a corporation to a lower or higher output.

Nevertheless, we seek quantitative predictions more frequently than qualitative predictions, because the latter is a kind of prediction that commonly cannot lead us very far. Qualitative predictions tend to focus normally on simple cases or on rather broad tendencies. In addition, the methodological weight of qualitative predictions in scientific research is ordinarily inferior to quantitative predictions. In the social sciences, in general, and in economics, in particular, quantitative factors are often deemed as more "objective" than qualitative ones, both in epistemological and methodological terms.[32] The influence of statistical economics and econometrics has reinforced the idea that quantitative predictions are, in principle, more "objective" than qualitative ones, both in their contents and in order to be tested.

Rosenberg connects generic predictions with qualitative ones and specific predictions with quantitative ones. He considers the existence of predictive content in economics as undeniable, but he sees that actual content is *de facto* limited to generic predictions. In addition, for him, they are almost "a necessary preliminary to specific or quantitative predictions" (1989, p. 67). Historically, classical economic theory predicted the important features: the existence, stability and uniqueness of a market clearing general equilibrium, insisting on the generic predictions.

But Rosenberg considers that afterwards "the shift from classical economic theory to Keynesian macroeconomics, and the rational expectations counter-revolution illustrate the degree to which economics as a discipline seems unable or unwilling to transcend generic predictions" (1989, p. 55). Even though it is a claim focusing on economic theory, it seems to be a strong claim if it is used as a view of economics as a whole, because the overwhelming presence of mathematical models in economics (i.e., statistical economics and econometrics) has increased the realm of "specific or quantitative predictions" in comparison with previous decades.

Within this epistemological–methodological context, where the scientific character of economic predictions is at stake, the issue for the scientific status of economics is clear: are generic predictions enough for economics to be a science? To state this question means that, against the critics of the possibility itself of scientific prediction in economics, it is assumed that economic theory has a predictive power. But the problem is to assess whether generic predictions have enough predictive power to be a science.

Generic predictions are not infrequent in economics, either due to the intrinsic difficulty of obtaining a specific prediction or for our present stage of knowledge about economic phenomena. Generic predictions are those of "the existence of a phenomenon, process, or entity, as opposed to specific predictions about its detailed character. Generic prediction is characteristic of most theories that proceed by establishing the existence of an equilibrium position for the system whose behavior

[32] This problem is connected with the topics of Chap. 5.

they describe, and then claim it moves towards or remains at this equilibrium value" (Rosenberg 1989, p. 53).

There is a relation in Friedrich Hayek (Nobel Prize winner in 1974) between generic predictions ("pattern predictions") and complexity of economics. In his later methodological work—the late 1960s—"Hayek emphasizes that while economics is capable of making certain types of empirical predictions, the complex nature of economic phenomena prevents economists from making anything more than generic, or what Hayek calls "pattern" predictions. These pattern predictions are associated with a particular type of scientific explanation: "explanations of the principle." The complexity of economic phenomena, for example, prevents economists from predicting what any particular consumer will buy, but it is possible to predict the general pattern of an individual consumption and how it is likely to change in response to taxes or subsidies. What an economist is explaining in such theoretical exercises is the general principle at work behind the scenes of the observed pattern of economic behavior" (Hands 2001, p. 47).

Usually, the lack of specificity is seen as a weakness in generic scientific theories. Commonly, in a "mature science" or "well-ordered" science, generic predictions are not considered good enough, because the scientific inquiry is guided by values such as *exhaustiveness*, and *cognitive progress* in science should not stop at a generic level. Moreover, scientific prediction is led by values such as *accuracy* and *precision*, which certainly are not generic: the former expresses correctness, while the latter points out detailed information.[33]

To improve scientific prediction and to get an increasingly specific stage, there are two ways which could be used by economics: "either supplement the theory with theories from other disciplines that will enable us to convert generic into specific predictions, or find measures of the independent or exogenous variables of the theory that will enable us to do so" (Rosenberg 1989, p. 54). This improvement affects economics not only as a "descriptive science" but also as an applied science, because the level of specificity in predictions in political economy could be crucial (for a country and for international trade). Therefore, to look for generic predictions in economics is not—in principle—good enough. It is a search that can be accepted as a starting point, but could hardly be an acceptable end for a science.

2.3.2 *Quantitative Prediction and the Differences Between Sciences*

Unquestionably, during the previous decades, economics has shown an increasing mathematical rigor, especially with the development of statistical economics and econometrics. The general characterization of *quantitative* predictions shows that they have a different character from qualitative ones. First, they require certain rules, within a model which receives a mathematical expression and makes these predictions more accurate and precise than the qualitative ones; second, the empha-

[33] The distinction "accuracy"–"precision" regarding economic prediction is analyzed in Chap. 9.

sis is on the model and its configuration, varying its features from a causal prototype to a non-causal one, and the role of the subject who predicts is not, in principle, relevant; and third, the prediction needs to make explicit how the available information is incorporated in it, and big differences exist, according to the control of the variables and the margin of error.

Are quantitative predictions in economics *similar* to quantitative predictions in other sciences? When this question arises in economics, a first answer is to consider—like Friedman (1953, pp. 4–5)—that there is no fundamental distinction between social sciences and natural sciences, but that economics has special difficulties and problems with data which are not obtainable by the physicist, due to the fact that the investigator—the economist—is also part of the subject matter. In addition, Friedman thinks that the problems of social sciences in conducting experiments does not "reflect a basic difference between the social and physical sciences both because it is not peculiar to the social sciences—witness astronomy—and because the distinction between a controlled experiment and uncontrolled experience is at best one of degree" (Friedman 1953, p. 10).

Another completely different answer to the same question is to establish a gap between both kinds of science: that is, to state—as Hicks does—that "the word prediction, as used in economics, commonly has a rather different meaning from what it has in experimental sciences. This is because our predictions are in time, in historical time, in a way that most scientific predictions are not. They are predictions about the future, the future from now, (…) Yet though the predictions relate to the future, the evidence on which we base them comes from the past" (Hicks 1986, p. 98). This view assumes that economics cannot be an experimental science, a claim also defended by some philosophers of science today, such as Tony Lawson (1997, pp. 199–226),[34] when there is *de facto* a tradition of decades of "experimental economics" (Roth 1988; Gonzalez 2007a).[35]

Several elements in these conflicting positions on quantitative predictions—absence of real distinction and deep division—require analysis. Firstly, a difference between prediction in economics and in natural sciences is often clear, insofar as they have many times a different degree of *regularity* of the events, due in part to the different degree of *complexity*. To some extent, regularity is a normal phenomenon in natural sciences (physics, geology, biology, etc.), in which the reproducibility of occurrences makes accurate predictability possible in many cases.

However, economic regularities are usually not derivable from "economic laws" (whose universality and even its existence are at stake).[36] In fact, some events in economics are completely unusual and even notoriously unexpected, like the great inflation of 1973 onwards, the economic crash in the stock markets in October 1987, the economic turbulences after 11 September 2001, or the depth of the ongo-

[34] His views on prediction are in Lawson (1985).

[35] In 2012 Alvin Roth was awarded with the Noble Prize in Economics.

[36] Even the notion of "law" in economics is under discussion, cf. Hausman (2000). The debate may be seen also in the context of the social sciences as a whole, where it is discussed if there can be laws of social science. In addition, it is commonly assumed that theories in the social sciences are less advanced than those of physics.

ing economic crisis (which started around the summer of 2007 and was noticeable on September of 2008).

Secondly, the *historicity* of factors that intervene in the economic predictions has strong weight. It might be considered *prima facie* that the feature is not in itself something inappropriate for natural sciences (like physics, chemistry or biology), insofar as the temporal aspects are not irrelevant in them (or even, there is a "natural history"). However, there are differences between "temporality" and "historicity" (Gonzalez 1996e, 1996d, 2011b). In addition, both kinds of sciences present a variance in the *type of link* between past and future events as well as in the "explanation" or "understanding" of what has happened and future occurrences: the link is usually weaker and more complex in economics than it is in natural science.[37]

Thirdly, the big difference is—in my judgment—in the problems of *accuracy* and *precision* of economic predictions, because of the complexity of the factors that are studied in order to predict scientifically (Gonzalez 2011a). So, even though the theory of chaos has shown an indeterminacy in natural dynamical systems which are usually deterministic, in economics—as well as in other social sciences and sciences of the artificial—to predict is commonly more difficult than in natural sciences: there are more levels at stake in social events (as will be seen with the distinction "economic activity" and "economics as activity") (Gonzalez 1994, esp., pp. 262–280). In addition, some economists think that economics could be a chaotic system (Simon 1989).

It seems clear that the differences in the kind of subject matter have incidence in the role of prediction. They make the economic case usually more difficult than the physical one, and they affect the possibility of prediction itself as well as the question of its accuracy and precision. Besides the epistemological and methodological factors, there is an *ontological* element, which Amartya Sen has pointed out. The notorious difficulties in making economic predictions—and especially making right predictions—"might be seen as resting on the fact, noted by Alfred Marshall, that 'no two economic events are exactly alike in all respects' (1949, p. 639). This diagnosis does, however, slightly beg the question because, strictly speaking, that characteristic is shared by, say, physics as well (…). The real difference lies in the enormous variety of 'respects' that could actually make an important difference in economics, and the complex ways in which these economic influences operate and interact with each other" (Sen 1986, pp. 4–5).

Besides the ontological element, there are at least two problems that concern intrinsic difficulties in social sciences: the *anticipation* of human actions and the *knowledge of the variables* that intervene now and in the future. Basically, the first problem is logico-methodological, which affects the possibility of predictions in social sciences, and it has received specific attention in the controversy over Popper's historicism (Gonzalez 1984; Urbach 1978, 1985; Chap. 3). The second problem is epistemological, which has been emphasized many times as the main obstacle for

[37] This affects the features of "causality" in social sciences, an issue discussed by philosophers as well as economists.

the accuracy and precision of predictions in social sciences and design sciences, in general, and of economics, in particular.

Unambiguously, the anticipation of human actions includes a wide collection of factors (social, historical, political, psychological, and biological), which constitute a source of its complexity and have a direct repercussion in economics. The knowledge of the variables depends on access to the results of interactions of human beings, dealing with each other in economic affairs with different values, objectives, motivations, expectations, and circumstances. Usually, all these elements together make prediction in economics more difficult than in the natural sciences. Specifically, this is the case in *predicting the choices* of economic agents and in *predicting the results of interactions* of many human and social entities in a wide variety of ways (Sen 1986, p. 5; regarding the underlying problem, cf. Buchanan 1987c). Therefore, quantitative predictions in economics are frequently more difficult than in mature natural sciences.

Within the social sciences, in general, and in economics, in particular, probabilistic predictions are especially important. They can be used as a tool for testing theories and as an instrument for guiding public policy. The second case has more practical consequences in the context of the social setting. It can also be connected to everyday life *conditional statements* like "if we do X, then very likely Y will happen" or, "if we do X, we will make Y's happening less likely." In addition, there are also *counterfactual predictions*: "if we had not done X yesterday, then Y would happen tomorrow" (or "if we had not done X yesterday, then Y would *very likely* happen tomorrow"). These kinds of predictions are relevant for public policy, even though they are hard to confirm and thus difficult for "science."

2.3.3 Types of Information for Prediction

Instead of the distinction qualitative prediction–quantitative prediction, which has a long tradition in economics as well as in other sciences, the idea may be accepted of the existence of *different types* of information understood as the basis to characterize economic predictions. Thus, some authors maintain that there are three possibilities of cognitive contents in analyzing predictions in economics: (a) subjective information; (b) statistical information regarding a concrete phenomenon through a lapse of time; and (c) statistical information that interconnects several phenomena or events.

(a) *Subjective information* (or even "subjectual" information)[38] is when the knowledge used for predictions comes from an individual perspective or has an institutional character (belong to a firm, a corporation, etc.) but is based upon ex-

[38] "Subjectual" expresses what is *objective in the subjects*, i.e., the factors that appear in the individual agents but they are not reducible to pure idiosyncratic elements of each one taking in isolation. In this sense, the need of decision-making by individual agents regarding the future is "subjectual," whereas the decisions as such of each one of the agents could be subjective (i.e., the decisions might be taken through biographical motivations or under specific circumstances).

periences, attitudes and expectations of the agents, either considered as individuals or by means of aggregations (i.e., "experts"). (b) *Statistical information* regarding *a concrete phenomenon through a lapse of time* is when the focus is on a time-series, searching statistical regularities based on the behavior of the variable that is analyzed (a variable that is studied via the analysis of frequencies of stochastic processes and probabilistic models). (c) *Statistical information* that interconnects *several phenomena* or *events* (e.g., causal relations) can be used to several aims: to seek analogies between similar phenomena, to search for statistical relations which can include causality or interdependence between events, and to look for structural components that derive from the dynamic of the variables through the time (i.e., econometric models) (Pulido and Lopez 1999, pp. 26, 52 and 55–58).

This tripartite distinction of information as a basis for economic predictions seeks to substitute, or put aside, the duality "qualitative prediction"–"quantitative prediction," where the former—qualitative—gathers basically the subjective information while the latter—quantitative—comprise the statistical information regarding a concrete phenomenon (time-series) as well as statistical information which interconnects several phenomena or events (analogies, statistical regularities of variables in their overall behavior, dynamic effects of variable and their incidence in structural changes, etc.).

Nonetheless, even the defenders of this triple distinction agree that "the utilization of opinions or expectations does not imply that the prediction cannot be quantified (for example, by means of the index of assent or an indicator of growth supported by the experts). In addition, the use of historical or relational information might end up (even though it is not the usual thing) in a merely qualitative prediction on the sense of the change or the relative levels of variation" (Pulido and Lopez 1999, p. 54).[39]

Therefore, even though the purpose was to overcome the distinction between qualitative prediction and quantitative prediction, this duality is still accepted *de facto*, presumably because it has a more basic character than the triple distinction of prediction pointed out here (prediction on subjective basis, of statistical nature on a concrete phenomenon and of statistical character on the interconnection of several phenomena or events). However, when the diverse predictive approaches—in science, in general, and in economics, in particular—are studied, three successive facets appear: first, subjective or judgmental; second, inferential (focus on a variable); and, third, formal or sophisticated (focus on the interdependence of variables, such as in relations of causality) (Rescher 1998, p. 88; see Chap. 10 here).

Rather than reduce economic prediction to a single methodological kind based on *a type* of information, it seems obvious that economic predictions include a variety of possibilities due to the twofold character of economics as a *basic science* and as an *applied science*. Thus, the characterization of "prediction" in the realm of economics is open to a diversity of possibilities. As a basic science, predictions of economic theory have been central in the methodology of this social science and

[39] See also Pulido (1989).

design science (Gonzalez 2008); and as an applied science, statistical predictions and econometric predictions have had a crucial role.[40]

Ultimately, the difference between statistical prediction and econometric prediction lies in the relevant use by econometric prediction of economic assumptions in addition to statistical assumptions. But statistical prediction and econometric prediction have a close relation insofar as they seek the estimation of the value of a variable (that may be one-dimensional or multidimensional) given the information of other variables that are known or are predictable. Such an estimate is obtained through the (conditional) expected value (or "expectation") of that variable, taking into account the information of the other variables previously defined. In this case, there is an overlapping between "expectation" and "prediction" (cf. Chap. 9).

2.4 Diversity of Economic Predictions

Undoubtedly, there are many kinds of economic predictions. From the philosophico-methodological point of view, which is the focus in this approach, the relevant cases can be located mainly in two different spheres: the first is directly connected with the *expected time horizon* and some *epistemological–ontological* aspects, whereas the second one highlights the *epistemological–methodological* considerations. The first group includes standard cases: the types of economic predictions according to important factors, such as the *length of time* and the *kind of event* predicted. The second group seeks new aspects in the field and comprehends the variety of economic predictions due to the *degree of control* of the variables, which can distinguish several predictive notions: foresight, prediction, forecasting, and planning.

2.4.1 *Types of Economic Predictions*

Within the sphere of the methodological distinction between qualitative prediction and quantitative prediction, it is possible to obtain many different types of predictions in economics. In this section some of the more relevant cases are pointed out. On the one hand, there is the very common differentiation of predictions according to the *length of time* or time horizon. On the other hand, there is the difference among predictions based on the *kind of event* predicted. Both cases are open to the methodological distinction between specific prediction and generic prediction, which has been discussed and affects the methods and limits of prediction in economics (on this issue, cf. Chaps. 10 and 11).

[40] According to Clive Granger (Nobel Prize in 2003), one of the controversies concerning the modeling process in economics is directly related to the use of economic theory: "Should the model specification be based on economic theory? Should the model be based on some well-founded theory, such as an optimizing typical agent theory?… What if there are several competing theories?" (Granger 1990b, p. 14).

There are *de facto* several *types of predictions* that can be made in economics and each requires, in principle, a different approach. The first classification is also common to other sciences, and has a clear presence in technology as well. It depends on the *length of time* in the future which the prediction looks to. (i) When the statement is about the near future, the prediction is in the *short run*. (ii) The intermediate case between the near future and a distant future is the instance of *middle run* prediction. (iii) When the content of the statement is in the horizon of a distant future, the prediction is in the *long run*.

According to this general presentation, what constitutes short, middle, or long run is not well defined, because it depends on several factors, such as the *variable* being predicted and the sort of *data available*. Thus, the short, middle, or long run in unemployment could be different from the case of business cycles. In this regard, it is assumed that, in general, the further ahead one predicts the less well one does it; in that larger periods errors are likely to turn out. The reason for this is clear: usually the information available for making predictions is more relevant in the short run than in the longer run (Granger 1989, p. 7).

A more sophisticated distinction on the *time horizon* of prediction typifies differences among five situations: immediate, short run, middle run, long run, and very long run (Firth 1977, p. 19). (1) The *immediate horizon* is between 0 and 3 months. It is used by stockbrokers or in some operative decisions (e.g., in management of inventories in small business). (2) The *short run* is from 3 to 12 months, and is practiced in decisions made by the government to control budget. (3) The *middle run* is between 1 and 3 years. This is used in some strategic decisions (e.g., leasing of technological equipment in some businesses). (4) The *long run* goes from 3 to 10 years, and is adopted in other strategic decisions (e.g., investments in research and development). (5) The *very long run* is beyond 10 years, and is the horizon used when deep changes are decided.

Another type of prediction depends on the *kind of event* to be predicted. (a) The *event outcome prediction* is used when it is known that an event will occur in the future with virtual certainty, but it should predict what the outcome of the event will be (e.g., a new product will be introduced in the computer market, what will its sales be?). (b) The *event timing prediction* is adopted when the prediction considers questions about when, if ever, an event will occur (e.g., when will the Federal Reserve modify interest rates? or when will be the next recession of American economy happen?). (c) The *time series prediction* comes when a prediction is made using a sequence of values usually recorded at equidistant time intervals (e.g., the weekly automobile production by the Opel division of General Motors or the monthly unemployment rate of British economy) (Granger 1989, pp. 7–12).[41]

Clive Granger maintains that the main problem with predicting the *outcome of a future event* is that "the event may be unique, so that really relevant information may be difficult or expensive to acquire" (1989, p. 7). The main approach to event outcome prediction is then to gather relevant data (e.g., to predict the success of

[41] In his analysis, he considers the words "prediction" and "forecasting" as completely interchangeable, cf. Granger (1989), p. 2, note.

the introduction of a new product for computers, the company will perform various market tests). The aim is to increase one's information set, and the usual limitations in doing this depend on the cost of gathering the information as well as the level of the relevant technology. In this regard, there is a connection between the scientific prediction and the technological prediction, because the capacity to compute some data depends on the availability of technological devices.

Event timing prediction depends on the existence of a sequence of similar events in the past, such as the timing of the Federal Reserve to modify interest rates or the signs of recession of American economy in previous occasions. By observing the pattern of the time between the events studied, it might be possible to predict when the next event will presumably occur. But it is more common to use the procedure of seeking the leading indicators, which are the events that are likely to precede the specific event that we are trying to predict (e.g., the figures of indicators such as unemployment or inflation).

Time series prediction makes statements about what value the economic series will take at some future time period $n+h$, where n is now and h is hence (h represents the number of time periods into the future that the predictor is looking at). In principle, there is little reason to suppose that it is possible to predict the value that will occur at $n+h$ with perfect accuracy and complete precision.[42] Thus, "$xn+h$ is a random variable, when viewed at time n, and so should be characterized in probability terms. In particular, one could talk about its distribution function or its probability density function, plus summary statistics such as mean and variance" (Granger 1989, p. 9). These distributions will then be conditional ones, given the information available at time n upon which a prediction is based.

Regarding time series prediction, there is an additional distinction among "interval," "point," and "trace" (Granger 1989, pp. 10–11). There is *interval forecast* when the forecaster puts limits on the value being forecast and has a reasonably high degree of confidence of being correct (e.g., 'I believe the price of tomatoes in Texas will be in the range of w cents and z cents per pound two years from now, with probability 0.96'). *Point prediction* is a single outcome $xn+h$ that, in some way, represents well the whole distribution of possible values (e.g., 'there will be 150 minor accidents in the main car manufacturing plant over the next four months'). Point predictions for the time series are specially used by the governments and also in many businesses. *Trace forecast* is the whole sequence of point predictions for $h=1, 2, 3, \ldots H$. A trace forecast is utilized in many cases, such as to decide the best time to enter in a specific market and purchase further stocks of a commodity, trying to buy at the lowest available price.

---

[42] On this issue of the distinction "accuracy"–"precision," see Chap. 9, Sect. 9.5. From a different point of view, there is an interesting analysis on the theoretical virtues of parsimoniousness, unification, and non *ad hocness*, on the dispute about Bayesianism, and on empiricism and scientific realism, cf. Foster and Sober (1994).

2.4.2 *The Distinctions between "Foresight," "Prediction," "Forecasting," and "Planning"*

Generally, the concept of "scientific prediction" is considered within the quantitative context rather than the qualitative. It is an expression that can appear in several ways with different senses and references, all of them with methodological consequences. This semantic and methodological diversity is particularly clear in economics, where an explicit distinction can be made between different notions related to future economic events: "foresight," "prediction," "forecast," and "planning" (Fernandez Valbuena 1990, pp. 388–389; Gonzalez 1996c). In this regard, if there are at least four kinds of scientific explanations (i.e., deductive–nomological, inductive–statistical, functional or teleological, and genetic or historical),[43] it could also be the case that prediction can also distinguish several possibilities, according to the degree of control of the variables made by the scientific prediction.

A *foresight* takes place when there is a clear control of the variables involved: it shows the state of a variable within a period of time, when that variable is directly or indirectly under our control (e.g., the interest rates on the immediate horizon; the collection of some kind of taxes in the short run, such as the VAT of some products; the number of civil servants next year in a country where this matter is regulated by the government, etc.). If there is a variation in the foresight, it could be as a result of a modification in the variable controlled (e.g., in the data used by the Federal Reserve, the Bank of England, or the European Central Bank; in the shortage of some products; new tax regulations, etc.).

Prediction concerns what, strictly speaking, is not known: it displays the state of a variable within a period of time, when the variable is not really under our control (e.g., the rate of inflation in the United Kingdom in the first term of next year or the price of fuel if there is a new war in the Middle East). In the determination of the predicted variable factors intervene which are beyond the control of the predictor (e.g., the level of inflation next year during the second semester; the number of unemployed in a year from now; the situation of car manufacturing in the European Union after some international agreements, etc.). In this regard, it can be pointed out that "in order to predict, foresight is needed, because the values that will be taken by the variables which we predict depend upon—although in a very partial way—the values that will be got by the variables which we control" (Fernandez Valbuena 1990, pp. 388–389).

Forecast is a prediction with a margin of error associated with it (e.g., the rate of unemployment in the United Kingdom next December will be between such and such per cent of the active population). It is not a mere quantitative prediction but rather a prediction where the level of knowledge of the variables offers a "weaker" situation than in "prediction" in the strict sense (e.g., the number of death casualties in car accidents next year in this region will be between 5 % and 10 % higher than

[43] This is the "classical" presentation of Nagel (1961, pp. 20–26). However, there are more types of scientific explanation, as it can be seen in the books Salmon (1990) and Gonzalez (2002a).

this year). The difference among these different cases in the future could be in the model chosen. Within an economic framework "that a particular presentation could be a prediction or a forecast depends on—almost always—the procedure used to make it. Thus, a determinist model (where there are no random variables) makes predictions, whereas a stochastic model (which includes random variables) makes forecastings" (Fernandez Valbuena 1990, p. 389).[44]

Finally, *planning* is a different concept about the economic future: it consists mainly in calculation and distribution. It assumes foresights, predictions and forecasts, using them to get some targets in space and time. Planning has a clearly teleological sense (i.e., it looks for a goal), whereas the others do not. Moreover, it is a concept of *action*: it is what should be done in a temporal schedule, taking into account the knowledge of the future (which is required in order to know possible ends and means). Thus, it is usually related to economic prescription and has an important role in economic organizations.

Planning has been a topic of deep controversies in economics in two directions. First, there is the question of the desirable scope of central planning in a modern industrial economy. Second, there is the issue of the relative merits of centralization or decentralization in large industrial concerns. Thus is studied in terms of the "planning process."[45] The reason is clear: it is a concept in the realm of decision theory (Granger and Machina 2006, p. 82). In fact, James March and Herbert Simon consider that *planning*, broadly defined, is "indistinguishable from other kinds of decision-making" (1993, p. 221).

Is this quadruple distinction on prediction too strict, even unrealistic? It suggests the idea of being something like a *genus* that becomes diversified in its *species*. From this point of view, a distinction between the general concept of "scientific prediction" and more specific characterizations, such as "foresight," "prediction," and "forecast" (which contribute to "planning") makes sense. In fact, it is possible to distinguish between these types of statements about future events; thus, the differences are relevant (especially in some cases). So, the distinction can avoid the objection of being too accurate or even redundant (Gonzalez 1996c).

Meanwhile, another objection arises: some sciences (e.g., economics) and some philosophers frequently use "prediction" and "forecast" without any distinction (Toulmin 1961). But this objection only takes into account a use that reflects a narrow scope. It only describes what *de facto* is and does not contemplate what *ought to be*, which is the other relevant side in methodological studies. These are dual—analytical and prescriptive—in the reflections on the processes of research.

Interestingly, Wittgenstein seems to accept the distinction between the notions of "foresight" and "prediction." *Foresight* includes a level of guarantee about the future that is the maximum possible (e.g., I can foresee my future actions accord-

---

[44] It seems rather obvious that there is no unanimity in this terminology, because very frequently the use of "prediction" and "forecasting" is completely interchangeable. On the use of "forecasting," see, for example, Anderson (1979), Irvine and Martin (1984), Klein (1984), Shim and Siegel (1988), and Woods and Fildes (1976).

[45] A detailed analysis of its role in this regard is in March and Simon (1993), pp. 193–233; esp., pp. 221–233. For a previous study from a different angle, cf. Holt et al. (1960).

ing to my intentions). Meanwhile *prediction* has fewer guarantees: it intrinsically has something not known. From this point of view, it is reasonable to have diverse predictions about the same action when the foundations are different (Wittgenstein 1982, nos. 232 and 923; pp. 34e and 119e). This phenomenon is important for science, in general, and for social sciences, in particular (mainly economics). It appears in Wittgenstein's mathematics, because the sense of prediction in his writings on this science is not a complete foresight, the absolute determination of the future result (Gonzalez 1996b, p. 304; cf. Wittgenstein 1974; Gonzalez 1993b).

Wittgenstein is against a subjective way of understanding prediction: he rejects the egocentric focus as starting point. At the same time, he recognizes differences between the first and the third person. "There are two different facts here: one, that in general I foresee my actions with greater accuracy than anyone else; the other, that my prediction is not founded on the same evidence as someone else's, and that it allows for different conclusions" (Wittgenstein 1982, no. 893, p. 114e; Wittgenstein 1953, II, xi/1976, p. 224e). For him, I foresee my actions mainly due to my intentions. When the prediction is contained in the expression of my intention, then it "has not the same foundation as another person's prediction of what I shall do, and (that) the consequences of these predictions are different" (Wittgenstein 1982, no. 905; p. 116e).

However, on the one hand, it should be pointed out that, from a *semantic* point of view, there is a qualification in the terms. "Foresight," "prediction," and "forecast" are used in these pages with a *scientific* sense and reference, which goes further than the ordinary one. These concepts can be distinguished from pre-scientific foresights, predictions and forecasts, insofar as they have a theoretical support and cannot be reduced simply to a matter of experience. The more precise nature of scientific language helps to clarify these activities concerning the future.

On the other hand, from an *epistemological* perspective, they go further than the intuitive conception based on individual or collective knowledge. So, according to the different degree of control of the variables, they give a diverse reply to the question: why can we anticipate (foresee, predict or forecast) such and such phenomena or events? The differences in the answers are conditioned by factors such as the *margin of error*. This is relevant, because the control of the variables is "maximum" for the foresight and "minimum" for the forecast. In fact, "the objective of forecasting is to reduce the forecast error: to produce forecasts that are seldom incorrect and that have small forecast error" (Abraham and Ledolter 1983/2005, pp. 1–2).[46] So, there appears a new aspect. To some extent, insofar as there is a mathematical "technique" which accompanies these activities, it is possible to assume that foresight, prediction, and forecast are sometimes an *application* of science rather than the kernel of science itself.

Foresight, prediction and forecast start from a specific language as well as knowledge, and can be subjected to rigorous mathematical tools (they seek to be accurate

[46] The question of level of error is always a crucial one, not only for social sciences but also for natural sciences: "we regard the total absence of error as radically implausible. Even if nature were completely deterministic, there still would be *observational* errors" (Foster and Sober 1994, p. 10).

and precise). These aspects—language, knowledge and mathematical tools—comprise progress of scientific knowledge: the first and the second are at the bottom of the methodological activity, and the third is an instrument for its measurement. Although there are links with them to ordinary language, the gap is increasing with respect to ordinary use, as can be seen in books and journals devoted to this topic. These publications have a strong tendency towards quantitative research and they give more weight to past events than to the present situation, considering the latter as one element more in a process.

Concerning the case of economics, Clive Granger recently proposed the use of "prediction" connected to theoretical models, broad empirical observations, non-specific contents and their evaluation. Meanwhile he suggests using "forecasting" for extrapolations based on empirical data, detailed observations of "actual economics" and specific contents related to the future.[47] Thus, for him, "prediction" seems to be in the realm of theoretical economics and the evaluation of its statements regarding the future, and "forecasting" is mainly in the field of applied economics, with a clear link to the policy-making (Granger 2012, pp. 312 and 314–315).

As a matter of fact, this solution regarding the predictive language is in tune with other influential econometricians, and it will be taken into account. But it seems better to follow a more sophisticated approach in philosophico-methodological terms. This is what has been developed here, where prediction is related to three levels of analysis, instead of just two: basic science (economic theory), applied science (applied economics), and application of science (actual policy-making). In addition, there are four concepts regarding the scientific study of future, instead of just two: foresight, prediction, forecasting, and planning.

To sum up, semantically "prediction" is a statement about the future: the sense of anticipation could be ontological or epistemological, and the reference may be a new fact and some non-observed phenomena.[48] Logically, scientific prediction and scientific explanation are structurally asymmetrical: a prediction cannot be an explanation insofar as an explanation is an argument. Epistemologically, prediction requires an empirical grounding, and scientific theories can offer reasonable bases for the practical prediction.[49] Methodologically, it is still an open discussion on whether prediction has more weight on confirmation than accommodation, but

[47] "Forecasting will be limited to the extrapolations based on empirical models or data exploration, whereas prediction will be formed from theoretical model" (Granger 2012, p. 312).

[48] Ontologically, the reality itself which is predicted do not require to have *eo ipso* posterior existence to the predictive statement, because it is legitimate to say in advance a social or economical event which, strictly speaking, is already going on (as was the case in astronomy with the prediction of Neptune or in quantum mechanics with the existence of neutrino). In human contexts, when a person is qualified as "predictable" could be seen as a "reliable person" and that means that the person is well known.

[49] "Typically there will be an infinite array of generalisations which are compatible with the available observational evidence, and which are therefore, as yet, unrefuted. If we were free to choose arbitrarily from among all the unrefuted alternatives, we could predict anything whatever. If there were no rational basis for choosing from among all the unrefuted alternatives, then, as I think Popper would agree, there would be no such thing as rational prediction" (Salmon 1981, p. 117).

mainstream economics (mainly economic theory) usually emphasizes prediction over accommodation. Axiologically, it has a clear value for science.

Predicting is used as a tool for testing theories and as an instrument for guiding the public policy. Both uses deal with qualitative predictions and, above all, with quantitative predictions. Thus, the duality qualitative–quantitative is maintained, even though there are several types of information to make predictions (e.g., subjective, statistical, and econometric). In addition, besides the diversity of economic predictions, which are commonly used (e.g., length of time, kind of event, etc.), there is a need for new categories that can enlarge the methodological role of prediction in economics: "foresight," "prediction," "forecasting," and "planning."

References

Abraham, B., and J. Ledolter. 1983/2005. *Statistical methods for forecasting*. New York: Wiley.

Achinstein, P. 1995. Explanation v. prediction: Which carries more weight? In *PSA 1994*, vol. 2, ed. D. Hull, M. Forbes, and R. Burian, 156–164. East Lansing: Philosophy of Science Association.

Anderson, O. D., ed. 1979. *Forecasting*. Amsterdam: North-Holland.

Bacon, F. 1620. *Novum Organum sive iudicia vera de interpretatione naturae et regno hominis*, London. (Translated into English by Peter Urbach and John Gibson, and edited by Peter Urbach 1994. *Novum Organum*. La Salle, IL: Open Court.)

Barnes, E. C. 2005a. Predictivism for pluralists. *British Journal for the Philosophy of Science* 56:421–450.

Barnes, E. C. 2005b. On Mendeleev predictions: Comment on Scerri and Worrall. *Studies in History and Philosophy of Science* 36:801–821.

Barnes, E. C. 2008. *The paradox of predictivism*. Cambridge: Cambridge University Press.

Blackburn, S. 1973. *Reason and prediction*. Cambridge: Cambridge University Press.

Brush, S. G. 1989. Prediction and theory evaluation: The case of light bending. *Science* 246:1124–1129.

Brush, S. G. 1995. Dynamics of theory change: The role of predictions. In *PSA 1994*, vol. 2, ed. D. Hull, M. Forbes, and R. Burian, 133–145. East Lansing, MI: Philosophy of Science Association.

Buchanan, J. M. 1987c. Is economics the science of choice? In *Economics: Between predictive science and moral philosophy*, J. M. Buchanan, 35–50. College Station: Texas A & M University Press.

Duhem, P. 1914. *La théorie physique; son object, sa structure* (2nd ed.). Paris: M. Riviere, Paris. (Translated into English by Ph. P. Wiener 1974: *The aim and structure of physical theory*. New York: Atheneum.)

Earman, J., and C. Glymour. 1980. Relativity and eclipses: The British expeditions of 1919 and their predecessors. *Historical Studies in the Physical Sciences* 11:49–85.

Fernandez Valbuena, S. 1990. Predicción y Economía. In *Aspectos metodológicos de la investigación científica*, 2nd ed., ed. W. J. Gonzalez, 385–405. Madrid-Murcia: Ediciones Universidad Autónoma de Madrid and Publicaciones Universidad de Murcia.

Firth, M. 1977. *Forecasting methods in business and management*. London: E. Arnold.

Foster, M., and E. Sober. 1994. How to tell when simpler, more unified, or less *ad hoc* theories will provide more accurate predictions. *The British Journal for the Philosophy of Science* 45:1–35.

Friedman, M. 1953. The methodology of positive economics. In *Essays in positive economics*, M. Friedman, 3–43. Chicago: The University of Chicago Press. (6th repr.1969).

Gonzalez, W. J. 1984. La interpretación historicista de las Ciencias Sociales. *Anales de Filosofía* 2:109–137.

Gonzalez, W. J. 1993b. The role of prediction in Wittgenstein's mathematics. In *Wittgenstein's philosophy of mathematics,* vol. 2, ed. K. Puhl, 126–132. Vienna: Hölder-Pichler-Tempsky.

Gonzalez, W. J. 1994. Economic prediction and human activity. An analysis of prediction in economics from action theory. *Epistemologia* 17:253–294.

Gonzalez, W. J. 1995. Reichenbach's concept of prediction. *International Studies in the Philosophy of Science* 9 (1): 37–58.

Gonzalez, W. J. 1996b. Prediction and mathematics: The Wittgensteinian approach. In *Spanish studies in the philosophy of science,* ed. G. Munevar, 299–332. Dordrecht: Kluwer.

Gonzalez, W. J. 1996c. On the theoretical basis of prediction in economics. *Journal of Social Philosophy* 27 (3): 201–228.

Gonzalez, W. J., ed. 1996d. *Acción e Historia. El objeto de la Historia y la Teoría de la Acción.* A Coruña: Publicaciones Universidad de A Coruña.

Gonzalez, W. J. 1996e. Caracterización del objeto de la Ciencia de la Historia y bases de su configuración metodológica. In *Acción e Historia. El objeto de la Historia y la Teoría de la Acción,* ed. W. J. Gonzalez, 25–111. A Coruña: Publicaciones Universidad de A Coruña.

Gonzalez, W. J. 2001e. Lakatos's approach on prediction and novel facts. *Theoria* 16 (3): 499–518.

Gonzalez, W. J., ed. 2002a. *Diversidad de la explicación científica.* Barcelona: Ariel.

Gonzalez, W. J. 2002b. Caracterización de la "explicación científica" y tipos de explicaciones científicas. In *Diversidad de la explicación científica,* ed. W. J. Gonzalez, 13–49. Barcelona: Ariel.

Gonzalez, W. J. 2004b. The many faces of Popper's methodological approach to prediction. In *Karl Popper: Critical appraisals,* ed. Ph. Catton, and G. Macdonald, 78–98. London: Routledge.

Gonzalez, W. J. 2005. The philosophical approach to science, technology and society. In *Science, technology and society: A philosophical perspective,* ed. W. J. Gonzalez, 3–49. A Coruña: Netbiblo.

Gonzalez, W. J. 2007a. The role of experiments in the social sciences: The case of economics. In *General philosophy of science: Focal issues,* ed. T. Kuipers, 275–301. Amsterdam: Elsevier.

Gonzalez, W. J. 2008. Rationality and prediction in the sciences of the artificial: Economics as a design science. In *Reasoning, rationality, and probability,* ed. M. C. Galavotti, R. Scazzieri, and P. P. Suppes, 165–186. Stanford: CSLI Publications.

Gonzalez, W. J. 2011a. Complexity in economics and prediction: The role of parsimonious factors. In *Explanation, prediction, and confirmation,* ed. D. Dieks, W. J. Gonzalez, S. Hartman, Th. Uebel, and M. Weber, 319–330. Dordrecht: Springer.

Gonzalez, W. J. 2011b. Conceptual changes and scientific diversity: The role of historicity. In *Conceptual revolutions: From cognitive science to medicine,* ed. W. J. Gonzalez, 39–62. A Coruña: Netbiblo.

Gonzalez, W. J. 2012a. La vertiente dinámica de las Ciencias de la Complejidad. Repercusión de la historicidad para la predicción científica en las Ciencias de Diseño. In *Las Ciencias de la Complejidad: Vertiente dinámica de las Ciencias de Diseño y sobriedad de factores,* ed. W. J. Gonzalez, 73–106. A Coruña: Netbiblo.

Gonzalez, W. J. 2013c. The roles of scientific creativity and technological innovation in the context of complexity of science. In *Creativity, innovation, and complexity in science*, ed. W. J. Gonzalez, 11–40. A Coruña: Netbiblo.

Granger, C. W. J. 1989. *Forecasting in business and economics*, 2nd ed. San Diego: Academic Press (1st ed., 1980).

Granger, C. W. J. 1990b. Where are the controversies in econometric methodology? In *Modelling economics series: Readings in econometric methodology*, ed. C. W. J. Granger, 1–23. Oxford: Clarendon Press.

Granger, C. W. J. 2012. The philosophy of economic forecasting. In *Philosophy of economics,* ed. U. Mäki, 311–327. Amsterdam: Elsevier.

Granger, C. W. J., and M. J. Machina. 2006. Forecasting and decision theory. In *Handbook of economic forecasting: Volume 1*, ed. G. Elliot, C. W. J. Granger, and A. Timmerman, 81–98. Amsterdam: Elsevier.

Grünbaum, A. 1962. Temporally asymmetric principles, parity between explanation and prediction, and mechanism versus teleology. *Philosophy of Science* 29:146–170.
Grünbaum, A. 1969. Explanation and prediction are symmetrical. In *The nature and scope of social science: A critical anthology,* ed. L. I. Krimerman, 126–132. New York: Appleton-Century-Crofts.
Hahn, F. 1993. Predicting the economy. In *Predicting the future,* ed. L. Howe, and A. Wain, 77–95. Cambridge: Cambridge University Press.
Hands, D. Wade. 2001. *Reflection without rules. Economic methodology and contemporary science theory*. Cambridge: Cambridge University Press.
Hanson, N. R. 1959. On the symmetry between explanation and prediction. *The Philosophical Review* 68 (3): 349–358.
Harker, D. 2006. Accommodation and prediction: The case of the persistent head. *British Journal of the Philosophy of Science* 57:309–321.
Hausman, D. M. 2000. ¿Necesita leyes la Economía? *Argumentos de Razón Técnica* 3:115–137.
Hempel, C. G. 1966. *Philosophy of natural science*. Englewood Cliffs: Prentice Hall.
Hempel, C. G., and P. Oppenheim. 1948. Studies in the logic of explanation. *Philosophy of Science* 15:135–175. (Reprinted in Hempel, C. 1965. *Aspects of scientific explanation and other essays*, 245–295. New York: Free Press.)
Hicks, J. 1986. Is economics a science? In *Foundations of economics. Structures of inquiry and economic theory,* ed. M. Baranzini, and R. Scazzieri, 91–101. Oxford: B. Blackwell.
Hitchcock, Ch., and E. Sober. 2004. Prediction versus accommodation and the risk of overfitting. *British Journal for the Philosophy of Science* 55 (1): 1–34.
Hogarth, M. 1993. Predicting the future in relativistic spacetimes. *Studies in History and Philosophy of Science* 24:721–739.
Holt, C. C., F. Modigliani, J. Muth, and H. A. Simon. 1960. *Planning production, inventories, and work force*. Englewood Cliffs: Prentice Hall.
Howson, C. 1989. Accommodation, prediction and Bayesian confirmation theory. In *PSA 1988*, vol. 2, ed. A. Fine and J. Leplin, 381–392. East Lansing: Philosophy of Science Association.
Howson, C. 1990. Fitting your theory to the facts: Probably not such a bad thing after all. In *Scientific theories*, ed. C. Wade Savage, 224–244. Minneapolis: Minnesota Studies in the Philosophy of Science.
Irvine, J., and B. R. Martin. 1984. *Foresight in science*. London: F. Pinter.
Klein, L. R. 1984. The importance of the forecast. *Journal of Forecasting* 3:1–9.
Lakatos, I. 1970. Falsification and the methodology of scientific research programmes. In *Criticism and the growth of knowledge*, ed. I. Lakatos and A. Musgrave, 91–196. Cambridge: Cambridge University Press. (Reprinted in Lakatos, I. 1978. *The methodology of scientific research programmes. Philosophical Papers* 1:8–101. Cambridge: Cambridge University Press).
Lakatos, I. 1974b. Science and pseudoscience. In *Philosophy in the open,* ed. G. Vesey. London: Open University Press. (Reprinted in Lakatos, I. 1978. *The methodology of scientific research programmes. Philosophical Papers* 1:1–7. Cambridge: Cambridge University Press).
Lawson, T. 1985. The context of prediction (and the paradox of confirmation). *The British Journal for the Philosophy of Science* 36:393–407.
Lawson, T. 1997. *Economics and reality*. London: Routledge.
Leibniz, G. W. 1678. Letter to Conring, 19 March 1678. In Leibniz, G. W. 1969. *Philosophical papers and letters*. Dordrecht: Reidel.
Lipton, P. 1990. Prediction and prejudice. *International Studies in the Philosophy of Science* 4 (1): 51–65.
Lipton, P. 1991. *Inference to the best explanation*. London: Routledge.
March, J. G., and H. A. Simon. 1993. *Organizations*. 2nd ed. Cambridge, MA: Blackwell.
Marshall, A. 1949. *Principles of economics*. 8th ed. London: Macmillan.
McIntyre, L. 2001. Accommodation, prediction, and confirmation. *Perspectives on Science* 9:308–232.
Mellor, D. H. 1979. The possibility of prediction. *Proceedings of the British Academy* 65:207–223.
Nagel, E. 1961. *The structure of science*. New York: Harcourt, Brace and World.
Pulido, A. 1989. *Predicción económica y empresarial*. Madrid: Pirámide.

Pulido, A., and A. M. Lopez. 1999. *Predicción y simulación aplicada a la Economía y gestión de empresas*. Madrid: Ediciones Pirámide.
Reichenbach, H. 1938. *Experience and prediction. An analysis of the foundations and the structure of knowledge*. Chicago: The University of Chicago Press.
Rescher, N. 1998. *Predicting the future: An introduction to the theory of forecasting*. Albany: State University of New York Press.
Rosenberg, A. 1989. Are generic predictions enough? *Erkenntnis* 30 (1–2): 43–6
Rosser, J. Barkley Jr. 1999. On the complexities of complex economic dynamics. *Journal of Economic Perspectives* 13 (4): 169–192.
Rosser, J. Barkley Jr., ed. 2004a. *Complexity in economics*, vol. 1. Cheltenham: Edward Elgar.
Rosser, J. Barkley Jr., ed. 2004b. *Complexity in economics*, vol. 2. Cheltenham: Edward Elgar.
Rosser, J. Barkley Jr., ed. 2004c. *Complexity in economics*, vol. 3. Cheltenham: Edward Elgar.
Roth, A. 1988. Laboratory experimentation in economics: A methodological overview. *The Economic Journal* 98:974–1031. (Reprinted in Hey, J. D., and G. Loomes, eds. 1993. *Recent developments in experimental economics*, vol. I, 3–60. Aldershot: Edward Elgar).
Salmon, M. H. 2002. La explicación causal en Ciencias Sociales. In *Diversidad de la explicación científica,* ed. W. J. Gonzalez, 161–180. Barcelona: Ariel.
Salmon, W. C. 1953. The uniformity of nature. *Philosophy and Phenomenological Research* 14:39–48.
Salmon, W. C. 1957. The predictive inference. *Philosophy of Science* 24 (2): 180–190.
Salmon, W. C. 1981. Rational prediction. *The British Journal for the Philosophy of Science* 32:115–125. (Reprinted in Grünbaum, A., and W. C. Salmon, eds. 1988. The limitations of deductivism, 47–60. Berkeley: University of California Press).
Salmon, W. C. 1990. *Four decades of scientific explanation*. Minneapolis: University of Minnesota Press.
Salmon, W. C. 1993. On the alleged temporal anisotropy of explanation. In *Philosophical problems of the internal and external worlds,* ed. J. Earman, A. Janis, G. Massey, and N. Rescher, 229–248. Pittsburgh: University of Pittsburgh Press.
Salmon, W. C. 2002a. Explicación causal frente a no causal. In *Diversidad de la explicación científica,* ed. W. J. Gonzalez, 97–115. Barcelona: Ariel.
Salmon, W. C. 2002b. Estructura de la explicación causal. In *Diversidad de la explicación científica,* ed. W. J. Gonzalez, 141–159. Barcelona: Ariel.
Samuelson, P. 1947. *Foundations of economic analysis. Cambridge*. MA: The MIT Press.
Scerri, E. R. 2005. Response to Barnes' critique of Scerri and Worrall. *Studies in History and Philosophy of Science* 36:813–816.
Scerri, E. R. 2007. *The periodic table: Its story and its significance*. Oxford: Oxford University Press.
Scerri, E. R., and J. Worrall. 2001. Prediction and the periodic table. *Studies in History and Philosophy of Science* 32 (2): 407–452.
Scheffler, I. 1957. Explanation, prediction, and abstraction. *The British Journal for the Philosophy of Science* 7:293–309.
Scriven, M. 1962. Explanations, predictions and laws. In *Scientific explanation, space and time*, ed. H. Feigl and G. Maxwell, 170–230. Minneapolis: Minnesota Studies in the Philosophy of Science. (Reprinted in Pitt, J. C. ed., 1998. *Theories of explanation*, 51–74. Oxford: Oxford University Press).
Sen, A. 1986. Prediction and economic theory. In *Predictability in science and society,* ed. J. Mason, P. Mathias, and J. H. Westcott, 3–23. London: The Royal Society/The British Academy.
Shim, J. K., and J. G. Siegel. 1988. *Handbook of financial analysis, forecasting and modeling*. Paramus: Prentice Hall.
Simon, H. A. 1954. Bandwagon and underdog effects and the possibility of election predictions. *Public Opinion Quarterly* 18:245–253. (Reprinted in Simon, H. A. 1957. *Models of man: Social and rational*, 79–87. New York: J. Wiley and in Simon, H. A. 1982. *Models of bounded rationality*, vol. 1: *Economic analysis and public policy*, 460–468. Cambridge, MA: The MIT Press).

Simon, H. A. 1958. The role of expectations in an adaptive or behavioristic model. In *Expectations, uncertainty, and business behavior,* ed. M. J. Bowman, Chap. 3, 49–58. New York: Social Science Research Council. (Reprinted in Simon, H. A. 1982. *Models of bounded rationality*, vol. 2: *Behavioral economics and business organization*, 380–399. Cambridge, MA: The MIT Press).

Simon, H. A. 1989. The state of economic science. In *The state of economic science. Views of six Nobel laureates,* ed. W. Sichel, 97–110. Kalamazoo: W. E. Upjohn Institute for Employment Research.

Toulmin, S. 1961. *Foresight and understanding. An enquiry into the aims of science*. Bloomington: Indiana University Press/London: Hutchinson.

Urbach, P. 1978. Is any of Popper's arguments against historicism valid? *The British Journal for the Philosophy of Science* 29:117–130.

Urbach, P. 1985. Good and bad arguments against historicism. In *Popper and the human sciences,* ed. G. Currie, and A. Musgrave, 133–146. Dordrecht: M. Nijhoff.

Urbach, P. 1987. The scientific standing of evolutionary theories of society. *London School of Economics Quarterly* 1:23–42.

Whewell, W. 1860. *On the philosophy of discovery, chapters historical and critical*. London: J. W. Parker and Son.

White, R. 2003. The epistemic advantage of prediction over accommodation. *Mind* 112 (448): 653–683.

Wittgenstein, L. 1953. *Philosophische Untersuchungen*. Edited by G. E. M. Anscombe and R. Rhees. Oxford: Blackwell. (Translated by G. E. M. Anscombe 1976. *Philosophical investigations*. Oxford: Blackwell, Oxford.)

Wittgenstein, L. 1974. *Bemerkungen über die Grundlagen der Mathematik*. Edited by G. H. von Wright, R. Rhees, and G. E. M. Anscombe. Frankfurt: Suhrkamp. (Translated by G. E. M. Anscombe 1978. *Remarks on the foundations of mathematics*, 3rd ed. Oxford: Blackwell.)

Wittgenstein, L. 1982. *Letze Schriften über die Philosophie der Psychologie*, vol. I. Edited by G. H. von Wright and H. Nyman, translated by C. G. Luckhardt and M. A. E. Aue: *Last writings on the philosophy of psychology*, vol. I. Oxford: B. Blackwell.

Woods, D., and R. Fildes. 1976. *Forecasting for business: Methods and applications*. London: Longman.

Worrall, J. 1989a. Fresnel, Poisson and the white spot: The role of successful predictions in the acceptance of scientific theories. In *The uses of experiment,* ed. D. Gooding, T. Pinch, and S. Schaffer, 135–157. Cambridge: Cambridge University Press.

Worrall, J. 2002. New evidence for old. In *In the scope of logic, methodology and philosophy of science,* vol. 1, ed. P. Gardenfors, J. Wolenski, and K. Kijania-Placek, 191–209. Dordrecht: Kluwer.

Worrall, J. 2005. Prediction and the "periodic law": A rejoinder to Barnes. *Studies in History and Philosophy of Science* 36:817–826.

Part II
The General Orientation in Methodology of Science and the Problem of Prediction as a Scientific Test

General methodology of science is directly connected with the study made in Part I, focused on the standpoint for prediction as a requisite for science, including the role of prediction in the distinction between basic science and applied science, followed by the analysis of the characteristics and main varieties of scientific prediction. Moreover, it deals with some crucial issues for the problem of prediction as a test for a science, because the general methodology of science goes to the basis of prediction as a criterion of demarcation insofar as it affects the progressive development of science.

On the one hand, a methodology of science assumes the constitutive elements of what is a "science." These constituents, according to some criteria, are distinguished from those of a "non science," a task that is developed by the philosophy of science (mainly, through epistemology). And, on the other hand, methodology of science looks at how to improve science in order to get progressive standards, because science is a human activity that should increase the reliability and depth of human knowledge. The interest for the *predictive process* is, then, a central issue, because either scientific knowledge can try to accommodate already known facts—which is characteristic of scientific explanation—or it can seek *anticipatory knowledge* about the future which is reasonably expected on the basis of present knowledge (as scientific prediction does).

These aspects receive a different emphasis according to the methodological orientation chosen. Part II of this book pays special attention to two of them, due to their influence on methodology of economics: (i) falsificationism, which is characteristic of Karl Popper, who highlights the role of deduction and creates with scientific prediction a real separation between general methodology of science and the methodology of social sciences (Chap. 3); and (ii) the methodology of scientific research programs, proposed by Imre Lakatos, who introduces historicity in the methodological realm, and stresses the notion of "novel facts" associated with scientific prediction (Chap. 4).

Falsificationism has been a pivotal orientation in general methodology of science for decades. In addition, it has been a clearly relevant position in the discussions on the methodology of the social sciences (including the possibility of long-term predictions in history) and, particularly, in the case of methodology of economics.

Besides some points of convergence with Friedrich Hayek's views on economics, Popper's falsificationism has also had a noticeable influence on a younger generation of economists, mainly through the London School of Economics, as well as on very well known authors in the methodology of economics (among them, Mark Blaug).

The methodology of scientific research programs tries to combine objectivity and historicity, seeking an approach beyond the limitations of Popper's views on methodology as well as the tendency towards relativism of Thomas Kuhn's initial conception of *The Structure of Scientific Revolutions* (1962). Lakatos' analysis of prediction and novel facts in science is of considerable interest from a general methodological viewpoint as well as because of its repercussion on the methodology of economics (see, in this regard, Gonzalez 2001).

Prediction appears in Lakatos' conception in at least three different levels: (a) as an important *aim* of the research programs; (b) as a key factor for increasing our scientific knowledge both theoretically and empirically; and (c) as the way to *assess* the scientific character of knowledge claims (i.e., a means for evaluating results). At all these levels he envisions a close connection between prediction and novel facts. In the case of economics, the methodology of scientific research programs has passed through three different stages in the degree of influence on economists, of which the second has been very influential in the methodology of economics (Gonzalez 2001b).

Even though these general orientations (falsificationism and the methodology of scientific research programs) emphasize the role of prediction in science, each has different theses from the methodological point of view. They are analyzed here in chronological order, which is also relevant from a thematic point of view, due to the conceptions of these thinkers. Moreover, in the case of Lakatos' methodology, he explicitly built it on the revision of the previous falsificationism.

References

Gonzalez, W. J. 2001b. Reconstrucción histórico-sistemática de la incidencia de Imre Lakatos en la Metodología económica. In *Ciencia económica y Economía de la Ciencia: Reflexiones filosófico-metodológicas,* ed. A. Avila, W. J. Gonzalez and G. Marques, 65–92. Madrid: FCE.

Kuhn, T. S. 1962. *The structure of scientific revolutions*. 2nd ed., 1970. Chicago: The University of Chicago Press.

Chapter 3
Falsificationism and the Methodological Levels on Prediction

Karl Popper is perhaps the most influential author on general methodology of science in the second half of the twentieth century, at least in Europe.[1] His views on scientific prediction, both in natural sciences and in social sciences, have also been influential. Moreover, his thought has had a direct repercussion on the methodology of economics,[2] due to his influence on well-known specialists (philosophers as well as economists). Eric Barnes goes beyond this position when he claims that "Karl Popper is probably the most famous proponent of the preference for prediction in the entire history of philosophy" (Barnes 2008, p. 9).

However, this evaluative statement on the preference for prediction is wrong as an overall picture if we analyze it in thematic terms, insofar as there is a clear difference between Popper's emphasis on prediction in the general methodology of science and his criticisms on prediction in the realm of the methodology of the social sciences (cf. Gonzalez 1984, 2004c, and 2010a). This different philosophico-methodological approach to prediction, which is very noticeable when he moves from Einstein's theory of relativity to his analysis of "historicism" (Popper 1957), is made explicit here.

In addition, if we see Popper's approach in a historical context of the philosophico-methodological conceptions of prediction in the twentieth and the beginning of the twenty-first century (Gonzalez 2010a), then Barnes' statement is also incorrect. At least Hans Reichenbach emphasizes more the role of prediction than Popper does even in the general case. This can be seen in *Experience and Prediction* (1938),[3] which can be considered as a more intense proponent of the preference for prediction

---

[1] Among the huge number of publications on Popper's views, for the analysis of his general philosophico-methodological approach see, for example, Schilpp (1974), Nola (1987), and O'Hear (1980, 1995). Regarding Popper's conception of the social sciences, there are interesting suggestions in Currie and Musgrave (1985), Flew (1990), Jarvie (1982), Koertge (1975), and Macdonald (1995).

[2] This can be seen, for example, in Hands (1993a). Popper's ideas have been compared with Hayek's proposals. On this Nobel laureate see, for example, Hayek (1964b, 1978).

[3] See also Reichenbach (1951a). He developed a logico-methodological conception of philosophy of science (Reichenbach 1936a, 1951a, 1978a, 1978b), which includes a direct criticism of Popper's *Logik der Forschung* (Reichenbach 1935). On his view see Putnam (1994).

W. J. Gonzalez, *Philosophico-Methodological Analysis of Prediction and its Role in Economics*, Theory and Decision Library A: 50, DOI 10.1007/978-3-319-08885-3_3

than Popper, because of the primacy that Reichenbach gives to prediction is clear on axiological, epistemological and methodological grounds (Gonzalez 1995).[4]

Given these thematic and historical factors at stake, after the coordinates of Popper's approach to prediction, the analysis will follow four steps in order to clarify his conception of scientific prediction: (i) the three methodological levels of his approach on prediction; (ii) the role of prediction in his general methodology of science; (iii) prediction in his methodology of social sciences: the problem of historicism; and (iv) his methodological conception of prediction and economics.

3.1 Coordinates of Popper's Approach to Prediction

Undoubtedly, Popper's approach to prediction should take into account several aspects: the variations of his philosophical trajectory (Gonzalez 2004c); the relevance of the methodology of science in his conception of prediction, which involves two main realms at stake—general and the social sciences—which has repercussions for the third sphere (the methodology of economics); and some characteristic features of his vision of scientific prediction. In these coordinates of his approach to prediction, it seems clear that methodology of science is a central theme in Popper's studies of science, insofar as he always puts special weight on the analysis of the growth of scientific knowledge.

But Popper did not accept the idea of "the" scientific method understood as a systematic way to achieve scientific results well founded (Worrall 2001a, p. 114). From this point of view, he is not supporting a kind of "methodological universalism" (Gonzalez 2012b), which is relevant to understand his position. In addition, as it has been pointed out in Chaps. 1 and 2, if we look from a general perspective on science, the methodological component is connected with other elements of science (language, structure, knowledge, activity, values, etc.). Therefore, it is opportune to begin this analysis with an *initial characterization* of Popper's views on *scientific prediction.*

Semantically, he distinguishes "prediction" and "prophecy," especially in social sciences (Popper 1948/1959): logically, prediction appears always in a deductivist sphere (i.e., a theory can have a predictive content and is structured in a deductive way), because he does not accept the scientific character of induction;[5] epistemologically, prediction is linked to future knowledge (for this reason corroboration has

[4] Barnes suggests that Popper's preference for prediction is mainly epistemological: "Popper linked the preference for prediction to his claim that a theory is scientific to the extent that it forbids certain observable state of affairs" (Barnes 2008, p. 11). On Reichenbach's epistemological approach to prediction, see his (1951b).

[5] The problem of induction has received attention from quite different perspectives. See, for example, Reichenbach (1936b), Neurath (1946), Boudot (1972), Niiniluoto and Tuomela (1973), Rescher (1980), Earman (1992), and Gillies (2000).

no predictive import);[6] methodologically, prediction is a feature of the growth of scientific knowledge (a mark of scientific progress); and axiologically, prediction is a characteristic aim of science. Here the analysis will emphasize the methodological aspects of prediction (Gonzalez 2004b).

Besides this thematic perspective (semantic, logical, epistemological, methodological, ontological, axiological, etc.), we can consider the historical dimension of Popper's approach to prediction. In this regard, if we leave aside his well-known differences with Reichenbach's philosophico-methodological perspective (see Gonzalez 1995) and look backwards on prediction, then a comparison can be made with William Whewell[7] and John Herschel. According to Barnes, like these authors, "Popper appeals to the predictions a theory makes as a way of separating the illegitimate uses of the method of hypothesis from its legitimate uses" (Barnes 2008, p. 10).

Historically, he also maintains that there is a big difference as well with these thinkers of the nineteenth century: "Whewell and Herschel pointed to predictive success as a necessary condition for the applicability of a theory that had been generated by the method of hypothesis. Popper by contrast focuses on his solution to the demarcation problem not in the success of the prediction but on the fact that the theory made the prediction at all" (Barnes 2008, p. 10). Nonetheless, Popper's philosophico-methodological approach to prediction has many nuances that should be considered, and they begin with the existence of several methodological levels of analysis at stake.

3.2 Three Different Methodological Levels

There are at least three different *methodological levels* which can be analyzed in Popper's approach: (1) the general methodology of science, where prediction appears as a usual element of scientific theories and one which is relevant for testing theories; (2) the methodology of social sciences as a whole, where he develops a strong criticism of the tendency articulated around the key role of prediction, which he calls "historicism" (and which has two different kinds: dualistic and monistic); and (3) the methodology of economics, a field which was not at the front line of his research (even though he was professor of a university center devoted to that field: the London School of Economics).[8]

---

[6] "It is not our corroboration statements but our *theories* which allow us to make predictions (in the presence of observed "initial conditions," of course), with the consequence that these predictions may be as hypothetical as the theories. *Thus our theories do have predictive import.* Our corroboration statements have no predictive import" (Popper 1974, p. 1029).

[7] On Whewell's approach, see Hesse (1971).

[8] An analysis of Popper's relation with the economists of his own school is found in de Marchi (1988b).

Prima facie, the analysis of Popper's approach to prediction seems paradoxical: he stresses the role of prediction within the general methodology of science, because he considers that it is a relevant element for the progress of scientific knowledge (i.e., it can be used to test scientific theories); but, at the same time, he criticizes the role of historical prediction as a scientific element within social sciences, as can be seen in his writings on "historicism," in which he rejects the existence of a logical basis for scientific prediction in historical settings (Popper 1957, p. vi). Consequently, this latter aspect affects economics, because this subject can only be seen within the realm of social sciences (even though some authors, such as Philip Mirowski, think that classical economics is built up following the schemes of Newtonian physics) (Mirowski 1989).

This tension between prediction in the general methodology of science and prediction in the methodology of social sciences can also be seen in the *wider framework* that underlies Popper's approach. In effect, he offers two different perspectives for the methodological problems: on the one hand, he holds the very well known position of *falsificationism*,[9] which is conceived to grasp the growth of scientific knowledge (the method of science in general, although it is frequently focused on the case of natural science); and, on the other, he defends a specific method for social science: the *logic of situation*, because he thinks that the proper method for the social sciences is based on rational decision making in a situation.

Among the elements to show the *divergence* in Popper between the general methodological framework—falsificationism—and the specific methodological approach to social sciences—the logic of situation—are two important features which he attributes to the latter: (a) that the method of explanation of the logic of situation is *unique* in the social sciences insofar as it is the way to grasp social events;[10] and (b) that the situational analysis comes from a specific field, because it is the *method of economic analysis*: "the analysis of situations, the situational logic, plays a very important part in social life as well as in the social sciences. It is, in fact, the method of economic analysis" (Popper 1945/1966, p. 97).

To accept the existence of that *dualistic* wider framework in Popper's methodological approach—falsificationism versus the logic of situation—is very damaging for his conception of the *unity of method* in science. In effect, by accepting such a divergence between the falsificationism and the logic of situation, it seems rather obvious that *de facto* natural sciences and social sciences will adopt different methodologies. In the case of falsificationism, there is no general principle that can be accepted always and by all, because *fallibilism* is essential to the growth of scientific knowledge; whereas in the case of logic of situation there is a *principle*

[9] Imre Lakatos emphasized that "falsificationism" can be understood in different ways, cf. Lakatos (1970).

[10] "That only in this way can we explain and understand what happens in society: social events" (Popper 1985, p. 358); cf. Caldwell (1991), p. 14. "In my view, the idea of a *social situation* is the fundamental category of the methodology of the social sciences. I should even be inclined to say that almost every problem of explanation in the social sciences requires an analysis of a social situation" (Popper 1994b, p. 166).

of rationality that cannot be removed and which throws light on what happens in society (Popper 1945/1966, p. 265).[11]

3.3 The Role of Prediction in Popper's General Methodology

Within the general methodology of science, Popper pays attention to prediction from his first book—*Die beiden Grundprobleme der Erkenntnistheorie*—[12] through to his later writings. Specifically, it is a topic which appears in his main works: *The Logic of Scientific Discovery*,[13] *Conjectures and Refutations* (Popper 1963a), and *Objective Knowledge* (Popper 1972), the books which reveal turning points in his career. These changes show that he does not offer a single conception of falsificationism.

3.3.1 Three Successive Conceptions

There is a clear evolution in his thought on science.[14] Moreover, there are—in my judgment—three successive conceptions of *falsificationism* in Popper: first, a logico-methodological approach, which is clear in the first period (from the 1930s to the 1950s); second, a methodological view in tune with an evolutionary epistemology, which is pre-eminent in the second period (during the 1960s); and third, a methodological perspective more open to the ontological component, which is dominant in the third period (from the 1970s to the 1990s) (Gonzalez 2004b).

Each one of these conceptions can be seen in these important books. *The Logic of Scientific Discovery* represents the methodological approach rooted in logic (with special emphasis on logical procedures such as the *modus tollens*);[15] *Conjectures and Refutations* offers an epistemological view of an evolutionary kind (an adaptive

[11] "I regard the principle of adequacy of action (that is, the rationality principle) as an integral part of every, or nearly every, testable social theory. Now if a theory is tested, and found faulty, then we have always to decide which of its various constituent parts we shall make accountable for its failure. My thesis is that it is *sound methodological policy* to decide not to make the rationality principle, but the rest of the theory—that is, the model—accountable" (Popper 1994b, p. 177).

[12] Although the book was written before *Logik der Forschung*, it was published much later: Popper (1979).

[13] Originally published in German: Popper (1935). It was translated into English by the author with the assistance of Julius Freed and Lan Freed, introducing some changes: Popper (1959).

[14] On the evolution of Popper's thought, cf. Gonzalez (2004c). About Popper's changes in his views on the problem of truth, cf. Martínez Solano (2005).

[15] "I suggest that it is the task of the logic of scientific discovery, or the logic of knowledge, to give a logical analysis of this procedure; that is, to analyse the method of the empirical sciences" (Popper 1959/1968, p. 27).

procedure of human knowledge) linked to methodology of falsificationism;[16] and *Objective Knowledge* shows a clear ontological perspective of science.[17] These successive conceptions of falsificationism—the logico-methodological approach, the position linked to an epistemological evolutionary view, and the more ontological perspective—have repercussions on his characterization of prediction.

Falsificationism—Popper's general methodology of science—is then connected with logic of science, epistemology (i.e., critical rationalism), ontology of science, and axiology of science, both in his main books and in other publications of the three main periods of his thought. *De facto,* the problem of scientific prediction appears, in one way or another, throughout all his writings. It can be found in those publications other than his main methodological books or his writings on historicism: "Indeterminism in Quantum Physics and in Classical Physics" (Popper 1950), *Unended Quest*,[18] "Replies to my Critics" (Popper 1974)[19] *The Open Universe. An Argument for Indeterminism*,[20] *In Search of a Better World* (Popper 1992, pp. 143–144), *The Myth of the Framework. In Defense of Science and Rationality* (Popper 1994a),[21] or *All Life is Problem Solving* (Popper 1994c/1999, pp. 14, 106, 131, and 135).

As is well known, Popper's main book—*The Logic of Scientific Discovery*—offers a deductive method for science. He thinks that basic sentences (such as predictions) are *deducible* from theories: it is from universal statements in conjunction with initial conditions that we *deduce* the singular statement called "prediction" (Popper 1959/1968, p. 60).[22] Prediction appears as a *test* of a theory: it could be used after the explanations and for theoretical reasons. In effect, "the theorist is interested in explanations as such, that is to say, in testable explanatory theories: applications and predictions interested him only for theoretical reasons—because they may be used as *tests* of theories" (Popper 1959/1968, p. 59, note 1). He offers a logico-methodological scheme with a theory-prediction link.

Hilary Putnam maintains that this view is not far from the "inductivist" account of the confirmation. In addition, he considers that the theory-prediction link is not

---

[16] "Criticism of our conjectures is of decisive importance: by bringing out our mistakes it makes us understand the difficulties of the problem which we are trying to solve. This is how we become better acquainted with our problem, and able to propose more mature solutions: the very refutation of a theory—that is, of any serious tentative solution to our problem—is always a step forward that takes us nearer to the truth. And this is how we can learn from our mistakes.

As we learn from our mistakes our knowledge grows, even though we may never know—that is, know for certain. Since our knowledge grows, there can be no reason here for despair of reason" (Popper 1963a, p. vii).

[17] His three worlds theory includes causal relations between them, and the world 3, which is the realm of science, has objective objects or entities, cf. Popper (1972), pp. 153–190, esp., pp. 155–158.

[18] Popper (1976) (enlarged version, Routledge, London, 1992), pp. 24–25, 35, 37–38, 43, 103–104, 117, 121–122, 158, 171–172 and 238 (note 283).

[19] Popper (1974), vol. 2, pp. 961–1197; esp., pp. 979–780, 997–998, and 1029–1030.

[20] Popper (1982), pp. 2, 6–7, 9, 11–12, 14–16, 32–37, 42, 62–78 and 129.

[21] Popper (1994a), pp. 89, 94, 133, 162–165, 168–169, 173 and 182.

[22] In addition, he points out: "the term 'prediction', as used here, comprises statements about the past ('retrodiction'), or even 'given' statements which we wish to explain ('*explicanda*')" (Popper 1959/1968, p. 60, note 2).

the decisive feature of a scientific theory: "it is because theories imply basic sentences in the sense of 'imply' associated with deductive logic … that, according to Popper, theories and general laws can be falsifiable by basic sentences. And this same link is the heart of the 'inductivist' schema. Both schemes say: *look at the predictions that a theory implies; see if those predictions are true.* My criticism is … a criticism of this link, of this point on which Popper and the 'inductivist' agree. I claim: in a great many important cases, scientific theories do not imply predictions at all" (Putnam 1974, p. 225).

Conjectures and Refutations combines an evolutionary epistemology and a falsificationist methodology. Thus, if the progress of science is to continue, we need positive successes in addition to successful refutations: "we must … produce theories that entail new predictions, especially predictions of new effects, new testable consequences, suggested by the new theory and never thought of before. Such a new prediction was that planets would under certain circumstances deviate from Kepler's laws; or that light, in spite of its zero mass, would prove to be subject to gravitational attraction (that is, Einstein's eclipse-effect). Another example is Dirac's prediction that there will be anti-particle for every elementary particle. New predictions of these kinds must not only be produced, but they must also be reasonably often corroborated by experimental evidence, I contend, if scientific progress is to continue" (Popper 1963b, p. 243).

Objective Knowledge stresses the indeterministic status of both natural and social reality, which directly affects the problem of scientific prediction: "evolutionary processes or major evolutionary changes are as unpredictable as historical processes or major historical changes. I hold this view because I am strongly inclined towards an indeterministic view of the world, somewhat more radical than Heisenberg's: my indeterminism includes the thesis that even classical physics is indeterministic, and is thus more like that of Charles Sanders Peirce, or that of Alfred Landé. And I think that evolution proceeds largely probabilistically, under constantly changing conditions or problem situations, and that every tentative solution, whether more successful or less successful or even completely unsuccessful, creates a new problem situation" (Popper 1972, p. 296).

3.3.2 Common Ground for the Conceptions of Falsificationism

Common ground for these successive conceptions of *falsificationism*—the logico-methodological approach, the position link to an epistemological evolutionary view, and the more ontological perspective—is the idea of elimination of error. Falsificationism is a general approach that systematizes the method of learning from our mistakes. Popper's view of scientific method "consists of these four steps:

1. We select some *problem*—perhaps by stumbling over it.
2. We try to *solve* it by proposing a *theory* as a tentative solution.
3. Through the *critical discussion of our theories* our knowledge grows by the elimination of some of our errors, and in this way we learn to understand our problems, and our theories, and the need for new solutions.

4. The critical discussion of even our best theories always reveals new problems.

Or to put these four steps into four words: *problems—theories—criticisms—new problems*" (Popper 1994b, p. 159). Falsificationism is then set by four main categories, and the one which is most relevant to science is that of error-elimination through criticism: we learn from our mistakes through critical discussion (which includes testability). It is a deductive procedure that uses experience as a negative test (as a means for refutation).

Emphasis on deduction and rejection of induction are two constant features of Popper's general methodology of science. This affects prediction directly, because he does not want to give elbow room to a predictive method based on *induction*: "Corroboration has no inductive aspect; and the logic of prediction consists, simply, in deducting predictions from hypotheses plus initial conditions. In other words, the logic of prediction is the ordinary deductive logic and nothing else" (Popper 1974, p. 1030). This position assumes that, among the array of generalizations that are compatible with the available observational evidence, there is a *rational basis in favor of one unrefuted generalization* (conjecture, hypothesis, etc.) instead of others for use in a predictive argument.

However, this claim gives rise to some problems, as Wesley Salmon has pointed out (Salmon 1981). Predictions are made for various purposes, such as to gain information in the theoretical context, which is useful in the *evaluation* of scientific theories—to test a theory—or to *make a decision* regarding a practical action (when the choice of an optimal decision requires the foreknowledge of future occurrences). This means that prediction is involved in a distinction between the *theoretical preference* and the *practical preference*. Salmon's emphasis is on the second case, and he analyzes the role of "corroboration" in it. He considers that the preferences between generalizations, which are to be used in the practical decision-making context, are not as Popper has maintained, because corroboration has not the role that he gives in the practical preference. In other words, it would be a mistake to defend, as Popper does, that corroboration reports past performance but that "*it could not be used to predict future performance*" (Popper 1976, p. 103).

Popper's idea is that statements of *corroboration* of conjectures have not predictive content as such, whereas *general statements* (conjectures, hypotheses, etc.) do have predictive content. Analyzing this view, Salmon holds that the problem is that there are many general statements (conjectures, hypotheses, etc.) "which make incompatible predictive claims when conjoined with true statements about past and present occurrences. The fact that a general statement has predictive content does not mean that what it says is true. In order to make a prediction, one must choose a conjecture that has predictive content to serve as a premise in a predictive argument. In order to make a *rational* prediction, … one must make a *rational* choice of a premise for such an argument. But from our observational evidence and from the statements about the corroboration of a given conjecture, no predictive appraisal follows" (Salmon 1981, p. 119). Therefore, for the purposes of *practical prediction*, corroboration does not furnish the rational basis for preference of one conjecture to another.

Induction and prediction appear here as connected problems: if Popper cannot provide a tenable account of rational prediction—given his emphasis upon objectivity and rationality of science—then we cannot credit him with solving the problem of induction. He maintains "our corroboration statements have no predictive import, although they motivate and justify our *preference* for some theory over another" (Popper 1974, pp. 1029–1030). But, in order to have a viable conception of *rational prediction* and an adequate solution to the problem of induction, the point is how corroboration can *justify* such preference of one theory over another.

When the question arises on how to select for the purposes of rational prediction in Popper theories, his solution is: "we should *prefer* the best tested theory … it will be 'rational' to choose the best tested theory … the best tested theory is one which, in the light of our *critical discussion*, appears to be the best so far" (Popper 1974, p. 1025). But he explicitly assures us that testing has no *predictive import*. Thus, according to Salmon, it is difficult to see "how it could be rational to judge theories *for purposes of prediction* in terms of a criterion which is emphatically claimed to be lacking in predictive import" (Salmon 1981, p. 122).

It seems that we need to distinguish *predictive content* and *predictive import*: even though corroboration statements have no predictive *content*, it does not mean that corroboration has no predictive *import*. For Salmon, "statements whose consequences refer to future occurrences may be said to have predictive content; rules, imperatives, and directives are totally lacking in predictive content because they do not entail any statements at all. Nevertheless, an imperative—such as 'No smoking, please'—may have considerable predictive import, for it may effectively achieve the goal or preventing the occurrence of smoking in a particular room in the immediate future" (Salmon 1981, p. 123). Continuing with this distinction, even if corroboration is lacking in predictive content, it does have *predictive import* (i.e., corroboration in some cases can provide the basis for deciding which theory—with its predictive content—is to be used to make practical predictions).

Therefore, there is a limit in Popper's general methodology of science: pure deductivism can hardly resolve the problem of rational prediction in contexts of *practical* decision-making. Salmon maintains that science is inductive in matters of intellectual curiosity as well as of practical prediction. Moreover, he considers that "Popper's adherence to the thesis that corroboration can provide a basis for rational prediction rests upon his realism, which embodies a version of a principle of uniformity of nature" (Salmon 1981, p. 124).[23] If this suggestion is correct, we can still legitimately wonder whether Popper's methodology is as far as from inductivism as he would have us believe.

After this analysis on prediction in his general methodology of science, it seems that he needs *induction* in order to have a consistent approach (a methodology in tune with his realist ontology) and, in addition, he must think his view that all prediction, aside from that involved in the testing of theories, is restricted to contexts in which practical action is at stake. Science is richer than that, because science gives explanations as well as predictions, and some of the predictions of theoretical

[23] On the principle of uniformity of nature, see Salmon (1953).

science have practical consequences whereas other do not (i.e., in scientific theories predictions can have both theoretical and practical interest, not only in natural sciences but also in social sciences).

3.4 Prediction in Popper's Methodology of Social Sciences: The Problem of Historicism

In spite of Popper's well-known general methodology of science—falsificationism—which he conceives as valid for any kind of empirical science, there is in his writings another methodology: the *logic of situation.* This approach is specific to the social sciences and introduces important methodological variations in comparison with the general falsificationist framework, because it relies upon a basically stable *rationality principle* (rather than upon the re-examinability of a potentially falsifiable theory)[24] and it is grounded in a *specific* case of science (the economic analysis).

3.4.1 Situational Analysis

Situational logic or *situational analysis* are two expressions which Popper uses to reconstruct the problem situation in which the acting person finds himself or herself and also to show how and why his or her action constituted a solution of the problem as he or she saw it. The method of situational analysis is conceived as an objectivist method: it looks for the critical discussion of our tentative solutions (i.e., it seeks our attempts to reconstruct the situation). It assumes the principle of acting appropriately to the situation, a rationality principle understood as a *methodological postulate* instead of an empirical or psychological assertion that the man in most cases acts rationally (Popper 1994b, p. 169).

Noretta Koertge has given us a systematic restatement of Popper's method of situational analysis: (a) *description of situation*: agent *A* is in a situation of type *C*; (b) *analysis of situation*: in a situation like *C*, the appropriate thing to do is *X*; (c) *rationality principle*: agents always act appropriately to their situations; and (d) *explanandum*: therefore *A* did *X* (Koertge 1975, p. 440; see also Caldwell 1994,

[24] In Popper, "(a) though potentially falsifiable, a theory may be currently untestable. (b) If a theory is potentially falsifiable, currently testable, and has been tested, then there are two possibilities: (i) If a test is positive, the theory is *corroborated.* … Corroboration does not mean *proven true*; Popper's *fallibilism* prohibits us from claiming that we have discovered the truth. (…) Nor should even consistently corroborated theory be viewed as *highly probable* or even *more probable*. This was the point of Popper's critique of inductive logic. It is a radical implication: Even perfect corroboration carries no evidential weight. (ii) If a test result is negative, the theory is *refuted* or *falsified.* Just as corroboration does not prove a theory true, refutation does not prove it false" (Caldwell 1991, pp. 3–4).

p. 142). In addition, Koertge also offers us a more extensive version of situational logic as Popper's proper method to follow in the social sciences:

1. *Description of problem-situation*: A thought he was in a problem-situation of type C.
2. *Dispositional law*: For all such problem-situations A would use appraisal-rule R.
3. *Analysis of situation*: The result of appraising C using R is X.
4. *Description of the agent's competence*: A did not make a mistake in applying R to C.
5. *Rationality appraisal principle*: All agents appraise their situations in a rational manner.
6. *Explanandum-1*: (Therefore) A concluded that X was the rational thing to do.
7. *Rationality principle*: People always act on the outcome of their rational appraisals.
8. *Explanandum-2*: (Therefore) A did X (Koertge 1975, p. 445; see also Caldwell 1994, p. 142).

Blaug, who labels himself as an "unrepentant Popperian," has made a devastating criticism of the "situational analysis," which leads him to the conclusion of incompatibility with the terms of the (general) methodology of falsificationism (Blaug 1994, p. 113).[25] For him, what is surprising is that (1) Popper claimed situational analysis to be *one* legitimate mode of explanation in the social sciences; (2) he admitted that situational analysis was false as a *universal law* of economic behavior, but nevertheless insisted that it should be maintained as an unexamined "metaphysical" principle; and (3) he virtually implied that it should be retained because situational analysis had shown itself to be *fruitful* in the past, particularly in economics (Blaug 1994, p. 112) (i.e., it resembles the concept of "rational choice" understood as the view that economic behavior is simply individual maximizing behavior subject to constraints).

According to Blaug, these three elements are not compatible with Popper's falsificationism: "(1) contradicts his 'unity of science' thesis, the doctrine that there is no difference in the structure of explanation in the natural and the social sciences and that all sciences must validate their theories in the same way. Likewise, (2) actually endorses one particular 'immunizing stratagem' in the face of refutations of rationality, namely to retain the rationality principle and to place the blame for refutation on, say, the constraints, the limited information available to agents or any other feature of the test in question. Finally, and most damningly, (3) provides an inductive argument on behalf of rational choice models of behavior—they have worked well in the past and so might work well in the future—which flies in the face of everything that Popper has ever written on induction" (Blaug 1994, pp. 112–113).

This logic of situation and the topics of the methodology of social sciences are central in Popper's writings from 1944 to 1957, when he publishes two influential monographs: *The Open Society and its Enemies* (Popper 1945) and *The Poverty of*

[25] Blaug's approach and its relations with Popper's philosophy are analyzed in Martínez Solano (2007).

Historicism (Popper 1957).[26] Both books belong to the period of predominance of the logico-methodological approach. Thus, when Popper deals with the problem of prediction in social sciences, his main focus of attention lies in the logical basis of prediction.

3.4.2 Concerns on "Historicism"

Unquestionably, the main reason that Popper gives to the refutation of "historicism" is logico-methodological: "*I have shown that, for strictly logical reasons, it is impossible for us to predict the future course of history*" (Popper 1957, p. vi; the italics are in the original). He insists in the logical feature of his methodological criticism: "this argument, being purely logical, applies to scientific predictors of any complexity, including 'societies' of interacting predictors. But this means that no society can predict, scientifically, its future state of knowledge" (Popper 1957, p. viii).

For Popper, the historicist doctrines of method are responsible for the unsatisfactory state of the theoretical social sciences (other than economic theory). He calls "historicism" to "an approach to the social sciences which assumes that *historical prediction* is their principal aim, and which assumes that this aim is attainable by discovering the 'rhythms' or the 'patterns', the 'laws' or the 'trends' that underlie the evolution of history" (Popper 1957, p. 3). Thus, he links historicism and prediction both in terms of social laws and in a softer sense of rhythms, patterns and trends. But he recognizes that it is a constructed position: "I hope that … I have succeeded in building up a position really worth attacking" (Popper 1957, p. 3).[27] In addition, sometimes he combines elements of "historicism" and "historism," which are two different views of social affairs (Gonzalez 1984, esp., pp. 131–132).

Historicism is clearly a technical term in Popper's writings.[28] Moreover, among historians it has a quite different meaning (Gonzalez 1996e), closer to what Popper calls "historism" (Popper 1945/1966, pp. 208 and 214). He conceives "historicism" as a view of the social sciences in which *historical prediction* is the principal aim, and that aim is attainable by discovering what underlies the evolution of history (laws, rhythms, patterns, or trends) (Popper 1957, p. 3). Thus, it is a perspective based on prediction that can altogether affect the interpretation of social sciences.

Three are the main features of his conception of "historicism": (i) its specific realm is the sphere of *necessity*, because the human being appears to be carrying on towards the future by irresistible forces (Popper 1957, p. 160); (ii) this view possesses a clear methodological character, which highlights impersonal factors in social change, and it is connected with a *non-relativistic* orientation, which tends to dogmatism (what is true is the "law of change"); and (iii) this position does not

[26] A preliminary paper on this subject was presented in Hayek's Seminar in the mid thirties and it was published in three parts in 1944–1945.

[27] "I have tried to perfect a theory" (Popper 1957, p. 3).

[28] On the terminological problems related with that methodological use, cf. Donagan (1974, esp., pp. 905–909).

accept the epistemological pluralism, because it assumes a *theoretical framework* to explain and to appraise the historical evolvement of society (Gonzalez 1984, p. 114).

Historism is in Popper the opposite conception to historicism. In fact, the features which he attributes to "historism" are quite different from historicism: (a) historism rejects a static view of the social world and criticizes the idea of "human nature" or *ontical structure* of the person (the human being—in the extreme version—does not have freedom: he or she *is freedom*); (b) this approach denies the existence of truth as an absolute value, which leads it towards a methodological *relativism* in the main advocates; and (c) it offers a defense of a *pluralistic epistemological* framework, which impedes the existence of a stable conceptual framework to appraise the contents of social sciences and increases the insistence in the importance of each historical period (Gonzalez 1984, p. 110).[29] Following this approach, it seems difficult to have scientific prediction in social sciences (among them, economics).

Although historicism and historism present quite different views on the role of prediction in social sciences, both have common roots in the past: (1) they share an *intellectual humus* in the European context of the eighteenth century and acquire their characteristic profiles during the nineteenth century; (2) both approaches rely upon the idea of change in human affairs, emphasizing the *historicity* of the human person as a social being; and (3) they are open to a methodological perspective of social sciences grounded in the history, but they show an important difference: historicism lacks the relativistic approach which is characteristic of historism, and in addition historicism exhibits a tendency towards dogmatism in the explanation of social events (Gonzalez 1984, pp. 111–112).

Concerning historicism—the thesis of *historical prediction* of social affairs as the main aim of social sciences—Popper distinguishes two methodological versions: dualistic ("anti-naturalistic") and monistic ("pro-naturalistic"). The point of separation between them is in the applicability of methods of physics in social sciences: for the dualists the methods of natural science cannot grasp the peculiarities of social sciences, whereas for the monists the methods of physics are applicable in the realm of social phenomena.[30]

Obviously, this methodological divergence affects the role of prediction. On the one hand, the *dualistic historicism* defends the inexactness of social prediction, due to the complexity of social structure as well as to the interconnection between prediction and the predicted events (Popper 1957, p. 13), and it accepts methodological essentialism, which makes social prediction more difficult than natural prediction insofar as this position includes a criticism of the use of quantitative methods in social science (Popper 1957, p. 31). On the other hand, the *monistic historicism* insists

[29] In economics, the importance of each historical period is emphasized by G. von Schmoller cf. Gonzalez (1991a).

[30] There are some peculiar remarks in Popper's analysis, because he finds similarities among philosophers of quite different tendencies in social sciences: "This historicist attitude was rather typical of the period [as] can be seen from the close similarity between the historicism of Marx and that of J. S. Mill (it is analogous to the similarity between the historicist philosophies of their predecessors, Hegel and Comte)" (Popper 1945/1966, p. 87).

on the need for causal analysis in social sciences, which is in tune with the dominant tradition in natural sciences, and it supports methodological nominalism, where the task of science is only to describe how things behave (instead of penetrating the essence of things in order to explain them) (Popper 1957, pp. 28–29).

Both historicisms—dualist and monist—are rejected by Popper as poor methods: he thinks that they do not bear any fruit. Afterwards, he presents a refutation of historicism in the Preface to *The Poverty of Historicism*, written more than a decade after the original publication of the book in *Economica*.[31] The argument may be summed up as follows: (i) the course of human history is strongly influenced by the growth of human knowledge; (ii) we cannot predict, by rational or scientific methods, the future growth of our scientific knowledge; and (iii) we cannot, therefore, predict the future course of human history (Popper 1957, pp. vi–vii).

But Popper's strong claims about the predictability of future events in the history of the predictor raise problems about human rationality and the rationality of science itself.[32] According to Peter Clark, "the arguments of the *Poverty of Historicism* to the effect that social trends and forces are unpredictable and that the growth of knowledge is inherently unanticipatable seem to fly in the face of ordinary human experience and apparently throw into doubt the rationality of activities which form the basis of social structures which are fundamental to modern society. Modern developed societies do behave in predictable fashion and we have good reasons for believing that to be so" (1995, p. 153), (e.g., insurance companies and government departments spend huge quantities of resources in time and money in trying to anticipate the environment in which they will develop in the future).

A careful interpretation of Popper's texts against historicism can show us that he does not exclude the *possibility* of prediction in social sciences as such, or even that he does not deny its *legitimacy* as a test for the theory (including economic theory). What he clearly rejects is the "historical prediction" understood as prediction of large-scale social phenomena,[33] such as the society without classes of Marxism or K. Mannheim's predictions for society as a whole (Gonzalez 1984, pp. 122–123). Furthermore, Popper also rejects the opposite extreme: the exactness of specific predictions in social realms, such as the financial predictions (e.g., the price of shares in the stock market). His main claim is the impossibility of anticipating today *what we shall know only tomorrow*, a position which he considers compatible with predicting that certain developments will happen under certain conditions (Popper 1957, p. vii).

Again, this approach has serious problems, because it diminishes the *rationality* of scientific activity. Besides the theoretical reasons in favor of future advancement of science, there are also practical reasons: the major research councils in science

[31] The book was first published in three parts in *Economica*, vol. 11, no. 42 (1944), pp. 86–103; vol. 11, no. 43 (1944), pp. 119–137; and vol. 12, no. 46 (1945), pp. 69–89.

[32] A strong criticism of his approach to historicism can be found in Urbach (1978); Urbach (1985), esp., pp. 137–139; and Urbach (1987), esp., pp. 30–32.

[33] "Theoretical science on which to base those large-scale forecasts whose confirmation would mean the success of social theory" (Popper 1957, p. 41).

appraise research projects and rate them worthy of support (or not, if they think that it is impossible in principle to anticipate how that knowledge will grow). "The rationality of the activities of the science research councils must, in part, hinge upon the correctness of the conception that it is possible to predict to some extent at least which projects are likely to be successful, and that fundamentally involves predicting how knowledge will evolve" (Clark 1995, p. 153).

Consequently, it seems clear that Popper does not succeed in his attempt to refute the possibility of predicting historical developments that may be influenced by the growth of our knowledge. However, both in terms of theoretical and practical reason, the intrinsic difficulties to get an *accurate* prediction of the growth of knowledge, especially in the realm of social sciences, should be assumed. This affects economics, both as basic science and as applied science.

3.5 Popper's Methodological Conception of Prediction and Economics

Regarding economics, Popper's methodological views have been influential for decades. This influence can be seen through relevant economists. The list of economists whose methodological writings reveal a Popperian influence includes well-known authors such as Chris Archibald, Jack Birner, Mark Blaug, Lawrence Boland, Bruce J. Caldwell, D. Wade Hands, Friedrich A. Hayek, Terence W. Hutchison, Joop Klant, Kurt Klappholz, Spiro Latsis and Stanley Wong (Caldwell 1991, p. 1).[34]

Among these economists, there are two names which are particularly influential: Blaug, a historian of economic thought who became especially interested in the methodology of falsificationism and its application to economics; and Hayek, a Nobel Prize in economics who has been influenced by Popper since the 1950s, if not earlier.[35] To some extent, these two authors represent two different perspectives within the methodology of economics: the broad scope and the restricted scope (Gonzalez 2000, esp., pp. 43–56). In effect, Blaug usually tries to connect in an explicit way the methodology of economics with the problems of the general methodology of science, whereas Hayek's primary interest is in the particular problems

[34] On the one hand, the list of economists whose general outlook has been influenced by Popper's work could be much longer, because there are also other well known names such as Richard Lipsey and Neil de Marchi; and, on the other hand, the level of influence varies clearly from one author to another (e.g., Spiro Latsis is more Lakatosian than Popperian, and Bruce J. Caldwell and D. Wade Hands are clearly critical of central tenets of Popper's approach).

[35] The relation between both authors starts earlier than the 1950s. In fact, Hayek got a position for Popper at the London School of Economics when he was in New Zealand (Popper 1976, p. 120), and previously—in 1937—he was invited to give a talk in Hayek's Seminar. It seems clear that Hayek has also influenced Popper, but it is still unclear who has more influence whom. In this regard, the conclusion that there are no influences between them is not reasonable, especially if it is accepted that Popper revised the last two parts of *The Poverty of Historicism* due to his intellectual relation with Hayek (Caldwell 2006).

of the methodology of economics, even though he also works on issues of the broad scope (and makes philosophical claims).[36]

3.5.1 Economic Prediction: Possibility and Inexactitude

Although Popper has had a clear methodological influence on economists (de Marchi 1988a, 1992), economics was not a subject of his special interest. Nevertheless, his writings on the methodology of social sciences point out some problems related with economic prediction, such as its *possibility* as scientific knowledge and its *inexactitude* as social knowledge related to the future. Besides his specific comments on economic predictions, we should take into account his approach to the methodology of social sciences—the logic of situation—and his position in general methodology of science, which is critical of instrumentalism and keen on realism.[37]

On the first problem of economic predictions—its possibility as scientific knowledge—Popper stresses that the argument against historicism does not refute the *possibility* of every kind of social prediction: "it is perfectly compatible with the possibility of testing social theories—for example, economic theories—by way of predicting that certain developments will take place under certain conditions" (Popper 1957, p. vii). For him, the argument only refutes the possibility of predicting historical (or economic) developments to the extent to which they may be influenced by the growth of our knowledge (and its affect on large scale economic phenomena).

The second issue—the problem of *inexactitude*—arises from the interconnection between social predictions and the predicted events.[38] Popper exemplifies it in economics: "suppose, for instance, it were predicted that the price of shares would rise for 3 days and then fall. Plainly, everyone connected with the market would sell on the third day, causing a fall of prices on that day and falsifying the prediction" (Popper 1957, p. 13). This means—for him— that an exact and detailed social scientific prediction (i.e., an accurate and precise economic prediction) is impossible.

Moreover, in the interconnection between social predictions and the predicted events Popper sees a threat to objectivity and valuation in social sciences. Thus, "it may, in an extreme case, even *cause* the happening it predicts: the happening might not have occurred at all if it had not been predicted. At the other extreme the prediction of an impending event may lead to its *prevention* (so that, by deliberately or

[36] On the relation between Hayek's methodology of the social sciences and Popper's philosophy of science, see Martínez Solano (2011).

[37] Realism is related to the aim of science in Popper (1983).

[38] The influence of a piece of information (historical or economic) upon the situation to which the information refers is what he calls the "Oedipus effect" (Popper 1957, p. 13). However, in a paper on physics, he wrote that it also occurs in the natural sciences: "One would expect the Oedipus effect to be a peculiarity of the social science and their subject matter, and that it is completely foreign to physics; but this is not the case" (Popper 1950, p. 189).

negligently abstaining from predicting it, the social scientist, it may be said, could bring it about, or could cause it to happen)" (Popper 1957, p. 15).

Even though Popper tries to deny that the *interconnection* between social predictions and the predicted events has a real effect in distinguishing the social sciences from the natural sciences (Popper 1976, pp. 121–122), his reflections on this issue show us—in my judgment—differences between social sciences (and, among them, economics) and natural sciences: on the one hand, in the social realm there is a clearer interplay between *predictions* (e.g., economic predictions based on a theory and previous empirical knowledge) and *expectations* (e.g., what the agents expect that could happen after the prediction); and, on the other hand, there may be an additional *second level* about the previous level of predictions and expectations (there could be the case of a metaprediction about the effects of the previous prediction and it is possible that the agents could have expectations about other agents' expectations).

Following Popper's example of the prediction of the rise and decline of the price of a share, it seems clear that it is a more complex event than a natural phenomenon insofar as *different* levels intervene. Above all, there is, firstly, an interaction between the observer's prediction and the agents' response to it; and, secondly, the agents are interested not just in the economic prediction but also in what other agents make of it (Hollis 1992, p. 41). In effect, in some economic areas, such as stock exchanges and financial markets, there are several levels due to a connection between economic factors and psychological components, which make economic prediction more complex than weather prediction. Thus, the problems of the possibility of economic prediction and the question of its inexactness should be analyzed in connection with the issue of *complexity*, which goes beyond the level of natural science.

Taking into account his remarks on social prediction (i.e., his criticism of large-scale prediction of human history by scientific or any other rational means as well as his objections to exactness of prediction of social affairs), economic predictions are still *possible* in Popper's methodology but they are also *unreliable*. The consequence for economics of his criticism of historicism is the rejection of two extremes: on the one hand, the scientific prediction of large-scale economic phenomena (such as the future triumph of proletariat in Marxism), and, on the other, the exactness of the scientific prediction of concrete economic events (such as the shares in the stock market).

Put differently, what Karl Popper actually accepts in economics is a kind of "generic prediction," that is, a prediction that is not specific in the details but that can be used as a test for economic theory. In this regard, it seems that his position is not far from some economists who defend the creativity and innovation of economic affairs, a view that is different from the mainstream conception in economic methodology.

3.5.2 Differences Between Predictions

Explicitly, Popper recognizes a difference between predicting a *singular event* (e.g., 'when will the next rise in the rate of unemployment in Western Ontario be?') and predicting a certain *kind or type of event* (e.g., 'why is there a seasonal increase and decrease of unemployment in the building industry?'). In the first case, natural science can succeed (e.g., 'when will the next lunar eclipse occur?'), whereas a social science, such as economics, is in a very difficult position: "the Newtonian method of explaining and predicting singular events by universal laws and initial conditions is hardly applicable in the theoretical social sciences" (Popper 1994b, pp. 165–166). But, in the second case, when the aim is to predict a kind or type of event, economics is in a much better position: it operates by the method of constructing *typical* situations or conditions (i.e., the method of constructing models).

Clearly, this distinction shows a resemblance with theses of the Austrian school of economics, as Popper himself recognizes (Popper 1994b, p. 166): the view is connected with von Hayek's idea that in the social sciences there is less "explanation in detail" and more "explanation in principle" than in the natural sciences (Hayek 1964a/1967). In endorsing this similitude, it is clear that Popper is assuming a methodological similarity between explanation and prediction, which supposes a version of the thesis of *symmetry* between both methodological processes.

Usually, when Popper quotes an economist with approval, the name is Friedrich von Hayek,[39] a leader of the Austrian school of economics, who was awarded the Nobel Prize in 1974. Both share a methodological individualism in social sciences and show a distrust of the accuracy and precision of economic prediction of singular events. In addition, they seem to adopt—to some extent—similar approaches to the rationality principle and in the issue of prediction of type of events.

Furthermore, there is recognition by Popper of the intellectual debt regarding the crucial notion of the *logic of situation*: "I was particularly impressed by Hayek's formulation that economics is the "logic of choice" (Hayek 1948, p. 35). This led me to my formulation of the "logic of situation" (Popper 1957, p. 149). This seemed to me to embrace, for example, the logic of choice and the logic of historical problem situation. (The origin of this idea may explain why I rarely stressed the fact that I did not look at the logic of situation as a deterministic theory: I had in mind the logic of situational choices)" (Popper 1994b, p. 181, note 1).

While he was in tune with some central claims of Hayek's conception, Popper made critical comments on instrumentalism, and instrumentalism is a methodological position that has been very influential in mainstream economic methodology, due to Friedman's views (Friedman 1953). "There is an important distinction which we can make between two kinds of scientific prediction, and which instrumentalism cannot make; a distinction which is connected with the problem of scientific discovery. I have in mind the distinction between the prediction of *events of a kind which is known*, such as eclipses or thunderstorms on the one hand and, on the other hand, the prediction of *new kinds of events* (which the physics call 'new effects') such as

[39] Popper dedicated *Conjectures and Refutations* to F. von Hayek.

the prediction which led to the discovery of wireless waves, or of zero-point energy, or to the artificial building up of new elements not previously found in nature. It seems to me that instrumentalism can account only for the first kind of prediction: if theories are instruments for prediction, then we must assume that their purpose must be determined in advance, as with other instruments. Predictions of the second kind can be fully understood only as discoveries" (Popper 1956/1963, pp. 117–118).

Anti-instrumentalism and defense of methodological realism are two sides of the same coin in Popper's approach. He accepts that a scientific theory may be applied to practical problems and, in this sense, they could be actual or potential instruments. But they are not *merely* instruments, because we may learn from science something about the structure of our world: they can include predictions that can lead us towards genuine discoveries. Moreover, "science aims at truth, or getting nearer to the truth, however difficult it may be to approach truth, even with very moderate success" (Popper 1994b, p. 174).[40]

Methodologically, Popper regards predictions (among them, economic ones) according to a realist approach: they can increase our knowledge and can be closer to the truth. In fact, he distinguishes *qualitative* predictions and *quantitative* predictions. The kind of test used can make the latter more reliable than the former: "tests can be graded as being more or less severe. Qualitative tests, for example, are in general less severe than quantitative tests. And tests of more precise quantitative predictions are more severe than tests of less precise predictions" (Popper 1963c/1994, p. 94). And it is clear that economics is, with social sciences as a whole, a discipline with a large number of quantitative predictions.

Another distinction in his writings, which also affects economics, is between *conditional* predictions and *unconditional* predictions. Certainly, both can be scientific. In the conditional case, they assert that certain changes will be accompanied by other changes: "we can learn from the economist that under certain social conditions, such as shortage of commodities, controlled prices, and, say, the absence of an effective punitive system, a black market will develop" (Popper 1948/1959, p. 279).

But, in the unconditional case, there are two possibilities: (a) *unconditional scientific predictions*, which derives from conditional predictions together with historical statements which asseverate that the conditions are fulfilled (e.g., the evolution of a disease in a patient or the collapse of an economic sector given its evolution); and (b) *unconditional historical predictions* or *prophecies*, when there is no justification in a theoretical science and these do not include conditional predictions. This last case—the historical prediction that he calls "prophecy"—constitutes the core of the historicism, the social methodology that he rejects (Popper 1948/1959, p. 279).

To sum up, Popper's methodological approach to prediction has been influential at three different levels: the general methodology of science, the methodology of social sciences, and the methodology of economics. However, each one of them has shown problems, such as the need for an initial *induction* for some predictions

[40] According to Barnes, "Popper's insistence that there is *absolutely no reason* to think that theories that survive rigorous testing are true undercuts his own solution to the demarcation problem" (Barnes 2008, p. 12).

(corroboration could have predictive import); the differences in the *framework* for prediction in natural and social sciences (falsificationism is not the same methodology as the logic of situation); and the *complexity* of economic events (rather than the distinction singular event-a type of event) as real bedrock for the problem of accuracy and precision of economic predictions.[41] These deficiencies leave the door open to posterior methodological approaches: among them, Lakatos's methodology of scientific research programs, which was conceived to circumvent problems of Popper's approach.

References

Barnes, E. C. 2008. *The paradox of predictivism*. Cambridge: Cambridge University Press.

Blaug, M. 1994. Why I am not a constructivist. Confessions of an unrepentant Popperian. In *New directions in economic methodology*, ed. R. E. Backhouse, 109–136. London: Routledge.

Boudot, M. 1972. *Logique inductive et probabilité*. Paris: Armand Colin.

Caldwell, B. J. 1991. Clarifying Popper. *Journal of Economic Literature* 30:1–33.

Caldwell, B. J. 1994. Two proposals for the recovery of economic practice. In *New directions in economic methodology*, ed. R. E. Backhouse, 137–153. London: Routledge.

Caldwell, B. J. 2006. Popper and Hayek: Who influenced whom? In *Karl Popper: A centenary assessment*, vol. I, eds. I. Jarvie, K. Milford, and D. Miller, 111–124. Aldershot: Ashgate.

Clark, P. 1995. Popper on determinism. In *Karl Popper: Philosophy and problems*, ed. A. O'Hear, 149–162. Cambridge: Cambridge University Press.

Currie, G., and Musgrave, A., eds. 1985. *Popper and the human sciences*. Dordrecht: M. Nijhoff.

de Marchi, N., ed. 1988a. *The Popperian legacy in economics*. Cambridge: Cambridge University Press.

de Marchi, N., 1988b. Popper and the LSE economists. In *The Popperian legacy in economics*, ed. N. de Marchi, 139–166. Cambridge: Cambridge University Press.

de Marchi, N., ed. 1992. *Post-Popperian methodology of economics*. Boston: Kluwer.

Donagan, A. 1974. Popper's examination of historicism. In *The philosophy of Karl Popper*, vol. 2, ed. P. A. Schilpp, 905–924. La Salle: Open Court.

Earman, J. 1992. *Bayes or bust*? Cambridge: The MIT Press.

Flew, A. 1990. Popper and historicist necessities. *Philosophy* 65 (265): 53–64.

Friedman, M. 1953. The methodology of positive economics. In *Essays in positive economics*, M. Friedman, 3–43. Chicago: The University of Chicago Press (6th repr., 1969).

Gillies, D. A. 2000. *Philosophical theories of probability*. London: Routledge.

Gonzalez, W. J. 1984. La interpretación historicista de las Ciencias Sociales. *Anales de Filosofía* 2:109–137.

Gonzalez, W. J. 1991a. Historismo y anti-historismo en la polémica metodológica entre G. Schmoller y C. Menger. In *Actas del V Congreso de la Sociedad Española de Historia de las Ciencias y las Técnicas*, eds. M. Valera and C. Lopez Fernandez, 2027–2041. Murcia: PPU–DM.

Gonzalez, W. J. 1995. Reichenbach's concept of prediction. *International Studies in the Philosophy of Science* 9 (1): 37–58.

Gonzalez, W. J. 1996e. Caracterización del objeto de la Ciencia de la Historia y bases de su configuración metodológica. In *Acción e Historia. El objeto de la Historia y la Teoría de la Acción*, ed. W. J. Gonzalez, 25–111. A Coruña: Publicaciones Universidad de A Coruña.

[41] The problem of complexity as a source for difficulties on scientific predictions, in general, and economic predictions, in particular, is addressed in Gonzalez (2011a, 2012b, and 2013b).

Gonzalez, W. J. 2000. Marco teórico, trayectoria y situación actual de la Filosofía y Metodología de la Economía. *Argumentos de Razón Técnica* 3:13–59.

Gonzalez, W. J. 2004b. The many faces of Popper's methodological approach to prediction. In *Karl Popper: Critical appraisals*, ed. P. Catton and G. Macdonald, 78–98. London: Routledge.

Gonzalez, W. J. 2004c. La evolución del Pensamiento de Popper. In *Karl Popper: Revisión de su legado*, ed. W. J. Gonzalez, 23–194. Madrid: Unión Editorial.

Gonzalez, W. J. 2010a. *La predicción científica: Concepciones filosófico-metodológicas desde H. Reichenbach a N. Rescher*. Barcelona: Montesinos.

Gonzalez, W. J. 2011a. Complexity in economics and prediction: The role of parsimonious factors. In *Explanation, prediction, and confirmation*, eds. D. Dieks, W. J. Gonzalez, S. Hartman, T. Uebel, and M. Weber, 319–330. Dordrecht: Springer.

Gonzalez, W. J. 2012b. Methodological universalism in science and its limits: Imperialism versus complexity. In *Thinking about provincialism in thinking*, Poznan Studies in the Philosophy of the Sciences and the Humanities, vol. 100, eds. K. Brzechczyn and K. Paprzycka, 155–175. Amsterdam: Rodopi.

Gonzalez, W. J. 2013b. The sciences of design as sciences of complexity: The dynamic trait. In *New challenges to philosophy of science*, eds. H. Andersen, D. Dieks, W. J. Gonzalez, Th. Uebel, and G. Wheeler, 299–311. Dordrecht: Springer.

Hands, D. W. 1993a. *Testing, rationality and progress: Essays on the Popperian tradition in economic methodology*. Lanham: Rowman and Littlefield.

Hayek, F. A. 1948. Economics and knowledge. In *Individualism and economic order*, ed. F. A. Hayek, 33–56. London: Routledge and Kegan Paul, The University of Chicago Press.

Hayek, F. A. 1964a. Degrees of explanation. In *Studies in philosophy, politics and economics*, ed. F. A. Hayek, 3–21. Chicago: The University of Chicago Press (Reprinted in 1967).

Hayek, F. A. 1964b. The theory of complex phenomena. In *Studies in philosophy, politics and economics*, ed. F. A. Hayek, 22–42. Chicago: The University of Chicago Press (Reprinted in 1967).

Hayek, F. A. 1978. *New studies in philosophy, politics, economics and the history of ideas*. London: Routledge and K. Paul.

Hesse, M. 1971. Whewell's consilience of inductions and predictions. *The Monist* 55:520–524.

Hollis, M. 1992. Historical prediction. In *Popper in China*, ed. W. H. Newton-Smith and J. Tianji, 37–54. London: Routledge.

Jarvie, I. C. 1982. Popper on the difference between the natural and the social sciences. In *In pursuit of truth*, ed. P. Levinson, 83–107. Sussex: Harvester Press.

Koertge, N. 1975. Popper's metaphysical research program for the human sciences. *Inquiry* 18 (4): 437–462.

Lakatos, I. 1970. Falsification and the methodology of scientific research programmes. In *Criticism and the growth of knowledge*, eds. I. Lakatos and A. Musgrave, 91–196. Cambridge: Cambridge University Press (Reprinted in Lakatos, I. 1978. *The methodology of scientific research programmes. Philosophical papers*, vol. 1, 8–101. Cambridge: Cambridge University Press).

Macdonald, G. 1995. The grounds for anti-historicism. In *Karl Popper: Philosophy and problems*, ed. A. O'Hear, 241–257. Cambridge: Cambridge University Press.

Martínez Solano, J. F. 2005. *El problema de la verdad en K. R. Popper: Reconstrucción histórico-sistemática*. A Coruña: Netbiblo.

Martínez Solano, J. F. 2007. La influencia de la Filosofía de Karl Popper en la Metodología de la Economía de Mark Blaug. *Laguna* 27:9–28.

Martínez Solano, J. F. 2011. La Metodología de las Ciencias Sociales de Friedrich Hayek y su relación con la Filosofía de Karl Popper. In *Ensayos de Epistemología contemporánea*, ed. Z. Saldivia Maldonado, 23–48. Santiago de Chile: Bravo y Allende Editores.

Mirowski, P. 1989. *More heat than light: Economics as social physics, physics as nature's economics*. New York: Cambridge University Press.

Neurath, O. 1946. Prediction and induction. *Analisi* 1 (3): 1–6 (Compiled in Neurath O. 1983. *Philosophical papers*, 1913–1946, 243–246. Edited and translated by R. S. Cohen and M. Neurath. Dordrecht: Reidel).

Nola, R. 1987. The status of Popper's theory of method. *The British Journal for the Philosophy of Science* 38:441–480.
O'Hear, A. 1980. *Karl Popper*. London: Routledge and K. Paul.
O'Hear, A., ed. 1995. *Karl Popper: Philosophy and problems*. Cambridge: Cambridge University Press.
Popper, K. R. 1935. *Logik der Forschung*. Vienna: Julius Springer (reprinted in J. C. B. Mohr—P. Siebeck—, Tübingen, 1994).
Popper, K. R. 1945. *The open society and its enemies*, vol. 1: *Plato*; vol. 2: *Hegel and Marx*. London: Routledge (5th ed., 1966, reprinted in 1992).
Popper, K. R. 1948. Prediction and prophecy and their significance for social theory. In *Proceedings of the tenth international congress of philosophy,* ed. E. W. Beth, H. J. Pos, and J. H. A. Hollak, 82–91. Amsterdam: North-Holland. Revised version: Popper, K. R. 1959. Prediction and prophecy in the social science. In *Theories of history,* ed. P. Gardiner, 276–285. London: Macmillan. Reprinted in Popper, K. R. 1963. *Conjectures and refutations. The growth of scientific knowledge,* 336–346. London: Routledge and Kegan Paul (5th revised ed., 1989).
Popper, K. R. 1950. Indeterminism in quantum physics and in classical physics. *The British Journal for the Philosophy of Science* 1 (2): 117–133, and 1 (3): 173–195.
Popper, K. R. 1956. Three views concerning human knowledge. In *Contemporary British philosophy: Personal statements*, 3rd Series, ed. H. D. Lewis, 355–388. London: G. Allen and Unwin (Reprinted in Popper, K. R. 1963. *Conjectures and refutations. The growth of scientific knowledge*, 97–119. London: Routledge and K. Paul (5th revised ed., 1989.))
Popper, K. 1957. *The poverty of historicism*. London: Routledge and K. Paul (reprinted by Routledge in 1991).
Popper, K. R. 1959. *The logic of scientific discovery*. London: Hutchinson (revised ed. in 1968). (Translation into English of Popper, K. R. 1935. *Logik der Forschung*. Vienna: Julius Springer).
Popper, K. R. 1963a. *Conjectures and refutations. The growth of scientific knowledge*. London: Routledge and K. Paul (5th revised ed., 1989).
Popper, K. R. 1963b. Truth, rationality, and the growth of scientific knowledge. In *Conjectures and refutations. The growth of scientific knowledge*, ed. K. R. Popper, 215–250. London: Routledge and Kegan Paul.
Popper, K. R. 1963c. Science: Problems, aims, responsibilities. *Federation of American Societies for Experimental Biology* 22 (4): 961–972 (Reprinted in Popper, K. R. 1994. *The myth of the framework. In defense of science and rationality*, 82–111. London: Routledge).
Popper, K. R. 1972. *Objective knowledge*. Oxford: Clarendon Press (revised ed., 1979, reprinted in 1989).
Popper, K. R. 1974. Replies to my critics. In *The philosophy of Karl Popper*, vol. 2, ed. P. A. Schilpp, 961–1197. La Salle: Open Court.
Popper, K. R. 1976. *Unended quest. An intellectual autobiography*. London: Fontana/Collins (enlarged version, 1992. London: Routledge).
Popper, K. 1979. *Die beiden Grundprobleme der Erkenntnistheorie*, ed. T. E. Hansen. Tübingen: J. C. B. Mohr (Paul Siebeck) (2nd revised ed., 1994).
Popper, K. R. 1982. *The open universe. An argument for indeterminism*. London: Hutchinson.
Popper, K. R. 1983. *Realism and the aim of science*. London: Hutchinson (2nd reprint, London: Routledge, 1994).
Popper, K. R. 1985. The rationality principle. In *K. R. Popper, Selections*, ed. D. Miller, 357–365. Princeton: Princeton University Press.
Popper, K. R. 1992. *In search of a better world*. London: Routledge.
Popper, K. R. 1994a. *The myth of the framework. In defense of science and rationality*, ed. M. Notturno. London: Routledge.
Popper, K. R. 1994b. Models, instruments, and truth. The status of the rationality principle in the social sciences. In *The myth of the framework. In defense of science and rationality*, ed. M. Notturno, 154–184. London: Routledge.
Popper, K. R. 1994c. *Alles Leben ist Problemlössen*. Munich: Piper (Translated by Patrick Camiller. 1999. *All life is problem solving*. London: Routledge).

Putnam, H. 1974. The "corroboration" of theories. In *The philosophy of Karl Popper*, vol. 1, ed. P. A. Schilpp, 221–240. La Salle: Open Court.
Putnam, H. 1994. Reichenbach and the limits of vindication. In *Words and life*, ed. J. Conant, 131–148. Cambridge: Harvard University Press.
Reichenbach, H. 1935. Über Induktion und Wahrscheinlichkeit. Bemerkungen zu Karl Poppers. *Logik der Forschung. Erkenntnis* 5 (4): 267–284 (Translated by E. Schneewind: Induction and probability. Remarks on Karl Popper's *The logic of scientific discovery*. In Reichenbach, H. 1978. *Selected writings*, vol. 2, ed. M. Reichenbach and R. Cohen, 372–387. Dordrecht: Reidel (it includes a postscript)).
Reichenbach, H. 1936a. Logistic empiricism in Germany and the present state of its problems. *Journal of Philosophy* 33 (6): 141–160.
Reichenbach, H. 1936b. Induction and probability. *Philosophy of Science* 3:124–126.
Reichenbach, H. 1938. *Experience and prediction. An analysis of the foundations and the structure of knowledge*. Chicago: The University of Chicago Press.
Reichenbach, H. 1951a. *The rise of scientific philosophy*. Berkeley: University of California Press (reprinting 1966).
Reichenbach, H. 1951b. Predictive knowledge. In *The rise of scientific philosophy*, H. Reichenbach, 229–249. Berkeley: University of California Press (reprinting 1966).
Reichenbach, H. 1978a. *Selected writings*, vol. 1, eds. M. Reichenbach and R. S. Cohen. Dordrecht: Reidel.
Reichenbach, H. 1978b. *Selected writings*, vol. 2, eds. M. Reichenbach and R. Cohen. Dordrecht: Reidel.
Rescher, N. 1980. *Induction*. Pittsburgh: University of Pittsburgh Press.
Salmon, W. C. 1981. Rational prediction. *The British Journal for the Philosophy of Science* 32:115–125 (Reprinted in Grünbaum, A., and Salmon, W. C., eds. 1988. *The limitations of deductivism,* 47–60. Berkeley: University of California Press).
Schilpp, P. A., ed. 1974. *The philosophy of Karl Popper*, 2 vols. La Salle: Open Court.
Urbach, P. 1978. Is any of Popper's arguments against historicism valid? *The British Journal for the Philosophy of Science* 29:117–130.
Urbach, P. 1985. Good and bad arguments against historicism. In *Popper and the human sciences*, eds. G. Currie and A. Musgrave, 133–146. Dordrecht: M. Nijhoff.
Urbach, P. 1987. The scientific standing of evolutionary theories of society. *London School of Economics Quarterly* 1:23–42.
Worrall, J. 2001a. De la Matemática a la Ciencia: Continuidad y discontinuidad en el Pensamiento de Imre Lakatos. In *La Filosofía de Imre Lakatos: Evaluación de sus propuestas*, ed. W. J. Gonzalez, 107–128. Madrid: UNED.

Chapter 4
Prediction and Novel Facts in the Methodology of Scientific Research Programs

Imre Lakatos developed the methodology of scientific research programs (MSRP) as an alternative to Karl Popper's philosophico-methodological approach to science (Lakatos 1970).[1] Nonetheless, Eric Barnes maintains that Lakatos' MSRP "followed Popper's falsificationist methodology in two crucial respects (among others): (1) risky predictions constitute the mark of scientific character (and, relatedly, the accommodation of data is scientifically suspect), and (2) successful predictions—aka novel confirmations—are the sole mark of scientific success" (Barnes 2008, p. 13).

But Lakatos' methodology of scientific research programs offers a conception of science, in general, and scientific prediction, in particular, that is completely inserted in the "historical turn" (Gonzalez 2010a).[2] Thus, his views on science emphasize the *historicity* of scientific activity instead of highlighting the content of science as Popper does in his different philosophico-methodological periods (Gonzalez 2004c). In addition, there is no equivalent in Lakatos to the criticisms made by Popper to "historicism," in general, and "historical prediction," in particular, which are the leit-motiv of his book *The Poverty of Historicism* (1957).

Concerning the views on scientific prediction, Ian Hacking thinks that Lakatos, through his MSRP, sides with William Whewell's emphasis on prediction against J. Stuart Mill's position, but "he does not give reasons. Rather he makes it true by definition that what matters to a theory is its ability to predict novel facts" (Hacking 1979, p. 389). Even though it seems clear that Lakatos assumes a predictivism on science, which can be seen as more intense than Popper's thought,[3] his position is more sophisticated that a dogmatic approach to prediction and requires a specific analysis.

[1] John Worrall sees ways in which the methodology of scientific research programs improves on Popper's methodology (Worrall 1978). However, he recognizes that Lakatos did not develop the "positive heuristics," which is an important aspect of his conception. For this reason, Worrall seeks advancements regarding Lakatos' proposals (Worrall 2001b).

[2] On Lakatos' philosophy see also Gonzalez (2001d) and Motterlini (2002) as well as on his differences with Feyerabend's philosophy (Lakatos and Feyerabend 1999).

[3] In addition to the difference due to the role of prediction in the methodology of social sciences, there is also in Lakatos a more intense emphasis on prediction within the general methodology of science, which accompanies his stress on the "novel facts."

W. J. Gonzalez, *Philosophico-Methodological Analysis of Prediction and its Role in Economics,* Theory and Decision Library A: 50, DOI 10.1007/978-3-319-08885-3_4

4.1 Three Different Levels on Prediction: Aim, Process, and Assessment

Overall, Lakatos' approach to prediction and novel facts is among the most interesting aspects of his MSRP. Even though his views on the importance of this issue have not remained at the center of attention in mainstream methodology of science in recent decades, mainly because other topics (explanation, progress, truth and truthlikeness, etc.) have received *more* attention, the study of the role of prediction of novel facts as a criterion of appraisal is an area where Lakatos tried to make a significant contribution. Moreover, it is an aspect of his thought that has enjoyed particular attention within the methodology of economics.

Besides the oscillations in the repercussion of Lakatos' methodology of scientific research programs on the methodology of economics (Gonzalez 2001b), there is another relevant aspect here: the controversies on prediction within the general methodology of science. In this regard, there are two controversial issues intertwined: first, whether accommodations or predictions provide superior evidential support for scientific theories;[4] and, second, if the prediction has actually more methodological weight than accommodation (Chap. 2, Sect. 2.1.2), which version of predictivism seems to be more reasonable, both in thematic terms and in historical ones (Hitchcock and Sober 2004; Barnes 2008).

Prediction appears in Lakatos' methodology of scientific research programs in at least three different levels: (a) as an important *aim* of the research programs;[5] (b) as a *process*—a key method—to increase the scientific knowledge both theoretically and empirically (as well as heuristically); and (c) as the way to *assess* the scientific character of the knowledge claims (i.e., a form of evaluating results). At all these levels—aim, process, and assessment—he sees a connection between scientific prediction and novel facts (Gonzalez 2001e).

This connection has a clear relevance for grasping in Lakatos' MSRP the semantics of *prediction* as well as for the logical relation between "explanation" and "prediction." Furthermore, the link between prediction and novel facts has an epistemological content, which affects the methodological procedure for *increasing* scientific knowledge as well as the methodological process of *evaluating* science according to the reliability of predictions.

Undoubtedly, these different aspects of prediction in Lakatos' conception—semantic, logical, epistemological, methodological, and axiological—require attention here in order to clarify his philosophico-methodological approach. They are also related to axiological issues (the cognitive value of prediction in the scientific research) as well as to ontological ones (due mainly to the role of novel facts).

The analysis in this chapter will be in four steps. (1) To examine his concept of "prediction" in Lakatos' methodology of scientific research programs, taking into

[4] This was one of the key issues at the 1994 meeting of the Philosophy of Science Association, cf. Stephen Brush (1995) and Peter Achinstein (1995).

[5] Prediction is not the main aim of science on Lakatos' view. Truth is the fundamental aim; predictive success is the indication that we may be approaching truth.

account different aspects (semantic, logical, epistemological, methodological, and axiological). (2) To clarify the notion of "novel facts," which requires the consideration of the various ways in which *new facts* can be understood. (3) To examine the prediction of novel facts as *criterion of appraisal* (theoretical, empirical, and heuristic). (4) To explore Lakatos' approach (i.e., the concept of prediction linked to novel facts) in connection with the field of *economics*, in order to shed new light on issues that have been discussed in recent years.

4.2 Prediction in the Methodology of Research Programs

An initial difference can be found in Lakatos regarding prediction and research programs. On the one hand, there is the prediction *about* the research program itself insofar as it is a *human undertaking*. His position is straightforward: "the growth of a research programme cannot be predicted" (Lakatos 1970/1978a, p. 69, note).[6] The reason for this is the creativity of the human mind which establishes a potentially unending stream of activity for which there is no saturation point: "there is no predictable or ascertainable limitation on human imagination in inventing new, content-increasing theories" (Lakatos 1970/1978a, p. 72, note).

On the other hand, there is the prediction *within* the research program: here there is mainly a methodological element that—for him—has a central role in the development and appraisal of the research programs: "all the research programmes I admire have one characteristic in common. They all predict novel facts, facts which had been either undreamt of, or have indeed been contradicted by previous or rival programmes" (Lakatos 1974b/1978a, p. 5).[7]

4.2.1 *A Pragmatic Characterization*

Although Lakatos uses the word "prediction" many times *within* the methodology of research programs, its meaning is not always clear. He does not offer a *semantic* definition of "prediction"—with a clear sense and reference—but rather a *pragmatic* characterization (a use within a specific realm): it is a proposition (a "particular hypothesis") supported by a theory (Lakatos 1968/1978b,, p. 192), whose content is related to novel facts. And, insofar as he links predictions to novel facts, it seems that he is connecting predictions and future events.

[6] Lakatos' references are to the reprints in his *Philosophical Papers*, vol. 1 (*The Methodology of Scientific Research Programmes*, 1978a) and vol. 2 (*Mathematics, Science and Epistemology*, 1978b).

[7] There is an inconsistent element here, because if the predicted novel facts were contradicted by previous or rival programs, then they would be already known. I owe this idea to John Worrall, *Personal communication*, 30 May 2004.

However, this is not always the case, as it can be seen in the discussion of the *sophisticated falsificationism*: "I use 'prediction' in a wide sense that includes 'postdiction'" (1970/1978a, p. 32, note. See also 1970/1978a, pp. 69–71 and 76; 1971/1978a, p. 114). Therefore, for Lakatos, prediction could also be backwards instead of being always forwards (i.e., related to the future). In addition, it means that he accepts that there could be "novel facts" of the past, which *prima facie* seems at odds with the notion (semantic and ontological) of *new* facts.

Nevertheless, Lakatos ordinarily uses the term "prediction" for the theoretical *anticipation* of a novel fact within a research program. This is a common usage in his writings, even though he maintains that "the novelty of a factual proposition can frequently be seen only after a long period has elapsed" (1970/1978a, p. 69). But this is a mysterious claim, because *prima facie* the novelty of a factual proposition does not require being seen after a long period.

Sometimes, Lakatos explicitly emphasizes his interest in *pre*-dictions (i.e., something said before it happens) which are successful, and he sees there a difference in comparison with other methodologies: "the successful *pre*dictions of novel facts which constitute serious evidence for a research programme and therefore vital parts of internal history, are irrelevant both for the inductivist and for the [naive] falsificationist" (1971/1978a, p. 114). Furthermore, he connects "prediction" and "unexpected fact" when he points out that a series of theories constitutes a theoretically progressive problemshift "if each new theory has some excess empirical content over its predecessor, that is, if it predicts some novel, hitherto unexpected fact" (Lakatos 1970/1978a, p. 33).

4.2.2 Logical Perspective: Proposition

From a logical point of view, prediction is—for Lakatos—a *proposition* of a theory rather than an argument. On the one hand, he maintains that prediction is a "particular hypothesis" which depends on the *theory* (1968/1978b, p. 192). In addition, Lakatos defends what he calls the "theoretical approach" to the reliability of predictions: "while theories may be said to be supported by evidence, 'predictions' are supported by theories" (1968/1978b, p. 192).[8] And, on the other hand, in the structure of the research program (hard core, protective belt, heuristic rules, etc.) he emphasizes more *prediction* than explanation.

Certainly, this position seems to favor an asymmetry between explanation and prediction (i.e., not a mere temporal anysotropy between them). However, for Lakatos, an adequate specific theory within a program must "explain" (i.e., entail) all known relevant facts (so, for example, Einstein's theory must entail all the facts already entailed by Newton's theory). What he had in mind was the *adjustability* of

[8] For Worrall, what Lakatos seems to have in mind in this statement is related with the issue of (so-called) "theory-ladenness" of observation. In this regard, Worrall considers that ultimately there must be sentences whose truth value we can decide *independently* of theory. (Otherwise the whole scientific enterprise would be without foundation). *Personal communication*, March 2000.

specific theories to any given finite set of data (i.e., Duhem's problem); and hence the intuitive judgment that only "predicted" evidence really tests. But the latter never meant that "explanation" of known facts was irrelevant.

Lakatos criticizes the logical empiricists who see scientific hypotheses purely from the point of view of concordance with experimental data, because for him the primacy of prediction is clear: "new scientific hypotheses are assumed not simply in order to patch up gaps between data and theory but in order to predict novel facts" (1970/1978a, p. 86). His conception considers a research program as degenerating when accommodating known facts, whereas he conceives that a progressive program is one that anticipates new facts.[9] Moreover, "when the program ceases to anticipate novel facts, its hard core might have to be abandoned" (1970/1978a, p. 49), which means that it should be replaced by a new one with a different hard core.

According to this prevalence of prediction over explanation, Lakatos criticizes those like Thomas Kuhn (1957, p. 224) who do not give special importance to a theory that happened to have anticipated a factual discovery. The criticism has implicit a clear difference between explanation and prediction: "like [J. Stuart] Mill and [J. Maynard] Keynes before him, Kuhn cannot understand why the historic order of theory and evidence should count, and he cannot see the importance of the fact that Copernicans *pre*dicted the phases of Venus, while Tychonians only explained them by *post hoc* adjustments" (Lakatos 1971/1978a, p. 115, note). So, besides the temporal anisotropy between explanation and prediction, there is in Lakatos a structural preference (i.e., "logical") in favor of prediction insofar as it is innovative.

4.2.3 Epistemological Component

Epistemologically, prediction is linked in Latakos to the possession of testable implications: it is an element of a theory that has *observable consequences* regarding some novel fact (1970/1978a, p. 83). In addition, prediction should be matched with the main epistemological problem of the methodology of scientific research programs, which is the connection of verisimilitude (i.e., the difference between the truth content and falsity content of a theory) with the scientific gambit of pragmatic acceptances and rejections. In other words, prediction is—for him—an epistemological rational exercise related to verisimilitude (Lakatos 1971/1978a, p. 113) (in Popper's technical sense and, therefore, it is an approach affected by the criticisms against the Popperian interpretation of verisimilitude) (Hands 1991a).

Where Lakatos departs epistemologically from Popper is in the *positive role* of experience: it is not a mere negative instance. Learning about a theory is—for him—primarily related to the new facts which it anticipates: "for the sort of Popperian empiricism I advocate, the only relevant evidence is the evidence anticipated by a theory, and *empiricalness (or scientific character) and theoretical progress*

[9] Lakatos qualifies once this position: "I define a research programme as degenerating even if it anticipates novel facts but does so in a patched-up development rather than by a coherent, preplanned positive heuristic" (1971/1978a, p. 112).

are inseparably connected" (1970/1978a, p. 38). In this regard, Mark Blaug holds that "Lakatos called the process of predicting novel facts 'theoretical progress' and the corroboration of these predictions 'empirical progress'" (Blaug 1991a, p. 504).

In addition to "theoretical progress" and "empirical progress," there is in Lakatos a *heuristic progress*—a progressive problemshift—which, in principle, depends on the successful prediction of some novel fact: a research program progresses when its theoretical growth anticipates its empirical growth (i.e., it keeps predicting novel facts with some success—progressive problemshift —),[10] whereas it stagnates when it gives only *post hoc* explanations of discoveries or facts anticipated by a rival program (Lakatos 1971/1978a, p. 112) (like the Cartesians, which explained what Newtonians predicted, but only *post hoc*).[11]

4.2.4 The Appraisal of Research Programs

It seems clear that, methodologically, prediction is used for the process of developing scientific research programs and for their appraisal both theoretically and empirically. Thus, for Lakatos, a scientific research program is "*theoretically progressive* if each modification leads to new unexpected predictions and it is *empirically progressive* if at least some of these novel predictions are corroborated" (Lakatos and Zahar 1976/1978a, p. 179).[12] In other words, he establishes an empirical criterion to place identity of what is theoretically progressive: the connection between excess of content and prediction of novel fact.

Lakatos' methodological approach offers an *appraisal* of scientific growth in terms of progressive and degenerative changes of problems ("problemshifts") in a series of scientific theories. Prediction plays also a key role in the interpretation of the scientific change—the *heuristic progress*—which is not seen from the point of view of incommensurability of theories but rather as the superseding of theories: "one research programme *supersedes* another if it has excess truth content over its rival, in the sense that it predicts progressively all that its rival truly predicts and some more besides" (Lakatos and Zahar 1976/1978a, p. 179). This was the case of Copernicus's program.

Yet Lakatos distinguishes in his own approach a *method*—the methodology of scientific research programs—and a *meta-method*—the methodology of *historiographical* research programs—that is a methodology of scientific research

[10] This "heuristic progress" could be interpreted as an anticipation of his acceptance of the Zahar–Worrall view. It means explanation/prediction of an old/new fact in a way that "cohered" with the general ideas underlying the program.

[11] Another case of heuristic progress is the following: "the progress is not even so much in the actual novel predictions which go beyond the premises—in this case that planets might move also in parabolas—but in the mathematical and physical novelty of problem-solving techniques which later lead to, and form part of, a progressive research programme" Lakatos (1961 and 1973/1978b, p. 101).

[12] Before this paper, Elie Zahar published an influential paper: Zahar (1973). Later on, he wrote another interesting contribution on Lakatos' MSRP: Zahar (2001).

programs of *second order* (1971/1978a, pp. 131–132). The former—MSRP—includes programs with a structure (hard core, protective belt, etc.) which is appraised mainly in terms of some excess empirical content over its predecessor; and the latter—MHRP—introduces a straightforward historical view: the research programs are appraised in historiographical terms (i.e., there is prediction of novel historical facts, unexpected in other historiographies, and those predictions should be corroborated by historical research) (Lakatos 1971/1978a, p. 133).

Pertaining to this distinction, Blaug maintains that "there is … no inherent connection between MSRP and MHRP and it may well be that the former is true and the latter is false" (1991a, p. 503). It seems to me that he goes too far in denying an inherent connection between "method" (the methodology of scientific research programs) and "meta-method" (the methodology of *historiographical* research programs), but Blaug is certainly right when he claims that scientists do not accept or reject methodologies according to Lakatos' historiographical criteria of appraisal.

4.2.5 A Value for Scientific Research

Axiologically, successful predictions have in Lakatos' conception a clear *value* for scientific research: "what really count are dramatic, unexpected, stunning predictions" (1974b, p. 6; see 1974b, p. 5). The anticipation of future events is an epistemic value, which in principle has for him more methodological weight than the explanation of already known facts. Scientific progress is seen above all as the process of reaching the *aim* of successful predictions, due to the stronger weight given to prediction over explanation.

Within this general framework, prediction has at least a quadruple role in Lakatos' philosophico-methodological approach: (i) it is the *aim* which is sought because of a superior epistemic value; (ii) it is what shows *theoretical progress* within a methodology of research programs (i.e., the procedure should lead towards an increasing number of reliable predictions); (iii) it is what counts as *empirical progress* insofar as the predictions are corroborated; and (iv) it is central in the *heuristic progress* when a research program is superseded by a new one.

Even though prediction plays a *crucial task* in Lakatos' approach (principally in the MSRP), which is even bigger than in the case of Popper's falsificationism, his characterization of this concept—including "prediction of novel facts"—is far from being thoroughly articulated in the key philosophical realms on science (semantic, logical, epistemological, methodological, and axiological), and so it presents some deficiencies and inadequacies. Let me enumerate the main ones:

Semantically, there is no definition of *prediction* in Lakatos. He offers a pragmatic interchangeable use of "prediction" and "postdiction," which are clearly two different notions (Gonzalez 1995, esp., pp. 53–54). Logically, he seems in favor of an asymmetry between explanation and prediction, and at the same time he shows an overwhelming preference for prediction that requires more attention. Epistemologically, prediction appears in a better context here in Lakatos than in Popper, insofar as the experience does not have a pure negative role, but that approach is affected by the problems related with the Popperian verisimilitude.

Methodologically, Lakatos advances in the process and appraisal of scientific progress when he sees three different perspectives (theoretical, empirical, and heuristic), but he excessively emphasizes the task of prediction. Axiologically, prediction is evaluated as a central value of scientific research when it seems to me more accurate to consider prediction as one important element among others, even though it could be more innovative and difficult from a heuristic point of view than explanation.

4.3 The Notion of "Novel Facts"

Due to the number of times that Lakatos mentions the expression *novel facts* in his methodology of research programs, it seems that it should be easy to identify what he means by "novel facts." This is not the case. Moreover, he himself recognizes that it is not obvious what a novel fact is: "there may be conflicting views about whether an accepted basic statement expresses a *novel* fact or not" (1971/1978a, p. 117). In addition, it is not completely clear what a *fact* is, because it is not something purely given but rather construed on the basis of the reality. Lakatos does not focus on the definition of *fact*, and in this point an idea of Peter F. Strawson could be useful: "facts are what statements (when true) state" (1950, p. 136).

4.3.1 Directions of Novel Facts

Regarding the concept of "novel fact," Lakatos' philosophico-methodological approach primarily oscillates between two directions. The first is *epistemologico-ontological*, which allows an ontological view of prediction, such as the anticipation of the existence of an entity (e.g., a planet or a satellite). The second is *epistemologico-methodological*, because the novelty is in the "reinterpretation," or in the use, of the knowledge already available.[13] Thus, it could be a temporal novelty, or the fact may be new, in the sense of not being used in the construction of the theory.

Commonly, Lakatos stands in the *first direction* in his strongest claims. For example, he maintains that novel facts are "facts improbable in the light of, or even forbidden," by a previous theory (1970/1978a, p. 32) (e.g., the phases of Venus).

---

[13] John Worrall maintains that Imre Lakatos was confused in this issue insofar as "predictions are always 'ontological': they always say that something exists or some effect occurs. Again the stuff about 'reinterpretation' is a reflection of the fact that Lakatos was vaguely aware of the correct Zahar-Worrall view [on novel facts] even when officially he was highlighting *temporally* novel facts. Hence he realized that there was no reason why, e.g., planetary stations and retrogressions should not fully support Copernican theory, despite [their] being known for centuries before Copernicus, and so he talked about Copernicus's 'reinterpretation' of stations and retrogressions (he may not actually use that example then, but it captures the point). But—according to Worrall—this confusion is shown to be quite unnecessary once the Zahar-Worrall's view is adopted," *Personal communication*, March 2000.

This case supposes epistemological incompatibility between old and posterior knowledge: "a new fact must be improbable or even impossible in the light of previous knowledge" (Lakatos 1970/1978a, p. 34, note).[14]

However, he follows the *second direction* in some cases, for example, when he holds that "*we should certainly regard a newly interpreted fact as a new fact*" (Lakatos 1970/1978a, pp. 70–71, emphasis added in the original). The difference is clear: here the expression "new fact" does not refer at all to an ontologically new fact (i.e., an undiscovered fact, something real unknown) but rather to an epistemological perspective which allows *reinterpretations* of known facts.

Even so, there is also the possibility of a pure *methodological* meaning: novelty regarding the *process of problemshift* of research programs. This third possibility arises from the existence in Lakatos of three criteria for appraising research programs: the criteria of theoretical, empirical, and heuristic progress (1978a, p. 189). The novelty regarding the process of problemshift of research programs can follow on from the third one: the *heuristic* progress. It can be connected with the heuristic power, "the power of a research programme to anticipate theoretically novel facts in its growth" (Lakatos 1970/1978a, p. 69, note).

The problem, however, is whether this *third direction* of novel facts—the "methodological novelty"—has life of its own in Lakatos' approach, or if, rather, it depends on its direct connection with the other two directions pointed out here (the epistemologico-ontological and the epistemologico-methodological). Before this third possibility on novel facts—a pure *methodological* meaning—is studied, the variety of views on "novelty" should be considered.

4.3.2 Different Kinds of Novelty

Today there is available a list of six different kinds of *novelty*. (I) Strictly temporal novelty: the fact was unknown when the theory was proposed; (II) heuristic view of novelty: the fact was not used in the construction of the theory; (III) novelty with respect to background theory (Alan Musgrave): the fact was not predicted by the best existing predecessor to the theory; (IV) novelty regarding background theory (John Watkins): a fact which has no counterpart among the consequences of the predecessors to the theory; (V) temporal novelty for the individual: the fact is unknown to the person who constructed the theory at the time the theory is constructed; and (VI) novelty with respect to design (i.e., facts the theory was not designated to explain; Hands 1991b, pp. 96–99; and Backhouse 1997, p. 115).

I think that the correspondence is clear between positions (I) and (II), and these two directions have been already pointed out here as the epistemologico-ontological and the epistemologico-methodological options. Moreover, in this regard, Lakatos

[14] It means that the fact could be an entity discovered later on (e.g., Neptune).

recognized that he changed his mind under Elie Zahar's influence (Zahar 1973; Lakatos and Zahar 1976/Lakatos 1978a, pp. 184–185).[15]

Initially, the novel facts were those which were never before observed (e.g., the return of Halley's comet, the discovery of Neptune, the Einsteinian bending of light rays, etc.) and which were forbidden by the rival program. After the acceptance of the modification, a novel fact could be a fact already known (such as Mercury's perihelion) which gives empirical support to a new theory (in this case, to Einstein's theory). This fact is not novel temporally speaking: its novelty consists only in its not having been used in the construction of the theory and, therefore, that novelty lies in the lack of methodological use of the knowledge already available (Gonzalez 2001e).

However, it seems more difficult to identify the third possibility that I mentioned before (i.e., a pure *methodological* meaning), because in Lakatos it is more implicit than explicit. It has resemblances with what Musgrave has in mind, insofar as the novelty of this third case is related to a *background theory* rather than a background knowledge like in kinds (I) and (II). His view, which corresponds to type (III), stresses that the basic question is not so much if evidence e confirms a hypothesis h but rather if an evidence e supports h' more than h''.

Thus the point of comparison is not the "background knowledge," in general, but rather the old theory that it challenges. "According to this view, a new theory is independently testable (or predicts a 'novel fact') if it predicts something which is not also predicted by its background theory" (Musgrave 1974, pp. 15–16). In other words, following this interpretation, there is a difference in the potential falsifiers: the new theory has some potential falsifiers that are not also valid for the old theory.

Musgrave thinks that his interpretation follows from the problem of *excess empirical content*, because—for Lakatos—to be independently testable or to have "some excess empirical content" over its predecessor supposes that a new theory must predict *novel* facts (i.e., facts improbable in the light of, or even forbidden by, the old theory). This interpretation includes another feature: a "novel fact" defined in that way—as improbable or forbidden—could be a *known* fact. Thus, it assumes that Lakatos does not *explicitly* adopt a strictly temporal view of novelty (Musgrave 1974, p. 16, note), which I think is wrong because sometimes he does.[16]

If Lakatos' criterion of heuristic progress consists of the acceptance of "problemshifts as 'scientific' only if they are at least theoretically progressive," and progress is measured by "the degree to which the series of theories leads us to the discovery of novel facts" (Lakatos 1970/1978a, p. 34),[17] then it could be a *heuristic novelty*

[15] See, in this chapter, the remarks on the Zahar–Worrall line on novel facts. John Worrall has developed many aspects related to prediction, both in historical terms and thematic ones (cf. Worrall 1989a, 2002, 2005).

[16] "Nobody had thought to make such an observation before Einstein's programme. Thus, in a progressive research programme, theory leads to the discovery of hitherto unknown novel facts" (Lakatos 1974b, p. 5).

[17] Following the Zahar–Worrall view on novel facts, "heuristic progress" can also be understood as some particular shift in theory "cohered" with the heuristic principles underlying the program. If you get increase of empirical content (whether new or old facts) in a way that "cohered" with the heuristic, then you have "heuristic progress."

when a new theory predicts something which is not also predicted by its background theory. Thus, in the progressive Newtonian problemshift, each successive link "predicts some new fact; each step represents an increase in empirical content: the example constitutes a *consistently progressive theoretical shift*" (Lakatos 1970/1978a, p. 48).

Does this methodological conception allow for the possibility of avoiding a strictly temporal view of novelty all together? It seems that here it is possible to apply Lakatos' principle of considering "a new interpreted fact as a new fact" (1970/1978a, pp. 70–71). Explicitly, he does not demand that "each step produce *immediately* an *observed* new fact" (1970/1978a, p. 49).

Hence, what Lakatos has in mind when using the expression "novel facts" could be distinguished—in my judgment—in three different aspects: (a) an *epistemologico-ontological* feature (the fact was unknown when the theory was proposed); (b) an *epistemologico-methodological* characteristic (the fact was not used in the construction of the theory); and (c) a *methodological* trait (the fact was not predicted by the best existing predecessor to the theory). Both (a) and (b) appear explicitly in his writings, whereas (c) is rather implicit.

Then it seems quite reasonable to expect that Lakatos would be open to the two sources of the *third aspect* (a methodological trait): (i) predictions that conflict with the previous theory, and (ii) predictions concerning phenomena about which the previous theory says nothing at all (Musgrave 1974, p. 16). The prediction of novel facts (unknown, known, and heuristically unused) is—for him—an aim, a procedure, and a result of science structured in research programs. Let us see if the other types of "novel facts" (those regarding the consequences, the individuals, and the design) belong to his methodology of scientific research programs or not.

4.3.3 From Six Options of "Novel Facts" to Four Choices

It should be considered that the list of six options can be reduced to four choices:[18] on the one hand, Musgrave and Watkins (i.e., approaches III and IV) were expressing basically the same idea; and, on the other hand, the "heuristic view of novelty" and the "novelty with respect to design" (i.e., the kinds of novelty II and VI) express at heart the same content. Thus, according to Alan Musgrave, "a new theory is independently testable (or predicts a 'novel fact') if it predicts something which is not also predicted by its background theory" (1974, pp. 15–16); meanwhile, for John Watkins, the new theory "breaks new ground here by making a predictive assertion in an area where its predecessor is silent" (1984, p. 295). Consequently, Watkins' proposal appears as a special case of Musgrave's position.

Furthermore, the "heuristic view of novelty" is already in Lakatos, who changed his mind under Elie Zahar's influence (Zahar 1973; and Lakatos and Zahar 1976/ Lakatos 1978a, pp. 184–185).[19] According to that view, "the explanation of Mer-

[18] Cf. Worrall, J., *Personal communication*, 30.5.2004.

[19] On novelty, cf. Leplin (1997), Chap. 3.

cury's perihelion gave crucial empirical support, 'dramatic corroboration', to Einstein's theory, even though, as a low-level empirical proposition, it had been known for almost a hundred years" (Lakatos and Zahar 1976/Lakatos 1978a, pp. 184–185). And Roger Backhouse's view of "novelty with respect to design" indicates that there are "facts which played no role in competing research programs. These facts must all be facts that the theory was not specifically designed to explain" (Backhouse 1991, p. 412).

Backhouse points this out in the context of the analysis of the neo-Walrasian research program in macroeconomics. Nevertheless, this economist previously recognizes that he is broadening the definition of novel facts in tune with what was accepted by Lakatos (1970/1978a, pp. 32, 70 and 71). He wants "to include new interpretations of already-known facts and facts which were not previously explained within the research program" (Backhouse 1991, p. 412). Consequently, I think that "novelty with respect to design" makes explicit an aspect of the "heuristic view of novelty".

Some of these types of "novel facts" are explicitly in Lakatos, and the other characterizations of novel facts can be seen as "enlargements" or alleged "improvements" (Gonzalez 2001e, pp. 505–508). On the one hand, there is now more clarity on the kind of *novelty* that he was thinking of (i.e., we have a better characterization of it, and several options available); and, on the other, there is still a key methodological question: what is the role that prediction should have for appraisal of the research programs?

Although this question can be connected with other philosophico-methodological aspects, such as the different options of scope and intensity of "predictivism" (see Chap. 2), it seems that there is a reasonable answer available. Because in recent decades there has been an increasing consensus among philosophers of science, in general, and philosophers of economics, in particular, that *prediction of novel facts* is not a necessary condition for scientific progress. Thus, prediction is only a *sufficient condition* for having progress in science (natural, social, or artificial). Hence, it is a relevant criterion for science, but as a sufficient condition of scientific evaluation of research programs.

Presumably, prediction of novel facts is the aspect of Lakatos' MSRP that is most in tune with how many economists see their methodology (Gonzalez 2001c).[20] In the case of economics as a basic science, we have in economic theorists such as Milton Friedman, who takes into account both the *temporal novelty* ["phenomena not yet observed" (1953, p. 7)] and the *heuristic novelty* [a test based on data not used in the derivation of the equations (Friedman and Schwartz 1991, p. 47)]. In the orientation of economics as an applied science, we can see that the cases such as econometrician David F. Hendry, who accepts the key role played by predicting novel facts and uses the expression "progressive research strategy," which is Lakatosian (Backhouse 1997, p. 116).

[20] Roger Backhouse gives three reasons on this relevance of Lakatos' prediction of novel facts for the economists. See Backhouse (1994b, pp. 187–188).

4.4 The Prediction of Novel Facts as the Criterion of Appraisal

Appraisal and structure (hard core, protective belt, etc.) are two elements intimately connected in the methodology of scientific research programs. Indeed, when Lakatos presents his categories of MSRP, he makes it explicit that the hard core of the program has to be abandoned when the program ceases to *anticipate* novel facts (1970/1978a, p. 49). Basically, the progress of a program consists of the success of the exercise of predicting new facts, which means an increase in the empirical content, and a degenerating problemshift occurs when there is no advance of novel facts (such a degenerating shift could lead to the abandonment of the hard core and, eventually, the whole program).

4.4.1 *Theoretical, Empirical, and Heuristic*

Both in his *method*—the methodology of scientific research programs—and in his *meta-method*—the methodology of *historiographical* research programs—[21] Lakatos uses the prediction of novel facts as the principal criterion of appraisal. In the case of MSRP, its role for scientific assessment follows—in my judgment—three different philosophico-methodological lines: theoretical, empirical, and heuristic.

First, the *theoretical* appraisal is progressive when it shows that the modification of the theories of the program lead to *new* unexpected predictions (i.e., each new theory has some excess empirical content over its predecessor), and the *theoretical* appraisal is degenerative when it only explains the given facts it was intended to explain. Second, the *empirical* appraisal is progressive when some of the novel predictions are *corroborated* (i.e., each new theory leads us to the discovery of a new fact), and it is degenerative when there is no such corroboration of novel facts. Third, the *heuristic* appraisal is progressive when *the problemshift* leads to the discovery of novel facts (i.e., the series of theories of the program show a positive degree in the changes of scientific problems that is at least theoretically progressive), and it is heuristically degenerative when the problemshift remains in the sphere of the accommodation of known facts (Lakatos and Zahar 1976/1978a, p. 179; Lakatos 1970/1978a, pp. 33–34).

When Lakatos evaluates his own criteria of appraisal in MSRP, he reaches the conclusion that in one sense his view is more liberal than Popper's appraisal of

[21] "Where Kuhn and Feyerabend see irrational change, I predict that the historian will be able to show that there has been rational change. The methodology of research programmes thus predicts (or, if you wish, 'postdicts') novel historical facts, unexpected in the light of extant (internal and external) historiographies and these predictions will, I hope, be corroborated by historical research. If they are, then the methodology of scientific research programmes will itself constitute a progressive problemshift" (Lakatos 1971/1978a, p. 133).

theories, which in another sense it is more strict.[22] On the one hand, it is more tolerant insofar as a research program can have anomalies and grow, despite inconsistent foundations and some ad hoc movements. And, on the other hand, it is more restrictive because it "demands not only that a research programme should successfully predict novel facts, but also that the protective belt of its auxiliary hypotheses should be largely built according to a preconceived unifying idea, laid down in advance in the positive heuristic of the research programme" (Lakatos 1974a/1978a, p. 149). The prediction of novel facts is linked to an excess empirical content of a theory over its predecessor.

What is involved here is double sided. It seems clear that these attempts made by Lakatos seek to offer a solid alternative to Popper's methodology. But, at the same time, they want to preserve some falsificationism in a sophisticated version (i.e., in research programs as "unit of appraisal"). This double side approach has drawn several criticisms. Two of them are relevant here: the first objection is the unnecessary reduction of the realm of appraisal (due to rely on "novel facts"), and the second is the overemphasis on the role of prediction.

According to the first objection, the realm of appraisal could be reduced unnecessarily if the theoretical, empirical, and heuristic appraisals rely only on novel facts. The criticism wants to avoid that "the only observational phenomena which have *any* bearing on the assessment of a research programme are those which are 'novel'" (Gardner 1982, p. 1). However, as has been pointed out earlier, it is the case that known facts are also relevant for Lakatos, not only for explanation but also for prediction. Nevertheless, his stress on novel facts could go beyond what he has in mind, especially when Lakatos maintains that "we must require that each step of a research programme be consistently content-increasing" (1970/1978a, p. 49).

4.4.2 An Overemphasis on the Role of Prediction?

Is there in Lakatos an overemphasis on the philosophico-methodological role of prediction? This question concerns the second objection and the very controversial issue of whether accommodation or prediction provide more evidential support for scientific theories. The controversy can lead to several views. (i) To give more methodological weight to prediction than to accommodation, according to the several possibilities of the *predictivist* option.[23] (ii) To reject that prediction has more weight than explanation and, hence, to accept the view that matching past or present evidence with hypotheses is good enough. This is the "accommodation" approach, also known as *explanationist* view, or even "retrodiction" perspective (Gonzalez 2010a).

[22] For Lakatos, "progress is marked by instances verifying excess content rather than by falsifying instances, and 'falsification' and 'rejection' become logically independent" (Lakatos 1974a/1978a, p. 150).

[23] Predictivism can follow options such as the "weak thesis" or the "strong thesis," as we can see in Lipton (1990). Later on more options have been presented, see for example Hitchcock and Sober (2004) or Barnes (2008). On this issue, cf. Chap. 2, Sect. 2.1.2.

Nonetheless, there is also another possibility: (iii) the "irrelevance" position, where it does not matter whether a particular hypothesis happens to be propounded before or after its examination. This position is usually seen within the second group (i.e., within the "accommodation" approach). But it could be interpreted as an intermediate conception, which asserts that the choice is an open question that depends on several factors and, therefore, there is no a priori methodological preference for prediction or for explanation (i.e., "accommodation").

Each side in this controversy on evidential support has some persuasive defenders. In the *predictivist* camp there are well-known philosophers of the twentieth century, such as Reichenbach (1938), Popper (1963b, pp. 241–243), and Lakatos (1970/1978a), and this camp can be enlarged with contemporary philosophers, such as Rescher (1998). They have highlighted the importance of prediction for the general methodology of science. Besides them, there are also other authors—philosophers as well as scientists—who have emphasized before the methodological role of prediction for scientific assessment: Bacon (1620), Leibniz (1678), Whewell (1860), Duhem (1914), Einstein (1920), etc. In addition, they can be considered within different philosophical schools (empiricist, rationalist, etc.).

Among the supporters of the alternative view—the *critics* of the predictivist thesis in different ways—there are some well-known philosophers too. Although they differ in the emphasis of their criticisms, they are J. Stuart Mill (1843/1973, vol. VII, p. 500), Stephen Toulmin (1961, pp. 22–23),[24] Carl G. Hempel (1965, p. 10), some Bayesians (Colin Howson and Peter Urbach 1989, p. 97/1993, p. 137), or those thinkers who, within the methodology of economics, choose "understanding" instead of "predicting" in the methodological debate between prediction and understanding (Gonzalez 2003a).[25]

Their views usually move in favor of the accommodation approach or retrodiction perspective—to match past or present evidence with hypotheses is good enough—but they can also lead to the *irrelevance position*, proposed by John Maynard Keynes. For this famous economist, "the peculiar virtue of prediction or predesignation is altogether imaginary… the question as to whether a particular hypothesis happens to be propounded before or after their examination [of its instances] is quite irrelevant" (1921, p. 305).[26]

Stephen Brush is a critic of the general predictivist thesis and adopts this last position. He points out three orientations of philosophy of science where "novel prediction" has played a dominant role in recent decades: Lakatos's methodology, Bayesian analysis, and scientific realism (Brush 1995). It seems clear that the Bayesian approach to scientific reasoning and the scientific realism have been very influential at least since 1980. As a matter of fact, there have been a rich variety of Bayesian conceptions as well as multiple versions of scientific realism, where

[24] Stephen Toulmin has a position with many nuances. On his views on scientific prediction, see Chap. 3 in Gonzalez (2010a, pp. 95–126).

[25] The methodological debate *prediction–understanding* is analyzed in Chap. 5, Sect. 5.2.

[26] This position is endorsed in Achinstein (1995, p. 163).

the "structural realism" proposed by John Worrall has also opened many lines of philosophico-methodological analysis on science.[27]

In the case of the Bayesian approach, which is based interpretations of probability that are applied to scientific reasoning, Brush thinks that their supporters have defended "all four possible positions: Bayesian analysis is (i) valid because it favors novel predictions, (ii) valid because it does not favor novel predictions, (iii) invalid because it favors novel predictions, and (iv) invalid because it does not favor novel predictions" (Brush 1995, p. 134).

Regarding scientific realism, Brush points out the well-known no-miracle argument: how can theories of electrons, space-time and DNA "correctly predict observable phenomena if, in reality, there are no electrons, no curved space-time, and no DNA molecules"? If there are no such entities, then it would be a miracle that there were a successful prediction about those phenomena (Putnam 1978, pp. 18–19; see also Worrall 1998).

Does novelty make a difference in terms of more empirical support? Brush thinks that there are semantic problems: he claims "what philosophers mean by explanation is just what scientists mean by prediction [sic]" (1995, p. 135). In addition, he sees historical problems. He considers the following case histories: (I) acceptance despite failed predictions; (II) rejection despite successful predictions; (III) acceptance independent of confirmation of novel predictions; (IV) retrodiction counts as much as novel prediction; (V) acceptance after novel prediction is confirmed but some problems remain; (VI) novelty does count but little; and (VII) novelty is crucial. His conclusion is clear: "the predictivist thesis gains little empirical support from the history of science" (Brush 1995, p. 141).

Yet Brush grants two methodological reasons in favor of novel prediction: "(a) the publicity generated by a successful novel prediction may lead scientists to *pursue* a theory that they would otherwise ignore; (b) a novel prediction may stimulate experiments designated to test the theory and thus contribute more to the advance of knowledge than a retrodiction" (1995, pp. 135–136). Therefore, even though he is a critic of the *predictivist* option in historical terms, he recognizes at the same time that there are some methodological values in novel predictions.

Two elements could be considered in evaluating Brush's criticism of the predictivist option: (1) the realm of research, and (2) the kind of argument. In the first case we have that, even though the methodology of science has a strong link with the history of science, it is not reducible to history of science (and vice versa): the methodology of science includes a prescriptive character (Gonzalez 1990a). Thus, Brush's analysis is obviously useful, but it is not the "last word" in this regard. Moreover, he himself says explicitly "I don't claim that philosophy of science must be validated by history of science" (Brush 1995, p. 133).

Meanwhile, in the second case, it should be pointed out that an important reason for placing more emphasis on the importance of making predictions comes from the no-miracle argument. Blaug stresses this factor of methodological evaluation: "a theory that successfully predicts out-of-sample data from sample data is likely to

[27] On these conceptions, with a large amount of bibliographical information, see Gonzalez (2006a).

have captured some aspects of objective reality because otherwise its record of predictive success is simply miraculous. Theories may also be simple, elegant, general and fruitful but none of these desirable properties in any way guarantees verisimilitude, that is, nearness to truth about objective world" (1991a, p. 502).

As a methodological criterion of scientific progress and appraisal, prediction of novel facts is important. In comparison to accommodation or retrodiction, prediction might have some methodological advantages from the point of view of the *process*—it can involve more novelty than the other procedures—; and from the perspective of *evaluation*, insofar as prediction seems to be more strict (its success or failure—e.g., in the case of Halley's comet—is determined in a comparatively simpler way). Methodologically, prediction has somehow more heuristic value than explanation, insofar as it is more creative and opens more possibilities of research than the other option (which seems to be implicitly accepted by some critics of the predictivist thesis, such as Brush).

Even so, to have *eo ipso* a superior evidential value is a different matter, and it is still under discussion if prediction has more confirmatory weight than accommodation (although nowadays there is a tendency in favor of a "pragmatic" or "weak" predictivism) (McIntyre 2001; White 2003). Furthermore, a successful prediction commonly cannot conclusively prove the theory involved: it is *one* criterion of appraisal but not the only one. In addition, there is another problem, which arises within Friedman's predictivist thesis in economics (1953): the possibility of successful predictions based on false assumptions in the hypotheses. This problem has received special attention in the methodology of economics and will be analyzed in subsequent chapters.

4.5 Lakatos' Criterion of Appraisal and Economics

Some authors have argued that Lakatos' ideas could be used legitimately to defend Friedman's instrumentalism, despite Lakatos' well-known opposition to that methodological approach (Klappholz 1991, esp., p. 53). In this regard, it has been emphasized that Spiro Latsis, his main follower in the methodology of economics at the beginning (Gonzalez 2001b), "used Lakatos's ideas to defend Friedman's instrumentalism" (Shearmur 1991, p. 40; cf. Latsis 1972, pp. 234–242). This assertion is correct insofar as it is made as a depiction of Latsis' views, but it is not fair if it implies that Lakatos himself was an instrumentalist rather than a realist in his methodology of scientific research programs.

Latsis holds that "Friedman's position is vindicated by Lakatos' methodology. False assumptions may be rich in true (and also in false) consequences, and long term progress may be founded on an intuitively false hard core" (Latsis 1972, pp. 241–242). Thus, he interprets the famous "F-twist"—the irrelevance of the absence of realism in the assumptions, which means accepting a descriptively false hypothesis—[28] as a mere "provocative formulation of the truism that the hard core of a powerful research programme may consist of counter-intuitive over-simplifications" (Latsis 1972, p. 242).

According to this analysis, the weakness of Friedman's approach would be its defensive character and the lack of a clear empirical criterion of progress. Therefore, Latsis accepts, to a large extent, an instrumentalist position—the predictivist thesis proposed by Friedman—which can be completed by filling in the gaps that he finds in that methodological view. For it is just the case that an instrumentalist approach could have a non-defensive character as well as a clear empirical criterion of scientific progress.[29]

Still, Lakatos did not reject realism and support an instrumentalist methodology based on the primacy of the prediction of novel facts as an aim in and of itself. Indeed, some of the criticisms that he received afterwards (for example, from Laudan) arose because he did not adopt an instrumentalist approach (Gonzalez 1990d, pp. 161–162). His methodology of scientific research programs should not be misrepresented. This requires taking into account some aspects:

He described the "research programs" as connecting the problemshift to new steps for increasing theoretical progress and empirical progress. For Lakatos, in his MSRP, each step in the research program requires a consistent content-increase (clearly, it is not a mere search for success in the accuracy of predictions). In addition, the positive heuristic should work to get a chain of ever more complicated models simulating reality, and thus it associates the models with the effort of grasping the reality (Lakatos 1970/1978a, pp. 48–50).

Unquestionably, it can be argued that Lakatos accepts the presence of inconsistencies in the case of scientific change or even progress based on inconsistent foundations.[30] Moreover, it might be stressed that he thinks that some of the relevant research programs in the history of science were grafted onto older programs with which they were inconsistent. But it seems clear that, in his approach, scientists tolerate the inconsistencies *only temporarily*: as the young grafted program strengthens, the supporters of the new program try to replace the old program altogether (Lakatos 1970/1978a, pp. 56–57). The reason for this competitive attitude of the champions of the new program is clear: the members of the inconsistent set cannot be all true, and therefore some of them must eventually be replaced.

To sum up, Imre Lakatos avoids the risks of a predictivist thesis based on the acceptance of false assumptions. Even though he stresses "the 'instrumental' aspect of

[28] For Latsis, the Chicago school's self defense includes that "even obvious falsity of the hard core in the standard interpretation need not deprive a research programme of its progressive character" (1972, p. 241).

[29] An example of an instrumentalist approach that does not have a defensive character and includes an empirical criterion of scientific progress is Laudan's methodology. This is made clear in his first conception of methodology, which has also a conceptual criterion of progress (cf. Laudan 1977), and it is even more patent in his second methodology, which relies on the concept of "evidence" (cf. Laudan 1996). On his views, cf. Gonzalez (1998e).

[30] He points out that Bohr's program had fast progress on inconsistent foundations, cf. Lakatos (1970/1978a, p. 67).

imaginative research programmes for finding novel facts and for making trustworthy predictions" (1970/1978a, p. 100), his framework is a critical realism directed towards a well planned building which matches the facts which are to be housed in them.[31] The repercussion of his conception in economics is clear, although it has suffered ups and downs.[32]

Here we have seen the problems of Lakatos' view on prediction in the methodology of scientific research programs and also the oscillations in his perspective on novel facts. His approach continues the predictivist line of Leibniz, Whewell, Reichenbach, and Popper, and it has a repercussion in the methodology of economics. However, despite the emphasis that Lakatos put on prediction of novel facts as criterion of appraisal, his position was insufficiently developed from the methodological point of view.

References

Achinstein, P. 1995. Explanation v. prediction: Which carries more weight? In *PSA 1994,* vol. 2, ed. D. Hull, M. Forbes, and R. Burian, 156–164. East Lansing: Philosophy of Science Association.

Backhouse, R. E. 1991. The neo-Walrasian research program in macroeconomics. In *Appraising economic theories,* ed. N. de Marchi, and M. Blaug, 403–426. Aldershot: Elgar.

Backhouse, R. E. 1994b. The Lakatosian legacy in economic methodology. In *New directions in economic methodology,* ed. R. E. Backhouse, 173–191. London: Routledge.

Backhouse, R. E. 1997. *Truth and progress in economic knowledge*. Cheltenham: Elgar.

Bacon, F. 1620. *Novum Organum sive iudicia vera de interpretatione naturae et regno hominis*. (Translated into English by Peter Urbach and John Gibson, and ed. Peter Urbach. 1994. *Novum Organum*). La Salle: Open Court.

Barnes, E. C. 2008. *The paradox of predictivism*. Cambridge: Cambridge University Press.

Blaug, M. 1991a. Afterword. In *Appraising economic theories,* ed. N. de Marchi, and M. Blaug, 499–512. Aldershot: Elgar.

Brush, S. G. 1995. Dynamics of theory change: The role of predictions. In *PSA 1994,* vol. 2, ed. D. Hull, M. Forbes, and R. Burian, 133–145. East Lansing: Philosophy of Science Association.

de Marchi, N., and M. Blaug, eds. 1991. *Appraising economic theories. Studies in the methodology of research programs*. Aldershot: Elgar.

Duhem, P. 1914. *La théorie physique; son object, sa structure*, 2nd ed. Paris: M. Riviere. (Translated into English by Ph. P. Wiener. 1974. *The aim and structure of physical theory*. New York: Atheneum).

Einstein, A. 1920. *Relativity: The special and the general theory*. London: Methuen. (Reprinted in 1994, London: Routledge).

Friedman, M. 1953. The methodology of positive economics. In *Essays in positive economics,* M. Friedman, 3–43. Chicago: The University of Chicago Press. (6th repr. 1969)

[31] It is the case that, despite Latsis' interpretation, there is nothing in Lakatos to support a *long-term* instrumentalism (as opposed to a short-term attitude of "we will eventually produce a theory that at least *might be* 'realistic' but give us one breathing-space in the meantime").

[32] Regarding the repercussion of Lakatos' approach in economics, cf. Gonzalez (2001b). An overview of his influence is in Gonzalez (2001c). Regarding Lakatos and economic methodology, see also Latsis (1976), de Marchi and Blaug (1991), Smith et al. (1991), Redman (1991), and Hands (1993b).

Friedman, M., and A. J. Schwartz. 1991. Alternative approaches to analyzing economic data. *American Economic Review* 81:39–49.
Gardner, M. R. 1982. Predicting novel facts. *The British Journal for the Philosophy of Science* 33:1–15.
Gonzalez, W. J. 1990b. Ámbito y características de la Filosofía y Metodología de la Ciencia. In *Aspectos metodológicos de la investigación científica*, 2nd ed., ed. W. J. Gonzalez, 49–78. Madrid: Ediciones Universidad Autónoma de Madrid and Publicaciones Universidad de Murcia.
Gonzalez, W. J. 1990d. El progreso de la Ciencia como resolución de problemas: L. Laudan. In In *Aspectos metodológicos de la investigación científica*, 2nd ed., ed. W. J. Gonzalez, 157–171. Madrid: Ediciones Universidad Autónoma de Madrid and Publicaciones Universidad de Murcia.
Gonzalez, W. J. 1995. Reichenbach's concept of prediction. *International Studies in the Philosophy of Science* 9 (1): 37–58.
Gonzalez, W. J. 1998e. El naturalismo normativo como propuesta epistemológica y metodológica. La segunda etapa del Pensamiento de L. Laudan. In *El Pensamiento de L. Laudan. Relaciones entre Historia de la Ciencia y Filosofía de la Ciencia*, ed. W. J. Gonzalez, 5–57. A Coruña: Publicaciones de la Universidad de A Coruña.
Gonzalez, W. J. 2001b. Reconstrucción histórico-sistemática de la incidencia de Imre Lakatos en la Metodología económica. In *Ciencia económica y Economía de la Ciencia: Reflexiones filosófico-metodológicas*, ed. A. Avila, W. J. Gonzalez, and G. Marques, 65–92. Madrid: FCE.
Gonzalez, W. J. 2001c. La Filosofía de I. Lakatos, 25 años después: Del "giro histórico" a la incidencia metodológica en Economía. In *La Filosofía de Imre Lakatos: Evaluación de sus propuestas*, ed. W. J. Gonzalez, 13–103. Madrid: UNED.
Gonzalez, W. J. 2001d. Lakatos's philosophy today. *Theoria* 16 (3): 409–413.
Gonzalez, W. J. 2001e. Lakatos's approach on prediction and novel facts. *Theoria* 16 (3): 499–518.
Gonzalez, W. J. 2003a. *From Erklären-Verstehen* to *prediction-understanding*: The methodological framework in economics. In *Realism in action*: *Essays in the philosophy of social sciences*, ed. M. Sintonen, P. Ylikoski, and K. Miller, 33–50. Dordrecht: Kluwer.
Gonzalez, W. J. 2004c. La evolución del Pensamiento de Popper. In *Karl Popper: Revisión de su legado*, ed. W. J. Gonzalez, 23–194. Madrid: Unión Editorial.
Gonzalez, W. J. 2006a. Novelty and continuity in philosophy and methodology of science. In *Contemporary perspectives in philosophy and methodology of science*, ed. W. J. Gonzalez and J. Alcolea, 1–28. A Coruña: Netbiblo.
Gonzalez, W. J. 2010a. *La predicción científica: Concepciones filosófico-metodológicas desde H. Reichenbach a N. Rescher*. Barcelona: Montesinos.
Hacking, I. 1979. Imre Lakatos's philosophy of science. *British Journal for the Philosophy of Science* 30:381–410.
Hands D. Wade 1991a. The problem of excess content: Economics, novelty and a long Popperian tale. In *Appraising economic theories*, ed. N. de Marchi, and M. Blaug, 58–75. Aldershot: Elgar.
Hands D. Wade 1991b. Reply to Hamminga and Mäki. In *Appraising economic theories*, ed. N. de Marchi, and M. Blaug, 91–102. Aldershot: Elgar.
Hands D. Wade 1993b. Popper and Lakatos in economic methodology. In *Rationality, institutions and economic methodology*, ed. U. Mäki, B. Gustafsson, and C. Knudsen, 61–75. London: Routledge.
Hempel, C. G. 1965. *Aspects of scientific explanation and other essays*. New York: Free Press.
Hitchcock, Ch., and E. Sober. 2004. Prediction versus accommodation and the risk of overfitting. *British Journal for the Philosophy of Science* 55 (1): 1–34.
Howson, C., and P. Urbach. 1989. *Scientific reasoning: The Bayesian approach*. La Salle: Open Court (reprinted in 1990). (Second edition 1993 *Scientific reasoning. The Bayesian approach*. La Salle: Open Court).
Keynes, J. M. 1921. *A treatise on probability*. London: Macmillan.
Klappholz, K. 1991. Comment on Shearmur. In *Appraising economic theories*, ed. N. de Marchi, and M. Blaug, 53–57. Aldershot: Elgar.

Kuhn, Th. S. 1957. *The Copernican revolution*. Chicago: The University of Chicago Press.
Lakatos, I. 1961/1973. The method of analysis-synthesis (1st part, 1961; 2nd part, 1973). Reprinted in Lakatos, I. 1978. *Mathematics, science and epistemology. Philosophical papers*, vol. 2, 70–103. ed. por J. Worrall and G. Currie. Cambridge: Cambridge University Press.
Lakatos, I. 1968. Changes in the problem of inductive logic. In *The problem of inductive logic*, ed. I. Lakatos, 315–417. Amsterdam: North-Holland. (Reprinted in Lakatos, I. 1978. *Mathematics, science and epistemology. Philosophical papers*, vol. 2, ed. J. Worrall and G. Currie 128-200. Cambridge: Cambridge University Press).
Lakatos, I. 1970. Falsification and the methodology of scientific research programmes. In *Criticism and the growth of knowledge*, ed. I. Lakatos and A. Musgrave, 91–196. Cambridge: Cambridge University Press. (Reprinted in Lakatos, I. 1978. *The methodology of scientific research programmes. Philosophical papers*, vol. 1, 8–101. Cambridge: Cambridge University Press).
Lakatos, I. 1971. History of science and its rational reconstructions. In *PSA 1970*, ed. R. C. Buck and R. S. Cohen, 174–182. Dordrecht: Reidel. (Reprinted in Lakatos, I. 1978. *The methodology of scientific research programmes. Philosophical papers*, vol. 1, 102–138. Cambridge: Cambridge University Press).
Lakatos, I. 1974a. Popper on demarcation and induction. In *The philosophy of Karl Popper*, vol. 1, ed. P. A. Schilpp, 241–273. La Salle: Open Court. (Reprinted in Lakatos, I. 1978. *The methodology of scientific research programmes. Philosophical papers*, vol. 1, 139–167. Cambridge: Cambridge University Press).
Lakatos, I. 1974b. Science and pseudoscience. In *Philosophy in the open*, ed. G. Vesey. London: Open University Press. (Reprinted in Lakatos, I. 1978. *The methodology of scientific research programmes. Philosophical Papers*, vol. 1, 1–7. Cambridge: Cambridge University Press).
Lakatos, I. 1978a. *The methodology of scientific research programmes. Philosophical papers*, vol. 1, ed. J. Worrall and G. Currie. Cambridge: Cambridge University Press.
Lakatos, I. 1978b. *Mathematics, science and epistemology. Philosophical papers*, vol. 2, ed. J. Worrall and G. Currie. Cambridge: Cambridge University Press.
Lakatos, I., and P. K. Feyerabend. 1999. *For and against method*, ed. Matteo Motterlini. Chicago: The University of Chicago Press.
Lakatos, I., and E. G. Zahar. 1976. Why did Copernicus's programme superseded Ptolemys? In *The Copernican achievement*, ed. R. Westman, 354–383. Los Angeles: University of California Press. (Reprinted in Lakatos, I. 1978. *The methodology of scientific research programmes. Philosophical papers*, vol. 1, 168–192. Cambridge: Cambridge University Press).
Latsis, S. 1972. Situational determinism in economics. *The British Journal for the Philosophy of Science* 23:207–245.
Latsis, S., ed. 1976. *Method and appraisal in economics*. Cambridge: Cambridge University Press.
Laudan, L. 1977. *Progress and its problems. Towards a theory of scientific growth*. Berkeley: University of California Press (edited in UK by Routledge and K. Paul, London, 1977).
Laudan, L. 1996. *Beyond positivism and relativism: Theory, method and evidence*. Boulder: Westview.
Leibniz, G. W. 1678. Letter to Conring, 19 March 1678. In *Philosophical papers and letters*, ed. Leibniz, G. W. 1969. Dordrecht: Reidel.
Leplin, J. 1997. *A novel defense of scientific realism*. New York: Oxford University Press.
Lipton, P. 1990. Prediction and prejudice. *International Studies in the Philosophy of Science* 4(1):51–65.
McIntyre, L. 2001. Accommodation, prediction, and confirmation. *Perspectives on Science* 9:308–232.
Motterlini, M. 2002. Reconstructing Lakatos: A reassessment of Lakatos' epistemological project in the light of Lakatos archive. *Studies in History and Philosophy of Science* 33:487–509.
Musgrave, A. 1974. Logical versus historical theories of confirmation. *The British Journal for the Philosophy of Science* 24:1–23.
Popper, K. R. 1957. *The poverty of historicism*. London: Routledge & K.Paul. (Reprinted by Routledge1991).

Popper, K. R. 1963b. Truth, rationality, and the growth of scientific knowledge. In *Conjectures and refutations. The growth of scientific knowledge,* K. R. Popper, 215–250. London: Routledge & K.Paul.

Putnam, H. 1978. *Meaning and the moral sciences*. London: Routledge & K.Paul.

Redman, D. A. 1991. *Economics and the philosophy of science*. New York: Oxford University Press.

Reichenbach, H. 1938. *Experience and prediction. An analysis of the foundations and the structure of knowledge*. Chicago: The University of Chicago Press.

Rescher, N. 1998. *Predicting the future: An introduction to the theory of forecasting*. Albany: State University of New York Press.

Shearmur, J. 1991. Popper, Lakatos and theoretical progress in economics. In *Appraising economic theories,* ed. N. de Marchi, and M. Blaug, 35–52. Aldershot: Elgar.

Smith, V. L., K. A. McCabe, and S. J. Rassenti. 1991. Lakatos and experimental economics. In *Appraising economic theories,* ed. N. de Marchi, and M. Blaug, 197–227. Aldershot: Elgar.

Strawson, P. F. 1950. Truth (II). *Proceedings of the Aristotelian Society* 24:129–156.

Stuart Mill, J. 1843. *A system of logic ratiocinative and inductive*. London: Parker. (Reprinted as Stuart Mill, J. S. 1973. *Collected works of John Stuart Mill,* vols VII and VIII, ed. J. M. Robson. Toronto: University of Toronto Press).

Toulmin, S. 1961. *Foresight and understanding. An enquiry into the aims of science*. Bloomington: Indiana University Press/London: Hutchinson.

Watkins, J. 1984. *Science and scepticism*. Princeton: Princeton University Press.

Whewell, W. 1860. *On the philosophy of discovery, chapters historical and critical.* London: Parker.

White, R. 2003. The epistemic advantage of prediction over accommodation. *Mind* 112 (448): 653–683.

Worrall, J. 1978. The ways in which the methodology of scientific research programmes improves on Popper's methodology. In *Progress and rationality in science,* ed. G. Radnitzky, and G. Andersson, 45–70. Dordrecht: Reidel.

Worrall, J. 1989a. Fresnel, Poisson and the white spot: The role of successful predictions in the acceptance of scientific theories. In *The uses of experiment,* ed. D. Gooding, T. Pinch, and S. Schaffer, 135–157. Cambridge: Cambridge University Press.

Worrall, J. 1998. Realismo, racionalidad y revoluciones. *Agora* 17 (2): 7–24.

Worrall, J. 2001b. Programas de investigación y heurística positiva: Avance respecto de Lakatos. In *La Filosofía de Imre Lakatos: Evaluación de sus propuestas,* ed. W. J. Gonzalez, 247–268. Madrid: UNED.

Worrall, J. 2002. New evidence for old. In *In the scope of logic, methodology and philosophy of science*, vol. 1, ed. P. Gardenfors, J. Wolenski, and K. Kijania-Placek, 191–209. Dordrecht: Kluwer.

Worrall, J. 2005. Prediction and the "periodic law": A rejoinder to Barnes. *Studies in History and Philosophy of Science* 36:817–826.

Zahar, E. 1973. Why did Einstein's research programme supersede Lorentz's? *The British Journal for the Philosophy of Science* 24:95–123.

Zahar, E. G. 2001. The interdependence of the core, the heuristic and the novelty of facts in Lakatos's MSRP. *Theoria* 16 (3): 415–435.

Part III
The Methodological Framework of Social Sciences and Economics: Incidence for Prediction as a Test

After the analysis of prediction within the general methodology of science, which has been made in Part II, there comes a new step: the study of the methodological framework of social sciences and the place of economics within it. The goal is to offer the methodological setting for prediction in economics, taking into account the methodology of social sciences. This study can be combined with the methodology of the sciences of the artificial—in the sense proposed by Herbert Simon—insofar as economics is a science of design as well.

Regarding the place of economics in the framework of social sciences, there is a dissection of the controversy between *Erklären* and *Verstehen*, which has been particularly influential in the methodological characterization of social sciences, mainly through the duality causality-teleology. And later on, there is an examination of the methodological debate *prediction-understanding*, which affects the overall view of economics as a science. In this regard, the focus is on the difference between the predictive emphasis—the line adopted by Alexander Rosenberg—and the position in favor of rhetorics (held by D. N. McCloskey).

The consideration of the dichotomy *Erklären-Verstehen* and the examination of the debate *prediction-understanding* have repercussions for the methodological scheme of economics within social sciences as well as for its own methodology as a discipline. Thus, Part III of this book pays special attention to the *broad approach* to methodology of economics: it starts in Chapter 5 with the methodological framework for prediction in economics within social sciences and continues in Chap. 6, which deals with the methodological approaches within economics, according to the perspectives of four Nobel laureates in this science (Milton Friedman, John Hicks, James Buchanan, and Herbert A. Simon).

For the problem of prediction as a test of economics as a science, it is particularly relevant to know the views of these prestigious economists. Chap. 6 emphasizes the clear differences between them when they analyze the role of prediction in economics. They present completely diverse approaches on the relevance of prediction to the status of economics as a science. In effect, the predictivist thesis (Friedman), the quasi-scientific option (Hicks), the dualist posture (Buchanan), and the wary attitude (Simon) represent different conceptions on this crucial issue for economics. In spite of the differences, it is also of interest to seek the underlying general methodology of these approaches.

Taking into account their contributions and the absence of consensus among them, Chap. 7 seeks to offer an alternative to their views using the perspective of action theory. In order to reach the goal of a new framework for the problem of prediction in economics there is an interplay between philosophy (mainly, semantics, epistemology and ontology) and methodology of economics. Thus, there is a scrutiny of the problem of prediction in economics from the viewpoint of action theory, because this philosophical realm combines the language of action, the knowledge of actions (as richer than the knowledge of behaviors), and the status of the human activity (connected with acts and actions).

To some extent, the perspective of action theory—with the distinction between "economic activity" and "economics as activity"—tries also to overcome the difficulties raised by the dichotomy *Erklären-Verstehen* and the debate *prediction-understanding*. As this view is conceived in this book—in connection with a theory of *social action*—it offers a methodological framework for the development of realistic economic predictions. These predictions are not usually based on mere "behavior" but rather on a more complex reality: human activity.

Chapter 5
From *Erklären–Verstehen* to *Prediction–Understanding*: The Methodological Framework for Prediction in Economics within Social Sciences

When the focus is on the methodological framework for prediction in economics, a relevant step is to take into account the methodology of social sciences. In this regard, the controversy between *Erklären* and *Verstehen* has a long tradition of over a century.[1] It offers us several options on how to see the relations between natural sciences and social sciences from a methodological viewpoint. Consequently, it gives several possibilities on where to place economics in methodological terms. In addition, the debate between *prediction* and *understanding*, which is within the science of economics, presents two different conceptions on how to see prediction in economics as a science (Gonzalez 2003b).[2]

Besides this line of research on methodology, where economics as a basic science has a key role (economic theory receives special attention), we can also think of economics as a science of artificial that is developed as a design science (Simon 1996). Thus, economics is human-made and can enlarge human possibilities through new aims, processes, and results. In this regard, economics can follow a methodology of applied science, where the designs are conceived in order to achieve new aims which get novel results through adequate processes (Gonzalez 2007b, 2008). Economics as applied science in this artificial domain also leads to aspects of complexity, which can be both structural and dynamic, and is mainly epistemological or ontological.[3]

---

[1] This methodological controversy has its roots in the nineteenth century. It was also a time when Carl Menger was making his investigations into the method of the social sciences with special reference to economics (1985). In addition, ideas on economic methodology from that century, such as J. Stuart Mill's proposals, have been thought on in recent decades. See, for example, Hausman (1992b).

[2] The debate between prediction and understanding belongs to the twentieth century. A panorama of the social sciences since the Second World War can be found in Bell (1982). Aspects of the context for philosophy and methodology of economics during that period can be seen in Hausman (1994b) and Caldwell (1993).

[3] These aspects of economics as an applied science of design and their connections to the problems of complexity are discussed in Gonzalez (2011a, 2012a, 2013b).

W. J. Gonzalez, *Philosophico-Methodological Analysis of Prediction and its Role in Economics,* Theory and Decision Library A: 50, DOI 10.1007/978-3-319-08885-3_5

5.1 From the Methodology of Social Sciences to the Methodology of Economics

Here the attention goes directly to the first line of research: it moves from the methodology of the social sciences to the methodology of economics.[4] In this regard, within the methodology of social sciences, there is a very influential controversy that opposes *Erklären* (explanation) to *Verstehen* (understanding). Meanwhile, within the methodology of economics, a more recent debate confronts *prediction* to *understanding*. However, to some extent, both disputes share some common ground: (a) the prominence of *Erklären* or the emphasis on *prediction* ordinarily goes in favor of the unity of science; and (b) the accent in *Verstehen* or the stress on *understanding* normally leads towards the diversity of science (i.e., a distinct characterization of science in the social sciences, in general, and economics, in particular).

On the one side, those who highlight the importance of *Erklären* and those who defend *prediction* as the goal and principal test of economics tend habitually to see the economic method as being in tune with the method of natural sciences. And, on the other side, those authors who insist on the role of *Verstehen* or stress the methodological function of *understanding* generally tend to distinguish social sciences (among them, economics) from natural sciences. Meanwhile, those who prioritize understanding the economic phenomena over predicting them tend to insist on the methodological difference between the social and the natural sciences.

Through the analysis of the controversy *Erklären–Verstehen*, which involves eight possible choices, we can get some methodological elements for the role of prediction in economics. In this controversy, among the set of options available, is Georg H. von Wright's conception. This view is in his famous book *Explanation and Understanding* (1971),[5] which deals with the methodology of social sciences with a Wittgensteinian inspiration and constitutes a sophisticated version of the dichotomy between *Erklären* and *Verstehen*.

This option is studied in Raimo Tuomela (1976).[6] His analysis is useful for clarifying that approach, the sixth in that methodological dispute. It has clear repercussions for the methodological framework of economics and, indirectly, affects the role of prediction in social sciences, in general, and in economics, in particular. Tuomela's position will be seen here from the point of view of causality and teleology, looking at its possible impact on the methodological structure of the social sciences and the problem of prediction in economics. In this regard, it should be

[4] Chapter 8 of this book analyzes Simon's approach to prediction in economics. He is the most influential author in the line of research centered on economics as a science of the artificial.

[5] Afterwards, he published several works connected with the problems of this book: von Wright (1973, 1974, 1983, 1984, 1985, 1986, 1987). His views receive special attention in the essays on explanation and understanding prepared by Manninen and Tuomela (1976).

[6] A commentary on Tuomela's criticisms of von Wright's book is found in Apel (1976), esp., pp. 164–166 and 173. In addition, the topic of "explanation" and "understanding" is analyzed in Tuomela (1988).

taken into account that prediction is frequently proposed as a test of economics as a science and, habitually, that character affects the issue of the scope of economics.[7]

After clarifying the methodological framework of *Erklären* and *Verstehen*, the attention will be here on the question of the methodological debate that specifically confronts *prediction* and *understanding*. The problem will be addressed following the dispute between Alexander Rosenberg and D. N. McCloskey. In this regard, the analysis is well aware of the methodological controversies within economics, which show clear differences between the mainstream tendency—the neoclassical economics—and the critics of this position (especially Herbert Simon, winner of the Nobel Prize in Economics in 1978 and the new institutional school).

In effect, there is a methodological dispute in economics between the mainstream tendency and its critics. This discrepancy involves a tension between two different methodological orientations: (i) emphasis on the importance of the success of economic predictions, mainly in economic theory;[8] and (ii) a more realistic attitude, which recognizes the insufficiency of prediction in economics to fill the whole subject-matter which is studied, insofar as prescription is also relevant—in applied economics—and acknowledges the frequent unreliability of prediction.[9]

5.2 The Methodological Controversy *Erklären–Verstehen* and its Repercussion for Prediction

Economics as well as other social sciences, such as history or sociology, has been involved in an uneasy situation between two different methodological options. On the one side, there is the approximation or even the identification with the dominant method in the sphere of natural sciences, which leads to a *methodological monism* (usually under the primacy of the method of physics). In a sophisticated version, it bears a position favorable to a methodological naturalism, which tries to subsume the patterns of social sciences within schemes acceptable in natural sciences. On the other side, the opposite conception seeks a proper *methodological identity* for social sciences that could be different from natural sciences or even completely incompatible with them. So, this methodological autonomy of science could adopt entirely different criteria from natural sciences when following a strict dualism.

These two poles—the pure methodological monism and the strict methodological dualism—underlie the *Erklären–Verstehen* controversy. Originally, the former is characteristic of physics, whereas the latter corresponds to the discipline of history. In this regard, physics appears as the key science within the natural realm, while

[7] "If economics is a science (…), it is a science whose powers of prediction and control are limited, largely because the phenomena it seeks to explain are subject to persistent change and often for reasons that may lie outside the traditional boundaries of the discipline" (Deane 1983, pp. 11–12).

[8] "The only relevant test of the validity of a hypothesis is comparison of its predictions with experience" (Friedman 1953, pp. 8–9).

[9] "Economic predictions are notoriously unreliable" (Sen 1986, p. 3).

history is considered as a central science in the social sphere. Moreover, from the chronological point of view, they are commonly presented as the first in their fields (Gonzalez 1996e).

Basically, *Erklären* is focused on the quantitative components of science, placing obliquely the qualitative ones. In addition, it insists on causal factors instead of attending to the teleological ingredients (goals, tendencies, rhythms, patterns, etc.). Thus, it is keen on causal explanations rather than of teleological explanations. Its realm characteristic—nature—can be commonly experimented and expressed in mathematical terms; and the phenomena with which it deals are, in principle, reproducible and predictable.

Meanwhile, the specific field of *Verstehen* is quite different: it is interested only in the human being, his or her interindividual relations, and their connections with reality beyond the mental sphere. Thus, by means of the activity of understanding (*Verstehen*), the aim is to grasp the meaning and purpose of human and social events (i.e., the relationship of human being with his entire environment), giving attention to the knowledge of the past and present. Thus, the qualitative components are, in principle, more relevant than the quantitative ones.

5.2.1 Eight Different Approaches

Undoubtedly, the methodological approaches of the dichotomy between *Erklären* and *Verstehen* have a long trajectory, which can be summarized in eight different approaches.[10] The first starts in 1858 with the publication of J. Gustav Droysen's *Grundriss der Historik* (1858/1958). There he proposes to separate three functions: "knowing," "explaining," and "understanding," which are—in his view—the methods of philosophy, physics, and history, respectively. This trichotomy, which was used to clarify the historical methods, is transformed into a dichotomy: "explanation" (*Erklären*) is opposed to "understanding" (*Verstehen*).

A fully fledged expression of this dichotomy, which is frequently considered as the actual first version of this methodological controversy, appears with Wilhem Dilthey's *Einleitung in die Geisteswissenschaften* (1983/1962). With him the duality *Erklären–Verstehen* gets a general character and obtains its influence in the methodological discussions. *Explanation* and *understanding* have quite different tasks. They configure two kinds of methods, which are completely different: the former only belongs to natural sciences (mainly, physics), whereas the latter is restricted to "moral sciences" (*Geisteswissenschaften*),[11] such as history.

---

[10] Most of these approaches are particularly clear in the case of the science of history, cf. Gonzalez (1996e, pp. 75–82). Seven of them are presented in Gonzalez (2003a), pp. 34–37.

[11] In this kind of sciences, the emphasis is on the mores or habits related to the expression of the human beings as endowed with mind or spirit (*Geistes*), who are able to do new things in a social setting. They produce forms of culture that, in principle, go beyond the abilities of the animals.

Max Weber—economist, sociologist, and political scientist—introduces a second approach around 1904. He presents *de facto* a modulation in this dichotomy insofar as *Verstehen* is not linked to a *Historismus*,[12] because he defends the objectivity of social sciences (1904/1968, pp. 146–214). His position is enlarged with the idea of the social sciences as a "value-free" enterprise (*Wertfreiheit*) (Weber 1917/1968, pp. 489–540). This approach goes beyond the province of economics—and even the region of social sciences—to get the general territory of science as a whole.

On the one hand, Weber's proposal of objectivity of social sciences (among them, economics) is associated with *Verstehen* as the adequate method. This is different and complementary to the method of *Erklären*. Thus, objectivity in economics could be compatible with a methodological differentiation with respect to natural sciences. On the other hand, his defense of social sciences (including economics) as value-free involves a methodological conception in favor of the unity of science. For him, it supposes that economics is "neutral" regarding the values in a similar way to the science which studies nature.[13]

A third approach regarding this controversy, quite different from the previous ones, is the monism proposed by the methodological verificationism, which was defended by the logical positivists at the beginning. Its precedent in the nineteenth century is August Comte's positivist monism. This methodological monism offered by the logical positivism during the Vienna Circle—and, in a more qualified way, by the logical empiricism of the Berlin school[14]— endorses the unification of science starting from the primacy of the idea of *Erklären*. It had its apogee between 1929 and 1942 but projected its influences for two more decades, earning many years later the title of "the received view."[15]

The most representative authors of this tendency maintain that disciplines related to the social world, such as sociology or history, should lead towards a scientific conception of the world based on physics. In his well-known "Manifesto of the Vienna Circle," Otto Neurath—with the contribution of Rudolf Carnap[16] and Hans Hahn—emphasizes that social sciences, beginning with history and economics, should carry out a logical analysis of their concepts and an epistemological examination of their

---

[12] On the characteristics of *Historismus* and its presence in Dilthey, cf. Gonzalez (1984), pp. 115-117. On the difference between *Historismus* and *Historizismus*, cf. Chap. 3, Sect. 3.4.2.

[13] On the central issue on science raised by Max Weber—the axiological neutrality or science as *Wertfrei* or value-free—see Gonzalez (2013a).

[14] These views could be distinguished according to their clear differences during this period. Hans Reichenbach, the leader of Berlin School, avoids Vienna's positivism because it impedes having statements of the future, which makes scientific prediction impossible. In addition, he rejects other central theses of the Vienna Circle, such as the "verification" principle; instead, he stands for the idea of "verifiability" according to his emphasis on probability (Reichenbach 1938, pp. 30, 38 and 304). On this issue, cf. Gonzalez (1995).

[15] This denomination, proposed by Hilary Putnam, is used as the central line of the interesting study of Frederick Suppe on the verificationist conception, cf. Suppe (1974).

[16] Carnap addresses the problem of prediction in science 17 years after the "Manifesto," cf. Carnap (1946).

foundations. According that view, such sciences should eliminate philosophical elements—the "metaphysical adherences"—to get to the level reached by physics.

Later on, the verificationist movement adopts a more flexible position. This happens when Carl G. Hempel acknowledges that "understanding" (*Verstehen*) is used by the experts in history. Nevertheless, he considers that its task is only psychological and heuristic: it consists merely to discern the motives of their performances. Thus, even then it should be integrated in a causal explanation. Furthermore, he develops a thesis, which is central in logical empiricism, of the need of general laws in social sciences. These laws should have analogous functions to those in natural sciences. In addition, social sciences, in general, and history, in particular, should use universal hypotheses, similar to those in the disciplines that deal with nature (Hempel 1942/1965, pp. 231–243).

Subsequent to this apogee for several decades of the idea of unification of science from the perspective of *Erklären*, there is a fourth approach, this time in favor of the specificity of human reality. It is a methodological turn that implies a diversification of the scientific disciplines. The new option stresses the distinctive character of social sciences. Thus, this change produces *de facto* a recuperation of the idea of *Verstehen*. This step is given under the influence of Ludwig Wittgenstein's "language of action" of *Philosophische Untersuchungen* (1953). Fundamentally, the new proposal was developed between the years 1957 and 1964.

During this period, the analytic philosophy of the ordinary language had a noticeable influence in the Anglo-Saxon world. In these years, new kinds of studies on language and action (intention, motive, etc.) were available. They developed a new sort of dualism in several authors: W. Dray (1957, 1964), G. E. M. Anscombe (1957), P. Winch (1958), Ch. Taylor (1964),[17] etc. Their positions, usually under the inspiration of the Wittgensteinian theory of meaning, recover the practical discourse: they consider it irreducible to physicalist language. Therefore, they see as impracticable the methodological verificationism of logical positivists (or even the "verifiability" linked to probability of logical empiricists). They highlight the meaning of human action and its connections with the uses of language. The analysis of language of action is then a new way to get *Verstehen*, because the variety of linguistic games expresses different "forms of life" (*Lebensformen*).

Almost at the same time as the Wittgensteinian perspective, there is another approach—the fifth—lead by Hans Georg Gadamer (1960–1965). His view proposes a revision of the idea of *Verstehen*. His position connects to some extent with Dilthey's hermeneutics, but Gadamer puts less emphasis on the methodological separation between the kinds of science. Moreover, he seems to accept that there is a first moment shared by the different sciences, be they natural or social. In addition, he made another contribution to the methodology of *Verstehen*: the relationship between understanding and interpreting requires the function of applying what is understood and interpreted.

[17] Afterwards, he published on this issue: Taylor (1980, 1981, 1985a, and 1985b).

Gadamer's approach offers *de facto* a general conception of social sciences, which is developed in his book *Wahrheit und Methode* (1960/1986).[18] But his perspective on the processes relies on the notion of "phronesis" rather than on the idea of a "method" (Martinez 1994). This involves a clear distance regarding *Erklären*. Moreover, in his perspective there is a link between language and historicity which is more intense than in Wittgenstein. In this new view of hermeneutics, there are elements of continuity regarding the hermeneutical tradition, but Gadamer includes also innovations in favor of intersubjective contents—and, therefore, some more objectivity—in the processes of understanding and interpretation.

Next comes Georg Henrik von Wright's proposal of a moderate version of *Verstehen*. He offers the sixth approach to this controversy in his book *Explanation and Understanding*, published in 1971. He presents new ideas on the dichotomy *Erklären–Verstehen* and gives elements to lay the foundations of social sciences in terms of human actions. He deals with the problems of explanation and understanding using notions regarding "causality" and "teleology" (such as intention, intentionality, or practical syllogism). Furthermore, he is interested in the question of how natural sciences are related with the study of man (the human being).

Unquestionably, von Wright's perspective received a direct influence from Wittgenstein, insofar as social sciences are "sciences of action." This feature distinguishes social sciences from the natural sciences, because human actions should be understood in terms of the reasons of the actors. By means of his analysis of explanation and understanding, von Wright offers a careful defense of the methodological dualism, which arises from a theory of action with a Wittgensteinian base and reaches new possibilities. This proposal stresses the irreducibility of the intentional or teleological components of human action, individual and social.

Following also a moderate line in favor of *Verstehen*, Karl Otto Apel presents in 1979 an alternative to von Wright's viewpoint. In this seventh approach to this controversy, the transcendental component has a role. This is mentioned in the title of the book: *Die Erklären–Verstehen-Kontroverse in Transzendental-Pragmatischer Sicht* (1979/1984).[19] Now there is a framework where the distinction between the methodological alternatives is made from the pragmatic and transcendental perspective. (a) Apel recognizes the differences among the diverse disciplines; but (b) he finds more common ground among the sciences than other dualist authors, including the Wittgensteinians.

Because Apel sees his view as "hermeneutical," he accepts aspects of Dilthey's philosophical tradition on understanding. He assumes the methodological dichotomy insofar as it makes possible a theory that distinguishes among sciences and is close to praxis. For Apel, on the one hand, his methodological option in favor of *Verstehen*—transcendental and pragmatic—allows us to assert that the reference is diverse (it changes from natural sciences to social sciences); and, on the other, his position endorses the differences among the internal interests of scientific knowledge (there are differences in the investigations made by each group of sciences) (Apel 1979).

[18] A posterior development of his thought about science is in Gadamer (1975, 1976). In addition, there are remarks on science in Gadamer (1989).

[19] In this regard, cf. Apel (1985).

Continuing with the idea of diversity in the kind of reference and in the type of interest, Apel considers that Gadamer ends up giving the monopoly of scientificity to the researches of natural sciences. This situation can be avoided expanding the conception of scientific rationality to get what is specific of social sciences. At the same time, more clearly than von Wright, Apel assesses elements of unity in science (1985). Certainly, he does not repeat the thesis of a single method or a unique way of raising scientific problems such as logical positivism does. He builds on other bases: the aspiration of truth of sciences and the possibility to find it in the argumentative discourse of them (Apel 1979).

Another possibility—option eight—related to this methodological controversy is the "double hermeneutics" approach. Anthony Giddens, a sociologist with a clear influence on British politics, uses this expression (1987, 1993, pp. 2, 9–15, 86, 164, 166–167, 170). However, several philosophers have used it as well. Thus, Charles Taylor, with a Wittgensteinian background, sees the social sciences as *doubly interpretative* (Taylor 1980; Rouse 1987, p. 170), and Roy Bhaskar assumes it within his philosophy of "critical realism" of open systems (Özel 2003, pp. 232–236).

Again, the idea is to emphasize a methodological difference between natural sciences and social sciences. Giddens maintains that, in the former, there is a single hermeneutic (i.e., understanding goes in one-direction), whereas in the latter the hermeneutic is double. Thus, in the social sciences, besides the "understanding" of the phenomena, people need to understand their own world. For him, "the concepts of the social sciences are not produced about an independently constituted subject-matter, which continues regardless of what these concepts are. The 'findings' of the social sciences very often enter constitutively into the world they describe" (Giddens 1987, p. 20).

Obviously, if Giddens wants to develop a scientific knowledge of social events, then he should be ontologically cautious and epistemologically prudent insofar as he states a mutual interpretative interplay between social science and those actions that belong to its subject matter. This is also relevant for economics, in general, and economic predictions, in particular, because the existence of a closer relation between the researcher and what is researched, due to the ontological character of the reality itself (we are, as society, object and subject of the research), should not lead to a lack of objectivity in the scientific status of the social sciences, in general, and each science, in particular.

Certainly, all these approaches on *Erklären–Verstehen* can have a correlate in the problem of prediction in social sciences, in general, and in economics, in particular. Those thinkers who insist on adopting methods akin to natural ones (the promoters of *Erklären*) usually end up giving a relevant role to prediction. Meanwhile, the supporters of strict *Verstehen* tend to consider prediction as less relevant for science (or even impossible as scientific knowledge of social affairs). What is important in the succession of the eight approaches is the progressive process of approximating the views by abandoning the radical positions.

Still, the roots of the controversy have not disappeared, as is seen in the debate in economics between *prediction* and *understanding* or in the increasing interest for qualitative methods of investigation, which are developed as complementary of the quantitative methods.[20] Regarding the methodological approaches in economics, there is a general tendency among the followers of the more dualist views to give less weight to the role of prediction. This is what happens with Ludwig von Mises, who, as Blaug has pointed out, maintains "the essential disparity in approach between social and natural science grounded in *Verstehen* doctrine and the radical rejection of any kind of quantification of either the premises or the implications of economic theories" (Blaug 1980, p. 92).[21]

To some extent, the controversy *Erklären–Verstehen* of methodology of social sciences is underneath the debate that confronts *prediction* to *understanding* in methodology of economics. Undoubtedly, this is in a new intellectual context, and the positions available have no direct relation with the problem of history, as in the case of *Erklären–Verstehen*. Even so, there is a common methodological ground between them. Thus, the debate *prediction–understanding* will be studied after clarifying some details on causality and teleology, because these concepts are relevant for prediction in economics, insofar as it is accepted that there is "economic activity" as well as "economics as activity" (see Chap. 7). This analysis takes into account von Wright's approach and Tuomela's criticisms.

5.2.2 Causality and Teleology

Regarding the philosophico-methodological framework of the social sciences, the problems of causality and teleology play a relevant part. They are connected to *Explanation and Understanding* like in von Wright's book (1971). Tuomela has analyzed it, paying attention to critical aspects. He focused his analysis on two topics: causality and practical reasoning (which connects with the more general issue of teleology). In both themes von Wright seems to support the position of *Verstehen*, insofar as he distinguishes his conception from characteristic approaches of *Erklären* and stresses the teleological elements of human action (Gonzalez 2003a, pp. 38–40).

As a matter of fact, von Wright maintains that the practical syllogism provides the social sciences ("sciences of man" in his terminology) with "something long missing from their methodology: an explanation model in its own right which is a definite alternative to the subsumption-theoretical covering-law model" (von Wright 1971, p. 27). Thus, he proposes to fill a gap of the methodology of social sciences following a *Verstehen* line. He thinks that it could be a real alternative to Hempel's *Erklären* approach of covering-law model: "what the subsumption-theoretical is to causal explanation and explanation in the natural sciences, the practical syllogism is to teleological explanation and explanation in history and the social sciences" (von Wright 1971, p. 27).

[20] Generally, this is still an area where a clear improvement to get the level of rigor of the publications on quantitative methods is needed.

[21] Blaug himself mentions von Mises (1949/1978), pp. 55–56, 347–349, and 863–864.

Predominantly, Tuomela's criticism of von Wright's position on causality goes against the idea that the notion of "action" precedes conceptually and epistemologically to the notion of "cause." Tuomela considers that "scientific theories in the 'pure' sciences (which aim at theoretical knowledge but not primarily at control, for instance) do not usually say anything—nor is needed—about the actions of scientists (or other agents) who use the theory for the purposes of testing, explaining, predicting, etc. Indeed I want to argue that there is an important type of cause in science which cannot thus instrumentalistically be analyzed in terms of potential or would-do manipulability" (1976, p. 190).

According to Tuomela's analysis, von Wright establishes a close connection between the problem of agency (freedom of the will) and the problem of causation (and determinism) within his "interventionist account," the result is that agency wins causality. Thus, Tuomela instead offers an alternative account where no such connection is to be found. He upholds "it is compatible that an agent acts freely (in an important sense) while his actions can be purposively caused by his effective intentions, wants or other effective pro-attitudes" (1976, p. 193).

But Von Wright does not find quite accurate the characterization that Tuomela has given to his "interventionist" position on causation. Nonetheless, he does not disagree with the alternative account proposed by Tuomela. The difference with the book *Explanation and Understanding* is that it conceives of the causal relation as subsisting, primarily, between individual events and not between event-types, which von Wright sees now as an improvement.

Moreover, he considers that there is a coincidence between both positions: the subsistence of the causal relation depends on the existence of a nomic or law-relation between event-types (i.e., generic features of the individual events). The key issue is when a relation between event-types is *nomic* (as distinct from accidentally universal). There is the difference: von Wright thinks the concept of cause presupposes the concept of action and that "Tuomela still has to show that he can give an alternative account of nomicity (lawlikeness) which substantially differs from mine" (von Wright 1976, p. 381).

Backward causation is another key issue that confronts these philosophers. This topic also has repercussions on the methodological problem of prediction (in the social sciences, in general, and in economics, in particular). According to Tuomela, von Wright tries to prove the existence of retroactive causation as well as to prove the independence of the cause–effect asymmetry of time considerations, and he considers the argument that is offered in *Explanation and Understanding* fallacious (Tuomela 1976, p. 186).

Yet, this idea of bringing about temporally prior events by means of some actions is *de facto* avoided by von Wright. His problem is a different one: the causal relation has a characteristic asymmetry or directedness (if p causes q in a particular occasion, then it cannot be the case that q causes p in the same occasion), and he does not think that the asymmetry of the causal relation can be derived from the asymmetry of the temporal relation before-after.

Thus, in *Explanation and Understanding* von Wright defended the retroactive causation as *thinkable* (logically possible) and not as something that exists. For him, the asymmetry of the causal relation is not merely a matter of before and after; moreover, he sees conceptual reasons against the possibility of retroactive causation (von Wright 1976, pp. 382–383). These difficulties for the backward causation could be used to argue in favor of the existence of an asymmetry between explanation and prediction.

Besides causality, teleology—“teleological explanation of action”—is another point of discrepancy between Tuomela and von Wright. But, in this case, the differences are clearly less intense. Both assume a *teleological framework* or standpoint of agency: the premises and the conclusion are dealing with something that the agent *does* rather than with something that “happens to him.” Action, as opposed to “mere” movement and the intention connected with and expressed by it, is intrinsically linked in a methodological sense as well as semantically and ontologically.

In order to describe something as *action means*, von Wright and Tuomela agree that there is a “practical syllogism” or “conduct plan” which matches the action. Both also concur in the logical independence between the premises of a practical inference and the action: the practical argument is constructed to explain or justify the action that is already there. The need of the practical inference schema is a necessity conceived *ex post actu* (Tuomela 1976, pp. 195–196).

Nevertheless, according to Tuomela, the theory of the practical syllogism deals with the “qualitative” philosophical foundations of rational deliberation and decision-making, being the alternative counterpart of the “quantitative” view of the statistical decision and game theory. He considers this somewhat unsatisfactory, whereas von Wright maintains that his theory of practical syllogism is not a theory of deliberation and decision making at all (von Wright 1976, p. 402). The differences go then to the problem of rationality.

Tuomela maintains that “a theory of competence or an intentionalistic theory of behavior assuming rationality is incomplete, if not vacuous, as a psychological theory (or theory of performance). This is because it assumes a strong kind of rationality (or intelligence) on the part of the behaving agent instead of explicating and explaining rationality and clarifying its conditions of applicability (which it should do)” (1976, p. 199). This issue has some similarities with the distinction between *substantive rationality* and *bounded rationality* in economics, a proposal of Herbert Simon (1976), insofar as the dominant tendency in economics tends to assume a strong kind of rationality (“substantive rationality”) instead of a procedural rationality (“bounded rationality”) (Gonzalez 1997b, pp. 208–213).

For Tuomela, “explaining actions by citing reasons and motives was then found to be a way of explanation which gives ‘sense’ or ‘meaning’ to them. This represents an aspect of explanation that can be called *understanding*. However, this is only one part of our explanation task. The other part is of course to explain actions by citing the real or actual reasons or motives for the agent’s actions” (1976, p. 201). Thus, for him, the question of what specific teleological conceptual framework is internalized (by a given society, for example) is not merely an *a priori* problem or a purely conceptual one. Nonetheless, he accepts *a priori* a general teleological framework that includes, among other things, the general idea that a behavior theory should explain actions by citing want-belief-type reasons and motives.

An overall picture of the criticisms seems to show that Tuomela wants to tip the balance towards *Erklären*, whereas von Wright tries to remain in the area of *Verstehen*. Hence, regarding the ideas concerning the key-role of "practical syllogism" as a pattern of explanation in the human sciences, von Wright says explicitly that "of this explanation model I maintain that it is not 'causalist' but genuinely 'teleological'" (1976, p. 373). The only aspect of teleology with which he has dealt at any length was "practical inference." von Wright recognizes that he has overrated the importance for the social sciences of this particular explanation pattern. In addition, he thinks that "practical syllogism" is not a good name, because of its misleading associations with the notions of deciding and planning (von Wright 1976, p. 373; cf. 1976, p. 394).

From the perspective of prediction in economics, von Wright's approach has interest insofar as he draws attention to human activity—social sciences as sciences of *human actions*—and recognizes the teleological framework (i.e., the intentionality in meaningful human actions). Clearly, economics is not merely a set of impersonal movements, at either in the microeconomic or in the macroeconomic level. There is a human intervention in economic parameters insofar as economics is a human activity (Chap. 7).[22]

As Amartya Sen has pointed out, "economic magnitudes are ultimately social magnitudes, and variables like prices, investments, consumption, money supplies and so forth do not, naturally, move on their own, untouched by human volition. To go no further than studying these aggregate macroeconomic magnitudes is to abstract from perhaps the most fundamental aspect of the social reality, namely the rich and inseparable relations between the society and the individual. One cannot ultimately understand movements of these macroeconomic magnitudes without taking note of the objectives, knowledge, reasoning and decisions of the members of the society" (1986, p. 14).

5.3 The Methodological Debate *Prediction–Understanding*

Through the several options on *Erklären* and *Verstehen* (in the methodology of the social sciences) and the reflection on "causality" and "teleology" (in the context of these disciplines as sciences of human actions) we have relevant features of the methodological framework for prediction in economics within social sciences. These features can be enlarged through the debate in the realm of economics between *prediction* and *understanding*. This debate directly affects the problem of prediction in economics, because offers two different methodological orientations. Moreover, *Erklären–Verstehen* and *prediction–understanding* are two methodological dualities that are not disconnected, even though their origins are different (i.e., they focus, respectively, in the main on history and economics).

[22] On this issue and its connection with the problem of prediction, cf. Gonzalez (1994).

5.3.1 The Former Controversy and the Latter Debate

Commonly, support for *Erklären* is associated with the compatibility with *prediction*. In fact, in the realm of "explanation" the predictability accompanies the task of giving explanations, because the *regularity* of the phenomenon could be assumed, and this allows predictions about future events. Furthermore, the predictability of phenomena appears as an ingredient in nomological-deductive explanations as well as in probabilistic-inductive explanations. (In addition, it has also a clear role in functional explanations and, to a lesser extent, in genetic explanations.)[23]

However, in the case of *Verstehen*, it seems clear that prediction cannot be in the first area of the understanding (and the interpretation) of the social affairs. Moreover, prediction may be diluted completely in that orientation if there is insistence either on the *singularity* of the phenomena studied or on the intrinsic *variability* of the interpretative schemes that are used to understand them (either by their dependence regarding the researcher or by their intrinsic variability as human undertaking). Thus, if it is assumed that the social events are unique (and, therefore, not repeatable), then any possibility of scientific prediction is more than doubtful.

The former controversy (*Erklären–Verstehen*) and the latter debate (*prediction–understanding*) can be used to distinguish two options: (1) a methodological *convergence* (the methods of social sciences akin to the methods of natural sciences or even identical to them), and (2) a methodological *divergence* (the separation between natural methods and social methods). That is many times the underlying issue between the positions of prediction and understanding, which has an additional corollary: to stress *understanding* usually includes a clear connection between economics and other social sciences (mainly psychology and law), whereas to emphasize *prediction* is normally a sign of autonomy of economics as a science (and a feature of similitude with natural sciences).

Both positions at stake here—the emphasis on prediction and the predominance of understanding—are clear when there is a comparison between Friedman and Simon. As is well known, Friedman highlights prediction as the aim of science, as a whole, and of economics in particular. Furthermore, he establishes a similitude with natural sciences: predictions in economics could be as reliable as predictions in physics. Thus, economics can be considered an objective science, in the same sense that physics is (Friedman 1953). This view has been highly influential within the mainstream tendency in economics. Moreover, according to D. N. McCloskey, this is one of the precepts of "the official methodology of economics": prediction is the *goal* of science, which is accompanied by second maxima: the predictions (or observable implications) of a theory are what matters to its *truth* (McCloskey 1983, p. 484, 1985, p. 7).

Starting from a critical point of view towards the mainstream tendency in economics, and consequently against Friedman's approach, Simon defends the priority

---

[23] Regarding the different kinds of scientific explanations, see Gonzalez (2002b).

of *understanding* the mechanisms of behavior in economics in past and present phenomena, instead of giving preference to predict the economic behavior of the future. In fact, he suggests that "we should be wary of using prediction as a test of science, and especially of whether economics is a science" (Simon 1989, p. 100). Thus, he does not emphasize prediction as the key issue for the demarcation of economics as science, even though he recognizes the importance of predictions understood as testable implications (Gonzalez 1997b, esp., pp. 213–222).

Furthermore, when Simon analyzes the relations between prediction and prescription in economics—the realm of applied economics—he highlights the role of prescription: "generally, modelling serves policy. We construct and run models because we want to understand the consequences of taking one decision or another" (1990a/1997, p. 122). In addition, when he develops economic theory—the sphere of basic science—he stresses the links between economics and psychology (Simon 1963a, 1987a), within his behavioral model of economics.

Other critics of the mainstream tendency in economics, such as the theorists of the new institutionalist school, also insist on the need for *understanding* economic phenomena.[24] They focus understanding from a contextual perspective: the important factors are social, cultural, and legal rather than directly behavioral (in the psychological sense). Hence, they emphasize the institutional and cultural aspects of the economic understanding (Dugger 1979). The neoclassic economist tries to test the success of the predictions of quantitative statements (mainly in the realm of prices), whereas the economist of the new institutionalist tendency tests the hypotheses against structural patterns,[25] usually taking into account a historical setting.

5.3.2 Predictive Emphasis and Rhetorics

Regarding the debate that confronts prediction to understanding, which appears as a "modern" proposal in front of a "postmodern" view, there is a clear dispute with methodological consequences for economics. The discrepancy appears expressly in Rosenberg's book *Economics—Mathematical Politics or Science of Diminishing Returns*?[26] He quotes from D. N. McCloskey that "the main achievement of economics is not prediction and control assigned to it by modernist social engineering, but the making sense of economic experience" (1985, pp. 174–175).[27]

This contrast between *prediction* and *understanding* is, for Rosenberg, the most basic in philosophy of social sciences: "philosophers and social scientist have long struggled over the question of whether the social sciences must choose between

[24] Ronald Coase, in his Nobel Prize lecture, stresses three times the aim of increasing our understanding, cf. Coase (1994a), pp. 3, 8 and 14.

[25] An example of the recognition of the difficulty of making predictions and, at the same time, a stress in the structural aspects of the firm is in the famous paper Coase (1937).

[26] Additional aspects of his conception can be found in Rosenberg (1994, 1998).

[27] "The best economic scientists, of whatever school, have never believed in profitable casting of the fores" (McCloskey 1990, p. 109).

affording interpretative understanding of human action—making sense of it—or subsuming it under predictive laws. Neither side in this debate ever surrendered the aim of providing knowledge—that is, justified true belief—about human action; both recognized that fallible people can be persuaded by artful though unjustified theory" (Rosenberg 1992, p. 43).

On the one hand, *prediction* appears in this debate as the "modern" methodology. Specifically, Rosenberg sees it as the key issue of the empiricist approach: "for certification as knowledge by means of observed predictions is the touchstone of empiricism" (Rosenberg 1995, p. 23).[28] And, on the other hand, *understanding* connects with the tradition of *Verstehen*, which has several different approaches (eight have already been pointed out). But McCloskey's position belongs to the "postmodern" setting rather than to a "modern" orientation. Moreover, that view represents—for Rosenberg—the latest version of the non-empiricist attempts to undercut the epistemic goals of the empiricist opponents (Rosenberg 1992, p. 43).

As a key methodological point, McCloskey has claimed explicitly "prediction is impossible in economics" (1983, p. 487, 1985, p. 15). This assertion is accompanied by the following arguments: (a) there are successful scientific theories, such as the theory of evolution, which have no predictions and, therefore, are unfalsifiable by prediction; (b) evolutionism is implicit in Friedman's most famous piece of predictivism; (c) predicting the economic future is, according to L. von Mises, beyond the power of the man; and (d) predictionism cannot be rescued by remarking that the economist makes only conditional predictions (McCloskey 1983, pp. 488–489, 1985, pp. 15–16).[29]

Rosenberg's arguments reject each one of these statements. (i) On the existence of important scientific theories that are not predictive at all, he points out "no theory has predictive content at all by itself, for no theory contains claims about the initial conditions to which it is applied for the generation of predictions. Theories have predictive content only when conjoined to such initial or boundary conditions" (Rosenberg 1992, p. 45). (ii) Friedman's position vindicates that "economic theory is deemed to have been predictively successful with respect 'to the class of phenomena which it is intended to explain'" (Rosenberg 1992, p. 57). (iii) The approval of von Mises's posture could be self-refuting: on the one hand, it issues a prediction about the future of economics which rests on a piece of present economic theorizing; and, on the other hand, to claim that economic prediction is unnecessary in economics goes against that certifiable improvements in knowledge of economic reality can derived only from predictions, successful and unsuccessful (Rosenberg 1992, pp. 54–55). (iv) Rosenberg defends the predictive success of economics and tries to show that McCloskey's last claim would be pointless except

[28] This claim contrasts sharply with the kind of supporters of the predictivist thesis, because many of them were rationalists, such as G. W. Leibniz and K. Popper, cf. Gonzalez (2001e), Sect. 3. They can be also idealists in the sense of Rescher (1992); see Rescher (1998).

[29] In the second edition of the book *The Rhetoric of Economics*, 13 years after the first one, the same ideas are repeated under the title "Profitable prediction is not possible in economics" (cf. McCloskey 1998, pp. 150–151).

against the background of failure to improve the predictive power of economic theory (Rosenberg 1992, p. 57).

Nevertheless, this debate between predictive emphasis and rhetoric cannot go further as a methodological dispute insofar as Rosenberg tries to develop *methodological thesis* regarding prediction and McCloskey maintains that "rhetoric is not a new methodology. It is antimethodology" (1998, p. 184). In this regard, the former has pointed out that generic predictions (i.e., those of the existence of a phenomenon, process or entity, as opposed to specific predictions about its detailed character) are not enough for economics and that economists should not be satisfied with them (Rosenberg 1992, pp. 69–70). Meanwhile, the latter stresses the *linguistic* approach. Thus, McCloskey holds that "the point of a rhetorical analysis is merely to read with understanding. (…) What distinguishes good from bad economists, or even old from young economists, is additional sophistication about the rhetoric" (1998, p. 5).[30]

It should be emphasized that the relations between prediction and understanding can lead to a position of *compatibility* insofar as it is accepted that *both* are necessary. On the one hand, prediction can provide a test-criterion for the adequacy of understanding; and, on the other, the success in predicting should be accompanied by a correct understanding of the phenomena involved. Thus, a predictive success can help to distinguish a correct understanding from misunderstandings, and a sound understanding of the processes that lead to a prediction is required to have a mature science. Therefore, the issue is not one of either-or but of conjoint collaboration.

5.3.3 Repercussion for Economics

When McCloskey maintains that economics is above all *discourse* and *conversation*, there is an important philosophical shift: the focus moves from methodology of science to semantics of science, which is the branch of philosophy of science that deals with the language of science. In this regard, persuasion, not truth, seems to be the main concern of the rhetoric study.[31] Moreover, it is recognized explicitly that "rhetoric does not claim to provide a new methodology, and therefore does not provide formulas for scientific advance" (McCloskey 1985, p. 174). Indeed, the sphere of study is not the method but rather pure language: "we wish to make plausible statements, whether 'scientific' or not" (McCloskey 1998, p. 175).

There is a clear difference between this view of *understanding* and the positions involved in the *Verstehen* stance: here the main aim is rhetorical, whereas the different options in favor of *Verstehen* have a clear *methodological* component in the main authors (Dilthey, Winch, Gadamer, Wright, Apel, etc.), even though in some hermeneutical traditions (especially in Gadamer) *Verstehen* is more a *phronesis*

[30] In order to complete the criticisms towards Rosenberg, see McCloskey (1994, pp. 247–264).

[31] The interest in the rhetoric of human sciences as focused on language and argument is in Nelson et al. (1987).

than a real method (Bernstein 1982, p. 829). In effect, in *Wahrheit und Methode* there is a connection between understanding, interpreting and applying, according to a practical knowledge that does not follow the precise rules of a method.[32] But it is still a *process*—a *phronesis*—that looks for the truth, whereas McCloskey only depicts a discourse—conversation—which seeks *persuasion*.[33]

Besides this methodological difference, which affects the aim and the process of economics, there is another relevant aspect which concerns the content: when the attention relies only in the *Verstehen* or in the *understanding*, interpreted as severed from and incompatible with the *Erklären* or with the importance of *prediction*, the final outcome is usually their own dissolution of the subject in question as a scientific discipline. Thus, the *Verstehen* in history from the point of view of *Historismus* and the rhetorically interpretative understanding in economics both end up discharging the possibility of a genuine science, because before they have abandoned the possibility of objective knowledge. Therefore, in the rhetoric approach what is at stake is the *scientific character* of economics.[34]

We can say that, in response to Terence Hutchison's question (1992b)—*to predict or not to predict?*—McCloskey's reply carries out rhetoric of interpretative understanding which avoids the "modern" interest in reliable predictions in order to have a science of economics. Against that "postmodern" conception of *understanding*, in addition to most of the methodologicians of economics, there is also the practice of the experts in methods of statistical economics and econometrics. There is in fact a line of research in this realm which not only assumes the *need* of making predictions to have the science of economics but that also stresses that *aim*.

Thus, there are authors like Clive Granger, who make a test of causality that is the base of economic predictions in multivariate models; Thomas Sargent, who with Robert Lucas, makes the test of contrast of rational expectations;[35] David F. Hendry, who constructs the major part of the model of dynamic prediction in macroeconomics; and Andrew C. Harvey, who presents the problems which arise from the specification of models to make predictions.[36]

These considerations offer some lessons for the methodological framework in economics that can be drawn from the controversy *Erklären–Verstehen* and the debate *prediction–understanding*. (1) The possibility of accepting *simultaneously* the unity and diversity of science. The controversy *Erklären–Verstehen* started with a dichotomy, which splits science in two separate branches (natural sciences and social sciences) and ends up with an attempt of mediation between them. However,

[32] There is a link between "understanding" and "interpreting" which is connected to applying. Thus, there are three aspects involved, cf. Gadamer (1960, p. 328).

[33] "Rhetoric is exploring thought by conversation" (McCloskey 1983, p. 483).

[34] Economics is seen as a rhetoric genre instead of a genuine science: "Grown-up economics is not voodoo but poetry. Or, to take other models of maturity, it is history, not myth; politics, not invective; philosophy, not dogma" (McCloskey 1990, p. 109).

[35] On the use of forecast evaluations to test the rational expectation hypothesis see Stekler (2002).

[36] I owe this idea to Carlos Fernández-Jardón, *Personal communication*, August 2005. On this issue, see Chaps. 10 and 11. A historical background is available in Morgan (1990), Qin (1993), and Epstein (1987). On the methodological aspects, cf. Poirier (1994) and Keuzenkamp (2000).

there is now a clear idea of the methodological *convergence* among sciences, even though there are some methodological divergences among them, due to the different kind of objects and problems that they dealt with. (2) Causality and teleology are two methodological issues which affect social sciences and, among them, economics. In fact, social sciences are open to causality, if this notion is conceived in a *purposeful* way instead of a mechanical one (i.e., to characterize human activity in causal terms does not undermine the intentional feature of human action). In this regard, these sciences can incorporate a teleological framework in their methodology. (3) The predictive aim of economics should be *compatible* with the interest in the realm of understanding, either in the sphere of rationality or in the context of cultural and institutional setting. Understanding could not be purely rhetoric, otherwise the scientific character of economics is at risk. (4) If the methodology of economics should deal with what economics *is* and what it *ought to be*, then predictions appear in an *important* place: it is a relevant aspect of the work of economics and is also needed to guide economic activity.

References

Anscombe, G. E. M. 1957. *Intention*. 2nd ed. Oxford: B. Blackwell.(2nd ed., 1963; reprinted in 1976)

Apel, K. O. 1976. Causal explanation, motivational explanation, and hermeneutical understanding. In *Contemporary aspects of philosophy,* ed. G. Ryle, 161–176. Stockfield: Oriel.

Apel, K. O. 1979. *Die Erklären-Verstehen Kontroverse in Transzendental-Pragmatischer Sicht*. Frankfurt: Suhrkamp. *Understanding and explanation. A transcendental-pragmatic perspective*. (trans: Warnke, G. 1984).Cambridge: The MIT Press.

Apel, K. O. 1985. La "distinción" diltheyana entre explicación y comprensión y la posibilidad de "mediación" entre ambas. *Teorema* 15 (1–2): 95–114.

Bell, D. 1982. *The social sciences since the second world war*. New Brunswick: Transactions.

Bernstein, R. J. 1982. From hermeneutics to praxis. *Review of Metaphysics* 35:823–845.

Blaug, M. 1980. *The methodology of economics: Or how economists explain*. Cambridge: Cambridge University Press.

Caldwell, B. J. 1993. Economic methodology: Rationale, foundations and prospects. In *Rationality, institutions and economic methodology,* ed. U. Mäki, B. Gustafsson, and C. Knudsen, 45–60. London: Routledge.

Carnap, R. 1946. Theory and prediction in science. *Science* 104 (2710): 520–521.

Coase, R. H. 1937. The nature of the firm. *Economica* 4:386–405. (Reprinted in Coase, R. H. 1988. *The firm, the market and the law*, 33-55. Chicago: The University of Chicago Press, Chicago).

Coase, R. H. 1994a. The institutional structure of production. In *Essays on economics and economists,* ed. R. H. Coase, 3–14. Chicago: The University of Chicago Press.

Deane, Ph. 1983. The scope and method of economic science. *Economic Journal* 93:1–12.

Dilthey, W. 1983. *Einleitung in die Geisteswissenschften*. Reprinted in Dilthey, W. 1962. *Gesammelte Schriften,* vol. 1 (5th ed.). Stuttgart-Göttingen: Teubner-Vaudenhoeck and Ruprecht.

Dray, W. 1957. *Laws and explanation in history*. Oxford: Oxford University Press.

Dray, W. 1964. *Philosophy of history*. Englewood Cliffs: Prentice Hall.

Droysen, J. G. 1858. Grundriss der Historik. Compiled in Droysen, J. G. 1937. *Historik. Vorlesungen über Enzyklopädie und Methodologie der Geschichte*, ed. Rudolf Bübner. Munich: Oldenbourg (3rd ed., 1958, Darmstadt: Wissenschaftliche Buchgesellschaft).

Dugger, W. 1979. Methodological differences between institutional and neoclassic economics. *Journal of Economics Issues* 13:899–909.

Epstein, R. J. 1987. *A history of econometrics*. Amsterdam: North Holland.

Friedman, M. 1953. The methodology of positive economics. In *Essays in positive economics,* M. Friedman, 3–43. Chicago: The University of Chicago Press (6th repr.1969).

Gadamer, H. G. 1960. *Wahrheit und Methode*. Tubingen: J. C. B. Mohr. (5th ed., 1986).

Gadamer, H. G. 1975. Hermeneutics and social science. *Cultural Hermeneutics* 2:307–316.

Gadamer, H. G. 1976. *Vernunft im Zeitalter der Wissenschaft*. Frankfurt: Suhrkamp.

Gadamer, H. G. 1989. *Das Erbe Europas*. Frankfurt: Suhrkamp.

Giddens, A. 1987. *Social theory and modern sociology*. Oxford: Polity Press.

Giddens, A. 1993. *New rules of sociological method*. 2nd ed. Stanford: Stanford University Press. (1st ed., 1976).

Gonzalez, W. J. 1984. La interpretación historicista de las Ciencias Sociales. *Anales de Filosofía* 2:109–137.

Gonzalez, W. J. 1994. Economic prediction and human activity. An analysis of prediction in economics from action theory. *Epistemologia* 17:253–294.

Gonzalez, W. J. 1995. Reichenbach's concept of prediction. *International Studies in the Philosophy of Science* 9 (1): 37–58.

Gonzalez, W. J. 1996e. Caracterización del objeto de la Ciencia de la Historia y bases de su configuración metodológica. In *Acción e Historia. El objeto de la Historia y la Teoría de la Acción,* ed. W. J. Gonzalez, 25–111. A Coruña: Publicaciones Universidad de A Coruña.

Gonzalez, W. J. 1997b. Rationality in economics and scientific predictions: A critical reconstruction of bounded rationality and its role in economic predictions. *Poznan Studies in the Philosophy of Science* 61:205–232.

Gonzalez, W. J. 2001e. Lakatos's approach on prediction and novel facts. *Theoria* 16 (3): 499–518.

Gonzalez, W. J. 2002b. Caracterización de la "explicación científica" y tipos de explicaciones científicas. In *Diversidad de la explicación científica,* ed. W. J. Gonzalez, 13–49. Barcelona: Ariel.

Gonzalez, W. J. 2003a. From *Erklären-Verstehen* to *prediction-understanding*: The methodological framework in economics. In *Realism in action*: *Essays in the philosophy of social sciences,* ed. M. Sintonen, P. Ylikoski, and K. Miller, 33–50. Dordrecht: Kluwer.

Gonzalez, W. J. 2003b. Rationality in experimental economics: An analysis of Reinhard Selten's approach. In *Observation and experiment in the natural and the social sciences,* ed. M. C. Galavotti, 71–83. Dordrecht: Kluwer.

Gonzalez, W. J. 2007b. Análisis de las Ciencias de Diseño desde la racionalidad limitada, la predicción y la prescripción. In *Las Ciencias de Diseño: Racionalidad limitada, predicción y prescripción,* ed. W. J. Gonzalez, 3–38. A Coruña: Netbiblo.

Gonzalez, W. J. 2008. Rationality and prediction in the sciences of the artificial: Economics as a design science. In *Reasoning, rationality, and probability,* ed. M. C. Galavotti, R. Scazzieri, and P. Suppes, 165–186. Stanford: CSLI Publications.

Gonzalez, W. J. 2011a. Complexity in economics and prediction: The role of parsimonious factors. In *Explanation, prediction, and confirmation,* ed. D. Dieks, W. J. Gonzalez, S. Hartman, Th. Uebel, and M. Weber, 319–330. Dordrecht: Springer.

Gonzalez, W. J. 2012a. La vertiente dinámica de las Ciencias de la Complejidad. Repercusión de la historicidad para la predicción científica en las Ciencias de Diseño. In *Las Ciencias de la Complejidad: Vertiente dinámica de las Ciencias de Diseño y sobriedad de factores,* ed. W. J. Gonzalez, 73–106. A Coruña: Netbiblo.

Gonzalez, W. J. 2013a. Value ladenness and the value-free ideal in scientific research. In *Handbook of the philosophical foundations of business ethics,* ed. Ch. Lütge, 1503–1521. Dordrecht: Springer.

Gonzalez, W. J. 2013b. The sciences of design as sciences of complexity: The dynamic trait. In *New challenges to philosophy of science,* ed. H. Andersen, D. Dieks, W. J. Gonzalez, Th. Uebel, and G. Wheeler, 299–311. Dordrecht: Springer.

Hausman, D. M. 1992b. *Essays on philosophy and economic methodology*. Cambridge: Cambridge University Press.

Hausman, D. M. 1994b. Introduction. In *The philosophy of economics. An anthology* (2nd ed.), ed. D. M. Hausman, 1–50. Cambridge: Cambridge University Press.

Hempel, C. G. 1942. The function of general laws in history. *Journal of Philosophy* 39:35–48. (Reprinted in Hempel, C. G. 1965. *Aspects of scientific explanation and other essays in the philosophy of science*, 231-243. New York: Free Press).

Hutchison, T. W. 1992b. To predict or not to predict? (That *is* the question)? In *Changing aims in economics,* T. W. Hutchison, 71–88 (notes in pp. 158–167). Oxford: B. Blackwell.

Keuzenkamp, H. A. 2000. *Probability, econometrics and truth. The methodology of econometrics.* Cambridge: Cambridge University Press.

Manninen, J., and R. Tuomela, eds. 1976. *Essays on explanation and understanding.* Dordrecht: Reidel.

Martinez, J. M. 1994. *La Filosofía de las Ciencias Humanas y Sociales de H. G. Gadamer.* Barcelona: PPU.

McCloskey, D. N. 1983. The rhetoric of economics. *Journal of Economic Literature* 21 (2): 481–517. (Reprinted in McCloskey, D. N. 2001. *Measurement and meaning in economics*, ed. S. Th. Ziliak, 16–203. Cheltenham: E. Elgar.)

McCloskey, D. N. 1985. *The rhetoric of economics.* Madison: University of Wisconsin Press.

McCloskey, D. N. 1990. *If you're so smart. The narrative of economic expertise.* Chicago: The University of Chicago Press.

McCloskey, D. N. 1994. *Knowledge and persuasion in economics.* Cambridge: Cambridge University Press.

McCloskey, D. N. 1998. *The rhetoric of economics.* 2nd ed. Madison: University of Wisconsin Press.

Menger, C. 1985. *Investigations into the method of the social sciences with special reference to economics.* New York: New York University Press.

Morgan, M. S. 1990. *The history of econometric ideas.* Cambridge: Cambridge University Press.

Nelson, J., A. Megill, and D. N. McCloskey, eds. 1987. *The rhetoric of human sciences.* Madison: University of Wisconsin Press.

Özel, H. 2003. Closing open systems: Two examples for the "double hermeneutic" in economics. *METU Studies in Development* 30:223–248.

Poirier, D. J., ed. 1994. *The methodology of econometrics.* 2 vols. Aldershot: E. Elgar.

Qin, D. 1993. *The formation of econometrics.* Oxford: Clarendon.

Reichenbach, H. 1938. *Experience and prediction. An analysis of the foundations and the structure of knowledge.* Chicago: The University of Chicago Press.

Rescher, N. 1992. Our science as *our* science. In *A system of pragmatic idealism,* vol. I: *Human knowledge in idealistic perspective,* N. Rescher, 110–125. Princeton: Princeton University Press.

Rescher, N. 1998. *Predicting the future: An introduction to the theory of forecasting.* Albany: State University of New York Press.

Rosenberg, A. 1992. *Economics-mathematical politics or science of diminishing returns*? Chicago: The University of Chicago Press.

Rosenberg, A. 1994. If economics isn't science, what is it? In *The philosophy of economics. An anthology* (2nd ed., revised), ed. D. M. Hausman, 376–394. Cambridge: Cambridge University Press.

Rosenberg, A. 1995. *Philosophy of social science.* 2nd ed. Boulder, CO: Westview.

Rosenberg, A. 1998. La Teoría Económica como Filosofía Política. *Theoria* 13 (32): 279–299.

Rouse, J. 1987. *Knowledge and power: Toward a political philosophy of science.* Ithaca: Cornell University Press.

Sen, A. 1986. Prediction and economic theory. In *Predictability in science and society,* ed. J. Mason, P. Mathias, and J. H. Westcott, 3–23. London: The Royal Society and The British Academy.

Simon, H. A. 1963a. Economics and psychology. In *Psychology: A study of a science,* vol. 6, ed. S. Koch, 715–752. New York: McGraw Hill. (Reprinted in Simon, H. A. 1982. *Models of bounded rationality*, vol. 2: *Behavioral economics and business organization*, 318-355. Cambridge, MA: The MIT Press.)

Simon, H. A. 1976. From substantive to procedural rationality. In *Method and appraisal in economics,* ed. S. Latsis, 129–148. Cambridge: Cambridge University Press.

Simon, H. A. 1987a. Rationality in psychology and economics. In *Rational choice. The contrast between economics and psychology,* eds. R. M. Hogarth, and M. W. Reder, 25–40. Chicago: The University of Chicago Press.

Simon, H. A. 1989. The state of economic science. In *The state of economic science. Views of six Nobel laureates*, ed. W. Sichel, 97-110. Kalamazoo, MI: W. E. Upjohn Institute for Employment Research.

Simon, H. A. 1990a. Prediction and prescription in systems modeling. *Operations Research* 38:7-14. (Reprinted in Simon, H. A. 1997. *Models of bounded rationality,* vol. 3: *Empirically grounded economic reason,* 115-128. Cambridge, MA: The MIT Press.)

Simon, H. A. 1996. *The sciences of the artificial.* 3rd ed. Cambridge: The MIT Press (1st ed., 1969; 2nd ed., 1981).

Stekler, H. O. 2002. The rationality and efficiency of individuals' forecasts. In *A companion to economic forecasting,* ed. M. P. Clemens, and D. F. Hendry, 222–240. Oxford: Blackwell.

Suppe, F., ed. 1974. *The structure of scientific theories.* Urbana: University of Illinois Press (2nd ed., 1977).

Taylor, C. 1964. *The explanation of behaviour.* London: Routledge/K.Paul

Taylor, C. 1980. Understanding in human science. *Review of Metaphysics* 34:25–38.

Taylor, C. 1981. Understanding and explanation in the *Geisteswissenschaften.* In *Wittgenstein: To follow a rule,* ed. S. Holtzman and C. Leich, 191–210. London: Routledge/K.Paul

Taylor, C. 1985a. *Human agency and language.* Cambridge: Cambridge University Press.

Taylor, C. 1985b. *Philosophy and the human sciences.* Cambridge: Cambridge University Press.

Tuomela, R. 1976. Explanation and understanding of human behavior. In *Essays on explanation and understanding. Studies in the foundations of humanities and social sciences,* ed. J. Manninen and R. Tuomela, 183–205. Dordrecht: Reidel.

Tuomela, R. 1988. Eine Pragmatisch-Nomologische Theorie des Wissenschaftlichen Erklären und Verstehens. In *Erklären und Verstehen in der Wissenschaft,* ed. G. Schurz, 125–170. Munich: R. Oldenbourg.

von Mises, L. 1949. *Human action: A treatise on economics.* New Haven: Yale University Press. (Reprinted in Hodge, W. 1978. London.)

von Wright, G. H.. 1971. *Explanation and understanding.* Ithaca: Cornell University Press.

von Wright, G. H. 1973. On the logic and epistemology of the causal relation. In *Logic, methodology and philosophy of science*, vol. IV, ed. P. Suppes. Amsterdam: North-Holland. (Reprinted in Sosa, E., and Tooley, M., eds. 1993. *Causation,* 105-124. Oxford: Oxford University Press.)

von Wright, G. H. 1974. *Causality and determinism.* New York: Columbia University Press.

von Wright, G. H. 1976. Replies. In *Essays on explanation and understanding. Studies in the foundations of humanities and social sciences,* ed. J. Manninen, and R. Tuomela, 371–413. Dordrecht: Reidel.

von Wright, G. H. 1983. *Practical reason.* Ithaca: Cornell University Press.

von Wright, G. H. 1984. *On human freedom.* Helsinki: University of Helsinki.

von Wright, G. H. 1985. Probleme des Erklären und Verstehens von Handlungen. *Conceptus* 19:3–19.

von Wright, G. H. 1986. Rationality: Means and ends. *Epistemologia* 9:57–71.

von Wright, G. H. 1987. Wissenschaft und Vernunft. *Rechtstheorie* 18:383–396.

Weber, M. 1904. Die "Objektivität" sozialwissenschaftlicher und sozialpolitischer Erkenntnis. In *Gesammelte Aufsätze zur Wissenschaftslehre,* ed. M. Weber, 146-214. Tubingen: J. C.. Mohr. (Foreword by Johannes Winckelmann., 1968, 1st ed., 1922).

Weber, M. 1917. Der Sinn der "Wertfreiheit" der soziologischen und ökonomischen Wissenschaften. In *Gesammelte Aufsätze zur Wissenschaftslehre,* ed. M. Weber, 489-540. Tubingen: J. C.. Mohr. (Foreword by Johannes Winckelmann., 1st ed., 1922).

Winch, P. 1958. *The idea of a social science.* London: Routledge/K.Paul. (reimp 1990).

Wittgenstein, L. 1953. *Philosophische Untersuchungen,* ed. G. E. M. Anscombe, and R. Rhees. Oxford: Blackwell. (Translated by Anscombe, G. E. M. 1976. *Philosophical investigations.* Oxford: Blackwell/Oxford).

Chapter 6
Methodological Approaches within Economics: The Perspectives on Prediction of Some Nobel Prize Winners

Through the analysis of the *Erklären–Verstehen* controversy and the debate *prediction-understanding* made in Chap. 5, we have obtained methodological elements for prediction in economics according to two main directions. First, the options available for the methodological framework of economics, based on its relation with the methodologies of groups of sciences, taking into account the methodological orientations in the natural sciences and the social sciences. Second, the place of prediction in the alternative between a conception of economics built on a methodological preference for the search of truth, which puts special emphasis on the role of mathematics, and a rhetoric vision of economic performance, where the prominence in the use of language gives the primacy to the role of persuasion.

After the methodological framework for economics, in general, and prediction, in particular, it is time to see the methodological approaches within economics that have a direct relation to prediction. Over the last decades both economic theory and applied economics have received increasing epistemological and methodological attention.[1] As has occurred with other sciences in the past, this philosophical interest appears as a consequence of the development of economics, which has enlarged its area of research and seems to be looking for clear progress in a more intense way than any other social science (or even science of the artificial) in recent times.[2]

[1] This can be seen in the large number of publications (books, articles, and journals especially devoted to this topic) prepared by philosophers of economics as well as by economists interested in methodological issues. In addition to the bibliography of this book, a good selection of publications in this regard is available in the three volumes edited by Daniel Hausman on *Philosophy of Economics* (1984, 1994a, 2008).

[2] On the publications related to economics as a science of the artificial, see Gonzalez (2007b).

W. J. Gonzalez, *Philosophico-Methodological Analysis of Prediction and its Role in Economics,* Theory and Decision Library A: 50, DOI 10.1007/978-3-319-08885-3_6

6.1 Development of Economics and Methodological Approaches

Many factors—both internal and external—intervene in this contemporary development of economics as a science, which has been accompanied by a strong expansion of applied economics through the econometric turn.[3] Its development as a science has given an impulse to the methodological approaches in economics—as basic science and as applied science—where there is a clear variety of options on prediction. Here the focus will be on prediction within the branch of economic theory, whereas the use of prediction in applied economics will receive more attention in following chapters (among them, Chaps. 10 and 11). The importance of economic theory should be emphasized, due to its special weight for the epistemological and methodological discussions in this discipline.

Economics is a science that receives a visible influence from internal and external values. On the one hand, it develops its own contents, to enlarge knowledge of economic activity and to solve specific problems, according to its aims and processes, in order to get results; and, on the other, economics is intertwined with other disciplines (psychology, law, sociology, ecology, politics, etc.), insofar as its activity is interrelated with other human activities. In addition to these aspects, which make it a complex science, economics is a social science as well as a science of the artificial (Gonzalez 2008). In spite of its complexity, the role of economic methods goes beyond economic science and has a clear incidence on other disciplines (Radnitzky and Bernholz 1987).

This preference for the economic dimension when studying human and social phenomena can lead us to what Blaug calls "economic imperialism" (1980, p. 248), as exemplified in Gary Becker, who—as is well known—researches social realities, such as families or prisons, from a purely economic view (Becker 1976, 1981).[4] However, economic criteria, beginning with the insistence on the correlation between cost and benefit, have also been applied to research methods in natural science (Rescher 1978, 1996).[5] They are used in connection with a key concept in methodology of science: scientific progress.

Within this general scope as an intellectual horizon, the emphasis here will be on the methodological concept of "prediction," which is crucial for economics and can be connected with "prescription." In this regard, the study will follow two steps: first, the role of prediction in economics will be examined through four Nobel Prize winners, focusing on it as a test for economics as a science; and second, the underlying general methodology of these approaches will be utilized to make explicit

[3] The turning point can be located in 1944, when T. Haavelmo publishes his paper "The Probability Approach in Econometrics." On the evolution of econometrics, cf. Morgan (1990). From the methodological point of view, Poirier (1994) should be emphasized.

[4] See also Becker and Stigler (1977). Regarding economic imperialism and its limits due to complexity, see Gonzalez (2012b).

[5] Moreover, this philosopher has also used the economic perspective to characterize the theory of knowledge: Rescher (1989).

several aspects: the absence of consensus which can lead to an alternative view around some central tenets, and the issue of the convergence between economics and physics.

Here, insofar as the attention goes above all to economic theory ("descriptive economics" or "positive" sphere), the focus will be on the relations between explanation and prediction, where the methodological problem of scientific test is commonly considered as crucial. Later on, the emphasis will be on applied economics ("normative economics"), and consequently on the nexus of prediction with prescription (the central topic of Chap. 12). This connection will be shown as well as the links of both—especially, the latter—with the specific values of "economic activity" and the values of "economics as activity" (i.e., values of economic undertaking as an activity interconnected with others in the social context) (cf. Chap. 7, Sect. 7.3).

6.2 The Role of Prediction in Economics: Four Methodological Options

Among prestigious economists, the characterization of *prediction* in economics from a philosophico-methodological viewpoint is still not entirely clear. The existing approaches to this task are far from coincident and, even worse, the concept itself of "prediction" is understood by economists in different ways. This divergence can be found in very influential economists, among them four Nobel laureates: Milton Friedman (1976), John Hicks (1972), James Buchanan (1986), and Herbert A. Simon (1978) (Gonzalez 1998b). The first of them addresses the issue directly, because—in his famous paper on "The Methodology of Positive Economics" (1953)—Friedman focuses the methodological discussion on the role of prediction in this science and its incidence for the duality "positive economics"–"normative economics."[6]

6.2.1 *The Predictivist Thesis: Milton Friedman*

Milton Friedman expresses a *predictivist thesis*. His conception of economic prediction is rooted in an instrumentalist methodology of science. For him, prediction is the goal of science as a whole. Thus, it is a constitutive feature of economics as scientific enterprise: "the ultimate goal of a positive science is the development of a 'theory' or 'hypothesis' that yields valid and meaningful (…) predictions about

[6] Among the expressions used in this regard are "positive economics" and "political economy" (Hutchison 1964). But here we have distinguished between "applied science" and "application of science," which means that "applied economics" is the knowledge for solving the specific problems, and "political economy" can be the use made of the knowledge by the agents in the changeable contexts of the policy-making.

phenomena not yet observed" (1953, p. 7). He highlights the scientific character of prediction in economics and subordinates the whole science to that aim.

From the perspective of substantive hypotheses, "theory is to be judged by its predictive power for the class of phenomena which is intended to 'explain' [sic]. Only factual evidence can show whether it is 'right' or 'wrong' or, better, tentatively 'accepted' as valid or 'rejected'" (Friedman 1953, p. 8). This *predictivist thesis*, where what is important is the success in making predictions, does not demand the realism of the assumptions. Friedman thinks that "the only relevant test of the validity of a hypothesis is comparison of its predictions with experience. The hypothesis is rejected if its predictions are contradicted (…); it is accepted if its predictions are not contradicted; great confidence is attached to it if it has survived many opportunities for contradiction" (1953, pp. 8–9).

Due to Friedman's enormous influence, this approach has had a strong impact on the debates on the methodology of "descriptive economics" and also a repercussion in "normative economics."[7] He sees his position in convergence with physics, because—for him—the task of economics is "to provide a system of generalizations that can be used to make correct predictions about the consequences of any change in circumstances. Its performance is to be judged by the precision, scope, and conformity with experience of the predictions it yields. In short, positive economics is, or can be, an 'objective' science, in precisely the same sense as any of the physical sciences" (1953, p. 4). Therefore, economics would be similar to natural sciences with respect to the quality of predictions, and both would have as a relevant test the comparison of their predictions with experience.

In spite of its influence, Friedman's predictivist thesis is too radical: neither scientific theories, in general, nor economic theories, in particular, can be reduced to the single goal of making predictions. The language, structure and knowledge of science are not *eo ipso* mere instruments to develop a methodology of prediction; they also seek to grasp the real facts, trying to give them either an "explanation" or an "understanding." Making predictions is then a relevant task that should be accompanied by other aspects, such as the description of human activity in the economic field or the evaluation of the result that it is convenient to obtain.

Furthermore, *to test* an economic theory through its predictions is, frequently, a difficult task (Caldwell 1982/1994, p. 174): first, part of the pertinent information—to evaluate the prediction made—might not be available and this contributes to the fact that the control of the observational process is sometimes a problematic issue; and, secondly, so-called "crucial experiments"—not only the "predictive," but also the "explanatory" ones—can raise a wide methodological debate dealing with the available data (as is usual in issues related to unemployment or economic crisis, such as the famous Depression of 1929).

[7] In fact, Friedman was prepared to countenance the use of positive economics to inform policy.

6.2.2 *The Quasi-scientific Option: John Hicks*

Another Nobel Prize laureate in economics—Sir John Hicks—argues in a very different vein,[8] with manifest discrepancy to Friedman: (i) Hicks rejects that the ultimate goal of economics is to predict, because this subject is more influenced by its past—its history—than its future; (ii) he does not accept a convergence between natural sciences—especially, physics—and economics, because he considers both sharply separated by the problem of prediction; (iii) he asseverates that economics is not, strictly speaking, a "science": he thinks that it is a "discipline" that is on the edge of science; and (iv) the scientific test of economic prediction should be abandoned, due to his conviction that it is not a kind of prediction of a genuine science.

The starting point of this *quasi-scientific option* is in the insistence on two separate levels: on the one hand, Hicks considers that economics as a discipline cannot be incorporated into the sphere of science, because—for him—it has no genuine scientific status (Hicks 1983c); and, on the other, he thinks that the confluence of economics and physics is not possible, because they belong to completely different domains of reality.

Moreover, Hicks thinks that "the word prediction, as used in economics, commonly has a rather different meaning from what it has in experimental sciences. This is because our predictions are in time, in historical time, in a way that most scientific predictions are not. They are predictions about the future, the future from now, (…) Yet though the predictions relate to the future, the evidence on which we base them comes from the past" (1986, p. 98).

Regarding the first aspect—a discipline rather than a science—Hicks points out that economics is a discipline "on the edge of science, because it can make use of scientific, or quasi-scientific, methods; but it is no more than on the edge, because the experiences that it analyses have so much that is non-repetitive about them" (Hicks 1986, p. 100). And, with respect to the second factor—the absence of confluence with natural sciences—he considers that there is a gap between physics and economics: "the facts which we study [in economics] are not permanent, or repeatable, like the facts of natural sciences; they change incessantly, and change without repetition" (1983a, p. 4).

Hicks assumes that the prototype of science is physics and that economics is always involved in changeable phenomena, making only weak predictions. In my judgment, he goes too far in denying economics a scientific character, because in economics there are foresights, predictions, and forecastings (Gonzalez 1996c, pp. 215–216), and therefore, not all economic predictions are *eo ipso* essentially weak predictions.

Even though scientific knowledge is, generally, more difficult in economics than in physics, we should take into account that it is a science of a different kind: it is of human and social character, and the model of the Newtonian mechanics is not valid for economics. The phenomena studied by economics are within the sphere of

[8] An analysis of Hicks' methodology of economics can be found in Blaug (1988).

events influenced by human action and contain specific conditions that the economists need to incorporate into their models.[9]

John Hicks maintains that there are *two kinds of predictions*: on the one hand, predictions of what will happen, and, on the other, predictions of what will probably happen (Hicks 1983c, p. 369). Physical predictions and economic ones are respective examples of the two types, where the former are more reliable than the latter. For him, the most that economic forecasting can do is to tell us what the value of a variable could be at some date in the future; what it is wisest to expect. These forecast expectations are formed as a basis for current action (Hicks 1983c, p. 369).

Besides the two kinds of predictions, Hicks also asserts the distinction between *unconditional* prediction, that something will happen just like that, and *conditional* prediction, which says that something will happen, if some conditions are satisfied.[10] He considers that some sciences are able to make some sorts of unconditional predictions, whereas the normal type of scientific prediction is the conditional (Hicks 1986, pp. 93–94).

Unconditional predictions can be made in astronomy, because the astronomer can tell us, with remarkable precision, just when there will be an eclipse of the sun. On the one side, the phenomena studied by the astronomer are beyond the range of being influenced by human action; and, on the other, the scientist can circumscribe his description of the phenomena and he or she can feel sure that there are no conditions that he or she has not taken into account.

Within the field of conditional prediction, Hicks establishes a distinction between *strong* and *weak* predictions. "If it is strong, it states that, given the stated conditions, the event will follow; if it is weak, it says no more than the event will follow, if there is no disturbance" (1986, p. 94). Thus, a conditional weak prediction requires only that some of the conditions for the event to follow have been identified, but there are others that cannot be specified or cannot yet be specified. He maintains that economic predictions are generally weak predictions. They are based on weak propositions and take the form 'This is what will happen, if something does not come up to prevent it'. The weakness is in its being subject to a *ceteris paribus* (other things being equal) clause (Hicks 1986, p. 97).

Clearly it is an acute weakness, because "a weak prediction, that the event will occur, if there are no disturbances, cannot be confirmed, nor can it be refuted, by what is found to happen" (Hicks 1986, p. 94). Moreover, according to Hicks, "if the event does occur, all we can say is that if the prediction was correct, there appear to have been no disturbances, or no sufficient disturbances. If the event does not occur, we can say no more than that if the prediction was correct, then there were disturbances. In neither case is it shown, at all directly, by experience that the prediction was right or wrong" (1986, p. 94).

---

[9] On the use of models in the social sciences, see Collins (1976).

[10] "Unconditional" does not mean here without "initial conditions": it expresses something which goes on its own, whereas "conditional" expresses the need of the existence of some phenomena that could or not happen.

If Hick's idea of the weakness of economic prediction is correct, then economics—and specifically, economic theory—is not a science or, at least, not yet. A mature science needs conditional strong predictions, where the predicted event will occur, under stated conditions, and the prediction will be either confirmed or refuted by the event. Otherwise, if prediction is so weak—as he maintains—such that its success or failure cannot be assessed by the experience, then we are on the boundaries of non-scientific prediction.

In my judgment, Hicks goes as far as he does, because we can find in economics a variety of possibilities: "foresights," "predictions," and "forecastings" (cf. Chap. 2, Sect. 2.4.2). In other words, economic predictions are not *eo ipso* essentially weak predictions. The internal and external limits do not imply such *essential* weakness; rather, they suggest that knowledge in economics is more difficult than in physics (or natural sciences, in general) and is a more complex reality than the physical one (in terms of interrelation of factors of economic activity and as a consequence of the connections with many other human activities).

Therefore, economics is a different kind of science: a social one as well as a science of the artificial. In this regard, the model of Newtonian mechanics does not seem to be valid for economics. The phenomena studied by economics are in the range of being influenced by human action and contain conditions that the economists could incorporate into predicting models. The problem can be raised by the prediction itself when this is published.[11]

6.2.3 The Dualist Posture: James Buchanan

Methodologically, James M. Buchanan—another Nobel laureate in economics—adopts a posture that is quite different from the predictivist thesis and the quasi-scientific option. He maintains that there exist two economic realms: on the one hand, there is an objective sphere that has predictions and, furthermore, possesses a scientific character; and, on the other, there is a subjective area and, in this second case, we have no scientific knowledge. Thus, in his book *Economics: Between Predictive Science and Moral Philosophy* (1987a),[12] he deals with the scientific character of this discipline, splitting it in two branches.

James Buchanan accepts the existence of a "subjective economics" whose domain is "defined precisely within the boundaries between the positive, predictive science of the orthodox model on the one hand and the speculative thinking of moral philosophy on the other" (1982/1987, p. 68). This subjective economics between science and philosophy cannot be predictive. Nevertheless, subjective economics "can offer insights into the dynamics through which a society of persons

[11] This question has been studied by Emile Grunberg and Franco Modigliani (1954, p. 478). See, in this regard, Chap. 1, Sect. 1.3.2.

[12] Additional aspects of his view are in Buchanan (1989, 1996). His perspective on what economists should do is in Buchanan (1987b).

who remain free to choose in a genuine sense develops and prospers" (Buchanan 1982/1987, p. 70).

Thus, the role of prediction would be restricted to a part of economics and only that part could be "scientific." Consequently, he assumes a coincidence with the predictivist thesis: there is at least a branch of economics—positive economics—that makes scientific predictions. Meanwhile he moves towards a quasi-scientific option with the notion of "subjective economics," but he introduces his own view: subjective economics "occupies an explanatory realm that is mutually exclusive with that properly occupied by positive economics" (Buchanan 1982/1987, p. 70).

For Buchanan, there are two kinds of economic discourse: the positive or predictive economics, which studies primarily what is more obvious in the human interaction, and the subjective (or non-predictive) economics, which seeks insights about the dynamics through which a society of persons evolves and prospers (a task related with choosing) (Buchanan 1982/1987, p. 70). Therefore, he accepts a *methodological dualism* within economics; besides, that cutting distinction (objective/predictive and subjective/non predictive) is seen as *necessary* in making the history of economic doctrines. Moreover, he considers that this *methodological duality* is needed to avoid confusion in making the history of economic thought.

Buchanan's methodological dualism is like a *tertium quid* between Friedman's predictivist thesis and Hicks's quasi-scientific option. In spite of their differences, these three positions on economic predictions endorse the idea of prediction as an *aim* of economics, but they disagree about its role as the scientific *test.*[13] Two of them agree on the existence of a realm—positive economics—where this discipline is an objective science, capable of predicting future economic phenomena in a reliable way (similar to natural sciences).

This acceptance of the possibility of scientific predictions in economics can be reinterpreted in terms of predictability of "economic activity," i.e., when the variables which are studied can be separated or distinguished ("isolated") with respect to other activities, or when they can be seen in an ideal context (such as some econometric theorems). In this case, the economic model can be precise, as a mere mathematical calculation, but it can put aside the usual variables that interfere in the real case. From this point of view, "prediction" (or, even, "foresight") of future phenomena can turn out to be viable, because it is possible to take into account the variable involved in the event and, thus, to have a precise knowledge of the outcome.

6.2.4 The Wary Attitude: Herbert A. Simon

There is, in Simon, a different conception of the status of prediction in economics. This approach can be seen in the context of two central problems: on the one hand, the possibility of prediction as the *main goal* of this discipline and, on the other, the

[13] It is convenient to emphasize that "the question of prediction in Economics involves, or brings together, most of the main questions as to what sort of subject Economics is" (Hutchison 1977, p. 8).

role of prediction as the *test* of economics as *science*. Regarding the first problem, he feels uncomfortable with the assumptions of economic models, especially in the case of Friedman (1953), which require substantive rationality and which emphasize reliable predictions as decisive. *De facto*, Simon rejects prediction as the main goal of economics, and he cannot accept that prediction could be the single aim of science. Thus, he criticizes the methodological primacy of prediction in economics.

Apropos the second issue—the role of prediction as the *test* of economics as *science*—the problem requires its diverse facets to be taken into account. An initial approach reveals that Simon considers that prediction does not belong to the set of characteristics that make economics a science. In fact, he suggests abandoning prediction as the test to ascertain whether economics is a science: "we should be wary of using prediction as a test of science, and especially of whether economics is a science, for an understanding of mechanisms does not guarantee predictability" (Simon 1989, p. 100). His interest is in *understanding* the processes that accounts for past and present phenomena rather than in the predictability of economic behavior.

Simon's scheme interconnects uncertainty, bounded rationality, and economic prediction (Gonzalez 1997b, pp. 216–217). His approach is based on the idea of economic behavior inserted in the context of uncertainty, which is seen as a crucial factor in human decision-making. In addition, economic actors possess bounded rationality and behave following it, because their power to compute information and to consider all the alternatives possible is limited (and not unlimited, as mainstream economics suggests). Then, economic predictions should be analyzed within the framework of these constraints.

a. Economic prediction cannot be made on the basis of a "perfect rationality," because Simon insists on the existence of clear limitations. Above all, there is uncertainty about the consequences in each alternative when an economic decision is made, where the information on the set of alternatives would be incomplete, and the complexity of situations can prevent us from making the necessary calculations to solve the problem (Simon 1972, p. 169). Therefore, epistemological limitations—the cognitive bases for rationality—have repercussion on the methodology of prediction in economics (which he analyzes in the case of microeconomics, mainly in organizations such as business firms).

b. Predictions are, for Simon, testable implications grounded in empirical knowledge. Thus, he maintains that insofar as the consequences of human behavior continue in the future we need to correct the predictions to objectively rational choices. But, on the basis of the realism of assumptions, prediction is not a pure inference based on optimal conditions,[14] because human decision-making is rooted in processes that seek the strategy of *satisficing* rather than of optimizing. Thus, in order to make an adequate economic prediction, we need to know some things which belong to the natural environment (e.g., the weather), others related with the social and political sphere beyond economics (e.g., a revolution), in addition to the behavior

[14] "Human beings (and other creatures) do not behave optimally for their fitness, because they are wholly incapable of acquiring the knowledge and making the calculations that support optimization" (Simon 1993, p. 156).

of other economic actors (consumers, competitors, suppliers, etc.) who can have an influence in our own behaviors (Simon 1996, p. 35).

c. Comparing the framework on prediction of mainstream economics (i.e., maximization of subjective expected utility) and the platform on economic prediction associated to bounded rationality, there is—for Simon— a clear difference in the final outcome, which goes in favor of his empirical account ("behavioral economics") (cf. Chap. 8, Sect. 8.4). Thus, he thinks that, in spite of their limitations, economic predictions based on a structure of bounded rationality *fit* with a great number of events (Simon 1992b, p. 18), because that framework looks for the reality of economic behavior as it can be observed in economic life (Simon 1992a, p. 3).[15]

d. Revisability of the predictive process should be taken into account in order to deal with forecast error. The sources of error could be in our bounded rationality or in the phenomena of economic behavior (i.e., new occurrences or different happenings from those previously predicted). Then, besides the assessment of the probabilities of predicted events, we need to use *feedback* to correct unexpected phenomena. For Simon, "a system can be steered more accurately if it uses feedforward, based on predictions of the future, in combination with feedback, to correct the errors of the past. However, forming expectations to deal with uncertainty creates its own problems" (1996, p. 36).

If we compare this scheme—the interconnection of uncertainty, bounded rationality, and economic prediction—with the mainstream economics (the expected subjective utility approach), the balance tilts in favor of Simon in several aspects (Gonzalez 1997b, pp. 217–218). These improvements do not exclude the existence of some deficiencies in his contribution to economics, such as the restriction in favor of an instrumental rationality that does not contemplate the evaluative rationality or his insistence in behavior instead of activity when dealing with the subject matter of economics (Gonzalez 2003d).

1. Behavioral economics is better off than mainstream economics with respect to the realism of *assumptions*, because Simon's stress is on reflecting the economic reality as it is, instead of privileging the predictive success beyond the adequacy of the assumptions (as Friedman does). He tries to avoid drawing strong conclusions from few *a priori* assumptions. The emphasis on uncertainty and bounded rationality is completely pertinent to the problem of economic predictions, and the attempt to predict economic behavior from a deductive inference based on an irrefutable set of premises is a failure (Simon 1976, p. 146).

2. The nexus between economics and psychology makes sense not only for the case of a rational choice but also for predicting the results of the interactions of economic actors (Simon 1963a/1982), because economics is above all a *human activity*. Explanation and prediction of economic movements are related to the actions of the members of society and the interaction of their activities (Sen 1986, p. 14). Moreover, the Nobel Prize awarded in 2002 to Daniel Kahneman reinforces the value

[15] "Because game theory is intrinsically unable to make specific predictions of behaviour from the postulates of rationality, in order to understand behaviour we must look at the empirical phenomena to see how people actually play games" (Simon 1992b, p. 25).

of this kind of research (Tversky et al. 1990; Kahneman et al. 1990). He is a firm supporter of bounded rationality and behavioral economics (Kahneman 2003), who analyzes the problem of prediction (Kahneman and Tversky 1973; Kahneman and Snell 1990), and works specifically in this field of interaction between economics and psychology (Tversky and Kahneman 1981).

3. Although prediction has an incisive role in economics, because the development of economic activities requires anticipation and, if possible, the control of future events; it seems clear that not all economics is related to prediction, even in the sphere of "descriptive" or "positive" economics. In addition, Simon has emphasized the need of *prescription* in systems modeling (1990a), which directly affects the characterization of economics and gives it a twofold relation. On the one hand, it is connected with the main characteristics of applied economics, insofar as economic policy-making requires prescriptions (as it is developed in Chap. 12); and on the other hand, prescription modeling reinforces the idea of economics as a science of the artificial.[16]

4. Even though the success of an economic prediction is very important (mainly the values of accuracy and precision), the crucial point in evaluating economic predictions is the reliability of the process—the *method*—used to make predictions, rather than the rigor itself of the result. Thus, prediction based on bounded rationality can avoid the main problems of the instrumentalist position (held, among others, by M. Friedman),[17] because it is possible to get success in the outcome without realism of the assumptions (as the logic of conditionals teaches us about the possibility of getting truth on false bases). The guarantee of reliability depends mainly on the predictive process and, therefore, in the kind of models used.[18]

Therefore, each of the four economists analyzed in this chapter has different views on central issues on prediction. (1) Semantically, in some of them prediction appears to be disconnected from the time factor: Friedman accepts the use of prediction to refer to an event in the past, and Simon agrees on testable implications that are not related to the future. (2) Epistemologically, there is a noticeable difference in regard to the acceptance of the absence of realism of the assumptions (Friedman) and the constant emphasis on empirical knowledge as a key element for economics (Simon). (3) Methodologically, the difference is even more remarkable: Hicks denies the scientific character of economics, Buchanan splits it into two domains (subjective and objective), and Friedman gives economics an equivalent status to physics. (4) Axiologically, there is also a clear difference between seeing prediction as a scientific aim *inter alia* (Simon) and considering prediction as pivotal to economics as a science (Friedman).

---

[16] Herbert Simon emphasizes economics as a science of the artificial, understood as a science of design, cf. Simon (1996, pp. 25–49, 111–138, 164).

[17] On the methodological instrumentalism on scientific prediction, cf. Gonzalez (1995, pp. 43–50).

[18] The analysis of predictive methods and the role of models in economic predictions is made in Chap. 10.

6.3 The Underlying General Methodology of These Approaches

Most of the discussions concerning the role of prediction in economics rely on the idea, expressly formulated by Friedman,[19] of prediction as the aim of science, in general, and of economics, in particular. This *predictivist thesis* upholds two important claims: (positive) economics is a science, and prediction is its ultimate goal. By contrast, Hicks maintains almost the opposite view: that economics still is not a science, because it is on the edge of science and on the edge of history. Thus, for him, it is more a discipline than a science, and "most, if not all, economic predictions are essentially weak predictions" (Hicks 1986, p. 97).

Between both authors is the option defended by Buchanan: he accepts the existence of *predictive science* of the "orthodox model" (positive economics) as well as a *subjective economics*, whose domain is located within the boundaries between the positive economics and the speculative thinking of moral philosophy (Buchanan 1982/1987, p. 68). This "subjective economics" is not a predictive one. Meanwhile, Simon's perspective—the wary attitude—assumes that economics is a science, but he has a concern regarding the use of prediction as a test for evaluating if economics (mainly economic theory) is a science. Therefore, they have very different conceptions on the role of prediction in economics.

6.3.1 *From the Absence of Consensus to an Alternative View*

Contrasting the views of these four Nobel laureates (Friedman, Hicks, Buchanan, and Simon) with *the* alternative to them will be the task of this section, followed by some central tenets of the alternative in the next section. Each of the conceptions analyzed here (predictivist thesis, quasi-scientific option, dualist posture, and wary attitude) has the support—implicit or explicit—of other economists and reveals the absence of consensus on this important issue of economics. The problems that they raise are basic, because they affect crucial points, such as the scientific character of economics as a whole, the existence of two different methodologies (objective or predictive, and subjective or non-predictive), or the status of economic predictions (similarity or non-similarity with physical predictions).

To put it differently, these conceptions on the role of prediction—especially as a scientific test of economics—raise the problem of the theoretical basis of prediction in economics, in general, and in economic theory, in particular. They also display the link between prediction and the subject matter of economics, because the underlying questions (such as the problem of the repetition of phenomena, the possibility

[19] "The ultimate goal of a positive science is the development of a 'theory' or 'hypothesis' that yields valid and meaningful (i.e., non-truistic) predictions about phenomena not yet observed" (Friedman 1953, p. 7).

of future alteration of predicted event, or the existence of diverse kinds of predictions) are directly connected with what could be its subject matter.[20]

My attempt here is to shed light on the theoretical basis of prediction in economics, taking into account the four positions (predictivist, quasi-scientific, dualist, and wary attitude) and to offer bases for an alternative to them from a methodological point of view, a conception that will be enlarged in other chapters (mainly, Chap. 9). This *alternative* has its axis in the idea of economics as a science whose subject matter is, primarily, actual human activity developing within a concrete sphere (i.e., exchanges, commodities, etc.) and is endowed with specific characteristics which makes it different from other connected activities (political, historical, sociological, ecological, etc.).[21]

Based upon that subject matter, only secondarily economics does prediction. Thus, this science emphasizes the study of phenomena not yet observed which are directly linked to present and past actions and, therefore, heavily dependent on mathematical calculus. But the access to future knowledge is possible by means of our present knowledge and depends upon it. Consequently, the research on future economic events is limited—at the very least—by present knowledge as well as by the reality itself that is predicted (i.e., the type of action and the existence of links with the economic activity which are known).

Certainly prediction, as a characteristic factor of scientific theories which can be diversified in three levels (aim, process, and result), requires making the constraints explicit—among them, the assumptions—because these are in some way their bedrock. This does not mean that generating predictions without the realism of assumptions would be impossible; it would be a risky activity, and in no way does lack of realism seem to be the usual element of scientific research. For these reasons, Friedman's proposals of a pure predictive effectiveness without realism of economic assumptions are clearly untenable (1953, pp. 16–30).

Moreover, a characteristic landmark of scientific theories—and this is valid for economic theories—is the progressive attempt of increasing truthlikeness, and this end is not attainable without trying to get the adequacy of assumptions to reality. Realism of assumptions does not guarantee by itself the goal of a successful prediction, but the risk of predicting without realism of assumptions is obviously greater.

For an adequate characterization of prediction in economics, it should be considered as a set of methodological elements. First, in contrast to the instrumentalist point of view, it seems that scientific prediction belongs to a wider context of several values (accuracy, precision, reliability, etc.) in order *to know* an economic reality, rather than to be an end that should be sought as such by itself. In addition, predictions need to be accompanied by the realism of assumptions. Second, every prediction includes an informative content: it can contribute to the *evaluation* of a hypothesis; so it is an important way for testing economic hypotheses, and it cannot be something alternative or substitutive for explanation: predictions have

[20] "The question of prediction in Economics involves, or brings together, most of the main questions as to what sort of subject Economics is" (Hutchison 1977, p. 8).

[21] A more explicit account can be found in Chap. 7.

a relevance of their own. Third, prediction is not *eo ipso* better than explanation from a confirmatory point of view. Nevertheless, prediction could have a special methodological attractiveness when it is successful.[22] Fourth, prediction is a human activity that cannot avoid the context in which it is made. This is specifically relevant in economics, where predicting is intrinsically connected with decision-making (Gonzalez 1996c).

With the emphasis on human activity, the problem of scientific prediction in economics appears more complex than in the predictivist thesis, and the primacy of the predictive aim does not seem to be necessary. But it is also more complicated than the wary attitude suggests, because "economic activity" is a richer concept than "economic behavior." (cf. Chap. 8, Sect. 8.4). In order to clarify this question, which may solve the controversy between the predictivist position and the other options—and, therefore, offer the alternative—the realm of scientific prediction should be clear (cf. Part I, mainly Chap. 2).

Is there "scientific prediction" in economics? The four different approaches to the problem of prediction in economics (predictivist thesis, quasi-scientific option, dualist posture, and wary attitude), in spite of their divergences, support the idea of prediction as *one important* aim among others in economics. In addition, they do not disagree regarding the presence of scientific features in economic predictions. Even more, three replies coincide in emphasizing the scientific character of prediction in economics, at least for positive economics; the other one deems the characteristics of prediction in economics insufficient to be considered as a "science," due to the problem of predictability of future economic phenomena.

Obviously, it is possible to predict economic activity insofar as the variables could be under our control. In my judgment, this possibility is clear in economic activity considered in "isolation" from other activities, or even as something which may be considered in purely ideal terms. In this case, the economic model appears to be more accurate and precise, like a mere calculation, usually putting aside the variables that presumably could interfere in the real case. From this point of view, the prediction (or even the "foresight," in the sense used in Chap. 2) of future phenomena is available, because it is possible to have an accurate and precise account of the variables related to the event and, therefore, a clear knowledge of the outcome.

But this kind of economic model is linked to "idealized" settings. Economics, as a real activity that is connected with many other activities, usually has more problems in giving an accurate prediction;[23] even more, the possibility itself of predicting could be argued. The variables that are under our control could be affected by other variables that are not, either because it is not possible at this moment to

[22] On this issue, cf. Chap. 2, Sect. 2.1.2, and Chap. 4, Sect. 4.4.

[23] Robert M. Solow has pointed out that "*much of the most interesting macroeconomic theory being done today* is an attempt to investigate coordination failures in the economy. They are much like external effects, or what in the U.S. academic circles are called thin market externalities" (Solow 1991, p. 25).

know of their existence, or for the (temporary) impossibility of getting information about them.

When this second possibility appears, it is said to be a "not predictable" phenomenon (on the basis of present knowledge) or even a strictly "unpredictable" event (in any time). Thus, economics as activity could have—at least, theoretically—not predictable events or even literally unpredictable events. However, if a phenomenon could be explained afterwards, then it could be predicted previously (for example, something extremely rare). Subsequently, the use of "unpredictable" should be restricted to the case of complete impossibility.

Economics has, then, two main kinds of problems in this field:[24] on the one hand, those derived from the present situation of our knowledge about economic affairs (i.e., the insufficient knowledge of a "knowable" reality); and, on the other, the intrinsic mutability of the economic reality, mainly when this is within the real sphere of economics as activity interdependent on others, which makes the knowledge defective due, precisely, to the complexity of economic reality. Both kinds of problems are not exclusive of prediction in economics, because—in some way or another—they are in other social sciences as well as in other sciences of the artificial.

Behind these problems is something basic which is frequently forgotten in economic predictions (and forecasting): the human and social character of economic activity and its interdependence with other human activities. So, as something *human* developing in the social environment, it cannot have the *same* characteristics as the natural phenomena. In other words, the continuous efforts to develop economic predictions, as a mere calculation, are not well focused due to the existence of human factors (qualitative ones), which cannot be expressed in "physical" (quantitative) terms.

6.3.2 Some Central Tenets

Following the theoretical basis of prediction in economics pointed out, based on a pragmatic realism combined with a methodological approach open to objectivity, there is an *alternative* to the instrumentalism of the predictivist thesis, the non-consideration of economics as a science by the quasi-scientific option, the acceptance of a "subjective (non-predictive) economics" by the dualist posture as well as the wary attitude towards the use of prediction as a test for economics as a science. In my judgment, the alternative should be articulated with some central aspects.

1. Economics is a science whose subject matter is primarily actual *human activity* developing within a concrete sphere and, only secondly, does it study the phenomena not yet observed. If economics is understood as a human activity, as a real interaction among the agents in this sphere (goods and services, exchange and commodities, etc.), then "prediction" should be just one of the aims to be considered and, presumably, not the first one. In other words, prediction is axiologically

[24] A more detailed analysis can be found in Chap. 11.

important for research in economic theory and also in applied economics, but it is not necessarily the main purpose of economics.

2. Scientific prediction is above all a methodological concept that is connected to a possible or real economic event. As such, scientific prediction needs to be based on a precise language, a logically well-formed structure, objective knowledge, and orientation towards an aim. Economics may have all these ingredients and may predict economic activity, insofar as the variables might be under (a sufficient degree of) control; meanwhile the situation is more complex in the realm of "economics as activity" (interwoven with other activities). The possibility of control is clear in economic activity considered in "isolation" from other activities, or even as something which may be considered in purely ideal terms; whereas in other cases it is more difficult or even completely problematic. Thus, the existence of limits in economic predictions is commonly accepted (cf. Chap. 11, Sect. 11.3).

3. Even though there could be some similarities, economic predictions are in principle different from physical predictions. This is based on the peculiarities of the subject matter of each one as well as the reality itself to be predicted (in one case originated by human activity, whereas in the other case it commonly has a complete independent origin). Thus, the question is not to maintain that it is not a science because it does not follow the patterns of physics, mainly Newtonian mechanics. The route should be another: it is a different kind of scientific endeavor (a social science and a science of the artificial). However, there is a methodological convergence through quantitative predictions of statistical economics and econometrics.

4. *De facto*, on the basis of the reality that is predicted, economic predictions are not reducible to merely quantitative ones. So, besides the quantitative predictions produced by mathematical calculations, economics needs qualitatively based predictions (mainly, in welfare economics). Both—quantitative and qualitative—can predict objective aspects of economic reality. In some phenomena, such as business cycles, the qualitative factors can have more relevance than in other economic events.

5. According to the control of variables—and, hence, its reliability—the role of prediction in economics has different possibilities. Among them are "foresights" (when the control is "maximum"), "predictions," and "forecasts" (when the control is "minimum") that accompany "planning." A *foresight* takes place when there is a clear control: it shows the state of a variable within a period of time, when that variable is directly or indirectly under our control (e.g., the collection of some kind of taxes). *Prediction* concerns what, strictly speaking, is not known: it displays the state of a variable within a period of time, when the variable is not under our control (e.g., the rate of inflation in the United States in the first term of next year or the price of fuel if there is a new war in the Middle East). *Forecast* is a prediction with a margin of error associated with it (e.g., the rate of unemployment in the United Kingdom in next December will be between such and such per cent of the active population) (cf. Chap. 2, Sect. 2.4.2, and Fernandez Valbuena 1990, pp. 388–389).

6. The basis for the methodological development of prediction includes the analysis of how economics progresses *de facto* and the indications about how it *ought to be* developed. (a) In the first case, it is the twofold use of economic predictions:

as a test for economic theories and as a guide for patterns oriented towards policy-making. The use of prediction as a means of testing economic hypotheses has been emphasized in the methodology of mainstream economics, as can be seen in Friedman's approach. The role as a guide for patterns oriented towards policy-making requires another methodological notion: prescription,[25] which is central in applied economics. (b) In the realm on how economics *ought to be* developed, a key place belongs to economic models, because they deal with the resemblance of economic reality and the construction of future designs in order to consider the appropriate policy. Economic models should be used to improve our knowledge of future events, mainly in the long term.

7. Generally, economic predictions are not unconditional but rather conditional and weak. However, economic predictions are not *eo ipso* essentially weak predictions (especially in the case of "foresight"). Instead of emphasizing the comparison with physics, and in order to recognize the existence of weak predictions in economics, the task should be how to make conditional and strong predictions in this social (as well as artificial) science. The bases are mainly semantic and epistemological: they are in the language and knowledge of objective elements of economic activity (cf. Chap. 7).

6.3.3 The Issue of the Convergence with Natural Sciences

By means of the development of statistical economics and econometrics, where probability calculus (classical and Bayesian) is crucial, there is a methodological convergence with natural sciences (among them, physics). Economic models (mainly in applied economics) and natural models (among them, physical ones) rely on probability calculus for predicting. To some extent, they share the problem of the accuracy and precision of predictions, depending on the kind of event that they predict (e.g., in earthquakes there is no accuracy on when they will happen, but there is a clear precision on where they could happen).

There are also some physical phenomena whose predictability is questioned (e.g., the turbulence movement of liquids, the "butterfly effect," Poincaré's problem of the three bodies, the movement of a pendulum out of its place, etc.). The Theory of Chaos focuses on the predictability of diverse physical events and gives reasons why the prediction of certain phenomena may be impossible (Cvitanovic 1984). It has led others to consider whether systems like economic ones may be chaotic.

Regarding this problem, Simon maintains that we "don't know whether the economy is a chaotic system" (1989, p. 99). He deems that the statistical tests applied to time-series (the money supply, stock prices or other economic series) to distinguish between simple randomness and chaos (and, then, unpredictability) are

[25] Cf. Chap. 12, which deals with methodological as well as axiological aspects of prescription in economics.

inconclusive. For him, the implications of the developments for the modeling of large socio-economic systems have hardly begun to be digested.

The main implication, for systems that we have reason to suspect are divergent or chaotic, is to give up prediction as the primary goal of modeling. "Chaos is essentially a statistical condition. It does not imply that *anything goes*. We may, for example, despair of tracing the future course of business cycles without renouncing the goal of making statements about the long-run development of an economy. For instance, we might make perfectly sound statements about the upper limits on per capita GNP without being able to say how closely, or when, these limits will be approached" (Simon 1990a, p. 8).

Terence Hutchison insists on the difference between economic and physical predictions: "economists cannot and will never be able to predict with the very high degrees of probability and accuracy which many natural scientists can achieve for their predictions" (1977, p. 10). In this comparison, he seems to assume that economics has both a lower knowledge of the reality that studies and a subject matter with a greater complexity than physics.

Hutchison sees increasingly important kinds of degrees of *interdependence* among economic factors, making economic prediction more difficult: (a) in regard to market activity, and (b) as between economic and social factors (Hutchison 1977, p. 31). His position stresses fundamental differences between economics and natural sciences.[26] At the same time, he emphasizes that "if all economic action or behavior was totally unpredictable, policy-making could only be sheer guess-work" (Hutchison 1977, p. 9).

It seems, therefore, that in spite of the cases where there is a convergence between economic and physical predictions, some important differences still remain. Usually, the differences are pointed out in the context of the comparison with Newtonian mechanics, which is considered by the economist as an excellent characterization of physics. Thus, the physical and economic spheres show an epistemological and ontological diversity. This diversity is reflected by scientific knowledge: human and social events depend on *our activity*, whereas the natural occurrences do not depend—at least, in principle—on our activity.[27]

Both can have unexpected phenomena, but their "unexpectedness" is different, because the human factor has its own peculiarities, and its spectrum of possibilities

---

[26] Hutchison considers that "in confronting and recognising such possibly serious difficulties looming over the future of economists' predictive performance and capacity, we are simply meeting up again with an aspect of the fundamental differences between economics and the more 'developed' natural sciences. Because of constancies in their basic materials, predictive capacity, once attained, regarding many physical or chemical phenomena, can be preserved, added to and accumulated to an extent significantly beyond what is possible in the social sciences. In economics and the social sciences it might well be that painfully and fleetingly achieved predictions and predictive capacity may not only lose practice relevance but may break down and even become more difficult to replace, because the basic material might be becoming more difficult, or impossible to predict" (Hutchison 1977, pp. 32–33).

[27] There are some cases, such as the evolution of climate change, where there is a repercussion of human activity on the natural phenomenon.

(due to its interrelation with other human activities) is wider than in the natural case. This difference can be assessed with the type of explanation that is offered after the phenomena. In effect, the reply to the question about why a physical phenomenon has happened could be unique (when the phenomenon is well known later on) and accepted by the scientific community as non-controversial (as the Newtonian laws which remain within the Einsteinian framework); whereas in the case of an economic phenomenon, it could have several replies (sometimes completely opposite) and moreover controversial ones (not only in that moment, but also later on).[28]

Stressing the differences between prediction in economics and physics has several consequences. One would be the necessity of studying the peculiarities of the subject matter of each one. The alternative to the four answers, which can be found in Friedman, Hicks, Buchanan, and Simon, not only needs to take into account such differences, but also has to go deeper into the specificity of the scope of economics. Simon has pointed out that Newtonian mechanics (and the law of falling bodies) is not the only model for a science and "it seems, indeed, not to be the right one for our purposes" (Simon 1979, p. 510).

In my judgment, economics can look for models in natural sciences, doing so without the mentality of pure imitation. Thus, instead of maintaining that it is not science because economics does not follow the Newtonian models, the solution should take another route: to consider other scientific models, seeing economics as a social science (as well as a science of the artificial), with specific characteristics which distinguishes it from a natural science. Within this context, it seems to me that the study of predictability in economics needs to take into account the distinction between "economic activity" and "economics as activity" among others activities (sociological, political, etc.). The scientific character of prediction in economics could be feasible in the first case, whereas it is difficult in the second, due to the interrelation with other human activities.

References

Becker, G. S. 1976. *The economic approach to human behavior*. Chicago: University of Chicago Press.

Becker, G. S. 1981. *A treatise on the family*. Cambridge: Harvard University Press.

Becker, G. S., and G. J. Stigler. 1977. De gustibus non est disputandum. *American Economic Review* 67:76–90.

Blaug, M. 1980. *The methodology of economics: Or how economists explain*. Cambridge: Cambridge University Press.

Blaug, M. 1988. John Hicks and the methodology of economics. In *The Popperian legacy in economics,* ed. N. de Marchi, 183–195. Cambridge: Cambridge University Press.

Buchanan, J. M. 1982. The domain of subjective economics: Between predictive science and moral philosophy. In *Method, process and Austrian economics,* ed. I. M. Kirzner. Lexington:

[28] A well-known example in Economics is the controversy about causes of the Great Depression of 1929: Keynesians and their opponents still have different explanations.

Lexington Books. (Reprinted in Buchanan, J. M. 1987. *Economics: Between predictive science and moral philosophy,* 67–80. College Station: Texas A&M University Press).

Buchanan, J. M. 1987a. *Economics: Between predictive science and moral philosophy*. College Station: Texas A&M University Press.

Buchanan, J. M. 1987b. What should economist do? In *Economics: Between predictive science and moral philosophy,* ed. J. M. Buchanan, 21–33. College Station: Texas A&M University Press.

Buchanan, J. M. 1989. The state of economic science. In *The state of economic Science. Views of six noble laureates,* ed. W. Sichel, 79–95. Kalamazoo: W. E. Upjohn Institute for Employment Research.

Buchanan, J. M. 1996. Economics as a public science. In *Foundations of research in economics: How do economists do research,* ed. S. G. Medema and W. J. Samuels, 30–36. Brookfield: Elgar.

Caldwell, B. J. 1982. *Beyond positivism: Economic methodology in the twentieth century*. London: Allen and Unwin. (revised ed., 1994. London: Routledge).

Collins, L. ed. 1976. *The use of models in the social sciences*. London: Tavistock.

Cvitanovic, P., ed. 1984. *Universality in chaos*. Bristol: Hilger.

Fernandez Valbuena, S. 1990. Predicción y Economía. In *Aspectos metodológicos de la investigación científica*. 2nd ed. ed. W. J. Gonzalez, 385–405. Madrid-Murcia: Ediciones Universidad Autónoma de Madrid and Publicaciones Universidad de Murcia.

Friedman, M. 1953. The methodology of positive economics. In *Essays in positive economics,* M. Friedman, 3–43. Chicago: University of Chicago Press (6th repr., 1969).

Gonzalez, W. J. 1995. Reichenbach's concept of prediction. *International Studies in the Philosophy of Science* 9 (1): 37–58.

Gonzalez, W. J. 1996c. On the theoretical basis of prediction in economics. *Journal of Social Philosophy* 27 (3): 201–228.

Gonzalez, W. J. 1997b. Rationality in economics and scientific predictions: A critical reconstruction of bounded rationality and its role in economic predictions. *Poznan Studies in the Philosophy of Science* 61:205–232.

Gonzalez, W. J. 1998b. Prediction and prescription in economics: A philosophical and methodological approach. *Theoria* 13 (2): 321–345.

Gonzalez, W. J. 2003d. Racionalidad y Economía: De la racionalidad de la Economía como Ciencia a la racionalidad de los agentes económicos. In *Racionalidad, historicidad y predicción en Herbert A. Simon,* ed. W. J. Gonzalez, 65–96. A Coruña: Netbiblo.

Gonzalez, W. J. 2007b. Análisis de las Ciencias de Diseño desde la racionalidad limitada, la predicción y la prescripción. In *Las Ciencias de Diseño: Racionalidad limitada, predicción y prescripción,* ed. W. J. Gonzalez, 3–38. A Coruña: Netbiblo.

Gonzalez, W. J. 2008. Rationality and prediction in the sciences of the artificial: Economics as a design science. In *Reasoning, rationality, and probability,* ed. M. C. Galavotti, R. Scazzieri, and P. Suppes, 165–186. Stanford: CSLI Publications.

Gonzalez, W. J. 2012b. Methodological universalism in science and its limits: Imperialism versus complexity. In *Thinking about provincialism in thinking, Poznan Studies in the Philosophy of the Sciences and the Humanities,* vol. 100, ed. K. Brzechczyn and K. Paprzycka, 155–175. Amsterdam: Rodopi.

Grunberg, E., and F. Modigliani. 1954. The predictability of social events. *Journal of Political Economy* 62:465–478.

Haavelmo, T. 1944. The probability approach in econometrics. *Supplement to Econometrica* 12:1–118.

Hausman, D. M., ed. 1984. *The philosophy of economics. An anthology*. Cambridge: Cambridge University Press.

Hausman, D. M., ed. 1994a. *The philosophy of economics. An anthology*. 2nd ed. Cambridge: Cambridge University Press.

Hausman, D. M., ed. 2008. *The philosophy of economics. An anthology*. 3rd ed. Cambridge: Cambridge University Press.

Hicks, J. 1983a. "Revolutions" in economics. In *Classics and moderns. Collected essays on economic theory,* vol. III, J. Hicks, 3–16. Cambridge: Harvard University Press.

Hicks, J. 1983c. A discipline not a science. In *Classics and moderns. Collected essays on economic theory,* vol. III, J. Hicks, 364–375. Cambridge: Harvard University Press.

Hicks, J. 1986. Is economics a science? In *Foundations of economics. Structures of inquiry and economic theory,* ed. M. Baranzini and R. Scazzieri, 91–101. Oxford: Blackwell.

Hutchison, T. W. 1964. *"Positive" economics and policy objectives*. London: Allen and Unwin.

Hutchison, T. W. 1977. On prediction and economic knowledge. In *Knowledge and ignorance in economics,* T. W. Hutchison, 8–33, 145–151. Oxford: Blackwell.

Kahneman, D. 2003. Maps of bounded rationality: Psychology for behavioral economics. *The American Economic Review* 93 (5): 1449–1475.

Kahneman, D., and A. Tversky. 1973. On the psychology of prediction. *Psychological Review* 80:237–251.

Kahneman, D., and J. Snell. 1990. Predicting utility. In *Insights in decision making,* ed. R. M. Hogarth, 295–310. Chicago: University of Chicago Press.

Kahneman, D., J. L. Knetsch, and R. H. Thaler. 1990. Experimental tests of the endowment effect and the Coase theorem. *Journal of Political Economy* 98 (6): 1325–1348. (Reprinted in 1993 ed. Hey, J. D., and Loomes, G. *Recent developments in experimental economics,* vol. I, 206-229. Aldershot: Elgar).

Morgan, M. S. 1990. *The history of econometric ideas*. Cambridge: Cambridge University Press.

Poirier, D. J. ed. 1994. *The methodology of econometrics,* 2 vols. Aldershot: Elgar.

Radnitzky, G., and P. Bernholz, ed. 1987. *Economic imperialism: The economic method applied outside the field of economics*. New York: Paragon House.

Rescher, N. 1978. *Scientific progress. A philosophical essay on the economics of research in natural science*. Oxford: Blackwell.

Rescher, N. 1989. *Cognitive economy. The economic dimension of the theory of knowledge*. Pittsburgh: University of Pittsburgh Press.

Rescher, N. 1996. *Priceless knowledge? Natural science in economic perspective*. Savage: University Press of America.

Sen, A. 1986. Prediction and economic theory. In *Predictability in science and society,* ed. J. Mason, P. Mathias, and J. H. Westcott, 3–23. London: The Royal Society and The British Academy.

Simon, H. A. 1963a. Economics and psychology. In *Psychology: A study of a science,* vol. 6, ed. S. Koch, 715–752. New York: McGraw Hill. (Reprinted in Simon, H. A. 1982. *Models of bounded rationality,* vol. 2: *Behavioral economics and business organization,* 318–355. Cambridge: The MIT Press).

Simon, H. A. 1972. Theories of bounded rationality. In *Decision and organization,* ed. C. B. McGuire and R. Radner, 161–176. Amsterdam: North-Holland. (Reprinted in Simon, H. A. 1982. *Models of bounded rationality,* vol. 2: *Behavioral economics and business organization,* 408–423. Cambridge: The MIT Press).

Simon, H. A. 1976. From substantive to procedural rationality. In *Method and appraisal in economics,* ed. S. Latsis, 129–148. Cambridge: Cambridge University Press.

Simon, H. A. 1979. Rational decision making in business organizations. *American Economic Review* 69 (4): 493–513. (Reprinted in Simon, H. A. 1982. *Models of bounded rationality,* vol. 2: *Behavioral economics and business organization,* 474–494. Cambridge: The MIT Press).

Simon, H. A. 1989. The state of economic science. In *The state of economic science. Views of six Nobel laureates,* ed. W. Sichel, 97–110. Kalamazoo: W. E. Upjohn Institute for Employment Research.

Simon, H. A. 1990a. Prediction and prescription in systems modeling. *Operations Research* 38:7–14. (Reprinted in Simon, H. A. 1997. *Models of bounded rationality,* vol. 3: *Empirically grounded economic reason,* 115–128. Cambridge: The MIT Press).

Simon, H. A. 1992a. Introductory comment. In *Economics, bounded rationality and the cognitive revolution,* ed. M. Egidi and R. Marris, 3–7. Aldershot: Elgar.

Simon, H. A. 1992b. Colloquium with H. A. Simon. In *Economics, bounded rationality and the cognitive revolution,* ed. M. Egidi and R. Marris, 8–36. Aldershot: Elgar.

Simon, H. A. 1993. Altruism and economics. *American Economic Review* 83 (2): 156–161. (Reprinted as Altruism and economics: Social implications. Simon, H. A. 1997. *Models of bounded rationality,* vol. 3: *Empirically grounded economic reason,* 257–265. Cambridge: The MIT Press).

Simon, H. A. 1996. *The sciences of the artificial.* 3rd ed. Cambridge: The MIT Press. (1st ed., 1969; 2nd ed., 1981).

Solow, R. M. 1991. *The rate of return and the rate of interest.* Stockholm: The Industrial Institute for Economic and Social Research.

Tversky, A., and D. Kahneman. 1981. The framing of decisions and the psychology of choice. *Science* 211:453–458.

Tversky, A., P. Slovic, and D. Kahneman. 1990. The causes of preference reversal. *American Economic Review,* 80:204–217. (Reprinted in J. D. Hey and G. Loomes, ed. 1993. *Recent developments in experimental economics,* vol. I, 147–160. Aldershot: Elgar).

Chapter 7
The Problem of Prediction in Economics from the Perspective of Action Theory

Undoubtedly, the problem of what economic prediction *is* and *ought to be* directly affects the central topics in economics. In this regard, the issue can be considered from different angles (semantic, logical, epistemological, methodological, ontological, axiological, and even ethical).[1] Commonly, it focuses on the *methodological* debate of the scientific character of economic predictions. Very often, the discussion follows two steps: first, on prediction as a test for knowing whether economics is a science or not and, second—if it is—as a means to establish the kind of science that it is.

This specification of the *scientific status* of economics is generally connected with the characterization of its *subject matter*. Both aspects are interdependent insofar as "the question of prediction in economics involves, or brings together, most of the main questions as to what sort of subject economics is" (Hutchison 1977, p. 8). This chapter seeks to outline elements of economic reality—the *clarification* of the subject matter of this science—in order to shed light on prediction in economics and to enlarge the analysis made in previous chapters. Here the aim is not to suggest a change of the subject matter of economics, rather to consider the *fundamental issues* of economics related to economic predictions.

7.1 Scientific Status of Economics and Action Theory

It seems clear that the methodological debate on prediction is linked to the controversy of the scientific status of economics. In fact, as pointed out in Chap. 6 (Sect. 6.2), the solutions given to this problem by important economists, including Nobel Prize laureates (such as Milton Friedman, John Hicks, James Buchanan, and Herbert Simon), are quite different: predictivist thesis, quasi-scientific option, dualist posture, and wary attitude. Furthermore, the crucial question—Is economics a science?—receives quite divergent answers.

[1] On the ethical dimension, see Granger (2012, p. 326). He is focused in what he calls "forecasting."

W. J. Gonzalez, *Philosophico-Methodological Analysis of Prediction and its Role in Economics*, Theory and Decision Library A: 50, DOI 10.1007/978-3-319-08885-3_7

Moreover, the characterization of the subject matter of economics is not neutral towards the interpretation of what an economic prediction is and ought to be.[2] In effect, the role of economic prediction is linked to the conception of the scope of economics. This point appears explicitly in Ph. Deane: "if economics is a science (…), it is a science whose powers of prediction and control are limited, largely because the phenomena it seeks to explain are subject to persistent change and often for reasons that may lie outside the traditional boundaries of the discipline" (1983, pp. 11–12).

7.1.1 The Bifurcation: Success versus Unreliability

Generally, in the methodological debate on the role of predictions in economics, there is a tension between two leading orientations among economists: on the one side, the stress on the importance of the success of economic predictions, which includes the acceptance of their reliability (Friedman 1953, pp. 8–9); and, on the other side, the more realistic attitude of recognizing not only the present insufficiency of prediction in economics to comprise the whole realm studied, but also its frequent unreliability (Sen 1986, p. 3).

Those who accept the first view see economics as a science, even one like physics (i.e., with precise predictions in conformity with experience); whereas the supporters of the second perspective are more critical and delimit the differences with physics (i.e., less reliable predictions within a different scope than natural science). Both tendencies concerning the role of prediction in economics have their roots in its subject matter. In effect, the emphasis on the importance of its success as well as on the recognition of its insufficiency and unreliability are related to elements of economic reality.

To be sure, the predictions of interest for the economists are the successful predictions. It does not mean that failures in predicting do not occur. On the contrary, failures in economic predictions are more frequent than successes. But, for economics to be a science, a *sufficient condition* is the presence of some successful predictions. Meanwhile, the expectation that scientific theories should improve in predictive precision has been considered "the most innocuous epistemological requirement of any science" (Rosenberg 1992, p. xiv). It assumes that even the best theories can include failures in predicting.

Nevertheless, the scientific test is, in principle, in the successful predictions not in the failed predictions (although it is quite possible to learn from predictive errors in order to improve economic models) (cf. Chap. 11). Thus, it is reasonable to demand that economic theories should show improvements in predictive power. It seems that the improvement is usually greater when successful predictions are made on the basis of the core of the theory rather than when they are made with the help of auxiliary hypotheses.

[2] A clear example is G. Shackle, who conceives economics as subjective and therefore non-predictive. Cf. Shackle (1972, 1979).

Furthermore, successful predictions should be seen in economics as basic science—economic theory—within a wider context of a human activity with ends and means, instead of merely focusing on the outcomes (as methodological instrumentalism does). In addition, in economics as applied science, prediction needs to take into account aims, processes, and results of the task of solving specific problems. Thereafter comes the facet of applying the economic knowledge in the variety of historically changeable settings, which also requires prediction (i.e., for the actual policy-making).

7.1.2 *The Realm of the Reality to be Predicted*

Once it is accepted that they could be scientific predictions, and that they might be made in the case of economics (Chap. 2), a problem arises concerning the specification of the realm of the reality that should be predicted in this science. Economic reality may, in itself, be one from an ontological point of view; but—in my judgment—it is possible to draw some important distinctions about that reality, such as a semantic, epistemological, and methodological distinction between "economic activity" and "economics as activity" (Gonzalez 1994).

In the former—"economic activity"—the language, knowledge, and methods are used to pay attention to the economic factors in themselves, putting aside its interrelation with others. In this sense, there is certain "isolation" of the economic reality. In the latter—"economics as activity"—it is necessary to take into account the interdependence of the activity of economics with respect to other factors (political, social, cultural, historical, etc.). This aspect opens economics to an interdisciplinary approach, which is used *de facto* in some cases (such as population economics). Thus, the study has a broad scope: the language, type of knowledge, and method used include contributions of other sciences (mainly human and social ones).

Methodologically, in some conceptions of this science—commonly, mainstream economics and the Austrian school—the first approach is leading; whereas in other cases (such as the German historical school, Marxism, institutionalism—old and new—or recent views on rhetoric of economics) the social and historical aspects are considered essential to understand the economic reality. These different orientations give grounds for methodological controversies, such as the famous one between Carl Menger and Gustav von Schmoller (Gonzalez 1991a).

Undoubtedly, to view economics as a purely economic activity has the direct consequence of reducing the field to be studied. Certainly, this reduction of scope goes beyond the mere "idealization" or "abstraction" which accompanies every scientific model, economic or not.[3] Meanwhile, to emphasize economics as *an activity among others*, stressing the social or historical aspects as crucial for understanding economic reality, can blur the specificity of economics as a science.

---

[3] On economic models, cf. Chap. 10, Sect. 10.3.

We need both "economic activity" and "economics as activity," because even if economic reality can have a character of its own, it is, at the same time, connected with other human realities. Following the distinction between "economic activity" and "economics as activity," the problem of prediction in economics receives new light. This duality allows us to distinguish between a type of event that could be predicted objectively (with higher or lower levels of accuracy and precision) from that of another type whose predictability would be more difficult or doubtful. The scientific character of prediction in economics could be clear in the first case; it might be difficult to accept in the second. In this line, the analysis of that duality—economic activity and economics as a human activity among others—can contribute to clarifying the role of prediction in economics.

Microeconomics and macroeconomics are two different considerations of economic reality. Actually, they work on two levels of economic reality; but there is a common ground for both as well as many interrelations between them (they can be seen as a system). To some extent, economics has a similitude with biology, because microbiology and "macrobiology" (zoology, botanic, ecology, etc.) may research the same reality—a system—but in different levels and following diverse methods.

Thus, the theories of economic actors (micro) and the theories of economic markets (macro) have some links which allow us to connect the macroscopic (the market) with the microscopic (the actors) taking into account some composition laws. The agents (individual and social) are the simple components of the complex market, and hence proper explanatory elements (Simon 1963b/1984, pp. 245–246).[4] Economic activities have their origin in the microeconomic level and can reach the macroeconomic realm, which is an aggregation and interrelation of economic activities. The development of microeconomics helps, in principle, macroeconomics.

Presumably, the conception of "economics as activity" is more important in macroeconomics than in microeconomics, because the influences of other fields (sociological, cultural, political, etc.) could be stronger in that case. However, macroeconomic activity has, in principle, its roots in microeconomic activity: complex social actions habitually have their starting point in less complex social actions, and these are at the very end and can be the result of interrelation of individual actions within the social sphere. Usually, the changes at the macroeconomic level (e.g., shifts in policy matters such as taxes or variations in the international trade) are not tested by direct observation or through an experiment.[5] Commonly, they require the repercussion on the microeconomic level, i.e., their incidence in concrete actions and tendencies of agents—individual and social—in markets and organizations.[6]

---

[4] According to Hicks, "the market economy, in practice, is a credit economy; so it depends upon trust between man and man. There are numerous ways which have been invented for diminishing that dependence; but it cannot be eliminated. Among the faceless individuals who populate our pure models there is place for it; but the market economy cannot exist, as anything more than a random sequence of bargains, without it" (1983b, pp. 351–352).

[5] Regarding the role of experiments in economics, see Gonzalez (2007a) and Chap. 9.

[6] On the distinction between "markets" and "organizations," see Simon (1991b).

7.2 Economic Prediction from the Viewpoint of Action Theory

An analysis of economic prediction from the viewpoint of action theory is legitimate insofar as the subject matter of economics is human action, and the economic method involves predictions regarding to human activity in this domain. In effect, the core of the subject matter of economics is, primarily, actual *human activity* developing within a certain sphere (i.e., exchanges, commodities, etc.) and is endowed with characteristics which makes it different from other connected activities (political, historical, cultural, sociological, etc.). Secondarily, economics studies the *phenomena not yet observed* which are directly linked to present and past actions. Here prediction plays an important role: it provides access to future knowledge by means of our present knowledge. In fact, "much of economics is concerned with prediction" (Sen 1986, p. 3). Moreover, it is indispensable for planning.

Apart from the methodological approaches to prediction in economics, studied in Chap. 6, there is another focus of attention: the relation of prediction with the subject matter of economics. From this point of view, the prediction of economic activity is seen as an element that connects with the core of the *subject matter* of this science. The differences in the way of conceiving the role of prediction in economics are linked to distinct conceptions of this science. This can be seen in the conceptions defended by four relevant economists (Friedman, Hicks, Buchanan, and Simon) analyzed before.

According to the *predictive thesis* of Friedman, prediction has the primacy as scientific element.[7] He sees prediction as a crucial element: it is the aim of science in general, and economics in particular. In addition, he considers positive economics as objective as physics (Friedman 1953, p. 4). The *quasi-scientific* option of Hicks breaks such congeniality between natural sciences and social sciences, emphasizing that in economics there are not real scientific predictions and, therefore, physics and economics are in quite different realms.[8] The *dualist posture* of Buchanan allows a middle ground, because there is a part of economics that makes objective predictions, whereas another cannot make predictions at all (1982/1987, p. 70, and 1959/1987); so it seems that natural sciences and social ones may have room for a methodological convergence. The *wary attitude* of Simon takes a different way: "we should be wary of using prediction as a test of science, and especially of whether economics is a science, for an understanding of mechanisms does not guarantee predictability" (1989, p. 100). His underlying perspective emphasizes the specificity of social sciences—the realm of decision-making processes—in its comparison with natural sciences.[9]

[7] "The ultimate goal of a positive science is the development of a 'theory' or 'hypothesis' that yields valid and meaningful (i.e., non-truistic) predictions about phenomena not yet observed" (Friedman 1953, p. 7).

[8] "The facts which we study are not permanent, or repeatable, like the facts of the natural sciences; they change incessantly, and change without repetition" (Hicks 1983a, p. 4).

[9] "The social sciences have been accustomed to look for models in the most spectacular successes of the natural sciences. There is no harm in that, provided that it is not done in a spirit of slavish

7.2.1 The Subject Matter of Economics: From "Behavior" to "Activity"

Simon has pointed out important elements of this science, which he explicitly defines: "*economics* can be defined as the science that describes and predicts the behavior of the various kinds of economic man" (1963a/1982, p. 320). Although he is not behaviorist and reaffirms the importance of motivations, his definition uses the term "behavior" which is not—in my judgment—the most appropriate for the present aim (cf. Chap. 8, Sect. 8.4).

The undesirability of using "behavior" is due to its stress on the outer component of economic activity that reduces the importance of the inner aspect (or even sees it as irrelevant), which opens the door to a behavioral interpretation of economic reality (including similarities between human beings and animals in the sphere of economics) (Kagel et al. 1981), which is clearly insufficient for grasping central aspects of economic phenomenon in real life. For this aim, it seems preferable to use the terms of *activity*, which include an outer element (what I call "action") as well as the inner factor (the "acts": mental activity).[10]

As an underlying presupposition, this proposal supports that *action* and *behavior* could be distinguished from a general point of view, with a direct application in economics. I suggest reserving the term "action" for genuinely human undertakings (in principle, deliberate), because it includes intentionality and is connected with mental acts, and to use "behavior" for the cases where there is no intentionality (or at least, the descriptions available do not include intentionality) and, therefore, can have resemblances with animal undertakings (or even to operations of artificial devices).

Consequently, "economic action" would be different from "economic behavior." In the first case, the undertaking may have a high degree of complexity, even though what is directly observable could be very restricted (e.g., to buy shares in the stock market). In the second case, the undertaking generally incorporates a more limited type of choice, which could be present to some extent in animals. These can have choices but they arise within a restricted range of variables.

With respect to the use of terminology like "market behavior" and "market action," there is a common ground because both can refer to the same reality. However, it seems to me that some nuances remain. The former expression could not be directly intentional, and it is habitually more descriptive and generic than the other. The latter is, in principle, more intentional and concrete than "market behavior." From a general viewpoint, the emphasis on action is not new.

---

imitation. In economics, it has been common enough to admire Newtonian mechanics (or, as we have seen, the law of falling bodies), and to search for the economic equivalent of the laws of motion. But this is not the only model for a science, and it seems, indeed, not to be the right one for our purposes" (Simon 1979, p. 510).

[10] See Sect. 7.3.1. Those acts include intentions, motivations, dispositions, memory, personal evaluations, decision-making, etc.

In effect, Alfred Marshall uses the terminology of action when he characterizes this science. He wrote at the beginning of his celebrated *Principles of Economics*: "Political economy or economics is a study of mankind in the ordinary business of life; it examines that part of individual and social action which is most closely connected with the attainment and with the use of material requisites of wellbeing" (Marshall 1949, p. 1).[11]

Frequently, this emphasis on individual and social action as *leit-motiv* of economics seems to have been overshadowed in the last decades with the impressive development of statistical economics and econometrics,[12] which has made significant strides in economics. However, in spite of its success, this phenomenon has been described in ambivalent terms: "Econometricians are stuffing suitably trimmed empirical data into the new economic boxes almost as fast as the theoretical innovations appear in print, though it is not obvious that the recent explosion of quantitative research in mathematical models has improved the explanatory or predictive power of the economist's 'engine of thought'" (Deane 1983, p. 11).

Hence, there is sometimes concern about the real incidence of statistical economics and econometrics for the role of economic prediction. *De facto*, the powers of prediction and control (knowledge of variables and their measurement) in economics are limited. In principle, the mathematical calculus for future economic events is limited—at least—by present knowledge as well as by the reality itself that is predicted (i.e., the type of action and the existence of links with the economic activity which is known). Very often, the economic phenomena are subject to changes, both as *economic activity* considered in itself and as an *activity among others*. In this second case, the reasons for change often lie outside the traditional boundaries of the discipline.

7.2.2 *Interdependence and Complexity*

Following the recognition of the interdependence between economic factors and other human and social elements (as well as artificial aspects), which should be taken into account, it seems clear that it makes sense that "economics is becoming more multidisciplinary in its methods, topics, and outlook. Branches of economics are incorporating techniques, knowledge and concepts from other disciplines in the social and natural sciences" (Sandler 2001, p. xii). This concern for those aspects of interdependence enriches economics methodologically.

However, we have seen in the recent past a quite different approach, which can be considered as a methodological extreme: "economic imperialism."[13] It is

[11] He added: "Thus it is on the one side a study of wealth; and on the other, and more important side, a part of the study of man. For man's character has been moulded by his every-day work, and the material resources which he thereby procures, more than by any other influence unless it be that of his religious ideals" (Marshall 1949, p. 1).

[12] On prediction in the realm of statistical economics and econometrics, cf. Chaps. 10 and 11.

[13] The limits of methodological imperialism are discussed in Gonzalez (2012b).

a well-known attempt to go beyond the traditional boundaries of the discipline in order to articulate economics dealing with phenomena of politics and social institutions (like prisons) and, above all, with questions about the family. This "economic imperialism" has been led by another Nobel Prize laureate: Gary Becker (1976, which includes Becker 1962).

In spite of his intellectual "imperialism"—the primacy of economic perspective—Becker recognizes that not all the aspects of human behavior can be studied by the economic approach with equal insight (1976, pp. 8, 9, 14). His focus goes from economic activity to economics as activity, studying what strictly speaking are not in themselves economic phenomena, like decisions on having children or marriage (Becker 1976, p. 169). He attributes to "the family the same dominant role in society traditionally attributed to it by sociologists, anthropologists, and psychologists" (Becker 1976, p. 169). From the point of view of prediction, Becker's proposals have been criticized, because if we follow him, "what we never do is to produce really surprising implications directing our attention to hitherto unsuspected 'novel facts', that is, facts that the theory was not specifically designed to predict" (Blaug 1980, p. 248).

Economists in favor of "economic imperialism" and their opponents agree generally in some aspects regarding predictions in economic models. Thus, among the different tendencies there is, to some extent, a consensus about *several features* of economic predictions. (i) What could be predicted is any economic variable. Generally, the focus is on macroeconomic variables (inflation, unemployment, etc.), because it is the field where we can obtain more reliable information, and the social pressure for predictions is more intense. (ii) How to predict scientifically is usually understood as how it is possible to design a statistical or an econometric model that could be evaluated according to the accuracy of predictions and realism of the assumptions in the hypotheses. (iii) Why predictions are made is a question commonly linked to the process of decision-making. The study of economic activity—its regularities and tendencies—could be able to realize in advance the consequences of the future evolution of the system and to modify the variables which could be of special interest. (iv) How much utility predictions can have—in spite of their presumed unreliability—is a question related to the problem of the reduction of economic uncertainty (Fernandez Valbuena 1990, pp. 386–387).

Interdependence is an issue that underlies a characteristic question: why are economic predictions so difficult? This central problem, crucial for explaining their unreliability, has a direct answer: the complexity of economic reality, which I condense in the duality "economic activity" and "economics as activity." In other words, there are an enormous variety of "respects" that could make a difference among economic events, and there exist complex ways in which the economic influences operate and interact with each other. "One source of this complexity lies in the difficulty in anticipating human behaviour, which can be influenced by a tremendously varied collection of social, political, psychological, biological and other factors. Another source is the inherent difficulty in anticipating the results of interactions of millions of human beings with different values, objectives, motivations, expectations, endowments, rights, means and circumstances, dealing with each other in a wide variety of institutional settings" (Sen 1986, p. 5).

Unreliability is a consequence of the complexity of economic reality, but it is also something due to the insufficiency of models (classic and time-series) of statistical economics and econometrics. (a) There are difficulties in transforming qualitative aspects into quantitative ones, in order to introduce those elements in the variables of the model. (b) Although a variable could be obtained, rigor in measurement is not always maintained. This inconvenience is increased by the difficulties there sometimes are in designing and conducting experiments in economics. (c) It is conceivable that with all the variables at hand a structural change might occur and, therefore, the mathematical calculus should be modified. (The economies of Eastern Europe countries after 1989 events or the performance of the banking system in Western countries, after the fall of Lehman Brothers in 2008, are two examples of this.) (d) The uncertainty in the endogenous variables (in the classic econometric model) could be possible and besides that we also need to predict the exogenous variables.

Complexity is, therefore, a typical feature of economic reality. It is something directly linked with the character of human activity. This complexity is different from that present in the weather, which makes it very difficult to forecast. In the weather, in spite of the difficulties of knowing the variables in advance, these belong mainly to a specific sphere: a physical one; meanwhile economic reality receives influences of diverse kinds of realms. In effect, there exists a wide spectrum of factors (ethical, social, political, psychological, biological, cultural, etc.) that affects economic reality as a human activity itself and as an activity connected with others.

To predict economic actions (individual or social) requires the consideration of the diversity of influences that condition those actions. This goes beyond mere behaviorist conceptions (above all the comparison with the rats)[14] to reinforce the *human* character of economic activity: we need the perspective of action theory. From this point of view, establishing the necessity and reliability of economic predictions—two issues at the core of the problem of prediction in economics—calls for clarifying the subject matter of this science, i.e., a kind of human activity developed within a concrete sphere and connected with other human activities. The study of the components and features of economic reality needs to analyze the distinction between "economic activity" and "economics as activity."

7.3 "Economic Activity" and "Economics as Activity"

Until now, I have been emphasizing the need to distinguish "economic activity" from "economics as activity," a human activity among others. The first is the *activity* of economics in itself, something that could be understood as autonomous regarding other human activities. It comprises economic activity which human beings carry out in their interrelations connected with goods and services, exchanges and commodities, innovation and plan optimizing decisions, and so on. The second

[14] The comparison with the rats is made by John Kagel (1987). For Herbert Simon, this author goes too far (Simon 1995b, pp. 359–366).

connects the links between economic activity and other human activities (cultural, political, sociological, etc.). In this case, economic activity appears integrated into the whole system of human relations; it is immersed in the set of activities developed by human beings in normal circumstances. Then, as an activity *among* others, economics has links with many activities (political, sociological, cultural, etc.).

Both economic activity and economics as activity should be considered in order to clarify the subject matter of economics, because this science explains and predicts human activities in the domain of a certain sphere (i.e., exchange, commodities, etc.). Those elements have direct implications on the realm of prediction. On the one hand, the normal aim of a human activity is more connected with the present circumstances than with a future not yet observed. On the other, the predictability of economic activity—which is, in principle, autonomous—is possible, and could be reliable; whereas predictability of economics as a human activity among others appears more unreliable, precisely due to the interdependence with other activities. Thus, prediction does not appear as the central aim of economics, in spite of the predictivist thesis, and its scientific character could be accepted in the economic activity.

Insofar as the economic enterprise is understood as a human activity, as a real interaction between the agents in this sphere (goods and services, exchange and commodities, etc.), "prediction" is just one more element to be considered and, presumably, not the first one, as Friedman claims.[15] In that case, as a science, it requires description and evaluation of phenomena, tasks that could be part of what is normally understood as "explanation." In addition, prediction is methodologically different from explanation,[16] not only by the mere fact of being related to the knowledge of future, but also for the process itself of making predictions. This process needs to consider the possibility of the future event as well as the concrete forms among the possible ones and their amount.

To make predictions in economics appears, then, as a somehow complex task that needs the previous knowledge of different variables, such as the ingredients of the human activity in that sphere, and the prognosis of future events on the basis of the present knowledge. Such economic activity has *inner* elements (i.e., self-interest, altruistic motives, etc.). It also has *outer* observable aspects: specific actions (in principle, consistent with respect to the inner elements). Above all, an economic prediction seeks what could be *testable* and, therefore, puts the attention in the realm of *economic actions* rather than in the non-observable acts which are supporting them.

Besides the "intrinsic" factors of economic activity, such as its purpose (i.e., self-interest, altruistic motive, etc.) and its repercussions (i.e., profit or cooperation), there are "extrinsic" factors, such as moral norms (or values) or social customs, with incidence in the purely economic commitments. Thus, the predictions of economic

[15] In fact, he seems to consider prediction as *the* aim of positive economics: "Its task is to provide a system of generalizations that can be used to make correct predictions about the consequences of any change in circumstances. Its performance is to be judged by the precision, scope, and conformity with experience of the predictions it yields" (Friedman 1953, p. 4).

[16] On the asymmetry between "explanation" and "prediction," cf. Salmon (1993).

activity should include the relevant "extrinsic" factors. This affects basic things, such as maximizing profits, because in some cases (e.g., in Japan) economic activity cannot be understood without moral norms and social customs that go beyond the profit-motive of the economic activity.[17]

These factors could be "external," in the sense of being of other activities but with incidence in economic ones. Properly speaking, external ingredients affect economics as activity (i.e., an action among other human actions). In that case, economics is related to different activities that can have an influence on it, and sometimes, can modify the economic activity (e.g., a political change). Let us analyze this activity and its features, which concerns the subject matter of this science, in order to clarify prediction in economics.

7.3.1 Act and Action: Activity

Any solution to the problem of scientific prediction in economics needs to consider economic activity. The present *alternative* to the four positions mentioned (predictivist thesis, quasi-scientific option, dualist posture, and wary attitude) includes several points. (1) The insistence of prediction as principal aim seems to be unattainable, insofar as economic activity should be explained (or described and evaluated) in the present in order to predict the future. (2) The emphasis on its human character—and, therefore, on its human and social status—establishes a specific character of economic predictions, which is commonly different from the predictions in the sphere of natural sciences. This aspect contributes to diminish the importance of the comparisons—made by the quasi-scientific option—with physical predictions: they are, in principle, in different realms. (3) The acceptance of human actions as objective, something that can be observable and, therefore, testable, avoids part of the problem of the dualist posture: actions could be used to test predictive hypothesis. (4) Prediction can have a central role in establishing the scientific status of economics, so it cannot be put aside as the wary attitude suggests.

For the alternative to those positions, the roots are in the very beginning: in the character of the economic activity. This conception maintains that to study economic activity and to work on economics as *activity*, a type of action among others, are complementary tasks. In the first case, economic reality is studied "directly": the research is carried out in order to make the features of the activity itself explicit—the central core of economic reality—which to some extent could be researched as an autonomous one. Meanwhile, in the second case, the investigation is made in terms of an "indirect study": it requires the connection and comparison with other actions (political, historical, sociological, etc.), insofar as the activity of this science is, among other facets, one more of human beings. However, the links with other types of actions are tighter in economics than in other sciences.

[17] Besides the profit-motive, the economic activity of individuals and their interaction can follow altruistic motives and be developed in terms of cooperation, cf. Thaler (1992).

Regarding the first case, emphasizing the content of the activity itself reveals the articulated structure of the economic activity. In effect, as other human activities, the economic one has two components. They correspond to the *inner* aspect of activity and the *outer* aspect of activity, the general distinction that Georg H. von Wright has highlighted (1971, p. 87), which I consider preferable to express as the duality "act" (the inner element) and "action" (the outer component), both within the field of "activity" (Gonzalez 1991c).[18] So, economic activity as such has an *act*—something mental that cannot be observed—which can be known only if it becomes an *action* (i.e., something observable). Act and action conform human activity: both intervene in its configuration.

Hence, the outer component of the activity ("action") is more than the mere observable behavior: it is connected with the internal element ("act") and is linked with other actions, with other "forms of life." In addition, economic actions can be seen as "modes of presentation"—in the Fregean sense—of economic reality. Thus, economic research can grasp the different modes of presentation of economic reality; each one of them should be studied in a specific branch of this science. The same action can receive a different treatment according to the perspective (e.g., the devaluation of the currency: economic history, political economy, business administration, etc.).

Acts and actions belong to the structure of the economic activity in the individual case as well as in the social one. The differences are clear from the point of view of prediction: the predictability of the *acts* appears as an *insolubilia*, insofar as the testability of what has been predicted is not warranted, because it cannot be observed; whereas the testability of the *actions* makes the predictability of future economic activities reasonable. The economic agents develop their activities in the social world, according to different levels that are now interdependent: local, regional, national, and international. This shows the complexity of the economic activity, which is an important factor for the possibility of a scientific prediction.

Consequently, among the features of the economic activity, there are several which make the prediction more difficult in this case than in other types of phenomena (mainly, the deterministic or quasi-deterministic ones). From the point of view of economics as activity, the difficulties can be seen as problems derived from being a social science (as well as a science of artificial), because that activity has—in one way or another—a common root with other social activities and human undertakings: the human self-determination in developing the activities (economic, sociological, political, etc.) related to human needs or as an enlargement of human possibilities.[19]

These difficulties do not exclude, in principle, the possibility of prediction in the economic field; on the contrary, that possibility is accepted. But they establish the

[18] This monographic issue of *Daimon* (Gonzalez 1991b), entitled "*Action Theory*/Teoría de la Acción," studies different aspects of human action, mainly in the context of social sciences. Previous studies on the philosophy of action can be found in White (1968).

[19] This second dimension is characteristic of the sciences of design, cf. Simon (1996) and Gonzalez (2008).

sphere in which that is possible: the economic activity in terms of *actions*, and not as mental acts. In other words, predictions have, as a normal field, something that could be objective and not something subjective. Thus, in spite of their differences, Friedman, Hicks, Buchanan, and Simon coincide in the interrelation between *objectivity* and *predictability*: they agree in something basic: only an objective science could be predictive.

In effect, science requires objectivity, which is related to a reality which could be *prima facie* measurable; and economics is not looking—at least, in principle—for something internal which could not be testable. So, what could be predicted in economics is the aspect of human activity that has observable consequences and not the inner act in itself (i.e., the mental act: intentions, motivations, plans and so on).

Nonetheless, the inner aspect of an activity is usually the first step for the outer action—the inner act yields the outer action—and, frequently, it is also the explanation of the activity that has been developed. This is what happens in the cognitive and motivational spheres, because both kinds of mental acts (e.g., expectations and motivations, which are initially subjective and could be intersubjective) are required in order to explain the economic activity, and they affect the predictive process.

Prediction looks at the actions of the agents and, at the same time, takes into account the mental acts which could originate such actions, but only from the starting point of the domain of what is observable (i.e., the action). The predicted economic activity, which is the articulation of acts and actions, needs to consider the internal factors (e.g., expectations and motivations) as possible or actual conditions of the future activity.[20] *Strictu sensu*, what could be predicted in economics are the observable activities of the economic agents.

Depending on those difficulties, what seems to be ruled out is the accuracy of the prediction in cases where internal factors or external circumstances make it nearly impossible to know with detail the future events, especially when the phenomenon is very specific.[21] So, what is affected is the *reliability* more than the possibility: they make the prediction more difficult than in any deterministic system, and they suppose the indeterminacy of the economic activity, even in the case of the assumption of the rational character of actions undertaken [i.e., to act according to the standards of rationality of mainstream economics, where the agent seeks to maximize, or to do so following Simon's bounded rationality (1972), where "satisficing" is enough].

Therefore, to accept economic activity as the basis for the subject matter of this science includes a wide spectrum of possibilities in the attempt to offer scientific predictions. This approach should take into account the self-interested activity and

[20] For Simon, "in a world of uncertainty, a theory cannot make a consumer's expenditure depend on future income, but only on *expectations* of future income. Hence the predictions of the theory will depend on assumptions about the formation of expectations" (1963a/1982, pp. 328–329).

[21] Hutchison maintains that "economists cannot and will never be able to predict with the very high degrees of probability and accuracy which many natural scientists can achieve for their predictions" (1977, p. 10).

the social interaction of the agents.[22] In addition, it needs to consider the connections with other actions that can interfere in the economic activity, both in the case of economic theory (i.e., as basic science) and of applied economics (i.e., as applied science).

7.3.2 *Economic Activity as the Basis for the Subject Matter of Economics*

Economic activity is developed by the agents interacting in the social context according to some mental acts, and with specific actions. This human activity receives internal and external influences. On the one hand, besides economic motivations that follow criteria of maximizing or satisficing, there are frequently noneconomic motivations (e.g., in the case of a manager or entrepreneur: status, prestige, power or a better position) (Simon 1963a/1982, pp. 331–332). On the other hand, the social character does economics as an activity among others and, therefore, under the influence of changing social and moral values within a historical context.

Since economics is related to other activities (historical, political, cultural, etc.), it does not seem reasonable to think of it as a mere mathematical calculation, severing it from its links with other human and social actions. These actions are not merely related to economics, because their influence could be decisive, especially in applied economics, where the political factors are heavily influential. Thus, the activity which is studied by this science—the present and the future—is influenced by other types of activities which make the prediction of a future event on the basis of the present knowledge harder and, consequently, could make the prediction of novel facts even more difficult, due precisely to the interdependence of the human and social activities.

If economic activity is considered in itself, instead of seeing it as an activity among others, then a characteristic element is its link with a specific use of language. It is—in Wittgensteinian terms—a type of language-game that relates to a way of living. Economic propositions depend primarily on actions (buying, selling, counting, etc.) of human beings (buyers, sellers, entrepreneurs, producers, consumers, workers, etc.). There is a connection between an economic concept, which could be expressed mathematically, and a concrete activity in human life. The development of this activity in the basic cases, as well as in the kind of work done by economists, is performed according to a specific use of language and a genuine sort of experience, which is a need of the human being. The sophistication of economic language involves a rich human and social experience.

Language and experience hold together in this activity. So, the clarification of economic language and economic experience can throw light on economic activity and, therefore, about its prediction. Both language and experience form the basis of

[22] On the characterization of action theory from the social perspective, cf. Tuomela (1991). See also Tuomela (1996a, 1996b, 1996c, and 1996d).

the subject matter of this science, because they are basic elements of economic reality. Experience in the case of economic activity shows that the reality that should be predicted is not to be accounted for by a handful of invariants. There is not a perfect adaptation of the human activity to the environment. Some mechanisms of economic activity may be relatively simple, but "that simplicity operates in interaction with extremely complex boundaries conditions imposed by the environment and by the very facts of human long-term memory and of the capacity of human beings, individually and collectively, to learn" (Simon 1979/1982, p. 491).

When the philosophy of science studies economic reality, it seeks primarily to clarify the features of economic activity that compound it and, secondarily, the relations of economics as activity with other human activities. Economic language and experience are studied by philosophy, taking into account the contributions of the semantics of science and the epistemology, respectively. The methodology of science, which is devoted to clarifying how scientific knowledge ought to be developed, suggests the ways in which the economic activity could be improved.

Although economic activity is the *basis* for the subject matter of economics, this is not sufficient to establish its object of study. It is clear that not every economic action receives the attention of this science: only some are researched scientifically. To some extent, this case is similar to history, where *historicity* of a human action—if it is understood merely as being an action *in* the history—does not guarantee, by itself, that the action is going to be an object of study for history as a science (i.e., to be a "historical action") (Gonzalez 1996e), even though it is an indispensable element. Accordingly, the mere characteristic of "economicity" of human activities—possession of the features of interest for economics—does not justify *eo ipso* that some activities are going to be an object for scientific research in economics, but without that characteristic economic science will not pay attention to them.

Prediction of future economic actions is based on similar premises: there is a subset of economic actions that are pertinent or relevant for scientific prediction and, therefore, will be predicted in economics. Above all, predictability commonly requires the assumption of a kind of repercussion or impact of the predicted action in other actions, otherwise scientific prediction appears useless, because not every future economic action is studied by economics as a science.

7.4 Economic Activity: Purpose, Content, and Repercussion

Any attempt to account for the *features* of economic activity needs to consider its purpose, content, and repercussion on other activities (economic and non-economic). These three features could be analyzed in different ways. First of all, the human activity that is called "economics" needs a *purpose*, because any activity bereft of purpose is by this fact bereft of sense. So, 'what is the aim of economic activity?' is a relevant question. Usually the answer has a wide spectrum of possibilities, among them competitive goals and cooperative ones. Both are actually in the microeconomic realm as well as in the macroeconomic one. Economics describes, evaluates, and predicts the different kinds of goals (self-centered or altruistic, etc.) in different systems (competitive and cooperative, etc.).

7.4.1 Purposive Character: The Distinction "Intention"–"Intentionality" and Prediction

Initially, an economic activity involves some purpose. Here "purpose" has a broader sense than "goal." The *purpose* of economic activity is not merely the possession of a concrete goal. The purpose is related to an experience that is, in principle, possible and could be expressed in propositions of future time. Using a language that is meaningful, the purpose looks forward to something future that makes what is going on intelligible. But this type of language and this sort of experience are not *eo ipso* equivalent to language and experience related with predictions. The difference is in the semantics and epistemology of "purpose" and "prediction." This could be clarified by means of Elisabeth Anscombe's distinction between "intention" and "prediction" (1957/1963, pp. 1–7, 90–94).

Her analysis of the language of action throws light here insofar as "purpose" and "intention" are similar, because to start an action with an intention includes that it possesses a purpose. The vice versa seems less direct: in principle, acting according to "purposes" supposes that the action makes sense: it has an orientation; whereas acting with an intention goes further: it requires a conscious intervention of the agent. In addition, we can distinguish between *intention* and *motives*: "A man's intention is *what* he aims at or chooses; his motive is what determines the aim or choice" (Anscombe 1968, p. 147).[23]

Intention and *prediction* have something in common: both have to do with the future. However, taking into account Anscombe's analysis, I think that the differences between "intention" and "prediction" are more important. (a) In an intention the event seems to be under our control: it appears as something which could be done by the agent (as in the expression of an intention like 'I am going to buy a share'); whereas, in a prediction, what is predicted may be out of our real domain (as it happens frequently in 'I am going to be ruined'). (b) The status of an intention is a mental act that can exist without a symbol; meanwhile prediction goes further into its initial mental status, because it is being something that can be tested. A prediction can have some proof or evidence in favor of it, whereas the intention can remain in the sphere of the agent and requires only having some reason for it. (c) The prediction could be linked to an intention, but the former is, or ought to be, objective; whereas the latter is in the subjective domain, connected with motives, wishes and obligations. So, the relation with the future is different in both cases;

[23] On the agent as subject of experiences, cf. papers of R. Chisholm (1991) and J. Margolis (1991) in Gonzalez (1991b).

what is more, an intention is not necessarily associated with a future event, because it makes sense to ask with what intention the thing was done.

Anscombe mentions "an action can be intentional without having any intention in it" (1957/1963, p. 1, see also p. 94). In my judgment, this could be understood by means of a distinction between "intention" and "intentionality." Basically, the difference lies in their status. *Intention* is a mental act that could be expressed in a statement or might be the origin of an action. It is something that cannot be observed and could be complete, although it remains in the sphere of the mind.[24] If intention is in the origin of an action, *intentionality* is a feature of the action and, therefore, it belongs to the realm of what is observable.

Intentionality is the orientation of the agents in their undertakings. It is usually a manifestation of an intention, but an action can be made according to diverse intentions (e.g., to buy a share in the stock market). The mere description of the behavior is not enough: we need to consider the intentionality of the action. For von Wright, "action is normally behavior understood, 'seen', or described under the aspect of intentionality, i.e., as meaning something or as goal-directed. Intentionality can quite rightly be said to be in the behavior. But not like a 'quality' inherent in the movements of limbs and other parts of the body. For these movements we can describe completely without mentioning intentionality. … To understand behavior as intentional (…) is to fit it into a 'story' about the agent" (1983, p. 42).

Following this distinction between "intention" and "intentionality,"[25] it is not possible to predict the intention of an agent in the realm of economics, but it is possible to predict the *intentionality* of an economic agent or a group (i.e., qualitative prediction). Economic activities require that intentionality in the actions is developed by the agents and, usually, the intention is the starting point for that intentionality. Nevertheless, it is possible for an action to be developed *intentionally* which has not been originated by a specific intention (this happens in many routine actions, like counting money in the case of a cashier).

From this point of view, in the sphere of economic activity, it is understandable that there exist social actions developed with intentionality by economic agents that have not initially made a "collective intention." The predictability of such social actions—economic ones—relies on the knowledge of social actions that are oriented towards goals, which possibly have not been deliberately chosen. Moreover, it should be considered that "individual rationality is not sufficient for collective rationality" (Sandler 2001, pp. 69–70).[26]

This emphasis on the *purposive character* of economic activity, as something that should be in the domain of actions rather in the realm of acts, is recognition of the interest of economics in "intentionality" rather than in "intention." It has consequences for the study of individual and social actions. Usually, economic actions

[24] "A man can form an intention which he then does nothing to carry out, either because he is prevented or because he changes his mind: but the intention itself can be complete, although it remains a purely interior thing" (Anscombe 1957/1963, p. 9).

[25] For further details on this distinction, cf. Elskamp (1986).

[26] In this regard, cf. Olson (1965).

are produced initially by the interaction of agents. Besides their intentions as individuals, they can have "we-intentions," i.e., intentions with others;[27] but the focus of this science, generally, is on the external aspect: the observable elements of the economic actions (even in cases like the theory of decision-making, whereas the attention is on the observable consequences). Thus, the field in which we can get scientific success is in the realm of the intentionality of economic actions.

Therefore, the predictability of economic activities depends on the capacity to say in advance the elements related with such purposive actions, actions which do not require an explicit intention to be included in the economic field. This point of view excludes the primacy of the "egocentric perspective," i.e., the attempt of explaining the economic actions (and predicting them) on the basis of their own case. The emphasis is more on the objective reality of actions developed by economic agents, rather than on subjective psychological acts.

Nevertheless, it is possible to get an objective study of the subjective elements of the human being (i.e., a "subjectual" study) (cf. Chap. 1, Sect. 1.3.1). This realm of something objective, which is present in the subjective dimension, comprises what is in the individuals but is not intrinsically individual (in the sense of being exclusively of him or her) and, for this reason, it is knowable by others. It allows us to have a scientific study of motivations and preferences (economic and non-economic ones), the subjective ingredients of human activities that have an objective repercussion in human actions. This is the way to know the motivations and preferences of economic activity. It is an indirect, not a direct way, contrary to "subjective economics" which G. Shackle has defended (1990; see also Ford 1983). The starting point is in the language and experience—something intersubjective that includes objective elements—and not in the egocentric perspective, the knowledge of the own case. This objective approach to the subjective dimension makes it possible to infer the intentions (mental acts) from the intentionality of actions.

7.4.2 The Content of Economic Activity

Secondly, and closely linked to the question of purpose of economic activity—its sense—another important problem appears: the *content* of economic activity itself and, therefore, the differences between its status and other human activities. In this respect, the question sets off a wide debate: "what are economic activities in themselves?," "what makes them different from other human activities?" On the one hand, the problem is the *specificity* of the kind of action that is studied by economics; and, on the other, the question is the *distinction* and *connections* between economic activities and other activities studied by other sciences, mainly human and social ones. Both aspects are ways to clarify the subject matter of this science. From the point of view of the theoretical basis of prediction in economics, they could be

[27] An interpretation of the intentions in the sphere of social actions has been developed in detail in Tuomela (1996a). See also Tuomela (1996b, 1996c, and 1996d).

interpreted as (a) the predictability of *economic activities* in themselves, and (b) the predictability of the *interferences* of other activities in economic ones.

Typically, both kinds of predictability are frequently interpreted from a quantitative perspective, rather than a qualitative one. Usually, predictability is understood in terms of empirical measurement. Generally, the key point is not what the content of economic actions is; rather, how it can be measured. Thus, it is assumed that mathematical calculus makes sense when it is predicting human actions. But, in fact, what is predicted is only an aspect of human actions, because there are some non-quantitative aspects to be taken into account. This has been pointed out by John Hicks: "Keynes was entirely right in emphasizing that there is an element in economic judgements about the future that is not reducible to mathematics" (1983b, p. 351). Hicks stresses that this element can be quite rational, without being expressible in terms of a probability calculus.

Understood as an activity, economics is concerned with goods and services within a concrete sphere of human life and connected with many others. This activity is developed by human beings—individually or in groups—in that sphere, acting according to their preferences and needs. This dynamic of economic activity avoids the presence of passive elements in the economic system, because the system itself arises through the interaction of individual and social agents. The human and social character of this activity introduces a new factor: the qualitative dimension. The economic reality is not merely something material and external to the agents. They intervene in the economic process and introduce some kinds of values by means of their personal evaluations (in the individual realm and in the social one). Buchanan has emphasized this: "goodness and badness are qualities that are assigned to physical things, to commodities or services, by personal evaluations" (1982/1987, p. 73).

Therefore, both quantitative and qualitative factors appear in economic activity. The recognition of the presence of the qualitative dimension has as a consequence the acceptation of difficulties for the predictability of this activity. It introduces an important element of variability, because personal evaluations can change from one person to another, according to different values (including the non-economic ones: ethical, cultural, social, etc.) and other circumstances (historical, political, demographic, etc.) external to that activity. These multiple aspects of variability have not been considered by the predictivist thesis (defended by Friedman), which adopts an instrumentalist position on prediction; instead, they could be attainable by an alternative view of prediction on a pragmatic realism ground.

Within a context of economic activity as central for economics, a *pragmatic realist* conception of prediction can be articulated as a combination of four ingredients: (i) realism of assumptions, (ii) confirmatory character of predictions, (iii) superfluity of the predictivist thesis, and (iv) inclusion in the field of decision-making. At the same time, the role of the social setting should be included in order to grasp the sphere of economic decision-making. Thus, action theory should consider collective action in institutions, in general, and in organizations, in particular. This framework can be useful to understand phenomena in economics like self-interest or the profit-motive, as well as cooperative or altruistic undertakings.

Quantitative and qualitative factors form the basis of the subject matter of this science, because both are relevant for the activity of the human being as *homo economicus*. They contribute to characterizing this science and influence its predictive aim. On the one hand, the purely predictive aim for this science is ruled out, insofar as it is not realistic to defend its primacy in the domain of human actions. Purely predictive economics requires an oversimplification of the real factors that interact in economic activity, including sometimes a deterministic behavior of human beings, who are oriented towards future targets. But this is not the case: usually economic agents develop actions intentionally following a bounded rationality rather than an omniscient rationality (Simon 1979/1982, pp. 499–503). The intentionality of the agents is oriented to choose according to some goals, and the goals could be changed. On the other hand, predictability is possible insofar as there is a continuity or stability that yields to a future regularity in the type of actions. The agents could have a common activity and share some goals. Then, economic activity is open to predictability, but as something which is not fixed by a deterministic behavior or a kind of oversimplified rationality.

Those elements of future economic activity that are predictable require the probability calculus. But calculation itself is a human activity developed by economists using mathematics. In effect, "the calculus makes no predictions, but by means of it you can make predictions" (Wittgenstein 1976, XV, p. 150). Commonly, predictions of economic events are usually made by means of calculations, but the *calculations* themselves do not make predictions. The calculations are right or wrong according to their result, whereas the predictions appear as an outcome on the basis of the present knowledge and, in themselves, predictions are not intrinsically dependent on a quantitative character.

To put it differently, the calculation is the normal means to make predictions in science, in general, and in economics, in particular; but neither are all predictions quantitative, nor is it sufficient to consider only mathematical factors in order to get a reliable prediction (in social sciences, in general, and in economics, in particular). The result of a calculation and the outcome of a prediction are different factors, insofar as the first has only a formal character, whereas the second includes—or could include—some qualitative elements (human or social).

From this point of view, as well as from the perspective of the intrinsic complexity of the economic affairs, the frequent unreliable character of the economic predictions becomes more understandable. The result of the calculation of the variables could be correct, whereas the outcome of the prediction could be different. One important reason for that difference is the autonomy of economic calculation and the dependence in the case of what is predicted. The process and result in an economic calculation follow their own rules, whereas the outcome predicted depends on something conditional: the fulfillment of the previous steps. In other words, economic predictions are commonly *conditional*, because the normal case establishes that "if *p* occurs, then *q* occurs": the future outcome requires previous activities. The conditional prediction is accepted when there is a justification for prediction, i.e., when it follows from a theory that has enough conceptual and empirical support.

7.4.3 Repercussion on Other Activities

Thirdly, after the problem of the economic purpose and the characterization of its content, the question to resolve is the *repercussion* or impact on other activities (economic and non-economic). It seems clear that the economic activity has repercussions to other economic activities (simultaneous and future) as well as to activities different from the economic ones, because it is an activity among others, and it is *eo ipso* related with other human actions. The first case, the realm of economic activity and its repercussions, directly affects the subject matter of this science. For the mere fact of being an economic activity is not enough to receive the attention of this science: the "economicity"—the economic dimension of a human activity—is a necessary condition for being an object of economics but is not a sufficient one. The repercussion or impact on other activities is necessary as well.[28]

Autonomy and objectivity of economic activities are the main problems related with the repercussion on others. They arise with a basic question: does economics depend on "internal factors" or require the presence of "external factors" to explain its content? This brings about the distinction between economic activity and economics as activity, distinction that comprises economic reality. Within the first dominion, economic activity is considered in itself, as something that could be developed following a specific track.

Thus, acts and actions—the components of the activity—should be autonomous, because they are not dependent on activities different from the economic ones. In effect, the inner and the outer elements of economic activity (acts and actions) are considered independently of other activities. The autonomy of the inner element (the "acts") and the outer one (the "actions") is then clear; the restrictions appear when this activity interferes with other activities. In effect, when economics is understood as an activity among others, the autonomy could have restrictions. Usually, the main constraints are political.

Prima facie, economics does not need "external factors" to explain the "internal factors" (i.e., its structure as economic activity), but internal and external factors intervene in the real process of economics as activity. Furthermore, the external factors (political, sociological, ethical or cultural) are sometimes crucial and the autonomy, in a strict sense, can disappear. The way to resolve this problem is by distinguishing the respective field of each facet that intervenes in that process. In that case, the autonomy of economics is limited by the interrelation with other activities. The recognition of its limits introduces an objective characterization of something usually intersubjective (such as the political influences, the sociological tendencies, the ethical values or the cultural preferences) which accompanies it. Thus, external factors condition the autonomy of internal factors, the development of economic activity according to its specific rules.

[28] There is an analogy with the case of history: the "historical actions" are not merely the actions developed on past time or in the present time; they need to have a repercussion on other actions in order to be studied by this science.

Even in the case of modifying the economic activity, the external modification could be objectively established and the boundaries delimited. But prediction appears, then, as a complex task, because it is difficult to say in advance what the incidence of such external influences on economic activity will be and even harder to foretell the precise changes which could be introduced in it. Predictability is not ruled out, mainly in the qualitative aspects, but it appears very imprecise in the quantitative domain. The existence of such unreliability of economics as activity means it makes sense to concentrate predictions in the short-term or the medium-term, and avoid the long-term. The source of the difficulties of prediction in this case derives from the absence of a complete autonomy of economics as activity. That lack of autonomy makes insufficient and inaccurate the attempts of purely mathematical predictions. In other words, it shows the deficiency of a conception of prediction based on mere econometric basis.

Concerning the economic activity in the basic cases, prediction is possible insofar as the phenomenon which is studied could be expressed in objective terms, i.e., when the objective dimension of the agents is considered. We need to know the objective ingredients of those who intervene in the economic activity. What is purely subjective and, therefore, *intrinsically variable* in the agents (among themselves and in each one as time passes by) is not scientifically predictable: there is a problem of applicability of a scientific theory.[29] This is the case of the inner element of the human activity (acts), which is not generalizable to other human beings. That dimension belongs to what, strictly speaking, could be called "subjective economics" and cannot be the object of study of economics as a science.

But what is objective in the agents and, therefore, has a specific content (either qualitative and quantitative or one of them) and possesses repercussion should be studied by this science. This does not mean converting economics into psychology; on the contrary, it includes the autonomy of this science, because the research field is precisely what is not merely psychological (i.e., specific characters of the individual *qua* individual or the idiosyncrasies of some groups). Economics as study of the objective dimension of the agents that make decisions researches the human agent as *homo economicus*, with a purposeful activity and content in the economic domain.

Now, economics appears as a science that considers the objective content and repercussion of human actions related to some purposes (buying, selling, investing, renting, leasing, saving, etc.). It is *science* insofar as can manage objective problems of those activities, either in the individual sphere or in the social one (micro and macro). In this regard, predictability is linked to that objectivity,[30] and it is excluded from those areas where objective knowledge is not possible. From this viewpoint, some claims of the quasi-scientific option, and the dualist position on economics are not attainable.

[29] "A general law or theory is applicable to certain body of data just in case the data satisfy the antecedent conditions of the law. (…) Attempting to confirm or disconfirm a general statement of theory presupposes its applicability to the data brought to bear on it" (Rosenberg 1984, p. 325).

[30] On the preconditions for rational prediction, cf. Chap. 10, Sect. 10.2.1.

On the one hand, the possibility of objective knowledge in the sphere of economics involves its scientific status in the present moment (or, at least, in a next future, depending on the kind of phenomena). So, the question is not—as asked by Hicks (1986)—whether economics is a science or a discipline; but, instead, it should be: what kind of science is it?; or at least: which part of it could be developed in order to make it a science? On the other hand, the presence of an objective domain in the field of economic activity avoids the problem of Buchanan (i.e., the question of a "subjective economics" non-predictive) (1982/1987). According to this alternative presented here, the question is not the existence of such field or branch of economics, because the possibility of an objective and predictive economics in the area of individual and collective actions is assumed. In addition, concerning the area of problems studied by so-called "subjective economics," it might accept the existence of another sphere that is not a science, or one that is another science, different from economics (perhaps, psychology).[31]

7.5 Economic Prediction and Human Activity

On analyzing economic predictions in the context of human activity, the scientific status of economics becomes clearer. In effect, the present analysis of prediction from the viewpoint of the action theory has shown enough elements to establish its scientific character as well as the difference with natural sciences, in general, and physics, in particular. Economics deals with an activity that, besides subjective elements, includes *objective components* in the domain of individual activities as well as in the field of social actions.

Individual activities have some subjective acts (like intentions) that belong to the sphere of the mind and cannot be knowable by observation and, therefore, are not predictable; but, when those acts are unfolded in actions (i.e., with intentionality), they become predictable. Social activities have an intersubjective origin, which in some cases could be explicitly shared (like "we-intentions" or intentions related with cooperative actions), and they are observable and sometimes knowable through experiments of different sorts (cf. Chap. 9; Gonzalez 2007a). The individual economic activities need to be developed into the social world, otherwise they cannot be an object for economics, which is a social science in the full sense of the word (and it is also a science of the artificial, which requires a social undertaking to be designed).

Within the social world, economics studies human agents who have mental "acts" (such as intentions, preferences, motives, expectations, dispositions, personal evaluations, etc.) as well as observable "actions" (social and individual ones) developed intentionally. Both aspects of economic activity—the inner acts and the outer actions—are under the influence of a great variety of factors (ethical, political,

[31] About the relations between economics and psychology, see Simon (1987a). See also the research made by Daniel Kahneman. Among his papers, Kahneman (2003) is particularly interesting.

cultural, sociological, ecological, etc.) that cannot be reduced to the kind of process study merely by observation and experimentation in the way that physics does. This science works basically within a realm of knowledge in connection with other realms (mainly, chemical and biological), whereas economics is a kind of knowledge which is heavily interdependent of other social sciences (history, sociology, psychology, etc.).[32]

Physical predictions, in spite of the problems generated by the theory of chaos,[33] work often with a range of events that, in principle, could be under our control, insofar as they are repeatable. Economic predictions have more difficulties: (a) the repeatability of the events could be questioned; (b) the number and variety of aspects which can intervene are bigger than in physics: on the one hand, there is a complex relation among factors traditionally considered as economic elements (e.g., in the economic decision-making: objectives, motivations, values, expectations, etc.); and, on the other hand, there also exists the influence of a collection of factors traditionally considered as non-economic ones (social, political, cultural, psychological, biological, historical, ecological, etc.) (cf. Chap. 11, Sect. 11.3).

If we take into account the diversity of the reality studied in science, it seems that the *concept* of "prediction" requires a differentiation according to the degree of control of variables (Gonzalez 1996a). Meanwhile, Hicks stresses another aspect: there are several kinds of predictions. For him, the main distinction is between the *conditional* and the *unconditional*. "A conditional prediction says that something will happen, if some condition is satisfied—a condition that we know how to describe. An unconditional prediction makes no such qualifications" (Hicks 1986, p. 93).

Hicks considers that "unconditional predictions" are possible in some sciences; above all, in astronomy: "the astronomer can tell us, with remarkable precision, just when there will be an eclipse of the moon; he can do quite unconditionally. He bases his prediction upon scientific laws, which are conditional; but he has similarly been able to satisfy himself that in the particular case the conditions must be met" (Hicks 1986, p. 94). The reasons are two: the astronomer can do this because the phenomena that he or she studies are, in general, beyond the range of influence of human action, and the astronomer circumscribes his or her description of the phenomena that he or she can feel sure that there are conditions which he or she has not taken into account.

But Hicks considers that "the normal type of scientific prediction is the conditional" (1986, p. 93). He thinks that this is obvious with experimental sciences, because every prediction of the result of an experiment is a conditional prediction; the steps that have to be taken to set up the experiment are the condition from which it is claimed that the results will follow. In this sense of "conditions," which is different from "initial conditions" (i.e., the special circumstances which the laws included in the explanatory premises are applied), "the action is the condition, or one of the

[32] There is also the realm of economics as a science of design. It is clear that, as a science of the artificial, economics has a dynamic trait in the sphere of complexity (Gonzalez 2013b) as well as a direct relation to scientific creativity and technological innovation (Gonzalez 2013c).

[33] An exhaustive study of the problems related with chaos is in Peitgen et al. (1992).

conditions, for the event to follow" (Hicks 1986, p. 93). Thus, for him, conditional prediction has helped us to foresee the consequences of human actions.

Nevertheless, Hicks deems that economic predictions are usually weak: the event will follow, if there is no disturbance. He goes too far with the underlying argument of the subjection of economic predictions to a *ceteris paribus* clause, because he regards as very difficult the strong conditional predictions in economics (i.e., that given the stated conditions, the event will follow).

What seems clear is that, ultimately, the difficulty of the methodological problem of prediction in economics—its necessity and unreliability—lies in the *complexity* of the human activity insert in the social setting.[34] This complexity contributes to the frequent unreliability of economic predictions, which have their roots in the subject matter of this science: economic reality is a social undertaking commonly mutable as a consequence of dependence of human activity. But "economic activity" is an objective and measurable reality. In addition, economics as an activity among others is also objective but more difficult to measure. Most of the econometric models of neoclassical economics focus on "economic activity," something that can be considered in itself (cf. Morgan 1990).

Such economic models—as happens with other scientific models—even though they use the empirical data available, many times study idealized settings (e.g., in order to have possible scenarios) rather than the complex real situation at hand. The economic reality always includes the influence of the other activities (political, cultural, etc.). Thus, besides this traditional source of difficulties for econometric models, shared by other models (i.e., a model usually simplifies reality), there is an intrinsic difficulty in the econometric models: to know all the endogenous and exogenous variables pertinent to the case that is researched. Another difficulty is the incapacity to grasp some qualitative aspects (to transform them into quantitative ones) that could interfere in the quantitative factors that the model considers.

Amartya Sen has emphasized that, in actual practice, many aggregate predictions are based on very simple structures. "Indeed, in some of the analyses, human beings hardly figure at all, and various economic magnitudes like money supply, the balance of trade, aggregate investment and the price level are seen as interacting with each other and having properties of their own" (1986, p. 14). This absence of human activity in the economic analysis deprives it of an ontological element that is important for epistemological and methodological considerations.

Although Sen recognizes that, for simple and immediate predictions, such short cuts do indeed have some usefulness, "they cannot provide a very deep explanation, nor supply a robust basis for a serious prediction. Economic magnitudes are ultimately social magnitudes, and variables like prices, investments, consumption, money supplies and so forth do not, naturally, move on their own, untouched by human volition. To go no further than studying these aggregate macroeconomic magnitudes is to abstract from perhaps the most fundamental aspect of social reality, namely the

[34] "The economy consists of the activities of many millions of decision makers, acting largely independently but sharing information used in forming their decisions: the economy is thus very complicated" (Granger 2001, p. 93).

rich and inseparable relations between the society and the individual. One cannot ultimately understand movements of these macroeconomic magnitudes without taking note of the objectives, knowledge, reasoning and decisions of the members of the society" (Sen 1986, p. 14). Thus, intentionality is not only present at the level of economic agents but also at the level of the theories of economic markets.

According to the analysis of prediction in economics from the perspective of action theory, it seems, first, that the problem of prediction is linked to the scientific status of economics. The characterization of its *subject matter* is not neutral for the interpretation of what economic prediction is and ought to be. Secondly, what may be predicted is economic reality as a result of *human activity*. The emphasis must be on the objective dimension of human activity, stressing the realm of actions rather than the sphere of mental acts. Prediction has, as a normal field, something that could be objective and not something subjective.[35] The scientific method is not to infer economic actions from introspection, asking how we ourselves would act if we found ourselves in such a position.

Thirdly, among the features of economic activity are its *purpose*, *content*, and *repercussion* on other activities (economic and non-economic ones). Fourthly, prediction in economics should enhance the different aspects of economic reality. So, in addition to the quantitative predictions produced by mathematical calculations, economics needs qualitatively based predictions (mainly, in welfare economics). Finally, the difficulty of the methodological problem of prediction in economics—its necessity and unreliability—lies in the complexity of human activity. Economic magnitudes are ultimately social magnitudes that do not move alone, untouched by human volition.

We need to consider the intentionality of economic agents within the theory of economic markets: scientific predictions in economics require taking into account collective action, especially when we are in public economics (cf. Sandler 2001, pp. 56–75).[36] (a) The focus of the analysis of the activities developed in economics should be in "intentionality" rather than in "intention." What can be studied and, consequently, predicted are the objective elements in the economic agents (either subjects involved in the decision-making or institutions as social organizations). (b) The content of prediction includes quantitative and qualitative factors, which should be reflected in economic predictions. (c) Besides the economic purpose and content, we need also to take account of the repercussion or impact of an economic activity in other economic activities for being subject matter of this science, because not every economic action is of interest for economics. To be sure, one source of the difficulties to economic predictions derives from the absence of a complete autonomy of economics as activity.

---

[35] This does not exclude the existence of something objective in the domain of the individuals and could be called "subjectual." Thus, what is "subjectual"—and, therefore, objective in the individuals—is predictable, whereas it is not the case in what is purely subjective.

[36] According to this author, "the theory [of collective action] is testable both in the laboratory (…) and from empirical data. As the theory has developed, novel insights about institutional design and other issues have emerged" (Sandler 2001, p. 75).

References

Anscombe, G. E. M. 1957/1963. *Intention*. 2nd ed. Oxford: B. Blackwell (reprinted in 1976).

Anscombe, G. E. M. 1968. Intention. In *The philosophy of action,* ed. A. R. White, 144–152. Oxford: Oxford University Press.

Becker, G. S. 1962. Irrational behavior and economic theory. *Journal of Political Economy* 70:1–13.

Becker, G. S. 1976. *The economic approach to human behavior*. Chicago: University of Chicago Press.

Blaug, M. 1980. *The methodology of economics: Or how economists explain*. Cambridge: Cambridge University Press.

Buchanan, J. M. 1959. Positive economics, welfare economics, and political economy. *Journal of Law and Economics* 2:124–138. (Reprinted in Buchanan, J. M. 1987. *Economics: Between predictive science and moral philosophy*, 3–19. College Station: Texas A&M University Press).

Buchanan, J. M. 1982. The domain of subjective economics: Between predictive science and moral philosophy. In *Method, process and Austrian economics,* ed. I. M. Kirzner. Lexington: Lexington Books. (Reprinted in Buchanan, J. M. 1987. *Economics: Between predictive science and moral philosophy,* 67–80. College Station: Texas A&M University Press).

Chisholm, R. 1991. The bearers of psychological properties. *Daimon. Revista de Filosofía* 3:7–14.

Deane, Ph. 1983. The scope and method of economic science. *Economic Journal* 93:1–12.

Elskamp, R. G. 1986. Intención e intencionalidad: Estudio comparativo. *Anales de Filosofía* 4:147–156.

Fernandez Valbuena, S. 1990. Predicción y Economía. In *Aspectos metodológicos de la investigación científica*. 2nd ed., ed. W. J. Gonzalez, 385–405. Madrid-Murcia: Ediciones Universidad Autónoma de Madrid and Publicaciones Universidad de Murcia.

Ford, J. L. 1983. *Choice, expectation and uncertainty*. New York: Barnes and Noble.

Friedman, M. 1953. The methodology of positive economics. In *Essays in positive economics,* M. Friedman, 3–43. Chicago: University of Chicago Press (6th repr., 1969).

Gonzalez, W. J. 1991a. Historismo y anti-historismo en la polémica metodológica entre G. Schmoller y C. Menger. In *Actas del V Congreso de la Sociedad Española de Historia de las Ciencias y las Técnicas,* ed. M. Valera and C. Lopez Fernandez, 2027–2041. Murcia: PPU-DM.

Gonzalez, W. J., ed. 1991b. *Teoría de la Acción/Action theory*, monographic issue of *Daimon. Revista de Filosofía* 3.

Gonzalez, W. J. 1991c. Mathematics as activity. *Daimon* 3:113–130.

Gonzalez, W. J. 1994. Economic prediction and human activity. An analysis of prediction in economics from action theory. *Epistemologia* 17:253–294.

Gonzalez, W. J. 1996b. Prediction and mathematics: The Wittgensteinian approach. In *Spanish studies in the philosophy of science,* ed. G. Munevar, 299–332. Dordrecht: Kluwer.

Gonzalez, W. J. 1996e. Caracterización del objeto de la Ciencia de la Historia y bases de su configuración metodológica. In *Acción e Historia. El objeto de la Historia y la Teoría de la Acción,* ed. W. J. Gonzalez, 25–111. A Coruña: Publicaciones Universidad de A Coruña.

Gonzalez, W. J. 2007a. The role of experiments in the social sciences: The case of economics. In *General philosophy of science: Focal issues,* ed. T. Kuipers, 275–301. Amsterdam: Elsevier.

Gonzalez, W. J. 2008. Rationality and prediction in the sciences of the artificial: Economics as a design science. In *Reasoning, rationality, and probability,* ed. M. C. Galavotti, R. Scazzieri, and P. Suppes, 165–186. Stanford: CSLI Publications.

Gonzalez, W. J. 2012b. Methodological universalism in science and its limits: Imperialism versus complexity. In *Thinking about provincialism in thinking, Poznan Studies in the Philosophy of the Sciences and the Humanities,* vol. 100, ed. K. Brzechczyn and K. Paprzycka, 155–175. Amsterdam: Rodopi.

Gonzalez, W. J. 2013b. The sciences of design as sciences of complexity: The dynamic trait. In *New challenges to philosophy of science,* ed. H. Andersen, D. Dieks, W. J. Gonzalez, Th. Uebel, and G. Wheeler, 299–311. Dordrecht: Springer.

Gonzalez, W. J. 2013c. The roles of scientific creativity and technological innovation in the context of complexity of science. In *Creativity, innovation, and complexity in science,* ed. W. J. Gonzalez, 11–40. A Coruña: Netbiblo.
Granger, C. W. J. 2001. Evaluation of forecasts. In *Understanding economic forecasts,* ed. D. F. Hendry and N. R. Ericsson, 93–103. Cambridge: The MIT Press.
Granger, C. W. J. 2012. The philosophy of economic forecasting. In *Philosophy of economics,* ed. U. Mäki, 311–327. Amsterdam: Elsevier.
Hicks, J. 1983a. "Revolutions" in economics. In *Classics and moderns. Collected essays on economic theory,* vol. III, ed. J. Hicks, 3–16. Cambridge: Harvard University Press.
Hicks, J. 1983b. Micro and macro. In *Classics and moderns. Collected essays on economic theory,* vol. III, ed. J. Hicks, 349–352. Cambridge: Harvard University Press.
Hicks, J. 1986. Is economics a science? In *Foundations of economics. Structures of inquiry and economic theory,* ed. M. Baranzini and R. Scazzieri, 91–101. Oxford: Blackwell.
Hutchison, T. W. 1977. On prediction and economic knowledge. In *Knowledge and ignorance in economics,* ed. T. W. Hutchison, 8–33, 145–151. Oxford: Blackwell.
Kagel, J. 1987. Economics according to the rats (and pigeons too). In *Laboratory experimentation in economics—Six points of view,* ed. A. E. Roth, 155–192. Cambridge: Cambridge University Press.
Kagel, J., et al. 1981. Demand curves for animal consumers. *Quarterly Journal of Economics* 66:1–15.
Kahneman, D. 2003. Maps of bounded rationality: Psychology for behavioral economics. *The American Economic Review* 93 (5): 1449–1475.
Margolis, J. 1991. Farewell to Davidson's theory of action. *Daimon. Revista de Filosofía* 3:65–79.
Marshall, A. 1949. *Principles of economics*. 8th ed. London: Macmillan.
Morgan, M. S. 1990. *The history of econometric ideas*. Cambridge: Cambridge University Press.
Olson, M. 1965. *The logic of collective action*. Cambridge: Harvard University Press.
Peitgen, H. O., H. Jürgens, and D. Saupe. 1992. *Chaos and fractals. New frontiers of science*. New York: Springer.
Rosenberg, A. 1984. On the interanimation of micro and macroeconomics. In *Philosophy of economics,* ed. D. Hausman, 324–343. Cambridge: Cambridge University Press.
Rosenberg, A. 1992. *Economics—Mathematical politics or science of diminishing returns*? Chicago: University of Chicago Press.
Salmon, W. C. 1993. On the alleged temporal anisotropy of explanation. In *Philosophical problems of the internal and external worlds,* ed. J. Earman, A. Janis, G. Massey, and N. Rescher, 229–248. Pittsburgh: University of Pittsburgh Press.
Sandler, T. 2001. *Economic concepts for the social sciences*. Cambridge: Cambridge University Press.
Sen, A. 1986. Prediction and economic theory. In *Predictability in science and society,* ed. J. Mason, P. Mathias, and J. H. Westcott, 3–23. London: The Royal Society and The British Academy.
Shackle, G. 1972. *Epistemics and economics*. Cambridge: Cambridge University Press.
Shackle, G. 1979. *Imagination and the nature of choice*. Edinburgh: Edinburgh University Press.
Shackle, G. 1990. *Time, expectation and uncertainty in economics*. Hants: Aldershot.
Simon, H. A. 1963a. Economics and psychology. In *Psychology: A study of a science,* vol. 6, ed. S. Koch, 715–752. New York: McGraw Hill. (Reprinted in Simon, H. A. 1982. *Models of bounded rationality*. vol. 2: *Behavioral economics and business organization,* 318–355. Cambridge: The MIT Press).
Simon, H. A. 1963b. Problems of methodology—Discussion. *American Economic Review* 53:229–231. (Reprinted in Simon, H. A. 1982. *Models of bounded rationality*. vol. 2: *Behavioral economics and business organization,* 369–371. Cambridge: The MIT Press; also reprinted as Simon, H. A. 1984. Testability and approximation. In *Philosophy of economics*. 1st ed., ed. D. M. Hausman, 245–248. Cambridge: Cambridge University Press).
Simon, H. A. 1972. Theories of bounded rationality. In *Decision and organization,* ed. C. B. McGuire and R. Radner, 161–176. Amsterdam: North-Holland. (Reprinted in Simon, H. A.

1982. *Models of bounded rationality*. vol. 2: *Behavioral economics and business organization*, 408–423. Cambridge: The MIT Press).
Simon, H. A. 1979. Rational decision making in business organizations. *American Economic Review* 69 (4): 493–513. (Reprinted in Simon, H. A. 1982. *Models of bounded rationality*, vol. 2: *Behavioral economics and business organization*, 474–494. Cambridge: The MIT Press).
Simon, H. A. 1987a. Rationality in psychology and economics. In *Rational choice. The contrast between economics and psychology*, ed. R. M. Hogarth and M. W. Reder, 25–40. Chicago: University of Chicago Press.
Simon, H. A. 1989. The state of economic science. In *The state of economic science. Views of six Nobel laureates*, ed. W. Sichel, 97–110. Kalamazoo: W. E. Upjohn Institute for Employment Research.
Simon, H. A. 1991b. Organizations and markets. *Journal of Economic Perspectives* 5 (2): 25–44.
Simon, H. A. 1995b. Comment on Kagel. In *Concept, theories, and rationality in the biological sciences*, ed. G. Wolters and J. G. Lennox, 359–366. Pittsburgh: University of Pittsburgh Press.
Simon, H. A. 1996. *The sciences of the artificial*. 3rd ed. Cambridge: The MIT Press (1st ed., 1969; 2nd ed., 1981).
Thaler, R. H. 1992. *The winner's curse. Paradoxes and anomalies of economic life*. New York: Free Press.
Tuomela, R. 1991. The social dimension of action theory. *Daimon* 3:145–158.
Tuomela, R. 1996a. *The importance of us*. Stanford: Stanford University Press.
Tuomela, R. 1996b. Intenciones conjuntas y acuerdo. In *Acción e Historia. El objeto de la Historia y la Teoría de la Acción*, ed. W. J. Gonzalez, 277–291. A Coruña: Publicaciones Universidad de A Coruña.
Tuomela, R. 1996c. ¿Qué es cooperación? In *Acción e Historia. El objeto de la Historia y la Teoría de la Acción*, ed. W. J. Gonzalez, 293–305. A Coruña: Publicaciones Universidad de A Coruña.
Tuomela, R. 1996d. Creencias de grupo. In *Acción e Historia. El objeto de la Historia y la Teoría de la Acción*, ed. W. J. Gonzalez, 307–332. A Coruña: Publicaciones Universidad de A Coruña.
von Wright, G. H. 1971. *Explanation and understanding*. Ithaca: Cornell University Press.
von Wright, G. H. 1983. *Practical reason*. Ithaca: Cornell University Press.
White, A. R., ed. 1968. *The philosophy of action*. Oxford: Oxford University Press.
Wittgenstein, L. 1976. *Lectures on the foundations of mathematics*. Hassocks: Harvester Press. (From the notes of R. G. Bosanquet, N. Malcolm, R. Rhees and Y. Smithies, ed. by C. Diamond).

Part IV
Epistemology and Methodology of Economic Prediction: Rationality and Empirical Approaches

The methodological framework of social sciences and economics of Part III have set the context for a new step in the way from the broad approach to the restricted perspective. In the previous chapters, there are central tenets for the problem of prediction in economics: (a) the methodological background of this issue within the social sciences (Chap. 5); (b) the methodological approach within economics, taking into account relevant conceptions of economic theory (Chap. 6); and (c) the bases for solving the problem of prediction in economics, considering the subject matter of economics in terms of activity (Chap. 7).

After these three steps, Part IV goes deeper into epistemological and methodological aspects. Thus, it deals with the epistemology and methodology of economic prediction in connection with rationality and empirical approaches. Following the overall path of this book, which goes from the general to the particular, these topics start from some considerations on human rationality in general to deal soon with the specific details on economic rationality. This move will emphasize the transition from the mainstream option for maximization to the more realistic characterization of "bounded rationality."

When the attention in Part IV goes to empirical approaches on economics, the focus moves towards some topics that belong mostly to the *restricted perspective* on methodology of economics. These features are commonly the case when Chap. 8 and 9 deal, respectively, with "behavioral economics," developed by Herbert Simon (Nobel Prize winner in 1978), and experimental economics, which has in Reinhard Selten (Nobel laureate in 1994) one of its most relevant specialists. Their approaches on epistemology are analyzed from the point of view of the relation to methodology of economic predictions.

Chapter 8 completes and enlarges the vision of Simon given in previous chapters. The study starts with "bounded rationality" as an alternative to classical and neoclassical conceptions of rationality. Now, the aim of economic decision making is *satisficing* certain goals instead of maximizing utilities or profits. In this context, he presents a new conception of the role of prediction in economics, because he rejects the primacy of prediction in economics, since he considers prediction as not being a basic element of the set of characteristics that make economics a science.

Simon's focus is in *understanding* the mechanisms that explain past and present economic phenomena rather than in the predictability of future events. In this regard, the chapter analyzes the philosophical basis of his "bounded rationality" approach and makes explicit the view of economic prediction that derives from there. This analysis focuses on the characteristics of his conception of "economic predictions" and evaluates its suitability in characterizing what economic prediction is and ought to be. After this critical analysis of his conception, a final section outlines an alternative concept of "prediction" based on action theory, where economics as "activity" replaces his perspective of economics as "behavior."

Sharing the epistemological basis of "bounded rationality," Selten has added important contributions to economics. His publications include criticisms of mainstream economics, especially of the principle of subjective expected utility maximization, and his work gives some deep comments questioning instrumental rationality. In this regard, Chap. 9 highlights these contributions to rationality in experimental economics, taking advantage of his analysis of game theory, where he shows the need for a bounded rationality supported by experimental evidence.

Selten's empirical approach goes beyond Simon's behavioral economics and presents "area theories," such as the theory of "equal division payoff bounds," which are based on a limited rationality. In addition, he offers us a series of phenomena that confirm experimentally the existence of a bounded rationality. These elements are important to the role of prediction in experimental economics, which Selten sees from game theory. In this realm, he provides relevant methodological proposals on "accuracy" and "precision."

Chapter 8
Rationality in Economics and Scientific Prediction: The Role of Economic Rationality in Prediction

Regarding the characterization of rationality in economics and the role of scientific prediction in it, there are many contributions made by Herbert Simon (Nobel Prize in economics 1978), mainly to economic theory. Among them is "bounded rationality," which he developed as *an alternative* to classical and neoclassical conceptions of rationality.[1] But, in his long intellectual trajectory, he presented three models of human thinking: (1) the administrative decision maker; (2) the universal decision maker, based on the approach to *homo economicus*; and (3) the symbolic problem solver, which is the conception related to cognitive psychology and artificial intelligence (Gonzalez 2007b).[2]

Initially, Simon focuses on the administrative decision maker, which is connected to his research on political science. This was in his times in Chicago, where he also was a member of the prestigious *Cowles Commision*.[3] Then he moved towards the universal decision maker, which he makes explicit in the first decade in Pittsburgh.[4] Later on, he enlarged his views with the symbolic problem solver, which is clear in his book *The Sciences of the Artificial*. This volume includes the idea of economics as a science of design, and in its three editions—1969, 1981, and 1996—is open to two models of thought: the universal decision maker, related to

[1] Regarding the context of the relations between rationality and predictability in economics see Bicchieri (1987).

[2] See also Dasgupta (2003, pp. 693–695) and Gonzalez (2007c).

[3] In the *Cowles Commission for Research in Economics* worked some of the most influential economists of the twentieth century: Jacob Marshak, Tjalling C. Koopmans, Oskar Lange, Kenneth J. Arrow, Lawrence Klein, Herbert A. Simon, Leo Hurwirz and Gerard Debreu. In addition, Franco Modigliani and Andreas Papandreou also attended their meetings. George J. Stigler and Milton Friedman, even though they were no members of the Cowles Commission, were related to the University of Chicago and they participated in some meetings as well. Occasionally, they received the visit of some scholars from abroad, such as Ragnar Frisch and Trygve Haavelmo, who came from Norway. This list of economists includes an important number of future Nobel Laureates in economics (Simon 1991a, pp. 101–102). It is interesting to point out that Klein developed a theory of economic prediction (1971), and Haavelmo made a study in the theory of economic evolution (1991).

[4] Cf. Simon (1957, p. 198). On the conceptual history of the expression "bounded rationality," see Klaes and Sent (2005).

W. J. Gonzalez, *Philosophico-Methodological Analysis of Prediction and its Role in Economics,* Theory and Decision Library A: 50, DOI 10.1007/978-3-319-08885-3_8

the *homo economicus*, and the symbolic problem solver, where cognitive psychology converge with artificial intelligence (Gonzalez 2007c).

8.1 An Alternative Approach to Rationality and Prediction

A central part of the universal decision maker is "bounded rationality," which is directly connected to the analysis of the economic agent (Gonzalez 1997b). The phrase "bounded rationality" involves a psychological setting and has an explicit concern for the *process* of making decisions, for procedural rationality and not just for substantive rationality.[5] Thus, the phrase focuses attention upon the discrepancy between a supposedly perfected human rationality—an assumption commonly held in classical and neoclassical economic theory—[6] and the reality of human behavior as it is observed in economic life, which has a bounded rationality.[7]

This distinction is an important one, because on its basis the strategy of economic decision-making becomes that of *satisficing* in pursuing certain goals instead of maximizing utilities or profits. In accordance with this attenuated kind of rationality, which is procedural and seeks the strategy of satisficing, there is in Simon's view a new conception of the role of prediction in economics. This new approach is consequently illustrated in the context of the central problems of prediction in economics: the possibility of prediction as the *aim* of this discipline, and the role of prediction as the *test* of economics as a science.

Considering the first problem (prediction as the *aim* of this discipline), Simon is uncomfortable with *assumptions* of economic models (such as Friedman's model 1953) that require substantive rationality and emphasize good predictions as decisive for adequacy. *De facto*, he rejects prediction as the main goal of economics and, therefore, he cannot accept that prediction is the sole goal of science. Hence,

[5] Simon's first major step towards formalizing the psychological theory of bounded rationality is his paper (1955a). It was mostly written in 1952 during his first RAND summer, and although the term "satisficing" was not used in that paper, "the satisficing concept—searching for 'good enough' actions rather than optimal ones—is already present" (Simon 1991a, p. 165).

[6] Classical and neoclassical economists have identified "rationality" with "maximizing"/"optimization" of some sort, and Simon has clearly switched to satisficing/adequation. According to Nicholas Rescher, philosophers never bought in on that identification of rationality with maximization. *Personal communication*, 24.5.2005.

Among the classical economists is John Stuart Mill (1836), and neoclassical economists are still mainstream in the profession. Regarding the neoclassical approach on economic rationality, Simon had a particular respect or special consideration for Kenneth Arrow's work (see, for example, Arrow 1972, 1987). Simon, *Personal communication*, 20.12.1993.

[7] "What Simon has labelled 'bounded rationality' is part of the human condition. Bounded rationality is natural rationality; it is the assumption of infinite capacity to handle infinite quantities of data which is artificial" (Loasby 1976, p. 3).

Simon criticizes the primacy of prediction in economics, a position held by some economists (especially, Milton Friedman).

Concerning the second issue (the role of prediction as the *test* of economics as a science), the problem requires taking into account its many sides. An initial approach reveals that Simon considers prediction as not being a basic element of the set of characteristics that make economics a science. In fact, he suggests abandoning prediction as a *test* to know if economics is a science insofar as it is currently practiced (Simon 1989, p. 100): his interest lies in *understanding* the mechanisms that explain past and present economic phenomena rather than in the predictability of economic behavior. He considers that prediction should not receive a special emphasis insofar as the time dimension is not—for him—relevant when we are dealing with the confirmatory value of evidence for a theory. In this chapter, this issue will be studied more closely.

A first approach is given by Hausman,[8] who maintains that is possible to distinguish three options of prediction (a) as testable implications regarding the future, (b) testable implications whose truth is not already known, and (c) testable implications. In his judgment, Simon does not deny the importance of prediction in sense (c) as the central test of science, whereas he denies that prediction in sense (a) is the crucial test of economics as a science.

In other words, economics needs testable implications drawn from past and present economic processes, but the crucial point should not be to test economics using the pure testable implications regarding the future. His main interest lies in understanding economic processes rather than predicting them. Thus, even when economic prediction is correct or successful, for Simon the important element is the understanding of the mechanisms that lead to those outcomes. Accordingly, in order to have a clear picture of his economic thought on prediction, there are two aspects that should be emphasized.

1. Simon considers that the economic theorist should get evidence regardless of its temporal character, because no preference is given to prediction: the confirmatory value of a theory does not depend on the time dimension (to be a new event or a future event). Thus, the stress should be on the gathering of evidence and on the use of empirical methods rather than on prediction as empirical or theoretical knowledge regarding the future. He is "someone who believes deeply in using empirical evidence to settle questions in science, including historical science" (Simon 2001, p. 504).9

2. Prediction is not—for him—a concept directly connected to the future. Simon thinks that prediction could be with regard to the past, the present, and the future. Predicting, in his mind, is to draw consequences from the theory, either about known phenomena or new ones, be it in the past or in the future. This perspective of atemporality of prediction makes it difficult to distinguish "explanation" from "prediction" and revives the very well-known controversy on the symmetry or asym-

[8] Daniel Hausman, *Personal communication* (21.1.1996). The option (b) can be in line with the heuristic view of novelty, i.e., some of the versions pointed out in Chap. 4.

[9] His views on economics from the point of view of its historical factors are in Simon (1998).

metry in explanation and prediction, which was in the front line of the philosophical debate in late fifties and early sixties, especially among logical empiricists.[10]

From a philosophical viewpoint, Chap. 8 studies the links between bounded rationality and economic predictions in Simon's work.11 It offers a critical reconstruction of his conception, because his behavioral tendency should be replaced—in my judgment—by a different position, based on the idea of activity. Firstly, there is an analysis of the philosophical basis of "bounded rationality," which includes his characterization of "rationality," in general, and what he calls "substantive rationality" and "procedural rationality." Secondly, after the concept of economic prediction deriving from Simon's "bounded rationality" is presented, there is an evaluation of his conception of "economic predictions" from the point of view of its adequacy in characterizing what economic prediction is and ought to be. Finally, after this critical analysis of his conception, the discussion offers an alternative, based on action theory, where economics as "activity" replaces economics as "behavior."

8.2 Rationality and its Varieties: The Place of Bounded Rationality

Basically, there are three successive epistemological levels of rationality that have a methodological repercussion. (a) Rationality of science as such, which is the widest realm possible, shared by the diverse scientific disciplines (at least, those that are empirical: natural sciences, social sciences, and sciences of the artificial). (b) Rationality of economics as a scientific endeavor (within the social sphere and the artificial domain), which is connected with other disciplines (psychology, sociology, political science, etc.). (c) Rationality of economic undertakings of agents in particular cases (e.g., those situations where the economic agent needs to make a decision and develop a sort of action in that regard). *De facto*, Simon has made contributions to these three levels related to rationality (Gonzalez 2003d). His main emphasis is on rationality of economic agents.

Recurrently, Herbert Simon conceives *rationality* in connection with the third level. According to his definition, it is a term that "denotes a style of behavior that is appropriate to the achievement of given goals, within the limits imposed by given conditions and constraints" (1972, p. 161; cf. Simon 1964, p. 573/1982, p. 405). The elements of this definition may receive more exact specification in particular contexts. Moreover, there are—for him—important specialized uses of rationality following those factors (style of behavior, goals, conditions and constraints) (Gonzalez 2003d, pp. 75–76).

[10] An interesting contribution to the thesis of asymmetry is Salmon (1993).

[11] His contributions to the philosophy of science and to economics (as well as the references of all his publications in both fields) are pointed out in Gonzalez (2003c). That presentation includes information from my conversations (1993, 1994, 1996, and 1999) with Simon on his conception of economics, in general, and his views on prediction, in particular.

Simon considers that there are several *uses of rationality* concerning the way of *achieving the goals*. (1) Within the sphere of the *utility function*, commonly dominated by the idea of maximization, he points out two types of rationality: (a) the strict species of rationality, customarily understood in terms of *optimality* (i.e., the rational consumer of formal economic theory maximizes his expected utility or the rational entrepreneur maximizes his expected profit); and (b) the more general kinds of rationality, called *adaptiveness* or *functionality*, where it is assumed that the pursuing of one's goals may not take the form of maximizing—or, in game theory, minimizing—the expected value of a utility function. (2) Regarding the *type of criteria* that are to be fulfilled in order to obtain a given goal, rationality can be seen in *dualistic* terms: the criteria should be consistent with the idea of the *all-or-none* way, such as happens in the case of attainment of the plain of aspiration, which is obtained or not obtained. (3) According to the *level of the goals* mentioned in his definition, rationality can take different forms: (i) goals of the choosing individual, (ii) goals of a social system to which he or she belongs, or (iii) goals imputed by the observer (Simon 1964/1982, p. 405).

From the point of view of *conditions and constraints* which appear in Simon's definition of rationality, he maintains that there are other two kinds: (i) rationality with *objective* conditions and constraints (i.e., objective characteristics of the environment external to the choosing organism); and (ii) rationality with *subjective* conditions and constraints, or *bounded rationality* (i.e., perceived characteristics or characteristics of the organism itself, which could be taken as fixed or beyond its own control). This last option corresponds plainly to his conception of human rationality as limited. In any case, Simon considers that an unambiguous use of the term "rationality" requires a specification by the user of the assumptions being made about goals and conditions (Simon 1964/1982, p. 405).

Those elements of the definition—the style of behavior, the achievement of goals, and the limits due to conditions and constraints—were pointed out before the specific case of economics comes out.[12] For, as Simon recognizes, "rationality" is a philosophical term previous to the emergence of the social sciences as independent disciplines. Moreover, he considers that "the modern usage of rationality is very close to Aristotle's concept of calculative or deliberative intellectual virtue" (Simon 1964/1982, p. 406).

This kind of rationality emphasizes the *process* of choice—to pick out or to single out one option from several—which requires the employment of the intellective faculty—to think about ends and means—. This view has a direct influence on the subjects that have their roots in Aristotle: logic, ethics, and psychology; whereas in other subjects, such as economics or sociology, the dominant kind of rationality prefers the emphasis on the *choices* themselves, i.e., the stress on the outcomes rather than on the processes.

[12] Frequently Simon insists on the need of a broad concept of "rationality" and criticizes "economic rationality"—the neoclassical model—insofar as it is a very particular and special form of rationality: the rationality of the utility maximizer, cf. Simon (1978, pp. 2–3).

In the fields that Simon has explored in greater depth (psychology and economics),[13] there is a difference in the predominant kind of rationality. This divergence is extremely relevant for him, and it is the starting point for one of his main contributions to economics: the distinction between *substantive rationality* and *procedural rationality*. Thus, in his contribution to the Nafplion Colloquium in honor of Lakatos, Simon points out that "substantive rationality" is the concept of rationality that grew up within economics while "procedural rationality" is the concept that developed within psychology (Simon 1976, p. 130). Although he recognizes that the two fields—economics and psychology—address two significantly different sets of research questions, and that each has adopted a view of rationality which, in principle, is more or less appropriate to its own research concerns, he criticizes substantive rationality in economics and stresses the importance of procedural rationality for this science.

When these concepts of rationality—the prevalent ones in economics and psychology—are compared and contrasted, several new differences appear, because economics has almost uniformly treated human behavior as rational, whereas psychology has always been concerned with both the irrational and the rational aspects of behavior. Simon is aware of this and pays attention to rationality instead of including irrationality as well. Nevertheless, he points out very frequently that economics sometimes uses the term "irrationality" rather broadly (mainly, in Gary Becker's papers: 1962, and 1974)[14] and the term "rationality" correspondingly narrowly. In fact, this restricted use of "rationality," which is dominant in the neoclassical economics—especially, in the Chicago school—excludes from the domain of the rational many phenomena that psychology would include in it and, consequently, he prefers to use the broader conception of rationality given by psychology (Simon 1987a, p. 25).

His economic theory includes an *alternative* to the rationality of the utility maximizer of neoclassical economics. He follows three steps (Simon 1978, pp. 2–3). First, the economists' notion of "rationality" should be *expanded* beyond their narrow view of "maximizing" to incorporate the view, held by most psychologists, that human behavior consists of a much larger rational component. For him, the outset is clear: people have reasons for what they do; they have motivations and use reason

[13] In fact, Simon began with political science, which connects with psychology and economics. His first book, which he quotes very frequently, is in that field: *Administrative Behavior* (1947/1997). He is also very well known for his contributions to computer science. In this area, in connection with our discussion, see his book *The Sciences of the Artificial* (1996). On the biographical aspects of these intellectual interests, cf. Simon (1991a), Chaps. 4, 9, 10, 12, 16, and 21. A complete enumeration of his intellectual activities is in that book: "the political scientist, the organization theorist, the economist, the management scientist, the computer scientist, the psychologist, the philosopher of science" (Simon 1991a, p. xviii).

[14] However, Simon has pointed out that what Becker calls "irrationality" in the first article, would be called "bounded rationality" in his own paper, cf. Simon (1978, p. 2, note 2). The argument is clear: Becker indicates that he denotes as *irrational* any deviation from utility maximization; thus, Simon's bounded rationality is "irrationality" in Becker's terminology, cf. Simon (1979, p. 497, note 2).

(well or badly) to respond to these motivations and achieve their goals (Simon 1987a, pp. 25–26). Second, economics should not limit itself to the narrower definition of "rationality," because a great part of much economic literature uses *weaker* definitions of rationality. Moreover, there is indeed much that economics could import from the other social sciences (especially, psychology). Third, economics has largely been preoccupied *de facto* with the *outcomes* of rational choice rather than the process of choice. However, the dynamics of choice under uncertainty makes it essential to consider choice processes.[15] Thus, the advances in the understanding of procedural rationality, particularly as a result of research in artificial intelligence and cognitive psychology, help to deepen our understanding of the dynamics of economic rationality.

Rejection of neoclassical treatment of rationality and defense of a broader concept of *rationality* open to other social sciences are two sides of the same coin. For Simon, neoclassical theories offer an abstraction and idealization of human rationality, because "they direct their attention primarily to the external environment of human thought, to decisions that are optimal for realizing the adaptive system's goals (maximization of utility or profit). They seek to define the decisions that would be substantively rational in the circumstances defined by the outer environment" (Simon 1996, p. 23). In addition, this *neoclassical treatment* of rationality, almost alien to the inner environment and the procedural aspects of rationality, differs from other social sciences: (i) it makes behavior objectively rational in relation to its total environment, including both present and future environment; (ii) it keeps silent about the content of goals and values; and (iii) it postulates the global consistency of behavior (Simon 1987a, p. 26).

Other social sciences, in their treatment of rationality, present a more *realistic framework*: (1) they seek to describe and explain the ways in which several non-rational processes (motivations, emotions, and the like) influence the rational processes (principally, in the focus of attention and the definition of the situation); (2) they seek to determine, through empirical methods, how the nature of values varies with time and personal experiences; (3) they seek to determine the processes—individual and social—whereby selected aspects of reality are noticed and postulated as the factual bases for reasoning about human behavior; and (4) they seek to establish the computational strategies which are used in reasoning, so that very limited information-processing capabilities can cope with complex realities.

These important differences regarding the conceptualization of rationality (mainly, in the elements of the definition—the style of behavior, the achievement of goals, and the limits due to conditions and constraints—) come back to the fundamental distinction: rationality in economics is seen from the *choices* which it produces, whereas in the other social sciences the emphasis is on the *processes* that it employs. To sum up, rationality in economics is "substantive," while the rationality in sciences such as psychology is "procedural" (Simon 1987a, p. 26).

[15] A well-known study on judgment under uncertainty is Tversky and Kahneman (1982). Daniel Kahneman's research on these psychological aspects led him to the Nobel Prize in Economics in 2002.

Both kinds of rationality—substantive and procedural—have been studied by Simon at length in his economic theory. *Substantive rationality* is built on classical and neoclassical economics as unbounded rationality: rational behavior is determined completely by the characteristics of the environment in which it takes place. The economic actor has the utility maximization or the profit maximization as goals, and the computational powers for his or her decision-making are unlimited.[16] Thus, in the rational person of neoclassical economics, there is no distinction between the real world and the decision maker's perception of it: he or she perceives the world as it really is.

Moreover, there exists a direct consequence for *economic predictions*: "we can predict the choices that will be made by a rational decision maker entirely from our knowledge of the real world and without a knowledge of the decision maker's perceptions or modes of calculation" (Simon 1987a, p. 27). To move from this kind of rationality to procedural rational requires—in his judgment—assumptions about matters of fact, because it is not enough to add theoretical postulates about the shape of the utility function or the way in which actors form expectations about the future (Simon 1987a, p. 28).

Procedural rationality depends on the process that generated it, and both the knowledge and the computational power of the decision maker are severely limited. When rationality is procedural, there is a distinction between the real world and the actor's perception of it; in addition, *economic predictions* are linked to problem situations (i.e., situations in which the subject gathers information of various kinds and processes it in different ways in order to arrive at a reasonable course of action) (Simon 1976, p. 132).

Here the shift is clear: from the best solutions and "easy" predictions—in substantive rationality—to the good solutions and complex predictions (in procedural rationality); in the former, there is an adjustment to its outer environment, whereas in the latter the ability to discover appropriate adaptive behavior is required. When rationality is substantive, then in order to predict the behavior of a system we need information about the outer environment and the goal, but we need no information about the process used to compute the optimal output quantity; while in the procedural rationality the adaptation process is itself problematic in ways that make predicting its behavior difficult (Simon 1996, pp. 25–26).[17]

I consider that these aspects on rationality pointed out by Simon (mainly, the distinction between substantive and procedural rationalities) constitute a better picture of rationality in economics than the neoclassical position and, consequently, the concept of "procedural rationality" makes it possible to make economic predictions more realistic than the neoclassical models. However, from a philosophical point of view, the underlying notion of "reason" is clearly deficient, because he conceives *reason* in purely instrumental terms: "we see that reason is

[16] With the assumption of substantive rationality, economics is free from any dependence upon psychology: this science becomes completely irrelevant to economics, cf. Simon (1976, p. 131).

[17] On this topic, see Simon (1978, pp. 8–9).

wholly instrumental. It cannot tell us where to go; at best it can tell us how to get there. It is a gun for hire that can be employed in the service of whatever goals we have, good or bad" (Simon 1983, pp. 7–8).[18] *De facto* that reason is very limited, because it is bounded by the situation and by human computational powers. Thus, the behavioral model—the alternative to subject expected utility—uses instrumental reason to make adaptive choices and sometimes survives in a complex world (Simon 1983, p. 34).

Following this conception, which has resemblances with David Hume's idea of reason exclusively linked to *means* (1739–1740/1964, book II, part iii, Sect. 3), we can see several problems. (a) With that position no elbow room appears in order to consider that reason should *evaluate* the ends—the goals—(Simon 1995a, p. 60), when it is patent that there is an evaluative rationality which informs us that certain preferences are absurd (i.e., preferences against our nature or clearly diminishing our chances) and establishes priorities regarding the ends (Rescher 1988, pp. 92–106). (b) Simon seems to be unaware of the need of a *rationality of ends* besides the pure instrumental reason with "given goals"[19] or with a rationality that depends exclusively on the "process" itself that generated it (Simon 1976, p. 131).[20]

The interest of having a rationality of ends has its roots in the limits of the other: the cognitive rationality related to means does not cover the whole field; furthermore, there is an important role played by the realm of will in choosing the end. Thus, although instrumental reason can provide appropriate means for the process towards the chosen ends, it represents only a part of rationality because the means could be oriented towards inappropriate *ends* (i.e., a person who embezzles company funds can be very efficient towards his given goals, but this does not convert his activities into rational ones in the full sense of the word) (Rescher 1988, p. 97).

[18] This instrumental character of human reason is also present in the field where Simon has worked more on goals: political science. In this area, he describes and analyses some problems (conflicting goals, salient goals, focus of attention, group identifications, etc.) and several goals (search of power, pursuit of private interest, etc.), but he does not offer an examination of the validity or not of those goals. Moreover, he seems to exclude any chance for an evaluative rationality of ends: "rationality can only go to work after final goals are specified; it does not determine them" (Simon 1995a, p. 60).

[19] He uses this phrase when he defines "rationality," cf. Simon (1964, p. 573/1982, p. 405); and Simon (1972, p. 161). Later on, he associates it to behavior that is substantively rational, cf. Simon (1976, pp. 130–131).

[20] This is the case also in Simon's papers on political science, a field where he pays more attention to goals: "the process of decision making aimed at securing or maintaining power are not fundamentally different from the process of decision making aimed at other goals" (Simon 1987b, p. 347).

8.3 The Role of Economic Predictions: Substantive Rationality versus Procedural Rationality

Within economic theory, Simon uses prediction as a *test* to compare substantive rationality and procedural rationality. First of all, he recognizes the importance of prediction when uncertainty is at stake: "because the consequences of many actions extend well into the future, correct prediction is essential for objectively rational choice" (Simon 1996, p. 35). Secondly, psychology has—for him—a key role when the discussion is about the procedures for rational choice. In this regard, a good method of testing a theory of rational choice is to exam choice behavior in relatively simple and well-structured laboratory situations where the theory makes specific predictions about how subjects will behave.

According to Simon, the experiments of subjective expected utility maximization, of Bayesian strategies for sequential decisions, and of other models of rational choice under uncertainty have shown that it is possible to construct sufficiently simple and transparent gambles that the subjects will respond to in a manner consistent with subjective expected utility (and, therefore, according to a substantive rationality); however, the smallest departures from this simplicity and transparency produce behavior in many subjects that cannot be explained by subjective expected utility or Bayesian models (Simon 1976, pp. 133–135).

8.3.1 Substantive Rationality and Procedural Rationality

On the one hand, substantive rationality and procedural rationality are useful, because we need to give an account not only of the extent to which appropriate courses of action are chosen by rational actors (substantive rationality), but also of the *effectiveness*, in the light of human cognitive powers and limitations, of procedures used to choose actions (procedural rationality). Nevertheless, on the other hand, "as economics moves out towards situations of increasing cognitive complexity, it becomes increasingly concerned with the ability of actors to cope with the complexity, and hence with the procedural aspects of rationality" (Simon 1978, p. 9). Thus, he emphasizes the deficiencies of a substantive theory of rationality (e.g., it has no place for a variable like focus of attention) (Simon 1987a, p. 31),[21] which makes it necessary to incorporate more ingredients than those of utility maximization in order to predict the behavior.

Additionally, Simon considers that there are some cases (the distribution of business firm sizes and the magnitudes of executive salaries) in which, with the

[21] In political science Simon studies this shift in attention in the case of public awareness and voting decisions. For him, regarding rationality of political behavior and the deficiencies of substantive rationality, "to predict the shift [in focus of attention], it is important to know what level of employment or inflation will attract attention; it is of no use to introduce a utility function to be maximized. Again, the auxiliary assumptions are doing all of the work, and these are empirical assumptions that cannot be deduced from the theory" (Simon 1995a, p. 52).

assumptions of substantive rationality, we can predict very little, and that little often incorrectly (1987a, pp. 34–38; esp., p. 35). Again, procedural rationality has the remedy, and a key point is empirical information: in order to predict behavior more precisely it is essential "to have good empirical information both about the kinds of information to which the decision makers have ready access and about their beliefs and opinions on the mechanisms of the world on which their decisions operate" (Simon 1987a, p. 38).

In following this procedural rationality—and, therefore, the behavioral model in economics—predictability is clearly restricted, because Simon's emphasis is on a bounded rationality in a way which creates difficulties for making predictions: "we are concerned with how men behave rationally in a world where they are often unable to predict the relevant future with accuracy" (Simon 1976, p. 142). It is a world characterized by the ignorance of the future, which prevents the economic actors from behaving in a substantively rational manner; they adopt a rational choice procedure that includes a procedural rationality for predicting the future.

Consequently, against neoclassical positions on predictions about phenomena not yet observed—mainly, Friedman (1953, p. 7)—Simon maintains that, "in this kind of complexity, there is no single sovereign principle for deductive prediction" (Simon 1987a, p. 39). For him, the evidence available reveals that a theory of substantive rationality and the assumptions of utility maximization do not provide a sufficient base for explaining and predicting economic behavior. Therefore, he suggests applying the procedural theory of rationality to economics, both at micro and macro levels.

Uncertainty has a key position in this issue. On the one hand, neoclassical economics defines rationality in the context of "perfect" prediction (i.e., "foresight") thus reducing uncertainty to certainty. Hence, its insistence on the importance of reliable predictions is built on the possibility of certainty of future economic events. It assumes that the economic theory can yield sufficiently accurate predictions, even though there is no realism in the economic assumptions (Friedman 1953, p. 15). On the other hand, Simon demands the realism of the assumptions in the theories of economic actors ("micro") as well as in the theories of economic markets ("macro") (1963b/1984), and both cases include uncertainty about the future.

In addition, Simon does not consider prediction as the central exercise with which economics is concerned: prediction is one economic exercise among others. Moreover, the main tenet is—for him—to *understand the mechanism* that enables one to make predictions (and to get reliable evidence to confirm the theory). Therefore, even though the economic prediction can be accurate, the important feature is the understanding of the mechanisms that lead us to precise results.

Again, this brings us back to rationality: our computational limits do not facilitate our having good models of the future, and even if we can get a good model of the future but our brain does not allow us to run the model as fast as time runs, then we would still remain uncertain about the future. Thus, for Simon, "bounded rationality is very closely related to uncertainty" (1992b, p. 15). He considers that this link between bounded rationality and uncertainty is especially important when there is a conflict of interests (e.g., the uncertainty of oligopoly) and in the case of scientific creativity. In the former, game theory has proved how difficult it is to define rationality in the multiperson game of incomplete information; and, in the latter, the uncertainty associated with scientific creativity (and technological innovation) is a part of this activity: the science is *our* science and this configures its limits.[22]

Quite correctly, Simon maintains that it is possible to separate "the ability to predict that things of a certain general kind are going to happen from the ability to predict in detail what they are" (1992b, p. 15). In effect, it is quite possible to predict that there will be faster supercomputers with new capacities 10 years hence while, at the same time, being unable to stipulate the specific designs of those supercomputers.

Taking into account the links between uncertainty, bounded rationality and prediction, *Simon's scheme* presents several elements in his economic theory, all interconnected with each other. (i) Economic prediction cannot be made on the basis of a "perfect rationality," because there are *limitations*: the uncertainty about the consequences that would follow from each alternative when a decision is made, the information about the set of alternatives could be incomplete, and the complexity of the situations can prevent us from making the necessary computations to solve the problem (Simon 1972, p. 169).

(ii) Insofar as the consequences of human behavior are extended into the future, we need *correct predictions* for objectively rational choices. But, on the basis of realism of assumptions, prediction is not a pure inference on the grounds of optimal conditions,[23] because human decision-making is rooted in procedures that lead to the strategy of *satisficing* rather than to optimizing.[24] Thus, according to Simon, in order to make an appropriate economic prediction, we need to know about some things that belong to the natural environment (e.g., the weather), others related to the social and political sphere beyond the economic (e.g., a war), in addition to the behavior of other economic actors (customers, competitors, suppliers) which may have influence on our own behaviors (Simon 1996, p. 35).

(iii) In spite of its limitations, economic prediction based on a bounded rationality framework *fits* with a lot of things (Simon 1992b, p. 18), because it focuses upon the reality of *human behavior* as it can be observed in economic life (Simon 1992a, p. 3).[25] (iv) Besides the estimation of the probabilities of predicted events, we need to use *feedback* to correct the unexpected phenomena. For him, "a system can be steered more accurately if it uses feedforward, based on predictions of the future, in combination with feedback, to correct the errors of the past. However, forming expectations to deal with uncertainty creates its own problems" (Simon 1996, p. 36).

[22] On this topic, see Rescher (1984) as well as Gonzalez (1996a, 2013c).

[23] "Human beings (and other creatures) do not behave optimally for their fitness, because they are wholly incapable of acquiring the knowledge and making the calculations that support optimization" (Simon 1993, p. 156).

[24] His vision of the future of bounded rationality is rooted in that idea, cf. Simon (2000).

[25] "Because game theory is intrinsically unable to make specific predictions of behavior from the postulates of rationality, in order to understand behavior we must look at the empirical phenomena to see how people actually play games" (Simon 1992b, p. 25). On his response to the evolution of game theory, cf. Sent (2004).

If this epistemologico-methodological scheme, which interconnects uncertainty, bounded rationality, and prediction, is compared with the approach of neoclassical economics (subjective expected utility), the scales tip in favor of Simon in four aspects. They are especially relevant for the central topic discussed in this part of the book, which is the relation between rationality and empirical approaches in the context of the philosophico-methodological analysis of economic prediction.

(a) There is an improvement with respect to the *realism of assumptions*, because he pays attention to economic reality as it is, avoiding drawing strong conclusions from a few *a priori* assumptions.[26] The emphasis on uncertainty and bounded rationality is quite pertinent to the problem of economic predictions, in addition to the insistence that the attempt to predict human economic behavior by deductive inference from a small set of unchallengeable premises is a failure (Simon 1976, p. 146). (b) The vinculum between economics and psychology makes sense not only for the case of rational choice but also in predicting the results of interactions of economic actors (Simon 1963b/1982), because—as we will see in the next section—economics is above all a *human activity* (Chap. 7).

(c) Prediction has a crucial role in economics: the development of economic activities requires anticipation and, if possible, the control of future events. However, *pace* Friedman, not all of economics is concerned with predicting. In fact, Simon has stressed the need of *prescription* in systems modeling (Simon 1990a), which affects directly the characterization of economics. (d) The crucial point for the assessment of economic predictions is the reliability of the *method* used to make predictions rather than the accuracy of the result. Thus, prediction based on the bounded rationality model avoids central problems of the instrumentalist position (adopted, among others, by Friedman).[27]

In this context, and with the role of prediction at stake, a key issue in Simon's characterization of this discipline appears. Because, on the one hand, he includes prediction as a central tenet in the *definition* of what economics is: "*Economics* can be defined as the science that describes and predicts the behavior of the various kinds of economic man" (Simon 1963a/1982, p. 320); but, on the other, he suggests putting aside this question where the discussion is about the *scientific character* of economics: "we should be wary of using prediction as a test of science, and especially of whether economics is a science" (Simon 1989, p. 100).

With this apparent contradiction—prediction is a basic *aim* of economic science, but it is not its main *test* as a science—he is again in the same theoretical line as in the case of uncertainty and bounded rationality: we need predictions in order to cope with future economic events and, at the same time, the economists "can even provide theoretical reasons why it should be impossible to predict the course of the business cycle or the stock market" (Simon 1989, p. 99). Thus, instead of insisting on the accuracy of the results—the predictions—as Friedman's instrumentalist model does, Simon's emphasis is on the understanding of mechanisms that do not

[26] The realism of assumptions was defended by other authors as well, especially Paul Samuelson in his direct criticisms of Friedman's methodology, cf. Samuelson (1963).

[27] On instrumentalism about scientific prediction, cf. Gonzalez (1995), esp., pp. 43–50.

guarantee predictability. Again, the stress is on the *procedure* rather than results, as in the case of procedural rationality versus substantive rationality.

8.3.2 Simon's Concept of Prediction in Economics

Predicting is—for him—neither the sole goal of economics nor the main goal of this science. Moreover, Simon seems to change Friedman's priorities: economics can be tested by assessing the *correctness of its assumptions* rather than by testing the empirical correctness of its predictions. This attitude is a consequence of his insistence on the need to look for the *facts*.[28] In addition, Simon seeks to *prescribe* human economic behavior, but not by means of a deductive inference from a small set of premises.

For Simon, prediction and prescription are interconnected: "predictive models are only a special case where we seek to predict events we cannot control in order to adapt to them better. We do not expect to change the weather, but we can take steps to moderate its effects. We predict populations so that we can plan to meet their needs for food and education. We predict business cycles in order to plan our investment and production levels. (…) When our goal is prescription rather than prediction, then we can no longer take it for granted that what we want to compute are time series" (1990a, pp. 10–11).

Philosophically, the concept of "scientific prediction" includes at least three basic aspects: semantic, logical, and epistemological, which have a direct repercussion on a fourth: the methodological aspect (Gonzalez 1994, 1996b). All of them have a presence in Simon's characterization of *economic predictions*. Semantically, "prediction" has in his writings a usual meaning: the sense is the anticipation of future events on the grounds of the present knowledge, and the reference is the complex human economic world that is, in principle, ruled by uncertainty.

However, Simon also accepts that prediction could refer to an event of the past or of the present, in consonance with his idea of linking prediction to any consequences of the theory, a position that diverges from the genuine sense and reference of prediction (Gonzalez 1996c, pp. 211–216). And he does not differentiate between "foresight," "prediction," and "forecasting," according to the degree of control of variables, but he distinguishes them from "planning,"[29] which is a concept directly connected with practical activity. Even though he avoids the problems of

[28] "The faith in *a priori* theory, uncontaminated by empirical observations, has been weakened—even among 'rational expectationists.' More and more economists are beginning to look for the facts they need in actual observation of business decision making and in laboratory experiments on economic markets and organizations" (Simon 1992a, p. 7).

[29] "Our practical concern in planning for the future is what we must do *now* to bring that future about. We use our future goals to detect what may be irreversible present actions that we must avoid and to disclose gaps in our knowledge (…) that must be closed soon so that choices may be made later" (Simon 1990a, p. 11).

Friedman's pragmatic-instrumentalist option,[30] Simon does not place clear boundaries between scientific and non-scientific predictions.

Logically, prediction has for Simon the generic role of drawing testable consequences, instead of being oriented towards testable implications regarding the future. His thought regarding the relations between "explanation" and "prediction" is not sufficiently clear. On the one hand, prediction is understood as any testable implication of a theory, which makes it practically indistinguishable from "explanation," because explanation cannot exclude *a priori* projecting testable implications. Moreover, explanation usually deals with past and present phenomena, a realm that Simon thinks can also be covered by prediction. On the other hand, his criticisms of neoclassical economics, usually embedded in logical empiricist claims, could be interpreted as a rejection of the symmetry between explaining and predicting.[31]

Obviously, Simon can follow patterns that are asymmetrical rather than symmetrical insofar as, for him, a decision-making theory understood as a nomological theory with strict predictions is not possible (the bounded character of economic rationality does not allow it). Uncertainty again has a special importance in order to skirt altogether the attempt of predicting economic behavior by a deductive inference from a small set of premises. Furthermore, he distinguishes between models for natural sciences and social sciences (Simon 1979, p. 510), and also accepts the existence of quantitative as well as qualitative predictions (Simon 1987a, p. 37).

Epistemologically, prediction belongs to a complex framework. Simon tends sometimes towards positions close to logical empiricism whereas in other cases he is very critical of that view. He moves in the first direction when he stresses the primacy of observations,[32] and rejects the preference for the theoretical component.[33] This anti-Popperian attitude (or anti-theory laden component) does not impede following a second direction and criticizing two forms of empiricism: the subjective Bayesian (Simon 1976, p. 134) and Becker's "casual empiricism" (Simon 1987a, p. 30).

Clearly, Simon adopts an epistemological foundation of prediction in economics on the grounds of rejection of any version of *a priori* in economic knowledge and the need for objectivity (which includes respect for reality: uncertainty, bounded rationality, and so on). He accepts Bayes model insofar as it is objective and it takes into account previous knowledge (i.e., the knowledge before the experiment is made). Thus, with these ingredients, especially his emphasis on the connection

[30] "The question whether a theory is realistic 'enough' can be settled only by seeing whether it yields to predictions that are good enough for the purpose at hand or that are better than predictions from alternative theories" (Friedman 1953, p. 41).

[31] The topic of symmetry and asymmetry of explanation and prediction has a long tradition in philosophy of science. Even the authors originally formed in logical empiricism have defended the asymmetry, cf. Salmon (1993), esp., pp. 241–246.

[32] "Assumptions to be supported by publicly repeatable observations that are obtained and analyzed objectively" (Simon 1987a, p. 28).

[33] "The only way to experience such a surprise is to go out and look at the world, perhaps with some presumptions about how the world is. It isn't necessary to have a theory, but just look at the world" (Simon 1992b, p. 23).

of knowledge with reality and the relevance of objectivity for scientific knowledge, his position assumes a kind of realism, albeit different from critical realism and internal realism.[34]

Methodologically, in Simon's conception, prediction has a well-defined framework: the insufficiency of pure deductions leaves a door open to induction; the need for realism in assumptions operates in favor of a non-instrumentalist view; and the importance of an interdisciplinary study (economics in connection with psychology, but also linked to the sciences of the artificial—artificial intelligence—and other disciplines) gives a broad scope for economic predictions within social sciences and develops it as a science of design (Gonzalez 2008).

Overall, this methodological aspect more than any other (semantic, logical and epistemological) has particular weight in his position, because he emphasizes the *processes*—the bounded rational procedures—that economic actors use to cope with uncertainty. The predicting procedures—the methods for anticipation future events—are demanded by the need to reduce such uncertainty. Besides the estimation of the probabilities of future events, he requires feedback to correct the expected phenomena or the incorrectly predicted events. In this sphere, he criticizes the methodologies of three important economists: Friedman, Becker, and Muth.[35]

An evaluation of these aspects (semantic, logical, epistemological, and methodological) of Simon's concept of prediction in economics requires us to emphasize several factors. (1) He has the merit of configuring a new framework for economic prediction where rationality has a key position. Economics is and ought to be a human activity, and it does not work on its own, untouched by economic actors. (2) Although to understand the mechanism of prediction is a crucial question, this is not enough; prediction should be used as a *test* for economics as a science: explaining and predicting are two decisive elements of science in this respect (they are more than aims of science). Prediction is a sufficient condition for a science, and this requirement needs testable implications regarding the future. Nevertheless, there is a difference between natural sciences and social sciences, and therefore economic predictions do not need to be like prediction in physics: they work on a different kind of reality. (3) There exists a link between prediction and prescription, and economics should attend to both. This link will depend on the capacity to get an increasing control of the variables (i.e., foresight rather than forecast) (Gonzalez 1996b, Sect. 5). (4) These semantic, logical, epistemological, and methodological bases of prediction constitute an advance in comparison with neoclassical economics, but it should be improved by taking into account economics as *activity*.

[34] On the kinds of scientific realism, see Gonzalez (1993a). On the issue of realism in economics, see Mäki (1989, 1998).

[35] Besides the criticisms of the Chicago school (to Friedman's methodology for positive economics and to Becker's "economic imperialism"), Simon does not accept the "rational expectations" of his former colleague John F. Muth (1961), cf. Simon (1976, pp. 142–143). Moreover, he considers that "the term is ill-chosen, for rational expectations in the sense of Muth are profit-maximizing expectations only under very special circumstances. Perhaps we would mislead ourselves and others less if we called them by the less alluring phrase, 'consistent expectations'" (Simon 1978, p. 2, note).

8.4 Rationality and Prediction in the Case of "Activity" and "Behavior"

To some extent, Herbert Simon's work is a long reflection on the concept of "human rationality," viewed from several angles (psychological and economic as well as political and computational). In fact, some of his main works are deeply concerned with this concept: in *Administrative Behavior* there is an examination of the implications of the limits of human rationality for organization behavior; in *The Sciences of the Artificial* he describes properties that are common to all adaptive (or "artificial") systems, looking for a basis for constructing a general theory of such systems; in *Reason in Human Affairs* he provides a framework for understanding the role of rationality in human affairs; … and even his *Models of my Life* could be seen from this perspective, because the book maintains that he has devoted "his scientific career to understanding human choice" (Simon 1991a, p. xvii).

8.4.1 Behavioral Conception

As far as bounded rationality and economic predictions are concerned,[36] four aspects of Simon's behavioral conception are particularly relevant. (i) Both—bounded rationality and economic predictions—are related to human *behavior*. This is intelligible and predictable as such, although it has many elements to be considered and, consequently, there is a serious problem regarding the reliability of prediction. *De facto*, several questions in the area of human behavior remain unresolved, and thus pose important difficulties for the reliability of predictions.

(ii) The accuracy of prediction depends on the *bounded* capacities to grasp the variables connected to the anticipation of future events. There are differences between prediction in the long run and the short run, due to the reality itself to be predicted and the different degree of control of its variables. Thus, it is possible that some phenomena are more predictable in the *long run* than in the short run (e.g., the demand of some new products or new services). However, that is not the most frequent case: the variables are, in principle, more knowable when they are close to the researcher (and, thus, within the field of experience and expertise to the researcher).

(iii) *Conditional* predictions are the normal case in economics, because it is quite rare to find predictions that, such as in astronomy, will follow from the general laws and initial conditions. The decision-making procedure includes an interdependence of variables: some of them are "exogenous" for us and others are "endogenous" within a specific model. Thus, when the problem is to predict the future price of petroleum (or the oil products), besides the endogenous variables of the economic

[36] The interest of Simon for the role of predictions was very clear. He studied prediction and hindsight as confirmatory evidence (Simon 1955b), economic expectations and plans of firms in relation to short-term forecasting (Simon and Cooper 1955), forecasting aggregate orders (Simon et al. 1960), etc.

model (the "genuine" economic variables), there are another variables that do not belong to the model (such as the decisions made by OPEC) that could be decisive for the final prediction. However, there are not—for Simon—*exogenous* variables in themselves: they may or may not be considered to be "exogenous" depending on the actual way the model is specified.

(iv) Economic predictions should consider *altruism*.[37] For, in order to predict properly on the basis of observation of real economic life, the strategy of maximizing utility—and its reduced form of maximizing economic reward—is not necessarily the dominant factor.[38] According to Simon, "human choice is driven by a number of motives, not limited to economic gain, that are based on anticipated consequences (pleasure and pain) for the chooser. Then one can call behavior 'altruistic' to the extent that it is influenced by expectations of pleasure and pain for other persons" (Simon 1993, p. 158).[39]

A special case is group loyalty, which has different forms, such as ethnicity. This feature has consequences in predicting attitudes and behavior of social groups. However, according to bounded rationality, there is a difference between knowing about ethnic desires to improve the condition of the group and predicting what policies will be supported by the group: "ethnic loyalties compete with many other loyalties, thereby making the prediction of choice further dependent on empirical investigation rather than a priori postulation" (Simon 1993, p. 158).[40]

Very frequently, Simon's economic theory insists on "human behavior" rather than "human activity." Although he uses the term "action," it often has the meaning of the operative result of behavior.[41] *Action* also appears in a "mechanical" context, according to the metaphors of computers: reason "goes to work only after it has been supplied with a suitable set of inputs, or premises. If reason is to be applied to discovering and choosing courses of action, then those inputs include, at the least, a set of *should*'s, or values to be achieved, and a set of *is*'s, or facts about the world in which the action is taken" (Simon 1983, p. 7).

Regularly, this procedural rationality—and, especially, the decision making process—is seen by him in the context of *behavior*: economics needs "to understand how human beings in fact behave in the face of uncertainty, and by what limits of information and computability they are bound" (Simon 1976, p. 144). Thus, he

---

[37] This approach goes directly against the neoclassical tendency in favor of self-interest and adds new elements for an alternative. A critique of the primacy of self-interest is in Sen (1976–1977).

[38] Simon himself recognizes that the possibility of non-selfish goals is not ruled out in economic theory, "for one person's pleasure may enter into another person's utility function; but since the utility function are givens of economic analysis, their content is irrelevant to the theory" (Simon 1963a/1982, p. 339, note).

[39] From a different philosophical perspective, a critique of maximizing is in Rescher (1987).

[40] This approach is connected to Simon (1990b).

[41] As a token of his paper on the topic: human beings "do not know all the alternatives that are available for action; they have only incomplete and uncertain knowledge about the environmental variables, present and future, that will determine the consequences of their choices; and they would be unable to make the computations required for optimal choice even if they had perfect knowledge" (Simon 1993, p. 156).

suggests replacing the over-simplified assumptions of the situationally constrained omniscient decision-maker (the neoclassical model) with "a realistic (and psychological) characterization of the limits of man's rationality, and the consequences of those limits for his economic behavior" (Simon 1976, p. 148).

Even though Simon's economic theory has advantages in comparison with the neoclassical economics or mainstream tendency on economic theory—as has been pointed out in this chapter—it is less complete than economics based on *human activity*. The complexity of economic reality is better analyzed in terms of the dual components "economic activity" and "economics as activity" than in "economic behavior."[42]

In effect, there is an *economic activity*, something that could be understood as autonomous regarding other human activities. It comprises economic activity which human beings carry out in their interrelations (interactions) involving goods and services, exchanges and commodities, innovation and plan optimizing decisions, and so. *Economics as activity* connects the links between economic activity and other human activities (political, sociological, cultural, etc.). In this case, economic activity appears integrated into the whole system of human relations; it is immersed in the set of activities developed by human beings in normal circumstances. Then, as an activity *among* others, economics has links with many activities (political, sociological, cultural, etc.).

8.4.2 Emphasis on Activity

Economic activity and economics as activity should both be considered in order to clarify the subject matter of economics, because this science explains and predicts human activities in the domain of a particular sphere (i.e., exchange, commodities, etc.). The elements of economic activity and economics as activity have direct implications for the realm of prediction. On the one hand, the normal aim of a human activity is more connected with present circumstances than with a future not yet observed. On the other hand, the predictability of economic activity—which is, in principle, autonomous—is possible, and could be reliable; whereas predictability of economics as a human activity among others appears more unreliable, precisely due to its interdependence with other activities. Thus, prediction does not appear as the central aim of economics, in spite of the predictivist thesis of neoclassical economics,[43] and its scientific character could be accepted in the economic activity (Gonzalez 1994, p. 263).

As basic science, economics has the mission of explaining and predicting human activities in the domain of a concrete sphere (i.e., exchange, commodities, etc.). As applied science, economics is related to the tasks of predicting and prescribing.

[42] This has been emphasized in Chap. 7.

[43] If we persist in using this predictivist thesis in evaluating the scientific character of economics, we may say that economics is a science due to the reliability of its predictions concerning its aspect as "economic activity."

When the basis is in the character of the *economic activity*, the components of human activity (act and action), the inner aspect of activity and the outer aspect of activity, should be studied. These features of economic reality include its purpose, content and repercussions on other activities (economic and non-economic).

(a) The analysis of the *purpose* of economic activity throws light on prediction, via an examination of the differences between "intention" and "prediction," which requires us also to take account of the distinction between "intention" and "intentionality." (b) The *content* looks at both the predictability of economic activities in themselves and the predictability of the influence or impact of other activities in economic ones. Both kinds need to be considered from the point of view of quantitative and qualitative predictions. (c) The *repercussion* on other activities (economic and non-economic) is relevant for the subject matter of this science and for the role of economic prediction. In addition, the human character of economic activity should be emphasized, distinguishing it from the realm of natural world. Thus, the relations between economic prediction and human activity highlight the differences between economics and natural sciences in general, and physics in particular (Gonzalez 1994, esp., pp. 262–280).

Between "human activity" and "human behavior" there are several relevant differences,[44] which can also be noticed in the ordinary language.[45] (1) Activity has an immediate *practical* character: it includes *praxis*—it is doing something which affects its reality—whereas behavior has a less diversified scope, mainly when it is understood as instinctive (close to animal behavior). (2) Activity has in itself *historicity*: human activity is *eo ipso* historical, not only in the sense of *having* time, but also in the deepest sense of occurring and developing precisely *with* time. This historicity affects the decision making process and it should be included among the elements to be studied. Behavior, on the contrary, has a more static constitution,

---

[44] On the features of "act," "action," and "activity" in the context of economics, cf. Gonzalez (1994, pp. 264–268). A bibliographic study of the philosophical perspective on action theory is in Elskamp and Gonzalez (1992).

[45] Regarding *action* and *behavior*, which are the closest terms among those just pointed out (act, action, and activity), the differences are also noticeable in American English, the language used in the works analyzed here. In effect, in the well-known *Webster's Dictionary* (ninth new collegiate edition), *action* appears with three main senses in the human case: (i) "an act of will"; (ii) "the manner or method of performing"; and (iii) "a thing done." In addition, it includes the sense of "a man of action," linked to the idea of *initiative*. Putting it all together, action is something human which could be carried out with initiative, but, above all, action is based in *an act of will*, which appears in a manner of performing and brings about a result (a thing done).

Meanwhile, "behavior," according to the *Webster's Dictionary*, has three senses: (a) "the response of an individual, group or species to its environment"; (b) "the manner of conducting oneself;" and (c) "the way in which something (as a machine) behaves." Thus, in *behavior* the *external* element prevails as in the starting point—a response to stimulation or to its environment—as in its form of evolving—the manner of conducting oneself— and it exhibits a regular pattern—the functionality of a machine or procedures which could be similar to it—. Therefore, the point of convergence between action and behavior is in the *process*—the manner of performing—insofar as there is involved a external factor and the performance could be repeated; whereas action—in the Dictionary—has *a broader scope*: its teleological character, with its starting in an act of will, goes to an end (a thing to be done) and gives more possibilities to human initiative.

because it can be considered without especial concern for historicity (a very well known example is behaviorism). (3) Activity has a very close link with *language*, more than behavior. So, there is no problem in the connection between action and language (such as in the case of "speech acts")[46] whereas there are criticisms regarding behavior and language (e.g., with Skinner's "verbal behavior" or Quine's proposals). (4) Activity has both a *descriptive* and a *normative* sphere, because there are genuine social actions which require norms to rule it properly (either ethically or legally), whereas behavior is more descriptive than normative.[47]

Although Simon is very critical of vision of rationality based on the human behavior of the neoclassical model,[48] his proposal receives the title of "the behavioral alternative" (Simon 1983, pp. 17–23).[49] Moreover, he defines economics in terms of description and prediction of "behavior" of economic man (1963a/1982, p. 320). This is not without a firm basis: his model of rationality works on human *behavior* rather than on human *activity*. But "neo-classical models of their essence concern economic *behaviour*," as M. Hollis and E. J. Nell assess in a chapter on "Behaviour and Prediction" (1975, p. 115). In effect, the main stream of neoclassical economics works on the concept of "behavior," and this is understood in a reductive way: the human being oriented towards given goals with an attitude of maximization under certainty. The primacy of self-interest and the difficulties for altruism are features of a model of man whose behavior is, in principle, predictable. In effect, the touchstone of economic behavior is subjective expected utility and this is predictable in accordance with some well-established premises.

Generally, neoclassical economics is compatible with a kind of behaviorist conception of the economic actor, whereas Simon's "behavioral model" is linked to a broader psychological picture of the human being (and connected to an approach to artificial intelligence). In fact, his alternative to the subjective expected utility

[46] As has been emphasized in analytic philosophy, when we speak we perform acts that are not the mere locutionary acts. Thus, the illocutionary and perlocutionary acts are not pure elements of behavior: to speak is a highly conscious ability that goes beyond the practical dominion of conduct which requires a previous learning (such as, how to use a calculator or an instrument in the laboratory). The effects of illocutionary acts and the consequences of perlocutionary acts are more complex than "verbal behavior."

[47] Simon tries to avoid the last problem in his theories of bounded rationality. For him, regarding the rational behavior itself, the focus could be in a descriptive perspective or in a normative one. In the first case, a conception may purport to describe how people or organizations do, in fact, behave, whereas in the second case the view may prescribe how people or organizations should behave in order to achieve certain goals under certain conditions, cf. Simon (1972, p. 161).

[48] Four components constitute the kind of rationally adopted by the subjective expected utility model. Simon himself has pointed them out (before he criticizes them in detail): a cardinal utility function; an exhaustive set of alternative strategies; a probability distribution of scenarios for the future connected with each strategy; and a policy of maximizing expected utility. In other words, this *homo economicus* is a decision maker with a well defined utility function; he or she has a well defined set of alternatives to choose from and can assign a consistent joint probability distribution to all future sets of events; and the *homo economicus* will choose the alternative or the strategy that will maximize the expected value in terms of his utility function. Cf. Simon (1983, pp. 12–17).

[49] On behavioral economics, see for example Baxter (1993), and Egidi and Marris (1992). On the role of prediction in the behavioral theory of the firm, see Cyert and Grunberg (1963).

model, which has a key point in the notion of "satisficing," is consistent with folk psychology, because this demands neither perfect consistency of preferences nor maximizing (Hausman 1992a, p. 253, note).

However, in spite of his important contribution to psychology (Newell 1989, esp., p. 401), mainly in cognitive psychology (in some ways, an alternative to behaviorism), the existence of *common roots* between both positions could be possible. In effect, these two approaches to economics actually share a common *starting point*, and Hausman points this out: the economists who explain behavior in terms of utility functions use beliefs and desires to clarify choices, and "Herbert Simon's theory of individual choice in terms of 'satisfacing' rather than maximizing still explains choices in terms of beliefs and desires" (Hausman 1992a, p. 322).

Nevertheless, there exists a *difference*: in the neoclassical model the outer component of the human being carries more weight than the inner component, because the observable factors of behavior are the key to establishing the decision making process as well as the future economic events which follow from that behavior within its external environment. Simon, on the contrary, pays more attention to the cognitive aspects of economic behavior. For him, "classical economics minimized its dependence upon motivational theory in psychology by taking utility maximization (for the consumer) and profit maximization (for the entrepreneur) as the sole motives of economic man. Similarly, economics got along almost without psychological hypotheses about economic man's intellective qualities by assuming him to be 'objectively' rational" (Simon 1963a/1982, p. 341). Thus, he considers that, given these basic assumptions (cognitive and motivational), "nothing more need be known about economic man to predict his behavior; it suffices to have information about its environment—e.g., the prices in the markets in which he trades, his production function, and so on" (Simon 1963a/1982, p. 341).

According to Simon's analysis, the predictive success in neoclassical economics is due to the adoption of quite simple assumptions regarding human behavior, but that success is also quite limited: it only covers a reduced area of economics. In his judgment, neoclassical economists can claim—with considerable justification—that "the classical model has had great predictive power in the areas of behavior with which they have been concerned. But economics has been moving steadily into newer areas where the power of the model has never been demonstrated and where its adequacy must be considered anew" (Simon 1963a/1982, p. 341). These are labor economics, oligopoly and imperfect competition, decision-making under uncertainty, and the theory of economic development. However, if we compare Simon's behavioral model on prediction with other models, including those formulated by some of his fellow Nobel Laureates, we can affirm that the discrepancy still continues and the differences are deep (see Gonzalez 1996c, 2006b).

Several significant conclusions follow from the present analysis of the relations between bounded rationality and scientific predictions. First, there are deficiencies in the neoclassical model, based on maximization under certainty with behavior ruled by optimism. Within this position, economic predictions can be accurate within certain parameters of "economic activity" but not really in the area of "economics as activity." Second, Simon's model constitutes a clear step forward when uncertainty is at stake, because uncertainty, bounded rationality and economic prediction are interconnected. His conception offers a real improvement in comparison with "perfect rationality" of neoclassical model, insofar as he proposes the strategy of satisficing, rather than maximizing, and the study of the limitations of predictions. However, he presents a behavioral model that still has some behavioral constraints that have precedents in neoclassical economics. Third, the model based on economics understood as a human activity reflects better the complexity of economic predictions and the necessity of combining the rationality of ends (goals) with the rationality of means (procedures).

References

Arrow, K. 1972. Exposition of the theory of choice under uncertainty. In *Decision and organization,* ed. C. B. McGuire and R. Radner, 19–55. Amsterdam: North-Holland.

Arrow, K. 1987. Rationality of self and others in an economic system. In *Rational choice. The contrast between economics and psychology,* ed. R. M. Hogarth and M. W. Reder, 201–215. Chicago: The University of Chicago Press.

Baxter, J. L. 1993. *Behavioral foundations of economics*. New York: St. Martin's.

Becker, G. S. 1962. Irrational behavior and economic theory. *Journal of Political Economy* 70:1–13.

Becker, G. S. 1974. A theory of social interactions. *Journal of Political Economy* 82:1063–1093.

Bicchieri, C. 1987. Rationality and predictability in economics. *The British Journal for the Philosophy of Science* 38:501–513.

Cyert, R. M., and E. Grunberg. 1963. Assumption, prediction, and explanation in economics. In *A behavioral theory of firm,* ed. R. M. Cyert and J. G. March, 298–311. Englewood Cliffs: Prentice Hall.

Dasgupta, S. 2003. Multidisciplinary creativity: The case of Herbert A. Simon. *Cognitive Science* 27:683–707.

Egidi, M., and R. Marris, eds. 1992. *Economics, bounded rationality and the cognitive revolution.* Aldershot: Edward Elgar, Brookfield: Edward Elgar.

Elskamp, R. G., and W. J. Gonzalez. 1992. Teoría de la Acción. Estudio bibliográfico. *Diálogo filosófico* 22:199–223.

Friedman, M. 1953. The methodology of positive economics. In *Essays in positive economics,* ed. M. Friedman, 3–43. Chicago: The University of Chicago Press (6th repr., 1969).

Gonzalez, W. J. 1993a. El realismo y sus variedades: El debate actual sobre las bases filosóficas de la Ciencia. In *Conocimiento, Ciencia y realidad,* ed. A. Carreras, 11–58. Zaragoza: SIUZ-Ed. Mira.

Gonzalez, W. J. 1994. Economic prediction and human activity. An analysis of prediction in economics from action theory. *Epistemologia* 17:253–294.

Gonzalez, W. J. 1995. Reichenbach's concept of prediction. *International Studies in the Philosophy of Science* 9 (1): 37–58.

Gonzalez, W. J. 1996a. Towards a new framework for revolutions in science. *Studies in History and Philosophy of Science* 27 (4): 607–625.

Gonzalez, W. J. 1996b. Prediction and mathematics: The Wittgensteinian approach. In *Spanish studies in the philosophy of science,* ed. G. Munevar, 299–332. Dordrecht: Kluwer.

Gonzalez, W. J. 1996c. On the theoretical basis of prediction in economics. *Journal of Social Philosophy* 27 (3): 201–228.

Gonzalez, W. J. 1997b. Rationality in economics and scientific predictions: A critical reconstruction of bounded rationality and its role in economic predictions. *Poznan Studies in the Philosophy of Science* 61:205–232.

Gonzalez, W. J. 2003c. Herbert A. Simon: Filósofo de la Ciencia y economista (1916–2001). In *Racionalidad, historicidad y predicción en Herbert A. Simon,* ed. W. J. Gonzalez, 7–63. A Coruña: Netbiblo.
Gonzalez, W. J. 2003d. Racionalidad y Economía: De la racionalidad de la Economía como Ciencia a la racionalidad de los agentes económicos. In *Racionalidad, historicidad y predicción en Herbert A. Simon,* ed. W. J. Gonzalez, 65–96. A Coruña: Netbiblo.
Gonzalez, W. J. 2006b. Prediction as scientific test of economics. In *Contemporary perspectives in philosophy and methodology of science,* ed. W. J. Gonzalez and J. Alcolea, 83–112. A Coruña: Netbiblo.
Gonzalez, W. J. 2007b. Análisis de las Ciencias de Diseño desde la racionalidad limitada, la predicción y la prescripción. In *Las Ciencias de Diseño: Racionalidad limitada, predicción y prescripción,* ed. W. J. Gonzalez, 3–38. A Coruña: Netbiblo.
Gonzalez, W. J. 2007c. Configuración de las Ciencias de Diseño como Ciencias de lo Artificial: Papel de la Inteligencia Artificial y de la racionalidad limitada. In *Las Ciencias de Diseño: Racionalidad limitada, predicción y prescripción,* ed. W. J. Gonzalez, 41–69. A Coruña: Netbiblo.
Gonzalez, W. J. 2008. Rationality and prediction in the sciences of the artificial: Economics as a design science. In *Reasoning, rationality, and probability,* ed. M. C. Galavotti, R. Scazzieri, and P. Suppes, 165–186. Stanford: CSLI Publications.
Gonzalez, W. J. 2013c. The roles of scientific creativity and technological innovation in the context of complexity of science. In *Creativity, innovation, and complexity in science,* ed. W. J. Gonzalez, 11–40. A Coruña: Netbiblo.
Hausman, D. M. 1992a. *The inexact and separate science of economics*. Cambridge: Cambridge University Press.
Hollis, M., and E. J. Nell. 1975. *Rational economic man. A philosophical critique of neo-classical economics*. Cambridge: Cambridge University Press.
Hume, D. 1739–1740. *A treatise of human nature,* ed. L. A. Selby-Bigge (1964). Oxford: Clarendon Press.
Klaes, M., and E.-M. Sent. 2005. A conceptual history of the emergence of bounded rationality. *History of Political Economy* 37 (1): 27–59.
Loasby, B. J. 1976. *Choice, complexity and ignorance. An inquiry into economic theory and the practice of decision-making*. Cambridge: Cambridge University Press.
Mäki, U. 1989. On the problem of realism in economics. *Richerce Economiche* 93(1-2):176–198.
Mäki, U. 1998. Aspects of realism about economics. *Theoria* 13(32):301–319.
Muth, J. 1961. Rational expectations and the theory of price movements. *Econometrica* 29:315–335. (Reprinted in Lucas, R. E., and Th. J. Sargent, eds. 1981. *Rational expectations and econometric practicem,* 3–22. London: G. Allen and Unwin).
Newell, A. 1989. Putting it all together. In *Complex information processing,* ed. D. Klahr and K. Kotovsky, 399–440. Hillsdale: Erlbaum.
Rescher, N. 1984. *The limits of science*. Berkeley: University of California Press.
Rescher, N. 1987. Maximization, optimization, and rationality. On reasons why rationality is not necessarily a matter of maximization. In *Ethical idealism. An inquiry into the nature and function of ideals,* N. Rescher, 55–84. Berkeley: University of California Press.
Rescher, N. 1988. *Rationality. A philosophical inquiry into the nature and the rationale of reason*. Oxford: Oxford University Press.
Salmon, W. C. 1993. On the alleged temporal anisotropy of explanation. In *Philosophical problems of the internal and external worlds,* ed. J. Earman, A. Janis, G. Massey, and N. Rescher, 229–248. Pittsburgh: University of Pittsburgh Press.
Samuelson, P. 1963. Problems of methodology-discussion. *American Economic Review* 53(2):231–236.
Sen, A. 1976–1977. Rational fools: A critique of the behavioural foundations of economic theory. *Philosophy and Public Affairs* 6:317–344. (Reprinted in Hahn, F., and M. Hollis, eds. 1979. *Philosophy and economic theory,* 87–109. Oxford: Oxford University Press).

Sent, E.-M. 2004. The legacy of Herbert Simon in game theory. *Journal of Economic Behavior and Organization* 53:303–327.
Simon, H. A. 1947. *Administrative behavior*. New York: Macmillan. (4th ed. (1997). New York: The Free Press).
Simon, H. A. 1955a. A behavioral model of rational choice. *Quarterly Journal of Economics* 69:99–118. (Reprinted in Simon, H. A. 1957. *Models of man,* Chap. 14, 241–260. New York: Wiley).
Simon, H. A. 1955b. Prediction and hindsight as confirmatory evidence. *Philosophy of Science* 22 (3): 227–230.
Simon, H. A. 1957. *Models of man*. New York: Wiley.
Simon, H. A. 1963a. Economics and psychology. In *Psychology: A study of a science,* vol. 6, ed. S. Koch, 715–752. New York: McGraw Hill. (Reprinted in Simon, H. A. 1982. *Models of bounded rationality,* vol. 2: *Behavioral economics and business organization,* 318–355. Cambridge: The MIT Press).
Simon, H. A. 1963b. Problems of methodology-discussion. *American Economic Review* 53:229–231. (Reprinted in Simon, H. A. 1982. *Models of bounded rationality,* vol. 2: *Behavioral economics and business organization,* 369–371. Cambridge: The MIT Press; also reprinted as Simon, H. A. 1984. Testability and approximation. In *Philosophy of economics,* ed. D. M. Hausman. 1st ed., 245–248. Cambridge: Cambridge University Press).
Simon, H. A. 1964. Rationality. In *A dictionary of the social sciences,* ed. J. Gould and W. L., 573–574. Glencoe: Free Press. (Reprinted in Simon, H. A. 1982. *Models of bounded rationality,* vol. 2: *Behavioral economics and business organization,* 405–407. Cambridge: The MIT Press).
Simon, H. A. 1972. Theories of bounded rationality. In *Decision and organization,* ed. C. B. McGuire and R. Radner, 161–176. Amsterdam: North-Holland. (Reprinted in Simon, H. A. 1982. *Models of bounded rationality,* vol. 2: *Behavioral economics and business organization,* 408–423. Cambridge: The MIT Press).
Simon, H. A. 1976. From substantive to procedural rationality. In *Method and appraisal in economics,* ed. S. Latsis, 129–148. Cambridge: Cambridge University Press.
Simon, H. A. 1978. Rationality as process and as product of thought. *American Economic Review* 68 (2): 1–16.
Simon, H. A. 1979. Rational decision making in business organizations. *American Economic Review* 69 (4): 493–513. (Reprinted in Simon, H. A. 1982. *Models of bounded rationality,* vol. 2: *Behavioral economics and business organization,* 474–494. Cambridge: The MIT Press).
Simon, H. A. 1983. *Reason in human affairs*. Stanford: Stanford University Press.
Simon, H. A. 1987a. Rationality in psychology and economics. In *Rational choice. The contrast between economics and psychology,* ed. R. M. Hogarth and M. W. Reder, 25–40. Chicago: The University of Chicago Press.
Simon, H. A. 1987b. Politics as information processing. *L. S. E. Quarterly* 1:345–370.
Simon, H. A. 1989. The state of economic science. In *The state of economic science. Views of six Nobel laureates,* ed. W. Sichel, 97–110. Kalamazoo: W. E. Upjohn Institute for Employment Research.
Simon, H. A. 1990a. Prediction and prescription in systems modeling. *Operations Research* 38:7–14. (Reprinted in Simon, H. A. 1997. *Models of bounded rationality,* vol. 3: *Empirically grounded economic reason,* 115–128. Cambridge: The MIT Press).
Simon, H. A. 1990b. A mechanism for social selection and successful altruism. *Science* 250:1665–1668. (Reprinted in Simon, H. A. 1997. *Models of bounded rationality,* vol. 3: *Empirically grounded economic reason,* 205–216. Cambridge: The MIT Press).
Simon, H. A. 1991a. *Models of my life*. New York: Basic Books-HarperCollins.
Simon, H. A. 1992a. Introductory comment. In *Economics, bounded rationality and the cognitive revolution,* ed. M. Egidi and R. Marris, 3–7. Aldershot: Edward Elgar.
Simon, H. A. 1992b. Colloquium with H. A. Simon. In *Economics, bounded rationality and the cognitive revolution,* ed. M. Egidi and R. Marris, 8–36. Aldershot: Edward Elgar.

Simon, H. A. 1993. Altruism and economics. *American Economic Review* 83 (2): 156–161. (Reprinted as Altruism and economics: Social implications. Simon, H. A. 1997. *Models of bounded rationality,* vol. 3: *Empirically grounded economic reason,* 257–265. Cambridge: The MIT Press).

Simon, H. A. 1995a. Rationality in political behavior. *Political Psychology* 16:45–63.

Simon, H. A. 1996. *The sciences of the artificial.* 3rd ed. Cambridge: The MIT Press (1st ed., 1969; 2nd ed., 1981).

Simon, H. A. 1998. Economics as a historical science. *Theoria* 13 (32): 241–260.

Simon, H. A. 2000. Bounded rationality in social science: Today and tomorrow. *Mind and Society* 1 (1): 25–39.

Simon, H. A. 2001. On simulating Simon: His monomania, and its sources in bounded rationality. *Studies in History and Philosophy of Science* 32(3):501–505.

Simon, H. A., and W. Cooper. 1955. Economic expectations and plans of firms in relation to short-term forecasting. *Studies in Inconme and Wealth* 17:352–359.

Simon, H. A., et al. 1960. Forecasting aggregate orders. In *Planning production, inventories, and work force,* ed. C. C. Holt, F. Modigliani, J. Muth, and H. A. Simon, 131–171. Englewood Cliffs: Prentice Hall.

Stuart Mill, J. 1836. On the definition of political economy and on the method of investigation proper to it. *London and Westminster Review,* vol. IV, 1–29. (Reprinted in Stuart Mill, J. 1967. *Essays on economics and society,* vol. IV, 309–339. Ed. J. M. Robson: Collected works of John Stuart Mill. Toronto: University of Toronto Press).

Tversky, A., and D. Kahneman. 1982. Judgment under uncertainty: Heuristics and biases. In *Judgment under uncertainty: Heuristics and biases,* ed. D. Kahneman, P. Slovic, and A. Tversky, 3–20. Cambridge: Cambridge University Press (reprint 1987).

Chapter 9
Rationality and Prediction in Experimental Economics: An Analysis of Reinhard Selten's Approach

Besides the approach to prediction based on the development of new aspects in rationality and empirical support which has been proposed by Herbert Simon's behavioral economics (Chap. 8), there is another interesting option where rationality accompanies experimental economics, and this gives new perspectives on prediction in this field. Many influential economists—such as the Nobel Prizes laureates Reinhard Selten (1994), Vernon Smith (2002), and Alvin Roth (2012)—have advocated this possibility. Among them, the work done by Selten, who uses ideas on bounded rationality in his epistemology, seems to me more interesting for the present research.

9.1 From Behavioral Economics to Experimental Economics

Behavioral economics is focused on observation of economic agents in markets and organizations (Simon 1991). This kind of empirical methodology has been the main interest of Simon's models on bounded rationality, which he always stressed as being empirically founded. Meanwhile, experimental economics goes further than that possibility in the research on economic phenomena.[1] It accepts the existence of "experiments" in social sciences, in general, and in economics, in particular. Thus, this branch of economics draws attention to new methodological aspects that can be relevant for the study of economic predictions (Gonzalez 2007a).

Experimental economics is a branch of economics that has received increasing attention since the mid-1980s to now. Nevertheless, Roth (1988/1993, p. 3) has set its first, informal, precedent as early as Daniel Bernoulli (1738). But it is only since the second half of the twentieth century that it has been clearly developed.[2] In fact,

[1] See, for example, Davis and Holt (1993), and Hey and Loomes (1993).

[2] Even though Volker Häselbarth in 1967 lists 20 publications before 1959, Selten stresses that "experimental economics as a field of economic research did not emerge before the 1960s" (Selten 1993, p. 118).

W. J. Gonzalez, *Philosophico-Methodological Analysis of Prediction and its Role in Economics*, Theory and Decision Library A: 50, DOI 10.1007/978-3-319-08885-3_9

it is in the period between 1975 and 1985 when experimental economics undergoes the transformation from "a seldom encountered curiosity to a well-established part of economic literature" (Roth 1987, p. 147). The process was consolidated around 1985, when the *Journal of Economic Literature* initiated a separate bibliographical category for "Experimental Economic Methods."[3]

Among its most influential specialists is Selten, who—as it is well known—along with John Nash and John Harsanyi received the Nobel Prize in economics for his work on game theory.[4] His relation with experimental economics appears to have its first expression when he publishes with Heinz Sauermann the paper "Ein Oligopolexperiment" (1959). A few years later, both—Sauermann and Selten (1962)—showed their approval of Simon's concept of "bounded rationality," which they use to develop an "aspiration adaptation theory of the firm" (Selten 1990, p. 649). Thereafter, the bounded rationality approach regarding human behavior and the methodological perspective of experimental economics have been closely related in Selten's intellectual trajectory (2003).

During all this period—at least, four decades—of his special interest in bounded rationality, Selten has made important contributions to economics.[5] Frequently, his papers include criticisms of mainstream economics, especially of the principle of subjective expected utility maximization. His publications are usually critical of assumptions of mainstream game theory,[6] which is deeply imbued with instrumental rationality. In fact, he links one of his most famous contributions to game theory—the chain store paradox (Selten 1978)—to the need for a bounded rationality supported by experimental evidence. He considers that the attempts to save the behavioral relevance of full rationality miss the point (Selten 1990, p. 651).

Furthermore, when Selten develops his economic approach, he presents area theories, such as the theory of equal division payoff bounds, which are based on a limited rationality (Selten 1987). In addition, he offers us a series of phenomena that confirm experimentally the existence of a bounded rationality (Selten 1998a). In this chapter, after the presentation of his approach to experimental economics, the emphasis will be on his conception of economic rationality as *bounded*. This contributes to an analysis of his views on prediction, which are clearly influenced by his position on bounded rationality, and it is a domain where he provides relevant methodological proposals (the role of the experiments is seen in a realm of "accuracy" and "precision").

---

[3] The same year—1985—the Fifth World Congress of the Econometric Society included a paper on experimental economics, cf. Roth (1986, p. 245).

[4] Selten has published with Harsanyi a general theory of equilibrium selection in games (Harsanyi and Selten 1988).

[5] Among a large number of publications, see Selten (1990, 1998a, 2001).

[6] John Nash considers that the book *A General Theory of Equilibrium Selection in Games*, written by John Harsanyi and Renhard Selten, "is very controversial" (Nash 1996, p. 182).

9.2 Selten's Approach to Experimental Economics

Epistemologically, Selten stresses the importance of *empirical knowledge* over theoretical knowledge, a position that is more in tune with an empiricist framework than with a rationalist one.[7] His views, furthermore, differ from the claims of critical rationalism, insofar as that he is dissatisfied with a negative role of experience and that he highlights the need for experience understood in positive terms (Gonzalez 2007a). In this regard, he maintains that "we know that Bayesian decision theory is not a realistic description of human economic behavior. There is ample evidence for this, but we cannot be satisfied with negative knowledge—knowledge about what human behavior fails to be. We need more positive knowledge on the structure of human behavior. We need theories of bounded rationality, supported by experimental evidence, which can be used in economic modelling as an alternative to exaggerated rationality assumptions" (Selten 1991a, p. 21).[8]

Selten's recommendation against the attempts to derive human behavior from a few general principles—either psychological or biological—[9]is the gaining of empirical knowledge. Furthermore, he is critical of unrealistic principles, thus opposing a view held by influential mainstream economists, and he does not accept criticism of the use of *ad hoc* assumptions insofar as they are empirically supported.[10] He maintains that successful explanations of experimental phenomena should be built up along the primacy of empirical knowledge. That knowledge reveals diversity: "experiments show that human behavior is *ad hoc*. Different principles are applied to different decision tasks. Case distinctions determine which principles are used where" (Selten 1991a, p. 19). Moreover, against the dominant position in favor of full rationality, he affirms that the "attempts to save the rationalistic view of economic man by minor modifications have no chance of succeeding" (Selten 1993, p. 135).

Methodologically, Selten seems to be sympathetic towards the research on induction (1990, p. 656).[11] His approach to experimental economics tends to identify some empirical regularities based on experimental data and thereafter to construe a formal theory to explain them, instead of beginning with a formal theory that is

[7] Some well-known economists, among them Simon and Selten, insist on the relevance of empirical knowledge and on the distinction between "empirical" and "theoretical," whereas many philosophers in recent decades have stressed that scientific knowledge is always theory-laden and give less importance to that distinction (Gonzalez 2013a).

[8] "The application of Bayesian methods makes sense in special contexts. For example, a life insurance company may adopt a utility function for its total assets; subjective probabilities may be based on actuarial tables. However, a general use of Bayesian methods meets serious difficulties. Subjective probabilities and utilities are needed as inputs. Usually these inputs are not readily available" (Selten 1991a, p. 19).

[9] "We have to gain empirical knowledge. We cannot derive human economic behavior from biological principles" (Selten 1991a, p. 9).

[10] "It is better to make many empirically supported ad hoc assumptions, than to rely on a few unrealistic principles of great generality and elegance" (Selten 1991a, p. 19).

[11] He is especially interested in the book Holland et al. (1986).

submitted to test in the laboratory. This kind of methodological approach is different from other *methodological possibilities* frequent among *experimental economists*, of which there are basically three: (1) experiments designed for testing and modifying formal economic theories; (2) experiments designed to collect data on interesting phenomena and relevant institutions, in the hope of detecting unanticipated regularities; and (3) experiments associated with having a direct impact in the realm of policy-making (Roth 1986, pp. 245–246).

The *fourth possibility* on experiments, which can be found in Selten's papers, stems from the dissatisfaction of a present theory in the light of the data and the need for an *alternative theory* based directly on observed behavior. The experimental results are used to identify some empirical regularities (and there is a similitude here with the second possibility). This evidence may suggest theoretical considerations that eventually may lead to the construction of a formal theory (and this is a difference in comparison with the second possibility). This theory is ordinarily of a *limited range*, because experimental results usually support only theories of limited range, whereas an empirical-based general theory of bounded rationality appears as a task for the future (Selten 1998a, p. 414).

This kind of methodological approach, which can be seen in Selten's theory of equal division payoff bounds (1982/1988; cf. Selten 1987, esp., pp. 64–80), is different from the methodological case of theory-oriented experiments insofar as the starting point is different. In one case—the first methodological view—the research starts with a body of formal theory and then proceeds to develop a set of experiments which allow some conclusions to be drawn about the theory, whereas in the other case—the fourth methodological view—the research starts with a body of data from experimental games, which leads to a theory (Roth 1986, pp. 266–267). The theory can take "the form of a hypothetical reasoning process which looks at the players in order of their strength" (Selten 1982/1988, p. 301).[12]

Underlying Selten's methodological approach on experimental economics is a rejection of key methodological views of mainstream economics: "the success of the theory of equal division payoff bounds confirms the methodological point of view that the limited rationality of human decision behavior must be taken seriously. It is futile to insist on explanations in terms of subjectively expected utility maximization. The optimization approach fails to do justice to the structure of human decision processes" (Selten 1987, p. 95). This methodological recognition of the need for a bounded rationality approach to human decision-making in the economic activity seems to me very relevant.

Nevertheless, we still have certain methodological problems in experimental economics, mainly in the sphere of *methodological limitations*: how much of what is obtained in the economic laboratory can be applied directly to the complex situation of economic activity within the real world? It is not a minor problem,

[12] He considers that "typically, game-theoretic solution concepts are based on definitions that describe the proposed solution by inner properties… The theory of equal division payoff bounds has a different character. The payoff bounds are not characterized by inner properties. They are constructively obtained by straightforward commonsense arguments based on easily recognizable features of the strategic situation" (Selten 1987, p. 78).

because—as Selten himself recognizes—"also field data are important, but they are more difficult to obtain and harder to interpret" (Selten 1998a, p. 414).

This aspect can have repercussions in two ways: on the one hand, in the characterization of *economic activity* as such (i.e., in giving the real features of human decision making in ordinary circumstances, instead of in an artificial environment); and, on the other, in the analysis of economic activity as *interconnected* with other human activities in a changeable historical setting, because economic activity is *de facto* connected with other human activities, and in a context which is also historical.[13]

9.3 Epistemic Rationality, Practical Rationality, and Evaluative Rationality

Within economics as a whole, the concept of "rationality" plays a key role, and experimental economics is not an exception. *Rationality* is a notion that is closely linked to "choice" and "decision making." In this regard, it is customary in economics to present rationality in twofold terms: on the one hand, *normative rationality*, which points to what one should do in order to attain some specific aim and, on the other, *descriptive rationality*, which is used to reflect human endeavors in order to explain them or to predict them. Both aspects—normative and descriptive—assume that human behavior—the conduct of *homo economicus*—is goal oriented, and the emphasis is usually put on the relation from means to ends. Thus, a rational economic choice appears frequently as a selection of *adequate means* to attain *given ends* (Gonzalez 2003b).

If the ends have more weight in the characterization of rationality and we understand that "rationality consists in the intelligent pursuit of appropriate ends" (Rescher 1988, p. 1), then the notion of *rationality* becomes wider than in the dominant tendency in mainstream economics. In fact, there are three different *dimensions of rationality* regarding choice and decision-making: (a) epistemic or cognitive rationality, (b) practical rationality, and (c) evaluative rationality.

From Kant on, the philosophical tradition "sees three major contexts of choice, those of *belief*, of accepting or endorsing thesis or claims, of *action*, of what overt acts to perform, and of *evaluation*, of what to value or disvalue. These represent the spheres of cognitive, practical, and evaluative reason, respectively" (Rescher 1988, pp. 2–3).[14] Thus, not all deliberative reasoning—including the economic one—is means-end reasoning: there are three kinds of rationality according to the objects of rational deliberation: *epistemic rationality*, which deals with what is possible to believe or accept in the realm of knowledge; *practical rationality*, which decides

[13] On the distinction *economic activity-economics as activity*, see Gonzalez (1994) and Chap. 7.

[14] According to Rescher, "for philosophers the crux of rationality is epistemic: making one's choices on the bases of the best available determination of the real/true/actual facts. So even in the light of imperfect information one can and should proceed rationally—by doing the best one can in the circumstances. So just this—imperfect information—is of great interest to economists but is nevertheless a topic that philosophers have neglected" *Personal communication*, 24 May 2005.

regarding actions; and *evaluative rationality*, which judges what to prefer or prize (it assesses values, goals or ends).

According to a characteristic analysis of rational choice (especially of a single-agent) within the mainstream tendency, there is first an attribution of *practical rationality* (the optimality of one's action is assumed, given one's desires and beliefs: if agent *a* desires *d* and believes that action *r* will secure *d*, the agent is practically rational in choosing *r*); and there is a second attribution of *epistemic rationality* to the actor (where rationality is then an attribute of belief, and consists in recognizing its correctness, given the evidence at the actor's disposal) (Bicchieri 1992, pp. 161–162). But ordinarily there is no mention at all of *evaluative rationality*: the ends are given—they are not evaluated—and a rational agent is instrumentally rational, i.e., he or she should make practical decisions on means to attain the given ends. This is also the case in Simon's conception of rationality,[15] in spite of his being clearly critical of the outlook on rationality of mainstream economics.

Although they share a common interest in bounded rationality, I think that Selten's views on economic rationality go beyond Simon's instrumental rationality insofar as Selten accepts the presence of *evaluative rationality* in addition to practical rationality and epistemic rationality. Even though he does not use that terminology in his papers, it seems to me that these three dimensions of rationality underlie what he calls "three stages of reasoning," which he finds in the boundedly rational strategy construction: (i) superficial analysis, (ii) goal formation, and (iii) policy formation (Selten 1990, p. 656).

In this differentiation, the "superficial analysis" is when there is easily accessible information, and the examination is qualitative rather than quantitative. Here, the presence of *epistemic rationality* is undeniable. The "goal formation" seems to have implicit (or even explicit) the use of an evaluative rationality: when some concept of "fairness" intervenes (be it in terms of equal profits, profits proportional to Cournot profits, etc.) in order to determine the quantities for players which can be called "an ideal point" (a cooperative goal), then a *rational evaluation* of the aim is made. The "policy formation" looks at the means to reach the end: it is necessary to determine a way in which the goal (cooperative at the ideal point) can be achieved. This case is a characteristic use of *practical rationality*.

Reinhard Selten and Alexander Ockenfels have offered us a good example of *evaluative rationality* through an experimental solidarity game (1998), because the other-directed motivations of the players can include reasoning about the *ends* themselves. On the one hand, solidarity aims at a reciprocal relationship, but it is a more subtle relation than giving after one has received. Solidarity is different from reciprocity insofar as the gifts made are not reciprocated. And, on the other hand, the subjects have to decide how much, in the case of their winning, they are willing to give to a loser, when he or she is the only one in the group, or to each one of the losers, when these are two.

[15] "We see that reason is wholly instrumental. It cannot tell us where to go; at best it can tell us how to get there. It is a gun for hire that can be employed in the service of whatever goals we have, good or bad" (Simon 1983, pp. 7–8). In this regard, see Chap. 8.

What Selten and Ockenfels have found is quite different from utility maximization: the players have "a decision process which first fixes the total amount to be sacrificed for solidarity and then distributes it (up to rounding) among the losers regardless of their number" (Selten and Ockenfels 1998, p. 525). The decision process that deliberates on the aim is based on the value of solidarity and it is different from a practical rationality of an instrumental kind.

9.4 Bounded Rationality in the Context of Experimental Economics

On the one hand, it is clear that Selten insists on the deficiencies of the dominant view on economic rationality: "experiments have shown again and again that the way in which human beings choose among alternatives is not adequately described by the theory of subjectively expected utility maximization" (Selten 1987, p. 43). Intransitivities in choice behavior and the phenomenon of preference reversal are mentioned as examples of the difficulties of the economic principle of utility maximization. In this regard, he is a critic of the philosophico-methodological approach of neoclassical economics.

Yet, on the other hand, it should be emphasized that he complains about the contemporary situation of experimental economics in this issue. He considers that "relatively few experimentalists contribute to the development of a theory of boundedly rational economic behavior. Too many experimentalists are in search for a confirmation of orthodox theory and go to great length in explaining away deviations that cannot be overlooked. Nevertheless the necessity for a radical reconstruction of microeconomic theory becomes more and more visible" (Selten 1990, p. 650).

9.4.1 Two Ways of "Bounded Rationality"

Bounded rationality in Selten can be understood in two different ways, because he distinguishes between cognitive bounds and motivational bounds. *Cognitive bounds* are the limits related to the human capability to think and to compute; whereas *motivational bounds* are the failures to behave according to one's rational insights (Selten 1993, pp. 132–133). The first kind—cognitive bounds—is stressed by Simon from his very first papers on bounded rationality to his latest writings on this issue (Gonzalez 1997b; cf. Chap. 8). The second kind—motivational bounds—appears more clearly in Selten.[16]

[16] Simon mentions "motivational constraints" in his writings, but he uses this expression in the context of a criticism to the traditional organization theory, which conceives the human organism as a *simple machine*. Thus, in his book with James March, he considers "the unanticipated consequences of treating an organization as though it were composed of such machines. This does not mean that the 'classical' theory is totally wrong or needs to be totally displaced. It means that under

As a matter of fact, Selten discovered these rational limits of motivational bounds along with the chain store paradox: it is not a lack of epistemic power but rather a failure to behave according to the rational insights. For him, "many phenomena of everyday life can be understood as caused by motivational bounds of rationality. Somebody who is convinced that it would be best for him to stop smoking may nevertheless find himself unable to do this" (Selten 1993, p. 133).

Between Simon's approach to rationality ("empirically grounded economic reason")[17] and Selten's conception (experimentally limited reason) there is a difference on bounded rationality: the former has accentuated the cognitive limitations (mainly as a limitation of computational capacity), whereas the latter offers a broader panorama insofar as *motivational limitations* are explicitly added to cognitive limitations.

Moreover, Selten considers that motivation is the mental process that acts as the driving force of human economic behavior (Selten 1998a, p. 414), and he emphasizes the second kind of rational limits—motivational bounds.[18] He maintains that "the motivational limits of rationality are due to the separation of cognition and decision. The problem is known in philosophy under the name of 'acrasia' or 'weakness of the will'. A person may know very well what action is best for him and yet may find himself unable to take it" (Selten 1990, p. 651).

Motivational limits are, then, experimentally based (the experimental research in recent years has dealt with questions of motivation, such as the influence of reciprocity, which affect rational decision making), and they are also analyzed philosophically (both in philosophy of mind and in ethics). Once their existence is accepted there is a problem: how to understand the role of "motivation" in economic behavior. In this regard, Selten explicitly recognizes: "I do not claim to be in possession of a valid theory of human motivation" (Selten 1994, p. 43). And his position includes an important assertion: "unfortunately we have no clear understanding of the interaction of different motivational forces. This is a serious difficulty for the development of a comprehensive theory of bounded rationality" (Selten 2001, p. 32).

Usually in philosophy, motivation is seen as something originally extrinsic to human will and which moves it towards a chosen end,[19] whereas in Selten it seems to be primarily intrinsic:[20] "the human motivational system determines the goal pursued by boundedly rational decision making" (2001, p. 32). His remarks on motivation

---

certain circumstances, which we will try to specify, dealing with an organization as a simple mechanism produces outcomes unanticipated by the classical theory" (March and Simon 1993, p. 53).

[17] This is the subtitle of Simon's *Models of Bounded Rationality,* vol. 3.

[18] Selten points out his own personal experience regarding his discovery of the chain store paradox, cf. Selten (1990, p. 651).

[19] "Motives" are not "reasons": the *motives* are what serve to impulse towards an action, but they are not the same as the *reasons* in favor of the action, cf. Rescher (1999a, pp. 88 and 91).

[20] Due to this feature, in the conversations held in Italy (mainly, on 2 October 2001), I proposed to Selten a change in favor of the expression "volitive bounds" and its correlate "volitional bounds," in order to emphasize the primarily internal character of these limits. This feature is not adequately grasped with the phrase "motivational bounds."

seem to suggest the idea of a human factor which is not in principle similar to "substantive rationality"—something more or less established in *homo economicus*—but rather as a *kind of process* related to "procedural rationality" (i.e., open to variability and in accordance with particular circumstances). Motivation appears as a process that includes human deficiencies: "motivation is concerned with what behavior aims at and how a multitude of fears and desires combine to determine human action" (Selten 1998a, p. 414). In his view, "motivation and bounded rationality are not completely separable" (Selten 1998a, p. 414).

Again, in comparison with previous economic views, I think it is an interesting improvement to maintain that cognitive bounds and motivational bounds are not disconnected. In other words, it seems to me that the limits of epistemic rationality and the limits of practical rationality are related in human economic activity, which is a process with a complex structure. In the example of reciprocity—I do unto you as you do unto me—Selten seems open to this nexus between a bounded rational *cognition* and a bounded rational *motivation*: "reciprocity means that there is a tendency to react with friendliness to friendly acts and with hostility to hostile acts. This requires an interpretation of acts of others as friendly, hostile, or neutral. Here, boundedly rational cognition enters the picture. Whether an act is perceived as friendly, neutral, or hostile depends on boundedly rational reasoning process" (Selten 1998a, p. 415).

For Selten, the *theory of decision making* has three levels: (1) the routine level, when routine decisions arise spontaneously without any thinking; (2) the level of imagination, which derives decisions from selected scenarios—the imagined courses of future play of limited length—and (3) the level of analysis, which requires abstract thinking (Selten 1993, p. 132). These three levels suggest the idea of increasing room for *more complex situations* for the economic decision-making than those situations that should be addressed by the relatively simple principle of bounded rationality based on cognitive bounds.

Regarding the issue of the relations between the *complexity* of possible cases (the recognition that different arguments can apply to different cases) and the idea of *simplicity* in economic decision being guided by bounded rationality, Selten points to a middle ground: "in theories of limited rationality one should not look for the simplicity of abstract principles of sweeping generality. A combination of complex case distinctions with very simple decision rules for every single case seems to be very typical for limited rationality decision making" (1987, p. 79).

Concerning the future, there is a constant thought in Selten's writings: the need for an empirically supported *general theory* of bounded rationality. In 1993 he foresaw it as an aim for the long run: "it will take decades of painful experimental research until an empirically defendable general theory of bounded rationality emerges" (Selten 1993, p. 118). In a later paper, dated in 2001, he insists on the necessity of that general theory: "a comprehensive, coherent theory of bounded rationality is not available. This is a task for the future. At the moment, we must be content with models of limited scope" (Selten 2001, p. 14). I think that bringing economic theory into line with empirical evidence is a project of great importance.

9.4.2 Economic Theories Based on Bounded Rationality: Theory of Equal Division Payoff Bounds

Frequently, Selten insists on his theory of equal division payoff bounds (Gonzalez 2007a. The original insight was that "equal shares of coalition values have a great significance for the thinking of the players" (Selten 1993, p. 120). He had the idea that players might tend to form a coalition with maximal equal share. In addition, the agreed upon pay offs would be determined by levels of aspiration derived from maximal equal shares of alternative coalitions. He was successful in the prediction of classroom experiments on a specific seven-person game, and he tried to generalize his theory to all superadditive characteristic function games.

After studying a great number of games, Selten saw that "equal share analysis was a better explanation of the data than its alternatives proposed by normative game theory, but it was not really satisfactory. As more data became available, I [Selten] developed a new descriptive theory for zero-normalized supperadditive three-person games in characteristic function form. This theory, called 'equal division pay-off bounds' (1993, 1987),[21] derives lower bounds for the players' aspiration levels based on simple computations involving various equal shares. The improved version of this theory (1987), in particular, has had a remarkable predictive success" (Selten 1993, p. 120).

The theory of equal division payoff bounds was thought of as *descriptive* in its character and *procedural* (i.e., it specifies the way in which the solution is determined). Selten considers that it is a theory "which fits the data much better than the bargaining set, at least for three-person games" (Selten 1998b, p. 12). It was designed as a three-person theory and only for zero-normalized games (i.e., games which have zero payoffs for one-person coalitions). The theory "describes a boundedly rational reasoning process which arrives at lower bounds $s1$, $s2$, and $s3$ for payoffs of players 1, 2, and 3 respectively, within a two-person coalition. These numbers are called *equal division payoffs bounds*" (Selten 1998a, p. 420).

According to Selten's approach, this "theorizing was no longer based on the idea of full rationality, but rather on that of bounded rationality" (Selten 1998b, p. 13). It is also a theory which seeks to be empirically based: "the reasoning process starts with the observation that player 1 has better coalition possibilities than player 2, and player 2 has better coalition possibilities than player 3. We express this by saying that the order of strength is $1>2>3$" (Selten 1998a, p. 420) where $>$ expresses the sense of "stronger."

Following the rationale of the game, there is a principle: "the stronger member in a two-person coalition should atw least get his or her equal share of the coalition value. Player 1 is stronger in 12 and player 2 is stronger in 23. This leads to the lower bounds $s1$ and $s2$ for players 1 and 2, respectively, $s1=a/2$, $s2=c/2$. From these

[21] Cf. Selten (1982, 1987, pp. 64–80).

lower bounds and upper bounds *h1* and *h2* for the payoffs of 1 and 2, respectively, in 12 are derived: *h1* = a—*s2*, and *h2* = a—*s1*" (Selten 1998a, p. 420).[22]

Player 3 is in a difficult situation insofar as "the coalition 12 with the highest equal share is the most attractive one. Moreover, in no two-person coalition player 3 is the stronger number. Therefore, for player 3, a lower bound cannot be derived in the same way as for players 1 and 2. In order to have a chance to be in the final coalition, player 3 may have to be willing to give both players 1 and 2 the upper bounds *h1* and *h2* they can obtain in 12. This leaves the minimum of *b*—*h1* and *c*—*h2* for player 3. However, player 3 also must get at least zero. This leads to the lower bound *s3* = max [0, min(*b*—*h1*, *c*—*h2*)]. We call *s3* player 3's competitive bound" (Selten 1998a, p. 420).

Concerning the issue of *prediction*, Selten's theory of equal division pay-off bounds "predicts that a two-person coalition *ij* will be formed in which both members receive at least their equal division payoff bounds *si* and *sj*, respectively" (Selten 1998a, pp. 420–421). This kind of descriptive theory is what he considers "casuistic" in the sense "that many case distinctions based on simple criteria are made; simple principles are applied in every single case. Casuistic procedural structures seem to be more adequate for the description of boundedly rational coalition formation than solution concepts based on abstract general principles" (Selten 1993, pp. 120–121).

9.5 Role of Prediction in Experimental Economics: The Influence of Game Theory

Prediction is always a key issue in experimental economics as well as in Selten's writings. In this regard, his approach stresses two methodological aspects: (a) the idea of prediction as a *significant test* for a theory; and (b) the need for a *method for comparing* the predictive success of different theories (Selten and Krischker 1982). The focus is often on designing new experiments to test the predictive value of a theory rather than on merely construing a new theory for describing the data observed. In addition, he proposes statistical tests to compare a new theory with the previously existing ones in order to show the superior predictive power for these experiments.

Selten often shows special interest in what he calls "area theory" (such as the theory of equal division payoff bounds), a kind of theory within a specific range of variables which can be checked in order to know whether the prediction is correct or not. This methodological approach improves the revision of the theory to fit the data, taking into account that—for him—there are variations from one case to another: "different theories often aim at different types of predictions" (1987, p. 43).

[22] The simple case of the fully asymmetric three-person quota game without a grand coalition and with zero payoffs for one-person coalition is illustrated in Selten (1998b, p. 13).

The *area theory* predicts a range of outcomes, whereas other kinds of economic theories predict only average outcomes, or are even less specific. The methodological advantage of area theory is then clear: for every single playing of the game, one can check the correctness of the prediction. This advantage is useful for improving theories in the light of experimental data. When prediction fails, it is possible to identify what went wrong. Therefore, Selten accepts a combination of *fallibilism* and *self-correctness* of economics in the methodological use of prediction within experimental economics.

9.5.1 Prediction as a Significant Test and as a Method for Comparing Theories

Besides the role of prediction as a *significant test* for a theory, which gives the data a crucial role in the revision of the theory, there is in Selten a particular emphasis on the need for a *method for comparing* the predictive success of different theories.[23] He proposes a method to solve the problem of different area theories predicting regions of diverse sizes. "A measure of predictive success is defined that is based on the relative frequency of correct predictions and a correction for the size of the predicted region" (Selten 1987, p. 44). It is a distinction reflected in the duality "hit rate"–"area," which seeks to show that the predictive success of a specific area theory (e.g., the theory of equal division payoff bounds) is superior to other theories (such as the theory of united bargaining set). This comparative methodology, based on prediction, seems open to the idea of an *improvement* in the science—in this case economics—which is *objective*, and not merely subjective or intersubjective.

Commonly, Selten's study of economic prediction is guided by game theory. As he has pointed out, game theory is no longer a specialty in economics but rather a common tool of economic theory (1993, p. 135). But, even though he has improved game theory throughout his career, he himself recognizes methodological limitations to game theory: "strictly speaking only finite games can be played in the laboratory" (Selten 1993, p. 130). Thus, the models of infinite games cannot be tested as such in the economic laboratory. These kinds of methodological constraints are relevant because Selten has a constant determination to connect game theory with experimental economics—*de facto* two crucial aspects of his career.

At the start, Selten's work on game theory was based on the Nash equilibrium, which belongs to the core of mainstream game theory. Harsanyi has summarized that influence: "one of Reinhard's important contributions was his distinction between *perfect* and *imperfect* Nash equilibria. It was based on his realization that even strategy combinations fully satisfying Nash's definition of Nash equilibria might very well contain some *irrational* strategies. To exclude such imperfect Nash equilibria containing such irrational strategies, at first he [Selten] proposed

[23] This will lead to him to the "accuracy"–"precision" distinction, which is developed in the next section. An analysis of the role of predictive accuracy in theory choice can be found in Eells (2000).

what now are called *subgame-perfect* equilibria. Later he proposed the even more demanding concept of *trembling-hand* perfect equilibria. Reinhard's work on *evolutionary stable strategies* was likewise based on the concept of Nash equilibria" (Harsanyi 1996, p. 160).

These are important contributions to game theory. The question of how to interpret them from a methodological point of view gives rise to some difficulties, because Selten is usually working with a limited rationality instead of a full rationality or strong assumptions of rationality (such as in the case of mainstream game theory). His intellectual attitude is clear when he analyzes his own contributions: "I do not believe in the descriptive relevance of strong rationality assumptions, I prefer to think of game equilibrium in empirically oriented models as the result of adaptive dynamic processes" (Selten 1993, p. 127).[24] In addition, he makes critical comments on claims of mainstream game theory, for example in the case of quotas, when he is analyzing strategic reasoning: "this kind of circularity is typical for rational game theory. However, subjects in the laboratory usually do not compute quotas. They seem to avoid circular concepts in their strategic reasoning" (Selten 1998a, p. 420).

Game theory is interpreted by Selten in terms of *methodological dualism*: normative game theory is very different from descriptive game theory. *Normative* game theory tries to mold a balanced mathematical structure of ideal rationality out of conflicting inherent inclinations of the human mind. Thus, for him, "the problem of normative theory is philosophical, not empirical. Only if you are a naïve rationalist can you think it is empirical" (Selten 1998b, p. 23). *Descriptive* game theory has a different aim: "the explanation of observed *behavior* of men, animals or plants, and has nothing to do with normative game theory. The problem here is empirical and *only empirical* arguments count, nothing else. The need for this distinction arises because there is experimental evidence from human game players which refutes naïve rationalism. Naïve rationalism could have been right, but it is not, it is refuted by experimental evidence" (Selten 1998b, p. 23). Following this sharp distinction, he develops a descriptive game theory on human players and focuses it on cases of microeconomics.

Using the theoretical design of descriptive game theory, Selten conducts economic experiments conceived to *test* the predictive value of the theory that he proposes. This is the case of his theory of equal division payoff bounds, the predictive success of which in the latter version, published in 1987, was understood as a guarantee of the *scientific character* of his theory (Selten 1993, p. 120). Nevertheless, he considers that the undeniable predictive success of a theory regarding the available data does not mean that the theory has the final answer to the problems that are studied. In other words, a theory should be open to revision, and that is a task that requires experimentation: "the development of successful descriptive theories is a slow process that must be guided by experimental evidence" (Selten 1987, p. 96).

[24] For Herbert Simon, "the chief contribution of formal game theory to our understanding of rationality has been to demonstrate rather convincingly (if not mathematically) that there is no satisfactory definition of 'optimal' rationality in the presence of opportunities for outguessing and outwitting" (Simon 2000, p. 28).

9.5.2 A Difference Between "Prediction" and "Expectation"

What seems to me less clear in Selten's concept of *prediction* in the analysis of experimental games, such as in the case of a solidarity game, is the use of "prediction" and "expectation." Sometimes he uses them as if they were synonymous or interchangeable. Such is the interpretation that can follow from this reflection: "it is possible that someone looks at his or her own behavioral inclinations in order to predict the behavior of others. We refer to this as 'expectations based on own behavior'. On the other hand, it is also possible that someone predicts the behavior of others with the intention of making his or her own behavior dependent on the behavior of the population. We refer to this as 'behavior based on expectations'" (Selten and Ockenfels 1998, p. 526).

Here it is possible to introduce some conceptual nuances. This is so not only on account of the possibility of predicting the expectations of others.[25] *Prediction* is a descriptive term: it is a cognitive content that could be related to "novel facts"[26] (in this case, to anticipate a possible behavior of others). It is understood as the expected value of something unknown, given the information available. *Expectation* can have—in my judgment—two senses in this context: a restricted version and a broad one. In the first sense, expectation converges with the idea of prediction,[27] because it is the expected value given the information available and has no relation with a subjective process; whereas, in the second sense, expectation requires the presence of subjective elements (and, in this case, it can include an attitude regarding what is expected).

Accordingly I think that, in the broad version, expectation is more generic than prediction and possesses a more subjective character than prediction. This seems to be recognized by John Muth, the inspiring author of the "rational expectations" hypothesis: the "expectations of firms (or, more generally, the subjective probability distribution of outcomes) tend to be distributed, for the same information set, about the prediction of the theory (or the 'objective' probability distributions of outcomes)" (Muth 1961/1981, pp. 4–5).[28]

Therefore, in this economic context, a prediction can be an expectation of some kind, whereas not all expectation is equivalent to a prediction even though it entails a prediction of a future event. At the same time, prediction could be a statement of the future related to a specific value at a particular moment, whereas expectation

[25] John Muth accepted this prospect explicitly: "it is often necessary to make sensible predictions about the way expectations would change" (Muth 1961/1981, p. 4).

[26] On "novel facts," cf. Gonzalez (2001, 2010a). In this regard, see Chap. 4, Sect. 4.3.

[27] "I should like to suggest that expectations, since they are informed predictions of future events, are essentially the same as the predictions of the relevant economic theory" (Muth 1961/1981, p. 4).

[28] The idea of "rational expectations" has received criticisms from the very beginning on its conception of economic rationality. It is an economic perspective that is completely different from the position based on bounded rationality. In fact, Simon has criticized it as a new expansion of the rationality principle as optimization. He has also pointed out that the rational expectations position was soon confronted with various conflicting empirical phenomena, cf. Simon (2000, p. 29).

could be more generic and might include a subjective factor. To sum up, although "prediction" and "expectation" refer to future phenomena, they offer subtle differences of conceptual character that have methodological repercussions.

9.6 The Measure of Predictive Success: Accuracy and Precision

When Selten deals with the issue of a measure of predictive success—a method to compare theories—the focus is placed on an area theory, in which he distinguishes two aspects: (i) the hit rate, and (ii) the predicted area (or region which covers the dispersion of predictions). The first one is presented in the following context: "a measure of the relative size of the predictive range is subtracted from the relative frequency of correct predictions. This yields the measure of predictive success. The term 'hit rate' is used for the relative frequency of correct predictions. If the outcomes are randomly distributed over the whole range of outcomes, the hit rate can be expected to be equal to the relative size of the predictive range. The measure of predictive success can be thought of as the surplus of the observed hit rate over the random hit rate" (Selten 1987, p. 80).

In addition to the hit rate, the measurement of the predictive success of economic theories also requires a consideration of the predicted area. The "area theory" has a range of outcomes that takes the form of a non-empty subset of the set of all configurations. Thus, for Selten, "in order to compare the predictive success of two area theories for a body of experimental data, it is not sufficient to examine which theory yields more correct predictions. A theory may produce many correct predictions simply because it predicts a very large range. An extreme example is provided by a theory which we call the *null theory*; the predicted range of the null theory is the set of all configurations" (1987, p. 80). Therefore, where area theories are to be compared in a meaningful way, the *size of the predicted range* or *area* is another aspect to be taken into account.

Put differently, Selten maintains that "area theories for prediction of experimental results delineate regions of predicted outcomes within the set of all possible outcomes. The difference measure of predictive success for area theories … is the difference between hit rate and area. The hit rate is the relative frequency of successful predictions and the area is the relative size of the predictive region within the set of all possible outcomes." (1991b, p. 153). He seems to give more weight to getting high hit rates than to obtaining small areas.[29] But, in my judgment, what should be emphasized is that his distinction between *hit rate* and *area* leads to another interesting distinction: "accuracy" and "precision," terms which are usually presented as synonymous, and here they acquire a new role in order to clarify the predictive success of theories.

[29] When Selten analyzes the theory of equal division payoff bounds, he maintains that "in view of the great variance of experimental results, it seems more important to aim for hit rates than for small areas in theory construction" (Selten 1987, p. 93).

Accuracy accompanies hit rate, which is the relative frequency of correct predictions. Moreover, “the hit rate is a measure of accuracy” (Selten 1991b, p. 153). But it could be the case that accuracy can reflect the mere fact of getting the predictive results themselves (i.e., achieving the aim of the correct predictions as such instead of the relevant subset of relative frequency). In other words, accuracy may be understood as a poor concept of predictive success in some cases: “no area theory can be more accurate than the trivial one, which simply predicts the set of all possible outcomes. This theory never fails to predict correctly, but it is useless in view of its complete lack of precision” (Selten 1991b, p. 153). Thus, it is not good enough for a theory to achieve the goal of correct predictions: it should be done in a refined manner—high hit rates—in order to be completely suitable.

Precision is related to the area (i.e., the size of the predictive region). It is the achievement regarding the predictive space: it has to be in the appropriate zone. There is a degree in this kind of exactness: “the precision of an area theory is related to the size of its set of predicted outcomes. The smaller the set is, the more precise is the theory” (Selten 1991b, p. 153). However, for Selten, there could be the case of a theory that is extremely precise but completely inaccurate (1991b, p. 161). This happens when a theory predicts a single point that never occurs as the outcome of an experiment. Thus, the hit rate–area combination for that theory is (0, 0), which converts it into a useless theory: it is extremely precise but fully inaccurate. Therefore, for area theories (i.e., specific theories with a subset of predicted outcomes), he stresses the need for accuracy and precision in order to measure the predictive success.

Following this distinction between accuracy and precision, Selten proposes this formula: $m = r - a$, where m = measure of predictive success, r = hit rate (i.e., the relative frequency of correct predictions), and a = the area (i.e., the relative size of the predicted subset compared with the set of all possible outcomes) (Selten 1991b, p. 154). The comparison between two theories from the point of view of predictive success depends on gains and losses in accuracy evaluated by hit rate differences and gains and losses in precision evaluated by area differences. A new theory T′ is more accurate than an older theory T″ when the hit rate of T′ is greater than the hit rate of T″, and the new theory is less precise than the older one when the area of T′ is greater than the area of T″ (Selten 1991b, p. 160).

As a methodological distinction, the difference between “accuracy” and “precision” seems an improvement in clarifying the degree of success of economic predictions, because it could be useful to distinguish between the relative frequency of successful predictions and the relative size of the predicted region within the whole space of possible outcomes. In addition, it contributes to avoiding certain extreme positions: “neither the prediction of a single outcome nor the prediction of almost all outcomes is a reasonable aim in the construction of area theories” (Selten 1991b, p. 166).

Even though “accuracy” and “precision” is a useful methodological distinction in comparing theories from the point of view of their predictive success, *two limitations* should be pointed out. On the one hand, this methodological proposal is restricted to measures of predictive success depending on only *two factors* (hit rate and area).

On the other, due to its *restricted realm*, these types of theories—area theories—are a kind of theory that has some advantages, when compared with other kinds of theories (for example, for every outcome observed it is clear in area theories if the prediction was correct or not). It seems, therefore, that further work should be done on the measure of predictive success of economic theories, in order to take into account the different cases that may arise.

Additionally, it may be the case that there is also a subjective content in Selten's distinction between "accuracy" and "precision": *accuracy* refers to a rate of successes in comparison with the total, whereas *precision* is a quotient between two quantities related to surfaces, the area of an experiment in comparison with the whole area. It may be understood as a uniform behavior for both cases (i.e., rates of success and amount of surface), and that is not clear enough.

To sum up, the role of experiments in the social sciences has been questioned or even neglected by those approaches that emphasized the methodological gap between natural sciences and social sciences.[30] Recent contributions in philosophy of science and new developments of the social sciences, such as economics, have led to an increasing presence of experiments.[31] There is a transition from the traditional notion to an enlarged vision. On the one hand, experiments are seen as a human activity oriented towards testing and evaluating scientific theories, both as an intervention in a material setting (i.e., laboratory experimentation) and as a creative procedure (computer simulations, thought experiments, etc.); and, on the other, experiments have enlarged the capacity of social sciences (mainly economics) to predict (cf. Chap. 11). Selten's approach to experimental economics has shown methodological improvements on prediction, such as in the measurement of predictive success in terms of accuracy and precision.

References

Bernoulli, D. 1738. Specimen theoriae novae de mensura sortis. *Commentarii Academiae Scientiarum Imperialis Petropolitanae* 5:175–192. (Trans. L. Sommer 1954. Exposition of a new theory on the measurement of risk. *Econometrica* 22: 23–36).

Bicchieri, C. 1992. Two kinds of rationality. In *Post-Popperian methodology of economics*, ed. N. de Marchi, 155–188. Boston: Kluwer.

Davis, D. D., and C. A. Holt, eds. 1993. *Experimental economics*. Princeton: Princeton University Press.

Eells, E. 2000. Prediction, probability, and pragmatics. *Canadian Journal of Philosophy* 30:183–206.

Galavotti, M. C., ed. 2003. *Observation and experiment in the natural and the social sciences*. Dordrecht: Kluwer.

Galison, P. 1987. *How experiments end*. Chicago: The University of Chicago Press.

[30] See, in this regard, Gonzalez (2007a, Sect. 1, pp. 275–277).

[31] On the recent approaches on observation and experimentation from a philosophico-methodological viewpoint, see Gonzalez (2010b). Previous studies can be found in Galavotti (2003), Galison (1987), Hacking (1983), and Radder (2003).

Gonzalez, W. J. 1994. Economic prediction and human activity. An analysis of prediction in economics from action theory. *Epistemologia* 17:253–294.
Gonzalez, W. J. 1997b. Rationality in economics and scientific predictions: A critical reconstruction of bounded rationality and its role in economic predictions. *Poznan Studies in the Philosophy of Science* 61:205–232.
Gonzalez, W. J. 2001e. Lakatos's approach on prediction and novel facts. *Theoria* 16 (3): 499–518.
Gonzalez, W. J. 2003b. Rationality in experimental economics: An analysis of Reinhard Selten's approach. In *Observation and experiment in the natural and the social sciences*, ed. M. C. Galavotti, 71–83. Dordrecht: Kluwer.
Gonzalez, W. J. 2007a. The role of experiments in the social sciences: The case of economics. In *General philosophy of science: Focal issues*, ed. T. Kuipers, 275–301. Amsterdam: Elsevier.
Gonzalez, W. J. 2010a. *La predicción científica: Concepciones filosófico-metodológicas desde H. Reichenbach a N. Rescher*. Barcelona: Montesinos.
Gonzalez, W. J. 2010b. Recent approaches on observation and experimentation: A philosophical–methodological viewpoint. In *New methodological perspectives on observation and experimentation in science*, ed. W. J. Gonzalez, 9–48. A Coruña: Netbiblo.
Gonzalez, W. J. 2013a. Value ladenness and the value-free ideal in scientific research. In *Handbook of the philosophical foundations of business ethics*, ed. Ch. Lütge, 1503–1521. Dordrecht: Springer.
Hacking, I. 1983. *Representing and intervening*. Cambridge: Cambridge University Press.
Harsanyi, J. C. 1996. The work of John Nash in game theory. *Journal of Economic Theory* 69:158–161.
Harsanyi, J. C., and R. Selten. 1988. *A general theory of equilibrium selection in games*. Cambridge: The MIT Press.
Hey, J. D., and G. Loomes, eds. 1993. *Recent developments in experimental economics*. Aldershot: E. Elgar.
Holland, J. H., K. J. Holyoak, R. E. Nisbett, and P. R. Thagard. 1986. *Induction: Processes of inference, learning, and discovery*. Cambridge: The MIT Press.
March, J. G., and H. A. Simon. 1993. *Organizations*, 2nd ed. Cambridge: Blackwell.
Muth, J. 1961/1981. Rational expectations and the theory of price movements. *Econometrica* 29:315–335 (Reprinted in Lucas, R. E., and Th. J. Sargent, eds. 1981. Rational expectations and econometric practice, 3–22. London: G. Allen and Unwin).
Nash, J. 1996. The work of John Nash in game theory. *Journal of Economic Theory* 69:182–183.
Radder, H., ed. 2003. *The philosophy of scientific experimentation*. Pittsburgh: University of Pittsburgh Press.
Rescher, N. 1988. *Rationality. A philosophical inquiry into the nature and the rationale of reason*. Oxford: Oxford University Press.
Rescher, N. 1999a. *Razón y valores en la Era científico-tecnológica*. Barcelona: Paidós.
Roth, A. 1986. Laboratory experimentation in economics. *Economics and Philosophy* 2:245–273.
Roth, A. 1987. Laboratory experimentation in economics, and its relation to economic theory. In *Scientific inquiry in philosophical perspective*, ed. N. Rescher, 147–167. Lanham: University Press of America.
Roth, A. 1988/1993. Laboratory experimentation in economics: A methodological overview. *The Economic Journal* 98:974–1031 (Reprinted in Hey, J. D., and G. Loomes, eds. 1993. *Recent developments in experimental economics*, vol. I, 3–60. Aldershot: E. Elgar).
Sauermann, H., and R. Selten. 1959. Ein Oligopolexperiment. *Zeitschrift für die gesamte Staatswissenschaft* 115:427–471 (Reprinted in Sauermann, H., ed. 1967. *Beiträge zur experimentellen Wirtschaftsforschung*, pp. 9–59. Tübingen: J. C. B. Mohr (Paul Siebeck)).
Sauermann, H., and R. Selten. 1962. Anspruchsanpassungstheorie der Unternehmung. *Zeitschrift für die gesamte Staatswissenschaft* 118:577–597.
Selten, R. 1978. The chain store paradox. *Theory and Decision* 9(2): 127–159 (Reprinted in Selten, R. 1988. *Models of strategic rationality*, 33–65. Dordrecht: Kluwer).

Selten, R. 1982. Equal division payoff bounds for three-person characteristic function experiments. In *Aspiration levels in bargaining and economic decision making*, ed. R. Tietz, 255–275. Berlin: Springer (Reprinted in Selten, R. 1988. *Models of strategic rationality*, 301–311. Dordrecht: Kluwer).
Selten, R. 1987. Equity and coalition bargaining in experimental three-person games. In *Laboratory experimentation in economics—Six points of view*, ed. A. E. Roth, 42–98. Cambridge: Cambridge University Press.
Selten, R. 1990. Bounded rationality. *Journal of Institutional and Theoretical Economics* 146(4): 649–658.
Selten, R. 1991a. Evolution, learning, and economic behavior. 1989 Nancy Schwartz memorial lecture. *Games and Economic Behavior* 3(1): 3–24.
Selten, R. 1991b. Properties of a measure of predictive success. *Mathematical Social Sciences* 21(2): 153–167.
Selten, R. 1993. In search of a better understanding of economic behavior. In *Makers of modern economics*, ed. A. Heertje, 115–139. London: Harverstern Wheatsheaf.
Selten, R. 1994. New challenges to the rationality assumption: Comment. *Journal of Institutional and Theoretical Economics* 150(1): 42–44.
Selten, R. 1998a. Features of experimentally observed bounded rationality. *European Economic Review* 42:413–436.
Selten, R. 1998b. Game theory, experience, rationality. In *Game theory, experience, rationality*, eds. W. Leinfellner and E. Köhler, 9–34. Dordrecht: Kluwer.
Selten, R. 2001. What is bounded rationality? In *Bounded rationality: The adaptive toolbox*, eds. G. Gigerenzer and R. Selten, 13–36. Cambridge: The MIT Press.
Selten, R. 2003. Emergence and future of experimental economics. In *Observation and experiment in the natural and the social sciences*, ed. M. C. Galavotti, 63–70. Dordrecht: Kluwer.
Selten, R., and W. Krischker. 1982. Comparison of two theories for characteristic function experiments. In *Aspiration levels in bargaining and economic decision making*, ed. R. Tietz, 259–264. Berlin: Springer.
Selten, R., and A. Ockenfels. 1998. An experimental solidarity game. *Journal of Economic Behavior and Organization* 34 (4): 517–539.
Simon, H. A. 1983. *Reason in human affairs*. Stanford: Stanford University Press.
Simon, H. A. 1991b. Organizations and markets. *Journal of Economic Perspectives* 5 (2): 25–44.
Simon, H. A. 2000. Bounded rationality in social science: Today and tomorrow. *Mind and Society* 1 (1): 25–39.

Part V
Methodological Aspects of Economic Prediction: From Description to Prescription

The previous chapters, especially those devoted to *economic rationality* (Part IV), have stressed the need for a change in the theoretical basis of prediction in economics in favor of more realistic assumptions. It is assumed that, in order to improve the *predictive success* of economics, the new approach should be supported by bounded rationality, both in economics as basic science and as applied science. Thus, this approach should be both in the descriptive (or "positive") realm of economics and in the prescriptive (or "normative") sphere of this science.

This new philosophico-methodological foundation to economics, which is different from the dominant view of mainstream economics—in relevant points—and also includes differences with several alternative positions (such as the views hold by Simon or Selten), should be accompanied by a research on "economic activity" rather than on "economic behavior." This proposal presupposes a *more complex approach* to economics from the methodological point of view, both in structural and in dynamic terms, due mainly to the interest in complexity and historicity of economics as human activity.

After the analysis of the methodological framework of economic predictions within the context of the social sciences (Part III) and the study of the epistemological background for the methodology of economic predictions (Part IV), the research now goes more deeply into specific aspects of the methodology of economics (Part V), but taking into account the philosophical perspective. Consequently, there is a clear connection with the previous contents, following the path of the book: from the general topics to the particular issues.

Thus, even though the analysis here pays attention to the *restricted perspective* on this methodological field—those issues on prediction that are the main concern of economists in areas such as statistical economics and econometrics—there is always a leading interest in the *broad approach* to methodology of economics (e.g., in the concluding considerations of the final chapter of this volume). Hence, Chaps. 10–12 deal mainly with the concrete problems of *methodology of economics* while keeping the interest in general methodological aspects (i.e., the connection of economics with a wider realm).

Initially, the focus of the analysis in Part V is largely on the realm of *description*—prediction as a methodological process related to economic theory—in order to reach later the sphere of *prescription* (the use of prediction to solve practical problems according to certain rules), taking into account that economics is applied science and not merely basic science. In the first case—the descriptive realm—there are several elements of the predictive process to be analyzed: a) the *aims* of the process (generic or specific); b) the type of *process* ("predictive procedures" and "methods of prediction"); and c) the *evaluation* of the methodological process according to the results. In addition, as a corollary, there are the problems of limits and obstacles of prediction as a process in economics. These are the topics of Chaps. 10 and 11.

Regarding the sphere of prescription (the "normative" dimension), the central issue is how should economic predictions—the knowledge about the future based upon past and present experiences—be connected with the prescription: the rules for the problem-solving in a concrete setting or environment. This crucial question serves as a main point of discussion in Chap. 12, where the character of economics as applied science is clearly emphasized. Thus, the focus moves here from prediction as a test of "descriptive" statements to prediction as a guide for patterns of policy-making (which later on can be implemented by agents and organizations in their variable settings).

Chapter 10
Methods of Prediction in Economics

Now that the general methodological framework for economic predictions (Chaps. 5–7) and the epistemological bases of economic predictions (Chaps. 8 and 9) have been considered, the analysis goes into more specific aspects of the methodology of predictions in economics. In this regard, the study of this methodological process requires us to focus on three central aspects: (i) the basis of the process, which leads to the reflection on the *kind of aim*—specific or generic—available to economic predictions; (ii) the type of the *process* for prediction, which includes a consideration of the difference between "predictive procedures" and "methods of prediction" (and, consequently, the role of observation and experimentation of economic phenomena); and (iii) the *evaluation* of the methodological process according to the outcomes, which requires an analysis of the results obtained using economic methods.

Furthermore, there are also associated questions on limits and obstacles of prediction in economics. They connect with the central issues related to the methodological realm (aims, processes, and results), as well as with epistemological and ontological problems. Here—Chap. 10—two of those aspects are analyzed: the basis of the methodological process according to the *kind of aims*, and the *type of process* of prediction in economics; whereas in Chap. 11 other aspects are studied: the evaluation related to the *results* and the issues on *limits* and *obstacles* of prediction in economics.

10.1 On the Methodological Scope for the Kind of Aim and the Type of Process

One initial methodological consideration should be pointed out: there are a variety of predictions according to the degree of control of the knowledge of economic variables. Thus, some variables can be predicted with considerable accuracy and precision (mainly in the short run), whereas others are almost entirely not predictable (above all in the case of specific economic predictions in the long run).

W. J. Gonzalez, *Philosophico-Methodological Analysis of Prediction and its Role in Economics*, Theory and Decision Library A: 50, DOI 10.1007/978-3-319-08885-3_10

For Clive Granger, who sometimes uses the term "forecast" interchangeably with "prediction,"[1] it should also be clear that "the methods that can be used to forecast can vary greatly and will depend upon data availability, the quality of models available, and the kind of assumptions made" (1989, p. 4). This last factor—the kind of assumptions—is directly related to the issue of economic rationality, a crucial epistemological element, analyzed in previous chapters. The data available depend on the type of process and the specific circumstances of each case; and the quality of models is a crucial element of the process, and one that requires special attention.

Taking into account these philosophico-methodological factors as well as the background of previous parts of this book, this chapter starts with the first aspect related to the methodological process in economics: the kinds of aims. Later on, it deals with type of processes for prediction, distinguishing "predictive procedures" and "methods of prediction" in economics. In this regard, the analysis starts with the preconditions for rational prediction.

Thereafter, the chapter emphasizes the diversity of predictive approaches (unformalized and formalized) and the need for a distinction between predictive procedures, in general, and predictive methods, in particular. Thus, following this distinction, there is a study of the predictive methods in economics. In connection with the methods of prediction in economics, the chapter pays particular attention to the role of models in economic predictions: the relation between characteristics and evaluation, the kind of economic modeling used in the predictive realm, and the relevance of predictive failure for economic modeling.

In this methodological scope related to economic predictions, which involves the kind of aim and the type of process, the leading focus is oriented mainly to those methodological aspects of economic predictions that commonly belong—or can be oriented—to the broad methodology of economics (see Chap. 1, Sect. 1.1.2). Certainly, there is also interest here in the features of economic predictions that are characteristic of the restricted methodology of economics. However, they are systematically developed in publications of a different sort, especially when their methodological targets are clearly specific within economics. This particular line of research is more noticeable when the attention goes to methodological issues of prediction in the sphere of applied economics and the central concern is problems in areas such as statistical economics or econometrics.[2]

---

[1] In other cases, he distinguishes between "prediction" and "forecasting." Then, he sees prediction as "formed from a theoretical model," and forecasting as "limited to the extrapolations based on empirical models or data exploration" (Granger 2012, p. 312).

[2] The list of publications in this regard is very long. Noteworthy contributions in these thematic contexts are Granger (1990a); Pagan (1990); Hendry and Ericsson (2001a); Clements and Hendry (2002a); Newbold and Harvey (2002); Elliott et al. (2006); Clements and Hendry (2011); Elliott and Timmermann (2013a, and 2013b); and Evans (2013).

10.2 Basis of the Methodological Process in Economics: The Kind of Aim

Regarding the kinds of aims sought by the methodological process in economics, there are some factors that are particularly relevant. (a) The question of the *level of concretion* of the aims: whether aims are (or even ought to be) *generic* or *specific*. This inquiry connects with the discussion on the distinction between qualitative predictions and quantitative predictions (Chap. 2, Sect. 2.3). (b) The issue concerning the *realm of the goal*, which could be located initially in a twofold option: the *descriptive* sphere or the *normative* domain. But they are interconnected, and the relation between both realms—"descriptive" and "normative"—shows us that the predictive weaknesses of economic theories can influence the applied economics to be developed by economic institutions (in the different areas: regional, national or international).

10.2.1 Level of Concretion of the Aims

On the question of the *level of concretion* of the aims, the debate of the methodological basis of the process of prediction in economics is primarily the distinction between "specific prediction" and "generic prediction." A characteristic *specific prediction* is normally related to detailed information (in principle, a definite time and date as well as a particular location), whereas a *generic prediction* is usually connected to a tendency or nonexclusive feature of a future phenomenon or event. Both kinds of predictions can be found in microeconomics as well as in macroeconomics. But "specific prediction" and "generic prediction" vary greatly in their degree of predictability, even though it seems, in principle, that generic prediction is more attainable than specific prediction.

Rosenberg maintains that "generic prediction is characteristic of most theories that proceed by establishing the existence of an equilibrium position for the system whose behavior they describe, and then claim it moves towards or remains at this equilibrium value. Classical examples of such theories are to be found in thermodynamics and evolution" (Rosenberg 1989, pp. 53–54). He holds that "some influential economists and philosophers of economics seem well satisfied with stopping at the point of generic prediction" (Rosenberg 1989, p. 67).

In this regard, in connection with the problem of how much predictive power a theory needs in order to have normative bearing on institutional design, Rosenberg sustains that "Buchanan gives us grounds to suggest that the most we need from economic theory for the purposes of political philosophy is generic prediction" (1992, p. 224). However, this is a position that is rejected at the conceptual level: "having assigned general equilibrium theory to contractarian political philosophy, we may still need a theory of economic behavior that transcends generic prediction" (Rosenberg 1992, p. 227).

From a descriptive point of view, it seems to me that the *predictive aim* of an economic theory cannot be good enough if it always remains in the sphere of generic prediction; and, in addition, economic prescriptions are ordinarily weaker if the bases are generic predictions instead of specific predictions. Thus, in principle, generic predictions are not enough as the usual aim of the methodological process: economic theories with generic predictions should be supplemented or improved in order to attain specific predictions. This improvement is a requisite of the *self-corrective* character of science: it encourages the revision of generic predictions and their mutation into specific ones.

Consequently, generic predictions can be commonly used as a starting point of economic theories to describe future phenomena or events, but normally this cannot be the final aim of a methodological process of economic theories. A generic prediction is appreciated insofar as it diminishes our uncertainty about an economic event, but usually the economic predictions are thought of in specific terms: a prediction for a concrete time and space, avoiding claims about an "ideal world" or statements that hardly can be tested in a conclusive manner.

There are two main ways of setting this *predictive improvement* in economics that will enable us to convert generic into specific predictions: (i) to "supplement the theory with theories of other disciplines," and (ii) to "find measures of the independent or exogenous variables of the theory" (Rosenberg 1989, p. 54). However, this predictive improvement is not only for the purposes of an economic policy, or for the attainment of a prescriptive aim, as Rosenberg insists (linking economic theory to a contractarian political philosophy) (1992, p. 227), but also for the descriptive purposes of *enhancing economic knowledge* to get predictive success on the phenomena or events.

For Rosenberg, economic theories in general have little predictive value: their predictive content is commonly limited to generic predictions. Nevertheless, he considers this as an important kind of prediction, and he seems to understand it like *qualitative predictions* insofar as he asserts that they are "almost certainly a necessary preliminary to specific or quantitative predictions" (Rosenberg 1989, p. 67). His critical comments on the predictive value of economics are usually focused on the general equilibrium theory, but his critique also applies to all rational choice models and to game theory. Hausman, however, rejects this position (1998a, p. 69), considering that this critique cannot be sustained, even though both agree that some economists are really mathematicians.

10.2.2 The Realm of the Goal

As regards the second issue, that concerning the *realm of the goal* (i.e., the *descriptive* sphere or the *normative* domain) receives more attention. The disagreement between Rosenberg and Hausman becomes clear, and it is directly related to the theoretical status of economics as a scientific discipline. The former argues why—in his judgment—rational choice and economic models are of interest for economics, even if they are empirically empty. His focus is on a normative argument.

Meanwhile, the latter rejects that normative argument in favor of representation of economic aims as more descriptively oriented.

For Rosenberg, economics forms part of a *normative argument* for the market: "general equilibrium theory is the formalized approach to the systematic study of this claim about how the unintended consequences of uncoordinated selfishness result in the most efficient exploitation of scare resources in the satisfaction of wants. (…) We can understand why economists continue to lavish attention on general equilibrium theory. It is not because they think it can be improved in the direction of a descriptively and predictively accurate explanation of economic activity, but because they believe it is already part of the best contractarian argument for the adoption of the market as a social institution and, more important, stands a chance of becoming an even better one, as its assumptions are weakened, changed, and varied" (1992, pp. 219–220). Instead, for Hausman, this normative argument is not valid at all: "Rosenberg's assertions here are incredible, if they are read as claims about the conscious beliefs of economists who value orthodox economic theory, including game theory" (Hausman 1998a, p. 70).

It seems that economists are increasingly aware of the *descriptive difficulties* with the axioms concerning individual rationality (that people's preferences are continuous, transitive, and complete, and that choice follows preference) as well as of the obstacles to the primacy of self-interest (that individuals care only for their own consumption bundles). Thus, some of the problems regarding the *predictive weaknesses* of economics rely on the assumptions that people are fully rational, instead of boundedly rational, and with a mere instrumental rationality, which therefore does not take into account an evaluative rationality. In addition, there are other problems for prediction, due to descriptive factors of economic activity: "incomplete futures markets, increasing returns of scale, indivisibilities, non-equilibrium trading, and so forth" (Hausman 1998a, p. 76).

But the predictive weaknesses of economic theories are not unrelated to the design of *institutions*, because the predictive value of a theory of individual economic activity within particular institutions affects the prescriptive value of a theory in the context of institutional design. Moreover, prediction and prescription are connected in economics: *prescriptive aims* require the contribution of economic predictions (Gonzalez 1998b). Therefore, predictive aims of economic statements cannot be reduced to the terrain of descriptive goals, either in themselves (to know the future) or as an evaluative tool (as a test for a theory), because the prescriptive goals should be considered as well. The reason is clear: prediction "serves as an aid to action and decision" (Hahn 1993, p. 84).

10.3 The Type of Process for Prediction: From Predictive Procedures to Methods of Prediction of Economics

Commonly, the methodological processes are directly connected to the aims (either generic or specific, descriptive or normative). This is also the case concerning the processes of economic prediction, either in economics as basic science or as applied science (which are relevant for the application of this science). In this regard, a close analysis of the characteristics of its *methodological process* of prediction in economics shows—in my judgment—two different possibilities.

Thus, from the point of view of the *type of process*, we should distinguish (1) predictive procedures (i.e., informal or less sophisticated ways of search), and (2) methods of prediction (or "predictive methods" according to a more rigorous path). Both processes are used *de facto* in the daily practice of economics. They can be employed independently or, as is more common, in a combined form. Moreover, the use of both kinds of approaches (judgmental and scientific) is explicitly assumed in econometrics.[3] Indeed, in addition to the contribution of the economists, the role of non-specialists is sometimes accepted for the adjustments.[4]

On the one hand, there are *predictive procedures*, such as guessing, "rules of thumb," "informal models," certain extrapolations, some surveys, etc. These are employed in economic areas (financial markets, business, etc.) as a practice based on "personal experiences," "knowledge of experts,"[5] and the like, but without a real methodological approach to the problem. Thus, they do not articulate the economic prediction on the basis of a clear scientific process, but rather in an unformalized way or inferential proceeding in a rudimentary sense (i.e., a somehow naive projection). On the other hand, there are *methods of prediction* (or "predictive methods") in economics that use scientific approaches in order to foretell possible events (e.g., in the short, middle, or long run).

Moreover, there are several *methods* available for constructing economic predictions. They are connected to *models*, as is the case in other sciences—mainly, applied sciences—where problem-solving requires models to predict the future. But important economists, such as David Hendry and Neil Ericsson, assume that "models are far from accurate representations of the economy, and their accuracy frequently changes abruptly. A model that closely represents the economy is good basis for forecasting only if the future economy is 'close' to the current one. The culprit of forecasting failure is not rapid evolution *per se*, as commonly occurs in technology, but abrupt changes, as may derive from legislative and political developments" (Hendry and Ericsson 2001b, p. 8).

Putting it differently, these authors are pointing to the existence of serious difficulties regarding economic models in their use within predictive methods.

---

[3] "There are numerous ways of generating economic forecasts. Many are a mix of science—based on rigorously tested econometric systems—and judgment, occasioned by unexpected events: the future is not always like the present or the past" (Hendry and Ericsson 2001c, p. 186).

[4] "Although progress is being made, we are still some way from a position where the model answers can be accepted without further human intervention. This is standard international practice. McNees surveyed the large U.S. forecasting organizations in 1981; they attributed between 20 and 50 % of the final forecast to judgmental adjustments (…). Adjustments are made in the light of other information, commonsense judgements, past model error, and a knowledge of its deficiencies. The useful exercise of this judgement is not limited to the specialists. Non-specialists may also make a valuable contribution providing that the issues are put to them clearly" (Burns 1986, p. 104).

[5] "Knowledge of experts" is understood here in the sense of human expertise rather than an "expert knowledge" run by a computer program.

The factors of concern are at least two: (a) economic models seem to have congenital problems in offering an *adequate representation* of economy, both in structural terms and in dynamic ones; and (b) some of the most important changes of the economic models are due to *external factors* (i.e., legal or political). The first aspect is mainly epistemological, whereas the second is more clearly methodological. Underneath both lies the issue of the *historicity* of economic phenomena, due to its being a human activity—and then with a historical framework—which is also an activity interconnected with other human activities (social, political, cultural, etc.).[6]

Hendry and Ericsson suggest that sometimes it could be better to use a simple strategy—extrapolation—than a model structured around past economic behavior: "If the economy stays on track, such extrapolative forecasts [from previous outcomes] are generally accurate. If the economy crashes, the extrapolative forecast will miss the crash itself (…) However, once the crash has occurred, the extrapolative forecast tends to come back on track, whereas many other types of forecast models continue to mis-forecast systematically. Consequently, it is desirable that forecasts from economic models 'adapt', with those forecasts adjusting rapidly to major changes, even when those changes are unpredictable" (Hendry and Ericsson 2001b, p. 8; on the rare events, see p. 9). Nonetheless, these authors are well aware of the criticism that forecast errors have been systematic, including the case of well-known economies like that of the United Kingdom.

10.3.1 On the Characteristics of the Methodological Process: Preconditions for Rational Prediction

Before the details on methods of prediction in economics are given, it is convenient to reflect on some previous steps. The first is in the preconditions for rational prediction. This question which emerges from the notion of "methodology" is related to how the processes *are* and how *ought to be*, and therefore contemplates the existence of frequent errors in economic predictions as well as the need for improvement (i.e., accuracy and precision).

Accordingly, taking into account the existence of difficulties for reliable predictions and, above all, the important phenomenon of the systematic character of the *predictive errors* which have appeared in relevant cases in economics, a general question arises: what are the main characteristics of the *methodological process* to be considered in economics in order to avoid or to diminish that phenomenon? In other words, is there a reasonable basis for skipping the methodological skepticism concerning the predictive improvement of economic methods dealing with predictive errors? The issue concerns *preconditions for rational prediction* to be considered in methodological processes in macroeconomics as well as in microeconomics.

[6] On the distinction between "economic activity" and "economics as activity," see Chap. 7. The historical character of economic activity is also pointed out in Sect. 8.4. The notion of "historicity" is analyzed in Gonzalez (1996e, 2011b). On the criticisms of the elbow room give to history within economic theory, cf. Hodgson (2001).

Rescher, thinking of the case for any science, offers a general conviction: "it is only where the future is somehow foreshadowed in the discernible stability patterns of the past-and-present that rational prediction becomes possible" (1998, p. 86). Thus, he considers three indispensable *preconditions* for *rational prediction*: (i) data availability (the relevant information about the past-and-present can be obtained in an adequately accurate and reliable way); (ii) pattern discernability (the body of data exhibits discernible patterns); and (iii) pattern stability (the patterns so exhibited are stable, and this structural feature manifests a consistency that also continues into the future) (Rescher 1998, p. 86).

Of these three preconditions, Rescher pays most attention to *pattern discernability*. He accepts the adaptation of our expectations of the future to the occurrence structure of the past according to rational criteria, which leads to an efficient pattern fitting. In addition, the predictive claims about the future have no other choice than to look to the past and present events, seeking not only the sameness but also the change (in human condition and its circumstances). Thus, "rational prediction pivots on the existence of some sort of approximative *linkage* that connects our predictive claims with the input data that provide for their justification. This linkage can be based either on explicitly articulated principles—explanatory regularities (…)—or on personal judgments that exploit a knowledgeable expert's tacit, unarticulated, and sometimes unarticulable background knowledge of the matter" (Rescher 1998, p. 87).

According to this analysis, which reflects a different level of rigor in the processes, there is a distinction between *predictive approaches*: (i) predictions which are *judgmental* or *intuitive* in proceeding via the unformalized, and occasionally unarticulable, processes of reasoning in the personal estimation of individuals; and (ii) predictions which are *discursive* in proceeding via formally rule-specified modes of reasoning (and, therefore, in a more demanding way than the other approach).

Hence, confidence in our predictions lies in the *correctness of our data* and the *kind of process* that is used (either the competence of the experts or the inferential principles, such as possible scientific laws). In the judgmental case, prediction is *personally mediated* (by "informed experts"), whereas the discursive approach on prediction is *methodologically oriented* (Rescher 1998, p. 86). In economics we can find both possibilities, although the level of reliability of the former (judgmental or intuitive in proceeding and personally mediated) is clearly lower than the latter (discursive in proceeding and methodologically oriented), because this can have a higher level of objectivity.

In this regard, it is generally assumed by many economists that "economists must resort to statistical inference" (Hahn 1993, p. 78) rather than to have special confidence in other resorts. Habitually, they rely on time-series and econometric models that "are based on statistical models, and therefore allow derivations of measures of forecast uncertainty, and associated test of forecast adequacy" (Clements and Hendry 1998, p. 16). Simultaneously, there is a wary attitude toward laws in economics (as regards their existence and characteristics) in some important authors (Hausman 2000).

Commonly, the methodological approaches in economics—as a social science and also as a science of the artificial—need to take into account different factors: on the one hand, the presence of *indeterminism* in human affairs (i.e., the diversity of variables, endogenous and exogenous, which are open towards the future), which is related to social choices and new designs to enlarge human possibilities (e.g., in financial economics); and, on the other, that the *predictive errors* are connected to variables from both sides (endogenous and exogenous).

These factors are associated with a quite prevalent conviction among economists: "our predictions cannot be exact and will be subject to error. This follows from inevitable errors of measurement and errors in the estimation of functional forms. In addition, one must bear in mind that the path of the exogenous variable which one takes as given may be a stochastic path" (Hahn 1993, p. 83). Nevertheless, economics needs successful predictions, and this requires us to work on the improvement of *reliability* at several methodological levels. This advancement includes *research* on data availability, pattern discernability, and pattern stability. To seek progress in reliability in these features could be seen as a key for the *success* of economic predictions.

Within this context, some *requirements* might be considered for successful predictions. Hendry points out four, whatever the source of the forecasts: "(a) there are regularities to be captured, (b) the regularities are informative about the future, (c) the proposed method captures those regularities, and yet (d) it excludes non-regularities" (Hendry 2001d, p. 24). He admits that items (a) and (b) are characteristics of the economic system (i.e., ontological and epistemological), whereas (c) and (d) are aspects of the predictive method. In addition, he recognizes that to achieve item (c) jointly with (d) is difficult in practice (this recognition is based on the history of economic forecasting in the United Kingdom).[7] Nevertheless, it is assumed that the methodological process can lead to successful predictions in economics.

10.3.2 Diversity of Predictive Approaches: Unformalized and Formalized Predictions

A second step after the recognition of the preconditions of rational prediction is to emphasize the diversity of predictive approaches. Thus, even though predictive approaches are attempts to offer *rational predictions*, some of them are *scientific* ("methods of prediction"), whereas others are not ("predictive procedures"). The need for rational prediction was already pointed out in the case of practical prediction as an element of criticism to Popper's methodological views on science.[8] Consequently, a rational prediction could be theoretical or practical.

[7] On economic forecasting, see, for example, Holden (1989), Mills (1999a, 1999b, 2002), and Newbold and Harvey (2002).

[8] The argument is based on Salmon's ideas on rational prediction, and it has been developed in Chap. 3, especially in Sect. 3.3.2.

In any case, Rescher stresses that rational prediction requires evidential validation from suitable data inputs. Furthermore, he sees three aspects involved here: "predictive approaches," "linking mechanism" (the connection of the predictive claim with the input data for its justification), and "methodology of linkage" (the kind of process followed when predicting). Using three aspects, he presents a detailed survey of predictive approaches (Rescher 1998, p. 88):[9]

A SURVEY OF PREDICTIVE APPROACHES

	PREDICTIVE APPROACHES	LINKING MECHANISM	METHODOLOGY OF LINKAGE
UNFORMALIZED/JUDGMENTAL			
	judgmental estimation	expert informants	informed judgment
FORMALIZED/INFERENTIAL			
RUDIMENTARY (ELEMENTARY)			
	trend projection	prevailing trends	projection of prevailing trends
	curve fitting	geometric patterns	subsumption under an established pattern
	circumstantial analogy	comparability groupings	assimilation to an analogous situation
SCIENTIFIC (SOPHISTICATED)			
	indicator coordination	causal correlations	statistical subsumption into a correlation
	law derivation (nomic)	accepted laws (deterministic or statistical)	inference from accepted laws
	phenomenological modelling (analogical)	formal models (physical or mathematical)	analogizing of actual ("real-world") processes with presumably isomorphic model process

Both unformalized and formalized predictions have a variety of possibilities within that detailed analysis. In the case of *judgmental mode of prediction* there are several options: (1) unformalized predictions, whose roots are in the *personal* estimation of individuals (in principle, people who have knowledge as experts about the issues involved); and (2) unformalized predictions made in a *multilateral* way, according

[9] Rescher's analysis includes more elements than those which appear explicitly in the table, mainly in the area of "unformalized/judgmental" prediction. *Sensu stricto*, scientific predictions are—for him—predictive validation by laws and modeling.

to different routes: (i) a combination of individual predictions in a mechanical manner (e.g., averaging), (ii) an integration of predictive information in more complex modes (like Delphi),[10] and (iii) the predictive expertise in other forms of informal judgment of experts as providers of information about processes (e.g., in the initial versions of "expert systems").[11]

Inferential (or "formalized") *modes of prediction* are those that dispense with personal estimation in favor of explicitly delineated processes. On the one hand, there are the elementary or less sophisticated formalized predictions, such as trend extrapolation (or projection), curve fitting, and analogy; and, on the other, there exist the more sophisticated formalized predictions, such as the use of indicators (either explained or unexplained, which includes the black-box prediction), law derivation (prediction with a nomic component), and phenomenological modeling (via analogy). The predictions made through the use of laws and models (elaborated by employing analogies) belong typically to the scientific sphere. In addition, there is also the possibility of using second order processes that combine the results of different predictive approaches (Rescher 1998, pp. 85–112).

All unformalized and formalized predictions are considered to be a general view on predictive approaches, but it seems to me quite clear that most of them are used in the case of economics (Clements and Hendry 2002a). From a methodological point of view, the key issue is the problem of establishing criteria to distinguish between "predictive procedures" and "methods of prediction" (or "predictive methods"). In other words, the underlying question is to separate the predictive approaches that are not scientific ("predictive procedures") from those which really are scientific ("predictive methods"). Rescher's analysis is general, because it was conceived for any science, but it does give guidance for this demarcation issue. It can be used for the study of economics as a science that employs habitually predictions.

(I) *Judgmental predictions*, including the unformalized made through *personal estimation*, are a very common case of rational prediction.[12] However, they are only "predictive procedures." Thus, they are not reliable for scientific purposes. The judgmental predictions are the product of insight and do not follow an explicit, methodically articulated way of predicting. In these cases we do not grasp the *modus operandi* of the process, and therefore we cannot provide any sort of cogent account of *why* the predicted result will be obtained.

Furthermore, reliance on informalized (judgmental) predictions made by experts includes a metaprediction: we predict that the expert will be right in the case that we are considering. But that reliance on "expertise" is risky, because it is based

[10] The Delphi procedure was developed in the 1950s by Olaf Helmer, Norman Dalkey, and Nicholas Rescher, cf. Helmer and Rescher (1959).

[11] According to Rescher, the difference between prediction by means of "expert system" and the informal judgment of experts lies in the *process* rather than in the data sources: the focus here is on the attempt to make explicit and systematize the *reasoning process* used by the experts themselves (a procedure used in medical diagnoses) (1998, p. 97).

[12] These predictions are commonly used in economics, cf. Önkal-Atay et al. (2002). In addition, there are several ways for improving the role of judgment in economic predictions, see Goodwin et al. (2011).

on available experience, while conditions and circumstances may change (Rescher 1998, pp. 88–91). This phenomenon—the risk of judgmental predictions—can be seen in the case of some predictions made by well-known stockbrokers of the New York Stock Exchange (Malkiel 1996).

Typically, a judgmental prediction is an informal assessment based on the experience of the predictor(s) and some kind of intuition that relies on the results of survey data. In this basic case, there is a clear dependence on subjective appreciation of an individual (or on intersubjective appraisal of a group). So, a major limitation of this judgmental prediction is in the *composing factors*: it could be the case that is not clear what elements have been taken into account in producing the prediction or what weight each factor has had. Another limitation is in the *testing* of the prediction, due to the difficulty in replicability: given the same information on a different day, the judgmental predictor(s) might come up with a quite different prediction.

Actually, there are two ways of difficulties here: (a) in the process of making a prediction again, either in order to obtain "the same" prediction or even a different one; and (b) in how to evaluate the content of the prediction, especially when we want to avoid epistemological biases and clear limitations.[13] Therefore, a judgmental prediction cannot be an adequate substitute for a formal quantitative analysis (Llewellyn et al. 1985, p. 124), even though it seems clear that a judgmental prediction may be considered as a complement for a final outcome (e.g., in economic decision-making).

Unformalized predictions made in a *multilateral way* also belong to the orbit of "predictive procedures." Thus, amalgamating expert predictions made through the aggregation processes (averaging), the Delphi technique, and the systematized expertise are still in the sphere of the judgmental mode of prediction. They offer valuable information, mainly subjective or intersubjective, which has difficulties in reaching the level of objective knowledge. This situation occurs with the amalgamations made mechanically by the combination of the results of questionnaires or surveys, or through the interactive procedure of consensus-formation in collaborative groups or panels.

On the one hand, a group average of economic predictions tends to be more accurate over time than any simple individual performance of prediction (although the parameter is important: commonly, economists perform better with production and employment levels than with interests rates); and, on the other hand, the consensus of experts is not a full guarantee of scientific character of any knowledge, because, as the history of science illustrates, there are many examples of consensus in error (Rescher 1998, pp. 91–96).[14]

(II) *Formalized predictions* are different from judgmental predictions, insofar as they include various routine modes of *pattern fitting*, such as trend projection (or extrapolation), curve fitting, cyclical analysis, and analogy exploitation (Rescher 1998, pp. 97–102). Habitually, these inferential predictive approaches have some

[13] "The accuracy of judgmental forecasts is, on average, inferior to statistical ones. This is because our judgment is often characterized by considerable biases and limitations" (Makridakis et al. 1998, p. 483).

[14] Consensus in error can be found in the times of Galileo Galilei and Charles Darwin.

advantages over the unformalized predictions, because they offer an explicitly delineated procedure and, therefore, the analysis of their processes can be made in a more objective way than in the case of judgmental predictions. Nevertheless, full confidence in a kind of "principle of continuity" in human affairs (i.e., that the observed patterns of the past will continue to predominate in the future) should be avoided.

a. *Trend projection* can contain the extrapolation of prevailing trends, which is commonly linear (but it might be of another kind).[15] Basically, this simple and naive procedure sees the future as merely continuing the lines of past developments. But the outcome of the trend projection is very sensitive to changes in prevailing conditions. The existence of those changes, which are often unforeseen, can originate visible mistakes such as those of the Club of Rome's study *The Limits of Growth* (Meadows et al. 1972).[16] Moreover, the premises used in the reasoning based on the continuation of present trends involve serious problems, because economics has a historical character, and economic activity is always open to new phenomena.

b. *Curve fitting* is a more sophisticated process than linear extrapolations. The projection of some patterns can provide the shape of a curve of some nonlinear sort (exponential, sinusoidal, S-shaped, etc.). Here statistics plays a crucial role because it is focused on providing mechanisms for patterns of order in masses of data (Arminger et al. 1995). There are "many powerful mathematical tools for fitting curves to temporally structured information: the data regarding the past can be projected by processes as varied as multiple regression analysis, time series analysis, envelope curve fitting, multimode factor analysis, correlation analysis, and various others" (Rescher 1998, p. 100). Nevertheless, there is still debate on the level of refinement of statistical sophistication that actually pays off in better predictive performance (it could be variations according to the kind of variables and the phenomena studied).

c. *Cyclical analysis* is a common predictive procedure in economics, where the interest for cycles has been the case (e.g., business cycles). The sequential stages can combine periods of different kinds: from rapid developments to relative stagnations, when the factors of innovation (such as the technological resources) seem exhausted. The application of the cyclical analysis for predictive purposes is problematic insofar as it is not easy to know where we are placed within a particular cycle. Frequently, the present position is seen only with the knowledge of hindsight. In addition, it could be that the end of the cycle is not clear enough.

d. *Analogy exploitation* or *circumstantial analogy* is when prediction is made through means of analogizing the pattern of developments from one domain to another. The analogies may rest on descriptive similarities, or they may also be based on shared structures or common developments. The procedure of analogy can place a particular case (e.g., a business firm or a nation) into a statistical "reference class" of others with which it shares some relevant features. In drawing predictive analo-

[15] Fernández-Jardón, C., *Personal Communication*, 25 January 2014.

[16] In my interview with Herbert Simon on 20 December 1993, he insisted on the *tremendous inaccuracy* of the variables predicted by the 1972 Club of Rome report. On this issue, see Chap. 1, Sect. 1.2.2. and 1.4.3.

gies there are potential weaknesses, because the situations that we analogize (either in microeconomics or macroeconomics) are never completely identical. It is very frequent to appeal to historical precedents, but this requires us to assume that history repeats itself, which raises methodological questions insofar as history is a science of human actions (Gonzalez 1996e, pp. 91–104).

A different kind of formalized prediction is prediction made by (leading) *indicators*. For Rescher, it is a more sophisticated process than the previous ones, and it is close to the scientific prediction (1998, pp. 102–104). Predictive indicators are based on two factors (usually quantitative) that are empirically correlated in such a way that the behavior of the first foreshadows the behavior of the second, either invariably or with statistical preponderance.

The relation presupposes the existence of causal linkages,[17] and this is how it is used in applied sciences, such as in medicine or economics (e.g., the increase in traveling between two regions and the rise in commercial activity between them). The causal relation between the predictive indicators might be rationalized or might remain (temporally) unexplained. In the last case, we have a predictive procedure vulnerable to the contingent changes in the world's course of events, because it does not offer firm ground for recognized stabilities.

Besides this plethora of predictive approaches, Rescher emphasizes that there are two main forms of *prediction grounded in scientific principles*: (i) law-based predictions, and (ii) model-based predictions (1998, pp. 105–110).[18] *Sensu stricto*, these belong to what I have called here "methods of prediction" in science. Hence, they are the predictive methods that go beyond the mere level of predictive procedures in order to guarantee the existence of science. Nevertheless, *predictive methods* can be complemented by the predictive procedures when the task is to give the whole picture of economic phenomena (Burns 1986, p. 104). Furthermore, model-based predictions can be seen as a broader concept than law-based predictions, insofar as scientific laws rely on scientific models.

1. *Law-based predictions* look for the most appreciated of the patterns: the scientific laws (or what we accept as such, either in the natural realm, in the social domain or in the sphere of the artificial). Thus, the inference from formalized laws (generally in mathematical form) is the most sophisticated predictive method. However, it is debatable whether we have genuine "laws" in economics, or rather some kind of broad generalization about certain economic phenomena (Hausman 2000). In addition, there are possible obstacles to a predictive reliance on potential lawful relationship: the intervention of choice and change (or even chaos) in the relevant phenomena may alter the *fabric of lawfulness* (on the ontological level), and the intrusion of change in those phenomena can *destabilize* the attempts to formulate descriptive laws (on the epistemological level).

2. *Model-based predictions* are focused on the artificially structured collection of processes that parallels the operations of the system. The idea is, in principle, to

[17] On causal order and statistical data, cf. Spirtes et al. (1993).

[18] "Of all predictive processes it is *scientific* prediction, by means of laws and law-exploiting models, that furnishes its user with the highest level of rational comfort" (Rescher 1998, p. 110).

exploit the presumed structural correspondence between the model and the system in question in order to base system predictions on modeling processes.19 Modeling national economies by computer simulation is one of these cases (a simulation that finance ministries commonly look to for policy advice).

Insofar as the model has more parameters, it needs more detailed information to operate. And when the models involve more parameters, the equations of the system will be more complex and elaborate. But computer simulation model of an economy, even though it is a potentially powerful instrument of prediction, can have problems: the data available may not be sufficient to support a workable model and the complexity itself of real world phenomena may be sometimes too complex for our inferential tools.

Beyond law-based predictions and model-based predictions there is an underlying feature to be discovered (if it exists): a *suitable structural character* of the phenomena (a kind of regularity). This is what is needed for something to be predictable using a particular scientific method. Due to the complexity of economic phenomena, it seems quite reasonable to combine the information from predictive procedures and the results of the predictive methods.

Nevertheless, this reasonable attitude leads us to a *metaprediction*: we should predict which kind of predictive would be more efficient in its role of foretelling future events (in this case, in the economic world). In other words: "predictive efficacy as such is something that can itself only be established by means of predictions" (Rescher 1998, p. 112). Therefore, the methodology of prediction can carry us on to a meta-methodology of predictions, where the different predictive processes are evaluated according to some criteria (effectiveness, efficiency, etc.).

10.3.3 Predictive Procedures and Predictive Methods in Economics

Until now—in the previous step, on the diversity of rational predictions—I have emphasized the existence of different predictive processes ("procedures" and "methods"), and that only some of them—"methods of prediction"—might be considered as scientific. In economics, some of these *predictive methods* are oriented towards qualitative predictions, whereas most of them are adjusted to quantitative predictions. Furthermore, the predictive methods can search for aims that may be divergent (either mainly descriptive or connected to a prescriptive goal).

Hence, there are several predictive methods in economics, among them what is commonly called "econometric methods of forecasting." In the list of "methods of forecasting" in economics made by Hendry, there is a large diversity of predictive processes: "guessing, 'rules of thumb', and 'informal models'; extrapolation; leading indicators; surveys; time-series models; and econometric systems" (2001d,

---

[19] On the relations between representation and models in science, see Gonzalez (2014).

p. 24).[20] Even though all are used in economic practice, it seems clear that not all of them are scientific.

What puzzles me is the presence of "guessing" in this list of "methods of forecasting," because it is not a *method* at all. There are no *rules* for guessing, and thus there is no real *process* to be followed in order to search for an aim. Furthermore, the path used in guessing could hardly be repeatable, even by the same person who makes the guess. And, although it is possible that a clairvoyant or an oracle might make a successful prediction, that statement could be completely fortuitous and, therefore, it is not a methodological achievement in any relevant sense.[21] It is a kind of "unformalized prediction," with no scientific value whatsoever. Moreover, "guessing" as well as "rules of thumb" and "informal models" are what I have called "predictive procedures." In economics they are employed *de facto* in some areas (e.g., in the decision-making of some firms), but they are not "predictive methods" according to a scientific process.

Likewise, I have also criticized the instrumentalist methodology of some authors, both in the general realm (Gonzalez 1995, in the case of Reichenbach's approach) and in the special domain of methodology of economics (e.g., analyzing Friedman's approach). They highlight the *predictive success* (even in the case of a clairvoyant or without the realism of assumptions), but success as such is not *eo ipso* a scientific feature (it could be completely random).

In addition to logical reasons (logic teaches us that a false statement may have a true statement as a consequence), there are methodological reasons already pointed out for the success of economic predictions, mainly that the proposed method should capture *regularities*. Thus, we are interested in the *methods*—the adequate processes—of scientific predictions in economics and not merely in the results *qua* outcomes (in spite of their being occasionally successful).

More rigorous than guessing, rules of thumb and informal models are the *predictive procedures* of extrapolation, forecasting based on indicators, and surveys of consumers and business. (i) *Extrapolation* is frequently used in economic matters (both in microeconomics and macroeconomics), and it is quite reasonable to do so, at least to some extent. This method could be successful when the present tendency persists in the future, but that is not habitually the case. Thus, extrapolation could be used to think of a possible outcome of a tendency, commonly in the short or middle run, but it is unable to indicate the change, or turning point, in economic tendency. Therefore, it is a limited predictive method. It would be more valid if the realm of study were "economic activity" rather than "economics as activity" (Chap. 7, Sect. 7.3). In addition, extrapolation is more reliable when the phenomenon is in the circle of a "foresight" than when it is in the orbit of a "prediction" or a "forecast" [in the specific senses and references already pointed out (Chap. 2, Sect. 2.4.2)].

---

[20] The details of these predictive methods extend beyond the scope of this book, which is focused on the philosophico-methodological approach. A large amount of information can be found in the bibliography cited in this chapter and in the following one.

[21] Commonly, an oracle gives a "close statement"—a result—whereas a scientist offers the process followed to reach the final result.

(ii) *Forecasting based on indicators* (mainly "leading indicators") has a long tradition, and it is also commonly used in economics. The emphasis is on identifying changes in directions in economic activity (i.e., "turning points"). In this regard, there are three groups of statistical indicators: "'leading indicators', or series whose peaks and troughs regularly precede those in general business conditions; 'lagging indicators', or series whose peaks and troughs regularly lag behind those of general business conditions; and 'coincident indicators', whose peaks and troughs regularly match those of general business conditions. Examples of leading indicators of general trends in economic activity typically include such variables as hours worked, new orders, wholesale prices, construction contracts, new business formation, and business failures" (Llewellyn et al. 1985, pp. 126–127).[22]

However, the predictive procedure of leading indicators "is unreliable unless the reasons for the lead are clear, as with orders leading production. As an example of their unreliability, the Harvard Barometer (a well-known leading indicator) missed the 1929 collapse. In practice, leading indicators need to be changed regularly, highlighting their inability to capture many of the underlying changes in the economy" (Hendry 2001d, p. 25).[23] Economic cycles are usually unequal: from a few months to a year or several years. Thus, insofar as leading indicators are located in the setting of the *historical character* of economics and need to deal with the *historicity* of economic events, they are less reliable than other predictive processes.

This can be seen when the composite leading economic indicator (CLI) focuses on the business cycle of market economies (understood as sequences of expansion and contraction in an economy). The research has two central problems of *identification*: on the one hand, how to establish clearly the reference of "business cycle" from the raw macro-aggregates on gross domestic product, unemployment, etc.; and, on the other, how to express the movements of the composite leading economic indicators in order to get predictions about turning points of the business cycle (Clements and Hendry 1998, pp. 13–14). In this regard, it is relevant to point out that economic time series are commonly *autocorrelated* and *intercorrelated*. Thus, a task is to predict chance correlations from the starting point of economic time series that capture persistent regularities.

Undoubtedly, there is an *interdependence* of economic variables and the theory should take this problem into account. Thus, even if our question is simply 'what will the British inflation rate be next year?,' the answer can include an interdependence of economic variables: "to predict inflation we must also predict interest rates; this in turn may require a prediction of exchange rates, and so on" (Hahn 1993, p. 82). The leading indicators are not in a mere "economic activity," but rather in "economics as activity," where contextual factors (social, political,

[22] A different kind of statistical indicator is the diffusion index. "This provides a measure of the proportion of a given set of leading indicators that are, at any time, moving in the same direction. The pooling of indicators in the form of a diffusion index reduces the risk that false turning points in economic activity may be signalled" (Llewellyn et al. 1985, p. 127).

[23] On the Harvard Barometer, cf. van den Bogaard (1999, pp. 289–290).

cultural, ecological, etc.) can have an influence (as can be seen in the indicators of business cycles).[24] And those factors have a historical dimension.

(iii) *Surveys of consumers and business* can also be used as a predictive procedure, mainly in microeconomics areas such as theory of the firm and industrial organization. Surveys can be useful to determine the point of departure for predicting because origins habitually play an important role in prediction (Clements and Hendry 1998, p. 15). But they can also give us relevant information about the future economic activity insofar as the intentions of the agents in the social setting—individuals or groups—become actions (i.e., their mental acts about the future may become, thereafter, empirically tested phenomena).

Considered as a procedure for economic prediction, surveys have the additional problem of being based on subjective decision-making rather than on objective content. Certainly, it is a kind of research on economic evaluation where there is a connection between expectations and predictions, but "expectations" are not identical to "predictions."[25] Thus, the key methodological issue with the surveys of consumers and business is how to get the relevant kind of regularity to be used by the predictive procedure (i.e., what is the data that can lead to pattern discernability and pattern stability).

Even though *extrapolation*, forecasting based on *indicators*, and *surveys* of consumers and business are three procedures used for prediction in economics, they are commonly considered less relevant than time-series models and econometric forecasting models. Moreover, in a well-known book on econometrics we can read: "economic forecasting methods can be classified into two broad categories. (1) *Causal forecasting/econometric models*," and "(2) *Time series models*" (Kennedy 1998, p. 288).[26] There is no mention of other predictive methods, presumably because it is assumed that these two are the main *methods of prediction* in economics.[27]

---

[24] "Our results also indicate that there is still much to learn about forecasting the business cycle. In particular, changes in the interest rate alone do not appear to have been sufficient to forecast the onset or length of the 1990s recession, even with the benefit of hindsight. (…) It still remains to be seen how well the implied composite leading indicator will forecast any subsequent UK recession" (Osborn 2001, pp. 122–123).

[25] See Chapt. 9, Sect. 9.5.2. On the specific approach of "rational expectations," an analysis is made in the papers collected in Frydman and Phelps (1983).

[26] Historically, "time-series analysts played the dominant role in developing theoretical methods for forecasting in the postwar period" (Clements and Hendry 1998, p. 9).

[27] It can be discussed if time series models, such as Box-Jenkins, should be considered in the group of "predictive methods" instead of being included in the set of "predictive processes." The difference between a Box-Jenkins model and an approach of a predictive process (e.g., trend projection or curve fitting) is mostly statistical: a Box-Jenkins model is more sophisticated than a regression on a linear tendency. But it seems that, from the economic point of view, they are somehow similar. Nevertheless, the superior statistical framework leads one to think of Box Jenkins models as methodologically more sophisticated than those cases pointed out within the "predictive processes."

(1) "Econometric forecasting models" seems a broader and better denomination than "causal forecasting models."[28] The *econometric model of forecasting* can be used to predict the dependent variable when the associated values of the independent variables are given. The model is employed according to a causal interpretation. From a mathematical point of view, it can have a wide range of sophistication: from a single equation with one or two explanatory variables to a large simultaneous-equation model with scores of variables (Kennedy 1998, p. 288). The last case is used in formal econometric systems of national economies. The aim is not only to predict the future of the economy, taking into account the available data, but also to provide knowledge in order to prescribe possible actions (i.e., policy advice).

Commonly, predictive methods based on econometric models work on relationships between variables such as GNP, inflation, money, interest rates, exchange rates,... These relations are expressed through equations based on available data, which are usually aggregate time series. According to Hendry, these econometric models have three *main components*: (a) deterministic terms, such as intercepts (taking the values 1, 1, 1,...) and linear trends (taking the values 1, 2, 3,...), which are introduced to grasp averages and steady growth, whose future values are known; (b) observed stochastic variables, such as consumers' expenditure, prices, and output, which have unknown future values; and (c) unobserved errors, all of whose values (past, present, and future) are unknown, although perhaps estimable in the context of a model (Hendry 2001d, p. 21).

From a historical perspective, the use of econometric models in forecasting macroeconomic developments and guiding the policy-making is more visible in the second half of the twentieth century. "Early applications of econometric methods were essentially microeconomic in orientation, involving the estimation of demand and supply relationships. The development and use of econometric methods in a macroeconomic context became widespread in the 1950s, although their initial application was, for most part, limited to the formal testing of hypotheses about the behaviour of economic agents. Examples were econometric studies of the determinants of consumption and investment behaviour, and of wage and price determination" (Llewellyn et al. 1985, p. 128).

(2) The *time series model* is focused on a time trend, a seasonal factor, a cyclical element, and an error term. The research seeks to break up a time series into these components and so to produce a means of predicting the behavior of the series. This kind of approach is based on the supposition that history provides some guide as to what expect in the future. Among the most sophisticated of these time series methods of research is the Box-Jenkins's analysis (Box and Jenkins 1970).[29]

---

[28] The causal models use "causal variables" as the variables that actually determine the outcome. Some authors consider that "models with no causal variables might outperform those with numerous correctly included causal variables" (Hendry and Ericsson 2001c, p. 190).

[29] Although there were a number of important contributions dealing with *AutoRegressive Integrated Moving Average* (ARIMA) class of models prior to 1970, that year marked the beginning of the popularization of this model and its associated predictive methodology, cf. Pedregal and Young (2002, pp. 71–72).

Indeed, these methods became so common in economic prediction that this analysis is usually referred to when economists (as distinct from business forecasters) talk about the "time series method" (Kennedy 1998, p. 288).[30] Nevertheless, Granger—in his lecture as Nobel laureate—points out his contribution in this regard: "cointegration," an important aspect missed in the previous work. Thus, methods to analyze a single integrated series had been proposed previously by Box and Jenkins and others authors, "but the joint analysis of pairs, or more, of such series was missing an important feature. It turns out that the difference between a pair of integrated series can be stationary, and this property is known as 'cointegration'" (Granger 2004, p. 361).

Predicting using time series models involves the identification of the components (seasonal, cyclical, etc.) on the basis of past movements in a given series, projecting them towards the future, and then aggregating them to obtain a projection for the series in question. In order to produce a projection using this method, there is no need for knowledge about causal factor or even economic theory. "Frequently-used methods of time series analysis are extrapolative forecasting (in which a variable is projected to continue growing or declining at its previous trend rate), regressive forecasting (in which a variable is projected to return towards a value observed in a preceding period), and adaptive forecasting (in which projections are revised upwards or downwards in light of the most recent forecast error). Box-Jenkins methods (…) are a particularly elaborate expression of time series analysis, integrating elements of extrapolative, regressive, and adaptive aspects of time series analysis in a general framework" (Llewellyn et al. 1985, p. 125).

Some authors highlight that the predictive methods in economics are not limited or confined to the specific aim of *foretelling* future economic events. Thus, they maintain that "formal econometric systems of national economies fulfill many useful roles other than just being devices for generating forecasts; for example, such models consolidate existing empirical and theoretical knowledge of how economies function, provide a framework for a progressive research strategy, and help to explain their own failures. They are open to adversarial scrutiny, are replicable, and hence offer a scientific basis for research" (Clements and Hendry 1998, p. 16). Consequently, predictive methods in economics can have several descriptive aims, but they can also be used for seeking prescriptive aims.

10.3.4 The Analysis of Their Predictive Methods by Economists

Basically, when economists analyze their predictive methods (mainly in the field of applied economics), they can follow two different paths: (a) an *empirical research*

[30] On time series econometrics, in addition to the book of Michael Clements and David Hendry (1998), already cited, cf. Granger and Newbold (1977); Abraham and Ledolter (1983/[2005]); Harvey (1990, 1991); Kacapyr (1996a); Kennedy (1998), Chap. 17, pp. 263–287; Clements and Hendry (1999); and Hendry (2000b). See also Kock and Teräsvirta (2011), and Koopman and Ooms (2011).

that can make comparisons, usually in the case of predictive competitions, looking at the performance of different methods for many time series; and (b) an analysis based on *computer simulations* which uses the artificially generated data (computer intensive numerical processes) to check the adequacy of econometric methods (Hendry 2001d, pp. 29–33). Both paths are widely used, but the former habitually has more advantages and difficulties than the latter. In addition, the analysis of predictive methods by empirical comparison could be made through controlled observations or using laboratory experimentation (cf. Chap. 9).

When the focus is on *empirical comparisons*, it is clear that the data generating process is not in the hands of the investigator and, in addition, the data will be imperfectly known. Thus, "the results of forecast comparisons for any one series could turn on idiosyncratic features of the series, so limit their general applicability. For this reason, many series are compared, and often series are selected which share certain characteristics, with the caveat that the results might only be expected to hold for other series with these characteristics. This highlights a 'circularity problem': until we know how empirical economic data are generated, we cannot know the appropriate framework for developing or analyzing methods, so cannot actually know how well they should perform" (Clements and Hendry 2002b, p. 7).

Computer simulations are widely used in statistical economics and econometrics. The predictive methods can be compared by stochastic simulations, where "replicas" of the concrete system and its initial conditions are created with a computer. Thus, an economist "generates artificial 'data' on which the models are compared in repeated trials, to calculate how well such methods perform in a controlled environment of their own choosing. However, the empirical relevance of such results depends on whether or not the artificial data 'mimic' the relevant properties of the 'real world', so may be open to doubt. This method of analysis is most useful when we know the large-sample behavior of statistics of interest for the forecasting methods (…), and wish to investigate the usefulness of these asymptotic results for samples of the size typically available to the applied researcher" (Clements and Hendry 2002b, p. 7).

Simulations—and, principally, computer simulations (Keller 2003)—have been characterized as "experiments" or, more appropriately, as "virtual experiments" (Gonzalez 2007a, pp. 284–285, and 2010b, pp. 35–36). They are a hybrid insofar as simulations can mix mathematical models with experimental ones. "This kind of experimental activity has a comparatively long tradition in economics, predating the computer simulations of the type so familiar nowadays. It consists of statistical or mathematical models that are simulated, or 'run', to generate output series with the aim of mimicking observed economic time-series data. For example, one of the most commonly available, but least understood, sets of economic data is that of stock market prices" (Morgan 2003, pp. 224–225).[31]

[31] Mary Morgan introduces the distinction between "virtual experiments" and "virtually experiments": "Virtual experiments (entirely nonmaterial in object of study and in intervention but which may involve the mimicking of observations) and virtually experiments (almost a material experiment by virtue of the virtually material object of input)" (Morgan 2003, p. 233).

Within this sphere of research—at least in the case of economics, mainly as applied science—there is an interweaving between the character of social science and the dimension of science of the artificial (in the sense of Simon 1996). On the one hand, simulations can use the *empirical information* of the world, which might be obtained through observations, or even through experiments (including laboratory experiments); and, on the other, simulations include a *nonmaterial component* that seeks to resemble aspects of the world (a virtual representation oriented towards a mimic of the real world). The point of this hybrid of the social and the artificial is clear: to produce new outcomes in areas where other kinds of research seem unfeasible or defective. Thus, they have an undeniable heuristic role that it is useful in areas such as econometrics.

Frequently it happens that simulations, in general, and computer simulations, in particular, can perform a similar task to that of thought experiments, insofar as they can contribute to establishing some phenomena as possible and in ruling out certain events as impossible. But not all thought experiments are *eo ipso* simulations: they can follow different heuristic routes.[32] Nevertheless, both share the consideration of nonmaterial elements (or, at least, non-tangible components). Methodologically, simulations are *virtual experiments*—they work on a hypothetical data stream in the case of economics—and ontologically they rely on constructed items within the artificial world (e.g., a resemblance of the real economic processes).

Methodologically, Alvin Roth—Nobel Prize with an important work on experimental economics—has pointed out rightly that there is a "distressing tendency to confuse computer simulations, and the kind of investigations one can do with them, with experiments involving the observation of real people in controlled environments. (…) Computers simulations are useful for creating and exploring theoretical models, while experiments are useful for observing behaviour" (1988, p. 1000/1993, p. 29). In fact, a difference can be pointed out between the conclusions obtained by computer simulation (e.g., in the case of computer "tournaments" reported by R. Axelrod (1980a, b, 1984) and the experimental results obtained in the laboratory (e.g., in the experiments made by R. Selten and R. Stoecker 1986)).

According to Roth, "the difference in results has a great deal to do with the difference between computer simulations and actual experiments. While the computer simulations which produce this result were conducted with an element of experimental flavour that is missing from conventional computer simulations (in that tournament entries were solicited from others), experiments with human subjects introduce a certain amount of open-ended complexity in the form of human behavior, that is absent from a tournament in which individuals are represented by short (or even moderately long) computer programs" (1988, p. 1001).

Clearly, the notion itself of "experiment" is commonly linked to the idea of something *artificial*, insofar as there is a human intervention to control a phenomenon or a set of phenomena (natural, social, or artificial). But there is an increasing

[32] Commonly, thought experiments are used to show the possibility and the impossibility of natural phenomena, social events, and artificial designs, as well as their limits in our world. See Gonzalez (2010b, pp. 37–38).

complexity in the study of the economic events, according to the scale of phenomena. The investigation may start from computer simulations—a clear artificial situation—and, through the analysis of controlled experiments in the laboratory environment—a less artificial case than the previous one—, the research of economic phenomena may reach the following steps of complexity: the real economic activity of human beings.[33] In this search the historical character of economics plays an important role,[34] which should be considered as well.

10.4 The Role of Models in Economic Predictions

When economists analyze their predictive methods, either by means of empirical research or using computer simulations, a central aspect is the role of models. Both the methods of prediction based on time-series models, including Granger's cointegration (Engle and Granger 1987; Granger 1986; see also Engle and White 1999), and predictive methods built upon econometric models need to revise their models according to the results of the empirical research and the contributions of the computer simulations. In addition, due to the different levels of complexity, the analysis can start from time series models and extend to econometric models that, from a more complex stage, incorporate the outcomes of time series models.

Moreover, the relation in economics between models and predictions is twofold. (1) There is the need for clarification of the *features of economic models* to be used in conforming economic predictions, taking into account the different kinds of aims of those predictions. (2) Economic predictions are outcomes that can be employed to *evaluate the models themselves* following some criteria (accuracy, precision, etc.), where the task of predictions is then to be a test for the economic models (on this second aspect, cf. Hendry 1986). The first problem is also associated with the characteristics of economic models themselves, an issue that has received intense attention.[35] Meanwhile the second question—the connection between the results of economic predictions and the quality of the models—is related to the evaluation and limits of predictions, which is a topic of Chap. 11.

---

[33] On complexity as a typical feature or economic reality, cf. Gonzalez (1994, p. 262). See also Gonzalez (2001a, 2013b).

[34] Roth sees a parallel between evolutionary biology and economics because they deal "largely with historical data" (1986, p. 270).

[35] See, for example, Boland (1989); Rubinstein (1998); Granger (1999); and Mäki (2002), part III: Economic Models and Economic Reality, pp. 105–228. The three volumes of *Models of Bounded Rationality* written by Herbert Simon (1982a, 1982b, 1997) offer a good example of the many aspects interrelated in the models.

10.4.1 A Twofold Relation: Characteristics and Evaluation

Both aspects of the twofold relation—the *characteristics* of economic models for predicting and the *evaluation* of the model according to predictions as a test—are interconnected: the former highlights the *process* itself of modeling economic predictions (i.e., elaboration of a mathematical model with an empirical content), whereas the latter insists on the *results* of economic modeling (which eventually can lead to reformulating the model if the outcome predictions are not good enough). Here, the attention goes initially to the elements to be considered in order to have an *adequate model* for a possible successful economic prediction, and later on—mainly, in Chap. 11—the emphasis will be on the use of predictions to evaluate economic models.

Terence Burns suggests five *characteristics of economic models* when he deals with the methodology of prediction. (i) Models are simplifications of a complex structure, and the task of the builder of an economic model is to devise a framework that captures the key interrelations. The new circumstances will require a number of adjustments. (ii) The data available is often insufficient to discriminate between alternative views of economic phenomena. It is sometimes difficult, statistically, to distinguish between models that are internally coherent in terms of different theories. (iii) Economic models are dominated by the range of historical experience. In this regard, the models are more suitable for analyzing relatively small changes from the current situation than for dealing with a large shock (such as a halving of oil prices). (iv) There are difficulties in measurement of the scale responses and the time lags involved: data limitations are a serious constraint for economic models. (v) It could be hard to cope with significant changes to the way expectations are formed. The issue is whether the process of formation of expectations built into the model is likely to change. This is more relevant in predictions that involve a sharp change of government policy (Burns 1986, pp. 104–105).

For statistical methods of economic prediction, such as time-series, being "model-based" is understood "in the sense that the forecasting operation is carried out subsequent to the statistical identification and estimation of a suitable (usually stochastic) mathematical model based on the available time-series data" (Pedregal and Young 2002, p. 69). So, *model* is seen here according to a first option, as some structural and dynamic *resemblance* or *representation* of an ongoing economic reality. The model relies on past and present data. This use of "model" focuses on the reality as such (mainly the past history of the time series itself), seeking a mathematical expression of a correlation of events (i.e., the patterns in the available economic data).

But there is another use of "model," which is quite different from an epistemological point of view, because of its reliance on more theoretical contents. The second use of model is when there is a somehow *ideal design* or *theoretical construction* that it is developed looking for new aspects in the economic realm (such as in the case of economics as a science of the artificial, e.g., where new "financial products" are developed to increase the gains in the investments, or as a social science, e.g., new macroeconomic scenarios created thinking of the solution of new immigration trends). The main goal of this second kind of model is not to be a "resemblance"—structural and dynamic—or "representation" of economic reality but rather to explore new domains of economic affairs following a theoretical design.

Models as "representations" (or structural and dynamic resemblances) and models as theoretical "constructions" (or ideal designs) are two different ways of seeing "economic activity" (and also "economics as activity" interwoven with other human endeavors). This epistemological difference has direct methodological consequences. On the one hand, predictive methods can use models as *representations* when the aim is to describe future outcomes of economic activity (e.g., consequences of present events). On the other, predictive methods may use models as theoretical *constructions* when they are dealing with future aspects that demand prescriptions (e.g., solutions to a possible novel state of affairs).

To *evaluate* economic models using economic predictions requires us to take into account what the *aim* of the model was.[36] If the purpose of the model was to describe with accuracy and precision the short run (or the middle or long run), then the data can be used to assess the realism of the *assumptions* of the model and its utilization in the methodological *process* of anticipation of unobserved events. However, if the aim of the model was to construct a possible solution to a concrete novel economic problem, thinking of the prescriptions that should be followed by that future design, then the evaluation of the economic model could be different, because the emphasis goes to the applicability of the prescriptions (Chap. 12). The empirical research has a clear role in the first case, whereas computer simulation gives more opportunities in the second option.

Burns insists on the idea of model as *representation* when he makes explicit his methodology of economic predictions: "The model plays a key role. It gives the analysts a consistent and comprehensive structure that captures the economic relationships that can be identified from historical data. A formal model ensures that the various interrelationships are taken consistently into account, both in forecasting and in policy advice. It makes possible many of the calculations that we do" (1986, p. 104).

But, at the same time, Burns accepts implicitly the existence of two kinds of models (i.e., "resemblance" and "theoretical construction"), each one connected with a type of prediction: "Macro-economists routinely produce two types of predictions; a forecast for the appropriate period ahead of the consequences of existing policies; and simulations of the effects of changes in policy instruments or states of the world" (Burns 1986, p. 104). Certainly, economics uses both kinds of models regarding prediction, because predictive methods are connected to descriptive aims as well as to prescriptive goals.

[36] "To evaluate an economic model, it is essential to know its purpose. Was it built to provide forecasts, to help with a policy decision, or test a specific economic hypothesis?" (Granger 2001, p. 94).

10.4.2 Economic Modeling in the Predictive Realm

How to *elaborate* an economic model and how to *evaluate* it are methodological issues that depend on aims. Economic models can be oriented in different directions and can be evaluated according to diverse criteria. Usually, the most basic case—both in economic theory and in econometrics—is the idea of model as "representation" or "resemblance" of economic reality. Thus, there is a clear rejection of Friedman's approach in favor of the absence of realism of assumptions in economic models. In this regard, due to their cognitive content models should have a relation to a possible correct *representation* (or structural and dynamic resemblance) of economic affairs, either in microeconomics or in macroeconomics. Moreover, models—in any science—are not pure "means" or "instruments," although they are mediators (Morgan and Morrison 1999), because a model could also be an ideal that is looked for.

Within the predictive realm, economic modeling is initially linked to the methods oriented towards accuracy and precision of future economic events. In the case of applied economics, the most sophisticated methodological processes are times series and econometric methods. Although both search this kind of "descriptive" aims, there are some differences between *time series models* and *econometric models*. The most important could be in the use of economic theory (at least in an explicit way). The time-series models (and, to a larger extent, indicator forecasting or "leading indicators") may not rely on economic theory, whereas econometric models have a clear connection to the models of economic theory.

This methodological difference between them is seen as an element in favor of prediction made with econometric models, because these models can be combined with a theoretically grounded economic explanation. Thus, even though econometric modeling is sometimes a precarious task (with unavoidable pitfalls and discouraging drawbacks), the models of econometrics have dominated the field of economic forecasting in recent decades, due to the reliance of the econometric models on economic theory, in addition to some advances in mathematical modeling and in computer simulations (Kacapyr 1996b, pp. 116–117).

When economic theory provides a reasonable account for economic activity, both in the cases of actors and markets, the econometrician stands on firm ground. Whereas if economic theory is ambiguous or has not a clear explanation of some phenomena, the econometrician is unsure about which mathematical formulation should offer to those events. Therefore, econometric models can develop insights into how the real world of microeconomics and macroeconomics functions. Nevertheless, "poor prediction" and "predictive error" are not the same, insofar as some economic variables may be inherently uncertain. In other words, *ontological uncertainty* is different from *methodological errors* due to epistemological mistakes in the knowledge of the variables.

Another interesting feature of econometric models in comparison with time series models is in their relation with the problem of *causality*. Thus, "in contrast to time series and statistical indicator methods, econometric methods involve the explicit representation of the presumed causality between the variable to be projected and its determinants. The nature of the relationships involved is based on economic theory, or other (…) bases, such as legislative or institutional arrangements. The parameter values of the equation, usually estimated by regression methods, are the quantitative expression of the way in which the variable whose behaviour is to be explained could be expected to respond to changes in each of its determinants. An important advantage of this approach to economic forecasting is that premises are made explicit, and lend themselves to generating forecasts which are conditional upon their assumptions" (Llewellyn et al. 1985, p. 129).

Nevertheless, there have also been improvements in *time series models*. Hence, "in contrast to 'classical' regression analysis, the more recent approaches to forecasting based on modern methods of time-series analysis allow inherently for the specification of dynamic relationships and automatically handle the statistical consequences of this. They began with a consideration of simple, univariate series, stimulated by the discovery that such models were not only simpler to estimate, but they could often produce forecasts that compared well with, and often outperformed, those generated by the large and expensive macroeconometric models. And univariate models do not, of course, require the concurrent modeling and forecasting of additional endogenous or exogenous variables, since the forecasts relies entirely on the past history of the time series itself" (Pedregal and Young 2002, p. 71).

An *evaluation* of economic prediction made using time series models shows us two main problems. On the one hand, that the methodological process works well for relatively short periods ahead (e.g., 1 month or one quarter), but predictive accuracy diminishes rapidly as the *time horizon* is extended. And, on the other hand, predictive methods using time series do not go deeply into how the *process being predicted*—economic activity—actually works. The knowledge of the model from the past is somehow "mechanical" and has a lagging response to changing events. And this becomes a serious limitation for economic prescriptions (mainly in the long run), because there is no clear picture of those factors that most likely will shape the economic future (Llewellyn et al. 1985, p. 125).

Comparatively, the *econometric model* is considerably more complex than the time-series model. Basically, the econometric model consists of the following stages. (i) That an appropriate theoretical configuration for the economic event (or the economy at issue) is chosen. This requires distinguishing between *exogenous* variables of the model (those determined outside it) and the *endogenous* variables of the model (those determined within it). (ii) That the theoretical configuration—structure and dynamics—is expressed in mathematical form. (iii) That the available data is used to assign numerical values to the parameters of the model. (iv) That those variables which are exogenous to the model need to be predicted (e.g., using time-series methods). (v) Conditional on those predictions of the exogenous variables of the model, the econometrician uses the model to generate prediction of the endogenous variables (Turner 2001, p. 45).

Methodologically, this predictive process includes more steps than the method for generating time-series predictions. However, it can afford some advantages to the econometric model in comparison with the time-series model. First, due to its connection to an economic theory, the econometric model can improve the *accuracy* of the predictions by adding the theory extra information to the model. Second, the econometric model could be used to set up *simulations* under different scenarios for the future state of the economy (Turner 2001, p. 45).

These advantages have a different epistemological ground. The first advantage of econometric models relies on the conception of a model as "resemblance" or "representation" of the economic reality; whereas the second advantage is open to the idea of a model as theoretical "construction" or "ideal design," and it can lead to the use of predictive models in connection to economic prescriptions. Thus, the econometric model can simulate the effects of alternative future scenarios, and each one can have a policy on the variables of interest.

Yet, econometric models also have had development, mainly in the case of *multi-equation* macroeconomic models. Thus, while representing an improvement over method of prediction based on time-series models (or even on leading indicators), single equation methods of econometrics "suffer from the limitation of being able to take into account only the direct influences on the variable being projected. Interactions and feedbacks of explanatory variables not explicitly represented in the equation are ignored. These considerations have led most, although by no means all, forecasters to use multi-equation macroeconomic models, as a basis not only for economic forecasting, but also for subsequent analysis of economy policy alternatives" (Llewellyn et al. 1985, p. 129). However, in spite of these advantages of the multi-equation macroeconomic models, there are also some disadvantages due to the complexity itself of the models with multi-equations and the possibility of a larger number of errors, because the number of variables taken into account is bigger than in single equation methods of econometrics.

10.4.3 Predictive Failure and Economic Modeling

Granger insists on the evaluation of predictive models according to the *aims* of the economic model: "the evaluation criterion should depend on the purpose of the model. This principle applies in particular to forecast evaluation: forecasts are made for a purpose. Forecasts typically provide the basis for economic decisions, and the resulting forecasts errors entail economic costs. Different models generate different forecasts, and the resulting economic costs have different distributions, which can be compared across models" (2001, p. 103).

Prima facie, predictive failure of economic models used in predictive methods comes from the main components of those models. In the case of time series analysis, the characteristics of these models commonly lead to an increment of the risk of error as soon as the *time horizon* is extended. Thus, "the predictive error of time series models over longer periods tends to accumulate, there being no exogenous data in the forecasting system after the first few periods. Hence over the longer horizon relevant for economic policy decisions the technical performance of time series models is unreliable" (Llewellyn et al. 1985, p. 125). Therefore, due to the difficulty in responding to changing economic events, time series model has problems being accurate when there is a structural change (endogenous factors) or a change in the general economic environment (exogenous factors).

If the predictive model is econometric, then there are three main *components* to be considered: (a) deterministic terms, (b) observed stochastic variables, and (c) unobserved errors. Their relations can be inappropriately formulated or inaccurately estimated, or might be altered over time in unanticipated ways. Some types of mistakes in these features of the model have pernicious effects on predictions, whereas other errors are relatively benign in many settings. "Surprisingly, the key to understanding systematic forecast failure depends on the behavior of the deterministic terms—even though their values are known—rather than on the behavior of variables with unknown future values" (Hendry 2001d, pp. 21–22).[37]

For that reason, Hendry insists on the *deterministic terms* of econometric models and points out five aspects which matter in practice: (1) the problem of inadequate representations or inaccurate estimates of intercepts and trends; (2) the issue of unanticipated changes in the values of deterministic terms; (3) the existence of deterministic shifts that reflect changes in the economy which are interacting with an incomplete model specification; (4) the need for reformulating models to minimize the effects of possible modifications in deterministic terms, even though it can lead to a poor representation of the data; and (5) the importance of emphasizing the modeling of changes in deterministic terms. In addition, he sees other sources of forecasting errors (such as mis-specifying the stochastic components or uncertainty due to estimating their parameters) as less relevant than the errors in the deterministic terms (Hendry 2001d, p. 22).[38]

But a methodological evaluation of economic modeling should take into account the *characteristics of predictive errors*, because the outcomes of economic predictions can be used to assess the quality of the model used. For Burns, the sources of those errors can be summarized in the following way. (i) The largest predictive errors occur when the economy moves most sharply relative to its trend. (ii) Frequently predictive errors tend to be correlated across variables (e.g., large forecasts errors for output are usually accompanied by significant forecasts errors for inflation). (iii) Predictive errors often reflect difficulties in coping with external shocks (either in the sense that events have a much bigger effect than previously expected or in the opposite case that the predictive effect does not occur). (iv) Sometimes a predictive error may occur because policy responded to the prediction itself (e.g., a predicted recession might not happen because policy was adjusted to counter it), even though he recognizes that this source of forecast error is not a big problem. (v) Predictive failures can arise because data about the recent past are inaccurate. (vi) Some economic periods may be intrinsically more difficult to predict than others (Burns 2001, pp. 173–175).

These characteristics of predictive errors as well as the recognition of predictive failures both in time-series models and in econometric models can be seen both historically and empirically. Again, the framework is the twofold relation between the

[37] *Prima facie*, the analysis has a hint paradoxical insofar as the deterministic terms are those that, in principle, have a more clear content. Underneath Hendry's considerations can be noticed the presence of historicity of economic phenomena.

[38] This author offers a detailed analysis in Hendry (2000c).

characteristics of economic models for predicting and the *evaluation* of the model according to predictions as a test, because they are interconnected. Thus, an *overall view* of the errors in using economic models for predicting can lead to connect aims (purposes of the models), means (methodological processes), and results (outcomes of predictions).

Historically, when the aim of the economic model is predominantly descriptive (which is commonly the case of basic science), the methodological conception of prediction that underpinned actual practice in economics (in general, and in applied economics, in particular) has relied on two central features: (a) an epistemological consideration of the possibility of getting *good representations* in *modeling* economic reality; and (b) an ontological assumption that the structure of the economy might remain *relatively unchanged.*

These epistemological and ontological features have three main consequences that can be proved in terms of theorems (Hendry and Ericsson 2001c, p. 186): (i) when the "best" model is available, the predictions are better produced, and so there is no need for an average of predictions across several models; (ii) predictive accuracy declines as the predictive horizon increases; and (iii) the calculated confidence interval around a prediction provides a good guide to the likely variation in the predictive error.

Empirically, the situation seems different than expected according to those two central features and their three corollaries. On the one hand, the epistemological consideration fails, insofar as many econometric models for predicting are known to be clearly mis-specified; and, on the other hand, the ontological assumption has its pitfalls, because the economy shows important but unanticipated shifts, which leads to failures in economic predictions.

In addition, Hendry and Ericsson maintain that "simple methods often outperform better-fitting ones, and pooling of forecasts (i.e., using an average of forecasts) can pay" (Hendry and Ericsson 2001c, p. 187; Makridakis and Hibon 2000). They also insist on the dependence of the quality of economic model upon the type of evaluation chosen, which comes back again to the evaluation of predictions according to the purpose of the model. This leads to a deeper evaluation and limits of predictions in economics, which are analyzed in the next chapter. In this regard, a central question is how to deal with *uncertainty* when making economic models for predicting.

To sum up, in economic predictions the kind of aim (generic or specific, descriptive or normative) and the type of process are interconnected. There are many different predictive approaches (unformalized and formalized), but only some of them are scientific (above all, time series method and econometric methods). Commonly, predictive methods can be tested by empirical research or through computer simulations. The role played by the models is crucial, both as "resemblance" and "constructive design." The relation with economic predictions is twofold: their characteristics are in connection with the features of the evaluation. The components of the time-series models and the econometric models (with a single-equation or multi-equation) are diverse and lead to a different evaluation.

References

Abraham, B., and J. Ledolter. 1983/[2005]. *Statistical methods for forecasting*. New York: Wiley.

Arminger, G., C. C. Clogg, and M. E. Sobel, eds. 1995. *Handbook of statistical modeling for the social and behavioral sciences*. New York: Plenum.

Axelrod, R. 1980a. Effective choice in the iterated prisoner's dilemma. *Journal of Conflict Resolution* 24:3–25.

Axelrod, R. 1980b. More effective choice in the prisoner's dilemma. *Journal of Conflict Resolution* 24:379–403.

Axelrod, R. 1984. *The evolution of cooperation*. New York: Basic Books.

Boland, L. 1989. *The methodology of economic model building: Methodology after Samuelson*. London: Routledge.

Box, G., and G. Jenkins. 1970. *Time series analysis, forecasting, and control*. San Francisco: Holden Day.

Burns, T. 1986. The interpretation and use of economic predictions. In *Predictability in science and society,* ed. J. Mason, P. Mathias, and J. H. Westcott, 103–125. London: The Royal Society and The British Academy.

Burns, T. 2001. The costs of forecast errors. In *Understanding economic forecasts,* ed. D. F. Hendry and N. R. Ericsson, 170–184. Cambridge: The MIT Press.

Clements, M. P., and D. F. Hendry. 1998. *Forecasting economic time series*. Cambridge: Cambridge University Press.

Clements, M. P., and D. F. Hendry. 1999. *Forecasting non-stationary economic time series*. Cambridge: The MIT Press.

Clements, M. P., and D. F. Hendry, eds. 2002a. *A companion to economic forecasting*. Oxford: Blackwell.

Clements, M. P., and D. F. Hendry. 2002b. An overview of economic forecasting. In *A companion to economic forecasting,* ed. M. Clements and D. F. Hendry, 1–18. Oxford: Blackwell.

Clements, M. P., and D. F. Hendry, eds. 2011. *The Oxford handbook of economic forecasting*. New York: Oxford University Press.

Elliott, G., and A. Timmermann, eds. 2013a. *Handbook of economic forecasting,* vol. 2A. Amsterdam: North-Holland.

Elliott, G., and A. Timmermann, eds. 2013b. *Handbook of economic forecasting,* vol. 2B. Amsterdam: North-Holland.

Elliott, G., C. W. J. Granger, and A. Timmerman, eds. 2006. *Handbook of economic forecasting,* vol. 1. Amsterdam: Elsevier.

Engle, R. F., and C. W. J. Granger. 1987. Co-integration and error correction: Representation, estimation and testing. *Econometrica* 55:251–276.

Engle, R. F., and H. White, eds. 1999. *Cointegration, causality and forecasting: A Festschrift in honour of Clive Granger*. Oxford: Oxford University Press.

Evans, M. K. 2013. *Practical business forecasting*. Oxford: Blackwell.

Frydman, R., and E. S. Phelps, eds. 1983. *Individual forecasting and aggregate outcomes. "Rational expectations" examined*. Cambridge: Cambridge University Press.

Gonzalez, W. J. 1994. Economic prediction and human activity. An analysis of prediction in economics from action theory. *Epistemologia* 17:253–294.

Gonzalez, W. J. 1995. Reichenbach's concept of prediction. *International Studies in the Philosophy of Science* 9 (1): 37–58.

Gonzalez, W. J. 1996e. Caracterización del objeto de la Ciencia de la Historia y bases de su configuración metodológica. In *Acción e Historia. El objeto de la Historia y la Teoría de la Acción,* ed. W. J. Gonzalez, 25–111. A Coruña: Publicaciones Universidad de A Coruña.

Gonzalez, W. J. 1998b. Prediction and prescription in economics: A philosophical and methodological approach. *Theoria* 13 (2): 321–345.

Gonzalez, W. J. 2001a. De la Ciencia de la Economía a la Economía de la Ciencia: Marco conceptual de la reflexión metodológica y axiológica. In *Ciencia económica y Economía de la*

Ciencia: Reflexiones filosófico-metodológicas, ed. A. Avila, W. J. Gonzalez, and G. Marques, 11–37. Madrid: FCE.

Gonzalez, W. J. 2007a. The role of experiments in the social sciences: The case of economics. In *General philosophy of science: Focal issues,* ed. T. Kuipers, 275–301. Amsterdam: Elsevier.

Gonzalez, W. J. 2010b. Recent approaches on observation and experimentation: A philosophical-methodological viewpoint. In *New methodological perspectives on observation and experimentation in science,* ed. W. J. Gonzalez, 9–48. A Coruña: Netbiblo.

Gonzalez, W. J. 2011b. Conceptual changes and scientific diversity: The role of historicity. In *Conceptual revolutions: From cognitive science to medicine,* ed. W. J. Gonzalez, 39–62. A Coruña: Netbiblo.

Gonzalez, W. J. 2013b. The sciences of design as sciences of complexity: The dynamic trait. In *New challenges to philosophy of science,* ed. H. Andersen, D. Dieks, W. J. Gonzalez, T. Uebel, and G. Wheeler, 299–311. Dordrecht: Springer.

Gonzalez, W. J. 2014. On representation and models in Bas van Fraassen's approach. In *Bas van Fraassen's approach to representation and models in science,* ed. W. J. Gonzalez, 3–37. Dordrecht: Synthese Library, Springer.

Goodwin, P., D. Önkal, and M. Lawrance. 2011. Improving the role of judgment in economic forecasting. In *The Oxford handbook of economic forecasting,* ed. M. P. Clements and D. F. Hendry, 163–189. New York: Oxford University Press.

Granger, C. W. J. 1986. Developments in the study of cointegrated economic variables. *Oxford Bulletin of Economics and Statistics* 48:213–228.

Granger, C. W. J. 1989. *Forecasting in business and economics*. 2nd ed. San Diego: Academic (1st ed., 1980).

Granger, C. W. J., ed. 1990a. *Modelling economic series: Readings in econometric methodology*. Oxford: Clarendon.

Granger, C. W. J. 1999. *Empirical modeling in economics: Specification and evaluation*. Cambridge: Cambridge University Press.

Granger, C. W. J. 2001. Evaluation of forecasts. In *Understanding economic forecasts*, ed. D. F. Hendry and N. R. Ericsson, 93–103. Cambridge: The MIT Press.

Granger, C. W. J. 2004. Time series analysis, cointegration, and applications. In *From les prix Nobel. The Nobel prizes 2003,* ed. T. Frängsmyr, 360–366. Stockholm: Nobel Foundation.

Granger, C. W. J. 2012. The philosophy of economic forecasting. In *Philosophy of economics,* ed. U. Mäki, 311–327. Amsterdam: Elsevier.

Granger, C. W. J., and P. Newbold. 1977. *Forecasting economic time series*. New York: Academic.

Hahn, F. 1993. Predicting the economy. In *Predicting the future,* ed. L. Howe and A. Wain, 77–95. Cambridge: Cambridge University Press.

Harvey, A. C. 1990. *The econometric analysis of times series*. Cambridge: The MIT Press.

Harvey, A. C. 1991. *Forecasting, structural time series models and the Kalman filter*. Cambridge: Cambridge University Press.

Hausman, D. M. 1998a. Rationality and knavery. In *Game theory, experience, rationality,* ed. W. Leinfellner and E. Köhler, 67–79. Dordrecht: Kluwer.

Hausman, D. M. 2000. ¿Necesita leyes la Economía? *Argumentos de Razón Técnica* 3:115–137.

Helmer, O., and N. Rescher. 1959. On the epistemology of the inexact sciences. *Management Sciences* 6:25–52.

Hendry, D. F. 1986. The role of prediction in evaluating economic models. In *Predictability in science and society,* ed. J. Mason, P. Mathias, and J. H. Westcott, 25–34. London: The Royal Society and The British Academy.

Hendry, D. F. 2000b. On the time-series approach to econometric model building. In *Econometrics: Alchemy or science? Essays in econometric methodology,* ed. D. F. Hendry, new ed., 119–128. Oxford: Oxford University Press (1st ed., 1993).

Hendry, D. F. 2000c. Predictive failure and econometric modelling in macroeconomics: The transactions demand for money. In *Econometrics: Alchemy or science? Essays in econometric methodology,* ed. D. F. Hendry, new ed., 246–269. Oxford: Oxford University Press.

Hendry, D. F. 2001d. How economists forecast. In *Understanding economic forecasts,* ed. D. F. Hendry and N. R. Ericsson, 15–41. Cambridge: The MIT Press.

Hendry, D. F., and N. R. Ericsson, eds. 2001a. *Understanding economic forecasts*. Cambridge: The MIT Press.

Hendry, D. F., and N. R. Ericsson. 2001b. Editor's introduction. In *Understanding economic forecasts,* ed. D. F. Hendry and N. R. Ericsson, 1–14. Cambridge: The MIT Press.

Hendry, D. F., and N. R. Ericsson. 2001c. Epilogue. In *Understanding economic forecasts,* ed. D. F. Hendry and N. R. Ericsson, 185–191. Cambridge: The MIT Press.

Hodgson, G. 2001. *How economics forgot history*. London: Routledge.

Holden, K. 1989. Macroeconomic forecasting. In *Current issues in macroeconomics,* ed. D. Greenaway, 163–181. London: Macmillan.

Kacapyr, E. 1996a. Forecasting with time-series techniques. In *Economic forecasting,* ed. E. Kacapyr, 92–115. Armonk: M. E. Sharpe.

Kacapyr, E. 1996b. Forecasting with econometric models. In *Economic forecasting,* ed. E. Kacapyr, 116–140. Armonk: M. E. Sharpe.

Keller, E. F. 2003. Models, simulation, and "computer experiments". In *The philosophy of scientific experimentation,* ed. H. Radder, 198–215. Pittsburgh: University of Pittsburgh Press.

Kennedy, P. 1998. *A guide to econometrics*. 4th ed. Cambridge: The MIT Press.

Kock, A. B., and T. Teräsvirta. 2011. Forecasting with nonlinear time series models. In *The Oxford handbook of economic forecasting,* ed. M. P. Clements and D. F. Hendry, 61–87. New York: Oxford University Press.

Koopman, S. J., and M. Ooms. 2011. Forecasting economic time series using unobserved components time series models. In *The Oxford handbook of economic forecasting,* ed. M. P. Clements and D. F. Hendry, 129–162. New York: Oxford University Press.

Llewellyn, J., S. Potter, and L. Samuelson. 1985. *Economic forecasting and policy-the international dimension*. London: Routledge and K. Paul.

Mäki, U., ed. 2002. *Fact and fiction: Foundational issues on economics and the economy.* Cambridge: Cambridge University Press.

Makridakis, S., and M. Hibon. 2000. The M3-competition: Results, conclusions and implications. *International Journal of Forecasting* 16:451–476.

Makridakis, S., S. C. Wheelwright, and R. J. Hyndman. 1998. *Forecasting: Methods and applications*. 3rd ed. Hoboken: Wiley.

Malkiel, B. G. 1996. *A random walk to Wall Street*. New York: Norton.

Meadows, D. et al. 1972. *The limits of growth. A report for the Club of Rome's project on its predicament of mankind*. New York: Signet/New American Library.

Mills, T. C., ed. 1999a. *Economic forecasting,* vol. I. Cheltenham: E. Elgar.

Mills, T. C. ed. 1999b. *Economic forecasting,* vol. II. Cheltenham: E. Elgar.

Mills, T. C. 2002. Forecasting financial variables. In *A companion to economic forecasting,* ed. M. P. Clemens and D. F. Hendry, 510–538. Oxford: Blackwell.

Morgan, M. S. 2003. Experiments without material intervention. Models experiments, virtual experiments, and virtually experiments. In *The philosophy of scientific experimentation,* ed. H. Radder, 216–235. Pittsburgh: University of Pittsburgh Press.

Morgan, M. S., and M. Morrison. eds. 1999. *Models as mediators*. Cambridge: Cambridge University Press.

Newbold, P., and D. I. Harvey. 2002. Forecast combination and encompassing. In *A companion to economic forecasting,* ed. M. P. Clemens and D. F. Hendry, 268–283. Oxford: Blackwell.

Önkal-Atay, D., M. E. Thomson, and A. C. Pollock. 2002. Judgmental forecasting. In *A companion to economic forecasting,* ed. M. Clements and D. F. Hendry, 133–151. Oxford: Blackwell.

Osborn, D. R. 2001. Forecasting and the UK business cycle. In *Understanding economic forecasts,* ed. D. F. Hendry and N. R. Ericsson, 104–123. Cambridge: The MIT Press.

Pagan, A. R. 1990. Three econometric methodologies: A critical appraisal. In *Modelling economic series, readings in econometric methodology,* ed. C. W. J. Granger, 97–120. Oxford: Clarendon Press.

Pedregal, D. J., and P. C. Young. 2002. Statistical approaches to modeling and forecasting time series. In *A companion to economic forecasting,* ed. M. Clements and D. F. Hendry, 69–104. Oxford: Blackwell.

Rescher, N. 1998. *Predicting the future: An introduction to the theory of forecasting.* Albany: State University of New York Press.

Rosenberg, A. 1989. Are generic predictions enough? *Erkenntnis* 30(1–2):43–68.

Rosenberg, A. 1992. *Economics-mathematical politics or science of diminishing returns*? Chicago: The University of Chicago Press.

Roth, A. 1986. Laboratory experimentation in economics. *Economics and Philosophy* 2:245–273.

Roth, A. 1988. Laboratory experimentation in economics: A methodological overview. *The Economic Journal* 98:974–1031. (Reprinted in Hey, J. D., and G. Loomes, eds. 1993. *Recent developments in experimental economics,* vol. I, 3–60. Aldershot: E. Elgar).

Rubinstein, A. 1998. *Modeling bounded rationality.* Cambridge: The MIT Press.

Selten, R., and R. Stoecker. 1986. End behavior in sequences of finite prisoner's dilemma supergames: A learning theory approach. *Journal of Economic Behavior and Organization* 7 (1): 47–70.

Simon, H. A. 1982a. *Models of bounded rationality*, vol. 1: *Economic analysis and public policy.* Cambridge: The MIT Press.

Simon, H. A. 1982b. *Models of bounded rationality*, vol. 2: *Behavioral economics and business organization.* Cambridge: The MIT Press.

Simon, H. A. 1996. *The sciences of the artificial.* 3rd ed. Cambridge: The MIT Press (1st ed., 1969; 2nd ed., 1981).

Simon, H. A. 1997. *Models of bounded rationality*, vol. 3: *Empirically grounded economic reason.* Cambridge: The MIT Press.

Spirtes, P., C. Glymour, and R. Scheines. 1993. *Causation, prediction and search.* New York: Springer.

Turner, P. 2001. Economic modeling for fun and profit. In *Understanding economic forecasts,* ed. D. F. Hendry and N. R. Ericsson, 42–53. Cambridge: The MIT Press.

van den Bogaard, A. 1999. Past measurements and future predictions. In *Models as mediators. Perspectives on natural and social science,* ed. M. Morgan and M. Morrison, 282–325. Cambridge: Cambridge University Press.

Chapter 11
Evaluation and Limits of Prediction in Economics

As emphasized earlier (mainly in Parts I and III), prediction has been proposed as the ultimate *test* of economics as a science. Thus, *economic theory*—and, in principle, also applied economics—can have its scientific test using predictions. This idea is defended by important economists, as well as by other relevant authors interested in the *broad approach* to methodology of economics, such as Mark Blaug. In this regard, he maintains that "economic hypotheses can be judged by their logical coherence, their explanatory power, their generality, their fecundity, and, ultimately, their ability to predict…" (2002, p. 49). In addition, within the *restricted perspective* of the methodology of economics, it is the case that "predictive ability has long played a role in evaluation of econometric models" (West 2006, p. 101).

Consequently, *applied economics* also gives special relevance to the evaluative task of prediction. Clive Granger recognizes the methodological importance of prediction in the actual realm of economics: "prediction plays an important role in the topic of model evaluation" (2012, p. 315). He considers that prediction should be formed from a theoretical model, which is connected to actual decision-making, in order to draw implications about the behavior of economics (Granger 2012, pp. 312 and 314). Furthermore, the evaluative position of economic predictions has repercussions for the *application of this science*. In effect, we need evaluations of economic predictions for the policy-making. The decision-making, which is a central part of the policy-making regarding a given setting, requires predictions. In this regard, it happens that "many of our decisions are based on predictions of future unknown events" (Abraham and Ledolter 1983/[2005], p. vii).

11.1 The Use of Prediction as a Test: Economic Theory and Applied Economics

Prediction is commonly used as a test of economic theory, in general, and of economic hypotheses, in particular. Moreover, for Blaug, prediction is the *ultimate test* of whether our economic theories are true and really capture the workings of the economic system (i.e., objective). Nevertheless, this position includes a clear

W. J. Gonzalez, *Philosophico-Methodological Analysis of Prediction and its Role in Economics*, Theory and Decision Library A: 50, DOI 10.1007/978-3-319-08885-3_11

caveat: to accept prediction as the *ultimate test* of economics "is not to say that we should always discard hypotheses that have not yet yielded empirically falsifiable implications but simply that theories such as general equilibrium theory, which are untestable even in principle, should be regarded with deep suspicion" (Blaug 2002, pp. 49–50).[1]

However, prediction is not the universal procedure for methodological *evaluation* in economics, as many economists have already pointed out, either from a historical point of view (e.g., in econometrics)[2] or from a thematic perspective (as Ronald Coase has emphasized for economic theory).[3] There are other processes for evaluation, for example those related to the understanding of economic phenomena, such as the statements on the institutional structure (e.g., in areas of price theory) (Coase 1994a).[4] Hence, it seems clear that prediction in economics has *internal* methodological *limits* in addition to *external limitations*.

Regarding the use of prediction as a test in economics, Blaug points to the issue of the focus of attention in the case of economic evaluation. He presents a criticism to the *restricted perspective* in methodology of economics: "economists have been unduly narrow in testing the falsifiable implications of theories in the sense that this is invariably taken to mean some statistical or econometric test. But history is just as much a test of patterns and trends in economic events as is regression analysis" (Blaug 2002, p. 50).

Furthermore, Blaug rejects an important aspect of the dominant predictivist thesis in methodology of positive economics (the possibility of avoiding the realism of assumptions): "Economists are loath to examine their assumptions by the use of survey techniques, by simply asking agents what they believe or what they do, because Friedman's methodology gave economists the false impression that nothing can ever be learned by such means" (Blaug 2002, p. 50; cf. Hausman 1997).[5] In other words, we need to know how realistic the assumptions made in the predictive models are, and that requires considering the empirical information (i.e., the correctness of our data) (cf. Chaps. 6–9).

---

[1] On the distinction between "predictive content" and "predictive import," see Salmon (1981), and Chap. 3, Sect. 3.3.2.

[2] It was not always the case that prediction was a main tool for evaluation, at least in the field of econometrics: it was in the mid-1930s that "economists had began to use economic forecasting for testing their models: Tinbergen (1939) was one of those responsible for developing forecasting tests of econometric models, partly in response to the criticism of Keynes (1939) and Frisch (1938)" (Clements and Hendry 1998, p. 7).

[3] "The view that the worth of a theory is to be judged solely by the extent and accuracy of its predictions seems to me wrong. (…) We are not interested simply in the accuracy of its predictions. A theory also serves as a base for thinking. It helps us to understand what is going on by enabling us to organise our thoughts. Faced with a choice between a theory which predicts well but gives us little insight into how the system works and one which gives us this insight but predicts badly, I would choose the latter, and I am inclined to think that most economists would do the same" (Coase 1994b, pp. 16–17).

[4] This content is the 1991 Alfred Nobel Memorial Prize lecture in economic sciences.

[5] On the special difficulties that arise in testing and appraising mainstream economic theory, cf. Hausman (1998b).

Both economic theory and applied economics use prediction as a test. Commonly, the focus is on evaluation of economic models, utilizing the predictive results to evaluate the validity of economic contents, either in the descriptive sphere or in the normative domain. In Chap. 10 the attention was on the basis of methodological processes of predictions—the kind of aims—and, above all, in the *type of processes* used for predicting. Then, the role of models in economic prediction was seen in the methodological orbit, emphasizing the *methods* for scientific predictions in economics and how those predictive methods are related to the characteristics of the model.

Following a complementary pathway, in order to stress the role of the *predictive results* for economic models, Chap. 11 highlights predictive outcomes in their evaluative task of economic theory and applied economics.[6] In this regard, there are three consecutive steps here: first, the evaluation of predictions in the context of economic models; second, the appraisal of economic predictions; and third, the limits and obstacles of prediction in economics.

(1) The analysis starts in the context of *economic models*, taking into account that models have purpose, content, and consequences, because the evaluation of predictions is related to each one of these aspects. In this regard, a central problem is uncertainty, due to its connection with the whole spectrum of elements of economic predictions: aims, processes, and results. (2) The criteria used for the *appraisal* of economic prediction receive attention according to its role to evaluate models. (a) Economic outcomes are used to evaluate the characteristics of the model (mainly through values such as accuracy and precision); but (b) it should be considered that there are several criteria in the appraisal of predictions and also different processes to assess predictions. These kinds of testing should be considered, and they also contribute to understanding the variety of predictive errors. (3) The *limits* and *obstacles* of prediction in economics also require attention in order to complete the picture of the boundaries of the predictive outcomes in this science.

11.2 The Evaluation of Predictions in the Context of Economic Models

An evaluation of economic predictions may be seen in the context of models, which involves several aspects: (i) the *purpose* of the model where the prediction is made, which could be of different kinds ("descriptive" or "normative," generic or specific, etc.); (ii) the *contents* of the economic model, which can emphasize a central factor

[6] According to Michael Evans, who is thinking of business forecasting, there are many ways in which the economic forecast can be presented in applied economics: point estimate or interval; absolute or conditional; alternative scenarios weighed by probabilities; asymmetric gains and losses; single-period or multi-period; short run or long range; forecasting single or multiple variables (Evans 2013, esp., Sect. 1.3, pp. 18–22).

(e.g., a unitary trend), or a set of components according to some criteria,[7] and requires one to consider its theoretical support as well as the empirical data available for the model; and (iii) the *consequences* of the model, both from an "internal" point of view (e.g., in order to reshape it to deal with new phenomena) and from an "external" perspective (i.e., the repercussion of economic prediction for the concrete economic sphere, e.g., prices, labor market, inflation, production, etc.).

11.2.1 Evaluation: From Economic Models to Predictions

First of all, in evaluating economic models, the evaluation criterion normally depends on the *purpose* of the model, and this applies to evaluation of predictions, because predictions are commonly made for a purpose (Granger 2001, p. 103). The criteria for "descriptive economics" (e.g., in order to test a specific economic hypothesis) can be different for "normative economics" (e.g., in how a prediction contributes to a prescription for policy-making).

Undoubtedly, the differences between economic theory and applied economics are relevant here, and they can lead to different criteria to evaluate economic predictions. Thus, the epistemic considerations (e.g., empirical adequacy) can have more importance in the former than in the latter, where the practical factors (e.g., the success of the corresponding decisions for solving problems) have a special incidence.

Secondly, the *contents* of the economic model can deal with structural (i.e., framework) or dynamic aspects of economics. They can be focused on economic theory or on applied economics, within a time schedule (e.g., in short, middle, or long run). When they are dealing with statistical economics and econometrics, the predictive methods commonly pay attention to the time series models as well as to the single-equation models and the multi-equation models.

In this regard, there could be a first "internal" evaluation, when the time series models are used as an initial step for econometric models. If this is the case, then there may be a second evaluation, which follows from the comparison of the contents of econometric model and the economic reality. When the evaluation concerns the contents of the economic model, the main criteria are epistemological values (i.e., accuracy, precision, reliability, etc.) and methodological values (i.e., the quality of the process itself, according to criteria of scientific progress).

Thirdly, the *consequences* of the model might be also epistemological and methodological. They can follow two directions: "internal" (when they have repercussion for the characteristics of the model itself) or "external," when the consequences are oriented toward the descriptive context (i.e., the sphere of the model as "resemblance" of the reality) or towards the prescriptive dimension (i.e., the terrain

[7] "Taking energy forecasting as an example, all of the following are possible components: (a) energy use for industrial, commercial, and residential purposes; (b) energy use per unit of each component of the GNP; (c) energy use per mode or form of energy (electricity, fossil fuels, etc.); and (d) energy use per capita, accompanied by a population projection" (Ascher 1978, p. 9).

of the model as "constructive design"). To a larger extent, the consequences depend on the results obtained by the model making predictions.

On the one hand, the results of predictions can be used to evaluate the *quality* of the model itself (i.e., its configuration). Hence, according to the twofold relation between characteristics of the models and predictions (cf. Chap. 10, Sect. 10.4.1), the predictive outcomes can contribute to reshape the models themselves. And, on the other hand, the results of predictions can also be assessed as scientific outcomes, according to their level of *success* (or failure) when they are describing the economic reality or, when pertinent, when they are used as bases for economic prescriptions.

Each of these three aspects of economic models (purpose, content, and consequences) can be in place when there is an evaluation of economic predictions, because predictions have aims, processes, and results in connection with economic models. The criteria of evaluation of predictions may be in tune with the different levels. Furthermore, for some economists, such as Simon (Chap. 8), the main point is the evaluation of the *process* of making predictions (i.e., the main criteria are related to procedural rationality), whereas mainstream economics—under the influence of Friedman—emphasizes the importance of the *results* of predictions.

Nonetheless, economic predictions very frequently differ from the actual outcomes that are obtained, both in microeconomics and in macroeconomics. These variances between economic predictions and actual outcomes are commonly analyzed in terms of *uncertainty*, which is a feature that affects aims, processes, and results of predictions. The "degree" of uncertainty is on many occasions what makes the difference between a useful economic prediction (i.e., highly informative) and useless one. Moreover, the measure of predictive uncertainty is a central methodological issue in this regard.

11.2.2 The Problem of Uncertainty

Commonly, statistical economics and econometrics worked in two kinds of environments in order to evaluate randomness.[8] On the one hand, they think of situations of risk when, regarding each variable involved in the case, the probability of occurrence of every variable can be established with exactness (i.e., there is a control of the data related to each variable considered). On the other hand, the usual situations of uncertainty, where the probability of each variable involved in the case cannot be clearly established (i.e., there is no exactness regarding the variables involved). This second option is what can be obtained ordinarily in real life, which is the focus of the present analysis and the main concern of economists.

De facto, "uncertainty" can be analyzed in each of the three aspects of economic models pointed out (purpose, content, and consequences). (a) When the purpose of the model is descriptive, it is common to inform of the predictive uncertainty

[8] Fernández-Jardón, C., *Personal communication*, 27 January 2014.

in addition to the prediction itself. A main *goal* is to diminish the margin of error, a characteristic aim of "economic forecast" (in the strict sense utilized in Chap. 2, Sect. 2.4.2). (b) A central concern of many economists—among them, Simon—is to decrease the level of uncertainty in economic models, stressing the knowledge of the factors that intervene in the *process* of predicting. This knowledge can be used to diminish the margin of error of forecasting. (c) Economic forecasts are outcomes which can be used to evaluate the models themselves, following some criteria (accuracy, precision, etc.), where the role of predictions is to be a *test* for the economic model (i.e., to evaluate its correctness).

This use of economic predictions to evaluate models is a key aspect of the twofold relation between *characteristics* of an economic model and *prediction as a test* that was pointed out in Chap. 10. Thus, once outcomes of economic forecasts are known, "the corresponding forecasts errors and the anticipated forecast uncertainty can be used to evaluate the models from which the forecasts were generated" (Ericsson 2002, p. 19). This evaluation of the model can lead to a revision of it, seeking to match economic predictions. Hence, a prediction is not merely "a consequence" of a model. It could be also the main reason to change a model or to elaborate a new one.

Uncertainty is a key problem in economics, both in economic theory and in applied economics. It contains many facets, because uncertainty could be seen at different levels. In the case of predictions, it can appear regarding *aims* (e.g., in international trade or in financial markets), in the area of *processes* (e.g., in the use of models), or in the sphere of *results* (i.e., in the interpretation of the outcomes). In each there could be uncertainty, insofar as it is an important feature of human knowledge in the domain of social activities and artificial endeavors. Uncertainty reveals lack of information, and this is a common ingredient of human knowledge regarding "economic activity" and "economics as activity" (in the sense pointed out in Chap. 7).

Due to the complexity of uncertainty in economics, it is possible to distinguish here at least two successive levels. The first one is the *initial methodological approach*, which corresponds to the degree of control of variables when an economic prediction is made. Thus, in Chap. 2, it was suggested that between "foresight," "prediction," and "forecasting" there is a clear difference on the degree of knowledge of the variables. Foresight shows the high stage of possible certainty, whereas forecast corresponds to a permanent presence of uncertainty, which should be diminished. But there is a *second methodological level*, where the approach is focused on a metaprediction, i.e., a prediction on the previous statement about the future economic event (commonly a forecast). This additional step is developed through calculations of predictable uncertainty.

Within this double methodological level at hand, it seems clear that uncertainty is not restricted to the realm of an economic model that makes predictions. Uncertainty could be also a feature of a *metaprediction*: we can distinguish between an uncertainty that is "predictable" and uncertainty that is "not predictable." In the first case it is possible to anticipate and calculate the level of uncertainty (e.g., the cumulation of future shocks to the economy), whereas in the second case the economic events belong to a shaky epistemological domain where "we do not know that we do not know" (Ericsson 2002, pp. 19–21). Even so predictable forecast uncertainty that belongs to the latter kind of forecasts can be calculated numerically in econometric models (Ericsson 2001, p. 91).

Forecast uncertainty—in economics, in general, and in econometrics, in particular—"reflects the dispersion of possible outcomes relative to the forecast to be made" (Ericsson 2001, p. 70). Thus, it is assumed that there is the habitual existence of forecasts errors (i.e., a difference between the forecast and the actual outcome). But this way of conceiving "forecast uncertainty" is somehow misleading, because "uncertainty" should be used in the epistemological context of something *subjective* or *intersubjective*, insofar as it is the opposite of "certainty." Meanwhile "error" is something *objective* and it can be established as what is contrary to "truth."

Therefore, it is a mistake to state that "'forecast uncertainty' should be called 'forecast error uncertainty' because the forecast error is what is uncertain, not the forecast" (Ericsson 2001, p. 70, note). Epistemologically, it is just the opposite: if eventually the forecast is an error, then its content can be *certain* (i.e., sure) and also *objective* (i.e., non-truth); whereas the forecast could be uncertain at the beginning (i.e., when it is made the statement that anticipates the future outcome). To be an error involves the recognition of something as *incorrect* on the basis of some kind of evidence, and this identification as error should include the certainty on behalf of the scientist or the scientific community.

Moreover, the methodology of economic forecast is built upon the idea of *diminishing the forecast error* in order to have an objective content.[9] Thus, the economist needs to deal with two aspects: errors and uncertainty. Initially, there are two main possibilities regarding economic errors: (I) an error can be theoretical, insofar as it is an expected error based on the knowledge available for the prediction; or (II) an error can be empirical, if it comes from a prediction that is made and the results actually do not fit with the economic reality (as a social event or an artificial occurrence).

Concerning uncertainty, we can think of several forms of uncertainty—epistemological, methodological, and ontological—and the existence of a "forecasting uncertainty" when the process of predicting starts. For example, it could be the case of an epistemological uncertainty (i.e., a problem in the level of knowledge available), a methodological uncertainty (i.e., the repercussion for the processes of the lack of information) or an ontological uncertainty (i.e., the event or occurrence might be uncertain as such). Meanwhile, to get an empirical error is to be in the terrain of *results*, which is a quite different issue. The evaluation of results belongs to the epistemological–methodological sphere and we can be *certain* regarding the result (and its content can be objective). Indeed, an error would be to point out when the outcome of the prediction is different from what we actually obtained (i.e., the real pattern of the event).

[9] In addition, "econometrics is not about measuring covering laws. It is about observing unobvious regularities" (Hoover 2002, p. 173). Regarding a taxonomy of forecast error measures, see Mathies and Diamantipoulos (1994).

What is correct is the connection between "uncertainty" and "ignorance." In this regard, uncertainty appears initially as an obstacle to predictive foreknowledge: "the limits of one's information set unavoidable limits to one's predictive capacities. We cannot foresee what we cannot conceive" (Rescher 1998, p. 135). Thus, we can distinguish between the uncertainty that we are aware of ("what we know that we do not know") and the uncertainty that is actually beyond us ("we do not know that we do not know"). Then, in the case of economics, it could be *predictable uncertainty* (such as in cumulation of future errors in the economy or in inaccuracies in estimates of parameters of the forecast model) and *not predictable uncertainty* (such as currently unknown future changes in the structure of economy, mis-specification of the forecast model, or mis-measurement of the base-period data) (Ericsson 2002, p. 22).

11.2.3 Forecast Uncertainty

Three modes of *uncertainty* can afflict economic predictions. Initially, uncertainty is an *epistemological* feature—the lack of information about the forecast—but it is connected to a *methodological* component (the economic model should consider the consequences of the ignorance). In addition, it might also be an *ontological* factor: the event could be random or even hazardous. Thus, uncertainty cannot be seen narrowly, as if it were a mere "defect" of an economic model.[10] In this context, it makes sense to maintain that is "by introducing uncertainty that economics can generate the most obvious features of a real economy: money, futures markets, shares and stock markets, bonds and interest rates, insurance, etc." (Rosenberg 1992, p. 175).

Basically, forecast uncertainty is related to two methodological components: a time horizon and a type of model. As it is commonly understood—in economics, in general, and in applied economics, in particular—*forecast uncertainty* depends on several interconnected factors: the economic variable to be forecasted, because some are more difficult than others; the type of model (static or dynamic, a single equation or a system) used for forecasting; the information available for preparing forecasts; the economic process which actually underlies the variable being forecasted; and the possible cumulation of errors or "shocks" to the economy (Ericsson 2001, p. 69; Clements and Hendry 1998, Sect. 7.3, Table 7.1). In addition, the way of estimating the parameters of the model also conditioned the error of prediction.[11] In other words, there are some elements to be taken into account in this regard:

[10] For Makridakis, Wheelwright, and Hyndman, "setting uncertainty at realistic levels, separating objective predictions from wishful thinking or the attainment of desired objectives, and realizing that unusual, threatening events have occurred and will continue to do so in the future are critical aspects that must be dealt with while forecasting" (1998, pp. 552–553).

[11] Fernández-Jardón, C., *Personal communication*, 23 February 2014.

a. Some *variables* considered in the economic forecast may be inherently more difficult to predict than others.[12] "For instance, imports and exports each might be highly predictable, and good models might exist for forecasting them. The trade balance—that is, the value of exports minus imports—might be quite difficult to forecast. In particular, by being the difference between two relatively large quantities (exports and imports), the trade balance is itself a relatively small quantity, whereas its forecast error reflects the forecast error of both imports and exports" (Ericsson 2002, p. 21).

b. The *model* that is used for forecasting has a crucial role for forecast uncertainty. Obviously, some economic models could be better than others, as emphasized in Chap. 10. The model has a purpose and, according to Granger, "the evaluation criterion should depend on the purpose of the model" (2001, p. 103). Within the descriptive sphere, the content of the model can offer a "resemblance" to the structure or dynamic of economic reality. Thus, a mis-specification of the model can involve a mis-representation of economic reality and, consequently, an inaccurate prediction.

c. Closely related to the previous element, the mis-specification of the *information* available for preparing forecasts could lead to forecast uncertainty. Insofar as "uncertainty" is based on some kind of "ignorance," to increase the level and quality of information is clearly beneficial for forecasting. Some approaches, such as behavioral economics (Simon) and experimental economics (Selten) (Chaps. 8 and 9), have stressed the importance of gathering empirical data in order to have a more reliable source of information than that of models of mainstream economics.

d. Within the domain of applied economics, a key role is played by the underlying "process of generating data" (mainly, in the case of econometric models). The process can place limits on the minimum forecast uncertainty obtainable from an economic model. "That distinguishes between the predicted forecast uncertainty—that is, the forecast uncertainty that one can anticipate, given the model—and the actual forecast uncertainty, which is the uncertainty arising from the combination of the model with the actual behavior of the economic data" (Ericsson 2001, p. 78).

e. Besides the type of model, another central methodological component for forecast uncertainty is a *time horizon*. In this regard, the predictive process is mediated by the time factor. Thus, the possible cumulation of errors or "shocks" to the economy leads to the consideration of the forecast horizon, which surely can influence the degree of forecast uncertainty. Moreover, "incorporation of time dependence into a forecast model implies that forecast uncertainty increases as the forecast horizon lengthens" (Ericsson 2001, p. 82).

Initially, two kinds of models may be used when forecast uncertainty is at stake: "static models" (i.e., trend models) and "dynamic models" (such as a random walk model). In the case of *trend models*, forecast errors are assumed to be independent across time, and forecast uncertainty is considered constant across different forecast horizons. When the models are *dynamic*, it is often assumed that forecast uncertainty increases with the forecast horizon. In other words, "static models commonly imply forecast uncertainty that is time-invariant or nearly so, whereas dynamic models

[12] On the origin of predictable behavior, see Heiner (1983).

typically imply time-dependent forecast uncertainty, often increasing the forecast horizon" (Ericsson 2001, p. 83). But, even though trend models and random walk models represent static and dynamic relations as a clear contrast, there is in practice a wide range of variety in economic modeling. *De facto*, there exist a whole spectrum of economic models that incorporate static and dynamic features.

11.2.4 Uses of Calculated "Predictable Forecast Uncertainty"

Pertaining to the issue of prediction as a *test* of economic modeling, it is worthy considering the uses of calculated "predictable forecast uncertainty" (which can also be of interest for not predictable uncertainty). This is the second methodological level, insofar as it includes a *metaprediction*: there is a prediction on a forecast in order to measure the degree of uncertainty. This measurement can be used to modify an economic model, in an effort to diminish the level of error observed.

Thus, several elements are involved here: first, a forecast could be made using an economic model; second, an outcome is obtained which eventually can have error in comparison with actual data; and third, an anticipated predictable uncertainty is also estimated by the economist (i.e., a prediction on the forecast already made). These elements are used to test the economic model and, where relevant, to reformulate it.

Methodologically, what it is important here is the combination of two methodological levels: an *economic forecast* and a *measure of forecast uncertainty*. The initial level includes uncertainty when the statement is made on a future economic event, and the second level provides an assessment of forecast error that is expected on the basis of the existing degree of uncertainty. Then, this additional information is obviously important in order to establish the quality of economic forecasts. When uncertainty appears with the lack of knowledge (i.e., an epistemological feature), then the degree of uncertainty of an economic forecast should diminish to the extent that the information available is more reliable.[13]

Calculations of *predictable uncertainty* serve relevant roles, both from a statistical point of view and from an economic perspective. "Statistically, calculations of predictable uncertainty are the basis for forecast confidence intervals, and for tests of a model's constancy over time. Prior to the realization of outcomes, confidence intervals provide an assessment of 'expected' or predicted forecast uncertainty, helping to qualify the forecasts themselves and to give a picture of expected range of likely outcomes. That is, information about forecast uncertainty is important to the forecast itself" (Ericsson 2002, p. 38). Both in a trend model and in a random walk model the confidence intervals are obtained from formulas used for the associated predictable uncertainty.

[13] Rescher has pointed out that, in some cases, too much information on something specific—such as a concrete event—makes thing harder for prediction: "the access of further information can sometimes make the future less predictable" (1998, p. 58).

Surely, a central role of the predictable forecast uncertainty is the *evaluation of the models* from which forecasts were generated. Thus, if the range of forecast error is large (i.e., errors lie well outside the area that was anticipated), then it seems visible that the model has problems of specification. In addition, predictable forecast uncertainty permits us to assess the extent in which "not predictable forecast uncertainty" is contributing to the realized forecast error. In this regard, statistical analysis of model-based forecasts, taking into account predictable forecast uncertainty, has played an important role in evaluating, and in improving, economic models (in the sense of representation or resemblance of economic reality) through test of parameter constancy (Ericsson 2002, p. 39).

Another consequence of the predictable forecast uncertainty (i.e., the recognizable presence and extent of uncertainty) is the broad context of *decision-making*, where there are many aspects to be considered. The issue at stake here is particularly relevant for economics as applied economics and for the application of this science. This is the case mainly because the predictable forecast uncertainty has repercussions for planning, where the knowledge regarding the future intertwines with the direction of the action towards chosen ends (Chap. 2, Sect. 2.4.2). In addition, it is a topic important for microeconomics as well as for macroeconomics.

Both in microeconomics and in macroeconomics the measures of predictable forecast uncertainty have many implications. In macroeconomics, it is very clear that governments and many institutions (national and international) need to consider the implications of forecast uncertainty, especially the costs of errors in policy.[14] Meanwhile in microeconomics, "if the forecast uncertainty for a certain variable is viewed as being considerable, insurance might be desirable as a mechanism for protecting against untoward outcomes; and different types of insurance might be available. Also, forecast uncertainty is inherent to many economic activities, such as business investment, with the possibility of large successes often being an attraction of such investment" (Ericsson 2002, p. 39).

11.3 The Appraisal of Economic Predictions: Criteria on Prediction as a Test

The appraisal of predictions is a task that could be made in different contexts: aims, processes, and results. Basically, the assessments are related to the purpose, content, or consequences of an economic model. In this regard, an economic prediction is commonly made with an *aim* (descriptive or prescriptive, generic or specific, etc.); it has a *process* in connection with structural (i.e., framework) or dynamic aspects of economics; and it can get a *result* with consequences for the model itself (or, in general, for the descriptive sphere of economic theory or the prescriptive terrain of

[14] Central Banks are among those institutions concerned with this issue, cf. Hatch (2001). The Bank of England uses "fan charts" in this regard.

applied economics). Thus, at least from the point of view of the results, prediction can be used as a *test* for a theory (either in macroeconomics or in microeconomics), or more specifically as a test for an economic model.

As regards the use of prediction for evaluating theories, taking into account the processes and the outcomes of economic predictions, there are sometimes economists with views somehow skeptical on the role of prediction *as a test* for an economic theory. This is the case of Hahn: "there are very large difficulties with prediction as a test for theory. Ultimately this stem from our inability to experiment scientifically, that is, adequately to control for the exogenous variable and for the intrinsic interrelatedness of economic phenomena. It has therefore proved hard to obtain decisive rejections of economic theories, a fact which means in turn that we must rely in the first instance on internal theoretical coherence in any evaluation" (Hahn 1993, p. 84).

But this approach assumes *de facto* several *criteria of evaluation* of economic predictions: internal coherence of the theory, adequate level of control of the variables (exogenous and also endogenous), and the possibility of a clear-cut refutability of economic theories. The internal coherence could be both in terms of consistency (i.e., a logical property of absence of contradiction) and systematicity (i.e., an epistemological feature of interdependence of the contents of the elements involved in the theory). Undoubtedly, these criteria—logical, epistemological, and methodological—should be considered when an appraisal of an economic prediction (both in economic theory and in applied economics) is at stake. In addition, some other evaluative criteria can be considered.

Simultaneously, there is the need for a clarification of *what a test for economics is*. In this regard, it is very clear that there is a branch of "experimental economics," which makes experimental tests and it was analyzed in Chap. 9. Thus, the claim of "our inability to experiment scientifically" should be qualified. (a) The author himself recognizes that some experiments have been undertaken following game theory, although he insists that "the scope for experiments in economics is rather limited" and the experiments already made are confined ("experiments of this sort [with students] provide insights but not certainty") (Hahn 1993, p. 78). (b) The notion itself of "experiment" should be expanded to go beyond some traditional boundaries insofar as new kinds of testing are assumed in the practice of economics (cf. Sect. 11.3.2 on different kinds of testing). In addition, the methodological discussion on testing in science has been very important in recent years, especially in the area of the problem of error.[15]

11.3.1 Main Criteria in the Appraisal of Predictions

Assessing predictive merit can be seen in the realm of *processes* or in the sphere of *results*. In Chap. 10 the focus was on the first dimension (i.e., the diversity of

[15] The debate has followed upon quite different lines, according to the diverse views on probability.

predictive approaches, in general, and predictive methods, in particular), analyzing the methods of prediction in economics and the use of models in this regard. The present chapter pays special attention to the predictive results. We can compare the predictive statements (commonly "forecasts" in the strict sense, i.e., with a margin of error associated to the statement on the future) and the outcomes that have been obtained. It is an evaluation where the predictive *aims* are important, because the results must be considered regarding the purpose of the models used.

Taking into account the need for an interconnection between aims, processes—mainly methods—and results, it makes sense to start with the existence of two different fronts in an evaluation: questions and responses. On the one hand, the evaluation of *predictive questions* focuses primarily on their importance and interest, their inherent resolvability and their difficulty. On the other, *predictive answers* can deal with a wide variety of aspects: relevance (to the question at issue), correctness (categorical alethic merit: true versus false), precision (informative merit in point of such contrast as specific versus vague, broad versus detailed), accuracy (comparative alethic merit: closeness to the truth), credibility (evidential merit or cogency: warranted versus unwarranted), and robustness (via agreement with the indications of other predictive resources) (Rescher 1998, pp. 113–131; esp., pp. 113–114).

Frequently, predictive answers are evaluated following the criteria of accuracy and precision. It is clear that a prediction could be *generic* or *specific*. In the case of being generic, a prediction might be correct (when it is proved to be true) or erroneous, either totally (the outcome is completely different from the real events) or partially (some mistakes are made in an overall adequate picture of the events). Meanwhile, when it is specific, there are fewer options: correct (i.e., a statement according to the phenomena observed) or erroneous (i.e., a wrong way of describing the fact studied). All these possibilities can be seen in economic theory as well as in applied economics, even though it is commonly easier to show that something is wrong than to prove that a statement is true.[16]

Accuracy is a different criterion of evaluation from correctness, insofar as it is a *matter of degree* instead of a question to be evaluated in absolute terms (as the case with assessments of correctness like all or nothing). Accuracy shows the level of exactness of a prediction. Thus, *accuracy* "pivots on the comparative extent to which a prediction 'misses the mark'. Even as we prefer correct predictions to incorrect ones, so we would—for obvious reasons—among correct predictions prefer the more accurate to the less so. Nonetheless, a predictive answer that is 'approximately correct' (…) can often render good informative and/or practical service" (Rescher 1998, p. 122).

[16] It is noticeable that Michael Dummett, who has developed an anti-realist semantics, where the notion of "proof"—a justified assertion—has more credentials than the concept of "truth," has written that "the defenders of truth-conditional theories of meaning are thus right to argue that the concept of truth is indispensable. The concept of truth is the pivot about which a theory of meaning is brought to bear on metaphysics. Metaphysics is concerned with the general nature of reality, and, as the opening remarks of the *Tractatus* state, reality is constituted not by the totality of objects that exists but by the totality of facts that obtain. Facts are true propositions: so metaphysics concerns itself with what truths hold good in general" (Dummett 2004, p. 35).

Precision is also a valuable asset in a statement about the future, but it is clearly more risky than a vague or less detailed one. "The more general a prediction, the safer; the more specific, the more problematic and risky" (Rescher 1998, p. 120).[17] *Precision* is a criteria used when the discussion goes on to the problem of "generic predictions" versus "specific predictions." In this regard, as pointed out in Chap. 3 (Sect. 2.3.1), generic predictions in economics are not good enough as an aim of a science. The search for generic predictions can be accepted as a starting point, but certainly not as an acceptable end for a science. In principle, economists should not be satisfied with generic predictions (e.g., in economic theory), because a "science requires persistent predictive improvement" (Rosenberg 1992, p. 20). Hence, precision is an important criterion when evaluating the quality of a predictive model.

Some ways to use "accuracy" and "precision" as measures of predictive success have been analyzed—in Chap. 9—in the context of experimental economics, due to the contributions made by Selten. But there are a remarkable number of ways of *measuring forecasting accuracy* in applied economics, and these predictive processes are used to compare between them. (1) *Mean absolute deviation* (MAD) or *mean absolute error* (MAE), which is the average of the absolute values of the forecasts errors; (2) *root mean square error* (RMSE), which is the square root of the average of the squared values of forecast errors; (3) *mean absolute percentage error* (MAPE), which is the average of the absolute values of the percentage errors and has the advantage of being dimensionless; (4) *correlation of forecasts with actual values*; (5) *percentage of turning points forecasts*; and (6) *conditional efficacy* (Kennedy 1998, p. 291).[18]

In these cases, "accuracy" is commonly understood as a goal to be obtained by the forecast as a consequence of diminishing the margin of error. But, simultaneously, it is accepted that the "best" way to improve accuracy using forecasting methods is a *combined forecast*, formed as a weighted average of a variety of forecasts, each made by a different predictive process. If the principles—on which there diverse forecasts are based—are sufficiently different from one another, then this average should prove superior to any single forecasting process, because the errors in the separate forecasts will tend to cancel one another. In addition, this suggests that good economic forecasts do not come from using a single model specification, but rather from *combining results* taking from a variety of reasonable models (Kennedy 1998, p. 292; on this issue, cf. McNees 1992).

Nevertheless, there are also "significant tests of forecast accuracy" (Mariano 2002, esp., pp. 284–295), thinking of the *quality* of economic models in order to make forecasts and the *adequacy* of economic models to elaborate policy analysis. "Tests of forecast accuracy can be either model-based or model-free. The first type

[17] Precision is important insofar as prediction cannot remain in the sphere of vague statements (i.e., in the realm of large confidence intervals). But it might be useless if there is a very precise statement whose actual value is outside of the confidence interval studied. Then, the criterion of accuracy is more relevant because combines precision (random errors) and bias (systematic errors) in a single measure. José Ramón Cancelo, *Personal communication*, January 2007.

[18] In this regard, see also Fildes and Ord (2002, esp., pp. 326–328), and West (2006).

assumes that the econometric model is parametric, estimated from a given data sample, and both the data and model are available for testing forecast accuracy. Tests of these genres have been developed for large macroeconomic models based on deterministic and stochastic simulations of the estimated model. (…) For model-free tests, (…) we assume that the information set at the disposal of the investigator consists only of a set of forecasts and actual values of the predictand. We also consider the case where we have two or more sets of forecasts from competing models, together with actual values, and wish to determine the relative accuracies of the forecasts" (Mariano 2002, pp. 284–285).

There are also empirical comparisons of competing methods of prediction, mainly seeking to assess the strengths and weaknesses in the search for accuracy (Fildes and Ord 2002, esp., pp. 334 and 340–341). *Comparative forecasting accuracy* has analyzed individual and multiple time series. Some conclusions have been obtained in this regard which are useful to improve the research on prediction and the practice of using predictions in economics:

"1 Statistically sophisticated or complex methods do not typically produce more accurate forecasts than simpler ones. 2 The ranking of the performance of the various methods varies according to the accuracy measure being used. 3 The accuracy of the combination of various methods outperforms, on average, the individual methods being combined, and does well in comparison with other methods. 4 The performance of various methods depends on the length of the forecasting horizon. (…) 5 The characteristics of the set of time series under analysis is an important factor in determining relative performance between methods. If the time series has a homogenous structure, that information should be exploited. That is, contextual knowledge should be utilized wherever possible. 6 A method specifically designed for the characteristics observed in specific data sets (such as telecoms data) may perform substantially better than the method selected as best in a broad-ranging competition using heterogeneous series. 7 Sampling variability of performance measures renders comparisons based on a single time-series origin unreliable; comparisons should be based on multiple origins. 8 The broad conclusions (listed above) of the M-Competition hold for time series drawn from a wide variety of economic and national contexts" (Fildes and Ord 2002, pp. 346–347).

11.3.2 Methodological Processes to the Assessment of Predictions: Different Kinds of Testing

Besides the recognition of the diversity of criteria for the assessment of economic predictions (accuracy, precision, etc.), the possibility of *different kinds of testing* of those scientific statements about future economic events should be emphasized. In this regard, there is an increasing methodological interest in the role of experiments understood in a broad sense (Gonzalez 2007a, pp. 280–281, and 2010b). The *criteria* used to distinguish the diversity of experiments are commonly features related to several elements—epistemological, methodological, and ontological—mainly

(i) the range of *controllability* of the variables, (ii) the level of materiality of the *processes* employed in the research, and (iii) the *sphere*—real, ideal, a hybrid, etc.—to be analyzed. Again economics is an interesting case study to see the differences between laboratory experimentation and other experiments, because it is a science that uses a variety of experiments.

1. As for epistemological issue of the *range of controllability* of the variables, there are at least three possibilities: (a) direct control; (b) indirect control (or statistical control); and (c) assumption in model. The last is the most complex, concerning the kind of *control of variables*, especially if we follow the analysis made by Alan Musgrave on Milton Friedman's approach on the lack of realism of the assumptions. For Friedman, an economic theory should not be criticized for containing "unreal assumptions" because the important point in order to evaluate a theory is successful predictions (Friedman 1953). Musgrave considers instead that Friedman's *dictum* (the so-called "F-twist") is false on the basis of three types of assumption: negligibility assumptions, domain assumptions, and heuristic assumptions (Musgrave 1981).[19]

2. Concerning the methodological issue of the level of *materiality of the processes* employed in the research, there are differences in the case of economics regarding several possibilities: (1) the empirical domain of *laboratory experimentation* (when a material realm is under direct control), (2) the "passive experimentation" of the *econometric case* (when a material realm receives an indirect control or statistical control), (3) the simulations and, above all, *computer simulations* (when the quasi-material realm or the pseudo-material sphere depends on the assumptions in the model), and (4) the *thought experiments* (when the non-material realm depends upon the assumptions in the model) (Boumans and Morgan 2001, p. 20).[20]

3. Both the range of controllability of the variables and the level of materiality of the processes employed in the research are connected to the *ontological issue* of the sphere—real, ideal, a hybrid, etc.—to be analyzed. Certainly the *sphere to be analyzed* by experiments varies from real (a direct tangible object of study or statistical data based on previous evidence) to clearly ideal (a thought experiment or a purely mathematical model). Between these poles—real, although artificially constructed,[21] and ideal—there is the realm of hybrids (e.g., in simulations) which could be quasi-material or pseudo-material.

If these distinctions (epistemological, methodological and ontological) that relate to the kind of experiments are basically correct, then there are clear differences in the *methodological processes* to appraise economic predictions (which is a central

---

[19] "*Negligibility assumptions* state that some factor has a negligible effect upon the phenomenon under investigation. *Domain assumptions* specify the domain of applicability of the theory. *Heuristic assumptions* are a means of simplifying the logical development of the theory" (Musgrave 1981, p. 386).

[20] Even though the origin of this distinction is in the analysis of *ceteris paribus* conditions, it seems to me that the main differences that are drawn in this differentiation have a rather general consideration for the methodological process.

[21] "In the laboratory an artificial economic reality is constructed, for example a market or an auction" (Selten 2003, p. 63).

issue in the methodology of economics). Experimental economics—mainly in the case of Selten—is well aware of this question and tries to emphasize the laboratory experimentation as the most reliable kind of experimentation to deal with the predictive success (and, therefore, with the notions of accuracy and precision).

Nevertheless, Selten also points out limits of this methodological approach: "experimental research (…) cannot replace field research. The institutional environment of economic participants must be investigated in the real world. Once we are sure we have modeled such an environment, however, we can and must test or redevelop the behavioral assumptions of theory in the laboratory" (Selten 2003, p. 68). Thus, the different kinds of testing in economics are related to its dual characteristic: it is a social science as well as a science of the artificial.

Consequently, we need testing according to the dual reality of economic phenomena—social and artificial—which also involves taking into account variability towards the future due to scientific creativity and technological innovation. In this regard, some phenomena of the future can fit into a correct identification of established patterns or relationships and their appropriate extrapolation, whereas other phenomena—mainly concerning the long run—can be in tune with "creative insights about forthcoming changes and their implications" (Makridakis et al. 1998, p. 568).

11.3.3 The Case of Econometrics: A Tertium Quid *between Laboratory Experimentation and Thought Experiments*

Econometrics may be seen as offering a *tertium quid* between the experimentation made in the economic laboratory and the thought experiments (Gonzalez 2007a, pp. 282–283). On the one hand, an econometric model shares with laboratory experimentation the *constructed character* of the process and the *artificial nature* of the environment, even though in the laboratory there are real agents (i.e., there is a direct control of variables) whereas in an econometric model there is a package of statistical data related to economic phenomena (i.e., the control of variables is indirect). On the other hand, an econometric model has no clear-cut relation to the circumstances of economic undertakings (mainly when the model relies on a process of generating data) as well as the thought experiments work in a sphere of *possibilities* (and also impossibilities) rather than in an actual environment.

Such a vision of econometrics as *a case of experimentation* between the laboratory experiments made in the context of the material world and the thought experiments related to a non-material world includes a peculiar notion: "passive experimentation," which accompanies the idea of "natural experiments" (and, therefore, a material environment). Thus, "unlike the lab experiment, the 'experiments' of econometrics are not actual ones but statistical ones, conducted on 'passive data': data thrown up by the uncontrolled experiments of Nature (the Economy), incorporating all the multiple variation of the interacting factors with which the econometrician must deal as best he/she can *ex post*" (Boumans and Morgan 2001, p. 18).

Compared with the methods of laboratory experimentation, the statistical methods of the econometric experiment—a passive one—might be interpreted as providing a substitute kind of control at the level of measurement process. It is an indirect control of the circumstances, and requires statistical assumptions that are sometimes unrealistic: econometrics cannot control the circumstances directly and accepts that we are *passive observers* of a stream of experiments that Nature (economic world) is turning out from within, like an enormous laboratory.[22]

Accordingly, the case of econometric experimentations relies on the possibility of "natural experiments" and their statistical control: "the econometric model is first built and estimated as a passive experiment and then is used as if it were a mathematical model" (Boumans and Morgan 2001, p. 19). The problem is, then, the application to the real economic world of those results obtained through this indirect way and, specifically, what the possible causal inferences regarding economic activity are. Not only is causality a debatable question in this context but so are the characteristics of reproducibility and replicability of econometric experiments ("passive experiments") in comparison with laboratory experimentation.

Some well-known econometricians, following a traditional notion of "experiment," have disregarded the possibility of experimentation in econometrics: "econometric theory is the study of the properties of data generation processes, techniques for analysing data, methods of estimating numerical magnitudes of parameters with unknown values and procedures for testing economic hypotheses; it plays an analogous role in primarily non-experimental disciplines to that of statistical theory in inexact experimental sciences (…). As expressed by [H. O. A.] Wold (1969), 'Econometrics is seen as a vehicle for fundamental innovations in scientific method, above all, in the development of operative forecasting procedures in non-experimental situations'. In Wold's view, econometrics needs to overcome both a lack of experimentation (which precludes reproducible knowledge) and the passivity of forecasts based on extrapolative methods" (Hendry 2000a, p. 13).

What is widely accepted in econometrics is the idea of "simulation experiments" (Hendry 1986, especially, p. 25), or computer simulations in order to test predictions. In this regard, even though there are many statistical and economic criteria for an *overall evaluation* of econometric systems, "success when 'predictive testing' seems to establish most credibility, perhaps because the data were unavailable to the modellers" (Hendry 1986, p. 25). Moreover, if the forecasts are accurate and the outcomes are known after the forecasts are published, then an econometric model seems "credible" or "adequate." Nevertheless, the ability of prediction tests to detect mis-specifications depends both on the structure of the chosen tests and on the properties of data process.

However, Hendry deems that there could be the case of no connection between the validity of an economic model (i.e., a representation of the economy) and any reasonable measure of its forecast accuracy. He points out *some caveats* concerning *model evaluation* using forecast performance. (1) "If some component has a 'large' variance, then poor forecasts will result even from the 'correct' model; whereas, if

[22] That is the idea of T. Haavelmo, cf. Morgan (1990, p. 245).

the error variance is 'small', one can obtain accurate forecasts despite of using an inappropriate information set" (1986, p. 26). (2) There is the possibility of forecasts that can have influence on the outcomes, and hence they might be self-invalidating. (3) It is the case that, in practice, the published forecasts from econometric models are the product of the model itself and the model's proprietors,[23] due to "intercept corrections" or "add-factors" which modify the pure model forecast.

Nevertheless, David Hendry thinks also "the third *caveat* (…) could be circumvented by acquiring access to a model's unadulterated *ex ante* forecasts. The second *caveat* places inherent limits on public forecastability, (…) although such limits are susceptible to economic analysis (…). The first issue is open to a more complete analysis" (1986, p. 27). But it is the second one that has commonly received more attention in the methodological debates regarding applied economics.

Moreover, this problem, which has received different names (effect Oedipus,[24] reflexive predictions,[25] contamination of the predicted by prediction, etc.), had a reply a long time ago (Grunberg and Modigliani 1954). In recent times, the response has been reinforced: "there is in any case no *logical* entailment of an impossibility to predict which is deducible from 'contamination'" (Hahn 1993). Therefore, the second caveat—the influence of a prediction on its outcome that eventually could be self-invalidating—should be a *possible effect* rather than a necessary effect. Thus, it should be analyzed in those concrete cases.

11.3.4 Predictive Errors and Economic Costs

Predictive errors (i.e., mistaken results)[26] can have quite different origins: epistemological (a deficient level of knowledge of variables, inadequate assumptions of the model, etc.), methodological (a defective characterization of the predictive process, an inadequate step in the process of predicting, etc.), ontological (a random behavior, an unexpected shift in an economic trend, etc.), axiological (a wrong selection of a target, an unbalanced scope),… Predictive errors can be found in economic theory and in applied economics, both in macroeconomics and in microeconomics. These can be seen in the descriptive sphere (e.g., when a theory is being tested in order to know its correctness) or in the prescriptive domain, where prediction combines with prescription and the economic policy is grounded on some predictions.

[23] A methodological question can be considered here: two independent analysts, using the same model, will they introduce identical corrections when the model shows that is not working properly?

[24] Popper uses this terminology (1957, p. 13). He gives the name "Oedipus effect" to the influence of an item of information (historical or economical) upon the situation to which the information refers to.

[25] Cf. Buck (1963), Grünbaum (1963), Grünbaum (1956), Romanos (1973), and Vetterling (1976).

[26] According to Granger and Machina, "forecasts are invariably subject to error" (2006, p. 89).

To put it differently, "forecasting error can have many causes, including unrealized assumptions, unexpected shocks, shifts in behaviour, and the inappropriate exercise of the forecaster's judgement. In some cases it may be found necessary, in the light of continuing evidence of poor predictive ability, to reformulate an equation, or set of equations. In this way, the model becomes not only an explicit representation of the forecaster's beliefs as to the key relationships among economic variables, but also a source of feedback which, in the light of experience acquired, may result in a rethinking of those relationships" (Llewellyn et al. 1985, p. 141).[27] Thus, it seems widely accepted that forecast errors are across variables and they might be originated by an unexpected feature of "economic activity" (e.g., a shock) or in the gathering of the data about recent past.

Clements and Hendry have proposed a taxonomy for all sources of predictive errors in economics (1999, Chap. 2). It underpins their conception of "economic forecasting" and is focused on econometric models. These models can have deterministic terms (such as intercepts and trends), stochastic terms (such as inflation and output),[28] and unobserved errors or shocks. Within this context, these authors conceive nine *sources of predictive error*, of which the first is considered the most pernicious: "(1) shifts in the coefficients on deterministic terms, (2) shifts in the coefficients on stochastic terms, (3) mis-specification of deterministic term, (4) mis-specification of stochastic terms, (5) mis-estimation of the coefficients on deterministic terms, (6) mis-estimation of the coefficients on stochastic terms, (7) mis-measurement of data, (8) changes in the variances of the errors, and (9) errors cumulating over the forecast horizon" (Hendry and Ericsson 2001c, p. 188; see also Keating 1985, pp. 120–134).

According to this plethora of sources of predictive errors, it seems clear that we should reject a possible version of "naive falsificationism": that a failure of an economic prediction can lead to invalidate an economic theory. It could be the case that some unexpected factor—a shift in one of the variables—can produce an outcome quite different from the predicted result. This can happen in areas of ordinary life, such as some prices of commodities (e.g., to raise the price of a particular item will lead to a decrease in the sold of that product, but an unexpected phenomenon—such as the publication of the discovery of a healthy property in it—can eventually carry out an outcome of more sold instead of less). This occurrence does not invalidate the general theory (e.g., on price formation).

From the point of view of the outcomes of economic predictions, there is a clear methodological difference between a kind of error that is to some extent *systematic*, due to a previous problem with the economic process used to make a forecast, and an *occasional* predictive error, even though it could be larger than expected, and then it might be particularly notorious. In other words, "poor forecast" is not the same than "forecast failure." This could be seen in the context of the measure of

[27] In the case of econometric models, among the potential sources of error are specification error, conditioning error, sampling error, and random error (Kennedy 1998, p. 289).

[28] It is odd that they have included "inflation" and "output" among the stochastic terms, because—in a strict sense—inflation and output are *statistical series* rather than "stochastic terms."

the forecast uncertainty: "a distinction exists between poor forecasts—ones that have associated numerically large forecast errors—and forecast failure, in which the forecast errors are larger than anticipated, given the forecast uncertainty associated with the forecast model" (Ericsson 2001, p. 90).

Furthermore, these "poor forecasts" and "forecast failures" might be really very expensive when the whole thing moves on the area of economic policy, especially when we are in the case of the application of this science in specific settings. By contrast, when the forecasts are accurate and precise, we can have important gains (especially in some economic areas). In other words, "within a given policy framework, forecast errors may increase economic instability and hence affect longer-term economic performance. Forecast errors are also important to consider in the conduct of policy: better forecasts will allow economic gains, so the search for improved forecasting models and methods should continue" (Burns 2001, p. 170).

Considering the question of the *costs of predictive errors*, "we should distinguish between the problems that forecast errors create when operating within a given policy framework, and the extent to which forecast error influence the choice of policy framework. The first situation is ongoing and concerns the role that forecasts play in the successful implementation of policy (…). The second situation arises only occasionally because the framework for conducting policy itself typically changes only infrequently. When it does arise, we need to decide whether the policy framework should be changed and, if so, what should replace it" (Burns 2001, p. 175).

Concerning the first situation—the effect of forecast errors within a given policy framework—the main cost of forecast error is commonly instability. Obviously, instability could be originated by different factors, but forecast errors can contribute clearly to economic instability, mainly in the cases of output, inflation, and public finances. "That instability can generate follow-on effects for some time and can have important effects on specific individuals and industries. Economic instability encumbers other government policies, particularly fiscal policy; and it can affect credibility of the policy framework and of the policymakers. Better forecasts can lead to gains in the conduct of policy" (Burns 2001, p. 184).

As for the second situation—the costs of forecast errors that can potentially influence the choice of policy framework—there are more practical concerns, insofar as it has a direct influence on national economies and in international trade. Thus, some decisions on economic policy, such as the euro as currency of thirteen countries of the European Union (in 2007), have many consequences. Hence, both forecasts themselves and forecast errors have relevance insofar as they contribute to making a success of policy innovations. But "forecasts do not typically play a decisive part in that choice, which focuses on a wider range of considerations. However, policy switches often do follow a period of difficulty with the previous policy regime, usually including significant forecasts errors, so confidence in the forecasting process is not usually high when designing the new framework" (Burns 2001, p. 183).

11.4 Limits and Obstacles of Prediction in Economics

Among the reasons to think on the limits and obstacles of prediction in economics is the recognition that economic models failed to predict some of the most important phenomena in recent decades, such as rising inflation and the severity of the post-1973 recession or later on—in the late 1970s and the early 1980s—the unusually large financial disturbances (including volatile exchange rates and high interest rates), or more recently the extent and depth of the economic crisis in the countries of the European Union and North America since the summer of 2007 to the present moment.

On the one hand, the available models commonly lacked the equations needed to represent these events (which, in the case of the ongoing crisis, involves other aspects also, such as two big deficiencies epistemological and ontological: the problem of the unreliable data regarding the economies of some countries and the structural problems of the banking system of several nations); and, on the other hand, it was also the case that the use of models by economic forecasters was not adequate, insofar as some models were utilized uncritically in circumstances for which they were not designed (Llewellyn et al. 1985, pp. 135–136).

"Internal" limits came ordinarily from the *characteristics* of the models used, mainly in the sense of structural and dynamic resemblance or representation of economic reality, but also in the sense of theoretical construction or ideal design on economic events. Models commonly incorporate a simplification of a complex economic reality and, hence, they have a limited range of application. The characteristics of models are according to some aims, and their use should be based on the kind of economic relationships that the models seek to represent or design. These internal limits could be epistemological (e.g., an insufficient knowledge of the variables), methodological (e.g., a deficit in the development of the processes related to the dynamic of economic activity) or ontological (e.g., the nature itself of the kind of event).

"External" limits came customarily from the *economic forecasters* insofar as they should have the skills to know in which circumstances the models at their disposal were to be used adequately. Thus, we can think of a Wittgensteinian view on prediction (Gonzalez 1996b), insofar as to predict in economics is to make *a use* of calculus as well as to utilize judgmental elements as a complement;[29] then, the economic prediction made it is an activity developed by someone using the calculation and looking for a rational result.

In other words, the external limits involve that "the model does not predict" (Llewellyn et al. 1985, p. 138; cf. McNees 1989), because the model is a content—a resemblance or a construction—which *is used* by the economist to make a

[29] According to Makridakis et al., "judgmental predictions must supplement the statistical ones when and where they can contribute the most: in identifying forthcoming changes and predicting the direction and extent that they will influence the future so that statistical predictions, which can more objectively and correctly identify and extrapolate established patterns and/or existing relationships, can be appropriately modified" (1998, p. 551).

prediction. Economists have also bounded rationality—in the sense of Simon and Selten—in addition to the economic agents, because they are not able to compute all the possible economic variables of "economic activity" and "economics as activity." Therefore, the external limits due to human bounded rationality should also be taken into account.

Besides the question of insufficiency of our knowledge, there is also the case that the reality itself, which often does not allow a precise prediction to be obtained. Both aspects—epistemological and ontological—take part in the methodological development of prediction. Insofar as the reality is characterizing the kind of prediction, the limits are mainly ontological. They may be related to the framework or the dynamic (or both) of the phenomena or events at stake. We can think, for example, that eclipses allow for strong predictions, whereas the floating of exchange rates allows only weak predictions.

Nonetheless there are also epistemological limits which affect the outcome of predictions: in eclipses, the whole of the information that is relevant to them can be collected and the prediction is accurate (a "foresight"), whereas the pertinent information on the floating of exchange rates could be altered by new variables (like in the case of European exchange-rate mechanism in September 1992) and the outcome of prediction could be quite different from what has been predicted.

11.4.1 Limits of Predictability: Epistemological and Ontological

A central distinction on limits was already pointed out in Chap. 1: the difference between limits as "barriers" (*Schranken*) and "confines" (*Grenzen*) (Radnitzky 1978). This was used in the case of science, in general, thinking of the cutting edge of the demarcation problem in the realm of economics. To some extent, that distinction can be also applied to predictions: there is an epistemological "barrier" or "frontier" between scientific prediction and non-scientific prediction. In addition, another epistemological problem is the possible "confines" or "ultimate point" to be reached by scientific prediction.

Originally, the distinction between "scientific" and "non-scientific" prediction is in Part I of this book, because the central tenet of this monograph is to clarify *scientific prediction* in economic science, taking into account economic theory and applied economics (mainly, statistical economics and econometrics). The issue of "confines" is also crucial. In many ways, it underlies the topics of this chapter, because the extent of predictive "confines" directly affects the problem of uncertainty and the efforts of diminishing the margin of error in seeking accuracy and precision. Moreover, "a science should show long-term improvements in the range of its confirmed predictions and in the precision of these predictions" (Rosenberg 1993, p. 161).

But within "internal" limits of prediction, we can think of a long list according to the constituents of a science: (a) semantic boundaries (difficulties in identifying a new phenomena—its sense and reference—); (b) logical limitations (structural boundaries of new theories to reflect economic activity and economics as activity); (c) epistemological limits in knowing future events; (d) ontological limitations (future unexpected changes and some new kinds of phenomena); (e) axiological frontiers (new goals to be predicted can appear); and (f) ethical limits as a consequence of the connections between prediction and prescription (in the context of applied science which leads to an economic policy).

These limits can be analyzed from different viewpoints: in the weak sense of our *present limitations* to predict (i.e., our boundaries in our historical setting) or in the stronger approach of the *intrinsic limits* to the human condition about predicting future events.[30] These are two different levels that have special relevance in the case of economics, because it is a social science as well as a science of the artificial (in Simon's terminological usage), and they have theoretical consequences as well as practical ones. Obviously, the real limits are those related to our capacities as human beings rather than to the limitations of our present economic models.

Rescher has focused on epistemological and ontological limits. "Epistemological limits on prediction exist insofar as the future is *cognitively inaccessible*—either because we cannot secure the needed data, or because it is impossible for us to discover the operative laws, or even possibly because the requisite inferences and/or calculations involve complexities that outrun the reach of our capabilities" (1998, p. 134). Meanwhile, "ontological limits exist insofar as the future of the domain at issue is *developmentally open*—causally undetermined or undeterminated by the existing realities of the present and open to the development of wholly unprecedented patterns owing to the contingencies of choice, chance, and chaos" (Rescher 1998, p. 134).

Both kinds of limits have repercussions on the methodological limits.[31] *De facto*, connecting to epistemological and ontological limits, we can think of methodological "confines," which have been clearly present here in several ways, such as in the cases of the predictable forecast uncertainty and the non-predictable forecast uncertainty. In addition, questions on choice or chance—and even chaos—can receive daily attention by economists (mainly in financial markets). The three of them are related to time and complexity, and economists have exhaustively researched them in the last decades.[32] But more work should be done, especially in order to deal with *historicity* of economics.[33]

[30] For Rosenberg, "the debate would threaten to be inconclusive, mainly because we have neither a natural unit of predictive power nor a good measuring device to calculate the changes in predictive power that we might expect over a period of a decade or even a century" (1993, p. 164).

[31] The methodological limits includes that the methodological universalism is untenable (Gonzalez 2012b). In this regard, it is quite interesting to see that Popper did not assume this idea of "the" scientific method (understood as a systematic way to achieve well founded scientific results), cf. Worrall (2001a, p. 114).

[32] An analysis of these issues can be found in Nieto de Alba (1998).

[33] Herbert Simon developed an initial attempt, when I explicitly asked him for a paper in this regard. The article was published in a monographic issue that I coordinated on philosophy and methodology of economics: Simon (1998).

11.4.2 Obstacles on Predictors

Limits on scientific predictions in economics could be on "internal" aspects related to scientific activity or on "external" factors of human capacities. The former belong to the sphere of the constituents of science and the limits pointed out (semantic, logical, epistemological, methodological, ontological, axiological, and ethical), whereas the latter are in human agents. Thus, within the framework of a social and artificial science, economic models needs to deal with the nature of things where choice or chance—and even chaos—can have a role, which can lead to creativity in human undertakings (e.g., creation of artificial products as "hedge funds"). In addition, our cognitive limitations are undeniable, as the bounded rationality approach has emphasized repeatedly.

For Rescher (1998), from a general point of view, the *principal impediments* to predictability are seven. (1) Anarchy, where there is lawlessness in the strict sense of the absence of lawful regularities to be linking mechanisms. (2) Volatility, when there is absence of nomic stability and then of cognitively manageable laws. (3) Uncertainty, which was analyzed previously. (4) Haphazard, when the lawful linking mechanisms do not permit the secure inference of particular conclusions: (a) *chance* and *chaos* (stochastic or random processes which make laws at issue irretrievably probabilistic); (b) *arbitrary choice* (determinations that are basically groundless are then rationally intractable), and (c) change and innovation (a kind of novelty that makes outcomes not foreseeable because prediscernible patterns are continually broken). (5) Fuzziness, which is data indetermination whether individually or in a collectively conjugate way. (6) Myopia, which is data ignorance in the sense of lack of sufficient volume and detail to be able to make a prediction. (7) Inferential incapacity, which is the infeasibility of carrying out the needed reasoning.

Economics tends to focus on some of them, where uncertainty has a key role from the methodological point of view (mainly in applied economics). According to the different economic schools, economists can point to some as central topics of relevance, i.e., obstacles for an adequate or reliable prediction. These issues are usually connected with central epistemological and methodological controversies: the possibility of economics laws, the way of understanding "causality" in economics, the role attributed to economic creativity of individual agents, etc.

But insofar as they are aware of doing science, the attitude of economists is to emphasize some "stable" elements: human rationality in the decision-making,[34] capacity to gather and observe unobvious regularities (Hoover 2002, p. 173), etc. Therefore, economists try to overcome these obstacles of predictability and, at the same time, they are well aware of the present stage of economic predictions (Clements and Hendry 2002c; see also Franses 2006), which includes the difficulties of correctly anticipating major future changes in economics (Makridakis et al. 1998, p. 570).

[34] On this issue, cf. Chaps. 8 and 9. Cf. Gonzalez (2003d).

Undoubtedly, there are serious obstacles to predictors from the angle of complexity, mainly epistemological and ontological, which have a direct repercussion in methodological aspects of prediction (Gonzalez 2012b). Complexity in this dual science of economics—social and artificial—can be both structural (i.e., framework) and dynamic. It can also concern different levels (such as micro and macro). In this regard, the dynamics of complex systems such as economics can be seen in terms of "historicity." This is the case insofar as economics as well as other complex systems have discontinuities in their changes (including catastrophes) (Rosser 1999).

On the one hand, there are aspects of economic dynamics that can be considered in terms of a linear system, which "is one you can understand by understanding its parts individually and then putting them together" (Mitchell 2009, p. 22). On the other hand, there are characteristics of economic dynamics that are of a nonlinear system, which "is one in which the whole is different from the sum of the parts" (Mitchell 2009, p. 23). Economics, as well as other social sciences, needs to address problems of nonlinear systems (Bertuglia and Vaio 2005). The studies of complexity in economics have evolved out of earlier work using nonlinear dynamics. They have been used to explain such phenomena as path dependence in technological evolution and regional development as well as "the appearance of discontinuities, such as the crashes of speculative bubbles or the collapses of whole economic systems" (Rosser 1999, p. 169).

According to Herbert Simon, nonlinear systems worked on "irregular phenomena" long before the chaos theory.[35] In this context, chaos "is a feature of certain dynamical models which exhibit sensitive dependence on initial conditions plus 'confinement' plus (typical) aperiodicity. Which is to say, roughly, that tiny differences in the initial states can exponentially inflate into big differences in later states, but the values of the relevant state variables eventually remain confined within the fixed boundaries although typically never exactly repeating" (Smith 1998, p. 20).[36] At the ontological level, Simon has pointed out that we "don't know whether the economy is a chaotic system" (1989, p. 99). Meanwhile, at the epistemological level, our cognitive limitations are undeniable, as the bounded rationality approach has repeatedly emphasized.

Within this context of complexity—epistemological and ontological, in the framework and the dynamic—a key way to address prediction in economics is through parsimonious factors (Gonzalez 2011a). The use of parsimonious factors, which give us the necessary and sufficient conditions to reach a given system or specific

---

[35] Simon, H. A., *Personal communication*, 31 July 1996.

[36] "Chaos in this sense ['sensitive dependence on initial conditions'] has been observed in cardiac disorders, turbulence in fluids, electronic circuits, dripping faucets, and many other seemingly unrelated phenomena. These days, the existence of chaotic systems is an accepted fact of science" (Mitchell 2009, p. 20). For a number of years the topic of chaos has received enormous attention, and exceeds the limits of this chapter: Brock (1991), Ruelle (1991), Winnie (1992), Kellert (1993), Batterman (1993), Stewart (1993), etc. Regarding its relation to complexity, besides the book by Smith (1998), see Bertuglia and Vaio (2005), Strevens (2003), and Rosser (2011).

whole,[37] are very useful in facing the problems due to the complex framework and the complex dynamics. They can give us the ontological elements (parts or phenomena), epistemological components (causes), methodological requisites (processes valid for development) and logical aspects (reasons) that are relevant for foretelling events in the economic realm (e.g., about the future of the financial crisis).

To sum up, the evaluation of prediction in economics has followed in this chapter two main stages: (i) the analysis of the role of prediction as an instrument to evaluate *economic models*, where uncertainty has a relevant place; and (ii) the appraisal of economic prediction as *an outcome* to be assessed according to several criteria (mainly, accuracy and precision), and through the existence of different kinds of testing (in special in the sphere of experiments) to make that appraisal. These stages have been complemented by a philosophical reflection on the limits and obstacles of scientific prediction in economics, which completes the study made in Chaps. 10 and 11 on aims, processes, and results of economic predictions.

Analyzing the role of prediction as an instrument to evaluate economic models, this chapter has offered a set of indications on how economists do work on these kinds of methodological problems. They try to improve the economic models, using predictions to increase reliability (and not only credibility). They have a special interest in the evaluation of economic forecasts, seeking to diminish the margin of error. So they deal with the predictive outcomes used as a test to assess the quality of economic models. This involves the question of uncertainty—the lack of knowledge—which is a crucial issue when economic prediction is at stake.

It is forecast uncertainty that forces economists—in economic theory and in applied economics—to work with criteria such as "accuracy" and "precision." In this regard, calculation of predictable forecast uncertainty is not only useful from the point of view of description of economic activity but also has numerous uses in economic practice. This includes the combination of statements about the future and, prior to the realization of outcomes, an additional estimation that helps to increase the quality of the forecasts themselves and offers a clear picture of the expected range of likely outcomes.

By means of the criteria of appraisal of economic prediction (mainly, accuracy and precision), the predictive outcomes of the models may be improved. The analysis of predictive errors may eventually make it possible to get better predictions. In addition, it is possible to reach a diversity in kinds of testing for economic predictions, where econometrics highlights the use of simulations, in general, and computer simulations, in particular. The development of new kinds of testing (mainly in the area of experimentation) is useful in order to have more reliable predictions.

A central concern is that "forecasting is more difficult when variables move sharply relative to trend" (Burns 1986, p. 178). This emphasizes the connection between epistemological factors (knowledge of variables), ontological elements

[37] Herbert Simon gave a lot of attention to parsimonious factors. See, for example, Simon (2001b). From a different perspective, there is also an analysis of parsimony and predictive equivalence (Sober 1996).

(the variability itself of the economic activity), and methodological components (the process to deal with that variability). Each one has certain limits, which in recent decades have been analyzed using increasingly sophisticated mathematical tools in statistical economics and in econometrics. In spite of all these advancements and improvements, the existence of complexity of economic phenomena places serious epistemological and ontological obstacles for the aims, processes, and results of prediction in economics.

References

Abraham, B., and J. Ledolter. 1983/[2005]. *Statistical methods for forecasting*. New York: Wiley.

Ascher, W. 1978. *Forecasting: An appraisal for policy-makers and planners*. Baltimore: J. Hopkins University Press.

Batterman, R. W. 1993. Defining chaos. *Philosophy of Science* 60 (1): 43–66.

Bertuglia, C. S., and F. Vaio. 2005. *Nonlinearity, chaos and complexity. The dynamics of natural and social systems*. Oxford: Oxford University Press.

Blaug, M. 2002. Ugly currents in modern economics. In *Fact and fiction. Models, realism, and social construction,* ed. U. Mäki, 35–56. Cambridge: Cambridge University Press.

Boumans, M., and M. S. Morgan. 2001. *Ceteris paribus* conditions: Materiality and the application of economic theories. *Journal of Economic Methodology* 8 (1): 11–26.

Brock, W. A. 1991. Causality, chaos, explanation and prediction in economics and finance. In *Beyond belief. Randomness, prediction and explanation in science,* ed. J. L. Casti and A. Karlqvist, 230–279. Boca Raton: CRC Press.

Buck, R. C. 1963. Reflexive predictions. *Philosophy of Science* 30:359–369.

Burns, T. 1986. The interpretation and use of economic predictions. In *Predictability in science and society,* ed. J. Mason, P. Mathias, and J. H. Westcott, 103–125. London: The Royal Society and The British Academy.

Burns, T. 2001. The costs of forecast errors. In *Understanding economic forecasts*, ed. D. F. Hendry and N. R. Ericsson, 170–184. Cambridge: The MIT Press.

Clements, M. P., and D. F. Hendry. 1998. *Forecasting economic time series*. Cambridge: Cambridge University Press.

Clements, M. P., and D. F. Hendry. 1999. *Forecasting non-stationary economic time series*. Cambridge: The MIT Press.

Clements, M. P., and D. F. Hendry. 2002c. Explaining forecast failure in macroeconomics. In *A companion to economic forecasting,* ed. M. Clements and D. F. Hendry, 539–571. Oxford: Blackwell.

Coase, R. H. 1994a. The institutional structure of production. In *Essays on economics and economists,* ed. R. H. Coase, 3–14. Chicago: The University of Chicago Press.

Coase, R. H. 1994b. How should economists choose. In *Essays on economics and economists,* ed. R. H. Coase, 15–33. Chicago: The University of Chicago Press.

Dummett, M. 2004. *Truth and the past*. New York: Columbia University Press.

Ericsson, N. R. 2001. Forecast uncertainty in economic modeling. In *Understanding economic forecasts,* ed. D. F. Hendry and N. R. Ericsson, 68–92. Cambridge: The MIT Press.

Ericsson, N. R. 2002. Predictable uncertainty in economic forecasting. In *A companion to economic forecasting,* ed. M. Clements and D. F. Hendry, 19–44. Oxford: Blackwell.

Evans, M. K. 2013. *Practical business forecasting*. Oxford: Blackwell.

Fildes, R., and K. Ord. 2002. Forecasting competitions: Their role in improving forecasting practice and research. In *A companion to economic forecasting,* ed. M. Clements and D. F. Hendry, 322–353. Oxford: Blackwell.

Franses, Ph. H. 2006. Forecasting in marketing. In *Handbook of economic forecasting,* vol. 1, ed. G. Elliot, C. W. J. Granger, and A. Timmerman, 983–1012. Amsterdam: Elsevier.

Friedman, M. 1953. The methodology of positive economics. In *Essays in positive economics,* M. Friedman, 3–43. Chicago: University of Chicago Press (6th repr., 1969).

Gonzalez, W. J. 1996b. Prediction and mathematics: The Wittgensteinian approach. In *Spanish studies in the philosophy of science,* ed. G. Munevar, 299–332. Dordrecht: Kluwer.

Gonzalez, W. J. 2003d. Racionalidad y Economía: De la racionalidad de la Economía como Ciencia a la racionalidad de los agentes económicos. In *Racionalidad, historicidad y predicción en Herbert A. Simon,* ed. W. J. Gonzalez, 65–96. A Coruña: Netbiblo.

Gonzalez, W. J. 2007a. The role of experiments in the social sciences: The case of economics. In *General philosophy of science: Focal issues,* ed. T. Kuipers, 275–301. Amsterdam: Elsevier.

Gonzalez, W. J. 2010b. Recent approaches on observation and experimentation: A philosophical-methodological viewpoint. In *New methodological perspectives on observation and experimentation in science,* ed. W. J. Gonzalez, 9–48. A Coruña: Netbiblo.

Gonzalez, W. J. 2011a. Complexity in economics and prediction: The role of parsimonious factors. In *Explanation, prediction, and confirmation,* ed. D. Dieks, W. J. Gonzalez, S. Hartman, Th. Uebel, and M. Weber, 319–330. Dordrecht: Springer.

Gonzalez, W. J. 2012b. Methodological universalism in science and its limits: Imperialism versus complexity. In *Thinking about provincialism in thinking, Poznan Studies in the Philosophy of the Sciences and the Humanities,* vol. 100, ed. K. Brzechczyn and K. Paprzycka, 155–175. Amsterdam: Rodopi.

Granger, C. W. J. 2001. Evaluation of forecasts. In *Understanding economic forecasts,* ed. D. F. Hendry and N. R. Ericsson, 93–103. Cambridge: The MIT Press.

Granger, C. W. J. 2012. The philosophy of economic forecasting. In *Philosophy of economics,* ed. U. Mäki, 311–327. Amsterdam: Elsevier.

Granger, C. W. J., and M. J. Machina. 2006. Forecasting and decision theory. In *Handbook of economic forecasting,* vol. 1, ed. G. Elliot, C. W. J. Granger, and A. Timmerman, 81–98. Amsterdam: Elsevier.

Grünbaum, A. 1956. Historical determinism, social activism and predictions in the social sciences. *The British Journal for the Philosophy of Science* 7:236–240.

Grünbaum, A. 1963. Comments on Professor Roger Buck's paper "Reflexive predictions." *Philosophy of Science* 30:370–372.

Grunberg, E., and F. Modigliani. 1954. The predictability of social events. *Journal of Political Economy* 62:465–478.

Hahn, F. 1993. Predicting the economy. In *Predicting the future,* ed. L. Howe and A. Wain, 77–95. Cambridge: Cambridge University Press.

Hatch, N. 2001. Modeling and forecasting at the bank of England. In *Understanding economic forecasts,* ed. D. F. Hendry and N. R. Ericsson, 124–148. Cambridge: The MIT Press.

Hausman, D. M. 1997. Theory appraisal in neoclassical economics. *Journal of Economic Methodology* 4 (2): 289–296.

Hausman, D. M. 1998b. Confirming mainstream economic theory. *Theoria* 13 (2): 261–278.

Heiner, R. 1983. The origin of predictable behavior. *American Economic Review* 73:560–595.

Hendry, D. F. 1986. The role of prediction in evaluating economic models. In *Predictability in science and society,* ed. J. Mason, P. Mathias, and J. H. Westcott, 25–34. London: The Royal Society and The British Academy.

Hendry, D. F. 2000a. *Econometrics: Alchemy or science? Essays in econometric methodology (new ed.).* Oxford: Oxford University Press (1st ed., 1993).

Hendry, D. F., and N. R. Ericsson. 2001c. Epilogue. In *Understanding economic forecasts,* ed. D. F. Hendry and N. R. Ericsson, 185–191. Cambridge: The MIT Press.

Hoover, K. D. 2002. Econometrics and reality. In *Fact and fiction: Foundational issues on economics and the economy,* ed. U. Mäki, 152–177. Cambridge: Cambridge University Press.

Keating, G. 1985. *The production and use of economic forecasts.* London: Methuen.

Kellert, S. E. 1993. *In the wake of chaos. Unpredictable order in dynamical systems.* Chicago: University of Chicago Press.

Kennedy, P. 1998. *A guide to econometrics*. 4th ed. Cambridge: The MIT Press.
Llewellyn, J., S. Potter, and L. Samuelson. 1985. *Economic forecasting and policy-The international dimension*. London: Routledge and K. Paul.
Makridakis, S., S. C. Wheelwright, and R. J. Hyndman. 1998. *Forecasting: Methods and applications*. 3rd ed. Hoboken: Wiley.
Mariano, R. S. 2002. Testing forecast accuracy. In *A companion to economic forecasting,* ed. M. Clements and D. F. Hendry, 284–298. Oxford: Blackwell.
Mathies, B. P., and A. Diamantipoulos. 1994. Towards a taxonomy of forecast error measures. A factor-comparative investigation of forecast error dimensions. *Journal of Forecasting* 13:409–416.
McNees, S. K. 1989. Why do forecasts differ? *New England Economic Review* Jan/Feb:42–54.
McNees, S. K. 1992. The uses and abuses of "consensus" forecasts. *Journal of Forecasting* 11:703–710.
Mitchell, M. 2009. *Complexity: A guided tour*. Oxford: Oxford University Press.
Morgan, M. S. 1990. *The history of econometric ideas*. Cambridge: Cambridge University Press.
Musgrave, A. 1981. "Unreal assumptions" in economic theory: The F-Twist untwisted. *Kyklos* 34 (3): 377–387.
Nieto de Alba, U. 1998. *Historia del tiempo en Economía: Predicción, caos y complejidad.* Madrid: McGraw Hill.
Popper, K. R. 1957. *The poverty of historicism*. London: Routledge and K. Paul. (Reprinted by Routledge in 1991).
Radnitzky, G. 1978. The boundaries of science and technology. In *The search for absolute values in a changing world. Proceedings of the VIth International Conference on the Unity of Sciences*, vol. II, 1007–1036. New York: International Cultural Foundation Press.
Rescher, N. 1998. *Predicting the future: An introduction to the theory of forecasting*. Albany: State University of New York Press.
Romanos, G. 1973. Reflexive predictions. *Philosophy of Science* 40:97–109.
Rosenberg, A. 1992. *Economics-Mathematical politics or science of diminishing returns*? Chicago: The University of Chicago Press.
Rosenberg, A. 1993. Scientific innovation and the limits of social scientific prediction. *Synthese* 97:161–182.
Rosser, J. Barkley Jr. 1999. On the complexities of complex economic dynamics. *Journal of Economic Perspectives* 13 (4): 169–192.
Rosser, J. Barkley Jr. 2011. *Complex evolutionary dynamics in urban-regional and ecologic-economic systems: From catastrophe to chaos and beyond.* Dordrecht: Springer.
Ruelle, D. 1991. *Chance and chaos*. Princeton: Princeton University Press.
Salmon, W. C. 1981. Rational prediction. *The British Journal for the Philosophy of Science* 32:115–125. (Reprinted in Grünbaum, A. and W. C. Salmon, eds. 1988. *The limitations of deductivism,* 47–60. Berkeley: University of California Press).
Selten, R. 2003. Emergence and future of experimental economics. In *Observation and experiment in the natural and the social sciences,* ed. M. C. Galavotti, 63–70. Dordrecht: Kluwer.
Simon, H. A. 1989. The state of economic science. In *The state of economic science. Views of six Nobel laureates,* ed. W. Sichel, 97–110. Kalamazoo: W. E. Upjohn Institute for Employment Research.
Simon, H. A. 1998. Economics as a historical science. *Theoria* 13 (32): 241–260.
Simon, H. A. 2001b. Science Seeks Parsimony, not Simplicity: Searching for Pattern in Phenomena. In *Simplicity, inference and modelling. Keeping it sophisticatedly simple,* ed. Zellner, A., Keuzenkamp, H. A., and McAleer, M., 32–72. Cambridge: Cambridge University Press.
Smith, P. 1998. *Explaining chaos*. Cambridge: Cambridge University Press.
Sober, E. 1996. Parsimony and predictive equivalence. *Erkenntnis* 44:167–197.
Stewart, I. 1993. Chaos. In *Predicting the future,* ed. L. Howe and A. Wain, 24–51. Cambridge: Cambridge University Press.
Strevens, M. 2003. *Bigger than chaos: Understanding complexity through probability*. Cambridge: Harvard University Press.

Vetterling, M. K. 1976. More on reflexive predictions. *Philosophy of Science* 43:278–282.
West, K. D. 2006. Forecast evaluation. In *Handbook of economic forecasting,* Vol. 1, ed. G. Elliot, C. W. J. Granger, and A. Timmerman, 99–134. Amsterdam: Elsevier.
Winnie, J. A. 1992. Computable chaos. *Philosophy of Science* 59 (2): 263–275.
Wold, H. O. A. 1969. Econometrics as pioneering in non-experimental model building. *Econometrica* 37:369–381.
Worrall, J. 2001a. De la Matemática a la Ciencia: Continuidad y discontinuidad en el Pensamiento de Imre Lakatos. In *La Filosofía de Imre Lakatos: Evaluación de sus propuestas,* ed. W. J. Gonzalez, 107–128. Madrid: UNED.

Chapter 12
The Relation Between Prediction and Prescription in Economics

Prediction has a direct relation to prescription in economics as *applied science*, because this branch of economics is oriented towards a solution of concrete problems, and this aim requires practical patterns. In addition, the *application of economics* by the agents in the variable settings requires the anticipation of the possible future and a set of prescriptions. Thus, the implementation of economic planning, either in microeconomics or in macroeconomics, takes into account the knowledge of the future and the prescriptions available for the achievement of specific targets.

These relations between prediction and prescription in economics—mainly, as applied science—involve at least three philosophico-methodological facets: epistemological, methodological, and axiological (Gonzalez 1998b). First, prescription is initially an epistemological concept, insofar as it is the intellectual content of the practical patterns to solve concrete problems. Second, prediction is a methodological concept when it is related to the scientific progress in the realm of applied science. Third, prescription is always made according to some values (Sen 1986, p. 3), either in a implicit or an explicit way, which are related to aims, processes, or results (Gonzalez 2013a).

Consequently, this chapter offers a philosophico-methodological approach to prescription connected with prediction according to the three aspects pointed out. It emphasizes the link with the problem of science and values, because the axiology of research is not disconnected from methodology of science. This relation is particularly relevant in the case of economics (Gonzalez 2001a), especially if we accept that economics is not a mere "technique," in the sense of a completely neutral undertaking, but rather a human activity interwoven with other human activities (see Chap. 7). In addition, the epistemological and methodological analysis of prediction in economics—its characteristics and limits—made in the previous chapters of this book is assumed.

Following these lines, the analysis will follow several steps: (1) the study of the interdependence of prediction and prescription, taking into account two sides: (a) that prediction is used in applied economics as a guide in order to think out the patterns of the policy-making (i.e., prediction gives information about the future that is needed for economic prescriptions), and (b) prediction is an instrument for the implementation of the chosen policy-making, within the realm of the application of

W. J. Gonzalez, *Philosophico-Methodological Analysis of Prediction and its Role in Economics,* Theory and Decision Library A: 50, DOI 10.1007/978-3-319-08885-3_12

economics; (2) the transition for prediction as a test (basic science) to a guide for policy-making (applied science); (3) the insufficiency of prediction in economics and the need for prescription in applied economics; (4) the consideration of the possible primacy of prescription over prediction, instead of the mainstream option in economics in favor of the prevalence of prediction; (5) the connection between methodology of science and axiology of research in the case of prescription, insofar as prescription needs values to select the goals (and also the means to reach them); and (6) the importance of a more clear characterization of "prescription" in order to meet the needs of future developments in economics as a science, mainly as applied endeavor.

12.1 Interdependence Prediction–Prescription

Following the analysis made on prediction in the previous chapters, the focus can now go to the role of *prescription* in economics, emphasizing its relations with prediction. Thereafter, the philosophico-methodological attention will be on the analysis of the internal and external values of prescription. Thus, these pages deal with the *nexus* between prediction and prescription in economics, trying to show that the relation is *bi-directional* and emphasizing the relevance of accounting for this factor. In addition, there is a special interest in making explicit the presence of values—internal and external—in economic prescriptions, which reinforce the idea of economics as human activity.

1. "Bi-directional" highlights the correlation between prediction and prescription. On the one hand, the usefulness of forecasts for policy-making is clear, because the reliability of the information about the future is very important for decision-making[1] (i.e., what to do and how to do it). This is the case mainly in macroeconomics, as governments and central banks (Federal Reserve, European Central Bank, Bank of England, etc.) are well aware of. On the other hand, the institutions related with policy-making may adjust policy variables (such as interest rates and tax rates) that can affect the course of economy. "Policy shifts thus can alter economic forecasts, provided that the forecasting model incorporates the policy variables" (Turner 2001, p. 42).

2. There is also a special interest in this chapter in pointing out the links of both prediction and prescription—especially, the latter—with the specific values of "economic activity" and also the values of "economics as activity" (i.e., values of economic undertaking as an activity interconnected with others in the social context) (Chap. 7, Sect. 7.3). These values can be used to complete the image of

[1] The policy-maker "is not only likely to be concerned with forecast error *on average*, but also with the maximum size of error that he is liable to be faced with. Hence, the main emphasis is on the overall *range* of forecast error" (Llewellyn et al. 1985, p. 96). On prediction and decision-making in economics, see also Granger and Machina (2006). A philosophical reflection on predicting and deciding can be found in Pears (1964).

economics as applied science, because they are in place when the economic models are constructed or designed to resolve concrete economic problems. It is clear that "numerous decision-making approaches are designed explicitly to calculate optimal policy choices (e.g., in terms of investment levels, project or product selections, or scheduling) on the basis of specific goal criteria and various elements of technical input, including forecasts" (Ascher 1978, p. 17).

12.1.1 Prediction and Prescription as Interrelated in Economics

Within this general scope as an intellectual horizon, the emphasis here will be on the notions of "prediction" and "prescription" as interrelated both in macroeconomics and microeconomics (Gonzalez 1998b). Economic models can be oriented towards descriptive aims, but also—and very frequently—to prescriptive ("normative" in the broad sense)[2] purposes. This feature is undeniable in economic forecasts when they search for accuracy and precision, because many times this is done in order to be used for policy-making. In this context, it is clear that "economic forecasting is not, generally, an end in itself. It is rather an input—an aid to those who make economic decisions, whether in the private or public sector. The value and usefulness of a forecast therefore depends fundamentally on the extent to which contributes constructively to that end" (Llewellyn et al. 1985, p. 93).

Moreover, economic models are not only prepared to "represent" or "resemble" real events,[3] but also to "construct" or "design" an ideal future outcome which needs to be considered for policy-making. This second kind of model is used in applied economics, and it is designed for introducing prescriptions related to future outcomes. Thus, predictive economic models made in econometrics are frequently accompanied by prescriptions for policy purposes. To put it differently: the possible scenarios—prediction—are followed by indications on how to deal with them (prescription).

Nevertheless, the operation of *policy rules* is sometimes put forward as the alternative to prediction. This idea of policy without predictions may be an attractive prospect but it is impractical. "In practice, the operation of policy rules themselves will involve the use of predictions. Even apparently straightforward policy rules, such as balanced budgets or monetary targets, require a considerable amount of technical expertise for their successful implementation. If the necessary predictions are not made in a systematic manner, they will simply be done in an *ad hoc* manner. The strength of model based predictions is that they bring consistency and attention to detail. It is likely that the operation of economic policy of any kind

[2] "Normative" is used here as opposite to "descriptive," but in economics these "norms" are—in principle—more flexible than in other sciences.

[3] On the philosophico-methodological issues related to representation and models in science, see Gonzalez (2014).

can be improved by the use of systematic model-based forecasts" (Burns 1986, pp. 117–118).[4]

However, it is difficult to find a clear *definition* of "prescription" in economics in the papers of influential economists (including those awarded the Nobel Prize) or among those authors who develop the philosophy and methodology of this science, even though there is a very interesting approach developed by Simon (1990a, 2002). Nevertheless, it is easy to put forward arguments in favor of economic prescription. In fact, even the staunchest defender of the predictivist thesis—Friedman—acknowledges such a necessity, but he seems to subordinate prescription to prediction, because he considers that normative economics "cannot be independent of positive economics. Any policy conclusion necessarily rests on a prediction about the consequences of doing one thing rather than another, a prediction that must be based—implicitly or explicitly—on positive economics" (1953, p. 5).

12.1.2 The Interdependence and the Distinction "Descriptive" versus "Normative"

Clearly, there is interdependence between "prediction" and "prescription." This characteristic can be seen in the context of the distinction between "descriptive" (positive) economics and "normative" (applied) economics. In this regard, normative economics is concerned with *ought to be*, but it is not totally independent of positive economics (Friedman 1953, p. 5). At first sight, the "positive"–"normative" distinction might appear to correlate a demarcation criterion between science and pseudo-science. But this is not the case, because positive and normative aspects of economics are frequently interrelated.

Normative economics is concerned with "ought to be" when we want to make "normative" judgments as to the most appropriate economic policy to pursue, even though such judgments will always be underpinned by positive economics. "Friedman's advocacy of strict monetary control is a good example of this and he argues, normatively, that monetary authorities ought to control the rate of growth of the money supply if they wish to control inflation. However, such advice, as far as Friedman is concerned, is founded upon positive economics which has 'established' the primacy of money supply increases in 'causing' inflation" (Pheby 1988, p. 85).

Hence, it is hard to imagine the analysis of economic policy without models with prediction and prescription (which can lead to planning, in the short, middle, or long run). Again, methodological criteria of evaluation, such as accuracy and precision, have an enormous importance here, as can be seen in macroeconomics, in general, and in international trade, in particular (e.g., in the case of oil prices). "Policy-makers need to know how dependable forecasts are—what degree of reliance it is appropriate to place upon them. Furthermore, it is necessary for forecasters to know

[4] In addition, "political and social changes taking place *pari passu* with developments in political economy must have affected the way political economy is interpreted" (Sen 1983, p. 95).

how much weight they should place on the accuracy of various forecast components when advising policy-makers" (Llewellyn et al. 1985, p. 94).

Methodologically, this is the terrain of prediction as a guide for policy making, first, and as an instrument for implementing it, later on. The sphere of what *ought to be done* in order to solve a specific problem (such as inflation, unemployment, deficit, etc.), due to the knowledge available about the possible future (applied economics), is different from what the agents (in business firms, in public organizations, or governmental agencies) *actually do* in the diverse historical settings available (regions, countries or continents), when they are using the knowledge to implement such solutions in those social environments (application of science).

Thus, even though these agents—in their various levels: firms, organizations, and governments—might share basically the same predictive content (i.e., the "descriptive" component about the future) and have received—to some extent—similar prescriptions (i.e., the "normative" facet of economics), they might end up proposing quite different applications of economics. This has been the case during the years of the ongoing economics crisis (especially from the summer of 2008 to 2013), both in microeconomics and in macroeconomics (including the bailouts of banks and countries of the Western economies).

12.2 From Prediction as a Test to a Guide for Policy-making

Underlying the present analysis, we can see that there are three fundamental uses of prediction in the social sciences, in general, and in economics, in particular: (i) as a *tool for testing theories*, in general, and hypotheses, in particular; (ii) as a *guide for the patterns of policy-making* (i.e., knowledge for the orientation of the solutions to practical problems); and (iii) as an *instrument for the implementation of the actual public policy* (i.e., the direction of human actions in the social world, which includes the knowledge regarding political economy). In this book the attention has been many times on the first case, where the methodological character is emphasized.[5] The focus has been on scientific progress (connected to autonomy, critical attitude, and objectivity) as well as on the criterion of reasonability in the process of making predictions and the success in the results predicted.

But there is also another important use of prediction: to be *a guide to shed light on the patterns* for policy-making. "There are an enormous number of economic policy issues that require a forecast. For example, the effects of changes in taxes and tariffs upon output and employment, the impact of legislation relating to retirement

[5] Frequently, the first use of prediction in the social sciences has received more attention than the other two. But Kaplan long recognized that "since events occurring at the human level are essentially the products of human effort and experience, it is reasonable to suppose that greater predictability in the social sciences will enhance man's control over his destiny as a social being" (1940, p. 492).

incomes upon savings behavior, questions relating to variations in regional growth rates and even the setting of greenhouse emission targets. This diversity is naturally associated with a corresponding diversity in what is forecast, the interval of time between which successive forecasts and the policy-makers, and the forecasting methods are deemed to be most suitable" (Pagan and Robertson 2002, p. 152).

In this sphere of applied economics, when economic prescriptions are at stake, there is an *institutional component* to use economic predictions for policy-making. Thus, "the prominence and acceptability of a forecast (…) depend in large part on the prominence and acceptability of the programs, procedures, and institutions that serves as their 'vehicles'. That is, the medium strongly influences the impact of the message" (Ascher 1978, p. 36). Consequently, there is a connection between the intellectual content of the prediction and the context where it is produced.

12.2.1 The Use of Prediction for Public Policy

From a methodological point of view, the use of prediction for public policy basically follows a process which might be summarized "as comprising of four elements: 1 A series of models or methods that are used to produce short-run (1–2 quarter ahead) forecasts. 2 A relatively small core model that produces forecasts of major aggregates of interest over a 1-3 year horizon. 3 A method for disaggregating the aggregated forecasts from the core model so as to utilize the insights of sector specialists. 4 A collection of auxiliary models that are designed to provide information about policy actions (such as policy simulations), or yield information relating to forecasts which are hard to analyze with the core model (such as the effects of unusual events). These elements are part of most of the forecasting systems we study although the emphasis given to each differs across institutions" (Pagan and Robertson 2002, p. 163).

This use of prediction for public policy highlights an additional aspect of prediction in social sciences (especially in economics): the direct repercussion in the sphere of social actions. It is a more practical case than the previous use of prediction, and in this sphere predicting is commonly heavily dependent on mathematical tools (statistical economics and econometrics). This is the field of applied economics, which has direct consequences for political economy—the implementation of economics—in its different levels (macroeconomics and microeconomics). But the uses of prediction as a tool for testing theories and as a guide for public policy need to take into account the preconditions of predictability, which include the problem of the regularity in human affairs (Chap. 10, Sect. 10.2.1; cf. Rescher 1998, p. 86).

Regularities in human and social affairs can be of different kinds. According to Simon, there "appear to be two quite distinct sorts of regularity in human affairs—the one represented by prediction of the arrival of a train, the other represented by prediction of the number of people who will die in auto accidents over Labor Day weekend. The latter depends, in one form of another, upon the law of large numbers; the former, upon a strict determination of behavior by program" (1958/1982, p. 390).

The existence of social regularities is indispensable for social life (in business firms, banks, international trade, public transportation, maritime traffic, etc.), and they could sometimes be more reliable than natural events.[6] But the regularities do not belong only to the camp of the sources for predictability: they can also be found in the effects of social predictions, such as the events known as *bandwagon effect* and *underdog effect* after a prediction has been published (Simon 1954).

Concerning this controversial issue of the effects of social predictions,[7] Herbert Simon has defended that "it is always possible in principle to take account of reactions to a publish prediction in such as a way that the prediction will be confirmed by the event" (Simon 1954/1957, p. 84). Thus, the "correct prediction requires at least some knowledge of the reaction function" (Simon 1954/1957, p. 87). In this regard, it is the case that there is special interest in the "bandwagon effect" (an announcement of a forecast positively influences the behavior of those concerned), in order to include it in the predictive model.[8]

In economics the uses of prediction as a test and a guide for patterns of policy-making are linked with two kinds of economic models ("representations" and "constructions"), which are connected to the distinction between "positive" economics and "normative" economics: the first type seeks a good resemblance of economic events, whereas the second is oriented towards generating forecasts under alternative policy regimes (Turner 2001, p. 44). Thus, there is an underlying methodological difference between both uses. In this regard, it is important to emphasize that what the methodological role of prediction in economics *is* and *ought to be* depends on the reality itself that is predicted. That reality comes from human actions in a social and artificial setting, which involves qualitative factors (such as those related to well-being or social security).

12.2.2 Quantitative and Qualitative Considerations

If the attention goes to the reality, then economic predictions should take into account quantitative and qualitative considerations in order to be *reliable* and *credible* (even though many times this is developed under the sphere of judgmental predictions, which are commonly less rigorous than other kinds of predictions). Moreover, it seems clear that, besides the quantitative predictions produced by mathematical calculations, economics needs qualitative predictions that have a repercussion on policy-making (mainly, in welfare economics). Both—quantitative and qualitative—can predict the *objective* aspects of economic reality (i.e., the observable

[6] In my conversations with Herbert Simon, he insisted several times on this idea: some social events (e.g., public transportation) can have a very strong regularity.

[7] According to Granger, economic forecasters can potentially have the ability to influence the actual economy "if the forecaster is particularly accomplished and has a previous good performance record" (Granger 2012, p. 326).

[8] "Provided that the response to the announcement varies continuously as the announcement alters, such a bandwagon effect could be in principle incorporated into the forecast" (Turner 2001, p. 34).

actions of economic actors and economic markets rather than the mental acts or *we-intentions*) (cf. Chap. 7).

By pursuing this perspective, which is mainly epistemological and methodological, it becomes easier to understand some views in economic theory: Friedman's emphasis on the objective dimension of the phenomena studied by economics, Hick's comparison with physics (which is usually considered much more objective than economics), Buchanan's distinction between subjective (non-predictive) and objective (predictive) economics, or Simon's concern for the lack of realism in economic assumptions and the insistence on the need for empirical grounding (Gonzalez 2006b). Even though they have different methodological approaches, they want—in one way or another—to guarantee *objectivity* in economics by linking prediction with objective knowledge. Moreover, it seems that all of them agree in something basic: only an objective science could be predictive, and this affects prescriptions, because the latter are usually connected with the former.

Many times the requirement of objectivity appears in a narrow sense, frequently connected only with quantitative predictions. However, according to the alternative based on the analysis of economic activity, one should recognize the existence of qualitative predictions in economics (and in the social sciences, in general) that complement the quantitative ones. They exist *de facto* in economics and they ought to be in this science,[9] insofar as economics works on economic actions which include qualitative factors differing in nature from those present in physics (and in the natural sciences, in general).

Taking into account these factors, predicting is as a complex task, especially when predictions are elaborated as bases for prescriptions for problem solving (i.e., the solution of concrete problems, either in macroeconomics or in microeconomics). The methodology of economic predictions needs to consider many elements: some come out of economic history,[10] because prediction cannot be detached from what has happened in the past (e.g., the econometric models are generally "backward-looking") (Redman 1989, p. 141; Streissler 1970, p. 18); and others come from theory, where economic agents and institutions are hypothesized to interact in a specific way. Both perspectives have their roots in the economic movements that arise from the actions of members of the society and their interaction. So, even when economic magnitudes are interconnected and have properties of their own, economic predictions depend on human factors that generate them and constitute the final source of its complexity.

Human factors are methodologically relevant when the problem of relation between theory and practice arises. As Sen—Nobel Prize winner in 1998—has pointed out, "economic magnitudes are ultimately social magnitudes, and variables like prices, investments, consumption, money supplies and so forth do not, naturally, move on their own, untouched by human volition. To go no further than studying

[9] The characteristics of *qualitative* predictions can be found in Chap. 2, Sect. 2.3.

[10] "A deep knowledge of the nature of (…) particular statistics as well as a grasp of the lessons of economic history is incredible important to being a successful forecaster for policy-makers" (Pagan and Robertson 2002, p. 153).

these aggregate macroeconomic magnitudes is to abstract from perhaps the most fundamental aspect of the social reality, namely the rich and inseparable relations between the society and the individual. One cannot ultimately understand movements of these macroeconomic magnitudes without taking note of the objectives, knowledge, reasoning and decisions of the members of the society" (Sen 1986, p. 14). In fact, economic activity depends not only on economic motivations, but also on non-economic ones. So, besides the profit-motive, there are other kinds of motivations, such as status, prestige or power (Simon 1963a/1982, pp. 331–332).

Methodologically, economists use "prediction" as a means of *testing hypotheses* and as a guide for political economy (e.g., ideas for planning, which eventually will be implemented). The first aim is widespread in the profession, but some economists (mainly of the Austrian school) criticize it. Among their reasons are, on the one hand, the argument that such testing is unnecessary, since the only way a false conclusion (prediction) can be generated in a system in which consequences are deduced from *a priori* premises is if a mistake is made in the verbal chain of logic leading from premises to conclusions; and, on the other hand, the predictions in the theories are unfalsifiable: it is senseless to try to falsify economic theories, because there are no "constants" in the social world similar to those encountered in the natural sciences (Caldwell 1982, p. 123).

These objections by some Austrians cannot get away from the necessity of checking if the economic predictions have support in the available evidence in order to develop our knowledge of economic reality; and the absence of "constants" similar to the natural world does not impede the existence of social regularities (among them, the economic ones) which could be systematically studied. Moreover, without social regularities, human society would be on the verge of collapse, because many ordinary economic activities (e.g., bank accounts, credit cards, mortgages, investments, etc.) are based on assumed regularities.

Certainly, the task of testing hypotheses by comparing their predictions with the data is an important one. Its contribution to progress in science depends directly on how this activity is understood. It requires a clear notion of what is the real content of predictions. The differences between "foresight," "prediction," and "forecast" (which contribute to "planning"), relevant from semantic and epistemological perspectives, can throw light on the methodological task. This study is incomplete if it only analyzes how economics progresses *de facto*, because, in principle, the methodology of science has a further aim: it seeks to give prescriptions about how economics *ought to be* developed (cf. Chap. 1, Sect. 1.1.1).

There is a clear risk in the task of converting prediction into a mere "technique" by emphasizing the perspective of mathematical calculus. In that case, prediction would occupy a place outside the core of science, insofar as it could be understood as an "extrinsic" application of science rather than a kernel of it. But this conception of prediction as a mere "extrinsic" tool of science is somehow reductionist, because, as it has been pointed out, *calculus* makes no predictions, but by means of it is possible to make predictions (Gonzalez 1996b). In this regard, it should be considered that economic predictions have aims, are made through processes and lead to results, and so they can be assessed from these three perspectives (Chaps. 10 and 11).

Moreover, the role of mathematics in science, in general, and in economics, in particular, is basically instrumental (although in different ways: to fix knowledge and to offer a heuristic device), and it has clear bounds from the theoretical point of view (as it happens in econometrics). (a) Both the "logic of discovery" and the "psychology of invention" prevent us from seeing mathematics as all-embracing, in spite of its very relevant role in the construction of hypotheses and in testing them. (b) Predictions in economics are not inseparably associated with mathematics, insofar as it could be possible to have qualitative predictions.[11] Nevertheless, mathematics are indispensable in cases such as forecasting, which necessarily includes the margin of error, and quantitative predictions.

12.3 Insufficiency of Prediction and the Need for Prescription

To circumscribe economics to the predictive task would be an unnecessary limitation, because prediction does not cover the whole field (Gonzalez 1998b, Sect. 2). In effect, as Sen has pointed out, "prediction is not the only exercise with which economics is concerned. Prescription has always been one of the major activities in economics, and it is natural that this should have been the case. Even the origin of the subject of political economy, of which economics is the modern version, was clearly related to the need for advice on what is to be done in economic matters. Any prescriptive activity must, of course, go well beyond pure prediction, because no prescription can be made without evaluation and an assessment of the good and the bad" (Sen 1986, p. 3).

Along with this objection, it is possible to add another regarding the criterion itself chosen by Friedman—that of *success* in predicting—because a very frequent criticism of economic predictions is their unreliability. Thus, what has been predicted by the economists should be compared with what actually happens (i.e., what is achieved by evidence). And, in consonance with the results obtained by this instrument, it is possible to argue in the way which "Professor R. Clower has written: 'If successful prediction were the sole criterion of a science, economics should long have ceased to exist as a serious intellectual pursuit'" (Hutchison 1977, p. 12). Consequently, the methodological instrumentalism of the predictivist thesis is indeed very problematic, as pointed out in different ways in this book.

Sen has emphasized that some of economics is *de facto* concerned with "evaluation as such, without being explicitly involved with either prescription or prediction. For example, in examining whether the British standard of living has been rising or falling over the last few years, the object of enquiry is assessment of what has been

[11] "The non-quantitative macroeconomic forecasting techniques are primarily concerned with predicting whether a cyclical turn will occur. Since the process of detecting business cycle changes is different from making quantitative predictions, forecasting methods based on indicators were designed to recognize and predict turning points" (Stekler 1991, p. 376).

happening, without being directly concerned with predicting what will happen, or prescribing what should be done. Other economic exercises are concerned with more clearly descriptive problems, e.g., measurement of the extent of unemployment, or construction of an index of inflation. Although implicit value elements may be present in these exercises, the primary purpose is to describe what has been happening in a way that relates to our interest in the matter. Any act of description does, of course, involve choice, but that does not make the act of description necessarily prescriptive or predictive" (Sen 1986, p. 3, cf. Sen 1980).[12]

On the one hand, it seems rather obvious that neither prediction, nor prescription can seek to cover the economic field as a whole. (i) In the "descriptive" sphere there are other methodological processes, such as scientific explanation—the response to a why question which includes accommodation to the available data—or understanding (in the sense used by Simon and Coase: to grasp the relevant elements of the decision-making in organizations and the structural elements of institutions) (cf. Gonzalez 1998b), where explanation is asymmetric regarding to scientific prediction (Chap. 2, Sect. 2.1), and understanding is seen as previous and more important than prediction in some cases (e.g., in the business firms as economic organizations). (ii) The "normative" domain cannot be filled completely by prescriptions, insofar as prescriptions are made after an evaluation of the goals to be achieved by them.

However, on the other hand, Sen's analysis is, in this case, philosophically messy, insofar as it contains two inaccuracies. (a) It is clear that "description" is semantically, epistemologically, and methodologically different from "prescription." From that point of view, an act of description never can be prescriptive in any relevant sense. (b) It happens that prediction has its roots in the descriptive realm but can also be used in a prescriptive context. Thus, there is an interdependence between prediction and prescription as applied economics shows everyday (e.g., in national economy to diminish the level of unemployment or to control inflation).

Evaluation has its environment in the axiology of research, because it is related to values to be used for the assessment. The combination of axiology of research with methodology of science can give reasons to recognize that mainstream economics has overemphasized the role of prediction. Moreover, the insistence on the predictive character of economic theory as a guarantee of its scientific make-up raises some clear problems, which are not concerned only with economics but also with other sciences. In effect, it is not always the case that the *predictive success* is a sufficient guarantee for having genuine "science."[13]

In this regard, Uskali Mäki has pointed out that "a classical example of this is, in the sixteenth century, the predictive superiority of Ptolemaic geocentric astronomy over its young challenger, Copernican heliocentrism, even though the latter was decisively closer to revealing the fundamental structure of the planetary system. The

---

[12] His position is not accurate from the point of view that it seems clear that "description" is quite different from "prescription" and that prediction has its roots in the descriptive realm although it can be used in a prescriptive context.

[13] On the characteristics of a science, cf. Chap. 2, Sect. 2.2.1.

difference between Copernican theory and economics, however, is that the former has indicated predictive progress, while the occurrence of such progress is controversial in the case of economics" (1994, p. 254).[14] The evaluation of economic theories should not be reduced to its mere predictive capabilities, because there are other aspects that must be taken into account, among them, prescription.

12.4 From the Predictivist Instrumentalism to the Possible Primacy of Prescription

Taking an opposing line to Friedman's predictivist methodological instrumentalism, important economists—among them, Simon (1963b) and Coase (1994a)—have adopted a critical attitude towards the primacy of success in prediction, stressing instead the "understanding" of economic processes (in social organizations and economic institutions). Furthermore, this is in tune with other economists, such as Paul Samuelson (1963, 1964, 1965a, and 1965b), Nobel Prize in 1970. Simon has criticized the absence of the realism of assumptions of the instrumentalist approach. His methodological position chooses ways that are different from Friedman's, insofar as Simon's insistence is on an economics empirically grounded and sees *prescription* as more relevant than prediction.

On the one hand, Simon considers that prediction is neither the single aim of economics nor the main task of this science (1989); and, on the other, he seems to give more importance to prescription than to prediction, insofar as the predictive analysis *serves* the prescriptive endeavor: "we construct and run models because we want to understand the consequences of taking one decision or another. Predictive models are only a special case where we seek to predict events we cannot control in order to adapt to them better. We do not expect to change the weather, but we can take steps to moderate its effects. We predict populations so that we can plan to meet their needs for food and education. We predict business cycles in order to plan our investments and production levels" (Simon 1990a, pp. 10–11; see also Simon 2002).

For Simon, in both cases—prediction and prescription—a good *understanding* of steady states can be more important than drawing time series, either predictive or prescriptive ones, and this affects microeconomics as well as macroeconomics. In addition, he sees that, in several cases, such as *models of competitive, confrontational situations*, or in *other models of international relations*, prediction seems

[14] Before the publication of Thomas Kuhn's methodological essays, the insistence on prediction as an evaluative criterion was common among economists: "an emphasis on prediction as the criterion by which to evaluate economic theories was also characteristic of the group of economists centred on [R. G.] Lipsey and [G. C.] Archibald working at the LSE around 1960. Their aims were the quantification and the testing of economic theory. As with the economists just mentioned, they started with a view of the nature of science, which was assumed to apply with minimal modifications (greater reliance on the law of large numbers) to economics (see Lipsey 1963: ch. 1)" (Backhouse 1994b, p. 183).

unfeasible: "it may be impossible to obtain answers to our predictive questions, and we may be well advised to ask a different set of questions instead" (Simon 1990a, p. 10).

Accordingly, Simon seems to change Friedman's priorities: on the one hand, economics can be tested by a judgment on the *correction of the assumptions*, instead of examining it through the probation of the empirical correctness of its predictions; and, on the other, the elaboration of models of complex systems is generally to *serve the policy* (Simon 1990a, p. 10), because he seeks the adaptation of economic behavior, which is a task of economic planning. Hence, Simon combines insistence on the attention to the *facts*,[15] beginning with the understanding of human behavior in the decision-making, and the existence of *specific goals* when the models of complex systems are built (Simon 1990a, p. 7).

In this regard, it is striking that an author so deeply involved in the theory of decision-making in the economic sphere (especially, in economic organizations) as Simon only takes into account, *de facto*, instrumental rationality.[16] Thus, due to his avoiding a *rationality of ends* (or evaluative rationality), the economic prescription seems in a precarious situation, since it requires a *delimitation of aims* according to rational criteria. In other words, prescription needs evaluative rationality to assess the ends or goals to be achieved.[17]

Simon keeps his distance towards the purely mathematical views, either from statistical economics or from econometrics: "when our goal is prescription rather than prediction, then we can no longer take it for granted that what we want to compute are time series" (Simon 1990a, p. 11). And he seeks to *prescribe* human economic behavior, but not by means of a deductive inference from a small group of premises: "our practical concern in planning for the future is what we must do *now* to bring that future about. We use our future goals to detect what may be irreversible present actions that we must avoid, and to disclose gaps in our knowledge (…) that must be closed soon so that choices may be made later. Our decisions today require us to know our goals, but not the exact path along which we will reach them" (Simon 1990a, p. 11).

Again the problem of the *nature* itself of economics appears here. In this regard, for many economists, Lionel Robbins's idea of economics as the science that studies human behavior as a relation between ends and scarce means with alternative uses is still in good shape (1935, p. 16). As Coase, Nobel Prize winner in economics (1991), maintains: Robbins's conception makes economics the science of human choices, even though most of economists restrict their work to a set of options

[15] "The faith in *a priori* theory, uncontaminated by empirical observations, has been weakened—even among 'rational expectationists'. More and more economists are beginning to look for the facts they need in actual observation of business decision making and in laboratory experiments on economic markets and organizations" (Simon 1992a, p. 7).

[16] "We see that reason is wholly instrumental. It cannot tell us where to go; at best it can tell us how to get there. It is a gun for hire that can be employed in the service of whatever goals we have, good or bad" (Simon 1983, pp. 7–8). Cf. Gonzalez (1997b).

[17] On evaluative rationality, cf. Rescher (1988, 1999a). On the case of rationality of ends and Simon, cf. Gonzalez (2003d), esp., pp. 79–83.

narrower than that suggested by that view (Coase 1988, Chap. 1). Thus, although that position leads to our carrying out a major relation of economics to *prescriptions* (which are a direct fruit of the decisions on choices), it seems that in economics the epistemic interest in favor of prediction prevails more than the practical dimension oriented to establish prescriptions.

When prescription predominates, there is a methodological shift in comparison with prediction, because prescription requires a methodological framework of an *imperative-hypothetical* kind, whereas prediction is usually within a hypothetical–deductive structure. In effect, prescribing needs to indicate an end to be achieved, and this aim demands the adoption of several means which should be used, otherwise the action which has been made cannot be considered as *rational.* The hypothetical imperatives seek to guide the economic activity and, hence, to orientate the decisions that have been taken—the choices made—to implement the adequate means of obtaining the ends sought. An important problem arises when the goal to be achieved is no longer available, due to some important changes that have led to consequences that were not predicted.

Through the incorporation of imperative-hypothetical methods, it may be an interwoven between the prescriptive facet of economics (which is then an applied science) and the normative character of social technology (an endeavor oriented towards transformation of reality). Applied science seeks the solution to practical problems, taking into account aims, processes, and results. Meanwhile technology is innovative when it is oriented towards certain *ends* (objectives) and considers that some *means* (operations developed through human undertakings) should be used, otherwise it would not be a rational technological behavior (Gonzalez 1997a, esp., pp. 263–264).

Technology is *conceptually different* from science insofar as it develops a creative transformation of the reality (natural, social, or artificial) which eventually gives a product or artifact. Technology uses scientific knowledge (know that), specific technological knowledge (know how) and evaluative knowledge (know whether) when it makes the *active transformation* of the reality (Gonzalez 2013c). It is clearly teleological: technology acts by pursuing some previously chosen ends and also selected specific means, which transform the reality available (Gonzalez 2005, esp., pp. 8–13). Thus, a *social technology* based on economics follows a planning, which requires the input of applied economics to give prescriptions that can be used to transform an economic reality (e.g., in social technologies of central planning). Besides knowledge, the social technology also involves an undertaking and a final outcome that should be tangible.

Therefore, prescriptions of economics can be connected with social technologies, either of a *piecemeal* kind—such as that proposed by K. Popper (1957)—or of a holistic class, such as the technologies for emancipation of the Frankfurt school. The nexus between both—applied economics and social technology—could be *planning*, which leads to making the prescriptive criteria to direct the economic agency in a specific direction operative. Both—the applied science of prescriptive economics and the social technology chosen—could be seen as *ontologically different* but *causally interdependent*, and their limits would be drawn, basically, by extrinsic evaluations (in principle, ethical, social, and political).[18]

12.5 Economic Prescription and Values

From the point of view of the scientific character of economics, a difficulty arises when prescription prevails (i.e., the normative dimension of economics, which is more connected to *evaluations* than to predictions), because it can introduce the "value judgments" in economics. In this issue, as Oskar Morgenstern has suggested, "economists have been admonished time and time again to leave their political and other value judgements out of their theories and outside their classrooms or, at least, to make it clear when they speak as scientists, and when as citizens, politicians, religious persons, etc. This advice is well taken and should be scrupulously followed, no matter how difficult" (1972, p. 711).

It seems clear that the advice was given in order to preserve the search for objectivity in economics, in tune with some views already analyzed in the methodological controversy *Erklären–Verstehen* (Chap. 5, Sect. 5.1). But epistemological objectivity is compatible with an axiology of research and, then, with the acceptance of values that can guide the methodology of economics [where the ethical values can have a role as well, especially in the case of the processes of prediction (Granger 2012, p. 326)].[19] From this perspective, the analysis requires taking into account the axiological context of prescription as well as the internal and external values of prescription.

12.5.1 The Axiological Context of Prescription

When the problem of *values in* science is studied rather than the *evaluations on* science, the issue is not merely a discussion of the personal, subjective difficulties, in separating his or her scientific attitude from the influences shaping his or her value judgments (Morgenstern 1972, p. 711). Nowadays it seems clear that there are values in scientific *activity*. And, in the present case—the science of economics—it is easy to appreciate that *prescription* deals with values in a more explicit manner than prediction. Moreover, prescription involves values in a dual form: internal (endogenous) and external (exogenous).

(a) There are *internal* values, which can be cognitive values—those of a neatly economic character—or methodological values (the sphere of the "economy of research"). Most of them usually evolve around the cost-benefit ratio. (b) There is a

[18] From a general point of view, this problem is studied in Niiniluoto (1993, 1997a, 1997b).

[19] Ethical values are a special kind of values. On the ethical values in science, in general, see Rescher (1999a) and Gonzalez (1999a). Regarding ethical values in positive economics and normative economics, see Gonzalez (2013a), pp. 1513–1516.

set of *external* values, especially social values (those related to the nexus between that activity and other human activities that have economic incidence) and political values (criteria of preference for practical actions regarding economics, which lead to priorities for ends and means). Both are particularly influential in the decision-making process regarding the aims to be obtained and the ways to achieve them.

Concerning economic prescriptions and their planning in time (mainly, the short, medium, and long run), these external values are not unfamiliar to the diverse factors which influence the economy as an activity interconnected with others in many ways (such as cultural, ecological, sociological, esthetical, etc.). This vision puts aside the perspective of economics as a completely autonomous activity (or even as isolated from the others) which would be entirely predictable (and, hence, easy for prescriptions). Even in the sphere of the reductive proposal, the analysis cannot be limited to the criteria such as the maximization of the subjective expected utility and some forms of cooperation, because the study of economic activity should be open to criteria of altruism (see Kitcher 2010; Schefczyk and Peacock 2010) and solidarity (see Selten and Ockenfels 1998).

Undoubtedly, values can have a link to reality, because they require some kind of support, either in human needs or in optional facets (Rescher 1999a). Values are not merely what we actually prefer as worthy; they are also what should be preferable for us. Economic values can be related to the economic reality as well as to human possibilities. In this regard, economics has a double side as human activity: (i) as an activity regulated by its own rules—*economic activity*—and, (ii) as an activity among others—*economics as activity*—interconnected therefore with other activities (social, political, etc.). This includes that we are assuming that there are or can be internal as well as external *values* in economics. In addition, economic values are related to the present, but they are also open to the future.

Consequently, instead of a human ongoing marked by variables which are totally quantifiable and mathematically expressible, from which the most strict econometric rigor can follow,[20] we have a human undertaking where the economic aggregates do not move on their own, untouched by the human agents. Hence, the presence of qualitative elements in economic models (Turner 2001, p. 46)—as happens in welfare economics—or the existence of cultural and social factors (such as in Germany and the mentality of saving or in Japan with the loyalty to the firm) mean that the prescriptions cannot be guided by purely econometric patterns which only have internal variables of the economic process.

This assumption of values in economics is a turn with respect to an influential tendency in methodology of economics, defended among others by Josep Schumpeter and Robert Solow (Nobel Prize in 1987), which insist on the methodological line of a *value-free* discipline. In this approach, economics (and other social sciences) has no more connection with values than any other science which studies nature. The difference would be in the level of repercussion, which is greater in economics than other fields insofar as it has influence in the actual policy, because normative economics provides the information relevant for political activity.

[20] On the different econometric conceptions, in general, and on the determinist position, in particular, cf. Morgan (1990).

Against this conception there are, nowadays, several philosophers of economics, such as Hausman and McPherson (1994, 1996),[21] who have pointed out the limitations accompanying this view of normative economics which converts it into "purely technical" or of a technological character: a mere practical knowledge which should be implemented in the domain of political economics. This axiologically neutral approach does not fit the actual configuration of applied economics, if it is thought of in terms of rationality (Gonzalez 2013a). In addition, it is incompatible with the attempts to take into account serious ethical aspects, such as altruism or solidarity.

Both authors think that the influence of social theorists, especially the economists, goes beyond the mere providing of "technical" knowledge to those who make the decisions, experts who had formulated the aims previously (Hausman and McPherson 1996). They consider that economists also intervene in (or help in the task of) *determining the goals* to be achieved. Thus, the picture of the economist as a mere supplier of technical or specific information does not match the fact, present in the last two centuries, of social philosophers who have found in economic theory ideas for their social design.

Underneath the economic prescriptions there are—in my judgment—a set of issues on the existence of an *evaluative rationality* with respect to ends; a rationality different from the instrumental rationality of means, which is the dominant both in the neoclassical authors and in Simon (Gonzalez 2003d, esp., pp. 77–79). Rationality of ends would take charge of drawing the aims of economic prescriptions. This includes several levels: first, the selection of possible *aims*; second, the elaboration of *priorities*, either in terms of a hierarchy of ends within a delimited field or through a consideration of the realms which are or should be priorities; and third, evaluation of the *consequences* which derive from those aims (in economic terms or in other terms: social, cultural, political, etc.).

A well-articulated *theory of economic prescription* should include—according to my proposal—several elements, in order to have an adequate status from an epistemological and methodological point of view. In addition, there is an underlying ontological dimension that goes with the idea of economics as a social science as well as a science of the artificial (i.e., a science of design), which deals with human activities in a multifaceted world. Among the elements of that theory of economic prescription, the following should be pointed out (Gonzalez 1998).

1. According to the rationality of ends, economic agents are neither mere searchers of maximization of subjective expected utilities (these are frequent in the methodological individualism of neoclassical economics), nor are they subjects whose full task is *satisficing*—in the sense of Simon—because the maximization is an ideal feature, not a real one, of economic agents (who have, in fact, a bounded rationality) and satisficing does not require that the aims are already given as Simon has defended. Moreover, the process of satisficing can be carried out following *different ways*, which can modulate the orientation towards the ends sought.

[21] The analysis of these topics was enlarged in the new version of the book of 1996: Hausman and McPherson (2006).

2. Incorporation of more qualitative factors at the moment of drawing the economic aims of prescriptions, since economic agents have not as a single goal to obtaining the maximum economic benefit: economic activity is linked to other economic strategies within the social world, which has its repercussion, as Sen has pointed out, in "the deep interdependence in the achievements of people's respective goals" (1986, p. 17). In addition, the publication of papers on the cooperative aspects in the domain of this discipline (Simon 1990a), and the research line about altruism in economics (Simon 1990b, 1991c, 1992c, 1993),[22] allow us to asseverate the existence of a break in the traditional neoclassical scheme of a utilitarian rationality of a very noticeable individualistic kind.

Furthermore, against the one-dimensional methodology of this orientation (i.e., mainstream economics), it should be emphasized that the economic activity itself is interconnected with other social and cultural elements (familiar, ethnical, national, international, etc.). This has influence on the prescriptions to be given (in a similar way as the social rejection to built up a motorway or a bridge motivates the modulation of a technology which is well oriented from the technological point of view). In addition, it has relevance for the implementation of those prescriptions by the agents in the diverse settings.

12.5.2 Internal and External Values of Prescriptions

The *internal values* of economic prescriptions depend, to some extent, on the knowledge provided by economic predictions, because, like any other conception that supposes the direction of human activity, prescription requires us to consider a *possible aim* and also that it might be *achievable*. Thus, some of the components of internal evaluations of economic prescriptions can be the simplicity of the goal, the consistency of means, the adequacy with respect to the agents, the ratio between cost and benefit, to avoid a biased viewpoint (especially if it has a political ingredient),[23] etc.

Regarding the *external values*, the list is wider: these go from evaluations of ethical and social character (repercussion to social groups, especially the labor dimension—i.e., in terms of employment: social discrimination versus social cohesion; integration in the working place versus emigration; labor dignity versus "junk contract," etc.) or of a social and cultural kind (i.e., social settling versus creation of minorities) to components of a different class (political, ecological, etc.). They can be at different levels, such as microeconomics and macroeconomics.

[22] See also the papers, such as Kitcher (2010) and Schefczyk and Peacock (2010), included in the monographic section on altruism of the journal *Economics and Philosophy*, vol. 26, no. 2.

[23] For Granger, this feature of avoiding a biased viewpoint is central for ethical values in economics (2012, p. 326).

Looking at the problem from a methodological angle, the complexity of economic reality seems more patent. In effect, the present general proposal assumes that the applied science which emerges—the "normative economics"—combines several things: (a) it is backed up by the predictive information of the descriptive or "positive" branch of economic science; (b) it should adopt a method different from the dominant methodological individualism of mainstream economics; and (c) that method will follow a position which is divergent with respect to the holistic methodology of narrow kind, such as that derived from the economic systems with prescriptions in terms of social planning, systems guided by a voluntarism regarding the economic aims (which do not contemplate that the rationality of means is not restricted to the mere economic activity but which is clearly affected by its character of being one *human activity* among others and, therefore, linked to ethical, social, and political factors which eventually affect productivity itself).

To look for that *tertium quid* between methodological individualism and holistic methodology in economics can lead us to stress the role of economic activity as *social action*, which is distant from the maximization of subjective expected utilities and different from the search of impersonal collective aims, planned extrinsically to the economic agents. This methodological option based on social action can be twofold: on the one hand, it can lead us towards economic models which "resemblance" in a better way economic undertakings; and, on the other, it can offer economic models which construct more credible possible scenarios to study the effects of changes in policy instruments.

Again methodology of science and axiology of research are connected. A possible enumeration of *internal* (or endogenous) *values* to *economic activity* as such can be the following: satisfactory relation between cost and benefit; efficiency and effectiveness, with predominance of the first; search of certainty, and consequently a diminution of the level of uncertainty; adequate correlation between means and ends, with the decrease of risk; profitability; competitiveness; etc. All of them could be interrelated insofar as they belong to a human activity developed in a social environment as well as in an artificial setting.

Concerning *external* (or exogenous) *values* to *economic activity* as such (extrinsic to economic knowledge and method) an important feature is the wide diversity of their possibilities, according to the human or social facet correlated with the economic undertaking: (i) on its socio-psychological dimension (trust, credibility, viability, …); (ii) as a socio-cultural phenomenon (to satisfy the needs, to cover the expectations, to synchronize with the social patterns, social welfare, …); (iii) insofar as it is a human activity capable of ethical valuation (dignity of the person, honesty, integrity, …); (iv) on the basis of its political scope (to reduce the inequalities, to increase freedom, …); (v) as it has a repercussion on the environment facet (protection of the milieu, to avoid ecological dangers, …); etc.

This taxonomy of values, as well as any other which could be offered, depends on a previous theoretical problem: the status itself of *values*. For modulation of the problem varies notably if an objectivity of values is defended (or, at least, some of them are), instead of considering that all values are intersubjective (or, even, merely subjective) and, then, under the acknowledgement by a collective (or, it is the case, by an individual) within a concrete framework of space and time. The way of characterization of the values influences in how to configure the axiology of inquiry,[24] because this marks the ends (in this case, economic) which will require adequate means (Gonzalez 2001a).

Thus, the reflection on the economic prescription exhibits several philosophico-methodological problems which are not easy to resolve: (1) the way of relating the values internal to economic activity and those external to economic knowledge and method but with repercussions in the economic science; (2) the status itself of the values involved (either in the human activity itself and in the study of economic events), and their weight in the priorities to be established by an axiology of inquiry; and (3) the form of evaluating the results of economic prescriptions, taking into account the internal and external values assumed.

12.6 Prediction and Prescription in Economics: A Central Tenet for Future Developments

Certainly, in economics as science related to the decision-making (especially as science of the artificial oriented to design better futures), "it is difficult to imagine the conduct of economic policy without predictions. Either explicitly or implicitly the conduct of any policy implies a view about the future" (Burns 1986, p. 103). A crucial task of applied economics (and specifically of econometrics) is "to predict the consequences of alternative hypothetical ways of administering government economic policy" (Sargent 1987, p. 1). This analysis should be followed by prescriptions on what should be done in order to solve concrete economic problems, and the consequences of those prescriptions are to be considered in future predictive models. In addition, there is an interaction of theory and practice: "forecasts typically provide the basis for economic decisions, and the resulting forecast errors entail economic costs" (Granger 2001, p. 103).

According to the analysis made in previous chapters (mainly, in Chap. 2), *prediction* could be seen as a generic term, insofar as it is open to a different level of control of the variables regarding the future and can be diversified into "foresight," "prediction," and "forecasting" (Gonzalez 1996c, pp. 215–216). It means that prediction—in the broad sense—is not *eo ipso* a deterministic notion. Thus, (a) the realm of prescription (patterns for policy, planning, practical measures, etc.) can be based on the sphere of prediction (e.g., in the case of a crop failure due to a drought, the practical measures that the authorities can sensibly take); and (b) the prescriptions need not be based on a "foresight" or strict prediction as to *what will*

---

[24] This expression is used in the sense now frequent after the publication of the book of Laudan (1984). But there are several differences from him, which come from the approach itself: he analyzes epistemic values, whereas here the realm is wider, both in the number of values (it includes, for example, practical values) and in the perspective, which is richer than his proposal (i.e., it includes a conception of a system). See, in this regard, Gonzalez (2013a).

happen, because it can be based on assessments about *probability* (what is likely to happen) or even be based on assessments about mere *possibility* (what may conceivably happen). In other words, rational action need not be predicated on basis of a strong prediction: it could be supported by a "forecasting"—in the sense used in Chap. 2—insofar as the statement about the future can rest on assessments of probability and possibility.

Taking into account the bi-directional relation between prediction and prescription as well as the non-deterministic context for them in applied economics, there are several elements that are relevant from a philosophico-methodological perspective and that should be emphasized. They are thought of in order to take stock of the complex task of articulate economic prediction with economic prescription:

Firstly, prediction is not the *leit-motiv* of economics, insofar as the aims sought by this discipline go beyond the range of descriptive tasks to go into the prescriptive functions of the axiology of economic research. Secondly, prediction can be distinguished from the mere *testable implications* of an economic model established. Prediction sees novelty in economics (ontological, epistemological, or heuristic) as commonly oriented towards the future. Furthermore, prediction looks at the future that, in principle, starts with the mark of uncertainty. Thus, the prescriptions can reduce the margin of uncertainty insofar as they select attainable aims and they associate the available means to them.

Economic prescription includes, basically, the following features: (i) in a form clearer than prediction, prescription takes place on a teleological horizon, because it appears directly related to *ends sought*; (ii) prescription exceeds the epistemological level which supports the predictive methodology and becomes a concept connected to the *direction of action*, an aspect which is more obvious when a planning of economic activity takes place; (iii) insofar as prescription leads towards an adaptation of the future of economic undertaking, it is supported by *the base of predictions* given by the economic science "positive" or "descriptive"; and (iv) there is an *asymmetry* between "prediction" and "prescription," because not all economic prediction is accompanied by the possibility of a viable prescription, due to the fact that it is possible to predict economic phenomena which we cannot actually control (i.e., predictions of economic cycles in the long run) and the economic prescriptions themselves are assessed with respect to their plausibility—as better or worse off economic policies—according to predictions, and thus predictions can be used to evaluate prescriptions.[25]

Due to the importance of prescription in economics, a detailed philosophico-methodological approach to it seems to be needed in order to complement the analysis made here on prediction in economics. Although the importance of prediction has been sometimes overemphasized (in the case of Friedman), it is quite obvious that prediction plays a crucial role, both in economic theory and in applied economics (and also in the application of economics). It can be seen as a central tenet of economics as a science.

---

[25] In this regard, Frank Hahn seems optimistic: "What occurs when we pass to the more distant future is that economics provides a fairly powerful tool for evaluating alternative policies" (1993, p. 93).

At the same time, the relations between prediction and prescription also require a more intense attention from a philosophical analysis that takes into account all the relevant elements (semantic, logic, epistemological, methodological, ontological, axiological, and even ethical) of a science. The methodological link between prediction and prescription is clear in economics (Pagan and Robertson 2002, esp., pp. 154–155 and 161–162). It seems to me that future developments should analyze prescription in the context of economics as a science that deals with "economic activity" and also with "economics as activity" interrelated with other social and artificial activities.

References

Ascher, W. 1978. *Forecasting: An appraisal for policy-makers and planners*. Baltimore: Johns Hopkins University Press.

Backhouse, R. E. 1994b. The Lakatosian legacy in economic methodology. In *New directions in economic methodology*, ed. R. E. Backhouse, 173–191. London: Routledge.

Burns, T. 1986. The interpretation and use of economic predictions. In *Predictability in science and society*, ed. J. Mason, P. Mathias, and J. H. Westcott, 103–125. London: The Royal Society and The British Academy.

Caldwell, B. J. 1982. *Beyond positivism: Economic methodology in the twentieth century*. London: Allen and Unwin; revised ed., 1994. London: Routledge.

Coase, R. H. 1988. *The firm, the market and the law*. Chicago: The University of Chicago Press.

Coase, R. H. 1994a. The institutional structure of production. In *Essays on economics and economists*, ed. R. H. Coase, 3–14. Chicago: The University of Chicago Press.

Friedman, M. 1953. The methodology of positive economics. In *Essays in positive economics*, M. Friedman, 3–43. Chicago: The University of Chicago Press (6th repr., 1969).

Gonzalez, W. J. 1996b. Prediction and mathematics: The Wittgensteinian approach. In *Spanish studies in the philosophy of science*, ed. G. Munevar, 299–332. Dordrecht: Kluwer.

Gonzalez, W. J. 1996c. On the theoretical basis of prediction in economics. *Journal of Social Philosophy* 27(3):201–228.

Gonzalez, W. J. 1997a Progreso científico e innovación tecnológica: La "Tecnociencia" y el problema de las relaciones entre Filosofía de la Ciencia y Filosofía de la Tecnología. *Arbor* 157(620):261–283.

Gonzalez, W. J. 1997b. Rationality in economics and scientific predictions: A critical reconstruction of bounded rationality and its role in economic predictions. *Poznan Studies in the Philosophy of Science* 61:205–232.

Gonzalez, W. J. 1998b. Prediction and prescription in economics: A philosophical and methodological approach. *Theoria* 13(2):321–345.

Gonzalez, W. J. 1999. Ciencia y valores éticos: De la posibilidad de la Ética de la Ciencia al problema de la valoración ética de la Ciencia Básica. *Arbor* 162(638):139–171.

Gonzalez, W. J. 2001a. De la Ciencia de la Economía a la Economía de la Ciencia: Marco conceptual de la reflexión metodológica y axiológica. In *Ciencia Económica y Economía de la ciencia: Reflexiones filosófico-metodológicas*, ed. A. Avila, W. J. Gonzalez, and G. Marques, 11–37. Madrid: FCE.

Gonzalez, W. J. 2003d. Racionalidad y Economía: de la racionalidad de la Economía como Ciencia a la racionalidad de los agentes económicos. In *Racionalidad, historicidad y predicción en Herbert A. Simon*, ed. W. J. Gonzalez, 65–96. A Coruña: Netbiblo.

Gonzalez, W. J. 2005. The philosophical approach to science, technology and society. In *Science, technology and society: A philosophical perspective*, ed. W. J. Gonzalez, 3–49. A Coruña: Netbiblo.
Gonzalez, W. J. 2006b. Prediction as scientific test of economics. In *Contemporary perspectives in philosophy and methodology of science*, ed. W. J. Gonzalez and J. Alcolea, 83–112. A Coruña: Netbiblo.
Gonzalez, W. J. 2013a. Value ladenness and the value-free ideal in scientific research. In *Handbook of the philosophical foundations of business ethics*, ed. Ch. Lütge, 1503–1521. Dordrecht: Springer.
Gonzalez, W. J. 2013c. The roles of scientific creativity and technological innovation in the context of complexity of science. In *Creativity, innovation, and complexity in science*, ed. W. J. Gonzalez, 11–40. A Coruña: Netbiblo.
Gonzalez, W. J. 2014. On representation and models in Bas van Fraassen's approach. In *Bas van Fraassen's approach to representation and models in science*, ed. W. J. Gonzalez, 3–37. Dordrecht: Springer.
Granger, C. W. J. 2001. Evaluation of forecasts. In *Understanding economic forecasts*, ed. D. F. Hendry and N. R. Ericsson, 93–103. Cambridge: The MIT Press.
Granger, C. W. J. 2012. The philosophy of economic forecasting. In *Philosophy of economics*, ed. U. Mäki, 311–327. Amsterdam: Elsevier.
Granger, C. W. J., and M. J. Machina. 2006. Forecasting and decision theory. In *Handbook of economic forecasting*, vol. 1, ed. G. Elliot, C. W. J. Granger, and A. Timmerman, 81–98. Amsterdam: Elsevier.
Hahn, F. 1993. Predicting the economy. In *Predicting the future*, ed. L. Howe and A. Wain, 77–95. Cambridge: Cambridge University Press.
Hausman, D. M., and M. S. McPherson. 1994. Economics, rationality, and ethics. In *The philosophy of economics. An anthology*, 2nd ed., ed. D. M. Hausman, 252–277. Cambridge: Cambridge University Press.
Hausman, D. M., and M. S. McPherson. 1996. *Economic analysis and moral philosophy*. Cambridge: Cambridge University Press.
Hausman, D. M., and M. S. McPherson. 2006. *Economic analysis, moral philosophy, and public policy*. Cambridge: Cambridge University Press.
Hutchison, T. W. 1977. On prediction and economic knowledge. In *Knowledge and ignorance in economics*, ed. T. W. Hutchison, 8–33 and 145–151. Oxford: Blackwell.
Kaplan, O. 1940. Prediction in the social sciences. *Philosophy of Science* 7(4):492–498.
Kitcher, Ph. 2010. Varieties of altruism. *Economics and Philosophy* 26(2):121–148.
Laudan, L. 1984. *Science and values. The aims of science and their role in scientific debate*. Berkeley: University of California Press.
Lipsey, R. G. 1963. *An introduction to positive economics*. London: Weidenfeld.
Llewellyn, J., S. Potter, and L. Samuelson. 1985. *Economic forecasting and policy—The international dimension*. London: Routledge.
Mäki, U. 1994. Reorienting the assumption issue. In *New directions in economic methodology*, ed. R. E. Backhouse, 236–256. London: Routledge.
Morgan, M. S. 1990. *The history of econometric ideas*. Cambridge: Cambridge University Press.
Morgenstern, O. 1972. Descriptive, predictive and normative theory. *Kyklos* 25:699–714.
Niiniluoto, I. 1993. The aim and structure of applied research. *Erkenntnis* 38:1–21.
Niiniluoto, I. 1997a. Ciencia frente a Tecnología: ¿Diferencia o identidad? *Arbor* 157(620):285–299.
Niiniluoto, I. 1997b. Límites de la Tecnología. *Arbor* 157(620):391–410.
Pagan, A. R., and J. Robertson. 2002. Forecasting for policy. In *A companion to economic forecasting*, ed. M. Clements and D. F. Hendry, 152–178. Oxford: Blackwell.
Pears, D. 1964. Predicting and deciding. *Proceedings of the British Academy* 50:193–227.
Pheby, J. 1988. *Methodology and economics*. London: Macmillan.
Popper, K. R. 1957. *The poverty of historicism*. London: Routledge (and K. Paul; reprinted by Routledge in 1991).

Redman, D. A. 1989. *Economic methodology. A bibliography with references to works in the philosophy of science, 1860–1988*. Westport, CT: Greenwood Press.
Rescher, N. 1988. *Rationality. A philosophical inquiry into the nature and the rationale of reason*. Oxford: Oxford University Press.
Rescher, N. 1998. *Predicting the future: An introduction to the theory of forecasting*. Albany: State University of New York Press.
Rescher, N. 1999a. *Razón y valores en la Era científico-tecnológica*. Barcelona: Paidós.
Robbins, L. 1935. *An essay on the nature and significance of economic science*, 2nd ed. London: Macmillan (1st ed., 1932).
Samuelson, P. 1963. Problems of methodology—Discussion. *American Economic Review* 53(2):231–236.
Samuelson, P. 1964. Theory and realism: A reply. *American Economic Review* 54:736–739.
Samuelson, P. 1965a. Professor Samuelson on theory and realism: A Reply. *American Economic Review* 55:1162–1672.
Samuelson, P. 1965b. Economic forecasting and science. *Michigan Quarterly Review* 4(4):274–280.
Sargent, Th. J. 1987. *Dynamic macroeconomic theory*. Cambridge: Harvard University Press.
Schefczyk, M., and M. Peacock. 2010. Altruism as a thick concept. *Economics and Philosophy* 26(2):165–187.
Selten, R., and Ockenfels, A. 1998. An experimental solidarity game. *Journal of Economic Behavior and Organization* 34(4):517–539.
Sen, A. 1980. Description as choice. *Oxford Economic Papers* 32:353–369.
Sen, A. 1983. Accounts, actions and values: Objectivity of social science. In *Social theory and political practice*, ed. C. Lloyd, 87–107. Oxford: Oxford University Press.
Sen, A. 1986. Prediction and economic theory. In *Predictability in science and society*, ed. J. Mason, P. Mathias, and J. H. Westcott, 3–23. London: The Royal Society and The British Academy.
Simon, H. A. 1954. Bandwagon and underdog effects and the possibility of election predictions. *Public Opinion Quarterly* 18:245–253. Reprinted in Simon, H. A. 1957. *Models of man: Social and rational*, 79–87. New York: Wiley and in Simon, H. A. 1982. *Models of bounded rationality*, vol. 1: *Economic analysis and public policy*, 460–468. Cambridge: The MIT Press.
Simon, H. A. 1958. The role of expectations in an adaptive or behavioristic model. In *Expectations, uncertainty, and business behavior*, ed. M. J. Bowman, ch. 3, 49–58. New York, NY: Social Science Research Council. Reprinted in Simon, H. A. 1982. *Models of bounded rationality*, vol. 2: *Behavioral economics and business organization*, 380–399. Cambridge: The MIT Press.
Simon, H. A. 1963a. Economics and psychology. In *Psychology: A study of a science*, vol. 6, ed. S. Koch, 715–752. New York: McGraw Hill. Reprinted in Simon, H. A. 1982. *Models of bounded rationality*, vol. 2: *Behavioral economics and business organization*, 318–355. Cambridge: The MIT Press.
Simon, H. A. 1963b. Problems of methodology—Discussion. *American Economic Review* 53:229–231. Reprinted in Simon, H. A. 1982. *Models of bounded rationality*, vol. 2: *Behavioral economics and business organization*, 369–371. Cambridge: The MIT Press; also reprinted as Simon, H. A. 1984. Testability and approximation. In *Philosophy of economics*, 1st ed., ed. D. M. Hausman, 245–248. Cambridge: Cambridge University Press.
Simon, H. A. 1983. *Reason in human affairs*. Stanford: Stanford University Press.
Simon, H. A. 1989. The state of economic science. In *The state of economic science. Views of six Nobel laureates*, ed. W. Sichel, 97–110. Kalamazoo, MI: W. E. Upjohn Institute for Employment Research.
Simon, H. A. 1990a. Prediction and prescription in systems modeling. *Operations Research* 38:7–14. Reprinted in Simon, H. A. 1997. *Models of bounded rationality*, vol. 3: *Empirically grounded economic reason*, 115–128. Cambridge: The MIT Press.
Simon, H. A. 1990b. A mechanism for social selection and successful altruism. *Science* 250:1665–1668. Reprinted in Simon, H. A. 1997. Models of bounded rationality, vol. 3: *Empirically grounded economic reason*, 205–216. Cambridge: The MIT Press.

Simon, H. A. 1991c. Altruism: Docility or group identification? (Response to L. R. Caporael and R. M. Dawes). *Science* 252:192.

Simon, H. A. 1992a. Introductory comment. In *Economics, bounded rationality and the cognitive revolution*, ed. M. Egidi and R. Marris, 3–7. Aldershot: E. Elgar.

Simon, H. A. 1992c. Altruism and economics. *Eastern Economic Journal* 18(1):73–83. Reprinted as Altruism and economics: A summary statement. In Simon, H. A. 1997. *Models of bounded rationality*, vol. 3: *Empirically grounded economic reason*, 241–255. Cambridge: The MIT Press.

Simon, H. A. 1993. Altruism and economics. *American Economic Review* 83(2):156–161. Reprinted as Altruism and economics: Social implications. Simon, H. A. 1997. *Models of bounded rationality*, vol. 3: *Empirically grounded economic reason*, 257–265. Cambridge: The MIT Press.

Simon, H. A. 2002. Forecasting the future or shaping it? *Industrial and Corporate Change* 11(3):601–605.

Stekler, H. O. 1991. Macroeconomic forecast evaluation techniques. *International Journal of Forecasting* 7:375–384.

Streissler, E. W. 1970. *Pitfalls in econometric forecasting*. London: Institute of Economic Affairs.

Turner, P. 2001. Economic modeling for fun and profit. In *Understanding economic forecasts*, ed. D. F. Hendry and N. R. Ericsson, 42–53. Cambridge: The MIT Press.

Index of Names

W. J. Gonzalez, *Philosophico-Methodological Analysis of Prediction and its Role in Economics,* Theory and Decision Library A: 50, DOI 10.1007/978-3-319-08885-3

R

S

Subject Index

W. J. Gonzalez, *Philosophico-Methodological Analysis of Prediction and its Role in Economics,* Theory and Decision Library A: 50, DOI 10.1007/978-3-319-08885-3

N

Q

R

MIX
Papier aus verantwortungsvollen Quellen
Paper from responsible sources
FSC® C105338

FSC
www.fsc.org

If you have any concerns about our products,
you can contact us on
ProductSafety@springernature.com

In case Publisher is established outside the EU,
the EU authorized representative is:
Springer Nature Customer Service Center GmbH
Europaplatz 3, 69115 Heidelberg, Germany

Printed by Libri Plureos GmbH
in Hamburg, Germany